EDUCATION
IN
VIOLENCE

To E. David Duncan

On behalf of the author
In memory of George Thomas
& an army that "could whip
the devil".

Best,
John S. Peterman

Major General George H. Thomas
The Rock of Chickamauga

EDUCATION
IN
VIOLENCE

The Life of George H. Thomas

and the History

of the Army of the Cumberland

---

by Francis F. McKinney

with a new introduction by
John S. Peterson

AMERICANA HOUSE, INC., Chicago, Illinois
1991

*"If this bill passes it is
a dissolution of the Union.
It will free the states from
their moral obligation and
it will be the right of all
to prepare for a separation
—amicably if they can,
violently if they must."*

—JOSIAH QUINCY, 1811

Preface

Two-thirds of the life of Major General George Henry Thomas is so thoroughly documented that it is possible to list every place he visited, why he went there and what he did. This documentation would seem to rule out any possibility of a synthetic reputation; yet such a reputation exists and has been accepted by historians. But the public has doubts about it. Theirs is a curious attitude. They are prone to make a statement about Thomas' military ability or patriotism and then deny it by asking for a confirmation. To answer this doubtful overtone, one book-length biography of Thomas has been published, written or projected for every eleven years which have elapsed since his death.

This doubt may be the result of the numerous contradictions which mark Thomas' career. He is best known for the greatest defeat suffered by the Union arms in the western fighting of the Civil War, while his most decisive victory, the only one to shatter a major army in battle, is forgotten. His native state of Virginia repudiated him, while Tennessee, which he scourged for four years, voluntarily cured his war-long state-lessness. He was no less a patriot because of his Southern birth than General Winfield Scott or Admiral David Farragut, yet his loyalty was much more suspect than theirs. He was under the compulsion of a burning professional ambition, yet he refused three promotions in-cluding that of the army's highest rank and command. He was full of humor but he rarely laughed. In public his tastes were simple and unostentatious, but in private he demanded that his appointments be complete and elegant. He was habitually prompt, but his reputation is for slowness. He was able to inspire faith in himself on the part of men whom he had just met, yet he is pictured as reserved and stand-offish. He strove to make his command into a perfect tool, yet he won his greatest victory with its broken remnant. He proved his gift for leadership on many fields, but he was branded as incompetent for a combat command. His physical energy was tremendous yet his closest professional friend only once saw him put his horse to its fastest gait. The *Official Records* show that he fought a nearly flawless campaign from Chattanooga to Atlanta, yet Sherman secretly blamed him for his failure to bag the Rebel army. Energy, ambition, persuasiveness and ability generally lead to attempts at domination, yet Thomas never tried to usurp a superior's command.

There are understandable reasons for these contradictions. Before the sound of Sumter's gunfire had died away, Virginia named Thomas as a traitor and his Southampton family and neighbors smothered and distorted the details of the first twenty years of his life. Thomas and his wife destroyed all records of his personal life and nearly all of whatever records there may have been of his motivations. To fill this vacuum military commentators supplied the motive which they thought would fit the facts. Two of Thomas' early and most widely read biographers described him in their own image. Chaplain Thomas B. Van Horne pictured him as being so pure and righteous as to seem sanctimonious. Piatt used Thomas' memory to belabor Grant, for whom he cherished a personal dislike.

Perhaps the thing which threw the image of Thomas farthest out of focus was Grant's belittlement of the man who, above all others, made his career a success. It is no inconsiderable part of military wisdom to know how much preparation should be tolerated. Grant and Thomas differed continuously on this subject from November 1863 until the end of the war. The matter came to a showdown with Lincoln and Stanton in December 1864 and Grant won his point. Thomas' military career was saved only by a telegraph operator who risked his job to suppress Grant's order for Thomas' relief.

When Thomas' victory broke down the Rebellion west of the Appalachians, Grant parried the implicit threat to his own professional standing by labeling Thomas as a picky commander who imperiled the Union cause while he perfected inconsequential details for his attack. Grant or his publicists coined a slogan to complete the destruction of

Thomas' professional reputation. "Thomas," they said, "is too slow to fight and too brave to run away."

A king's power is greatest just after he saves it from a rebellion. The South's rebellion ended in 1865 but Thomas was not of the King's Party. Records could have been and apparently were tampered with. The King's Men took unearned credits from other men and were powerful enough to weave them into history. Thomas was dead and could make no rebuttal.

Yet a military leader so sluggish, cold and lacking in toleration of the human race as Thomas was supposed to be could never have created that superb military tool—the Army of the Cumberland. It was conceived in chaos around Thomas' tavern headquarters in the Kentucky blue-grass country. Through the great swinging campaigns of 1863 it was trained to fight, pursue and annihilate. It applied the absolute degree of military violence to the enemy without permitting the effort to verge onto savagery. In striving for perfection its crowning victory was robbed of the drama and color which is the stuff of military history. The Army of the Cumberland is the lengthened shadow of its leader and its memory is plain and undistorted. It is impossible for this army to be recognized as one of the nation's best while its creator has the self-annulling reputation which history has fastened on him. The unity of a man and his creation is such that an attempt to tell only a part of the truth tears a seamless fabric and its broken threads cannot be hidden.

Thomas nourished the first units of this army before they had been brigaded—some of them before they had been mustered into the federal service. He led its first division through the mud to Mill Springs and surprised himself and his men with the success of this jeweled tactical miniature. In the tangled cedar thickets bordering Stones River his regular brigade discharged the awful responsibility of saving the entire army. At points some ten miles apart on a little known ridge it staged one of the war's epics of defense and its most magnificent assault. Its furled flags now slowly dropping to pieces in capital rotundas across the nation still seem to retain some sensuous reminders of those great days —the taste of the dust of Kelly's field, the smell of the charring ground fires of Snodgrass Ridge, the tiny flashes of light thrown back from polished brasses as the color sergeants dodged up the steeps of Missionary Ridge.

For more than three years Nathan Bedford Forrest, the foremost leader of mounted troops in the English-speaking world, taught the Union commanders in the west the fine points of horse-fighting. Grant,

Thomas, Sherman and Sheridan were four of his pupils. What they accomplished with Forrest's lessons is the history of the last months of the Civil War. Thomas, punitively stripped of most of his infantry, built a cavalry corps whose like had never before been seen on the American continent and with it he stung the Rebel power from Virginia to Florida.

His was an army of many skills in addition to those of combat. The Army of the Cumberland was the first to fight exclusively along the line of a railroad and the way it harnessed that facility to military use gave to the science of transport and supply a division of time and a multiplication of tonnage never seen before. Its officers practiced the rudimentary use of map coordinates. Its signallers took the first halting steps toward the concept of remote fire control. Its folding Cumberland pontoon increased the mobility of the Blue armies. It was a tempered tool of many talents. The Army of the Cumberland caught fire when Thomas led and wept when he died.

Introduction

In the winter of 1942-43, Douglas Southall Freeman paused in the midst of his labors on LEE'S LIEUTENANTS to draw an historical parallel and express his hopes for American forces then fighting round the world— "Ours may it be in 1943 to duplicate the experience of the Army of Northern Virginia from Seven Days to Chancellorsville. In this next phase of this Second World War, the period from our Gettysburg to Appomattox, may the fortunes of our men be not those of the Army of Northern Virginia but those of its gallant adversary, the Army of the Potomac."

Surely, one can appreciate the grace of Dr. Freeman's sentiment and sympathize with his desire to draw an inspiring parallel between our Civil War armies and their World War II descendants. The American Civil War furnished innumerable examples of heroism on both sides, as well as an expanded political creed and a fund of experience that would prove useful in helping us cope with 20th Century mass violence. One regrets only that Freeman's angle of vision precluded his mentioning any armies of the West. In retrospect, it may be that the Union Army of the Cumberland was the most modern of our Civil War armies and the one that most appropriately links the armies and commanders of the 1860's with those of the Second World War.

The Abraham Lincoln Book Shop is to be congratulated for bringing us this excellent reprint of Francis F. McKinney's EDUCATION IN VIOLENCE:

A BIOGRAPHY OF GEORGE H. THOMAS AND A HISTORY OF THE ARMY OF THE CUMBERLAND. Long out of print, written during the Civil War biographical renaissance of the 1950's, this work continues to be the classic, well-nigh definitive study of George Thomas and his forgotten army. Indeed, considering the difficulties its author was forced to surmount, it deserves to rank among the finer literary performances in modern Civil War writing.

Not the least of McKinney's problems was his subject. Of the major Civil War commanders, Thomas is easily the toughest nut to crack. For example, what to do with a Virginian whose state disowns him and whose family does everything in its power to erase him from memory? How to treat a subject who completes the process by destroying all papers in his possession relating to personal affairs? Thomas justified his action in the following terms: "All that I did for my government are matters of history, but my private life is my own and I will not have it hawked about for the amusement of the curious."

McKinney's task was further complicated by Thomas' premature death. Curiously, both Thomas and Robert E. Lee died in the same year, 1870, each without leaving memoirs or a sustained body of writing concerning their wartime activities. As a consequence, their post-war reputations would be fashioned by other men, other generals, writing usually for highly partisan purposes. For Lee, the controversies would elevate him to the status of a near-God. For Thomas, the results were altogether different. On the day of his death, among his papers was a partially completed letter written in response to a newspaper article attacking his conduct of the Nashville Campaign.

Thomas' problem was essentially political, and at the heart of the politics was his peculiar position within the Union command. Up until 1861, his career had been nurtured by powerful Virginia influences and connections, or, as an Ohio officer once put it, before the Civil War the merit of a United States army officer was measured in the inverse ratio of the distance of his birthplace from Fairfax Courthouse. In the wake of Ft. Sumter, Thomas was suddenly homeless, stateless and without a power base. Within the Lincoln cabinet and the army, the Ohio influence became paramount. Secretaries Stanton and Chase worked to advance the career interests of Ohio's native sons—officers such as McClellan, Buell, Sherman, Grant, Rosecrans, and Sheridan.

During the post-war phase—the period corresponding with the Grant, Hayes, and Garfield administrations—the Ohio influence became dominant. Sherman's memoirs were published in the mid-'70s, followed by Grant and

Sheridan's in the mid- and late-'80s. By then, Thomas was long dead, unable to reply to the cumulative myths concerning "Slow-Trot Thomas", the army commander "too slow to fight, and too brave to run away."

This is not to suggest that Thomas was without literary defenders. On the contrary; within the Society of the Army of the Cumberland and among Union veterans at large were a number who resented Sherman and Grant's characterizations of Thomas as being "slow of mind," fit only to command and fight from a defensive position. Unfortunately, most of Thomas' champions tended to write overblown eulogies and describe him in terms— "massive, fully rounded"—that only tended to reinforce the prevailing stereotype. In our time, there is also what might be called the Chickamauga problem. Thomas' stand on Snodgrass Ridge is one of the epic defense actions in American military history. So much so that it warps the modern perspective. We tend to view him as the eternal "Rock of Chickamauga", ignoring his other battles and forgetting that he could indeed take the offensive and even annihilate an army.

Yes, Francis McKinney faced substantial problems in writing this book. And he solved them in a manner common to all master biographers— by conducting years of extensive and painstaking research; by absorbing a mountain of facts and putting them through the reducing valve of a highly-gifted and discriminating intellect; and, by taking and shaping the remainder into a balanced narrative, written with precision and grace.

On the biographical side, McKinney makes up for the dearth of personal data by expertly fleshing-in the army context of Thomas' pre-war years. His West Point chapter illustrates perfectly what a skilled "life and times" biographer can do when operating in an informational void. One of Thomas' roommates, Stewart Van Vliet, was unable to recall a single anecdote beyond once watching Thomas throw an obstreperous cadet out of his room. Nonetheless, one leaves the chapter with a strong sense of Thomas and of what lies up the road for his generation of West Pointers.

The author's analysis of the power struggles within the Union command is a superb reminder of just how impossible it is, in a democratic societal context, to separate politics from war. It is also a refreshing antidote to much of the worshipful literature surrounding Sherman and Grant. McKinney scores a number of hard points against these men, and yet, one senses that his motive in doing so is not so much to even old scores as to obtain justice for Thomas and his army. Furthermore, on the strength of the evidence, even the most ardent Army of the Tennessee camp follower will admit that some justice is long overdue. Sherman himself, near the end of his life, conceded that his West Point roommate and old friend had been treated shabbily.

At the heart of the book is McKinney's analysis of Thomas' leadership of the Army of the Cumberland, a role for which the author believes he had been long preparing. Each phase of Thomas' military education—the Seminole War, Mexican War, frontier Indian fighting—contained a set of lessons that would bear fruit at his Tavern headquarters at Camp Dick Robinson in Kentucky Bluegrass country in the autumn of 1861. As he patiently organizes, equips, and trains his raw citizen-soldier volunteers, one senses the emergence of a highly professional, highly modern commander. This sense is heightened as one grasps the import of his innovations in the use of railways, the science of tonnage, map co-ordinates, and the concept of remote fire control. McKinney is correct in describing the Army of the Cumberland as an army of many talents. Many modern talents, that is.

The author's battle writing is on a par with the best in the field, and from Chickamauga on, nothing less than riveting. After the Battle of Nashville, many readers may wish to reconsider Douglas Southall Freeman's choice of Civil War armies as role models for armies of a later time. In 1943 or any year, U.S. forces afield may be better advised to duplicate the experience of the Army of the Cumberland from Chickamauga, through the battles for Chattanooga, the Atlanta Campaign, and pursuit and annihilation of Hood's army at Nashville.

On May 26, 1865, the Union armies of the West led by General Sherman paraded in the last Grand Review. Bismarck's ambassador, basking in the pomp, went agog in bestowing compliments on the various corps marching past. "Here is an army that can whip all Europe! ...Here is an army that can whip the universe!" Behind Grant and Sherman's armies, at the very tail of the column, was George Thomas' old 14th Corps, his best. As Cumberlanders trooped by in an eerie presentiment of things to come, the German outdid himself. "Now here...here is an army that can whip the devil!"

George Thomas once remarked, "History will do me justice." History, a German ambassador and this book have done just that.

John S. Peterson
Gettysburg, Pennsylvania
March 1991

PUBLISHERS NOTE: *We are deeply grateful to Mr. Peterson for saving our original edition of this book when his house recently caught fire. "I grabbed my guitar, banjo, and a book for which I am writing an introduction." We admire him for his priorities!*

Contents

Illustrations

* All ranks listed are the highest attained for Civil War services. No distinction has been made between regular army officers and volunteer officers. The former outranked the latter.

Maps

EDUCATION
IN
VIOLENCE

1

Early Days

The Civil War made George Henry Thomas a national figure, but it erased from the records nearly all details of his youth.

He was born in Southampton County, Virginia, July 31, 1816, and spent his boyhood on a farm six miles southwest of the town of Jerusalem, now called Courtland. His parents, Elizabeth Rochelle and John Thomas, were married February 9, 1808, in Southampton County by Joseph Gurley, an Episcopal clergyman. Six girls and three boys were born to them. His father died of a farm accident on February 19, 1829, at approximately forty-five years of age. His mother died January 27, 1856, at the age of sixty-eight. Her death, too, was apparently accidental.

The Thomas home, now known as Thomaston, is a mile or so west of the Nottoway River, not far from the North Carolina boundary. The residence today is one of the most pretentious in the neighborhood, shaded by a magnificent oak. The foundations indicate that the house originally consisted of two rooms on the first floor and one on the second. The room in which George was born was the smaller of the downstairs rooms, measuring about nine feet by eleven. The kitchen at that time was housed in a separate building. The bricks used in the two-foot thick foundation walls were made on the place and the oversize pine sills and joists were hand sawed. Both jobs were done by slaves. The first addition to this house, which doubled the living space, must have been made about the time George was born. A second addition, which again doubled the living space, was made possibly before 1831.

In the year of George's birth, John Thomas, with the aid of Edmond Spencer and nine taxable slaves, was working 438 acres. In addition to the acreage and slaves, his taxable estate comprised six draught animals and one two-wheeled riding chair. By the time of his death his estate had more than doubled. He was neither the wealthiest man in St. Luke's parish nor the poorest. He was probably a hard worker. He held the confidence and esteem of his neighbors and was a member of the political faction that controlled Southampton County. With farming he combined the profession of accounting. In at least one of these activities—probably in both—he was successful. He carried his share of the burden of making local government work. Undoubtedly the example he set young George was a combination of integrity, industry, patience and dependability. These are not glamorous attributes. Their possession often carries with it a lack of joyousness and an inability to create or to partake of the froth of life.

His mother's contribution to George's character is not so clear. In the records of early Virginia, no minute books recorded the details of family life. No order books set forth the customs of local society. No property lists registered the growth of family assets in terms of human behavior. No records were ever kept to show how the traditional lightness of Elizabeth Thomas' French touch leavened the introspective virtues of her Welsh husband. For more than a quarter of a century after her husband's death, Elizabeth met the expenses of the family and created a modest addition to the family assets. She carried her brood safely through the Nat Turner uprising.

Her grandfather was a Huguenot who emigrated to Virginia in 1690. Her father married Judith Gilliam, one of the beauties of Southside Virginia. Elizabeth was one of their nine children. Two of her brothers, James and Clement, lived in Southampton County at the time young George was growing up. James was undoubtedly one of the foremost figures of the community. As its clerk, he was the chief executive officer of the county. Some of the national figures of the day corresponded with him. His local friends, while traveling, kept him in touch with matters political and economic. The tenth president of the United States was glad to have one of his sons marry James Rochelle's daughter. What this Huguenot blood contributed to George Thomas' character is now conjecture, but the Rochelle name was highly thought of in Virginia and the family connections were of great value to George's early career.

The Nottoway River, with its smooth, strong current, was the principal feature of that part of Southside Virginia. Being navigable to small boats nearly as far upstream as Jerusalem, it provided easy egress to the south—toward Albemarle Sound and the Dismal Swamp. Farm produce went down this stream and trade goods came back. Escaped slaves heading for the haven of the Dismal Swamp found an easier, safer flight route along its lower reaches than over the upland roads where telltale signs would be left at every soft spot. In addition, the Nottoway tended, in the early days, to break up Southampton County into small units. The river's backwaters everywhere laced the flat, yellow, arable lands with heavily brushed cypress swamps which had to be avoided by the traveler until they were filled or bridged. It was a country that discouraged its dwellers from congregating. It forced them to get along with what they had or could make for themselves, and made them self-reliant. In those who successfully met this challenge, self-confidence was nourished until it became a notable characteristic.

The Nottoway River may also have been the main reason why the Southside Virginians turned their backs upon the glamorous plantation area of the Tidewater. They never came within the orbit of that part of Virginia's culture and magnificence. In space the two were only fifty miles apart. In time the difference was a hundred years. But the end products of each were nearly equal.

Two crises are known to have occurred during Thomas' youth. The first, occasioned by the death of his father, came when he was twelve years old. It was met promptly by his mother, who kept the farm going, secured the remission of taxes on two of her infirm slaves and sold off some of the land to take care of the more pressing debts. Her brother James handled the details of the land sale and found a job as deputy county clerk for her son John, then nine months married. The second crisis came two years later. It was the Southampton Insurrection, when the slaves, under Nat Turner, rose against their masters. Sixty-nine years later, Judith and Fanny Thomas, sisters of George, retold the story of how they were warned of the approach of the armed slaves; how their mother hitched up a team and attempted to drive her children to Jerusalem for protection; how the slaves threatened to frustrate her plan and finally how she abandoned the carriage and led her family on foot through the pine and oak ridges to the safety of the town.

But in this interview the name of George Henry Thomas was never mentioned. Nor is there any record of what he may have done to help the family over the hurdle of his father's death.

The educational facilities of Southampton County were equal to the demands of that time. The day of the public school in this area was still in the future, but some progressive neighbor was always available to furnish schooling in his own home for his family and make instruction available to the community. During Thomas' school days, two such public spirited citizens were Thomas Pretlow and James Parker.

Along with his book learning, Thomas acquired a practical education. In this he was self-taught. Because the family's cash revenues were meager and the price of store goods was high, most of the products required by the Thomases were made on the place by slave artisans. The only anecdote of his boyhood ever related by Thomas illustrates his devotion to the study of practical mechanics, but even more reveals his character. It does not deal with a dramatic adventure, but with a prosaic task which stamps its hero as a painstaking apprentice. During his boyhood, Thomas decided to appraise his powers of observation and manual dexterity by as severe a test as he could devise. He visited the harness shop and watched, step by step, the making of a saddle. Then, with only this experience to draw on, he built one for himself. In telling the story, Thomas understated his motive. He was proud of the results of the stiff test he gave himself but, for fear of appearing boastful, he disguised the point.

With such ability it is not surprising that Thomas had no trouble with his education. By the time he was nineteen he had exhausted the facilities of the local schools and his inclination ran to the study of law. There was no better place in Southampton County for such study than the office of the county clerk. The county court was responsible for law enforcement. It levied taxes, collected them and disbursed them. It was the chief administrative agency of the county and its clerk proved, recorded and registered its documents. All the court records, from pleadings to executions, flowed across his desk. It offered a broader opportunity for a student than the office of the busiest lawyer.

Thomas' uncle, James Rochelle, was dead, but there was no difficulty over the appointment as deputy county clerk. November 18, 1835, one month after Rochelle's successor assumed his office, George was sworn in as his deputy. The small brick building in which he went to work is used today as the vault for the county records. It is in a beautiful, well shaded spot midway between Courtland's main street and the Nottoway River and within a stone's throw of each.

Close beside it today, a monument to the soldiers of the Confederacy records that this tiny community supplied four companies of infantry, one squadron of cavalry and one battery of artillery to the Southern cause. But on the records of the Senate of the United States stands the opinion that this community's contribution to the Northern cause was a single individual who stood second to none in the Northern armies as a military leader and a man.[1]

Before Thomas had been three months at his new duties, John Y. Mason, who represented Southampton County in Congress, visited Jerusalem. He had been a deferential friend of James Rochelle, and was a surety on the bond of Rochelle's successor. He was undoubtedly well acquainted with the Thomas family if not with George himself. Whatever the reason, he offered the young deputy an appointment to West Point and the offer was accepted.

On March 1, 1836, Mason formally recommended the appointment to the Secretary of War in a letter wherein he described Thomas as of fine size, of excellent talents and having a good preparatory education. His age was given as several years younger than it actually was. Biographers have labored to find a connection between this appointment and the slave uprising of five years before. There would seem to have been none. The time lapse was too long and Mason's interest in the boy was too scant for Thomas to have been an object of popular or official solicitude. Less than four weeks later Mrs. Thomas signed her consent for her youngest son to bind himself to serve five years as a cadet in the United States Military Academy. A month later Thomas was at West Point and his acceptance of his conditional appointment as a cadet was in the mail.

These fragmentary facts are all that remain upon which to reconstruct the boyhood of George H. Thomas. They are scanty for two reasons. One was Thomas' reticence. He left no written record of his private life and refused inquirers the use of his private papers. As he put it in later years, "All that I did for my government are matters of history, but my private life is my own and I will not have it hawked about in print for the amusement of the curious."

The bitterness engendered by his part in the Civil War was the second reason. His home people were convinced that Thomas had sold his talents to the Yankees. His sisters even refused to acknowledge his existence. They would not permit the mention of his name in their presence. Most of the people in Southampton County followed the family's lead. His ostracism was so complete that inquiries in the vicinity of his boyhood home forty-six years after his death revealed none who remembered him. To Virginians he was a traitor. Outside of his traitorous acts they had no interest in him.

One laconic boyhood biography of Thomas was purportedly written by his sister Judith to a Philadelphia newspaper. "General Thomas," it stated, "had many friends, a comfortable home and a native state until he deserted them." She might have said, and probably truthfully, that as a boy George was as playful as a kitten; that he loved sugar; that he spent more of his play time with the Negro boys around the slave quarters than around his father's house; that he was constantly giving the slave boys presents, and that he tried to teach them how to read and write.[2]

2

West Point Cadetship

Thomas was eager to start his military career. He apparently made two trips to West Point between the first of March and the first of June. On one of them he stopped in Washington to thank his sponsor, but Mason's sour and pessimistic greeting must have dampened the boy's enthusiasm.

Whether Thomas realized it or not, West Point was then the foremost engineering school in the country. Its graduates had a choice between two professions springing from the same education—engineering and soldiering—one constructive, the other essentially destructive. It is a matter of record that engineering appealed to the Northern cadets more than to those from the South. In later years Thomas appraised the school in these words: "I venture unhesitatingly to say . . . that no other institution of learning in the country has contributed more to the advancement of science and literature than the Military Academy at West Point."

In those days, West Point was an easy school to get into. The entrance requirements were not high enough to bar a boy whose father was too poor to send him to school or whose education had been limited by the location of his pioneer home. But its early administrators had set high educational standards, and it was not an easy school to stay in. To an undisciplined boy with little interest in scientific studies it was not a pleasant place.

The entrance examination, given about the middle of June in 1836, was confined to reading a few passages of prose or verse, writing a few sentences on the blackboard from dictation and working out, again at the blackboard, a few elementary arithmetical problems. At about this time Thomas and the other candidates were measured, weighed and examined for physical blemishes.

On June 21, all the candidates were arranged in a line facing an officer who read an order stating, "The following named individuals, candidates for admission into the Military Academy, having been examined by the Academic Board and found duly qualified, are conditionally admitted as cadets into the Military Academy, to rank as such from the first of July next." Raising his eyes, he continued, "When you hear your name called, step three paces forward." Well toward the end of the alphabetical list of seventy-one, Thomas heard his name and stepped forward.

With these three steps Thomas ceased to be a civilian. His life from now on was ordered by military regulations and he was held strictly accountable for every delinquency. Specified textbooks channeled his mental processes just as rigidly as military routine compartmentalized his time. At the same time, his life was broadened by contacts, either official or social, with some of the leading dignitaries of his lusty young country, and with cadets from every part of the Union representing every shade of political and social opinion, by the historically rich locale of West Point, and by a curriculum frankly patterned after the most advanced French and Swiss schools.

He was given a list of clothing and ordered to purchase the items necessary to complete his wardrobe. He was assigned to a mess squad, marched to and from his meals, told where to sit at table and when, told not to talk unnecessarily during meals, not to address the waiter, told when to rise from the table. Yet if, in his opinion, the butter was unpalatable or the meat tainted or insufficient there was a remedy available to him. This he was told about, too. His rights and privileges were protected as scrupulously as his derelictions were punished.

His pay was twenty-eight dollars per month. His rations cost him twelve dollars. A monthly stoppage of two dollars was made for books and drawing instruments, another of the same amount for the purchase of uniforms and equipment upon graduation. Only in exceptional cases did he get his hands on any of the balance. He bought an account book in which he recorded the detail of every purchase. Periodically this book was audited by the superintendent. On his approval, the treasurer paid the debts and Thomas' record was cleared. He was not permitted to receive any money from home, nor sell any clothing, books or equipment, nor contract any debt without the superintendent's permission, nor keep a waiter nor a horse nor a dog, insult a sentinel by word or gesture, answer for another at roll call, send or accept a challenge to fight with deadly weapons, nor upbraid another for declining to fight. In all, there were 304 separate regulations covering 53 pages. Most of them were "shall nots." In addition, his conduct and the routine of his life were ordered by the general army regulations and by the rules and articles of war—three volumes in the aggregate forming a book as thick as a dictionary.

In July 1836 the plebes (freshmen) were ordered into camp to orient themselves to their new way of life. The third and first classes went with them. The second class, except for a few unfortunates, was on leave. Going into camp meant moving out of the barracks, marching northeast four or five hundred yards, setting up tents in orderly rows over wooden floors, and moving in for the months of July and August. Thomas shared his quarters in South Barracks with Stewart Van Vliet, twenty-one years old from New York state, and William Tecumseh Sherman, sixteen years old from Ohio.

During the two months of camp the cadets were drilled in military formations and routines. No studying was done except by a few who obtained permission to take preparatory work under one of the academy instructors. The plebe at first was put into a squad without arms and taught the facings and squad movements. He learned how to wear his uniform, how to keep it in proper condition, what to do at the various commands and the proper tempo for doing them. Later he received a flintlock musket a little lighter than the arm issued to the troops and with a shorter barrel and smaller caliber, learned how to load, aim and fire it, how to keep it clean and how to care for his other equipment and his tent. At the same time he learned the manual of arms and the duties of a sentinel and was assigned to guard duty eight hours out of every twenty-four. This meant that he rarely got eight hours of uninterrupted sleep.

It was especially during the tours of night guard duty that the plebes received a great deal of unofficial attention from the old cadets. The plebe sentinels became the butts of all sorts of practical jokes. Occasionally someone would take this horseplay personally and physical collisions resulted. Thomas once threw one of these jokers out of his room. The penalties for fighting and its formal counterpart, dueling, were heavy but the records are full of arrests for fighting and of punishments assessed against the offenders. The regulations attempted to provide a safety valve for these excess animal spirits by encouraging the cadets

to demand a board of inquiry when their character was impugned or
their honor sullied.

At the end of August, the tents were struck and the cadets moved
into the barracks—inconvenient, cold, ill-arranged, overcrowded struc-
tures, unfit for the purposes for which they were designed. The second
classmen returned and classes began. The change was celebrated by a
cotillion. Nearly six hundred cadets and their guests danced until 3:00
A.M. to music by the post band.

Thomas and his two roommates occupied a room on the south side
of South Barracks. It was approximately eight feet by ten, heated by an
open fireplace, lighted by three candles, meagerly furnished with a
table, three straight-backed chairs, a looking glass, wash stand, wash
basin, pitcher, pail, broom and scrubbing brush. Each bed was rolled
inside a canvas cover in the daytime. After tattoo at night, the cadet
unrolled it on the floor and turned in. He was supposed to be in bed
with his candle out at taps. Water came from a pump outside the barracks. If hot water was wanted it was heated at the fire. Thomas took
his bath out of the wash basin and then cleaned up his own splashings.
There were demerits for sweeping these splashing into the hall. Fear
of retaliation prevented him from leaving a wet spot where a roommate's bed would be unrolled. Slops were emptied into the bucket
and the bucket was emptied into the latrine, which was located behind
an enormous pile of fire wood. It was as close to the barracks as sanitary
rules would permit and, when guards were posted, each cadet reported
his use of it. Winter nights such trips were not popular so whenever
possible the cadets took advantage of the narrow porches outside their
rooms, a custom repugnant to the sentries and the passing post officers.

Each cadet was charged with the care of his own gear. They took
weekly turns as room orderly. An order tacked on the inside of their
door specified the place and arrangement of every article. Rooms were
inspected at least twice a day to see that these orders were obeyed. One
of the most important duties of the room orderly was to see that the
heavy iron fender was put in front of the fire when the room was vacant.
Despite this mandate, fires were frequent, but the well trained bucket
brigades kept them under control. Once a week all the roommates
turned to, scrubbed the floors, washed the woodwork, dusted and
generally spruced up. Their handiwork was inspected by the commandant of cadets. If he was like many such inspecting officers he ran
his white-gloved fingers over the more inaccessible surfaces for definite
proof that the housecleaning was well done.

At dawn the cadets were aroused by the sound of drum and bugle.

By sunrise they had answered roll call, cleaned their muskets and accoutrements and stood room inspection. From then on, except for one short recreation period, study alternated with recitation. At 9:30 tattoo was sounded, a final inspection was made of the cadet rooms and at 10:00 all lights were out.

All violations of the regulations that were discovered were punished. In answer to charges made against him the accused was permitted to file a written excuse. If satisfactory, the charge was withdrawn. If not, he was tried by a court martial and punishment inflicted in accordance with its findings. For the more severe offenses, the violator was put under arrest. Technically this meant that he was confined to his room and went to his meals under guard. He attended classes, however, but was restricted to certain areas of the post. The superintendent tried and punished cadets for lesser offenses. His punishment generally consisted of additional guard duty. For being late once at reveille roll call Thomas got off with the lightest punishment, one hour of ordinary, or weekday, guard duty. Extra guard duty was imposed on Saturdays or holidays for more serious infractions. All punishments carried with them, however, a certain number of demerits which were posted to the cadet's record and reduced his final class standing. If they totaled more than two hundred in a year the cadet was dismissed. Most offenses were breaches of military rules. In the records that are still available for Thomas' class, the major penalties were given for disobedience of orders, fighting, drinking, and gambling. None involving moral turpitude was recorded. Infractions of the strict code of personal honor were frequently punished by the cadets themselves without waiting for a court martial. Such action generally resulted in the resignation of the accused cadet, so the official records remained startlingly free of major breaches of discipline. During his first year, Thomas collected twenty demerits.

But cadet life for Thomas was not all work and punishment. Swimming, skating, dancing, hiking, football and such indoor games as chess and backgammon were all legitimate pastimes, but they were rigidly controlled as to time, place and duration. Then there were the forbidden pastimes which caused many of the offenses that appeared on the punishment book. Chief among these were off-limits visits to the local inns, swimming at the wrong time and place, foraging (West Point slang for stealing fruit, poultry and edibles of all sorts for midnight snacks before the open fire in some cadet's room), card playing and visiting. The latter was a crime only when indulged in at unauthorized times—generally after lights out.

The differences between the North and the South, although a quarter of a century away from open rupture, were even at this time noticeable to at least one of Thomas' cadet acquaintances. "Many of the cadets," he observed, "especially those from the slavery states, have a great contempt for our Yankee farmers, and even pretend to compare them with their slaves. They have the greatest contempt for all those who gain a subsistence by the sweat of their brows." [1] Richard Stoddert Ewell, Thomas' classmate and a Virginian, sounded a note of jealousy. "There are several Yankees here," he complained, "who know the whole mathematical course. Of course they will stand at the head of the class. A person who comes here without a knowledge [of mathematics] has to contend against those who have been preparing themselves for years under the best teachers and who have used the same class books. The Yankees certainly take the lead in almost every class." [2] That Ewell spoke more from prejudice than from fact is evidenced by the scholastic attainments of Cadet Paul Octave Hebert of Louisiana, who graduated first in the class of 1840—a slave state resident who consistently showed his scholastic heels to the Yankees.

Class work started immediately after the cadets moved into barracks. The cadets were divided into sections of from twelve to fifteen men each and were marched to and from classes by the best student in each section, called the marcher. As the course progressed, the cadets were transferred from one section to another, until the first section, under the direct tutelage of the ranking professor, contained the best students in that particular study. The members of the last section were understandably called the "goats."

This section system automatically graded the cadets on scholastic ability. It provided a group small enough so that each cadet could have individual instruction at each meeting of the class. Most important, it enabled the instructor to give each cadet a thorough examination daily in his assigned work. Each cadet was required to give a daily demonstration of each subject at the blackboard, an infallible test of his preparation. Thomas was reported to have been one of the most imperturbable of men, but his classmates saw him go pale with suffering when he could not do his work at the blackboard.

Thomas took two studies during his plebe year, French and mathematics, but the mathematics covered algebra, geometry, trigonometry, the application of algebra to geometry, and mensuration, so actually he studied six courses. Assignments were heavy. The 390-page algebra textbook, for example, was covered in five weeks.

Thomas' first section assignment was, of course, arbitrary, but as the scholastic year moved along he began to evidence the slow, steady, unostentatious progress that was characteristic of his entire life.

Albert E. Church, who taught Thomas mathematics, was the only faculty member to leave an appraisal of him. "He never allowed anything to escape a thorough examination and left nothing behind that he did not fully comprehend," said Church.

In January 1837 Thomas passed his midyear examinations, received his warrant as a cadet and signed the articles pledging himself to five years of service. His scholastic showing, coupled with his soldierly appearance, general aptitude and good conduct, resulted a few days before his June examinations in his appointment as corporal, the highest rating open to a third classman. He proudly took his uniform coats to the post tailor, where two chevrons of one-half inch gold lace were sewed on each sleeve below the elbow with their points up.

June examinations were more formal than those in January. Both were oral and both were held before the academic board, which at that time was made up of assistant professors of mathematics, natural philosophy and engineering. But when Thomas stood before the academic board in June, he found the room crowded with strangers. They were members of the board of visitors, officially appointed each year to inspect and report upon the Military Academy. Thomas' textbooks had been placed before the visitors and they were invited to choose the portion for his examination and to put to him such questions as they might select.

In June of 1837, Thomas, Van Vliet and Sherman were moved out of their room to make way for the incoming class of cadets, which they must now drill, discipline and supervise. In a few weeks the battalion moved into camp and Thomas' class, now old cadets, took up their traditional role of baiting the plebes. The plaintive tone of the plebe letters and diaries of that day, however, arose more from homesickness and the irritations and discomforts of a new routine than from any mistreatment at the hands of the old cadets.

As the eleventh ranking corporal in the battalion, Thomas' responsibilities were broadened to cover the military smartness and efficiency of a squad of his brother cadets. Here he learned that rank of itself does not make a military commander. To gain the confidence of his men the commander must earn his authority. This was a lesson Thomas never forgot.

So far as can be learned, Thomas and his roommates continued to live in South Barracks during the winter of their second year. Now their room was on the north side overlooking the Plain and a breathtaking view of the Hudson where it cut through Storm King Mountain.

His studies, too, were expanded. Military instruction covered the school of the company, the duties of a corporal and preliminary work in artillery. Classroom work included analytical geometry, integral and differential calculus, French and drawing. It may have included geography, grammar and rhetoric, but no marks were given in these subjects. Thomas' instructor in artillery was Lieutenant Robert Anderson.

In December 1837 there occurred one of those odd outgrowths of the West Point honor system so intriguing to the non-military mind. Cadets Gardiner, Thompson and Sevey of Thomas' class were placed under arrest for gambling. When the entire membership of their class and the one below it pledged themselves to refrain from gambling, the arrest was lifted. This code was generous to the cadet who respected it but unrelenting to its transgressor. There is a story told of a later class that voluntarily donated the cash to take up the bad debts of one of its members, while a committee appointed by the class secured the cheat's written resignation and put him on the train for home.

A partial list of Thomas' delinquencies, probably from April 22, 1838, to April 25, 1840, has been preserved on page 129 of Punishment Book Number 1834, kept in the West Point Library. It reads:

April	22	Late at Reveille	1 demerit
April	29	Introducing citizens in quarters 5 & 6 P.M.	5 "
May	13	Visiting north side of S.B. [South Barracks] 8 & 9 P.M.	5 "
May	28	Loitering 7 & 8	2 "
June	7	Floor not swept 5½ & 6 A.M.	3 "
June	9	Ord. [Orderly] Room not policed 5½ & 6 A.M.	3 "
Oct.	4	Absent from drill roll call	3 "
Dec.	24	Out of bed after taps	3 "
Mar.	13	Not in bed at taps	3 "
April	7	Neglect duty as file closer not reporting men looking to rear at inspection	3 "
April	15	Late at 2, class parade	1 "
May	21	Visiting study hours 9 & 10 A.M.	5 "
July	9	Late at tatoo roll call	1 "
July	9	Late at reveille	1 "
Sept.	10	Coat not buttoned at 4 & 5 P.M.	1 "
Feb.	15	Visiting 12 & 1 P.M.	5 "
Feb.	17	Late at 8, Class Par.[ade]	1 "
April	25	Visiting 11 & 12 P.M.	5 "

History has labeled Thomas as a wooden, unemotional, unfriendly recluse. But the penalty of three demerits for a Christmas Eve offense hints that this appraisal may be wrong. Half of the eighteen criminalities reported above are for tardiness and visiting. Yet throughout his military career Thomas was noted for his punctuality and his disinclination to initiate social contacts. It is possible that the visiting was not social but was concerned with classroom work, which would partly reconcile his cadet and his later-day habits.

The three demerits for neglect of duty on April 7, 1839, are worth some attention. West Point regulations demanded that cadets acting as sentinals, file closers, marchers, carvers, etc., report the military and disciplinary breaches of their fellow students. At this time Thomas was a sergeant and officially responsible for certain of the actions of his men. This regulation which, in a way, made tale bearing mandatory, put many a cadet in a dilemma. The board of visitors, in their report for 1837, recognized this embarrassment and went on record as opposed to the application of this rule to a court martial. Thomas may have been slovenly in the performance of his duty and deserved the demerits. On the other hand, he may have noticed some mitigating circumstance and taken the blame himself rather than let it fall upon his subordinates. If the latter be true, it evidences an aptitude for command, a subject in which Thomas later excelled.

By June 1838, two years had passed since Thomas and his classmates had begun their professional training. Those who had not received more than 150 demerits for the year, and whose parents requested it, were granted a furlough during the period of the summer encampment. On June 23, 1838, Thomas left for his home. Prior to his departure, the Academy treasurer advanced him the cash needed for his trip. This furlough was one of the few occasions in a cadet's career when he received cash instead of credit.

The change in physical environment from the rocky heights and bracing air of the Catskills to the loamy, level tidelands of Virginia, shimmering in the heat waves and oppressively humid, was no greater than the change from the self-serving barrack life of West Point to the slave-served life of the well-to-do Southern family. This contrast may have had some effect on Thomas, because his class standing during the ensuing year was lower than at any other time and he was given more demerits than in any other year. He returned to the Academy at the end of August in time to join the battalion in its removal to barracks. He and his roommates were probably quartered now in North Barracks. Here the rooms were nearly twice as large as those in South Barracks and more efficiently heated.

The curriculum, too, for the second classmen was enlarged and broadened. It embraced natural and experimental philosophy (physics), optics, magnetism and electricity, astronomy, chemistry, drawing, school of the battalion, duties of sergeants, and instruction in artillery.

West Point's specialization in science and mathematics made it a school based on textbook work where outside reading was not necessary for a satisfactory mark in the day's recitation. Withdrawals of library books could be made only during two hours a week and were limited to books calculated to assist the cadets in their classroom work. In addition, there was a widespread belief, both in the army and out of it, that reading was neither manly nor soldierly. In February 1839, Thomas drew his first book from the library. It was Williams' *Florida*. At this time the army was seeing active service in that state. The year before Thomas entered the Academy, Major Francis L. Dade and his detachment had been wiped out by the Seminole Indians of Florida. It is probable that Thomas, with his habitual foresightedness, was preparing himself against the time when he might be ordered there. One month later, Thomas withdrew Thomson's *Botany,* indicative of his lifelong interest in this science.

Years after Thomas had left the imprint of his genius upon the national history, a commentator said that there had been no trace in him of a responsiveness to literature, art or the beauty of nature.

Following his midyear examination in January 1839, Thomas was appointed one of eighteen cadet sergeants and assigned to Company A. He had been eligible for this appointment the preceding June. It may be that a temporary slackness in his work and conduct caused this delay in his promotion.

Shortly after June examinations, he received his appointment as cadet lieutenant and was assigned to Company C. All through his final year, he wore three chevrons of single gold lace on each arm above the elbow with their points up. This designated him as one of the eighteen cadet officers assigned that year to the battalion.

During the summer encampment, Thomas received instruction in riding and fencing. But the riding instruction carried none of the glamour generally associated with the cavalry. The wide-seated, embossed dragoon saddles were ill suited to the smaller frames of the cadets. Unable to brace themselves effectively against the movements of the horse, the cadets were chafed until their legs bled.

It is possible that about this time Thomas gave up the blanket laid on the floor that had been his bed for more than three years. If he obtained one of the new iron bed stands, he was charged a rental of twenty cents per month for its use and an additional amount to cover any repairs that had to be made on it. There were other signs, too, of a changing world. The article of clothing worn by Thomas to cover his legs now became known officially as "trowsers" instead of pantaloons and he was permitted to use a lamp instead of a candle.

The studies prescribed for the first classmen looked easy, but the cadets found this supposition wrong. They covered the evolutions of the line, duties of commissioned officers, infantry tactics, artillery, geology and mineralogy, engineering, science of war, rhetoric, moral philosophy, political science, and the use of the sword.

Dennis Hart Mahan, thirty-six-year-old professor of civil and military engineering and the father of Alfred Thayer Mahan, probably had a greater influence upon Thomas than any other member of the West Point faculty. Mahan had spent four years in Europe and had studied at the French engineering and artillery school in Metz. For lack of suitable textbooks in his chosen subjects, Mahan, at the beginning of his teaching career, supplied lithographed notes of his lectures so clear and meaty that they were adopted as texts by other schools in the United States and exerted their influence abroad. From these notes, formal textbooks were later prepared. Thomas' class used Mahan's notes on military science, which were lithographed in 1835.[3] The French, mathematics and science taught the cadets for their first three years were the foundation for Mahan's courses.

In his class in the science of war, Mahan taught the elements of strategy, ways and means of moving men and supplies to "validate the selected strategic conception," and the tactics needed to translate the strategy into victory. He stressed the seven principles necessary to an operation with superior forces against a decisive point: (1) Assume the initiative. (2) Direct the attack against the enemy's weak point. (3) Attack only against one wing unless the attacking forces are so superior that all cannot be brought into action against one wing. (4) Force the enemy to secure his position by detaching troops so that his principal mass is weakened. (5) When masses are concentrated bring them into action with effect. (6) Give a defeated army no rest. Frederick and Napoleon never fought for paltry towns and villages, it was pointed out, but fought to destroy utterly all means of further resistance. A general who fights with any other view may win the field but he will never gain an advantage to his country. (7) Officers must inspire confidence in themselves and emulation of themselves; all troops are brave when their leaders set them the example. The soldier must have confidence in the wisdom and talents of his commander and in the valor of his comrades, and the commander must make himself loved, esteemed and feared. Not many of Mahan's students realized the importance of principles six and seven.

The classroom work in political science caused the bitterest discussion about the West Point curriculum. Publicists have claimed that West Pointers were taught Rawle's theory that the Union was dissoluble and that if it were dissolved allegiance reverted to the state. Secretary of War Cameron in 1861 threw the whole matter into political controversy by asking whether the widespread treachery of the Southern West Pointers might not have been promoted by a defect in West Point's system of education. Left-wing Republicans grabbed the intimation and built it into an accusation that the Military Academy caused the rebellion. Apparently Rawle's theory was taught, but only in the year 1826. It was not taught to Thomas' class. If that be true, the only West Pointer so taught who rose to prominent command in the Rebel army was Albert Sidney Johnston.

Thomas' quiet pursuit of his studies throughout the winter of 1839-40 was interrupted by a threat to abolish West Point which took the form of a bill introduced into Congress. The school was continually under suspicion by the public, which feared the establishment of a military clique. The bill was defeated, but some of the cadets were understandably upset.

In June the final standings for the whole four years of work were published and Thomas ranked as twelfth in his class. Class standing, in that day, did not rule promotion. Thomas' promotion in the early part of his military career was based upon his seniority in his regiment and later in his arm of the service. During the Civil War, promotion of general officers was at the discretion of the President.

Thomas was never under arrest during his four years at West Point. This means that he was never accused of any serious breach of military discipline. He never asked for a court of inquiry to clear his reputation or to rectify a personal affront. Nor is there any record that he was involved in any such inquiry brought by another cadet.

The members of Thomas' graduating class were picked men, thoroughly screened by four years of difficult study, the demerit system, and the West Pointer's code of honor. They knew they were receiving a specialized engineering training worth, in civilian life, from $5,000 to $15,000 a year. They knew that the market for their services was growing rapidly and that their diploma made them preferred applicants for the choicest jobs. They were not in the mood to jeopardize this opportunity by scholastic failure or disciplinary penalty. The exhibitionists, the perennial juveniles and the young men-about-town were the ones who were generally in trouble. Their names, as a consequence, appeared most frequently in the records.

Thomas' progress had been steady and continuous. He was quiet, industrious, thorough, and did a better than average job. He refused to show off his physical or his mental assets. After his death, when biographers were combing his record for color and anecdotes, one of them wrote to Stewart Van Vliet asking his help. Van Vliet's reply was significant. He could recall only one incident, that in which Thomas threw a practical joker out of his room.

The evening of the day his course was completed, Thomas called at the adjutant's office and picked up his diploma—his credentials to violence. At the end of June he was relieved of duty at the Military Academy and ordered home. He was recommended for a commission as second lieutenant in the United States Army and President Van Buren acted favorably upon the recommendation. On July 1, 1840, he was assigned to Company H of the Third Regiment of Artillery and was ordered to report to Fort Columbus on Governor's Island in New York Harbor on or before September 30, 1840.

3

The Seminole War and Garrison Duty

Thomas reported to Governor's Island on September 25, nearly a week ahead of time. He learned that the Third Regiment of Artillery was fighting as infantry in small detachments scattered along the Florida coast. The regiment needed 300 replacements to bring its numbers up to war strength. These were being recruited at Fort Monroe, Lynchburg and Fort McHenry. Fort Columbus was the head-quarters for the recruiting service. When Thomas arrived, he found officers from most of the artillery companies, who were collecting men for their own units or for general service. Among them were Braxton Bragg, Joseph Hooker and F. O. Wyse, all of whom he had known at West Point. Wyse was the first lieutenant of Company D, to which Thomas had been reassigned in August.

Fort Wood, on Bedloe's Island, was the principal recruiting depot. The raw recruits were forwarded there to be set up as soldiers and drilled. This was Thomas' job and he was put at it as soon as he re-ported. Here he spent the first month and a half of his career as an army officer.[1] It is probable that he was in command of the recruits intended for Company D. He mustered, inspected and drilled them, appointed lance sergeants and corporals, and read the Articles of War to them each week.

By the middle of November, Thomas was at sea with 205 recruits on their way to war. Their destination was Fort Lauderdale with stops at Savannah and St. Augustine.

The settlement of Fort Lauderdale was small, primitive and dirty. It consisted of a cluster of cane-built huts and a few wigwams. One room with a thatched roof resting on cane walls and a floor of rough boards laid on the sand served as quarters for an officer. A similar but larger hut housed the officers' mess. Two unplaned planks resting on stakes driven into the sand formed the mess table. Blocks of wood were used for seats. Table furniture consisted of tin plates, pewter spoons, rusty knives and two-tined forks. A typical breakfast was coffee without milk, brown sugar, hard bread, buckwheat cakes and rancid butter. For dinner, bean soup and salt pork replaced the buckwheat cakes and commissary whisky was substituted for the coffee.

Shortly after Thomas arrived, the regimental commander made an inspection of Fort Lauderdale and directed that a scout be made once a month for the purpose of combing the country around the Indians' old camps. In a campaign through such country the problem was transport and supply and, as though to set a pattern for future campaigns, the problem began to fall into Thomas' lap. In short order he acquired the responsibilities of commissary, quartermaster, adjutant and ordnance officer. During the first six of these scouts, Thomas' monotonous staff work kept him in camp.

On June 22, however, Captain R. D. A. Wade assumed command of the post. Immediately Thomas went out on his first scout. A month later another scout was ordered but again Thomas' staff duties kept him in camp. He went along on the next four scouts, the second of which, in November 1841, made history.

Wade commanded this scout and Thomas was his second. Its objective was to capture seventy Seminoles who were resisting the government's efforts to transfer them to a reservation in the Indian Territory. The troops moved out in twelve canoes with provisions for fifteen days.[2] It was planned as a surprise attack. Their route was northward and it took them as far as the present city of Palm Beach. In Hillsboro Inlet they captured a lone Seminole fisherman who was induced to lead the troops to his village fifteen miles west. This they reached in the morning after an overland march. Here they surprised and captured twenty Indians and six muskets and destroyed fourteen canoes and all the stores that could be found. Eight Indians were killed. Troops and prisoners returned to their canoes that same forenoon and proceeded northward to the orange grove haulover where camp was made that night. Next morning the command continued northward, but after traveling three miles, the water became too shallow for the canoes. Camp was established and canoes and prisoners were left in charge of the post surgeon, who was the third officer on the scout, and a camp guard. The rest of the party took up the line of march through deep bog and saw grass, pine barren, hammock and cypress swamp. Their objective was another village thirty miles to the north. Again their guide was a captured Indian. The attack, this time made at dusk, was a complete surprise and was perfectly executed. The following morning the troops began their return march to their canoes. On the way, they destroyed another canoe, a field of pumpkins and an old hut on the shore of Lake Worth.

As Indian raids went in this feckless war, this one was successful. Wade had solved the problem of locating the enemy by the use of captured warriors. He might have been led into an ambush and lost his entire command, strung out as they were in single file and waist deep in mud and water. It was a calculated risk and it worked. But what was more important to Thomas' military career was that it proved the workability of the plan of operation devised by Colonel William Jenkins Worth, in over-all command of the Seminole War, who pressed its success upon his superiors in justification of his own strategy. The troops moved rapidly, achieved a tactical surprise and exploited it completely. Eight Seminoles were killed and sixty-three captured with thirteen muskets, twelve powder horns and quantities of buckshot and ball. Thirty canoes and a large collection of stores were destroyed. The troops had traveled about 150 miles. In his official report Captain Wade thanked Thomas for his valuable and efficient aid and Colonel Worth recommended him for the brevet rank of first lieutenant. The episode created quite a stir at the command level in the army. At least four reports and letters mentioning Thomas by name crossed the desks of the Adjutant General, the General-in-Chief and perhaps the Secretary of War.[3] Yet in spite of the Secretary's implied promise, Thomas' brevet was not granted for thirty-one months and it may have been only Worth's insistence that finally forced action. At any rate, Thomas had seized the first opportunity that came his way, eye-witnessed the efficacy of a complete follow-through to an attack, and achieved, in a little more than one year, an honorary advance in rank that normally would have required four years or more. In addition, he shared the professional leadership of his class and was a marked man among the army subalterns.

Thomas' account of this affair makes no reference to his own part in the action nor to the official recognition accorded it. "I was on the expedition under Maj. Wade," he wrote in 1859, in reply to a query about his part in the Florida War, "which captured something like sixty-nine or seventy Indians." The unwritten law of the Virginia gentleman abhorred bragging, and Thomas was one of its devotees. He failed to mention that during part of the raid, he kept a musket pointed at the back of a hostile guide wondering who was being betrayed—the Seminoles or the army.

Less than three months before this scout, Worth had sent a confidential order to all of his district commanders offering a bounty for every Indian killed or captured. The blood money earned by Wade's detachment would have been $1,790.

When Thomas returned to Fort Lauderdale from his fifth and last raid, he found a new captain in command of Company D. He was Erasmus Darwin Keyes, a socially inclined, observant and articulate New Englander. He first saw Thomas as he stepped ashore from a canoe at the conclusion of a two-week scout. He must have been wet, muddy, bearded, well greased for protection against mosquitoes, and bone tired. Thomas served as one of Keyes' subalterns for two years and in that time Keyes learned much of his character. Keyes described the young officer as he came to know him in those days. He was twenty-six years old, six feet in height, in form perfectly symmetrical inclining to plumpness, with a blonde complexion, and large, deep blue eyes. The shape and carriage of Thomas' head and the expression on his handsome face reminded Keyes of a partrician of ancient Rome. He had an even temperament, was never violently demonstrative, seldom much in advance of the appointed time in arriving at his post of duty, never late, never impatient, never in a hurry, having supreme self-possession yet devoid of arrogance. He received and gave orders with equal serenity, did his duty and kept his appointments precisely. His deportment was dignified. In the presence of strangers and casual acquaintances Thomas was reserved, yet he was social and possessed a subtle humor which showed itself in similes and illustrations of character. He was an accomplished officer. His turn of mind inclined him more to science than to literature and his reading was extensive and varied. But the qualities which exalted him were judgment, impartiality, and integrity. In all of these, Keyes observed, Thomas had no superior.

Tucked away in his description of the physical Thomas is an observation that is significant because it has been made by so many of the men who knew Thomas but has been explained by none. Keyes says that his own confidence in Thomas was at once complete, and he acted upon it by using Thomas' advice to fill in his own lack of knowledge about the practical side of a company commander's duties and to appraise the officers with whom he had to work. Several major Civil War figures were not impressed with this characteristic of Thomas'— Schofield because of jealousy, Grant (he and Thomas must always have circled each other stiff-leggedly like suspicious dogs), and Sherman, who was just as erratic in this reaction as he was in so many others. But the immediate result of this facet of Thomas' personality was to make him the recipient of ever-widening duties and responsibilities.

Thomas' humor, as described by Keyes, was the result of his faculty for observation combined with his bent for connecting what he observed with something utterly dissimilar. His location of a slovenly officer at the geometrical intersection of two lines of tobacco-stained spit was typical, even though a little too subtle for the appreciation of an army camp.

Less than three weeks after Keyes reported to Fort Lauderdale, the Third Regiment of Artillery was ordered out of Florida. Thomas moved with his company by sea. They reached New Orleans in February 1842 and stayed there nearly five months. Then a partial concentration of the Third Artillery was being made at Fort Moultrie in Charleston Harbor, and Company D was ordered to join it. They embarked on June 30 but failed to reach Moultrie for more than thirty days, having been becalmed on the way. Regimental headquarters were already established in the fort when they arrived. The remaining space had been pre-empted, so Company D made its quarters in the gun sheds outside the fort which had been remodeled into barracks. Bragg, who also came in late with his company, shared the gun sheds with them.

Charleston was the center of violent political discussion. This time it concerned the extension of slavery by the annexation of Texas. It took official warnings from their superior officers to keep the hotheads on both sides from airing their opinions too belligerently. Out of it came a distinct impression of Thomas which seems to have been held generally throughout the army. He loved Virginia and showed that the bias of his affections was toward the South. He was also warmly attached to the Union. He argued against secession and he was one of the fairest of the Southern officers in his judgment of Northerners. In this fiery throng, where duels were narrowly averted, Thomas was calm, just, sympathetic and genial.

In March of 1843, he received his long-deferred brevet of first lieutenant, but it was dated to take effect at the time of Wade's raid. Army regulations provided that a brevet entitled its holder to the pay of its rank as long as the holder discharged the duties of that rank. So

Thomas, having served as first lieutenant, charged the additional money into his pay accounts and the paymaster general's office promptly threw out his claim. Thomas protested and asked that the matter be referred to the Attorney General if the paymaster general did not see fit to uphold his protest.[4] The paymaster general's finding was reversed and Thomas got his extra pay. Seven years later the case of Lieutenant Thomas was being cited by the Adjutant General to help swell the pocketbook of some other underpaid subaltern. Thomas' pay as a second lieutenant was $25.00 a month with an additional allowance of eighty cents a day for rations. He was allowed one servant and $2.50 a month for the servant's clothing. If he had been mounted he could have drawn $8.00 a month for forage, but Company D had not been mounted since Thomas had been assigned to it. When he acted as adjutant, Thomas received an extra $10.00 a month.

While on his holiday leave in December 1843, Thomas was transferred to Light Company C at Fort McHenry, Baltimore. He found there Captain Samuel Ringgold, First Lieutenants E. J. Steptoe and W. H. Shover, and Second Lieutenant R. S. Ripley. From the army's point of view, Baltimore was socially one of the most desirable posts in the country. But this assignment was even more desirable from a professional point of view. It was Thomas' first assignment to a fully equipped battery.

The artillery, once the favored arm of the service, had lost its prestige. It had come under the control of the ordnance department and the staff had swallowed the line. Under staff control the artillery had functioned as garrisons for forts along the Atlantic coast and the shores of the Great Lakes. It had lost all feeling of unity. During the Florida War it had fought as infantry. While Thomas was at West Point a strong effort was being made to break this bureaucratic stranglehold. An old act of Congress designating the formation of one company of light artillery for each artillery regiment was seized upon. These companies were mounted during Thomas' second year in the Military Academy and were equipped as light batteries. They were also called flying batteries and later field batteries. Through them, the artillery began to take ceremonial precedence over all other arms.

Captain Ringgold, the leader in this movement, had studied artillery organization and tactics in France and England. He had selected and trained the officers that were to command the other three light batteries —Braxton Bragg, Randolph Ridgely and John Marshall Washington. Thomas was now a hand-picked junior member of this group and he was to get his first training under Ringgold himself.

In March 1844, Thomas and Company C were in Washington, detailed as part of the honor escort for the funeral of five government officials killed by an accidental explosion aboard the *U.S.S. Princeton.* Thomas, with a crape band on his left arm and a bow of black on his sword hilt, rode with his battery ahead of the hearses. It is not unlikely that sometime during this month he was a guest at the White House. John Tyler, Jr., son of the President, was living in Washington as a member of his father's official family. His wife was Thomas' first cousin.

In July, Thomas was promoted to the rank of first lieutenant and in September he received a twenty-day leave, which gave him a chance to go home and show his new trappings to his friends. Less than a month after returning from this leave he was ordered to join Company E at Fort Moultrie. Bragg was acting as his new captain.

In February 1845, Thomas helped open a recruiting rendezvous in Charleston and remained on this duty a little less than a month. Within two weeks after rejoining his company he left on a seven-day leave. It was a good-bye leave. The regular army was concentrating in Texas for war with Mexico.

That country was being pressured into war by the territorial hunger of the American people. The hunger was mostly for slave territory to offset the free territory acquired by the Louisiana Purchase. The immediate objective was to insure the annexation of Texas. Even before the annexation took place Brevet Brigadier General Zachary Taylor was ordered to occupy Corpus Christi, a town at the mouth of the Nueces River in the area claimed by Mexico. Taylor's orders were to defend Texas from invasion, and the American interpretation of invasion covered many of the things Mexico would have to do to protect her own sovereignty. By autumn of 1845 Taylor had concentrated at Corpus Christi all but four regiments of the regular American army.

This was the first offensive war fought by the United States. To complicate the problem President James K. Polk elected to fight it on two widely separated fronts—southward across the Rio Grande and far to the west in southern California. In the United States' military perspective it was a rehearsal for the Civil War, still sixteen years in the future.

4

The Mexican War

Thomas' company commanded by Bragg reported, without its horses, to Taylor in New Orleans on July 19, 1845. Except for this company and one other, the Third Artillery fought without their guns. U. S. Grant was a subaltern in one of the infantry regiments.

While Thomas and his battery were sailing toward New Orleans, the Congressional resolution of annexation was accepted by Texas. In December 1845, while Thomas and the other subalterns at Corpus Christi were collecting the ingredients for their New Year's eggnog, Texas was admitted as a state. The following month Taylor's army was ordered to the Rio Grande.

Meanwhile Thomas' professional duties kept him busy.[1] His artillery horses were purchased from the Mexicans and had to be branded, broken and trained. His gun, gun carriage, limber, caisson, forge wagon, battery wagon, supplies and ammunition had been lightered ashore, most of them thoroughly soaked in the process. The gun was his first concern. It was made of bronze so rust was no worry, but he had to test the trunnions to see that they had not been bent by rough handling. He had to water-check the gun barrel for leakage. Axles were lubricated. Shot were gauged for size and dropped twenty feet onto an iron block to disclose hidden defects. Then they were lacquered for protection against rust. Powder came packed in hundred-pound barrels —oak, hickory or cedar staves with copper hoops, nailed with copper nails and closed with a screw plug and a leather washer steeped in beeswax. The barrels were broached and the powder measured into woolen bags. These were sewed, gauged and covered with paper cylinders for protection. Slow matches that burned at the rate of four inches an hour and quick matches with a burning rate of one yard in thirteen seconds were provided. The finished ammunition was stowed in the ammunition chests with an allotment of slow and quick match. Forge and battery wagons were packed in accordance with a standardized plan, so that the trained artilleryman in the dark, or during the stress of battle, could put his hand on the part he needed without fumbling. Thomas also wanted a furnace for heating his cannon balls to turn them into incendiary projectiles, but he didn't get it.

Taylor, in command of the United States field army, completed his plans early in March 1846 for his advance to the Rio Grande. He had selected the town of Matamoros as his objective. His base was Point Isabel at the mouth of the Rio Grande. To that place he shipped his supplies and equipment. The troops would march with their camp equipment, rations for the men, grain for the horses, and ammunition. Their route was across the flat coastal plain.

On March 8, Colonel David Emmanuel Twiggs, a Georgian with a high professional rating, moved out of Corpus Christi with the First Brigade, Army of Occupation. The other brigades followed in sequence. Thomas and Company E marched on the eleventh with the last brigade. By that date the entire army, numbering 2,500 men, was in motion. The march averaged fifteen miles a day. On the twenty-fourth, the army halted while the empty wagons went to Point Isabel for supplies. They returned shortly and on the twenty-eighth, Taylor's advance reached the Rio Grande opposite the fortified town of Matamoros. Work was begun on the fort that was to neutralize the Mexican stronghold and to open the Rio Grande to Taylor's transport.

In retaliation, General Arista, the Mexican commander, who had already burned Taylor's base, put his cavalry across the river, captured Hardee [2] with sixty-three American dragoons and threatened to cut Taylor's communications with Point Isabel. This was the overt act Washington had been waiting for and war was declared. But Taylor did not learn of the declaration until after he fought three battles.

To counter the Mexican threat, Taylor moved to cover his base, leaving one regiment of infantry and two companies of artillery under the command of Major Jacob Brown to defend the partly finished fort, then called Fort Texas. It was poorly located and was large enough to house the whole army, but was defended now by a force of about 500 with four eighteen-pounders and four light six-pounders. The latter group was Bragg's battery and one of the six-pounders was commanded by Thomas.

The Mexican effort to reduce the fort started on May 3. The construction of the fort was continued under fire and on May 7 the last bombproof was finished, giving the personnel complete protection. The Mexicans opened their bombardment with seven guns and were answered by the Americans. The range was too great for the six-pounders, however, and their fire was discontinued. The eighteen-pounders continued their counter-battery work and dismounted some of the Mexican guns. This stopped the direct fire of Arista's artillery-men and they opened with their howitzers and mortars which were out of reach of Brown's flat trajectories. From that time on the Mexicans held the fort under this vertical fire.[3]

The crisis of the beleaguered garrison came on May 6. The fort was invested and its 500 defenders were cut off from Taylor's army by 8,000 Mexicans. Major Brown received a wound that resulted in his death three days later. At 10:30 A.M., several rounds of canister from Bragg's guns drove off the Mexican infantry from the rear of the fort. At 4:30 in the afternoon, the Mexicans sent in a surrender demand. It was refused by a council of the company officers.

At noon on May 7, four of Bragg's horses were killed and one caisson disabled. The accuracy of the Mexican artillery was increasing. Half of their shells were dropping inside the fort. But this was the day the bombproofs were completed and the troops were safe from everything except an assault. After dark a sortie by the garrison cleared away some cover that was being used as protection by the Mexican sharpshooters. By midafternoon on May 8, the Mexican guns were playing on the fort from the north, south and west but the sound of gunfire from the northeast heralded the approach of Taylor's army and heartened the garrison. On this day the fort took from 150 to 200 shells and from 75 to 100 round shot.

Shortly after Major Brown's death at 2:00 P.M. on the ninth, the garrison could hear the fire of Taylor's second battle. And at 5:45 P.M., the Mexican retreat could be seen.

A military blunder during the first two weeks of May 1846 nearly made trouble for Taylor. His line of communication from Point Isabel to Fort Brown was not perpendicular to the enemy's front, with the result that his army could not cover it. The enemy had the choice of time and place for breaking it. When they exercised this choice Taylor had three alternatives. He could sacrifice his fort and secure his base.

He could save his fort and sacrifice his base. Or he could defeat the Mexican army and protect them both. He elected to save his base and sacrifice his fort, if necessary. But the Mexicans made more mistakes than Taylor, who not only saved both fort and base but drove the Mexicans off the soil of what is now Texas. The beaten army was permitted to cross the Rio Grande unmolested.

Although most of the Northern commanders in the Civil War fought in Mexico and presumably profited by its mistakes, Grant and Thomas profited the most. Both fought to destroy their opponents. They reaped the full harvest of victory. One fact, in particular, must have impressed Thomas. In spite of Taylor's military shortcomings the public showered him with their plaudits. It was plain to be seen that a military commander need not do a thorough professional job to win a military reputation. Pursuit was more difficult than battle. The additional hard work that it entailed added nothing to the length of a general's stilts.

In the first battle of the Mexican War, Ringgold put to the test his theory that artillery was not primarily a defensive arm and that it could fight with better results from the front than from the rear. He took a mortal wound while fighting his guns from Taylor's front line at the Battle of Palo Alto, on May 11, 1846. Upon Ridgely, Washington, Bragg, Thomas, and the others Ringgold had picked to be trained in his new tactics, fell the responsibility of carrying on his work.

Some 200 miles west of Matamoros, the city of Monterrey guarded a pass through the Sierra Madre Mountains. Through this pass went the road that connected with Tampico to the southeast, San Luis Potosi to the south and Chihuahua to the northwest. Taylor wanted the control of that road to open his way to Mexico City and Chihuahua. Halfway between Matamoros and Monterrey, near the junction of the San Juan River with the Rio Grande, was the town of Camargo. It could be supplied by boat from his base at Point Isabel, so Taylor picked it for his supply depot in the move against Monterrey. On June 6, an advance guard was started out from Matamoros to take and hold Camargo. It consisted of a battalion of infantry, some cavalry and two guns from Bragg's battery. Thomas was in command of the guns.

The trip was a difficult one. The worst thing they had to contend with was the heat. Frequent halts had to be made to unharness and unsaddle and to rub dry the horses' backs and shoulders to prevent scalding. It finally became necessary to march at night and rest during the day.

In spite of these difficulties, Thomas must have been glad to get away from the camps around Matamoros. There it was even worse. Sand blew into everything. Dysentery was raging. Measles had become epidemic and was proving fatal in many instances. Worst of all, the volunteers were out of hand. A regiment of Louisiana planters refused to do their work and demanded that the regulars cut their wood, carry their water and clean their camp. When the regular officers refused to turn their men into servants, the volunteers mutinied. Maryland and Ohio volunteers threatened to shoot out their differences with their muskets, a sort of wholesale duel. Training and discipline were needed but the volunteers wanted neither. Ammunition was wasted despite orders. Volunteer officers were untrained and often afraid to enforce discipline. Regular officers were too few to control them. Robbery, rape and murder terrorized the Mexicans and for the most part went unpunished. The citizens of Matamoros liked the steady, well disciplined troops of the line, as they called the regulars, but they hated and feared the volunteers.

Thomas found Camargo a city of 5,000, but by the end of August, 15,000 men were camped there. They occupied a strip of land several hundred yards deep for three miles along the river bank. But Thomas' section of Bragg's battery enjoyed preferential quarters. It occupied some of the buildings on the town's plaza with comfortable lounging space during the heat of the day. His mess was excellent and officers invited to it fared well. Stores in quantities to dumbfound the Mexicans slowly piled up. General Worth commanded and discipline was enforced. No traders were allowed and no liquor. But one-third of the volunteers were sick and there were many deaths. The camps were built on flooded ground, and when the mud deposits dried, every breeze raised clouds of dust. The temperature sometimes reached 112 degrees. Scorpions, tarantulas, mosquitoes, centipedes, ants and small frogs were pests. Impure drinking water made more trouble. The wagon trains which had proved adequate for the army's transport over the coastal plains were inadequate for mountain work and pack mules were being trained to take over their functions. This was the first campaign ever fought by an American army without either boat or wagon transport.

Four months had gone by since Taylor's victories near Matamoros and the newspapers were criticizing him for his slowness. On September 5, Taylor's infantry advance moved out of Camargo. Company E, with Thomas, J. F. Reynolds and S. G. French as lieutenants, marched the next day. The artillery comprised four light batteries made up of one twelve-pounder and three six-pounders each, and one battery of two twenty-four-pound howitzers and one ten-inch mortar. Monterrey, a little more than a hundred miles up the San Juan River, was defended by General Ampudia and an estimated 10,000 men. Taylor's force numbered 6,500. The Americans concentrated twenty-seven miles from Monterrey and moved to Walnut Springs on the northern outskirts of the city. The main force went into camp while the engineers made a reconnaissance. Taylor's battle plan was based on the engineers' report. Worth's augmented division was to swing wide to the west and get astride the Mexican communications while the rest of the army demonstrated against their northern and eastern fronts. If these moves were successful the Mexicans were to be trapped by a pincer movement and captured or destroyed.

During the four days of the battle, Bragg's guns worked with Twiggs' division on the northern and eastern sides of the city. On the morning of the twenty-first, Twiggs' division was ordered to demonstrate at the northeast corner of the city in favor of Worth's main attack. Twiggs remained in camp that morning trying to loosen his bowels in the belief that a bullet striking his belly under such circumstances had a better chance of passing through the intestines without cutting them. This effort kept him off the field until noon, and the movement was launched under Garland's direction. "Lead the head of your column off to the left," he ordered the colonel of the leading regiment, "keeping well out of reach of the enemy's shot, but if you think you can take any of them little forts down there with the bayonet, you better do it." The order was not obeyed.

What was intended for a demonstration turned into an assault against Teneria, a strong Mexican redoubt mounting four guns. It was an ill-starred movement. The Mexican artillery in the Citadel scourged the right of the column. Teneria hammered at its left and completely protected the Mexican infantry, just inside the edge of the town, who poured a heavy small arms fire into their faces. Garland's attack stalled barely inside the town.[4] A call went back for Bragg's battery, which came in at a full gallop. For half a mile its four guns were exposed to the fire from the Citadel. The leading section jammed into the narrow street and halted. There was no room to unlimber. An appalling fire poured into them from both sides and the front. The infantry had to help manhandle the gun around so that it could be withdrawn. The battery got off only a few shots.

Meantime one of the volunteer brigades had moved around the left of Garland's stalled assault and had taken Teneria. Supports were sent in and the gain was widened and consolidated. Bragg had repaired

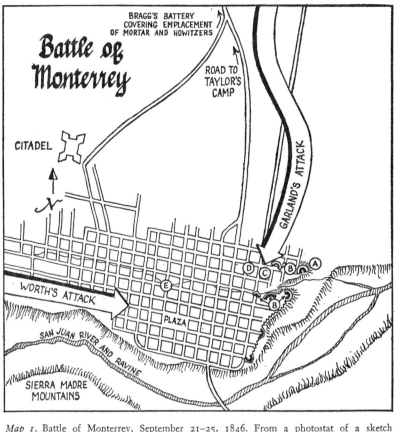

Map 1. Battle of Monterrey, September 21–25, 1846. From a photostat of a sketch (*RG 77, Records of the Office of the Chief of Engineers, Headquarters Map File, Map Ama 105, No. 3, National Archives*) prepared by Lt. George Gordon Meade, assisted by Lt. John Pope and Col. Jefferson Davis. The army spelled the name of the city and the battle Monterey.

    A—Teneria
    B—Mexican gun emplacements
    C—Where Garland's attack stalled
    D—Where Bragg's battery jammed in the street
    E—Thomas' gun on September 23

his losses and his and Ridgely's batteries were ordered in to support the infantry. By evening of the twenty-first, Monterrey was invested.

    There was a lull in the fighting on the eastern side of Monterrey on the twenty-second, but Worth was pounding steadily ahead at the western defenses. Bragg's battery was posted north of the town to discourage any sorties from the Citadel by the Mexican lancers. Bragg had smothered a similar attempt near the Citadel on the preceding day with a few rounds of canister while the supporting infantry formed a hollow square. From where the battery lay they could see the Mexicans a couple of miles off to the west running toward the town under the pressure of Worth's advance. The battery was within range of the Citadel's guns, but a slight rise of ground in front of them served as protection against direct fire. Nothing was as demoralizing to the troops in those days as exposure to artillery fire of solid shot. Thomas, very probably, was apprehensive of this and did everything in his power to minimize its effect upon the men of his section. Guns, horses and men were dispersed to reduce the casualties from the cannon balls which the Mexicans were bouncing at them over the ridge. The scattering of sand and gravel added to the men's nervousness. The ammunition chest of one limber was shattered. Finally the guns were withdrawn, one at a time.

During the night of the twenty-second, all of the Mexican strong points except one in the eastern end of the city were abandoned. At daylight they were occupied by Taylor's troops.

On the twenty-third, the pincers began to close. The volunteers went into the city to breach the barricades around the plaza near the center of the city where Ampudia's ammunition was stored. The Mexicans were now concentrated in a ring around this position. Every street leading to this plaza was blocked with masonry and raked by Mexican fire. The house tops were crowded with Mexican riflemen. At noon, French's piece was ordered into the city to breach one of these barricades. Thomas came in with Taylor shortly after French had taken his position. An informal council of war was held in the protection of one of the Mexican houses to plan for the final assault. The plan was built around the two pieces of artillery. French was to dominate with his fire the street at which he was already located. Thomas was to cross this street under cover of the smoke from French's gun, move one block west, train his gun to the south and pound to pieces the barricade that was barring the American infantry from reaching the plaza along this route.[5] But his shot were too light for this job. Using canister he could force the Mexican defenders to lower their heads. This, and the smoke from the gun's explosion, gave the infantrymen a chance to advance by short rushes to the relative safety of a doorway or window embrasure.

But the Mexican riflemen on the house tops were so well protected that the Americans in the street could not shoot them down. No scaling ladders or storming equipment had been provided. After two or three hours of this close work, Taylor, who did not know that Worth's troops were within one block of the west side of the plaza, gave the order to retire from the lower end of the city. Thomas received the order, reloaded, fired a farewell shot and retreated under a shower of bullets.

The artillery was carefully handled during this street fighting. The guns were loaded and leveled in the protection of a building. Then they were drawn into firing position with ropes while the artillerymen remained well protected from the Mexican fire. A match on the end of a long handle would be held against the vent and, as soon as the gun fired, it would be drawn back under cover for reloading.

It was the other jaw of the pincer that finally forced Ampudia to ask for terms. This was Worth's division moving in from the west. Worth was a better street fighter than Taylor. He put his troops through the houses instead of through the streets and captured a building which commanded the plaza. The Mexicans gave up. On September 26, Ampudia's army marched out of the city under the terms of an armistice.

As a result of being named in two official dispatches, Thomas was brevetted captain to rank from September 23, 1846.[6] He was at the head of his class in battle honors.

Monterrey was Thomas' third engagement. For the second time he had seen a beaten enemy escape destruction. He had observed the penalty of reckless command. When Bragg's guns jammed in the narrow street they were out of action. The infantry, lacking the support it needed, failed then to take Teneria. He had learned how to calm men under fire and had visual proof of Ringgold's theory that artillery was a front-line offensive weapon. It should have convinced him that the classic principles of military operation had no more application to street fighting than to guerrilla-like raids in the Everglades.

Bragg was promoted and transferred. Thomas West Sherman, who succeeded to the command of the battery, was in Tampico. With this change, the responsibility of command fell temporarily upon Thomas. The War Department wondered if this was advisable. Taylor thought it was and said so in a letter to the Adjutant General. In it he was highly complimentary to Thomas and the junior officers of the battery.[7]

Taylor had given the American people their first successful American offensives. He had raised American military morale to a respectable level. He was a Presidential candidate and the anti-Administration politicians were pushing his fortunes at home. The Administration planned to nullify Taylor's threat to its own future by removing him from further active fighting. The main American attack was to be inland from Vera Cruz toward Mexico City. General Winfield Scott was to command it and troops from Taylor's army were to be put under his command. Taylor was to remain in the north with nothing to do but command the northern garrisons.

Meantime, Thomas remained at Monterrey refitting and reorganizing. His battery had suffered the heaviest casualties in the artillery battalion and the inevitable problem of filling the vacancies caused by desertion and expired enlistments had to be met.

Taylor now proposed to establish his defensive line from Parras through Saltillo, Monterrey and Victoria to Tampico. Acting on this proposal he started on the two-hundred-mile mountain march toward Victoria. Thomas and his battery went with him. It was not an easy march and the heat increased the discomfort. Mountain marching presented problems never met in the flatlands, but Thomas' caution saved men and horses. He trained his wheel drivers to recognize the early signs of collapse and to take steps to avert it. At one point he had to double-team his guns to get them up a grade.

Victoria was occupied December 29 without resistance. On January 4, Major General Robert Patterson came up from Matamoros. His was also a two-hundred-mile mountain march but he failed to treat it as such and broke down his command. His troops were nearly mutinous.

While Taylor was at Victoria, Scott, unknown to him, arrived at Camargo. The purpose of his visit was to talk over his plans with Taylor. Under the circumstances, Scott withdrew the troops he wanted without consulting Taylor. To make matters worse, one of the messengers who was carrying Scott's written instructions to Taylor was captured. In this way, Santa Anna, who had been returned to command of the Mexican army by American connivance, learned how Taylor's army was being stripped and of the projected movement against Vera Cruz. Perhaps because of this information, he decided to crush Taylor before any additional forces could be recruited for him. Late in January 1847, the Mexican general started his forces northward from San Luis Potosi.

Taylor elected to meet Santa Anna where the ranges of the Sierra Madre pinched the valley of one of the San Juan's tributaries to a width of two miles. The pass or defile was near the hacienda of Buena Vista about six miles south of Saltillo. His position was naturally strong. His right was made impregnable by the contours of the ground and by artificial barricades. His center was well protected by natural defenses, but his left was weak and drew the brunt of the Mexican attack. No effort was made to strengthen it. Santa Anna was threatening with 20,000. Taylor counted less than 5,000 and fewer than 500 of these were troops of the regular army. The light batteries of Washington, Bragg and T. W. Sherman made up a large part of these regulars. Thomas fought as Sherman's first lieutenant with Reynolds and French acting as the other subalterns. Sherman had taken over the command from Thomas on February 14.

This battery, which had been in such excellent condition early in

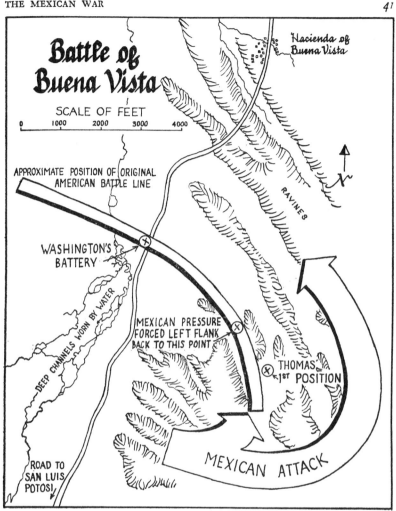

Map 2. Battle of Buena Vista, February 22–23, 1847. From a photostat of a contemporaneous sketch (*RG 77, Records of the Office of the Chief of Engineers, Headquarters Map File, Map Ama 114, No. 6, National Archives*).

November, was now reported as feebly manned and greatly reduced. The disintegration took place on the march to Victoria and back during the period of Thomas' command, but the way in which the battery fought a few weeks later mitigated any possible censure.

At nine o'clock in the morning of February 22, 1847, the massed squadrons of the Mexicans, with flashing lances and colored pennons, could be seen. They were followed by dense columns of infantry that crowded into the narrow valley in front of Taylor's battle line.

Brigadier General John Ellis Wool, Taylor's second in command, had already deployed the Americans—his right protected by barricades,

Washington's battery astride the road and the balance of his forces between the road and the foothills on the left. Taylor approved the deployment when he came in from Saltillo with Bragg's battery, the First and Second Dragoon Regiments and Jefferson Davis' regiment of Mississippi riflemen. These units he held in reserve. They, with Washington's and Sherman's batteries, were all the regular troops Taylor had. The Mississippians were volunteers.

At 2:00 P.M., the Mexicans began their deployment in an effort to outflank Taylor's left. Through a misunderstanding, this flank fell back. There was firing all along this wing for several hours and by dark the Mexicans occupied the sides and summits of the protecting mountains. Taylor's left was outflanked. That night a gentle breeze wafted the melodies of Santa Anna's personal band across the American lines. The music ended after an hour and the air grew cold. There were spits of rain during the night and strong winds. The Americans slept without fires and with their arms close at hand.

The twenty-third dawned cloudlessly. The breeze was cool, the sunshine radiant. Action was opened on the extreme left by the Mexican light troops. By 8:00 A.M., Santa Anna put his heavy assault columns in motion. The pressure was too much for the Second Regiment of Indiana Volunteers. They broke and their retreat uncovered the left flank of the Illinois volunteers. Taylor's position was turned.

The battle was barely started and the American situation was perilous. Taylor was at Saltillo with most of the American reserves. Wool was in command, facing one of the most difficult of defense problems. He had to bend back the left end of his line at a right angle so that some of his men faced the Mexican attack that was coming from the south and others faced that which was coming from the east. This angle, called the salient, was the weakest spot in his line. It was the classical position for artillery. The assignment went to Thomas with a six-pound gun and French with a twelve-pounder. Bissell's Second Regiment of Illinois Volunteers supported the guns. These two guns and the single regiment took the weight of Santa Anna's attack, which was directed at their front, their left and their left rear. Each artillery discharge cut a swath through the dense Mexican ranks but failed to stop them from moving more men farther to the rear of the American position. To counter this, Bissell was ordered to fall back to take advantage of the protection of a ravine to his left and rear. The guns went back with him and came into battery again on his flanks, but the American position was deteriorating.

Bragg was now ordered to the salient from his position on the far right. He came up fast and went into action on Thomas' left. Sherman's other two guns arrived and went into position on Thomas' right.[8] Two-thirds of the American artillery was now defending the salient. Three regiments of infantry arrived to stiffen Bissell's line. Taylor, who was now on the field, threw in all the reserves he had and made the salient secure.

Meantime the pressure of Santa Anna's main attack shifted north-ward and Taylor began stripping elements from the salient to stop it. This called for a reorganization. Thomas remained where he was. French, who had been wounded, was replaced by Garnett. O'Brien brought up two guns from Washington's battery. These four guns covered an arc of 180 degrees. Shortly after noon, Garnett's gun was sent northward where the Mexican pressure was still building up.

Thomas' gun crew was using canister at point blank range. They were probably firing once every twenty seconds. At this rate their original supply of ammunition would have been exhausted in an hour —probably less when allowance is made for breakage and for losses when the gun changed ground.[9] Replacement ammunition during the fighting was supplied by wagons which also brought up food and water and removed the wounded.

Meantime, farther north, Taylor was in a tight spot. All his reserves were committed. If they could not hold, there was no help nearer than Saltillo six miles away, and that garrison was busy fighting off the Mex-ican cavalry. Fortunately, his men held. The Mexicans faltered, stopped and balanced nervously on the edge of a rout. A white flag appeared from the Mexican headquarters. The American fire slackened. Santa Anna's flag inquired what Taylor wanted. It was a ruse but it worked. By the time the truce conversations were over the Mexicans were out of danger in an orderly withdrawal.

This withdrawal now flowed around the salient and across the muzzles of the guns of Thomas and O'Brien. Its direction was the reverse of the one the Mexican advance had followed in the morning. The two young officers advanced their guns well to the front to bring the Mexicans under fire. At the same time, Santa Anna's reserves were sent to meet and support their harried comrades. The two Mexican forces concentrated in front of and slightly to the right of Thomas' gun. The place got too hot for the volunteer infantry, who took cover in the middle ravine. Washington, some 1,500 yards to the right, turned his guns to cover the infantry's flank but failed to stop the Mexicans.

It was the crisis of the battle. Nothing but the guns of Thomas and O'Brien could stave off defeat until Taylor could get up some help from the less threatened portions of his line. The artillerists fell back with the recoil of their guns, saving valuable seconds at each discharge, which they used to increase their rate of fire. Both of O'Brien's guns were captured. Cool, intrepid Thomas kept his fire going in spite of losses. Nearly every cannoneer was down. Just in time, the hard-fought Battery Bragg came up and opened fire without infantry support. Taylor himself arrived. "Double shot your guns and give 'em hell, Bragg," he ordered. (History toned this down to, "A little more grape, Captain Bragg.") The Mexican advance was hard hit but not stopped. Then the rest of Sherman's battery and Davis' Mississippians came up. Elements of the Indiana brigade came in from the extreme left. The crisis was over. The Mexicans were repulsed and fell back in disorder. Late that afternoon Santa Anna began his retirement.

Buena Vista nearly wore out Taylor's light batteries. In his final swing from the extreme left to the salient, Bragg reported that his horses were so exhausted that he could not force them into any gait faster than a walk in spite of everything his drivers could do with whip and spur. If Santa Anna had ordered forward his whole line at almost any time after the American left was turned, Taylor's force would have had to retreat. Taylor saved himself by transferring batteries and infantry from one threatened point to another, a tactic he could not have used if Santa Anna had pinned down his whole line. This was a demonstration of the obvious, but most West Pointers disregarded it.

A military critique of the battle written sixty-two years after its occurrence says, "In all the annals of American warfare no other such victory as Buena Vista can be pointed out. Upon ground unprepared for defense, with its left flank practically in the air . . . this little body of well trained volunteers successfully resisted from daylight till dark the assaults of an enemy three times its own strength, and at last repulsed him and kept the field." But "keeping the field" was a result disapproved of (as Mahan had repeatedly pointed out) by Frederick and Napoleon. It was destined to become the costly habit of United States army commanders for the next twenty years.

Thomas was proud of the American feat of arms but he would not permit himself to brag about it even indirectly. He was slightly apologetic, however, over Taylor's failure to consummate the victory.[10]

Three batteries of light artillery, expertly and courageously handled, had saved the American army from defeat. On the basis of reports by Wool and Thomas West Sherman, Taylor paid official tribute to them. "The services of the light artillery," he wrote, "always conspicuous, were more than usually distinguished. Moving rapidly over the roughest ground, it was always in action at the right place and the right time, and its well directed fire dealt destruction in the masses of the enemy." He mentioned the skill, gallantry and name of every artillery officer.

Such praise, combined with Virginian influence, was certain to bring Thomas official recognition. It came in the form of the brevet rank of major and was dated February 23, 1847.[11] Thomas kept the single silver bar on each end of his shoulder straps but he wore the gold oak leaf of his brevet rank between them. Three brevets in seven years marked Thomas as one of the outstanding junior officers in the army. Coupled with his political heritage, this seemingly assured his military future.

At the close of the Mexican War, fourteen of Thomas' classmates had won one brevet, three had won two brevets and Thomas and Oscar Fingal Winship had won three each. It is interesting to note that Robert E. Lee, although superior in rank to Thomas, received his brevet rank of major nearly two months after Thomas had been awarded his.

The paradox of the volunteer must have been of high interest to Thomas at this time. The volunteer was the raw material of the American fighting army. The regular army, the professional fighting force, was pushed into the subordinate role of a peacetime army. On Buena Vista's plateau, Thomas saw that the raw, unruly volunteers were turning into first-class fighting men. Some three months after the battle, he watched the officers of a mounted regiment of volunteers vainly trying to form their men on the Buena Vista battlefield for a review by that stickler for military formality, General Wool. As a review it was not a success. The men were dirty, verminous, bearded, long haired and weather-beaten. Some had no clothing to cover their underwear. They lounged in their ranks and gibed at the reviewing officer. Yet their battle honors comprised one of the military sagas of the continent. Their title was the First Missouri Mounted Volunteers, their commander, the fabulous Alexander Doniphan. The dust of the Santa Fe Trail and El Camino Real was ground into their skins. They had just swung the greater part of a thirty-five-hundred-mile circle from Kansas through Mexico on their way back to Missouri. March discipline they endured; hunger and thirst they accepted; victory they could improvise from the materials at hand. But the formalities of army life in garrison they could not abide.

The suspicion of a standing army that made Congress so hostile to the Military Academy sprang, of course, from the people. The popular theory was that volunteers would save the nation in time of need. There was a fundamental social cleavage between the regular and the volunteer. Men who enlisted in the regular army were predominantly social misfits who had failed at every other attempt to make a living. Civilians instinctively distrusted them and carried this feeling with them when they volunteered. This led to friction. Yet both made good soldiers.

Basically, the regular was as much a volunteer as the man enlisted for ninety days or for the duration of the war. No drafted troops fought the Mexicans. Both were subject to the same fears. They were equally courageous, equally tenacious. Some of the Civil War officers disagreed with this theory. They claimed that the regular was too smart to stand fast when the odds against him were great. Yet the battle records do not bear this out. Although they fought each other in camp and overclaimed one another in battle, the volunteers brought the army the numbers it needed, and the regulars brought it the knowledge necessary to save time and lives. The successful commander understood them both.

Comparison between professional and volunteer officers in the Civil War, however, was far less favorable to the volunteer. His failing was apparently due to a lack of military aptitude. In the last campaign of the Army of the Cumberland, only two of the ten officers exercising a command above that of a division had not attended West Point or had not had at least ten years of army experience before the outbreak of the war.

Whether or not the lesson was plain to Thomas then, at some time he reached the conclusion that volunteers could be turned into a first-class fighting force if their officers wanted it that way. Confidence was the basis of a proper relationship. The men gave it to the officer who could bring them victory, who was conscious of their own individual dignity, who used discipline for mutual protection and not to demonstrate his personal power, who used drill to ready his men for battle and not to show himself off on the reviewing field, and who demonstrated a military competence that would protect them from unnecessary loss and hardship.

From February 1847 until July 1848, Thomas divided his time between Buena Vista and Monterrey. The war in the north was ended. At this time, the commissary general of subsistence put in a bid for Thomas' services.[12] His proposal was approved by the Secretary of War but the transfer was never made.

Also at about this time, Thomas received a letter from Southampton County, Virginia, dated February 8, 1848. It advised Thomas that a testimonial sword in honor of his record in the Florida and Mexican wars was being sent to him. Its cost had been met by subscriptions by his boyhood neighbors.[13]

Thomas acknowledged the fulsome praises of the formal resolution of his Southampton neighbors with a stilted, uncharacteristic letter written from Buena Vista on March 31, 1848.[14]

The sword was patterned after the dragoon saber with basket hilt, solid silver grip and an amethyst set in its gold pommel. The scabbard was of solid silver. Scabbard, hilt and grip were enchased and engraved with scrollwork, military insignia, the names of Florida, Fort Brown, Monterrey, and Buena Vista, and a vignette of the Battle of Monterrey. This sword, evidence of the esteem of his fellow Virginians, was withheld from Thomas after he chose to remain with the Union in the Civil War. It had been left for safekeeping with his sisters, who refused his requests for its return. They presented it instead to the museum of the Virginia Historical Society at Richmond, and succeeded in perpetuating a memory they had once tried hard to destroy.

In July 1848, Company E, with Thomas riding at the head of his section, left Monterrey and marched by easy stages to the mouth of the Rio Grande. At Fort Brown on August 9 they learned that a formal peace had been signed with Mexico. In September, Thomas received his brevet as major. The next month Company E left Texas but Thomas remained behind in charge of the commissary depot at Brazos Santiago. This was an island off the Texas coast eight miles from the mouth of the Rio Grande where ice sold out of the hold of a Boston ship at a dollar a pound. Thomas remained here five months. Bragg tried to get this professional exile cut short by obtaining for Thomas a detail to West Point,[15] but the effort brought no immediate results. On February 1, 1849, Thomas left Texas for Jerusalem, where he spent a six-month leave and was welcomed by his neighbors as a returning hero. The ten Thomas slaves [16] must have greeted him with a mixture of curiosity and anticipation.

On August 1, he reported to Fort Adams at Newport, Rhode Island, and assumed command of Company B in the absence of its regular captain. Six weeks later he was at sea in command of an artillery battalion of four companies with combat orders. Trouble with the Seminoles was brewing again in Florida. Twiggs was in command. His instructions were to safeguard the settlements and to remove the Indians. He was to use bribery if possible, force if necessary. Thomas stopped for a week at Savannah, Georgia, evidently for a regrouping of the Third Artillery, and finally disembarked at Palatka, Florida, on the twelfth of October. His command was acting as infantry.

Twiggs' safety buffer between the Indians and the settlements extended from Fort Pierce to Tampa. Thomas made the trip in nine months. During that period he was working closely with George Gordon Meade, who was locating a line of protective forts. Thomas followed on his heels, garrisoning and supplying each fort as it was located.[17] When this work was completed, Thomas evidently reported in person to Twiggs at Tampa and was sent southward to Fort Myers. Twiggs considered this the most important post in his department. It was also one of the most unhealthy. Here, on September 20, 1850, Thomas received the orders detailing him to duty at the Military Academy. This was the assignment Bragg had tried to secure for him two years before. His orders, however, were contingent upon his relief, a contingency not satisfied until more than six months later.

5

West Point Instructorship and Marriage

On September 7, 1850, Brevet Major William H. Shover died, leaving vacant the post of instructor of artillery and cavalry at the United States Military Academy. There was stiff competition for the position. At least four candidates were using influence to push their claims.

The day after Shover's death the superintendent asked that Thomas be detailed to fill the vacancy. Thomas was then in Florida and there is no record that he ever applied for this assignment. That his candidacy was preferred over the claims of four brilliant or politically powerful officers argues that someone in a high place was pushing him. It is possible that the superintendent of the Academy ran his finger down the list of artillery subalterns and picked his man on rank and merit. Thomas was the ranking first lieutenant with the brevet of major, although four lieutenants in the artillery outranked him in seniority. Probably the Virginia Congressional delegation also wanted the assignment for Thomas.

Nearly two years before, Bragg had suggested Thomas' name for this duty in a letter to John Y. Mason. The suggestion was made without Thomas' knowledge to a man with whom Bragg was unacquainted. "He [Thomas] is certainly entitled to some consideration from his government," Bragg wrote. Mason, then a member of Polk's cabinet, knew that his protégé was one of the distinguished junior officers in the army and a marked favorite of the citizens of his old Congressional district. The implication that the government was not doing right by one of Virginia's deserving sons, especially when that implication came from a North Carolinian, may have stirred the Virginians to action and the quick appointment in 1850 came as a balm to their disappointment of 1848. In the case of at least one officer from Virginia, when tangible recognition of his services seemed overdue, petitions were circulated among the prominent men of the state asking for rectification of the slight. When these were signed in sufficient numbers they were forwarded to the President of the United States. It took a hardy politician to ignore the rights of an army officer from Virginia.

At any rate, there was quick action by the War Department. Ten days after the instructorship became vacant, Thomas was ordered to West Point as soon as he was relieved of his command. On November 20, 1850, becoming nervous about the delay in getting relieved, Thomas wrote to the adjutant of the United States Military Academy saying that he might not be able to carry out his orders for a month.[1]

It would appear from his letter that Thomas was anxious for the detail. Public demands for economy were crippling the army. Thomas saw what the future held for the artillery. In March 1851, his battery was dismounted, as were all the other light batteries but one in the Third Artillery. At West Point, Thomas could worry through the army's low period. He would command the West Point light battery, one of the few left in existence. His work would put him in a position to make contributions to the science and practice of gunnery. On top of this he would receive a relatively substantial pay increase.

Meantime the superintendent waited. On March 18, 1851, impatient and exasperated, he wrote to Brigadier General Joseph G. Totten calling his attention to the fact that although Major Thomas had been at Boston Harbor with his regiment for two months, he had failed to carry out his six-month-old order to report to West Point.[2]

This time he got results. Thomas reported and on April 3, 1851, was assigned to duty as instructor of artillery and cavalry and received from Fitz John Porter the funds and public property of his department.

During his instructorship Thomas served under two superintendents, Captain Henry Brewerton until the end of August 1852 and Brevet Colonel Robert E. Lee thereafter. It is noteworthy that the officially recorded progress in bettering the equipment for the artillery and cavalry was all made under Lee, evidence that these Virginians worked well as a team.

Some of the officers with whom Thomas was in daily contact during this tour of duty were George B. McClellan, then commanding a company of engineers; Captain George Washington Cullum, army biographer and Halleck's wartime chief-of-staff; Brevet Major Fitz John Porter, who innocently made trouble for Mrs. Thomas a decade after Thomas' death; Captain A. H. Bowman, who was superintendent of West Point during the Civil War; Lieutenant Henry Coppée, who wrote a full-length biography of Thomas; Lieutenant Charles C. Gilbert, whose promising career was blasted at Perryville by his overreaching ambition; Lieutenant E. Kirby Smith, who nearly undid the work of Thomas' Mill Springs campaign; and Lieutenant Absalom Baird, who won the Medal of Honor while fighting south of Atlanta as one of Thomas' division commanders.

As his title implied, Thomas was responsible for teaching artillery tactics according to the approved system. The cadets were taught the school of the field piece but the emphasis was given to heavy and mountain artillery. An insufficient number of textbooks for this instruction were on the post when Thomas reached there and he asked for more.

Despite the official emphasis, the cadets preferred the glamour of the light battery—the rattle of the gun carriages, the clamor of the section officers, the sound of the trumpet and the rapid fire of the six-pounders that rolled their din and smoke around them. Thomas added to this glamour. He was tall, but so well proportioned that the students hardly noticed his height. He was full-built without corpulence, had a large head, short brown hair, short moustache, large limbs, firm tread, and a brown and ruddy complexion. His voice was properly suited to command and carried well. His seat in the saddle was solid. Major George H. Thomas of Virginia, who had been in bloody battles and three times brevetted, was not a figure to pass unnoticed.[3]

Cavalry instruction, when Thomas took up his duties, was confined to practical work. The course was not one of the major parts of the curriculum and the cadets were not graded in it. During Thomas' tenure, however, he persuaded the academic board to recommend the substitution of the study of cavalry tactics for practical lessons in riding and induced Professor Mahan to turn over some of the hours devoted to engineering drawing to this study. At the same time, the cadets were to be graded in their cavalry studies.

Thomas applied the cavalry instruction to the two mounted arms of the service—the dragoons and the mounted rifles. The first was a heavy-striking force and to that end the troopers were selected for their size and power. This called for large, heavy equipment, so their mounts had also to be large and heavy. The mounted rifles were light troops for mobility and celerity of movement. Both fought dismounted and the cadets had to be schooled in these tactics. The dragoons fought mounted as well as dismounted and Thomas taught the shock tactics of massed horsemen. Jeb Stuart, one of Thomas' students and later Lee's cavalry leader, followed this indoctrination until the end. He fought dismounted when he had to but preferred to lead down his Gray squadrons in a mass, horses stretched out on the run, troopers standing in their stirrups with bare steel flashing overhead. Thomas schooled his pupils, too, in the management and care of their horses and in the nomenclature and use of mounted equipment.

Thomas and his fellow Virginian, Philip St. George Cooke, who was commanding the cavalry school at Carlisle, Pennsylvania, were ordered in April 1852 to report on a new method of horsemanship under consideration for the use of the mounted forces. General Scott advised the Secretary of War, "Their opinion [that of Thomas and Cooke] would no doubt have great weight with their fellow officers." What their report stated is now, unfortunately, not known.

It was only three years since the end of the Mexican War and therefore doubtful that artillery instruction had been up-dated by the experiences of that fighting. The classical military principles were of European origin, founded on the strategy and tactics of Frederick the Great and Napoleon. What occurred in the border skirmishes in America was of little significance to European military students who wrote most of the books. But Thomas, as one of the outstanding artillerists in Taylor's army, had proved some new concepts of logistics and tactics for that arm of the service. Whether West Point artillery texts had caught up with Thomas or not, it is safe to assume that his students had all the benefits of his practical experience.

The West Point Registers show how the cadets fared under Thomas' instruction. Some felt that Thomas gave high marks for indifferent recitations. Yet if it be true that the competence of a teacher is measured by the success of his students, then it is significant that one outstanding Civil War cavalry leader of each side came from the Thomas-taught group. They were Phil Sheridan and Jeb Stuart. Another was one of the conspicuous artillerists of the Confederate forces, Stephen D. Lee—no relation of Robert E. Lee.

Not all of Thomas' students absorbed his instruction so well. John Bell Hood was a gaunt, uncouth, unintellectual youth who developed into a handsome, blue-eyed giant, with a personality that made him one of the best assault commanders in the Rebellion. But he never learned how to get the potential striking power from his guns. In one battle, one of the bloodiest for its duration of any in the Civil War, his men fought without artillery.[4]

If Thomas' instruction, combined with cadet aptitude and the opportunity afforded by the Civil War, produced some outstanding military leaders, it was not because of a lack of discouragements. Serviceable horses, suitable saddles and adequate stabling were needed. The beasts were advanced in age, worn out and broken down or diseased. Some were far gone with glanders. One was nineteen years old and lame, and so sullen and unmanageable that the cadets could use him at but few of their exercises; another was scrofulous and so uncontrollable that the strongest cadet in the academy could not manage him; another suffered from an affliction that caused him to fall down on all occasions, and the blindness of still another made him unsafe to ride.

Thomas had not been at West Point a week before his request for artillery horses was on its way to the Quartermaster General with Brewerton's letter of transmittal. This was followed by requisitions for curry combs, brushes and lighter saddles for cadet use.

The saddle requisition led Thomas into one of the few official reprimands of his career. Brewerton's method of forwarding Thomas' requisitions was evidently too wishy-washy to get results. So Thomas resorted to direct methods, short-cutting official channels. Thomas S. Jesup, the Quartermaster General, reported the dereliction to General Joseph G. Totten, and Thomas was officially reminded of his violation of military procedure. He sent a lame excuse to Totten but apparently healed the matter with a promise. "For the future my letters shall be sent through the proper channels." [5]

Thomas' drive for the betterment of his department met with little success under Brewerton, but under Lee he began to get action. On October 9, 1852, Lee was warning Totten that the public stables in which the academy's twenty-nine artillery and cavalry horses were kept were dangerously inadequate and that there was no shelter of any kind for the thirty additional horses he was trying to buy.

With progress being made on the procurement of horses, Lee switched his pressure to saddles. This was a problem Thomas had been trying to solve for more than a year. Lee, instead of merely forwarding his subordinate's requisition, took a definite position on the matter and put all the prestige of his rank and position behind it. He wrote to the Quartermaster General objecting to the use of the dragoon saddles, "because they are so large and harsh in the seat that the cadets become chafed and excoriated to such a degree as to be incapacitated for riding. . . . I am informed by an officer now on duty at the Academy that, when a cadet, his legs were frequently so excoriated as to bleed after the usual lesson of instruction on the saddles in question." [6]

Six months went by and Thomas and Lee raised their sights. Horses, dragoons and officers sufficient for the instruction of the cadets were now provided. The cadets were receiving practical instruction each day the weather permitted. What the instructor of artillery and cavalry needed now was a new riding hall. Cadets were injured by being knocked out of their saddles by the iron columns in the building they were then using or by skinning their knees against the walls. The project was initiated, but not carried to its conclusion until after Thomas had been detailed to other duties.

On his world tour, after serving as President of the United States, Grant told how Thomas won one of his many nicknames. He was re-emphasizing the point that Thomas was too slow to make a competent military commander. When Thomas was commanding the cadets in cavalry drill he would never permit them to go beyond a slow trot. Just as soon as the line of mounted cadets began to gain a little speed, Thomas would order, "Slow trot," and the cadets began to call him "Slow Trot Thomas." [7] It may be that Thomas did not object to speed in his cavalry drills, but had in mind the advanced age and physical infirmities of his horses and the danger from the narrowness of the hall. Nicknames are generally a sign of popularity and it is a matter of record that Thomas was popular with many of his cadet students. A Southern cadet, however, writing fifty-six years later, found him cold, phlegmatic, unimpressionable, but a born soldier. [8]

The Schofield court was one of the disciplinary measures in which Thomas became involved during this tour of duty. The enmity of John M. Schofield toward Thomas is a matter of history. It probably started at this time.

The trouble began on June 18, 1852, when the class of 1856 were presenting themselves as candidates for admission. Schofield had been detailed to instruct a section of these candidates in mathematics so that they could pass their entrance examinations. Four of the candidates failed in this course and three of these had been members of Schofield's section. The record of the Schofield court is restricted material because its publication might embarrass the descendents of the accused, but from the correspondence that passed between West Point and the chief engineer of the army it is evident what happened. Schofield permitted his class to be turned into a burlesque by making the uses of their procreative and eliminative organs the subject of a blackboard examination. In reporting the affair to the Secretary of War, Schofield's offense was called disgraceful and exemplary punishment was recommended.[9] The Secretary agreed and Schofield was dismissed from the Academy. Two weeks later this decision was reconsidered and the matter was referred to a court of inquiry. Thomas served as a member of this court.

In his autobiography, Schofield states that he was sentenced to be dismissed, and that Thomas and one other officer were the only ones of thirteen members who declined to vote for remission of the sentence. The identity of these votes, however, Schofield claimed he did not learn until two years before Thomas' death when, as Secretary of War, he gained access to the transcript of the court's proceedings.

Among the guests at the West Point Hotel during Thomas' tour of duty was Mrs. Abigail Paine Kellogg, a widow from Troy, N.Y. With her were two daughters, Frances Lucretia and Julia Augusta. The thirty-one-year-old Frances kindled a gleam in the eye of the Major. A brother officer who knew the lady, and was an eye-witness to the courtship, described her as large and of a stately presence, having an attractive appearance and possessing culture and conversational charm. Another said that in height Thomas and his bride were completely matched, and that she was a beautiful and accomplished woman. To Meade, who saw her at the West Point Hotel in the late 1850's, she was a tall, good-natured woman and quite civil. Fourteen years later the Attorney General met her at West Point and wrote in his diary that she was a lady of plain worth and dignity.[10]

She was one of a family of eleven children. Her forebears on both sides were prosperous, substantial and highly regarded. Her father, a hardware and grocery merchant, died when she was fourteen. Her mother, either from her husband's estate or from her own family, or both, controlled a modest fortune of about $100,000.[11]

At the age of eight Frances was enrolled as a day student in the famous Troy Female Seminary, afterwards renamed the Emma Willard School, and she remained there as a student for seven years.[12] During this period the school was under the direction of Mrs. Emma Hart Willard, a poet, historian, scientist, teacher, and ardent Unionist. There was no better girls' school in the United States. Miss Kellogg's background was compatible with that of her admirer in education, culture and living standards.

She and Brevet Major Thomas were married on November 17, 1852, at St. Paul's Episcopal Church in Troy by the Reverend Dr. Van Kleeck. The parish register shows that John F. Kellogg, the bride's brother, and Daniel Southwick, her uncle, were the witnesses. One of these probably acted as best man. If a friend accompanied Thomas on his boat trip up the Hudson, or if some member of his family came north for the ceremony, the record is silent in the matter. Had the bridal pair desired it, they could probably have had a goodly representation of wedding guests up from West Point merely by issuing invitations. If Brevet Colonel and Mrs. Lee had headed such a group, leave for the occasion would perhaps have been granted freely to the younger officers. It would have been in character, however, for Thomas to go alone to claim his bride. He did strap on for the ceremony—the only recorded time he ever wore it—the jeweled sword presented to him by his Southampton neighbors.

Probably he dressed for the occasion in a new uniform—a dark blue frock coat ornamented by gold epaulettes with crimson centers, and a crimson sash; dark blue trousers with a red stripe on each side seam; a red horsehair plume on his cap, its front ornamented by crossed cannon with a "3" in the angle between them; the gold leaf of his brevet rank between the single silver bars of his regimental grade; a black patent leather sword belt with a brass "A" worked into its buckle; and ankle boots with gilt spurs.

Two days before the wedding, Thomas obtained a twenty-six-day leave. Undoubtedly sometime during this leave he took his bride to Virginia, where she met her husband's family and friends and was dutifully greeted by the Thomas slaves. When the leave was over, bride and groom made their home on the post. There, in accordance with army protocol, Thomas took his bride to call upon his superiors and the junior officers came to his quarters to meet Mrs. Thomas formally.

Less than three months after the end of Thomas' honeymoon, with the accession of Franklin Pierce to the Presidency, Jefferson Davis was named Secretary of War. In his plans for the betterment of the army he was not to forget the brilliant young artillerist he had learned to respect on the field of Buena Vista. The day before Christmas of 1853, Thomas was made a captain. His first promotion had come to him three years and ten months after his graduation. It took him nine years and eight months to climb the regimental ladder behind the twenty first lieutenants who were ahead of him to gain his second promotion. He was now the junior captain on the regimental list of twelve, and at the bottom of the list of some forty-eight captains in the artillery.

On May 1, 1854, Thomas was relieved of his duties at West Point. It was Mrs. Thomas' first experience with the routine uprooting of army families. She returned to her mother's home after living with her husband for sixteen months. She was not to rejoin him for two years.

Before Thomas' transfer was completed, however, Lee registered an emphatic protest at the change. On April 13, 1854, he asked Totten not to relieve Thomas, adding that he knew no officer who was more capable. Lee did not feel that Thomas was irreplaceable but he objected, with good reason, to the relief of a key instructor less than two months before the end of the academic year. Totten denied his request on the ground that the decision was that of the Secretary of War and Lee dropped the matter.[13]

Thomas probably did not relish the change any more than Lee. He was kissing his beloved Fanny good-bye and was exchanging the comforts of West Point for the hardships of that Siberia of the United States army posts—Fort Yuma, California. But first he had to solve a problem in troop psychology.

6

Fort Yuma and the Organization of the Second Cavalry

In the spring of 1854, the War Department was having trouble moving a battalion of the Third Artillery to the Pacific coast. The movement had been started the previous December. Four months later the troops had moved only as far as Virginia. The situation was embarrassing. The first embarkation had been made from New York Harbor but the transport *San Francisco* had been wrecked in a storm off Cape Hatteras the day before Christmas. Two hundred out of the six hundred men of the Third Artillery were lost. By the middle of April the battalion had been recruited and concentrated at New York for its second embarkation. The steamer *Falcon* was at the dockside. Wyse, Thomas' first lieutenant during the Fort Lauderdale campaign, was in command. He got his men aboard but, becoming suspicious of the *Falcon's* seaworthiness, abruptly refused to go with them. Another officer was given the command and the ship sailed. But Wyse's presentiment proved correct. The *Falcon* was disabled off the Chesapeake Capes and the troops had to be disembarked at Fort Monroe.

In those days the army contracted for the transportation of troops but it had not set up a reliable method of determining the seaworthiness of the vessels offered by the contractor. Neither were the shipmasters always reliable. Ringgold, on his way to Mexico with his battery, suspected that the captain was deliberately trying to wreck his vessel for the insurance. Thomas once had to put a drunken master under arrest and turn the command of the ship over to the mate. Under the best conditions it was doubtful whether boating beat marching from the point of view of the troops. They generally came aboard drunk and worked off their hangovers amid the fumes of burning sulphur, used as a disinfectant, on a vessel that rolled like a doughnut in a pot of violently boiling fat. In addition to these hazards, the voyage seemed jinxed. Even their commanding officer had preferred the risk of ruining his career to facing the peril with his men. Now the firm hand of an officer who had the complete confidence of his men was necessary to complete the long-contemplated troop movement.[1]

Thomas was chosen and, at his request, was quickly relieved of his West Point duties so that he could see his command before it was to embark. In a few days the crisis was resolved and Thomas, with his new command, was aboard the steamer *Illinois,* Panama bound. In ten days they had crossed the isthmus and re-embarked on the steamer *Sonora.* May 20 they were at San Diego and by the end of the month at San Francisco. Using sail in 1842, it had taken Thomas one day longer than this to make the trip from New Orleans to Charleston.

While waiting for the battalion baggage to arrive, Thomas was assigned to the command of the Presidio. Meantime he located Sherman, his old West Point roommate, who had forsaken the army for banking and was living in San Francisco with a newly acquired wife. Living expenses were high. Cab fare for two from the steamboat dock to a hotel was twenty dollars in gold. To offset this increase in living costs Thomas was entitled to an addition of two dollars a day to his pay during his stay in California. In a fortnight the Presidio interlude was ended by orders to take over the command of Fort Yuma in the southeast corner of California at the junction of the Colorado and Gila rivers. He was to go by ship to San Diego, pick up two companies there and make the 208-mile overland march to his new post.

This was a famous trail but a hard one, peopled by the ghosts of thousands of wayfarers. Chief among them were the crack First Dragoons under General Stephen Watts Kearny on their way from Missouri to San Diego. It had been the worst part of their eighteen-hundred-mile march. A bundle of grass tied on each saddle gave scanty forage the first night. There was a two-day march between waterholes. After that the mounts were being led or pushed by their riders. Uniforms were shredded by cactus and shoes by rim rock. Red eyed, crack lipped, cotton mouthed, Kearny's command crossed the Southern California desert in November. Now it was July.

Thomas was forced to improvise to get his men through without severe losses. The last six days of the march were through the desert. Water was scarce. The midsummer sun raised the temperature to 115 degrees and above, and there was no natural shade. Thomas remembered the midsummer march to Camargo along the Rio Grande and took a lesson from that experience. He marched his men only at night and kept them quiet and out of the sun in the daytime, probably by using the shade of the wagons and canvas tarpaulins. But even so they showed increasing signs of exhaustion. Thomas cached his heavier stores, loaded his men into wagons and, by forced marches, got them to the fort. His report to the Pacific division headquarters bluntly stated that troops should never be marched across the desert during the summer.

Fort Yuma had been established in 1852 by Samuel P. Heintzelman, the officer Thomas was relieving. Its purpose was to protect the ferry across the Colorado River, an important link in the long trails from New Mexico and Sonora over which livestock were driven to supply meat for the California mining camps, where prices were high and quality not too closely scrutinized. Now the Yuma Indians were showing signs of unrest. They were at war with the Cocopas to the south and the Maricopas to the west. The Colorado River had failed to overflow in its annual freshet, which meant that there would be no planting and therefore no crops. Lacking food, the Yumas were expected to make trouble.[2]

The traffic at this isolated crossroads was amazing. At the height of the gold rush 10,000 persons a year were crossing. In 1856, 28,000 sheep were crossed in a month. A toll of fifty cents was charged for a horse and man. The travelers fought and robbed each other and intermittently fought the Indians. A map printed in the *Quarterly of the Historical Society of Southern California*,[3] shows that the westbound trail followed the south bank of the Gila River to its junction with the Colorado, crossed the Colorado and followed what is now known as the Emigrant Trail to San Diego, San Bernardino and Los Angeles. Six years before the fort was established, the Mormon Battalion crossed, short of food and sullen over clashes between their own celestial discipline and the mundane brand imposed by army regulations.

Here on the California side of the river, on a rocky hill that was an island during flood water, stood Fort Yuma. Its site was originally occupied by a Spanish mission. The bricks from the mission buildings subsequently were used to build comfortable quarters for the troops. This conversion of material from a facility for promoting peace through spirituality to one for promoting peace through force may well have given Thomas food for reflection. Thomas' peace was accepted by the Indians who had refused the peace presented by the padres, although they did accept the dramatic crucifixion and used it enthusiastically on their captives.

Water at the fort was pumped seventy feet from the river onto the parade ground by horses on a treadmill. The water settled overnight and was distributed by carts in the morning. The steamer *General Jessup* ran irregularly between the fort and the Gulf of California. Much of the fort's supplies came in by this route although wagon trains from the California seaports and pack trains from Sonora supplemented this river-borne traffic.

It was the unrelenting heat that Thomas seemed to remember most vividly in after years. It made the skin dry and harsh, the hair crisp. Furniture brought in from the north would fall apart. A leather trunk would contract so that the tray could not be lifted out. Ink would dry so fast that the nib of the pen would have to be washed off every few moments. Soap would lose one-sixth of its weight by evaporation and eggs their watery content. Whenever the subject of climate or temperature was brought up in Thomas' hearing he was liable to repeat the story about one of his men who died at Yuma. His ghost came back to the fort's guardroom looking for the dead man's blankets, as he found it too cold for comfort in hell.

In addition to making improvements at the post, Thomas sought to interest the army in operating its own river steamers. He investigated the navigability of the Colorado River upstream from the fort with a view to using it as a waterway to supply the army in Utah, but the white water and sheer walls of the Grand Canyon demonstrated the impracticability of his plan.[4]

In March 1855, he distributed long-range rifles to his command and inaugurated a two-month rifle practice, the result of which he was to report to the Department of the Pacific headquarters.

Along with his military duties, Thomas taught himself the Indian language. Seventy-seven words were phonetically spelled out in a paper entitled, "Vocabulary of the Kuchan Dialect of the Yuma Linguistic Family." It was perhaps the first attempt to give a written form to the speech of these Indians. The vocabulary was compiled at the risk of personal danger and is one of the most valuable manuscripts of the Bureau of American Ethnology. It is evident that the work was done by Thomas for his own amusement. His field notes were never arranged until 1868 when the work was done evidently at the request of George Gibbs, at that time the greatest authority in the United States on American Indian languages. Thomas was apologetic over the fact that his compilation was incomplete. He had misplaced the complete list of names of the different parts of the human body.

At the same time he made an important contribution to knowledge of the zoology of the Mexican border. A leaf-nosed bat, closely related to the true vampire, which he sent to Washington, was the first of its family ever found in the United States.[5] Outstanding scientists of the day credited Thomas and his assistants with making the zoology of the Pacific coast better known to the public than that of the more populous Atlantic seaboard. This work was a continuation of his field studies in botany during the second Florida campaign, which had brought him to the attention of several of the nation's foremost authorities in this branch of science. Thomas was not merely a collector of flora and fauna in accordance with War Department orders. He was well informed on many scientific subjects. Few men better understood the value of a microscope.

Interests of this kind were eyed suspiciously by army officers of the 1850's. The legends of the army are full of stories of how a commanding officer refused to find room in his crowded transport for a subordinate's meager library but had no trouble locating storage space for a case of whisky.

How near Thomas came to frustration in his tour of duty at Yuma may be inferred from the fact that he made application to the War Department for a transfer to an Eastern post as army paymaster. He may have wanted to avoid the discomforts of frontier garrisons. He may have sought duty at a post where his wife could be with him. Whether he failed to push his application aggressively or neglected to rally to its support the influence of his Virginia friends, nothing came of it. It may have been that the army hierarchy had other things in mind for Thomas at the time and opposed his transfer from the line to the staff, because on May 12, 1855, he was promoted to major and ordered to duty with the Second Regiment of Cavalry. This was rapid promotion. It came less than a year and a half after he was made captain. It jumped him over every captain in the Third Artillery and over every captain but three in all of the artillery regiments. It also increased his pay from sixty dollars a month with four rations and one servant to eighty dollars a month with four rations, forage for four horses, and two servants.

Thomas learned of his promotion on July 21, 1855. He left Fort Yuma and arrived at Jefferson Barracks, Missouri, on September 22, 1855, to take up his new duties. He probably started growing a moustache as he journeyed eastward since the mounted regiments were the only ones at this time that could legally wear such ornament. It is certain that the post tailor replaced the single row of brass buttons on his uniform coat with two rows of seven each, evenly spaced.

The Second Regiment of Cavalry became famous for the number of its officers who achieved high rank in the Confederate armies. They were hand picked by Jefferson Davis and, in a way, his reputation ran with their fortunes. From the beginning of his administration as Secretary of War, Davis pressed for a larger army. Ultimately Congress gave him four more regiments. One of these was recruited as the Second Cavalry. It became the crack unit of the army, a prestige long held by the First Dragoons.

The assignment of the Administration's political supporters to important commands in newly formed regiments was a custom that had become a precedent. Davis broke this custom when he staffed the Second Cavalry. Albert Sidney Johnston was named colonel. Robert E. Lee was induced to give up his staff duties and take a line appointment as lieutenant colonel at no increase in pay but with a chance for more rapid promotion. His record, stiff with honors, entitled him without question to the appointment. Hardee, whose capture just before the siege of Fort Brown caused the declaration of war with Mexico, was named the senior major. Two years' study of cavalry tactics in Europe and two brevets were the basis of his right to the command. The other appointment as major went to William Helmsley Emory of Maryland. He had resigned in 1836, been reappointed to the army in 1838 and won two brevets. As an officer of the famous First Dragoons and as chief of General Stephen Watts Kearny's topographical engineers, Emory's name was on most of the maps of the Southwest. He had marched with Kearny from Missouri to the Pacific when the troopers out-footed their horses through a fog of dust and took California for the Union. But Emory gave up the appointment shortly after receiving it in order to take equal rank in the First Cavalry, and the position was tendered to Braxton Bragg. Bragg refused.

In a way, the guns of Bragg and Thomas had blasted Jefferson Davis' way to power and Davis was not one to forget. When Bragg suggested Thomas for the appointment, Davis listened and Thomas became the junior major.

Junior though he was, his record ranked with the best. Mess table opinion credited him with being one of the three foremost of the younger officers in the service. The five men who controlled the army [6] had written their appraisals of him into the record. Four of these were favorable and one was censorious. The Secretary of War promoted him over most of the captains. Major General Winfield Scott, General-in-Chief and a fellow Virginian, made official the unofficial opinion of the rank and file. The senior brigadier general, T. S. Jesup, also a Virginian, reprimanded him for a breach of military procedure. Wool named him as one of the five to whom the nation was mainly indebted for the victory at Buena Vista. And Twiggs testified to his ability as a combat leader and approved his capability as a military administrator. Behind all this was the civil power of Virginia, whose authority was recognized by every state in the Union.

Half the company officers of the Second Cavalry were picked from the regular army. Among the captains were Earl Van Dorn, E. Kirby Smith, George Stoneman and Richard W. Johnson. Some of the lieutenants during Thomas' command were John Bell Hood, Kenner Garrard and Fitzhugh Lee. These officers played prominent parts in Thomas' later career.

The selection of these officers was almost entirely Davis' work. There is only circumstantial evidence that Davis selected them with the idea that they would fight for the South if the occasion arose, although Thomas believed that he did. It is safe to assume, however, that Davis felt he must please the Southern politicians, whose votes had augmented his army, by his selection of the new officers. The Virginians were gratified at the treatment accorded their state and as long as Davis was able to keep the Virginians happy he could keep himself politically strong. It should not be overlooked that the First Cavalry, organized by Davis at the same time, contained a high ratio of Northern officers.

Of the four field officers of the Second Cavalry, the appointments of Johnston and Thomas were most open to criticism, Johnston because he had been so long out of the army and Thomas because he lacked seniority. Thomas' record could sustain his appointment but apparently the justification for Johnston's appointment was that he had been a hero to the youthful Davis during the Secretary's undergraduate days at West Point.

The men of the Second Cavalry were picked as carefully as the officers. Most of them, too, came from slave states. Nine troops were recruited, one each from eight selected states and the ninth from the nation at large. Even its equipment had to be beyond reproach. The army routine of purchasing horses at or below a maximum price fixed by the War Department was waived. The Second Cavalry was permitted to buy the best horses obtainable regardless of price. Officers went into the horse country of Kentucky to find their mounts, which averaged $150 a head. The animals were matched for color and horses of the same color were assigned to the same troop. One of Thomas' troops had bay mounts, the other gray. One squadron was armed with a new breech-loading rifle. An officer unlucky enough to be thrown fairly from his saddle supplied his mess with free champagne, and good horsemanship became a commonplace in the regiment.

During the month that he was with the regiment prior to his departure Thomas was kept busy. About half of the company officers had come to the Second Cavalry direct from civilian life and Thomas had the job of training them. This regiment and the First Cavalry were the first purely mounted troops in the United States Army. The tactics Thomas taught now were different from those he had taught at West Point. Mounted reconnaissance was the cavalry's prime job. They pursued and demoralized a defeated enemy. They screened the movements of their own forces and held the enemy's communications under constant threat. They even stood guard while mounted, in advance of the pickets, and were known as vedettes. Their most glamorous role was that of a striking force aimed suddenly at an enemy's weakened point. Personally Thomas denied the axiom that the cavalry should not fight dismounted. Northern commanders generally shared this view and the Blue squadrons did their best work dismounted.

Ten companies of the Second Cavalry, 710 strong, moved out of Jefferson Barracks for Fort Belknap, Texas, on October 27, 1855. From here they would be deployed along the border. The wives of four officers rode with the command, probably in ambulances. Thomas rode at the head of his squadron, the three black feathers in his hat moving with the motion of his horse. Because the cavalry were not permitted to fly the colors, the regiment carried a blue flag with an adaptation of the arms of the United States. Twenty-six days later the command reached Fort Washita where Bragg was commanding. There was a big reunion. The Texas-bound officers were handsomely feted and sent on their way lacking their allotted amount of sleep. But Thomas did not go with them. He was detached at Fort Washita for court martial duty. His arrival had been delayed by high waters in Missouri, and the court, which had been sitting for three days when he arrived, refused to seat him.[7] He remained at Fort Washita until the following month when, in compliance with his own request to be permitted to rejoin his regiment by way of New York City, he left for the East and the arms of his bride. Probably because he was already in the East, his regimental commander asked that Thomas be detailed to the recruiting rendezvous in New York City to enlist a principal musician, two buglers and a band for the Second Cavalry. Thomas acknowledged the receipt of these orders from West Point on January 26, 1856.[8]

The following day his mother died suddenly in Southampton County, Virginia. Since Thomas' personal papers have been destroyed, there is no way of telling how he reacted to this news. Neither is it known how or when he received it. There is no record showing that he applied for leave to go home, and it is certain that he went on with his recruiting duties. Undoubtedly, having no time to attend her funeral, he wrote asking for details and what he could do about expenses, settling her estate and helping his sisters. This is one of those facts which give color to the theory that Thomas was an unemotional man devoid of ordinary human reactions.

It is possible that bandsmen were easier to recruit than the other ratings, for they were exempted from the height and age specifications. Music boys between the ages of twelve and fifteen could be taken. But even with these relaxations Thomas did not get all the men he needed. Rather than stay in New York City until the job was done he asked permission to turn the work over to the regular recruiting service so that he might rejoin his regiment.[9]

While in New York, Thomas made a routine report to the Adjutant General on the subject of target practice with small arms. In it he set forth his philosophy of command as follows: "My experience teaches me that soldiers usually shape their conduct according to the characteristics of their officers and that the reputation of a command for efficiency and skill depends almost entirely upon the interest which their officers take in their instruction. I therefore do not think it advisable or necessary to offer any inducements or rewards to acquire skill. It is sufficient for the soldier to be convinced that his officer takes pride in pointing him out as one of the most skillful and efficient of his command."[10] Good officers, in Thomas' opinion, made good troops.

7

Campaigns Against the Texas Comanches

The Texas frontier was moving westward faster than the army could establish and garrison the forts to protect it. By 1856 the forts in north Texas, set up by the treaty of annexation, had been engulfed by the settlements. Fort Mason was the westernmost post of this defense line. In less than five years the frontier pushed westward the distance of ten days' travel time. This had crowded the Indians, driven off their game, increased their debauchery by the whites and set up a situation which rapidly was becoming explosive.

The army determined to establish an equilibrium of force along the famous California Mail Route. This four-hundred-mile stretch of border between the Red River and the headwaters of the Concho River became Thomas' patrol.

The Office of Indian Affairs, with some niggardly cooperation from the state of Texas, had established two inadequate reservations to help quiet the Indians. One reservation of twenty-eight square miles stretched downstream from Camp Cooper along the Clear Fork. This was known as the Comanche reserve. The Brazos reserve, three times as large, was located some fifty miles to the east near the junction of the Clear Fork with the main stream of the Brazos. It housed representatives of half a dozen tribes less aggressive and more sedentary than the Comanches. Camp Cooper, so inhospitable that it was designated as a double-ration post, guarded the Comanche reserve, and Fort Belknap kept order on the Brazos.

Thomas' trip to New York and his recruiting assignment had kept him from his regiment some six months. When he returned the Second Cavalry had not been deployed. Lee commanded four troops at Camp Cooper, and Hardee commanded the balance at Fort Mason. Thomas was directed to relieve Hardee. His orders were to protect the settlements from the hostile Indians, protect the reserve Indians from the greedy whites, help the Indian agents discharge their duties, survey railroad routes, construct military roads, and safeguard mail and travelers. Fort Mason was well behind the new defense line. Its housing facilities were preferable to those of the new posts. When Thomas relieved Hardee of his command of the post and garrison on June 21, 1856, he moved into a three-room house. Colonel Johnston was in San Antonio acting as the commander of the Department of Texas.

There were between 500 and 600 Indians on the Comanche reserve when Thomas reached the plains country. John R. Baylor, the Indian agent in charge of the reservation, had succeeded in inducing them to plant their first crop. This was ruined by grasshoppers and the replanting was killed by a drought.[1] Some of their hunting parties, out looking for buffalo by the agent's permission, were overdue. When they did return they came on foot, destitute and starving. The buffalo were leaving the country. Many of these Indians were blood relations to the Northern Comanches, who were then raiding the settlements for revenge, horses and captives. Trouble between the troops and either group of Indians upset the other. Terror on the border was the result.

It was a good thing that Jefferson Davis and the four field officers of the Second Cavalry had determined on making that regiment one of the elite in the service. It was to be combat-sharpened on a harsh grindstone. The Comanches were the most terrible savages of the plains. They killed and captured more whites than any other western Indians and stole more horses and cattle. They had greater skill in inflicting pain, and human agony was their highest enjoyment. Man for man the Second Cavalry outweighed them but the Comanches often chose hand-to-hand combat. Their small, wiry, fleet, and durable ponies were more than a match for the $150 mounts of the troopers, and superb horsemanship increased their superiority. When retreat became hopeless they dismounted and kicked off their moccasins as evidence of their determination to stand and fight. Their bows had a faster rate of fire than the musket, but repeaters made them obsolete. The modern marine,

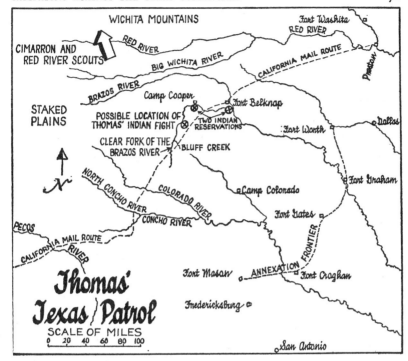

Map 3. Thomas' Texas Patrol. The Second Cavalry worked from Richardson's map, which can be seen at the Library of Congress. The present map is a composite of four different maps, none of which agree on the location of natural features.

with his automatic rifle, would be proud to equal the records of some Comanche marksmen with their arrows. These arrows were capable of a true flight of three hundred yards and were exceptionally accurate up to fifty yards, one authority says seventy-five yards. They could be fired at the rate of eight or ten aimed shots in half a minute.

The horse made the Comanche. It was his combat transport. It fed him when other food failed. Together with the captives it helped him take, it was his trading stock. Horses stolen from the Texas settlements were sold at a good price to the Santa Fe caravans out of Fort Bent. There was generally a ready market for captives but, if not, they were good for two and sometimes three days of torture. It took several years for the Second Cavalry to learn its lessons. In the meantime the Comanches scourged portions of the Texas border as it had never before been scourged.

Before Thomas had time to deploy his five troops, he was ordered to court martial duty at Ringgold Barracks on the Rio Grande, opposite Camargo. Lee was ordered to the same duty and at his suggestion they pooled their transport, escort, servants and supplies and divided their mess bills. Each officer probably had one servant. Lee furnished the cook. A six-mule wagon and nine troopers completed the party as it set out on the three-week trip. Once, stopped by high water, they chanced a crossing and made it by floating their wagon. Uniforms, bedding and food were covered with a film of mud.

Ringgold Barracks was so crowded that there was no room for them in the officers' quarters. Thomas and Lee therefore ate and slept in the same tents that had provided them shelter on the trip. The court was convened on October 1, 1856, to try Major Giles Porter and it did not rise until four and a half months later.

Sometime between November 1 and Christmas, Mrs. Thomas joined her husband. Lee was their guest for Christmas dinner and probably for other meals. Undoubtedly they entertained several officers, for there were at least four other wives on the post at the time. Mrs. Thomas was aided in her housework by two white women whom she had brought with her from New Orleans.

An hour after the court's adjournment, the Thomases left for the north. Three weeks later they rode into San Antonio where they probably entertained and were entertained by Colonel and Mrs. Johnston. But another court martial was being convened at Indianola and Thomas was named as a member of it. At this point, Mrs. Thomas' domestic establishment broke down. One of her white servants had fallen in love with a soldier and now wanted to leave her employ and get married. The major solved the difficulty by buying a slave.

On April 6, 1857, the Thomases were back at Fort Mason, but in two weeks they were off to Camp Cooper and another court martial. Here the troops were under canvas. Lee pitched a tent for his own use and one for the Thomases. He invited them to his own mess and was embarrassed because of the meagerness of his food supply and the inexperience of his servant. Three weeks served to dispose of this trial and then a court of inquiry was convened at Fort Mason to hear the troubles of Lieutenant Wood, one of the junior officers of the Second Cavalry.[2] Colonel Johnston, Lieutenant Colonel Lee and Major Thomas were members and since Fort Mason was Thomas' post, he and his wife would act as hosts. They saw to it that the hospitality extended to their visitors was as generous as the circumstances permitted. The Fort Mason Derby was the key social event. It was run for one thousand yards and repeat. Entries were officers' service mounts ridden by their owners. The ladies watched from their carriages and bet gloves and handkerchiefs. Baskets of champagne and here and there a pay account changed hands between the officers.

But Lieutenant Wood's business was more serious. He had been informed by Captain William R. Bradfute, also of the Second Cavalry, that rumors were being circulated accusing him of having stolen money from a drunken civilian. Wood asked for a court of inquiry to clear his record, his request was granted by the President of the United States and the court met. But before their work was completed an express rode into Fort Mason with urgent orders. Johnston was wanted immediately in Washington to confer with the government on the Mormon troubles in Utah. Lee was to succeed him in command of the regiment and the Department of Texas and was ordered to San Antonio. Thomas carried the case to its conclusion. He ruled that Wood's reputation had not been damaged because no rumor had ever existed and that furthermore there had been no foundation for such a rumor.

With the exception of a short tour of recruiting duty, Thomas had spent a year serving on courts martial. One thing he learned was that military legal proceedings were used for a weapon almost as frequently as for a shield. As a result, he henceforth read or had examined for him every case prepared for court martial relative to his command. If the slightest trace of malice was evident he often tore up the papers.

By the time the Wood court of inquiry was completed, Twiggs had assumed command of the Department of Texas with his headquarters in San Antonio. The deployment of the Second Cavalry had been completed and they were now garrisoning a cordon of posts from the Red River to the Pecos.[3] It was Twiggs' old scheme that had worked so well for him in Florida where he had also had Thomas to establish and garrison his defense line. But here his cordon was too thin. To defeat the rawhide-tough Comanche, with his commissary in the form of strips of raw meat laid across a pony's back, required different tactics than to defeat the Seminole moving on waterways between fixed bases. Contention was rife on the Indian reserves. Baylor had been succeeded by Mathew Leeper as agent of the Comanche reservation, and he was retaliating by stirring up the settlements to demand a much harsher treatment of the Indians and to oust the incumbent administrators. It was a political brawl and Twiggs sided with the Texans. This dissention was an invitation to the Comanche raiders and they seized it with a raid on the reservation itself. If they had ridden into Twiggs' headquarters and stolen his sword out of its scabbard, their challenge to his authority could hardly have been more insolent. With each violation of the border, Twiggs' embarrassment increased.

The Second Cavalry, too, was unhappy. Their quarters were uncomfortable and inadequate. No supplies were available except the uninteresting staples handled by the commissary. Their duty was arduous and there were no compensating recreations. On behalf of his command, Thomas complained bitterly of perpetual banishment.[4] There were professional lapses, too, that hurt the men's pride, mortified their commanding officers and supplied the infantry with material for many a caustic remark.

One such incident involved Cornelius Van Camp, a junior second lieutenant in the Second Cavalry who commanded the detachment guarding the Comanche reserve. On August 31, 1858, Agent Leeper notified Van Camp that two renegade Comanches were on the reserve in defiance of his orders to leave, and he asked for help. Van Camp paraded his detachment, twenty-five strong, and marched them down to the seat of the trouble. His purpose was to capture the renegades, but the reserve Indians misread his intent. Fearing for their own lives they moved out to meet the troops. The excitement was intense. Dogs were barking, women screaming and the warriors yelling and stringing their bows. Outnumbered four to one, Van Camp halted with the warriors facing the cavalrymen in an opposing line. They could level as many muskets as the soldiers. There was a parley but it came to nothing and Van Camp ordered an advance. The excited Indians prepared to attack and roughly handled their own chief, who tried to stop them. Both sides had gone too far to back down. Van Camp gave the order to load and his sergeant informed him that the men had only one round of ammunition and that there was no more back at their camp.

Thomas reported the bare facts to Twiggs. Twiggs forwarded the report to Washington. His covering letter used the words "deeply mortified . . . at loss what to do . . . distressing . . . ordered an investigation . . . criminal neglect. . . ." A month later Van Camp's record was cleared by the soldier's requiem, "killed in action."

There was no doubt that the morale of the Second Cavalry was sinking. A few months prior to the Van Camp episode there had been a more subtle indication of this. Lieutenant George Stoneman had sent armed troopers onto the reserve without the agent's permission. When the agent objected Stoneman replied arrogantly, "I claim the privilege of refusing to answer the demands of anyone to whom I am not subordinate, in regard to my official acts or the motives by which I am actuated."[5] The corruptive influence of violence was subverting Stoneman's duty. The cause of the trouble may have been indicated by an official complaint to the Commissioner of Indian Affairs condemning Twiggs for his prejudice against the Indians.

Thomas was keeping his head but his position was difficult. Since

October 21, 1857, when Lee had left Texas on leave, Thomas had been in command of the regiment. He was in just the right position to take the blame if things blew up. He was facing the stiffest test, so far, of his career. His physical courage had been proved. Moral courage, diplomacy and the art of persuasion were what he needed now. Thomas sought a partial escape from his troubles in the extension of his scientific studies to the Texan fauna.[6]

To make matters worse, Twiggs was riding him. Apparently the riding started with the Wood court of inquiry. Bradfute, who had convinced Wood that his character had been maligned by rumors, now felt that his own honor was compromised because Thomas had found the rumors nonexistent. He asked Twiggs for a court of inquiry for his vindication and Twiggs granted it. It convened in San Antonio in November 1857 and Thomas was ordered down from his duties as regimental commander to testify. A court appointed by a brigadier general to clear a captain whose honor had been sullied by a major would not be easy on the major.

The Bradfute court reversed Thomas' findings of the preceding July. As Thomas rode back to Fort Mason from San Antonio he was probably thinking bitter thoughts. To his towering problems of command was added his public repudiation by the Department commander and the implication that he had dishonored his oath. He knew the army code. As a Virginian, he knew too well what his hot-spurred juniors were thinking. It was two troubled months before the Second Cavalry learned that Twiggs' backhanded slap at Thomas had drawn a stinging reprimand from the Secretary of War.

While Thomas was testifying at the Bradfute court he received orders from Twiggs to detail an officer to recruiting duty in New Orleans. He complied by selecting Lieutenant Wood. The following day Twiggs ordered Thomas to make a new detail that would not do "manifest injustice to the other subalterns in Second Cavalry." This is the only accusation of favoritism ever recorded against Thomas.[7]

Early in the spring of 1858 the Second Cavalry was ordered to Fort Leavenworth as the first leg of a march to Utah where Colonel Johnston was running into serious trouble with the Mormons. Thomas ordered the concentration of his regiment at Fort Belknap and began pulling in all his units from detached duty. Even though the grazing was poor at Fort Belknap it was the nearest spot to Leavenworth so he took the chance of gaunting his horses.

Just about the time the concentration was completed, however, the movement to Fort Leavenworth was countermanded. For a short period in the middle of June, Twiggs was under the impression that the Second Cavalry was no longer under his command. During this period Thomas received orders direct from Washington to send a detachment to pick up 400 horses at Fort Smith. Thomas ordered an officer and twelve men to this duty. With the promulgation of this order Twiggs learned that the Second Cavalry was still under his command. He immediately ordered Thomas to increase his Fort Smith detail by 120 men. Thus augmented, the detachment must have run pretty close to 25 per cent of the regiment's effective strength. Thomas complied with the order without protest but his covering letter which accompanied a copy of Twiggs' order advised the Adjutant General of the change. It was a typical Thomas protest, Virginian in its propriety and restraint.

But the Second Cavalry, with a large train of hired wagons on demurrage, and with inadequate grazing, had to move. On August 12, 1858, orders had come out from the Adjutant General to return the units to their former stations, "subject to such changes as the Department Commander might direct." The change that the Department commander directed was a raid into the Wichita country. Twiggs stripped from the garrison all its combat troops and put them under Earl Van Dorn's command for the raid. It was common knowledge in the army that Thomas was entitled to this command by virtue of seniority alone, yet Twiggs' defiance of this military precedent had been condoned by the Adjutant General. Thomas gazed over a deserted, sunbaked parade ground as he pondered his problem.

Shortly after October 1, the news came in of Van Dorn's battle. During its four years on the Texas border the Second Cavalry fought thirty-two different engagements with the Indians. Van Dorn's was their greatest victory. It confirmed the wisdom of Twiggs' choice of command and put Thomas in more of a hole than ever. Twice he applied to Twiggs for leave and twice his application was turned down.

There is only one known piece of evidence that gives a picture of Thomas' state of mind at this time. It is a copy of a letter written by him to his sister Fanny, dated at Fort Belknap two days before Christmas 1858. This was less than three weeks after his second application for leave had been refused. It was two and a half months before he started his counterattack against Twiggs. The letter reads:

My dear Fanny
    Yours of the 7th ult. has been in my possession for some time. I have been waiting to learn if Col. Lee will join the regiment before answering it, as I had previously written that we would go on leave when he joined. A few days ago I learned that his leave had been extended until the first of

May next.[8] So we shall have to wait until that time unless some other field officer joins the Regiment. It does not make a great deal of difference now, as Mrs. Kellogg's [Mrs. Thomas' mother's] health has improved so much that Fanny is no longer anxious about her. However, I must manage somehow to get out next May, as she is not only almost out of clothes but I promised her mother to take her north this last spring and should not like to delay it any longer than the next.

You must have had a hustling and noisy time of it during the visit of Ben's [Thomas' oldest brother's] family. I hope they all enjoyed themselves. I should have liked very much to have been with you too.

I do not know when we can ever visit Ben or have his family with us.

He wrote me that he would have come with his family to Fort Leavenworth to see us, had we been so fortunate as to get there, and I am in hopes still that we may be able to invite them some day.

This place continues as wretchedly dull as ever, and we have had one or two as cold spells as I have ever experienced in New York even at this season of the year.

The high winds during the whole winter here are as bleak and disagreeable as the March winds in Virginia and it frequently and very unexpectedly turns excessively cold. So we are constantly uneasy about the weather all winter. Please tell Judy [his oldest sister, then operating the homestead farm] that I will send her the $100 for the church as soon as the paymaster comes up from San Antonio. If she cannot get the neighbors to join in building one, I wish her to expend it in charitable purposes among the needy in the neighborhood.

I hope she has made a good crop this year.

Fanny joins me in wishing you all a happy Christmas and sends much love.

Yours truly

George H. Thomas [9]

On March 11, 1859, seven months after Van Dorn had been given command of the Wichita expedition, Thomas wrote Twiggs accusing him of an injustice in disregarding his seniority and requesting that Twiggs forward his complaint to the General-in-Chief. Twiggs acknowledged the receipt of this letter on March 29, saying that he considered Thomas' criticism uncalled for, improper and unmilitary. A week later Twiggs advised Thomas that he would not get a field command until July 13, on which date Colonel Lee's leave would terminate. He referred again to Thomas' letter of March 11 and called it uncourteous and inconsistent.

On May 3, Thomas' case received a severe setback when Winfield Scott advised Twiggs that he approved the action of which Thomas had complained. Three weeks later, Thomas appealed from Scott's decision with a request for a court of inquiry. The Secretary of War reversed Scott's finding on July 7, 1859, and closed the case by refusing the court of inquiry.[10]

The Texans were now making nearly as much trouble for Thomas as the Indians. Baylor, at the head of a hundred whites, moved to invade the Brazos reserve. But Captain John H. King of the First Infantry, with his detachment and a single piece of artillery, dissuaded him. Two months later Baylor tried it again, this time with a force two and a half times as large. They killed and scalped one old Indian, after putting a rope around his neck, and threatened a general assault on the rest of the reserves, but thought better of it before hostilities actually began, and withdrew. But the Indians, now thoroughly aroused, followed them, probably off the reservation. A fight ensued with the Indians getting the best of it. Thomas reported the affair to Twiggs. He added that the whites were arming for the purpose of breaking up both reserves, that all civil authority seemed to be at an end, and that the May term of the district court of Young County could not be held because the judge and other officers feared to travel through the excited district.

Thomas asked Twiggs for authority to take two companies from Van Dorn so that he might restore order and protect the reserves until the Indians could be removed. Twiggs denied the request on the ground that the argument between the whites and the reserve Indians was a civil matter in which the troops should not interfere. It took three and one-half months for this divergence of policy to come up to the Secretary of War for a ruling. When it did, he held with Thomas.

By that time, however, orders had already been issued to move the reserve Indians out of Texas and Thomas was placed in charge of the escort of four troops of cavalry and one company of infantry. Twiggs vainly protested its size. Eight hired ox teams hauled the Indians' goods and their sick and feeble. A company of infantry held the Red River crossing just below the mouth of the Big Wichita until the Indians were safely across. The march was something less than four hundred miles and Thomas was away from his post twenty-two days.

At the time of the removal, Twiggs reported that Texas was free of Comanches except for small parties that were raiding for horses. He had now been two years in command of the Department but there was yet no peace on the border. At least two of his moves had stirred up the Indians to greater retaliation. Van Dorn's attack on the unsuspecting Comanche village east of the Wichita Mountains had destroyed 120 lodges and slaughtered 58 Indians. It was a military victory but a diplomatic error, because these Indians were on their way to attend a peace council. In Indian eyes, peace movements now were suspect. Van Dorn's violence broke down the shield to the Texas settlements which it sought to maintain. The forced removal of the Texas reserve Indians was another convincing fact, from an Indian point of view, that peace with the white man did not pay. As a result, the Comanches coordinated their attacks with those of the Arapahoes and Cheyennes and struck with greater violence against the whites.

Twiggs' forward planning, so far as the Second Cavalry was concerned, was a fall raid against any Northern Comanches who might follow the southern migration of the buffalo. This, he sanguinely assured the Adjutant General, would drive back the Indians and rid Texas of the Comanches for some time. The raid was to cover the headwaters of the Red and Canadian rivers. The records fail to show whether Twiggs was lulled into a feeling of false security or whether he was putting the best possible face on things to help his pending application for a twelve-month leave.

Five companies were detailed for the Red River-Canadian River duty and Thomas commanded them. They followed an Indian trail into what is now northwestern Oklahoma to a point near the Cimarron River but finally lost the trail when it was obliterated by buffalo. He returned to Camp Cooper on November 22, having been out nearly eight weeks without finding any recent signs of Indians. While he was gone Twiggs left on leave.

During the winter of 1859–1860, the Indians were operating a systematic raiding plan worked out in cooperation with other tribes. In the middle of February 1860, this policy reached an audacious climax. Almost simultaneous raids were made at Camp Colorado, Camp Cooper and Fort Mason. This was a hundred-mile line which formed the heart of Twiggs' original defense cordon. The mule yard at Camp Cooper was raided on February 17 with the apparent collusion of the sentry. Picket stakes were pulled up, the bell cut from the neck of the bell mule and the whole herd driven off. No alarm was given for fifteen or twenty minutes. The trail of the raiders was picked up the next morning and followed for sixty miles. Twenty-three animals were recovered. The following night all the animals from the agency near Camp Cooper, except those locked in the stable, were stolen.

This was the situation that faced Lieutenant Colonel Lee when he took command of the Department of Texas on February 20, 1860. Almost immediately the effective cooperation between Lee and Thomas, which had been evident at West Point, began to function. Lee's first task was to quiet the uproar of protest that swept the Texas settlement and echoed in the halls of Congress. John N. Reagan told Congress, referring to the rape of the Camp Cooper mule yard, that the Second Cavalry couldn't even protect its own mounts. Lee pointed out that the difficulties arose from worn-out horses and was not a matter of poor morale.

From May 2 to June 2, 1860, Thomas was scouting some one hundred miles west of Camp Cooper in the northeast corner of the Staked Plains. His mission was probably two-fold—retaliation for the Indian raids of the preceding February and an attempt to learn where, along the upper reaches of the Brazos, Big Wichita and Red rivers, the raiding Indians stopped for water and grass.

A little less than eight weeks after he returned, Thomas was off on another scout, this time to the southwest. Again he was searching for the grass and water oases that the raiding Indians required to support their animals in their long, fast rides over the arid stretches of the state. The most painstaking part of his search covered the region between the 31st and 33rd parallels of latitude and the 101st and 102nd meridians. It embraced the source of the North Concho River and the upper valleys of the Main or Middle Concho and the Colorado. On his way back to Camp Cooper from this scout, not far from where Bluff Creek empties into the Clear Fork on the California Mail Route, his Delaware guide discovered a fresh Indian trail. Thomas immediately split the party, sending his sick with his wagons and baggage on to Camp Cooper. The remainder of his detachment, some twenty-five men, followed the trail under Thomas' command. The Indians were headed west-northwest and Thomas followed them until darkness made the tracking impossible. The troops had covered forty miles since picking up the Indian trail and farther than that since they had broken camp in the morning. Their horses were jaded.

At seven o'clock the following morning, August 26, 1860, Thomas' advance scout and the Indian trail guard made contact. Thomas received the signal agreed upon and at once moved out his men at a gallop. The Indians, eleven in number, were a mile and a half ahead, breaking camp on the right bank of the Clear Fork. The attack was a surprise except for the eight- or ten-minute notice given them by their guard. With their expert knowledge of mounted tactics, however, the Indians had their back trail blocked by a deep ravine that was impassable to mounted troops. Here the cavalry lost considerable time searching for a crossing. They finally made it by dismounting and leading their horses over. The Indians had used the time to round up their loose animals and begin their flight. By the time Thomas had his men remounted the Indians were half a mile ahead of him. Although his horses were tiring fast, he pressed the pursuit at full speed. The Indian ponies were relatively fresh and their loads were lighter, but the necessity of herding ahead of them some twenty-eight loose horses slowed their pace and the cavalry began to close in. To save themselves the Indians abandoned their herd and a lone warrior to act as a rear guard. If the chase followed the patterns of most of these cavalry skirmishes, the stronger cavalry horses drew ahead of the weaker ones and the pursuit gradually tailed out as this distance increased.

How many of the pursuers remained in the forefront the record does not say, but there must have been at least seven and probably more. Thomas was one of them. Suddenly the Indian rear guard slid off of his horse, kicked off his moccasins, dropped to one knee and unslung his arrows. The troopers, still mounted, charged in on him in a mass, firing as they moved. A hail of bullets filled the air around him. More than twenty of them took effect.

A charging horseman offers only a small target—face, shoulders, arms and legs—the rest of his body being masked from a dismounted man by the horse's head, neck and chest. A galloping horse could cover the effective range of an arrow in fifteen to twenty seconds. Yet the Indian's arrows found these moving targets four times. They inflicted one face wound, one shoulder wound and two leg wounds on four different men. These were all aimed shots and the rapidity of his fire was extraordinary. When the fight closed to hand-to-hand combat the Indian inflicted two more casualties with his lance but, weakened by his numerous wounds, he lacked the strength to drive home his steel. The odds against him were greater than those faced by Custer and by the defenders of the Alamo. A gallant warrior died that midsummer morning on the grassy plain beside the Clear Fork.

The pursuit was discontinued, Thomas reported, because the retreating Indians had opened a two-mile lead and his own animals were exhausted. He rounded up the captured ponies while his second in command attended to the wounded. Thomas, who must have been in the forefront of the charge with his body bent low along the horse's neck, took an arrow in the face.[11] It pierced the fleshy part of his chin and drove hard into his chest. Acting as a skewer it held his head in a strained position while his horse jarred to a stop. Thomas pulled it out with his own hand, probably before he dismounted. There was no professional medical attention until the hospital steward in the spring wagon met the detachment two days later. Even then Thomas, whose wound was officially reported as serious, refused to quit his saddle. The weather turned for the worse the afternoon of the skirmish as the detachment slowly retraced its steps. Thomas rode at its head, his awkward bandage soggy from the rain. Three months later the details of his scout were published to the army in general orders.

It is probable that Thomas' detachment divided among themselves the money received from the sale of the twenty-eight captured animals, but there was an intangible gain with far-reaching implications. Thomas' emotion had led him into an acceptance of the tactic of attrition. His recklessness had corrupted his talent. There were less expensive ways of disposing of a lone warrior, but to practice them he needed to conquer himself.

Thomas had now examined the frontier from the Cimarron to the Pecos and his abnormally keen observation had spotted the possible points of departure for the war parties planning to pillage the west Texas settlements. Lee and Thomas conceived a system of spot defense which would deny to the raiding bands the rendezvous they needed for pasture and water.[12] One of these spots was the head of the Concho and while Thomas was examining it in detail, Lee was recommending to army headquarters the construction of a fort there. But the plan died almost as soon as it was conceived. On July 23 Thomas applied for a twelve-month leave, which was granted on August 28. It went into effect on November 12 and Thomas started for the East.

It would seem reasonable to assume that Thomas discussed the national political situation with Lee. In Texas in the fall of 1860, men everywhere were talking of secession. The fear and anger caused by the John Brown raid had not abated. The strain of the Presidential election was tearing down what little feeling remained of pride in the Union. These things were apparent to Lee. They must have been to Thomas. If he saw any of the Virginia newspapers, he read of the growing dissatisfaction and more and more talk of secession. The extreme positions of radicals on both sides led to heated arguments. These Thomas probably tried to avoid if one can judge by the tactics he used in Charleston in 1842. Lee, subjected to the same tensions, became noticeably reticent. No written record of Thomas' state of mind at this time survives, although others have spoken for him. Fitzhugh Lee, who was with him at this time, says that Thomas' feelings were Southern to an almost bellicose degree. Grant said practically the same thing, but he had not seen Thomas since the Mexican War. Both witnesses testified after Thomas' death.

As the time for Thomas' departure from Texas grew closer, his problem of what to do with the female slave he had purchased for

Mrs. Thomas became more pressing. He wanted to free her but she objected. The economical move would have been to sell her but this solution ran counter to his conscience, so he took her with him to his home in Virginia.

This distaste for selling was the result of one common Southern justification for slavery. Under this theory the slave willingly gave his services in return for the protection of the master. Thomas, having assumed this responsibility, was loath to divest himself of it even by manumission. After the war when the woman, then free, claimed his protection he recognized his responsibility, even extended it to include the woman's husband and children, and brought the family to Nashville. Here he tried unsuccessfully to train them for the life of freedom. When he was ordered to the Pacific command, Thomas induced his brother Benjamin to give them employment and, with their consent, sent them to him. In keeping with this stubborn moral sense that rejected three legal but unilateral solutions of an awkward situation, was Thomas' stubborn refusal ever to accept any compromise of measures that he had determined upon as right. To superiors this trait was maddening; to his adversaries it was a thrust-proof armor; to the soldiers under his command, who had temporarily given him custody of their lives and liberties, it was a guaranty that their sacrifices were not to be in vain.

8

Civil War and Personal Decision

On his way home from Texas, Thomas met with an accident. He stepped off the train in the darkness at Lynchburg, miscalculated the distance to the ground and wrenched his back so badly that the journey was halted at Norfolk. Mrs. Thomas, who had left Texas several months earlier, was summoned by telegraph to his aid.[1] His injury proved stubborn and it was nearly eight weeks before he could continue his trip to New York. With considerable effort he managed to travel the fifty miles from Norfolk to his Southampton home to spend Christmas. As his sister Fanny forty years later recalled the details of his visit, the Major and his wife arrived December 15 and left January 8. "He had much of his army baggage sent here and left it, wishing it to be stored in the house, implying that he would return for it and it would be ready for his use; he also brought his servants and left them in my sister's care until such time as he and his wife might require the services of the cook, whom Mrs. Thomas wished to retain."[2] Sister Judith recalled that her brother spoke of returning in March.

During this visit South Carolina seceded. This seemed of little moment at the time. The North derided the idea and the South doubted South Carolina's method and timing.

Leaving Southampton County, Thomas visited Washington. He called on General Scott and allegedly reported to him that Twiggs was not to be trusted.[3] There is some doubt that Thomas made this accusation, but the conversation probably did touch upon his experience with Twiggs.

In any event, the Thomases were in New York City registered at the New York Hotel, 721 Broadway, between Washington Place and Waverly Place, by January 18. Meantime three more states had seceded —Mississippi, one of whose counties in turn seceded from the state because of its Union sympathies; Florida, where several of the delegates elected as Unionists switched their votes to secession; and Alabama, where one county with an overwhelming Union sentiment maintained its freedom of opinion with a military organization.

Because of his back injury, Thomas was seriously concerned about his physical ability to continue in the army. In addition, he saw little hope for the prosperity of the service, as Northern men were now in possession of the government and they had always been unfriendly to the armed forces. Such a state of mind would account for his anxiety for employment outside of the army. He also was disgusted at the weakness shown by the national government at this time and confessed that he had little hope of its maintaining itself. It appeared to him to be falling apart for want of capacity, integrity or firmness, or perhaps all of them. But most pressing of all was the necessity to find some means of support if, as he believed, his back was permanently injured. He and Mrs. Thomas were talking over their future prospects when she saw an advertisement in the *National Intelligencer* which she read to him. It seemed to offer a solution to their problem.

In response to the advertisement, Thomas immediately wrote to Colonel Francis H. Smith, Superintendent of the Virginia Military Institute at Lexington.

Dear Sir:

In looking over the files of the National Intelligencer this morning, I met with your advertisement for a commandant of cadets and instructor of tactics at the Institute. If not already filled, I will be under obligation if you will inform me what salary and allowances pertain to the situation, as from present appearances I fear it will soon be necessary for me to be looking up some means of support. Very respectfully, your obedient servant, Geo. H. Thomas, Major, U. S. Army.[4]

The office he inquired about was just then being vacated by Major William Gilham, who had been a classmate of his at West Point. Thomas availed himself of this relationship by sending his letter to Gilham for transmission to Colonel Smith and perhaps by giving Gilham some of the reasons why he was thinking of leaving the army. A reply advised Thomas that the instructorship was not to be his.[5]

As for the national news, part of it was more disquieting, but there were also encouraging signs. Three more states had split away from the Union—Georgia, after seriously questioning the timing of the move; Louisiana, with a New Orleans paper charging fraud; and Texas, where there had been rumors of intimidation. The Confederacy was organized with Thomas' admirer Jefferson Davis at its head. Offsetting this news, the peace conference called by Virginia was meeting in Washington under the leadership of ex-President Tyler. His own state was taking the lead in holding the Union together and, if it were successful, Thomas knew that Virginia's voice would still carry weight in the national councils even though the control of the army might be in Northern hands. In addition, Maryland's governor refused to call a convention to consider secession. North Carolina and Tennessee were holding back, and secession fever in Arkansas was cooling noticeably. Missouri voted eighty thousand against secession and the Kentucky legislature was refusing to listen to that state's vocal secession minority.

About this time, Thomas heard that one-fourth of the regular army, including the Second Cavalry, had surrendered to the Texans without a single casualty. This he found hard to believe. It didn't seem to be in character for hotbloods like Van Dorn, Hood and Fitzhugh Lee. Then the real news began to come through. Twiggs had surrendered all the United States posts and stores in Texas. The troops had been disarmed and ordered out of the state. Thomas' indignation flamed. He regretted that he had not been on duty when the surrender took place. "I would have taken command of the men," he said, "marched them north until they reached the loyal states, and the rebels should not have taken a prisoner or captured a cannon or a flag." Flagrant disobedience of Twiggs' orders under such circumstances would have been balm to his sores.[6]

Perhaps it was his wrath over Twiggs' surrender that caused him to write the following letter on March 1, 1861, to the Adjutant General:

I have the honor respectfully to ask to be detailed as Superintendent of the mounted recruiting service for the next two years.

My reason for making this application is: I am still quite lame from an injury which I received last November in Lynchburg, Va., and although I could attend to all my ordinary duties I fear that I shall not have sufficient strength to perform every duty which might be required of me if with my regiment.[7]

Three days later Lincoln was inaugurated. For the first time there was no slaveholder in the President's Cabinet. Thomas began to regain his confidence in the national government. His back was healing, too, enough so that he could walk outdoors and extend the length of his route a little each day. Old army friends dropped in with news. Sherman had quit his job in Louisiana when that state seized the United States arsenal at Baton Rouge. A dozen officers ahead of Thomas had resigned or been dismissed. Lee had accepted a commission as colonel in the United States army. Hardee had resigned and Thomas may have speculated upon his chances for moving into Lee's vacated command. Altogether things did not look too gloomy. There was plenty of discussion, too, as to what an officer should or should not do about resigning. One officer saw Thomas many times in New York and heard him discuss the state of the nation with other officers who afterwards went into the Rebel army. Later he maintained that Thomas never agreed, in his hearing, to the proposition that an officer in the United States army must go with his state if it seceded.[8]

On March 12, Thomas wrote as follows to John Letcher, the Governor of Virginia. . .

Dear Sir:

I received yesterday a letter from Major Gilham of the Virginia Military Institute, dated the 9th instant, in reference to the position of Chief of Ordnance of the State, in which he informs me that you had requested him to ask me if I would resign from the service, and, if so, whether that post would be acceptable to me. As he requested me to make my reply to you direct, I have the honor to state, after expressing my most sincere thanks for your kind offer, that it is not my wish to leave the service of the United States as long as it is honorable for me to remain in it, and, therefore, as long as my native state remains in the union, it is my purpose to remain in the army, unless required to perform duties alike repulsive to honor and humanity.

The position of chief of ordnance of the state of Virginia carried with it the rank and pay of a colonel. If, as Thomas firmly believed, there was to be no civil war, here was his chance to use his professional skills at a substantial increase in pay and without the active field duty ruled out by his injury. Yet he declined it. His refusal, however, was not absolute.

On April 4 a test vote in Virginia showed that state opposed to secession. Two days later, and more than six months before his leave expired, Thomas was ordered to active duty and accepted. The orders came from General Scott. The Second Cavalry was being brought back from Texas to be recruited and re-equipped. Scott wanted Thomas to take command of the men when they landed at New York City, entrain them for Carlisle, Pennsylvania, and get them ready quickly for active duty.

Thomas took care to advise his superiors that he was physically unfit for such service. Mrs. Thomas wanted to dissuade her husband from the course he had chosen but since he had not discussed the matter with her she kept silent. Her dissuasion, if it had been expressed, would have been based upon his physical disability, but Thomas had already answered this argument. "I can attend to the remounting of the regiment," he said, "although I cannot ride on horseback." Mrs. Thomas' unexpressed reply was, "Not one in a dozen, injured as you are, would have reported for duty." [9]

But even if Thomas refused to ask his wife's advice, he felt that he needed her help. When he said good-bye to her in New York, it was understood that she would join him in Carlisle in a few days. Thomas also had to break his promise to his sisters, for there was no chance now for a leisurely trip through Virginia to pick up his duffle and his slave.

The trip to Carlisle was a fateful one for Thomas. At Harrisburg he was startled by the newsboys running through the cars shouting their extras. The headlines announced that Sumter had been fired on. Five days later, Virginia seceded.

Thomas had probably been asked many times, directly or indirectly, what stand he intended to take between the Union and the South. So far as his personal testimony is known he never committed himself. His commitment now was so prompt as to indicate that his mind had been made up in advance. It also seems probable that he reached his decision without asking the advice of anyone. At least he never consulted his immediate family, for his wife, writing of the matter on November 5, 1884, said, "There was never a word passed between myself or *any one* of our family upon the subject of his remaining loyal to the United States government. We felt that whatever his course, it would be from a conscientious sense of duty, that no one could persuade him to do what he felt was not right." At the same time, however, Mrs. Thomas affirms that she knew all along what her husband intended to do.[10] His sister Fanny also was certain that she knew what he intended to do. Their opinions are irreconcilable.

Thomas wired his wife not to come to Carlisle and wrote her that he was remaining with the Union. Later she recalled his words, saying that "turn it every way he would, the one thing was uppermost, his duty to the government of the United States." [11] At the same time

Thomas notified his sisters of his decision. So far as is known they never acknowledged his letter.

A captain of the Second Cavalry intimately acquainted with Thomas maintained that Thomas always felt that a majority of his fellow Virginians agreed with him regarding loyalty to the federal government. He believed that Virginia never would have left the Union if her political leaders had not jockeyed her into a position of disloyalty. Thomas never ceased to feel that, up to the outbreak of fighting, he was more properly representative of Virginia than the secessionists.[12] How right he was soon became apparent when forty of Virginia's western counties refused secession and organized the state of West Virginia.

When the officers of the Second Cavalry assembled for the distribution of their weekly mail there was always an airing of individual opinions as to the ultimate course of events political and military. During these discussions none ever heard Thomas indicate that in the event of war his sympathies would lie with his state as against the Union. If such a stand would cut the ties of friendship and blood Thomas expressed himself as ready to pay that penalty. His sisters disagreed totally with these ideas and exacted the penalty he foresaw.

Rightly or wrongly, his sisters had believed that he would be their contribution to The Cause. When he failed them their only defense was to disown him. Their bitterness was deep. It was printed in the papers at the time of Thomas' death that he had sought to relieve some of his sisters' more serious shortages after the war by sending them packages of food and clothing but his effort was ignored. Benjamin did not share his sisters' attitude. He told Mrs. Thomas that he did not see how his brother could have done otherwise.[13]

A variant of the foregoing story is told even today in Southampton County. After Appomattox, some Union officers learned that Thomas' sisters were destitute. They loaded an army wagon with household supplies and accompanied it to the Thomas homestead. The sisters received them with stately courtesy but icy coldness, listened to their story and then assured the officers they had no brother. This fiction was maintained for years. They could not be trapped into admitting the relationship. A very young boy who used to visit the sisters with his father was always cautioned beforehand never to ask to see the general's sword.

Another story is that when a Confederate soldier from Southampton County was stranded in Tennessee after the war, Thomas provided him with funds for getting home. He was quick to call on the sisters with the news of their brother's kindness. A stormy scene followed, the sisters declaring they had no brother and never wanted the name of George Henry Thomas mentioned in their presence.

Hand in hand with these stories is the firm belief that Thomas in some way prevented Southampton County from being pillaged by the Yankees. Citizens of Sussex County, whose smokehouses and livestock were continually levied on during the Petersburg fighting, used to drive their hogs and cattle across the Southampton County line where they were never touched.[14] There is evidence to support this feeling. In reply to a query from Grant as to the best way to get an armed force to Raleigh, Thomas detoured him around Southampton County, though a march route through Southampton would have been more direct.[15]

Lee is alleged to have made his choice of allegiance by instinct. If this is another name for the impulse that springs from the ties of place and the accepted beliefs of a community, this statement is probably true. Lee never lost close touch with his Virginia home. More than half of the time the Second Cavalry was in Texas prior to the Civil War, Lee lived at Arlington.

The ties that bound Thomas to Virginia and his neighbors of Southampton County were much looser. In the quarter century preceding the outbreak of the Civil War, the aggregate of the time Thomas spent at home was less than eighteen months. Although his Northern wife denied having influenced him, she pulled him unconsciously but steadily into a Northern environment. The percentage of naval officers who left the United States service when war became a reality was much smaller than that of the army. Service afloat kept them away from home. They, like Thomas, may have been affected by the loosening of their home ties.

At any rate, Thomas apparently made a rational choice. Men, wealth and natural resources, he knew, were controlled by the North. He reasoned that the South could not overbalance these advantages. He was unwilling to believe that the South would be so crazy and unjust to herself as to start hostilities.[16]

To many, however, Thomas' reasoning was unsound. Many thought Lee had chosen wisely and Thomas had made a bitter mistake. European military critics writing from the cold, scientific point of view demonstrated almost unanimously that the South would win. Horace Greeley believed this was so and did not change his mind until the war was more than two years old. Up to the middle of April 1861, many Northerners were full of doubts and misgivings. It was the arrogant blast of the Rebel guns at Sumter that convinced the Unionists they could conquer the South.

Thomas was not the only Virginian who fought for the North. The Virginians in his own class at West Point split evenly. Forty-one per cent of the West Point graduates born in Virginia or appointed therefrom who were in the army at the outbreak of the war left it to join the Confederacy. The five Virginians with the most outstanding military accomplishments to their credit in 1861 also split in favor of the North—Scott, Thomas and Cooke remained loyal, Lee and Joseph Johnston switched their allegiance. This was close to the over-all average.

Scott, as General-in-Chief of the army, would have been the prestige catch for the Rebels. He was approached cautiously. "I now inform you," said Virginia's emissary, "that I am officially charged with a communication to you from the Governor of Virginia. . . . I shall not make that communication unless you answer me that it will be received without offense." Scott growled some words to the effect that he had been a Union man all his life and expected to remain one, and went on with the job of winnowing his officers.

The North's angling for Lee was a high pressure endeavor. Veiled offers were made to him that he might eventually have the top Union command. His answer was a courteous refusal. Realizing that Lee was lost to the North, Scott suggested that he resign. The details of Joseph Johnston's resignation are uncertain, but it was accepted three days before Lee's.

Philip St. George Cooke had won his spurs in 1846 when General Stephen Watts Kearny called him out as his best captain, jumped him over all the majors and put him as lieutenant colonel in command of the Mormon Battalion then in Sante Fe on the verge of mutiny. His orders were to march his command to California and on the way to pick out a practicable wagon road. He succeeded, and the Southern Pacific and Santa Fe railroads thought enough of his route to use it for getting into southern California. His family split over the question of secession even wider than did Thomas'. One of his sons became a Confederate brigadier general, one daughter married Jeb Stuart, another followed her husband South, and another daughter cast her lot with the North. That Mrs. Stuart's son, originally named after his grandfather, had his name changed in 1861, reminds one of the legend that Thomas' sisters asked him to change his name in that same fateful year.

Not all the officers who resigned their commissions to go with the

South were Southerners. The Adjutant General of the army, Samuel Cooper, the man for whom Camp Cooper was named, although a New Yorker by birth, resigned in favor of the Confederacy shortly after Lincoln's inauguration. John Clifford Pemberton, a Pennsylvanian, resigned in April and saw his loyalty come into question after he surrendered Vicksburg. Pemberton's decision was perhaps the most painful of all. His wife, a Virginian, threatened to repudiate him if he joined the North. His wealthy mother threatened to disinherit him if he joined the South.

Thomas' decision to continue in the Union army was an expensive move. As a result of it his property in Virginia was confiscated; his family, with one exception, repudiated him; the South named him traitor; and among many in the North he was suspect. Most damaging, however, was the fact that all his political support was lost. Ohio moved into the political vacuum left by Virginia's withdrawal and worked hard to advance the interests of her own sons—McClellan, Buell, Sherman, Grant, Rosecrans and Sheridan. Chase and Stanton swung the wheel-horse load for Ohio in the cabinet. This virile state clinched its control of the federal government during the administrations of Grant, Hayes and Garfield, all native sons. Their military favorites had a wide-open opportunity to enhance the reputations they brought from the battlefields.

In the beginning, this lack of political support was negative rather than positive in the retardation of Thomas' personal fortunes. Officers commissioned from civil life went ahead of him in grade because their states demanded their recognition. But the day soon came when Thomas stood in the way of some powerful politician. Then the whisper arose in the political councils, "He's a Virginian. Do you think he's safe?" It is rumored that Lincoln himself was inclined to "let the Virginian wait."

9

Carlisle and the Shenandoah: Thomas Wins His Star

Thomas reported his arrival at Carlisle on April 13 and sent army headquarters another official notice that his lamed back would prevent active field service. Within three weeks, however, his injury had healed enough to permit him to ride. Such rapid improvement may have been due partly to his ambition to get to Washington, where the Second Cavalry was wanted to guard the Treasury and White House.

At the same time that Thomas went to Carlisle, Fitz John Porter, Assistant Adjutant General acting for Simon Cameron, the Secretary of War, went to Harrisburg to aid in recruiting the Pennsylvania regiments and to protect the railway leading from Harrisburg to Washington. There was a tacit understanding that if regular troops, commanded by officers in the regular service, led the volunteers through Baltimore on their way to Washington there would be no trouble.[1] Thomas and the Second Cavalry were picked for this duty.

Thomas' immediate job, however, was to recruit the Second Cavalry and re-equip it for active service. While he was thus engaged, Virginia adopted a contingent resolution of secession and her political leaders immediately went to work to implement it. Up to this moment, Thomas' army career had been sanctioned by the place of

his birth. As an Ohio officer put it, before the Civil War the merit of a
United States army officer was measured in the inverse ratio of the
distance of his birthplace from Fairfax Courthouse. Thomas soon was
to be asked for a repayment of past favors that had come to him because of this fact.

Less than a week after Thomas reached Carlisle Barracks, rebellion
flamed in Baltimore and Thomas received his first combat orders for
the Civil War. He and his regiment were to report to Harrisburg
dismounted but equipped for combat. They would go on to Washington as soon as they had opened Baltimore for the passage of troops.
Late in the afternoon of April 21, Thomas with 400 troops, nearly half
of them recruits, reached Harrisburg and reported to Fitz John Porter.
There were 3,400 unorganized militia at Cockeysville, Maryland, a few
miles north of Baltimore, waiting for a bridge to be repaired. Porter
wanted Thomas to take command of them and get them through to
Washington. Meantime he was having a train made up that would
take the Second Cavalry and a bridge repair crew to Cockeysville.

A few days before this, Governor Curtin of Pennsylvania had referred to Porter the case of one of Thomas' junior officers who, while
on leave, had been arrested on suspicion of disloyalty. Thomas had
already reported that another of his subalterns had resigned the service
just before leaving Carlisle. Porter was worried. He had no doubt of
Thomas' loyalty but he feared that some or all of his company officers
would refuse to go any farther with their troops. They were holding
private conferences over their problem and it was evident to Porter
that they were looking to Thomas for guidance. Thomas listened
unconcernedly while Porter worried the subject but did nothing to
relieve his apprehension. It was dark when their train was called. As
Porter and Thomas moved out to board it one of the anxious young
officers was waiting at the car steps for his commander.

"What shall we do, Sir?" came his anxious inquiry.

"We are ordered to Washington and there we go." Thomas' reply
was matter of fact and soothing. "There will be time enough after
getting there for you to decide what to do."

At midnight the train reached York, where it was stopped by an
approaching locomotive bearing a man who claimed to be a courier
from Washington. He had orders for the Cockeysville troops to return
to York. These orders were verbal and their validity was suspect but
there was no way to get a verification from Washington. Secretary of
War Cameron's actual orders to bring the troops through to Washington at all hazards were never delivered. Because Porter failed to carry
them out, he incurred the enmity of Salmon Porter Chase, Secretary

of the Treasury. Perhaps Chase at the same time lost confidence in Thomas. If Thomas had been permitted to force his way through, Washington would not have suffered the nightmarish week that dismayed Lincoln into pacing the White House and asking himself, "Why don't they come? Why don't they come?"

Four thousand militia under conflicting orders were now billeted on the residents of York while Thomas tried to bring order out of chaos. In the midst of it all Thomas got orders to bring his own command into Washington but they were to come mounted and fully equipped. Entangled in the confusion, there was nothing he could do to work out his own problems so he asked to be ordered back to Carlisle.[2] On the twenty-fifth his orders reached him and he shepherded his men back to their starting point. Nearly a week had been wasted although he had managed to get requisitions out for horses, saddles, bridles, blankets, horseshoes, and the multifarious equipment that goes to outfit a cavalry trooper. A special train was ordered to bring on the horse furniture. Arms were ordered from New York, but New York had to look for them in Pennsylvania. One of Thomas' captains was sent to Harrisburg to inspect the horses as the contractor brought them in. His orders reflected the urgency of the times. ". . . It perhaps will be better not to be too critical, confining yourself to the fact of their being serviceable." The eyes of the sergeants schooled in the choosiness of the old Second Cavalry must have bugged out in astonishment at the tug marks on the flanks of some of their new mounts.

Thomas finally got the first four companies of his rejuvenated regiment off to Washington but that did not end his work. While he was waiting at York the remaining squadrons of his regiment disembarked at New York City and came on to Carlisle. Supplies were more and more difficult to obtain, mostly because no system had been worked out for issuing them. Thomas' troops, destined for the defense of the Capital, had a high priority. When the desperate effort was being made to outfit the Cockeysville troops it was found that unnecessary duplications were delaying the filling of requisitions. Fitz John Porter, Governor Curtin, and the major general in command of the Pennsylvania militia were all trying to get arms and equipment for the same troops from the same sources at the same time, and none of them agreed on minor specifications.

While getting his regiment ready for field service, Thomas received two promotions. On April 25 he was made a lieutenant colonel and eight days later he was promoted to colonel. Both promotions were orthodox advancements on the basis of seniority as the result of resignations of senior cavalry officers in the regular service. Between these promotions, each of which required him to renew his oath of allegiance, a general order was published requiring all officers in the service prior to April 1 to take the oath anew. As a result, Thomas took three oaths within a short time and caused one of his captains to wonder audibly at the performance. "I don't care," was Thomas' reply, "I would just as soon take the oath before each meal during my life if the department saw proper to order it."

Pennsylvania had furnished sixteen regiments of three-month men in answer to Lincoln's call and this entitled her to two major generals. One of these was Robert Patterson. Fourteen years before, Thomas had watched him march into Victoria at the head of 1,500 overdriven and maltreated volunteers. Now he was ordered to report to Patterson at Chambersburg with four companies of the Second Cavalry and the First City Troop of Philadelphia, and take command of the First Brigade of Patterson's army.

Scott, who considered Patterson a good officer for second in command, was questioned as to the advisability of giving him the chief command of the upper Potomac. He pointed out to his inquisitor that there were so many Pennsylvania troops in the Army of Pennsylvania that he could not do otherwise. "But," he added, "I have flanked him by two good army officers [Thomas and Abercrombie] and I have but little fear that he can go very far wrong." [3] McClellan, who agreed with Scott's opinion, considered Thomas one of the best officers in the army.

This was Thomas' first command of volunteer troops.[4] They were the only means at hand for fighting the war and Thomas proposed to use them. Fitz John Porter believed them altogether inefficient. But Thomas reminded him that their opponents were using the same type of men. He had watched Worth enforce discipline on the identical troops at Camargo that had defied Twiggs at Matamoros. He had seen Doniphan receive obedience from his Missouri volunteers while they jeered at Wool and his West Point precision. Once they could be made to take soldiering seriously, volunteers could be handled like regulars. Thomas waited for the opportunity to drive this lesson home. It came when one of his volunteer officers excused his neglect of duty on the ground that the matter in question was a joke. Thomas brought him stiffly to heel and took care to let the ranks learn of the incident.

Thomas knew from his Mexican War experience that discipline could not be ordered from the volunteers. They detested orders since these implied a superiority on the part of the giver. At the same time, their common sense told them that a military operation must be directed by someone. So they compromised this warfare between instinct and reason. If the order seemed trivial, unnecessary or unreasonable they obeyed it jeeringly or defied it. If they judged it reasonable they accepted it. The officer who understood this viewpoint and acted upon it won the respect of the volunteers. Once he had this they would obey almost any of his orders. Within a short time the skeptical Fitz John Porter revised his opinion. "Thomas' brigade," he reported, "is in fine condition."

Along with the problem of the volunteer went much speculation on the length of the war. Among the officers of the Army of Pennsylvania, Thomas stood almost alone in the belief that it would be long. He understood the South better than most Northerners and the North better than most Southerners. He could see both points of view and realized that the struggle had to be fought out to the bitter end. The seceded states had to be whipped back into the Union. This meant conquest and conquest took time.

The Rebels, however, might win by a stalemate out of which would grow a negotiated peace when the price of conquest proved too high for the invader. Strategic defense could lead to a Rebel victory.[5]

Conquest meant the destruction of the Southern armies' will to fight. This single fact set the pattern for the war. The majority of the Northern commanders fought to win the field. As Sherman put it, "The trouble was that the [Northern] commanders never went out to lick anybody, but always thought first of keeping from being licked." This was a winning tactic for the South but never for the North. Only a few of the Northern commanders recognized this fact. But the South underestimated its opponent and eventually lost its main armies. One was destroyed by Thomas, the other was captured by Grant.

Harpers Ferry was seized by the Virginia troops when that state left the Union, but Joseph E. Johnston, who had been ordered to the command at that point, considered it untenable and on June 14 retired toward Winchester. Patterson was watching him from Hagerstown, Maryland, where he had moved on June 7. On June 16 he ordered his vanguard, with Thomas in command, to cross the Potomac.

The crossing was made at Williamsport well upstream from Harpers Ferry. John Sherman, a member of Patterson's staff, and his brother, Thomas' old West Point roommate, sat on a large stone and watched the cavalry splash through the waist-deep water where the ford angled sharply upstream to reach the Virginia shore. The night before at the Williamsport tavern, where John had his headquarters,

Thomas and W. T. Sherman crawled over a large-scale map spread on the floor and talked professionally of communications, lines of operation and strategic points as they singled out Richmond, Vicksburg, Nashville, Chattanooga and Knoxville as the probable vital points of the war. Writing of the event thirty-four years later, John marveled that their predictions should have been so accurate and inclusive. If he was impressed by the fact that these two officers, attached to the eastern armies, picked the west as the main area of maneuver, he didn't say so. W. T. Sherman took advantage of the situation to ask his old roommate how he felt about the idea of abandoning the Union and going south. Thomas answered, "I have thought it all over and I shall stand firm in the service of the government." [6]

This was Thomas' opportunity. The political support that had served him so well before the war was now gone. John Sherman, Ohio's political clerk of the works, could have and probably would have supplied part of this lack. William Tecumseh was ready to help. He had to have a pace setter, for he was not a front runner. Eight days before this he had written John, ". . . There are two A-1 men there [with General Patterson], George H. Thomas, Col. Second Cavalry and Captain Sykes, 3d Infantry. . . . I would name such as them for high places . . . but Thomas is a Virginian from near Norfolk and say what he may he must feel unpleasantly at leading an invading army. But if he says he will do it, I know he will do it well. He was never brilliant but always cool, reliable and steady, maybe a little slow." [7] But Thomas let the opportunity pass.

This invasion did not last long. The following day Thomas and his men were ordered back to the Maryland side. Scott had detached all of Patterson's regular troops, including Thomas and the Second Cavalry, for duty in Washington, and the Pennsylvanian did not feel strong enough to maintain his position in Virginia without them. Patterson finally managed to hang on to Thomas but he lost half of the companies of the well-trained Second Cavalry.

On July 2, with Abercrombie in advance and Thomas in support, Patterson again crossed the Potomac and pushed Stonewall Jackson out of the way at Falling Waters. It was an action between Johnston's screen and Patterson's leading elements that succeeded in checking the Union advance until Thomas deployed and, with infantry and artillery, threatened to turn Jackson's right. Thomas surprised his subordinates by accurately interpreting, from the sound of the firing, what was happening on the skirmish line out of range of his vision. Compared with Monterrey and Buena Vista it was a puny affair but for the numbers engaged it was the most important action to date in the war. Thomas and Abercrombie handled their brigades admirably and the fact was officially noted. But news of the action was smothered by the publicity that was given to the Union defeats at Big Bethel three weeks earlier and Bull Run three weeks later.

The affair at Big Bethel presented Thomas with a disciplinary problem involving the bitterness that had split the country. One of his captains, hearing the news of the defeat, gave out with the opinion, "I'm glad the damned old abolitionist [the Union commander] was whipped." Whereupon a junior officer replied, "It seems to me, sir, that you are fighting on the wrong side." A challenge was issued and accepted and the camp buzzed with speculation. That evening at dinner the blue-clad officers stood at attention behind their chairs as Thomas entered the mess room and made his dignified way to the head of the table. Instead of seating himself and releasing them from this customary courtesy Thomas began to talk. He had heard rumors of a duel in the brigade and he wanted to remind those concerned that this was no personal matter to be decided with smoking pistols. If the captain had meant what he said, then he *was* fighting on the wrong side and that was a matter no duel could settle. "Let there be no more talk about this being a damned Abolition war," Thomas admonished. "Gentlemen, take your seats." Chairs scraped, waiters moved, china clinked, the sound of conversation filled the room. There was no duel and no more criticism of the war aim where Thomas could hear of it.

With Thomas in the van, Patterson moved on July 3 to Martinsburg. Some forty-five miles southeast of here the main armies were converging on Bull Run. Some twenty miles to the southwest was Johnston's main force at Winchester, and Patterson was to prevent him from joining the Bull Run concentration. He was in poor shape to do it. If he moved toward Johnston he left the railway, and his wagons were inadequate to supply his needs. His ninety-day men whose time was nearly up had served notice that they were leaving when it expired. Patterson put the problem up to a council of war and the vote, including Thomas', was to move to Charlestown. This was closer to Bull Run and no farther from Johnston.

On July 10 Patterson was advised that he had six days to get to Bull Run before Johnston or to keep Johnston from getting there.

In response to his orders of July 17, Johnston began his movement toward Manassas Junction. One of Thomas' junior volunteer officers, while on a reconnaissance, saw the dust raised by marching troops

headed from Winchester to the fords of the Shenandoah and was sent
at once to report to Patterson. Thomas was at headquarters at the time
and, when nothing happened, sent for his junior and asked him what
he had seen. After hearing his story, Thomas strode without a word
to Patterson's command post and told him that there was still time to
intercept Johnston. But Patterson refused to follow his advice.

Behind Jeb Stuart's cavalry screen, Johnston was moving out of
Winchester with Jackson in the lead. All day, while the infantry
marched seventeen miles and forded the Shenandoah, the Gray cavalry
bedeviled Patterson's outposts, driving in his pickets first here and then
there, covering every road and path between Patterson and Johnston's
old camps. After sunset Stuart picked up his wearied troopers and
marched them through the darkness to Front Royal. By 8:00 A.M. of
the nineteenth, Jackson's brigade was entrained. On the twentieth
Stuart's horse and the artillery jingled into Manassas under their own
power. Johnston, with the rest of the Second Brigade, came in by train
that same day. Johnston was up and Patterson's goose was cooked.

Patterson moved to Harpers Ferry on the twenty-first. On the
twenty-fifth, when his time expired, he was relieved by Nathaniel P.
Banks and shouldered with a large part of the blame for the loss of
Bull Run.

Combat is the direct measure of troop training and leadership, but
in Patterson's short campaign there was no opportunity to apply this
yardstick to Thomas' command. There is a collateral test of an officer's
ability, however, and the way in which Thomas measured up to this
is worth noting.

Samuel J. Randall was a trooper in the Philadelphia city cavalry
while that unit was under Thomas' command. Subsequently he served
as speaker of the United States House of Representatives. His written
testimony is evidence that sometime between the end of May and the
first of August, Thomas' volunteers came to the realization that he
was competent for higher command. Because of this and what it meant
to their individual safety, Thomas won their confidence. Under such
an officer, Randall pointed out, an army takes on renewed vigor and
courage. This appraisal came from a man who had no relations with
Thomas other than the customary ones between a private and a brigade
commander.

So far as is known Thomas never summarized his technique of
command. Others have done it for him.[8] He believed in a thorough
training of his troops but limited this training to essentials. He was

a disciplinarian but got his results without harshness. He was a master of detail without permitting its onerous demands to dominate his time or energy. He believed in the dignity of the individual soldier and took pains to see that it was not belittled. Above all he was a conservator of his men. He protected their rights, guaranteed their comforts and husbanded them against wounds and death. He thought highly enough of this technique to want to multiply his forces in his own hands rather than to take organized units from another command.

Lincoln at this time was working on the problem of holding the border states. The problem was political but the threat of military force was needed to back up his political maneuvers and counter those of the Confederates. Kentucky was one of those problems and Lincoln decided to turn over its military responsibility to Brigadier General Robert Anderson. Anderson accepted on the condition that he could name his principal assistants, who would rank as brigadier generals of volunteers, and the President agreed. He chose W. T. Sherman, Thomas, and Ambrose Burnside, although Don Carlos Buell was later the fourth choice when McClellan refused to release Burnside. The slate was referred to some members of Congress representing Kentucky and Tennessee,[9] who wanted Thomas replaced by Simon Bolivar Buckner. Perhaps their desire arose not from distrust of Thomas but from their belief that such a prominent Kentuckian as Buckner would have a greater influence on the political situation. Lincoln left the decision to Anderson and Thomas got the appointment.[10] On August 17, 1861, Thomas was commissioned brigadier general of volunteers, placing him fifty-fifth on the list of officers of that rank. This promotion entitled him to wear a single star on each shoulder, two rows of eight buttons each on his uniform coat, spaced in pairs, and a gold embroidered spread eagle with one star on each flank corner of his dark blue saddle blanket. But for some reason he continued to wear his colonel's uniform.

This may have arisen from his sensitiveness about his position in the army since the secession of Virginia. Thomas knew that his promotion would not be consummated until Lincoln's nomination was approved by the Senate. His name was not sent up to that body until December 6, 1861, and not approved until the end of January 1862. As the result of his promotion his pay was $124.00 a month. In addition he was allowed twelve rations a day, forage for five horses, food and uniforms for three servants, $30.00 for fuel, $80.00 for quarters, $90.00 for transportation of baggage and $15.00 for stationery.

In later years Thomas wrote that he was indebted to General Anderson for the promotion and that it came to him without any solicitation on his part.

After Thomas' death, Sherman contended that Lincoln questioned Thomas' loyalty, and he frequently mentioned this theme. He reflected an extensive gossip campaign. Thomas' reputation had a definite value to anyone able to capture some of its effulgence and Sherman overlooked few opportunities to lengthen his own shadow. In 1890 Sherman enlarged his role in the struggle to gain the credit for Thomas' loyalty. He is reported to have said at that time that Lincoln called on him for advice on the nominations for brigadier general and when he said to Lincoln, "Why don't you nominate old Thomas?" Lincoln demurred until Sherman agreed to be responsible for Thomas' loyalty.

Thomas M. Anderson flatly contradicted Sherman and their argument became another part of the public discussion over Thomas' suspected disloyalty. Anderson's statement is credible. "I have reason to believe," he wrote, "that Mr. Lincoln did not urge a word of objection to Thomas. Not three months before he had made him a colonel. He was himself born in the South. The general he was sending out to command the Department of Kentucky was a Southerner. . . . It would have been simply inconceivable that he would have refused to promote an officer who had served actively through one campaign because he had, like himself, been [born] in a Southern state."

"I know," Anderson wrote in another connection, "that the President made no objection to the appointment of Thomas as a brigadier general in August 1861." [11] To penalize men because of their Southern birth certainly would not have been much help to Lincoln's program for holding the border states. Lincoln was too astute a politician to have missed this point.

Thomas, with the right to fasten the yellow sash of a general officer around the waist of his blue uniform, had now regained some of the rank he had lost by reason of the appointment early in the war of scores of colonels from civil life. But, more important, he was now enrolled as a volunteer. He still remained a colonel in the regular army but his dual commission freed him from the strangling toils of his regular rank.

Lincoln was probably the nation's most militarily awkward President. Much of his trouble stemmed from his inability to organize his military forces. A ready-made solution for this problem lay in the fullest use of the trained officers of the regular army. These men had what the volunteers lacked, the experience that comes from a specialized training like West Point or from long experience in the army. Lincoln could never have filled all of his commissions with officers so trained but there were approximately 630 of them available at the start of the war and he could have recruited all of his regimental commanders and officers of higher rank from this reservoir. McClellan favored this plan, Cameron endorsed it, but Lincoln refused it. He maintained a substantial separation of the regular and volunteer armies. It is estimated that the government discarded two thousand years of officer training. If the regular officer, who had made the army his career, could not contrive to move into the broader field of command of the volunteer troops, most of his talents were wasted and his career was penalized in favor of officers who had resigned from the army before the war or of men without officer training. Those who had resigned were now appointed with high rank to the volunteer forces by the state governors. Grant, McClellan, Halleck, Sherman, Rosecrans and Hooker were examples of this kind of salvage.

State influence resulted in quick promotion. Sherman's star came to him as a result of Bull Run. He was sitting with a group of officers in the Adjutant General's office (then in Lee's former home in Arlington) when an aide came in with a list of the newly promoted colonels and read it aloud—Sherman, Porter, Heintzelman and others. There were thirty-eight in all. The men couldn't believe it. Promoted for losing a battle—unheard of! "By Jesus Christ, it's all a lie," Heintzelman's nasal voice twanged in derision. "Every mother's son of you will be cashiered."

"We felt he was right," wrote Sherman later, and added with evident relief, "but, nevertheless, it was true."

Sometime prior to this, Grant had read of his promotion in a St. Louis paper. "I found," he wrote, "the President had asked the Illinois delegation in Congress to recommend some citizen of the state for the position of brigadier general, and that they had unanimously recommended me as first on a list of seven. . . ." The political power of Lincoln's state was beginning to focus on Grant.

On August 24, Thomas M. Anderson handed his colonel an envelope that he had brought out from Washington as the courier of his uncle, General Robert Anderson. In it was Thomas' new commission and a covering letter from the general asking Thomas to meet him in Cincinnati on September 1 for further instructions. At the same time Thomas was assigned to duty in the Department of the Cumberland, but Nathaniel P. Banks, who had succeeded to Patterson's command, delayed his relief in fear of an impending attack. About the thirtieth,

Thomas left Hyattstown, Maryland, on the first leg of his western journey. The route he took led him to New Haven, Connecticut, for a Sunday stopover with his wife.[12] If he had followed Sherman's example he would have taken her with him to Cincinnati. He undoubtedly reassured her about his back injury and picked up all the little details of her activities since he had left her in New York. Perhaps they laughed together at their fears of six months gone regarding his ability to continue to make a living.

10

Westward to Camp Dick Robinson

Thomas reached Cincinnati just in time to move on to Louisville. He missed the conferences between Anderson, Sherman, Andrew Johnson, influential Kentucky Unionists, and representatives of the governors of Ohio, Indiana and Illinois. Kentucky affairs were at their crisis. Bishop General Polk had invaded the state, anchored his western flank at Columbus and closed the Mississippi. Grant, without orders, had seized Paducah and gained control of the mouths of the Ohio, Tennessee and Cumberland rivers. Troops and supplies were by-passing Kentucky in favor of Fremont in Missouri and the Union commanders in West Virginia and farther east. Efforts to remedy the situation were aborted by the failure of the War Department to keep the promises of men, money and materiel made to Anderson a few weeks before.

But Kentucky was for the Union. Lincoln had traded the military initiative on the Kentucky front for the state's refusal to secede. It was a master stroke but was marred by the blundering of Cameron and Scott. Instead of concentrating adequate troops north of the Ohio to be thrown into Kentucky as soon as its political status was resolved, they had ordered them off to the flanks. The Rebels moved northward through a military vacuum and masses of Kentuckians wavered in their allegiance as they came under the bayonets of the Southern troops. While Polk strengthened his grip on the Mississippi, Zollicoffer [1] struck through the Cumberland Gap three hundred miles to the east.

This was war on a grand scale. The theologian shook the folds out of his war maps three years before the Northern commanders did.

The Rebel defense line now stretched westward from the southern cape of the Chesapeake until it lost itself somewhere in the Rocky Mountains, although for all practical purposes the left flank ended in southern Missouri. The location of this defense line approximated 36° 30′ north latitude, the division between slave and free territory set up by the Missouri Compromise. It crowded north of this line at the Virginia salient which thrust boldly toward Pennsylvania and the Great Lakes.

There were several weak spots in this line. Its right flank could be turned from the Atlantic coast. It could be split along the line of the Mississippi River. It could be pierced along the line of the Tennessee and Cumberland rivers. The Virginia salient could be pinched off. The attack on Virginia was adopted as the Northern offensive effort in the fall of 1861 and Thomas was picked to lead it.

The salient would be difficult to defend and its successful liquidation promised a dazzling reward. The loss of Virginia, the strongest state in the Confederacy, would be irreparable. The mountain range along its western border was dominated by Union sympathizers so that the Northern armies, if they could base there, would be in friendly territory. From the southern limit of this mountain range these armies could segment the Confederacy by drives toward Mobile and Savannah. By controlling the eastern passes through the mountains a Union army could strike with impunity against the flank of enemy forces moving between Richmond and the Carolinas. Of the three railroads that supplied Virginia, one ran through this mountain range from Chattanooga to Richmond by way of Lynchburg.[2] Another railway from Richmond to Wilmington, North Carolina, was vulnerable to an attack from the seacoast. Simultaneous threats against these two communication lines would force an enemy withdrawal from Richmond. A build-up of Union pressure southward from the Norfolk-Washington-Harpers Ferry line would hasten this retrograde movement.

Thomas was one of the early proponents of the idea of a strike eastward from the fastnesses of the southern Appalachians and urged it upon Scott before leaving for Kentucky. It is not known today how far Thomas' plan went but it did give a military justification for the political redemption of East Tennessee, a subject close to Lincoln's heart. At any rate a detailed directive for the East Tennessee movement was drawn up by Lincoln and sent to the headquarters of the army. The directive was undated but the editors of the *Official Records* have fixed it between September 25 and October 4, 1861. It has been called one of the famous documents of the war. It began: "On or about the 5th of October (the exact date to be determined hereafter) I wish a movement made to seize and hold a point on the railroad connecting Virginia and Tennessee, near the mountain pass called the Cumberland Gap."

Lincoln wanted the military movements from the coast against the eastern flank of the Virginia salient to be simultaneous with that through the Cumberland Gap. McClellan called Ambrose Burnside to his headquarters almost immediately and put him to work preparing for the movement. When the time for the advance arrived all the forces at Louisville and Cincinnati, and on the railroad between them, were to be placed under Thomas' command. He was to concentrate, equip and train this force for a movement into East Tennessee through the Cumberland Gap to cut the railroad between Chattanooga and Richmond and to hold the mountain region for the Union. McClellan and Fremont were to take advantage of whatever opportunities Thomas' main attack might offer.[3]

With this end in view, Anderson ordered Thomas to the command of the largest collection of troops in Kentucky. These were Kentucky and Tennessee volunteers, about 6,000 in number, currently under the command of Lieutenant William Nelson [4] of the United States navy, encamped on the farm of Richard M. Robinson near the town of Bryantsville. The rendezvous was named Camp Dick Robinson. On September 15 Thomas took over this command.

He found the troops an unorganized mob. They lacked supplies, equipment, transportation and adequate food and shelter. No staff existed for the correction of these shortages. No money was at hand for supplying them. Most of the men had not been mustered into the Union service, so the new commander found himself in actual command of state levies without a commission to make that command legal. The rolls were so sketchy that Thomas could only guess at his actual strength. Federal credit in the amount of six million dollars had been used without any records to show how or why. He had to bring two and one-half months of paper work up to date while he pushed ahead with his own plans.

The only trained officer he had in his command had been schooled in the tactics and procedures of the navy. The next one, who arrived three weeks later, had received his training in Europe. Thomas pledged his personal credit for money to clothe, feed and shelter his men. Sorely needed wagons were collected for him at Cincinnati but before they could be forwarded they were commandeered for the West Virginia troops. One of his inexperienced colonels asked for help in laying out the fortifications of his outpost but Thomas had no engineer officers to send him. Contractors, committed to supply his force with overcoats, welshed when the Governor of Ohio offered more money per garment. Measles brought to camp by a young recruit multiplied in two days to 120 cases and the need for extra medical help was urgent. The safety of Camp Dick Robinson required that Thomas seize the railroad that brought up his supplies, but the Kentucky legislature demurred. To add to Thomas' troubles, Kentucky Unionists with influence enough to entitle them to an audience took up his time with their plans for winning the war. He was discouraged enough to think seriously of asking to be relieved from his command.[5]

One day, with his camp full of visitors and his undisciplined soldiers calling for speeches, Thomas' feelings burst through his iron self-control. He left the porch where the speakers were and retired to his office. Here he paced up and down waiting for the time when he could go back to business. The speaker finished and the soldiers demanded their commander with cries of "Thomas! Thomas!"

"Damn this speech making," an aide heard him say. "I won't speak. What does a man want to make a speech for?" He slammed the door behind him as he retreated farther into the building.

However much the confusion centering around Dick Robinson's woodland pastures might have irritated Thomas, it failed to exasperate him. He was the most patient of men. He wasted no time in complaints or useless upbraidings. Through it all he remained as respectful and attentive to a remark by a subordinate as he did to one made by General Anderson.

It was at this time that the differences between the military thinking of Thomas and that of the officers of the limited-objective school became apparent. Thomas expected to whip the seceded states back into the Union, to break down the Rebellion, to destroy the Southern armies. "We end the conflict either at Boston or New Orleans," he is reported to have said. "There is no boundary between." The limited-objective school counted it a victory when they pushed southward that imaginary boundary called a military line. Early in 1862 Halleck presented the Union with the tremendous land area of southern Kentucky, middle and western Tennessee and the northern parts of Mississippi and Alabama. But the Southern army, which he permitted to escape, had it all back in 120 days.

Thomas' objective set the pattern for an integrated army which was

not intended for show or parade. There are no records of grand reviews at Dick Robinson, no requisitions for white gloves or paper
collars. Thomas did not believe that his commission gave him an army
or invested him with any more than the symbols of command. He
looked upon it as an order to find an army and to build it into a power
that would make his campaign plans effective. He knew that only his
troops could invest him with the substance of leadership. So he covered
the fields for miles around Dick Robinson with squads engaged in
company drill; attended the dress parades of each regiment; inspected
their clothing, arms and equipment; instructed the probationary
quartermasters, commissaries, ordnance officers, engineers, signalmen,
scouts, spies and provost marshals.

On the day Thomas assumed the responsibility for the chaos at
Camp Dick Robinson, Albert Sidney Johnston succeeded Polk in command of the Rebel forces in Kentucky. Within thirty-six hours he was
threatening Thomas from front, flank and rear. The frontal attack was
commanded by Zollicoffer and destroyed Thomas' camp at Barbours-
ville. Zollicoffer was moving northward along the historic Wilderness
Road,[6] his thrust aimed potentially at Frankfort and Louisville, the
political and economic centers of the state. Actually it was a demonstration in favor of Buckner, who was moving north to Bowling Green,
also with the ultimate objective of Frankfort and Louisville. This
combination was a grave threat to Thomas' security.

Zollicoffer's thrust had driven Thomas' men back to London, but
Thomas decided to make his main stand on the Rockcastle River. It
was some twenty miles farther north but a splendid natural fortress
for blocking the invasion route. The alternate road from the mountains
to the center of the state he could block with rocks and trees and defend with light forces. These moves checkmated the threat from his
front. Anderson disposed of the threat to his right flank by moving
Sherman with 3,000 men south to meet it.

The strike at his rear aimed at breaking his communications with
Cincinnati and Louisville by an uprising of Kentucky secessionists.
Thomas smothered it with a regiment of infantry. These checks gave
him time to complete his defensive plans. For 100 miles off to the
southwest, he placed scouting forces to guard the few passes in the
irregular line of the Cumberland foothills and to prevent by delaying
actions any surprise of his main body. This defense cordon took advantage of the rugged declivities of the Cumberland escarpment. The
relatively few routes for an enemy debouchment into the lowlands
could be guarded with patrols. Since Zollicoffer had chosen the main

ramparts of the Cumberlands for his defense line, the forty-mile-wide plateau between the mountains and the flatlands was left as a no-man's land where the raiders of the two forces harried each other. To protect his left flank Thomas suggested a movement up the Big Sandy River. This area was under the control of another military department but the cooperation Thomas requested was given.

There were half a dozen skirmishes along the line of Thomas' frontier within the next thirty days. The largest took place at London. It was a feint to cover Zollicoffer's raid on the Goose Greek salt works off to the east, but it had its repercussions on the highest military level. Thomas' field commander misinterpreted Zollicoffer's design and notified Thomas that the enemy had taken London. Thomas notified Anderson and Anderson telegraphed Lincoln asking for all the troops the North could raise. Military inexperience on a dirt road in south-eastern Kentucky was affecting the command decisions of the army's highest echelons. None of these skirmishes took place under Thomas' eyes. He remained at Dick Robinson working on the solution of his basic problems.

Since an offensive aimed at East Tennessee was his first obligation he gave it all the attention he could and within twelve days after assuming his command sent his plan to Anderson.[7] He proposed to enter Tennessee by way of Somerset, Kentucky, cut the railroad between Knoxville and Greeneville by destroying the bridges and then turn upon Zollicoffer while he was in the passes of the Cumberland Mountains. This would put Thomas between Zollicoffer and his supplies. In his opinion, Zollicoffer's force could soon be captured or dispersed. His plan was a departure from orthodox military thinking. He proposed to cut loose from his base, subsist his army in the enemy's country and defeat his forces in detail. It was a workable plan. Grant used the same strategy two years later at Vicksburg to bring the North its greatest military victory to that date. Thomas advised that Zollicoffer's position could be turned by a rapid march of three days, most of which could be made through a thoroughly Union section of Tennessee. The accuracy of this forecast was also borne out later when first a Union force and then a Confederate force accomplished what Thomas prophesied. Since this was actually a flank attack against Albert Sidney Johnston's right as well as a strike against Richmond, Thomas' success would immediately relieve the Union forces of the Rebel pressure northward from Columbus and Bowling Green.

He also advised his superior, "I have learned today [September 27] that Nashville has been made the depot for the army in Virginia and that Zollicoffer only occupies the Cumberland ford to operate the road to best advantage." Even under ordinary conditions this would have been a handsome piece of intelligence work, for Thomas knew the location of the Virginia supply depot before Johnston was advised officially of it. That he accomplished it in spite of the confusion at Camp Dick Robinson is amazing.

Thomas asked for 20,000 men to make his strike successful. His specification proved to be close to the mark. Two years later Burnside went in with 15,000. This was a little short of his actual need and he got into trouble. Naturally Thomas expected the men to be properly equipped to take the field. Although there was little he could do to equip them until he was supplied with at least $100,000, he laid immediate plans for raising the additional troops. By early October he had approximately 9,000 men and he planned to recruit eight additional regiments at different points along his frontier. Meantime he proposed to put the troops he already had into an efficient condition for taking the field.

When Thomas spoke of an efficient condition he envisioned for the future many things in addition to the troops and their equipment. He saw in his mind a complete and self-sufficient striking force that could be expanded into an army—a fully equipped staff for its administration, the proper balance between the various arms of the service, pioneers and mechanics who were the forerunners of the army engineers, map makers, scouts, guides, hospital corps, and a secret service group which probably approximated the present intelligence section. In these beginnings, before its First Brigade was organized, Thomas was giving shape to that formidable military machine that was later to be the Army of the Cumberland.

Within less than two weeks after assuming command, Thomas had secured, tested and appraised the facts that were the basis of his decisions. He evaluated the problem of defense by raw, under-equipped troops and made his dispositions accordingly. He calculated the risks of a successful movement and specified the requirements for victory. In addition he laid the foundation for a modern army.

One Monday late in September 1861 there came to Thomas' headquarters on secret business the Reverend William Blount Carter. He was an East Tennessean who had been a leader in the movement to separate from Tennessee. For the meeting, Thomas brought together his brother, S. P. Carter,[8] Andrew Johnson and Horace Maynard, one of Tennessee's representatives in Washington. Carter unfolded a plan to raise a revolt in East Tennessee in conjunction with Thomas' advance. He promised to seize and hold the railroad until the army's arrival. Would Thomas accept his aid and supply the money? Thomas was willing and he expected to get the money from Andrew Johnson. When Johnson refused, Thomas sent Carter to McClellan and urged that officer to approve the idea and supply the funds.[9]

Monday, October 11, began no differently for Thomas in his tavern headquarters at Camp Dick Robinson than the four or five days that had immediately preceded it. He was still acting as his own quartermaster and discharging the duties of the brigade commissary officer while attending to the supervision of his various combat units. The need for men was not pressing but the need for a competent medical staff was. The usual weekend disciplinary problems required attention. One of his cavalry units was not where it should have been. Some of the East Tennesseans were reported drunk on the picket line. Some of the more intractable men from the front were being sent down for chastening.

Andrew Johnson was coming up from Cincinnati and that always meant interminable arguments about East Tennessee. The preceding Friday Thomas had learned that Anderson had been relieved on account of his health and that Sherman had succeeded him. Now he had at hand a queer dispatch from that mercurial officer. It read, "It is very important that you should make an advance movement in the direction of the Cumberland. I know your means of transportation are insufficient but our adversaries are no better off, and we should fight with similar means. Can you hire some wagons and show a force in the direction of London? Of necessity I cannot give minute directions and can only say that if your men simply move the effect will be good." [10] This was no order. As a serious suggestion it made no sense. Whatever information it was intended to reveal was perplexingly guarded. The puzzlement remained in the back of his mind as he went on with his work.

When Johnson arrived he seemed a little embarrassed but Thomas was relieved that he didn't start in with more demands for East Tennessee. Thomas opened the letter that Johnson handed him from Mitchel in Cincinnati and read, "Under orders of the Secretary of War of this date [October 10] I am directed to repair to Camp Dick Robinson, and there prepare the troops for an onward movement, the object being to take possession of Cumberland Ford and Cumberland Gap and ultimately seize the East Tennessee and Virginia railroad. . . ." [11] Had Thomas connected the letter with Sherman's puzzling dispatch, things might have begun to clear up a little. Johnson undoubtedly could have added some details since it seems evident that he intrigued in some way to give Mitchel Thomas' command. Whatever he learned, Thomas decided to ask to be relieved from his command since the Secretary of War had seen fit to supersede him without any just cause. Mitchel and Sherman were so informed.

Thomas Van Horne, who had access to all of Thomas' papers, never was able to learn the reason for Cameron's action. At this date it is impossible to reconstruct the affair. Politics were being played in Lincoln's Cabinet. Cameron's time was running out and he had joined forces with Chase in a desperate effort to stave off his deserts. As a result, the War Department had two heads. Which was responsible for the supersession of Thomas is unknown, although it has been established that Mitchel and Chase had a close personal relationship. Mitchel had been ordered to Cincinnati in command of the Department of Ohio to quiet the alarm there over Zollicoffer. He soon got into a dispute with Anderson over departmental jurisdiction. The matter was referred to Washington and Mitchel went there in person to present his case. He was accompanied by the Governor of Ohio, which served notice that he had the backing of that puissant state. The dispute was decided in his favor.

While there Mitchel spent the night of September 16 discussing with Andrew Johnson and Horace Maynard the cutting of the East Tennessee and Virginia railroad. On September 26 Mitchel wrote the War Department, "I therefore urge the necessity of placing in supreme command of this expedition to Kentucky and to Tennessee an experienced general, who will command the entire confidence of the government." On September 29 he was personally expressing the same idea to a "person sent out by the Secretary of War." Cameron called on Mitchel in Cincinnati on October 10 and ordered him to the command at Camp Dick Robinson. Sherman was advised by the Adjutant General, who hoped Sherman's judgment would accord with the views of the Secretary of War.

It happened that Sherman's judgment did not accord with that of the Secretary and he so informed Thomas. Sherman sent no orders to Mitchel to activate his new command and failed to keep an appointment with him in Lexington. Cameron talked with Sherman in Louisville, and later on his way back to Washington he told Mitchel that Sherman refused to cooperate with the East Tennessee expedition as they had planned it. Four months later Chase wrote to Mitchel, "It is deplorable that you were ever recalled from your movements in East Tennessee."

Sherman had spoiled Cameron's plan but the Secretary of War had the last word and he used one with the bark on it. Within a month after meeting with Sherman in Louisville, he relieved Sherman and let it be known that he thought him insane. Whatever the real story was, the most surprised participant probably was Andrew Johnson. He was a master of the technique of political knifing and the quick parry that saved Thomas must have won his admiration. At any rate, he and Thomas discussed in detail the East Tennessee movement and Johnson made notes of the specifications for victory that Thomas set up.[12] For more than a week it was touch and go whether Thomas would hold his command. Sherman working for him in Kentucky and Anderson in Washington finally won him the chance to go ahead with his plans.

The close-mouthed Thomas said nothing about the affair that has ever become public. It seems fairly certain that the attempt to unseat him rankled. He wrote Maynard a letter which has been lost but which brought forth the following admonition: "You do wrong in allowing personal indignities, come from what quarter they may, to diminish your activity in her [the U.S.] service." [13]

Just after Thomas had been informed that Mitchel was to take command, but before the situation had been resolved, Anderson visited Thomas on his way to Washington. Sherman had expected to be present but was prevented by Cameron's visit to Louisville. Anderson found Thomas surrounded by difficulties and exposed to labors of the most serious character. He was threatened by an attack from the east and another from the south. A secessionist uprising could cripple his supply line at any time. His main force at Rockcastle River was too far from its depot. His troops were only partially supplied, they refused to touch the uncouth European muskets sent them by the War Department, and he was much troubled for want of money. All his regiments except one lacked transportation. Mules had been purchased on credit for his Kentucky regiments but there were no wagons or harness. He had two batteries but one of them lacked caissons, harness and horses. He had contracted for clothing and tents but could not get delivery until they were paid for. There were no hospital supplies, no quartermaster and no commissary officer.

Thomas and Anderson made up a list of his minimum requirements for a successful forward movement. Thomas was to push for its fulfillment through official channels while Anderson pressed the matter in Washington. They decided to ask for the following: two brigadier generals for field commands; staff officers—quartermaster, commissary, engineer and topographical engineer; $100,000 in cash;

arms and ammunition to supply the demand which would arise among the Tennesseans; permission to recruit one company of men for duty as engineers; a small pontoon train (this was Anderson's suggestion); some regular troops to steady the raw volunteers and afford rallying points in case of reverses; authority to arrest and try evil-doers who might molest his advance, and to call for troops from Indiana, Ohio and Illinois. Above all, speed was urgent.

Anderson, in addition, urged that Thomas be promoted to major general of volunteers.[14]

Having failed to win Sherman's help in changing the command of the East Tennessee expedition, Cameron ordered him to inspect the situation at Camp Dick Robinson and get a forward movement under way. The threat of being relieved of his command was still hanging over Thomas but Sherman found that he was not a man to be convinced against his better judgment. Thomas refused to move until he had been equipped to move successfully. Sherman was caught squarely in the clash of wills between Thomas and Cameron. He resolved his dilemma by agreeing with Thomas and writing a record that would satisfy Cameron. The next day Sherman assured the Secretary that Thomas had been ordered to advance; but even before he received this intelligence, Cameron admitted that matters in Kentucky were in a much worse condition than he had expected to find them.

While Sherman was making his inspection at Camp Dick Robinson, William Blount Carter returned from his visit to McClellan. He was on his way with $20,000 and the blessings of the Administration to light the fires of revolt along the railway in East Tennessee, and this revolt would fix the time for Thomas' advance. Carter recalled afterwards that Sherman opposed the idea but that Thomas talked him out of his objections. The East Tennessee plan had nearly reached the point of no return and the pressures were bearing hard upon Sherman. In addition to Thomas' requisitions for troops, supplies, money and transport and Cameron's pressure for action, Andrew Johnson and Horace Maynard were in camp to make sure there were no slip-ups in the deliverance of their homeland.

Between the twenty-second and the twenty-seventh of October, Carter was within fifteen miles of the vital railroad, keeping Thomas informed by courier. There was a ten-day lag between the writing of Carter's dispatches and Thomas' receipt of them. Even today these messages are alive with urgency and apprehension.

The revolt was scheduled to begin the night of November 7. Thomas' advance units were in London with their points thrown out toward Cumberland Ford, twelve or fifteen miles from the Gap. He was moving cautiously because of the rawness of his troops and the shortage of transport. Zollicoffer had concentrated his inadequate force at Cumberland Gap. Every other pass was unguarded. Sherman was apprehensive and cautioning against a forward movement.

Andrew Johnson was with Thomas' forward elements. In some way he learned that Thomas was to be ordered back towards the Kentucky River and that the advance was off. Johnson's heated and intemperate objections and his attempts to get the East Tennessee brigade forward, even if no other troops went, nearly forced Thomas to order his arrest.[15]

Also while Sherman was making his inspection of Camp Dick Robinson in accordance with Cameron's order, Zollicoffer was stirring. On October 16 he moved out of Cumberland ford towards London with 4,500 men. His objective was north and west of that town, where he hoped to trap some hit-and-run raiders who had recently retreated from Albany, but he could not spring his trap as long as the Union force at Camp Wildcat, on the Rockcastle River, remained on his flank. This force had just been augmented by two new Ohio regiments and Brigadier General Schoepf[16] had taken command. Zollicoffer's force was traveling light. Food and supplies were being collected for them at Jamestown, but they would have to march 150 miles, fight twice, and get to their supplies before the food and ammunition they had with them gave out. It was a pretentious plan for untrained troops, and it came to grief at the first obstacle. Schoepf's men refused to budge and Thomas, acting as his own quartermaster at Dick Robinson, kept feeding Schoepf supplies, ammunition and encouragement. On the twenty-second, his plan hopelessly fouled up, Zollicoffer was falling back to fortify Cumberland Gap. Schoepf advanced to London.

Thomas was elated and anxious for a further advance. He believed that Zollicoffer now could be driven easily out of Kentucky. He established a supply depot at Crab Orchard and shortly thereafter moved his headquarters to the same point. He asked for permission to shift his supply line so as to avoid the difficult haul through the Rockcastle hills and to take advantage of a road which would be usable all winter. Again he asked for trained regiments, cash and supplies. This was the ninth such request he had made in a little more than thirty days. Schoepf wanted to advance, believing he could scatter Zollicoffer and take the Gap, but Thomas would not unleash him until he learned how fast clothing and ammunition could be sent forward. He had heard rumors, also, that Lee was to supersede Zollicoffer. "If he does,"

Thomas advised Sherman, "I should wish to be prepared for him fully."

Sherman, who wanted nothing to do with East Tennessee in any event, feared flank attacks on Thomas' extended communications and objected to a farther advance. Thomas was still insistent that East Tennessee should and could be invaded in accordance with his original plan but Sherman was beginning to develop the premonitory symptoms of a nervous breakdown. Out of these arose the fears that numbed his energy and robbed him of his sleep. He saw Thomas as overwhelmed on his front while his communications were cut at the Kentucky River bridge. Sherman admitted that he had no control over his future movements. All these fears were poured into the ears of the imperturbable Thomas in one anguished dispatch.

Thomas answered it immediately. Cold facts were the only antidote he knew for such fever and he gave them without reassuring generalities. It was reported that Zollicoffer was retiring—that disposed of the danger to his front. The enemy on his flank had fallen back to Virginia—that disposed of the threat to the Kentucky River bridge. Thomas had no facts to give about the Bowling Green front, another source of Sherman's fears, so he sent him a good spy. Sherman would have to help himself to some extent.

Between the time Sherman was notified of his relief and the time he actually gave up his command, his fears broke clear of restraint. To his sick imagination Albert Sidney Johnston was preparing to throw Buckner's heavy force between Bowling Green and Somerset, paralyze Thomas by cutting his communications, seize Cincinnati and threaten the invasion of Ohio. He telegraphed Thomas to retreat.[17] Thomas remonstrated but obeyed. The East Tennesseans mutinied. The debacle that followed was called by the Rebels the Wildcat Stampede. Thomas made no attempt to clear himself of the storm of denunciation that broke over him. Too late Sherman accepted Thomas' recommendation and countermanded his retreat order. Months later Sherman was still trying to justify this indefensible retrogression. Wherever the blame lay, Thomas three years later formally accepted the responsibility for the failure of the East Tennessee plan.

11

Victory at Mill Springs

Don Carlos Buell had been recalled from California for assignment to Anderson's Department of the Cumberland, but on September
12, 1861, he was transferred to the Department of the Potomac, a move
that was indicative of the way in which the Kentucky army was
neglected. Nor were its swelling troubles assuaged by Anderson's
feeble administration or Sherman's panic. The field commanders were
blamed for the failure of the East Tennessee plan but the real fault lay
with the Secretary of War.

McClellan had replaced Scott as General-in-Chief. He ordered Buell,
who was one of his close friends, to Louisville and at the same time
sent Henry W. Halleck to St. Louis. The common boundary of their
rival departments was the Cumberland River, one of the main invasion
routes of the South. With Halleck, a major general, commanding the
west bank and Buell, a brigadier general, commanding the east, it is
one of the miracles of the war that the North made any military
progress on this front.

The orphan army in Kentucky (its official name was the Army of
the Ohio) now was to get the care and nourishment that would result
in the incomparable Army of the Cumberland. Buell was ordered to
its command to take and hold East Tennessee, with Thomas as his
strike commander. To this end everything else was subordinated.

Buell found his new army in an almost hopeless state of disorganization but he had one leverage that had been denied to his predecessors. He was given what Thomas had asked for a month previously, control of the new troops that were being raised for his department. This was a preventive of future evils but not a cure for those already existing.

The shortages and disorganization of his command were scandalous. Men without rank were acting as general officers. Some regiments had arms of three different calibers. There were not enough wagons and teams to supply 20,000 men at a distance of two days' march from their depot. His command was a dispersed mob without mobility or equipment. It could be called an army only by courtesy.

Buell was a precisionist and his command soon began to show it. General Order Number 3 was a profound shock to his regimental commanders, who were accustomed to appearing on parade out of uniform, living away from their commands, accepting the resignation of their company officers and discharging their own men. These practices were now forbidden.

Then he came to grips with his touchiest problem. The state governors who raised his troops considered them their own. They exchanged their arms, ordered them to other commands, supplied them with special rations, called upon them for military reports and advised them on matters of military routine, discipline and strategy. Buell met the issue head-on and incurred the bitter enmity of Oliver P. Morton, Governor of Indiana. This doomed his military career but freed the western armies from interference by the governors who raised the troops.

Winter transport difficulties were shifting both sides westward from the Cumberland Gap. Zollicoffer was reported moving by the end of November. He wanted to substitute the water route up the Cumberland River from Nashville for the road haul through the mountains. But after reconnoitering three sides of Mill Springs he finally halted there on November 29. It was a tiny place on the south bank of the Cumberland River just below the fall line. There was a gristmill to supply one of his staple foods and a sawmill for cutting the lumber he needed for his winter quarters. The surrounding country was fertile and well stocked. Wood and water were abundant. His position commanded the ferry and was well sited to repel an attack from the north. He had placed himself squarely in the path that Thomas had chosen for getting into East Tennessee. Thomas had no chance now to turn his position and attack him from the rear.

Sometime previously Thomas had requested Sherman's permission to set up a supply depot at Lebanon. Buell gave Thomas the orders to make the shift. This moved his base from Cincinnati to Louisville, cut his supply line about one-third and gave him a rail haul for the entire distance. Schoepf was pulled out of London and put in at Somerset. The East Tennessee brigade remained on the Wilderness Road watching Cumberland Gap.

About the same time, Thomas was placed in command of all Buell's forces east of New Haven, Kentucky. This foreshadowed his division command, which came to him December 2. His was the First Division in what was to be the Army of the Cumberland and his brigade commanders were Schoepf, Carter, Colonel M. D. Manson, who had come to the division in command of the Tenth Regiment of Indiana Volunteers, and Colonel Robert L. McCook, one of Ohio's famous fighting McCooks, who had just reached Lebanon in command of a regiment recruited from the Germans living in Cincinnati. Four other division commanders were named at the same time. They were Alexander McD. McCook, O. M. Mitchel, William Nelson and T. L. Crittenden.

While Buell was organizing and equipping and Zollicoffer was moving into winter quarters, active campaigning practically ceased. There were several threats against the Union force at Somerset but Buell countermanded Thomas' orders for an offensive movement. Buell's eyes were fixed on the main rebel force blocking the line of the railroad and the Cumberland River to the south. They were defending the city of Nashville which Buell wanted to occupy before attempting a major strike against East Tennessee. Any threats from the direction of Nashville would bring immediate countermeasures from Buell but he would not permit Thomas to dissipate any of the Union strength by moving around the Rebels' right flank.

The East Tennessee plan, however, was far from dead. Thomas' division was being organized for this special purpose and Buell reported officially that he hoped to have the preparations completed soon. At this same time, Lincoln proposed to Congress the construction of a military railway to transport an army into East Tennessee and to supply it after it got there. The fate of this railway suggestion is the key to the strategic puzzle of the Civil War. It could have been finished in six or eight months but the idea was dropped after three months' consideration because it could not be completed within the period of military operations.

Less than a year later it became evident to the Northern command that the control of East Tennessee was essential to victory by either side. Lee wanted to occupy it after the fall of Petersburg had pinched off the Virginia salient in the hope that with his army in its mountain fastnesses he could still force a negotiated peace.

Meantime defensive measures alone forced the North to launch ten major attempts to win control of this strategic bastion. Once this control was theirs, the three great drives that hopelessly segmented the South were launched from its southern end and the movement of Thomas' horsemen northeastward along its railway backstopped Grant's trap for Lee at Appomattox.

While Buell was watching Nashville and Thomas was watching Zollicoffer, ships, troops and supplies for the simultaneous strike proposed by Lincoln against the east base of the Virginia salient were being concentrated in Chesapeake Bay. Their orders were to secure a lodgement on the North Carolina coast, penetrate the interior and threaten the lines of transportation in the rear of Richmond's defenders. Buell now seemed to be the only one who was dragging his feet and his reluctance seemed to stem mainly from the fact that, principally because of transportation difficulties, he saw his military objective as the army of Albert Sidney Johnston rather than the left flank of the army in front of Richmond.

At Christmas time Buell went up to Lebanon to look over Thomas' division and Thomas showed him, although Buell may have been already aware of the fact,[1] that Zollicoffer's destruction would not only threaten the Richmond supply lines but would also turn Albert Sidney Johnston's right and threaten his base at Nashville. Buell was convinced and ordered Thomas forward to clear Zollicoffer out of the Somerset front. If successful in capturing or destroying him, Thomas was to stop and await further orders.

It was to be a joint assault against troops behind fortifications. While Thomas struck Zollicoffer's left, Schoepf was to assault his front. This plan called for a tactical combination of widely scattered bodies of troops in front of the enemy. Schoepf did not like the idea of such a frontal attack and said so plainly. He suggested a plan for maneuvering the enemy out of his fortified camp and Thomas thought well enough of it to forward it to Buell. Buell wisely left the matter to Thomas' judgment.

Thomas started his sixty-five-mile march January 1, 1862, and reached Logan's crossroads, eight miles west of Somerset and nine miles north of Zollicoffer's camp at Beech Grove across the Cumberland River from Mill Springs, on January 17. This was an average of less than four miles a day for the head of his column. The mud in places was two feet deep. There were 600 wagons to be hauled with unbroken teams and some of the rear elements failed to get up in time for the battle. The rain, the mud, the stalled artillery, the endless double teaming of his ammunition and commissary train cooled off Thomas' ardor for a move against Knoxville and converted him to Buell's main idea, which was to move south on Nashville. On January 13 he suggested to Buell that a move down the Cumberland River toward the Tennessee capital was more in order but Buell made no change in his immediate plans for Thomas.

Thomas' halt at Logan's crossroads was to give his four straggling regiments time to get up and to instruct Schoepf in the details of his part in the attack. Schoepf visited him on the day of his arrival. Thomas revised his map so that roads, fords and place names agreed with Schoepf's, and directed Schoepf to send three regiments and a battery to replace his mud-bound units. That evening Thomas sent two of his regiments out to capture one of Zollicoffer's foraging trains encamped about six miles away.

Despite the march fatigue, wet and muddy clothes and bedding, and short rations, Thomas had not neglected his command's morale. He let it be known, when he had made contact with Schoepf, that his command had many advantages over the enemy. They had a numerical superiority. They were better equipped. They had a tactical advantage. His announcement worked. His raw troops were afraid the Rebels might get away without a battle. They were confident of licking them.

How Thomas inspired his men is not known but the way he handled his officers has been recorded. On the first night of the march to battle Thomas gave his staff their positions at the mess table. He sat at the head. The quartermaster was placed at the foot and the adjutant at Thomas' right. There were still two volunteer officers and a civilian aide to be seated. The civilian had served with the army in Texas and knew that the military took precedence but Thomas thought otherwise. Beckoning to the civilian he said, "Come, you're the oldest soldier; you take my left ahead of the volunteer aides."

Later, when the volunteers complained of the mud and the cold, Thomas used the civilian as an object lesson. He recalled how the old army had overcome worse hardships in the Texas mountains, "with not a human being in sight but grasshoppers." [2]

Fishing Creek flowed in a southerly direction between the forces of Schoepf and Thomas. At best it was a considerable obstacle to quick communication. Its gorge was from 200 to 300 feet deep and the dis-

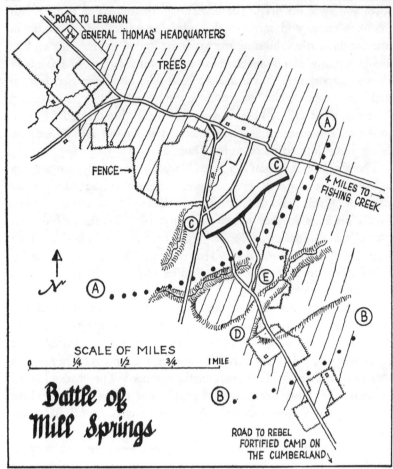

ROAD TO LEBANON

GENERAL THOMAS' HEADQUARTERS

TREES

Ⓐ

FENCE→

Ⓒ

4 MILES TO →
FISHING CREEK

Ⓒ

Ⓐ

Ⓔ

Ⓑ

Ⓓ

SCALE OF MILES

0   ¼   ½   ¾   I MILE

Battle of
Mill Springs

Ⓑ

ROAD TO REBEL
FORTIFIED CAMP ON
THE CUMBERLAND

Map 4. Battle of Mill Springs, January 19, 1862. From a sketch of the battlefield (*War of the Rebellion: Official Records of the Union and Confederate Armies. Atlas, Plate 6, No. 3*).

　　AA—Thomas' picket lines
　　BB—Line of vedettes
　　CC—Approximate position of Thomas' line when he came on the field
　　　D—Charge of the Ninth Ohio
　　　E—Rail fence where the Second Minnesota fought

tance from rim to rim varied from half a mile to thrice that distance. There were only two places in the vicinity of Somerset where it could be crossed by trains and artillery. Now it was in heavy flood from the rains that had impeded Thomas' march.

　　Major General George Bibb Crittenden,[3] who had recently taken command of the Southern force (Zollicoffer was commanding one brigade and Carrol the other) was in a quandary. His army had crossed to the north side of the Cumberland River in defiance of orders and now occupied a bad defensive position. With Schoepf and Thomas separated by Fishing Creek, Crittenden decided to strike Thomas before the two could unite and move against his fortified camp.

But Thomas was not to be caught with his guard down. He had thrown out strong picket companies a mile in front of his camp. Nearly a quarter of a mile in front of them were the pickets themselves, patrolling an arc wide enough to detect any enemy advance. Three-quarters of a mile ahead of these were the vedettes of the cavalry. If this defensive plan worked his main body would have an hour's notice of an enemy advance.

The Mill Springs battle began before dawn on January 19 when Crittenden's advance element ran into the cavalry vedettes. It was raining hard and had been most of the night. The Rebels, armed mostly with flintlock muskets, were having trouble keeping their priming powder dry.[4] The collision brought a few scattering musket shots which alerted Thomas' camp. The vedettes fell back on the pickets. Both fell back on the picket companies, which forced the deployment of Zollicoffer's leading regiment. The picket companies fell back slowly, buying time at a low price. Their line was soon stiffened by another company sent to their support. Crittenden's regiments began to flow out on both sides of the road, feeling for the Yankee flanks. Soon they developed the Yankee position and began building up pressure against its right. The action so far was confined to the Tenth Regiment of Indiana Volunteers which had had the picket duty. The Fourth Regiment of Kentucky Volunteers came to its support but, not being battle-wise, deployed to the left instead of the right.[5] As the Rebel pressure slowly forced back the Tenth Indiana, the Fourth Kentucky was left alone with the enemy in front and on both flanks.

This was the situation that Thomas found when he came on the field and he knew it could easily lead to disaster. He sent the Tenth Indiana, which had not been panicked, back into the line on the right of the Fourth Kentucky. Then he ordered the Tennessee brigade and a section of artillery into position on the left of the Fourth Kentucky. The Rebel advance was stopped at this new line and was in some confusion over the death of Zollicoffer. He had been killed while suggesting to the colonel of the Fourth Kentucky that that officer's command was firing on friendly troops. The uniforms of both were covered by rubber ponchos and recognition was slow.

Thomas was ready for his counterstroke. The Second Regiment of

Minnesota Volunteers came on the field and he ordered it to take over the combined fronts of the Tenth Indiana and the Fourth Kentucky. A single musket shot followed by five or six in quick succession had aroused the Minnesotans from their sleep. It was the first Rebel fire they had ever heard. Wet, cold and hungry, the companies formed to the summons of the rolling drums. The rain had ceased but the air was thick with mist and smoke. On Thomas' orders the troops pushed their way through the dense underbrush and came suddenly to a rail fence at the edge of an open field. Dimly seen through the mist and smoke a hundred yards from the fence was the Rebel battle line. In their inexperience, however, they did not notice that another line of Rebel infantrymen were lying on the ground on the opposite side of the same fence. The surprise was mutual but the Minnesotans recovered first and drove off the enemy.

Close behind the Second Minnesota came the Ninth Regiment of Ohio Volunteers—the Bully Dutchmen they were called, already blooded in the West Virginia fighting. They deployed on the right flank, overreached the Rebel left and swung against it like a gate. From this position they launched a bayonet charge which drove the Rebels from the field.

Thomas kept on their heels. For the seven or eight miles of the pursuit the Union line was kept as straight and even as if the movement were a drill. Every regiment and battery was in its proper place, while Thomas, visible to the troops, appeared "as cool as a cucumber." A half-hearted rear guard action delayed him but not for long. During this pursuit his force was augmented by the raiding party that had been sent after Zollicoffer's train and by more of Schoepf's brigade from Somerset. With this expanded force he invested the Rebel fortifications at the Cumberland River and held them under his artillery fire until dark. The next morning he marched into their empty camp.

Leaving everything behind—even their colors and their wounded—Crittenden's army had crossed the Cumberland during the night and dissolved into small groups and then into individuals as they made their way to their homes. Since the object of a conquering army is to destroy the force opposed to it, this was a model victory and the most consequential, so far, to the Northern arms. Its completeness was a surprise to Buell. The battle had been fought in accordance with the classical military principles which Thomas never forsook. Observers have called Mill Springs one of the most remarkable Union victories of the war.[6] So far as the Kentucky campaign was concerned it was decisive, for it smashed the eastern anchor of Albert Sidney Johnston's defense cordon and made the rest of his line untenable. Furthermore, it revealed to the Northern commanders the myth of the Rebel offensive strength in the west.[7]

The victory was greatly appreciated by Lincoln, who was in one of his moods of dark discouragement at this time. Public confidence in the currency was ebbing, the Treasury was empty and foreign relations were delicate. His armies had known little but defeat. In his phrase, the bottom was out of the barrel. His depression may have lightened on Washington's birthday when the captured battle flags sent by Thomas to Buell and by Buell to the capital were presented to Congress by the Adjutant General after the reading of Washington's Farewell Address. Most of the Administration officials were present for the first ceremony of this kind.

Others, too, stressed the completeness of the victory. Said Buell, "The defeat of the enemy was thorough and complete." Stanton said that the enemy was completely routed in accordance with the purpose of the Union army to attack, pursue and destroy. Crittenden reported, ". . . many officers and men, frightened by false rumor . . . shamelessly deserted, and . . . fled to Knoxville, Nashville and other places in Tennessee." Thomas reported that Zollicoffer's forces were entirely dispersed and that there would be no enemy encountered in East Tennessee.

Yet the action was not without its critics. T. L. Livermore in 1895 stated his belief that if Thomas had called Schoepf's men to him on the seventeenth and had advanced immediately against Crittenden, he might have captured or destroyed the Confederates. He also pointed out that while Thomas was taking seventeen days to march sixty-five miles, 4,000 men of Grant's army marched seventy-five miles in four days in western Kentucky in the same inclement weather.[8]

Mill Springs, like most well fought battles, was colorless. There were no tactical mistakes to be remedied by desperate countercharges. Frontal assaults would have wasted lives that Thomas' more skillful tactics saved. This was one of the few battles of the war in which the South was not outnumbered; yet Thomas kept his casualties low, approximately 6 per cent of his effectives. Eight Union regiments were engaged in the battle itself. Two more came on the field in time for the pursuit and three more in time for the investment. Thomas' effective force on the field numbered about 4,000. Crittenden marched with eight regiments of infantry, approximately one regiment of cavalry and two batteries of artillery. He too had about 4,000 effectives on the field. The battle was fought with numerically equal forces but the reserves Thomas had near the battlefield or coming up gave him a distinct superiority. Losses of killed, wounded, captured or missing were 262 for the North and 533 for the South.

Crittenden's artillery was not used effectively. Thomas' batteries, according to his opponents, swept the field with shell, grape and canister. Their fire was decisive in forcing the evacuation of the Rebels' fortified camp. Eleven pieces of artillery (one other piece was captured during the retreat), more than 150 wagons and more than 1,000 horses and mules were abandoned, together with camp equipment, small arms and stores.

Thomas' skill in handling his men is attributable to three things. First, he deployed his picket company to avoid a surprise, often a disastrous shock to inexperienced troops. Since he expected an attack, however, it is not clear why he used no intrenchments. Second, he was on the field himself to reassure his men and to learn firsthand what was going on. Third, he was able to foresee what was to happen, so he could guard against the blows before they fell and take full advantage of the opportunities as they were presented. Having done these things, he left the troops to fight the battle their own way. They took the first collision and alerted themselves before Thomas was out of bed. Driven off the field, the Tenth Indiana re-formed without panic and was perfectly willing to go back into the line when Thomas gave the order. He did not order and, so far as is known, did not suggest the charge of the Ninth Ohio that won the battle for him. But it was perfectly timed. The men, sensing that fact, drove it home. Thomas' contribution lay in putting his best regiment at the right time in the one spot from which a decisive counterattack could be mounted. There was undoubtedly mismanagement by Crittenden in not getting more of his regiments into action in the early part of the fight, and there were two breaks, both of which favored the Yankees—the rain which made the Rebel flintlocks miss fire and the death of Zollicoffer.

There is a mystery about the dispositions at Mill Springs which the written messages of the official records do not explain. When Thomas planned a battle he never took chances. He always tried to crush his opponent with overpowering force. The disposition of his pickets indicated that he knew an attack was imminent. Why, then, did he put his depleted force of green troops into camp within a few miles of the enemy and with the swollen waters of Fishing Creek between himself and Schoepf? Why, above all, did he send two regiments of this force away after a wagon train? One theory is that he was doing everything possible to entice Crittenden out of the protection of his fortifications. Thomas was anxious for a fight but he is also on record as not wanting to make an assault on troops behind breastworks.

Thomas was not as unflustered and self-possessed as many biographers have made him out to be. Speed S. Fry, colonel of the Fourth Kentucky and one of those who shot Zollicoffer, said to Thomas as they stood in the abandoned fortification looking at the evidence of headlong flight, "General, why didn't you send in a demand for surrender last night?" Thomas looked at him a moment as if reflecting. "Hang it all, Fry, I never once thought of it." He had forgotten in the excitement of his first combat command, the main point of Mahan's teaching. He won a total victory by dispersing his enemy but the victory was accidental. He learned in the process that pursuit was too difficult a tactic to be improvised.

For their victory Thomas and his men received the congratulations of the army commander, the thanks of the states of Kentucky and Ohio and those of the President. The first three mentioned Thomas by name. Lincoln did not but promised suitable recognition as soon as the battle reports were received. The first newspaper accounts of the battle gave Schoepf credit for the victory. Lincoln notified Andrew Johnson that Schoepf had killed Zollicoffer and routed his army. Less than a month after the official battle reports were forwarded to Washington, Lincoln nominated Thomas for the commission of major general of volunteers.[9] Six other officers who had distinguished themselves at Mill Springs were also named for promotion. Four were confirmed on March 24. Thomas' was not confirmed until April 25 and his commission was not dated back to the day of the battle. Two of the nominations were never confirmed.

Buell had recommended that Thomas be rewarded by brevet, leaving the full promotion to the grade of brigadier general (i.e., in the regular army) to flow exclusively from fitness for the office as shown by service. Horace Maynard sent Thomas his congratulations and added a postscript, probably with his tongue in his cheek, "Yesterday the Senate confirmed your nomination as brigadier general." This referred to his commission as brigadier general of volunteers dated the preceding August.

On reading of the Mill Springs disaster in the Louisville papers, Johnston reported to his superiors, "If my right is thus broken as stated, East Tennessee is wide open to invasion, or, if the plan of the enemy be a combined movement upon Nashville, it is in jeopardy, unless a force can be placed to oppose a movement from Burkesville. . . ." Thomas favored the Nashville movement. On January 23 he reported to Buell that the roads to East Tennessee were impassable, that there would be difficulty in foraging his animals, and that Crittenden's force had disbanded and thrown away their arms. He suggested that Carter go into East Tennessee to encourage the citizens and take them arms and that he himself be permitted to move down the Cumberland, fortify Burkesville and cooperate in a move against Bowling Green. Lincoln, however, disagreed. "Could not a cavalry force from General Thomas . . . dash across and cut the railroad at or near Knoxville, Tennessee?" was his query to Halleck and Buell.

On February 6 Thomas was ordered to move with all possible dispatch from Somerset to Lebanon in support of Buell's movement south along the railroad through Bowling Green. The next day the capture of Fort Henry by the navy was announced. The drive by Halleck and Buell up the Tennessee and Cumberland rivers was on in earnest. From Lebanon Thomas was ordered toward Munfordville as part of the general movement against Bowling Green but so rapid was the disintegration of the Rebel defense line under the alternate blows of Thomas at Mill Springs and Grant at Fort Donelson that these orders were countermanded. He was sent to Louisville by forced marches, where transports would pick up his division and carry it to Nashville. From a position as the prime mover of the Western armies, Thomas was now sucked into a current which swept him off to play a supporting role in an entirely different movement dominated by Halleck and aimed at the occupation of Rebel territory.

The first East Tennessee campaign was a record of frustration in spite of the fact that time proved it to be inevitable.[10] The first frustration was Sherman's panic retreat order which halted Thomas' advance in the fall of 1861. The next was the weather, which drove both contenders from the mountains as soon as winter closed in. The railroad which Lincoln proposed to have built from middle Kentucky to Knoxville would have overcome this objection. The later Union drives into the area were made in the summer or fall. The Battle of Mill Springs was fought in the winter but it was fought in the lowlands. The weather kept it from being the preliminary to a drive toward Knoxville. Its military significance lay in the fact that it broke the eastern end of Johnston's defense line and gave strength to Buell's contention that his primary objective was the army of Albert Sidney Johnston rather than that of Joseph Eggleston Johnston in front of Richmond.

The controlling frustration arose from Halleck's ambition to become the commander of all the Northern armies in the west. When he achieved it in March 1862 the attention of his combined force was focused on the sterile strategy of occupying Rebel territory.

So it happened that the first East Tennessee campaign, which ended at Mill Springs, became the beginning of an entirely different movement which ended in northern Mississippi, in which Grant was the principal actor and for which Halleck received the principal credit. This was the campaign against Forts Henry and Donelson and the piercing of the entire width of Tennessee along the Tennessee River. In this operation Buell and Thomas played minor roles.

12

The Corinth Campaign and Buell's Failure

When Thomas and his veterans disembarked at Nashville, its population was something less than 20,000. It was the first seceded capital to be reoccupied and it was the best provisioned military depot in the South. Its percussion caps had helped whip the Yankees at Bull Run. It housed one of the few machines in the Confederacy for rifling gun barrels and its factories turned out sabers, muskets, saddles, harness, knapsacks and uniform cloth.

Its occupation, however, accentuated the evils of a divided command. As Grant, Thomas and the navy fought southward through Kentucky, the command areas of Halleck and Buell were divided by the channel of the Cumberland River. If the southern boundary of Kentucky was crossed, Halleck's troops could not officially engage the enemy. In anticipation of this, Lincoln detached an area called West Tennessee from Buell and gave it to Halleck. But his plan was so ill considered that Halleck's field commander did not know the boundaries of his combat area.[1] On March 13, 1862, nearly a month later, he cured this defect by giving Halleck the over-all western command.

"Old Brains," as Halleck was sarcastically called by his troops, was fat, sluggish, careless, indolent and inexact. He could not ride his horse out of a walk and he lacked command energy but not the ability to advance himself. The combat talents of Grant, Thomas and the navy masked his military incapacity. He used the results of their victories to advance his claims to over-all command and at the same time increased his professional stature by pointing out the obvious inefficiency of a divided command. Before accepting his advice, however, Lincoln moved to nullify in part its gains.

This was his appointment, over Buell's protest, of Andrew Johnson as military governor of Tennessee with the rank of brigadier general. The day before Halleck accepted his new command, Johnson reached Nashville. His ideas about winning the war differed from Halleck's. He wanted to liberate East Tennessee and, with its manpower, form a provisional state government which in the end would bring Tennessee back into the Union. While this provisional government was being organized he demanded that Halleck disperse his army to police the state. Halleck's plan was to concentrate his force, move it against the Rebel army and win the war. In one of the few bits of humorous writing to be found in the *Official Records,* Halleck interpreted the situation. He wrote Buell, "Governor Johnson will release our grasp on the enemy's throat in order to pare his toenails." In some way which is not now apparent, Halleck managed to shift Johnson's irritation over the military situation from himself to Buell.

While this infighting was taking place in the high echelons of the western command, Albert Sidney Johnston was concentrating and supplying a Rebel army at Corinth, Mississippi. In the middle of March, Grant was watching them from Pittsburgh Landing on the west bank of the Tennessee River, nine miles upstream from Halleck's concentration point, the village of Savannah. Buell was under orders to move to Savannah but first he had to rebuild a bridge over the Duck River at Columbia, Tennessee. This job was completed on March 30 after two weeks of work. The same day the bridge was finished the water level in the Duck River dropped enough so that the fords became usable. On this day Buell began his march. For the head of his column at Columbia the distance to Savannah was ninety miles. Thomas, because his division had been in action most recently, was at Nashville assigned to the rear of Buell's column. This made his march distance in the neighborhood of 150 road miles.

Buell's problem was to move 37,000 men with their artillery and trains over a narrow, ungraded, dirt road. He estimated that the head of his column would reach Savannah on April 5 or 6 and neither Grant nor Halleck disagreed with this schedule. It was March 20 when Thomas moved his division out of Nashville. Nelson's division, which had Buell's advance, was two days' march beyond Columbia.[2] Thomas inched forward as the long column opened out due to the accidents, breakdowns and delays which always slow such a march. His men made cheerless camps in a country churned into mud and stripped of forage and firewood. On April 3 Nelson's cavalry was in touch with Grant at Savannah but no orders to hurry came down the long, sinuous column. On April 4, Buell, from Waynesborough, asked Grant for an appointment in Savannah on April 6. Nelson himself reached that waterbound village on the fifth and was supplied with guides to get his division through the flooded lowlands to the ferry terminal across the river from Pittsburgh Landing. The Battle of Shiloh began the following day and Thomas received orders to move by forced marches to Grant's aid.

That afternoon his men heard the rumble of Shiloh's artillery. They covered twenty-two miles before dark and continued marching after sundown, when it began to rain. At 11:00 P.M., the troops filed off the road to rest in the mud of a plowed field. There were no fires. The next morning at 4:00 A.M. they started out again. These were march-weary men hurrying to relieve the battle-weary. On the ninth they stacked their arms on the battlefield of Shiloh, too late to fight but just in time to bury the dead.

In the military sense they were fresh troops. They expected to be sent south in pursuit of the Confederacy's western army, which was in full retreat. Its commander was dead, it had lost heavily in the first day's fighting, and had been defeated the second day. But Grant never gave the order.

Halleck came down from St. Louis in the middle of April to take the field command of the combined armies of his new department. His staff and headquarters troops watched him pacing back and forth in the texas of a river steamer scolding Grant. Halleck was dressed in civilian clothes—swallow-tailed coat and velvet slippers. Grant sat listening, red faced, deferential and undistinguished, his uniform covered with mud. Grant's relations with his superior had been so strained a few weeks before that he had asked to be relieved of his command. Now trouble between the two was working up to another crisis.

With Grant's military career under threat, Thomas' prospects began to improve. Lincoln's nomination of him as major general of volunteers, which had been stalled for a month by a Senate committee, was confirmed by Halleck's urgent solicitation of the Secretary of War. It was a tardy recognition of his Mill Springs victory but a substantial jump in rank. Only seventeen volunteer officers were senior to him.[3]

Halleck reorganized his army into four divisions—Right Wing, Left Wing, Center and Reserve. Buell commanded the Army of the Ohio, which was the Center; John Pope, the Left Wing; and John A. Mc-Clernand, the Reserves. As soon as Thomas' new rank was published, Halleck named him to the command of the Army of the Mississippi, which was the Right Wing. This consisted of Thomas' favorite Mill Springs division and four divisions of Grant's Shiloh veterans. His division commanders were Thomas West Sherman (Mill Springs division), William Tecumseh Sherman, J. A. Davis, S. A. Hurlbut and T. J. McKean.

Grant was made second-in-command to Halleck, stripped of his troops and officially ignored. It was some time before Thomas became aware that he had actually been used to deprive Grant of his command. Thomas and Halleck were much together during the ensuing campaign and when Grant happened to be with them Halleck was overly solicitous of Thomas' suggestions. He was like the spiteful hostess who makes a fuss over one guest in order to emphasize her neglect of another. Grant apparently held Thomas partly responsible for this slight and relations became strained. This was a situation that Thomas would not tolerate for long. He could not ask to be relieved of his command in the face of the enemy but he would do so at the first opportunity.

Although Thomas was the junior major general, only Halleck and Grant were his superiors in command. This mix-up between rank and command was an outgrowth of the Northern politicians' antagonism to a standing army. The highest rank in the army was that of major general, with the result that major generals commanded divisions (the regular command for a two-star general), corps and armies. McClellan and Halleck were major generals while commanding as generals-in-chief.[4]

At about this time, Thomas was handed a petition from the officers of one of his brigades for the removal of their brigade commander. Such action strikes at the heart of military discipline. The routine procedure for Thomas would have been to prefer charges against the insubordinate officers and let a military court assess the blame and fix the penalty. But Thomas chose a different course. He called the disaffected officers to his headquarters, pointed out the error of their way and the punishment to which it exposed them. As a result there were apologies to the brigade commander. This velvet-glove policy seemed to work for Thomas. It kept the volunteer prima donnas under control as long as he commanded them but without destroying their spirit.

The control, however, was Thomas' own. His division for a long time refused this forbearance to its other commanders.

Halleck was plainly miscast as a field commander. He knew little about living in the field and his camp arrangements were inadequate, uncomfortable and irritating to himself and his staff. He did unify the command, concentrate his forces and point them for the Rebel army at Corinth, all proper moves. But he was unable to inspire confidence and lacked the energy to exploit them. Instead of using his greatly superior force to outflank and trap his opponents, he crept forward to a frontal assault which he never launched.

His army, in overwhelming force, advanced twenty-two miles between April 29 and May 30. During that time one of Thomas' divisions built seven intrenched camps. This was probably the slowest uncontested advance ever made by a major military force on the North American continent. The officers under Halleck's command garnered little military prestige. There was a spirited debate between Buell and Pope over the sterile honor of having put the first troops into Corinth but Thomas, with a stronger claim than either,[5] kept out of the discussion.

Halleck won the rail junction of Corinth but the Confederates won the time needed to reorganize their shattered army. They were able to slow the momentum of their long retreat from Mill Springs. With the Confederacy fighting for a stalemate this was winning strategy.

Halleck was at a loss for his next move. Buell and Pope were ordered south in half-hearted pursuit, but this movement petered out halfway to the Rebels' entrenched camp at Tupelo. Thomas was stopped at Corinth and put in command of its garrison. It had been an unhealthy camp for the Confederates and his biggest job was to sanitate the area. One colonel reported later that the health of his men was never better.

Thomas took advantage of this lull to ask Halleck to relieve him of his command of Grant's army and return him to the command of his Mill Springs division. With scores of major generals frozen in their rank by the inflexible rule of the War Department, there was considerable competition for higher command. Thomas' renunciation, therefore, must have raised quite a few eyebrows. He evidently had two reasons. One was that he wanted to secure for himself the opportunity to multiply his well-trained division into a corps and then into an army of his own. The other was that he wished to restore to Grant the command that Halleck had taken from him.[6] Thomas never knowingly permitted himself to be used to inflict an injury on another and he was undoubtedly opposed to an actual violation of the rule of seniority, even if technically the rule was observed. He may have remembered his own feelings when Van Dorn was given the field command of the Second Cavalry while he as regimental commander had no troops except the band and the headquarters company.

It is possible that Sherman had something to do with Thomas' stepping aside, for he was one of his intimate friends and had been drawn into Grant's orbit during the Donelson movement. Sherman and Grant were then army outcasts. Their mortification gave them a common outlook.

Grant must have felt bewildered, frustrated and insecure. No matter how many battles he won, he must have thought, the army seemed to distrust him. No matter how much his rank increased the responsibilities that went with promotion were denied him. Now, with the best combat record in the army, his superiors were trying to ease him out of the service.

How much of this state of mind Thomas knew can only be conjectured, but he probably sensed most of it. His step-down from a corps to a division command should have brought reassurance to Grant. One mutual friend thought it did, that Grant in his deprecatory way was ready for a complete accord but that the Virginian's attitude smothered it.[7] Another observer, however, says that Thomas was not actuated by such a sentimental weakness as justice for a wronged officer, but rather by his own ambition. He wanted to return to his original command because through its careful organization and its confidence in his leadership he was building an army that was to be irresistible.[8]

Thomas had spent most of his military career in restoring the lost morale of his field commands or remedying the deficiencies of their former commanders. He had prevailed upon a mutinous battalion of the Third Artillery to face the hazards of a sea voyage. At Carlisle Barracks he had rebuilt the Second Cavalry after its morale had been destroyed. At Camp Dick Robinson he had organized out of a rabble the First Brigade of the Army of the Cumberland. Within four months he had expanded it into a division which became recognized as the best of the six under Buell's command,[9] and with it he had won the first significant Union victory. He had confidence in his ability to train a force that could destroy the enemy without great losses to itself. These things he did without disciplinary violence. He did not feel that his obligations were discharged simply by taking from some other commander an army that was already organized.

There is no known record of Thomas' statement of his motive in stepping aside, although his wife's testimony supports the belief that it was his sense of justice. In any event, it proved the truism that one way to make an enemy is to put him in your debt, although its final effect, coupled with Sherman's efforts, may have been to keep Grant in the army.

It was now more than four months since the Union strategy in the west had been turned away from the Rebel army in front of Richmond and directed toward the one in front of Nashville. The effort had been successful if measured by the distance of the Rebel retreat but it was now faltering under Halleck's sluggishness. An enemy retreat is never proof of conquest. As long as a Confederate army remained in existence, conquest was only a dream.

Halleck's army, nearly 100,000 strong, had a choice of movements aiming at an eventual conquest of the South. If its commander had no stomach for the short, quick way—the destruction of the Rebel army—Vicksburg to the west or Chattanooga to the east would fall without resistance to the first major military force to threaten them. Vicksburg's capture would open the Mississippi; Chattanooga's would give the North control of the mountain ramparts.

Early in June there were at least five officers within riding distance of Halleck's headquarters qualified to handle successfully this double objective. An officer of more than average ability, and Halleck's aides could have talked to a score of them in a single afternoon, could have secured at least one of these objectives. But Halleck fumbled away his opportunities. The Confederate command was watching his army anxiously. Jefferson Davis' query to Tupelo regarding that army's plans for the future brought this reply: "The plan of the future operations must depend to a great extent on the movement of the enemy. Should he divide his forces, the offensive must to taken . . . but should he keep his forces together, he must be made to divide them. . . ."[10] That dispersion of the Federal forces for which the Rebels would have been forced to fight, Halleck gave them for nothing. In the face of this demonstrated ineptitude, he was called to Washington on July 11 to be the General-in-Chief of all the armies.

The strategic importance of East Tennessee was plain to both sides. It was the starting point for aggressive campaigns, without which neither side could win. Its fortresses provided the Rebels with a base for their strikes against the Ohio River frontier. They would provide equal security for Northern moves southward toward Atlanta and east-

ward into the Carolinas and Virginia. Next to the destruction of the
Rebel army, the occupation of East Tennessee was perhaps the North's
most important military objective.

Halleck looked at the problem as he settled lethargically into his
Corinth camps and decided to turn the mountain ramparts into a Union
bastion. On June 9 he recalled his halfhearted pursuit of the Rebel
army and sent Buell eastward with verbal orders to occupy East Tennessee. Buell was willing and his army was in motion two days later.
Two of his divisions, with some 8,000 effectives each, were already in
the area. One, under Brigadier General George W. Morgan, was
threatening the Rebel position at Cumberland Gap and took it nine
days later; the other, under Major General Ormsby M. Mitchel, was
lobbing shells across the Tennessee River into Chattanooga in an un-
coordinated diversion which helped Morgan's advance 120 miles to
the north.[11] Between these Federal threats Major General E. Kirby
Smith, with approximately 3,000 men, stood at Knoxville and watched
apprehensively.

Buell had all he needed to make good his occupation of East Tennessee. With Morgan and Mitchel snapping at Kirby Smith's flanks,
Buell aimed to cross the Cumberland Plateau at McMinnville, swing
across the head of the Sequatchie valley at Pikeville, drop down to the
Tennessee River from the 1,200 foot heights of Walden's Ridge and
cross its waters in the vicinity of Kingston, where Kirby Smith would
be hopelessly trapped. This was a route march of perhaps 350 miles.
His Corinth troops could cross the Tennessee River at Eastport, where
there were plenty of facilities, and move with light trains toward their
supplies instead of dragging them behind them. The broad Tennessee
River would guard their right flank. The rail lines from his supply
depot at Nashville to Stevenson and Decatur, Alabama, would supply
his divisions as they came up to its single line of track at preordained
sidings. His heavy combat supplies would be picked up from the rail-
heads at Tracy City and McMinnville. Thirty days, perhaps, would be
a comfortable time for executing this movement so that by the middle
of July he could present Halleck and the nation with the gift of this
strategic area which in the end proved decisive in the outcome of the
war.

But this was not to be. Halleck feared that the Rebels might move
into Chattanooga before Buell could occupy it so he ordered Buell to
move directly there and to supply himself by means of the Memphis
and Charleston railroad. Buell tried unsuccessfully to point out the
fatal drawbacks of this plan. His railroad communication must be

secure from his supply base to Stevenson. To reach Stevenson by Halleck's route would mean that his supplies would move from Louisville by boat to Eastport, Mississippi. Here they would be transshipped and moved by wagon to Iuka, transshipped again and moved by rail to Decatur, ferried across the Tennessee River at Decatur and reloaded on another train which would carry them to Stevenson. It was a time-consuming operation. Each pound of freight—and Buell required 100,-000 pounds of provisions daily in addition to forage, quartermaster's and ordnance supplies and ammunition—would have to be manhandled six times. To make matters worse, the Memphis and Charleston railroad had been completely wrecked during the Corinth campaign and its rolling stock had been removed or destroyed. Furthermore, the stretch of the Memphis and Charleston from Iuka to Decatur lay south of the Tennessee River. Rebel raiders could break it at will. Bridges could be burned; cuts could be filled; rails could be torn up at almost any place and laid on a pile of burning ties to twist themselves out of shape; half a dozen rifle bullets could empty a water tank; split rifle cartridges could be wedged into the firewood piled beside the right-of-way and fires kindled to destroy the fuel for the locomotive boilers; the jerry-built telegraph line beside the track could be cut with little effort and rail operation would be crippled until the break could be located and repaired.

Since Buell had no choice, he moved in accordance with Halleck's orders. Thomas, with Buell's best combat division, was held by Halleck at Tuscumbia to get the vital sixty-five miles of railroad between Iuka and Decatur operating and guard it against enemy raids. For more than six weeks, one fifth of Buell's striking force labored with picks and shovels to bring into operation a piece of railroad that retarded, rather than aided, their military campaign. Eventually it actually crippled Buell's alternate plan for carrying out his military mission.

There were two lines of railroad running south to the Tennessee River from Nashville. The one to the west passed through Franklin and Columbia and connected with the Memphis and Charleston across the river from Decatur. The eastern one ran through Murfreesborough to Stevenson where it made a junction with the Memphis and Charleston only a few miles from Bridgeport on the Tennessee River. As soon as Buell was convinced that Halleck's operation order was irrevocable he gave orders to have both these north-and-south railroads made operational and supplies stockpiled at Stevenson for his Chattanooga advance. Both these railroads were perpendicular to the enemy's front and therefore more easily defended. But Halleck's orders were con-

trolling and Thomas in obedience to them began calling for freight
cars and locomotives. The quickest way to get them was to rob the
Nashville-Decatur railroad, which was already in short supply, so the
Nashville-Decatur began to pillage its connecting lines. The shortage
spread northward along the communication arteries until it infected
the vital link between the Louisville base and the Nashville depot. This
error in military planning along the Tennessee River crippled the
stockpiling of Buell's supplies far to the north.[12] Thus Buell had the
impossible task of repairing, operating and guarding 500 miles of railroads in order to make a 200-mile march.[13] With this handicap he lost
the race to Chattanooga.

While the futile task of railroad repair went on, Braxton Bragg,
whose light battery had fought beside Thomas at Buena Vista, took
command of the Confederate army at Tupelo and made his plans for
moving into East Tennessee. He, too, planned to use the rail lines and
he made what was perhaps the world's first mass movement of troops
for a significant distance by this new military transport medium. His
route was south from Tupelo to Mobile, thence north to Montgomery,
after a short march between non-connecting lines, and thence through
Atlanta to Chattanooga. Two days after Thomas finally got his section of the Memphis and Charleston working, Bragg's advance was
detraining in Chattanooga. Buell's opportunity had been frittered
away and Halleck, already appointed General-in-Chief of all the Northern armies but not yet clothed with that authority, decided to clear
himself and let the blame rest on Buell. He was aided by Andrew
Johnson.

"Nashville," Johnson wrote to Halleck on June 17, "had been left
to a great extent in a defenseless position." He wanted Buell's inept
subordinates relieved and asked that Thomas and his division replace
the present garrison.[14] On July 10 Johnson wrote Lincoln that Buell
was not the man to redeem East Tennessee and suggested that a change
must be made.[15] Incidentally he remarked that if the army had started
work on the railroad from Kentucky to East Tennessee, which Lincoln had suggested a year earlier, it would have been completed by
now and would have saved its construction cost in troop fares and
freight bills.[16] Lincoln, upset by McClellan's defeat in front of Richmond and Jackson's campaign in the Shenandoah Valley, felt that
Buell should move more rapidly and Halleck used this admonition
to lay the groundwork for Buell's professional destruction,[17] although
he had promised that Buell's movements would be properly explained
to the President when he got to Washington. But if his attitude then

was the same as when he convened the Buell Commission, he made no mention of his own crippling specifications which had smothered Buell's advance.[18]

With 27,000 Rebel troops in Chattanooga and 18,000 more in Knoxville (Kirby Smith had been reinforced) Buell had to revise his strategy from maneuver to assault. But Bragg had already snatched the initiative. His problem was to stop the tide of disaster which had been running since the Confederate defeat at Mill Springs and reverse it if possible. He and Kirby Smith decided to occupy middle Tennessee as the first step and they called on two of the South's ablest cavalry leaders to help. East Tennessee began to boil with military activity. On July 4 John Hunt Morgan moved out on his first Kentucky raid.[19] He crossed the Tennessee River and climbed the steep, 2,200-foot escarpment of the Cumberland Plateau by way of Sparta. He was probably checking the grades and noting the available water and grass for Bragg's army if it chose to take this northern route. Morgan was halfway across Kentucky by the eleventh. Excitement was rampant in Cincinnati and Lincoln tried to calm Louisville's panic by wire. Morgan swung a great loop to within fifty miles of Cincinnati before returning to East Tennessee by way of Somerset, Kentucky, breaking Buell's rail line wherever he touched it and upsetting the Kentuckians with fake telegraphic reports of his whereabouts and accomplishments. It may have been his exultant report to Kirby Smith of July 24 to the effect that Kentucky could be taken and that 25,000 to 30,000 Kentuckians would join the Rebel army which gave Bragg the idea he finally acted upon.

On July 9 Forrest ferried 1,400 horsemen over the Tennessee and crossed the Cumberlands by way of Altamont and McMinnville. This was the southern and alternate route for Bragg's army to follow and Forrest reported back its assets and liabilities. The day after the first through train from Nashville, loaded with Buell's supplies, whistled for the crossing at Stevenson, Forrest rode into Murfreesborough. His troops were ready down to the last horseshoe nail and his silver spurs winked in the rising sun as he struck the Federal garrison. The surprise was complete. Forrest took more prisoners than he had men and Buell's supply line was ruptured for two weeks more. He had ten days' rations on hand—and it would take him ten days to cross the Cumberlands and the Tennessee River if he met no opposition. This was too big a risk to be hazarded.

Buell accepted his defensive role and dispersed his army in a seventy-five-mile arc from Battle Creek to McMinnville to wait for provisions

and to watch Bragg. Halleck's false strategy, combined with the wrecking of his supply line, lost Buell his chance to keep Bragg off balance;
but it was in August that Buell's difficulties began piling up to a dangerous climax. They were of three kinds—those caused by the enemy,
those caused by a breakdown of the servomechanisms of his own command and, unbelievably, a major blunder on the part of Lincoln and
Stanton.

There were alarms from enemy probings all along Buell's defense
arc and the stories which poured into Buell's headquarters magnified
the realities they reported, but there were other signs which were more
definitive. Morgan moved out of East Tennessee early in the month
to paralyze the railroad between Louisville and Nashville. This was
a sensitive area. Louisville was the base of supplies for most of the
Union armies in the west and Buell drew his requirements from it
and stockpiled them in his forward depot at Nashville by rail because
low water prevented the use of the Cumberland River. On August
12 Morgan seized the twin tunnels near Gallatin and held them long
enough to run into them strings of freight cars filled with combustibles.
These were set on fire and the wooden shorings were burned out.
Tunnel roofs and sides collapsed, burying the rails under six feet of
debris. This rail rupture was not repaired for nearly four months and
the wagon road around the tunnels was next to impassable.

Four days after the tunnel destruction, Bragg started to move his
main pieces. The campaign upon which he now embarked was brilliant. His advertised objective was to add Kentucky to the Confederacy.
His proclamation in aid of it was probably written with tongue in cheek
but it was excellent propaganda to use in the foreign offices in Paris
and London and it had its effect on the Northern defeatists. If he could
annihilate Buell's army his victory might be decisive. His minimum
objective was to win back to Rebel control northern Alabama and as
much of Tennessee as was possible. While doing these things he was
preventing the Northern armies of the west from making any moves
toward a further conquest of the South. He achieved his minimum
objective, yet the blame which fell on his shoulders at the end of the
campaign was almost as heavy as that which fell on Buell.

Buell rightly suspected that Bragg would cross the Tennessee and
enter the Sequatchie Valley. From here he could move up toward
Pikeville to turn the Yankee left or down toward Battle Creek to turn
their right. Buell was almost sure that he would use the valley as a
ladder to climb to the top of the Cumberland Plateau and would
move up through Pikeville. Thomas agreed and did everything in his

power to induce Buell to concentrate to meet this threat. But Buell had the crushing responsibility of command and he rightly elected to be certain of Bragg's intentions before committing himself. He knew, too, that a screen of Brigadier General Joseph Wheeler's[20] excellent cavalry would be thrown out ahead of the marching infantry to prevent Buell from reading Bragg's intentions. To pierce this screen and to locate Bragg's mass of maneuver he sent McCook, with Crittenden in close support, up the Sequatchie River to the Therman road to watch and wait. When he located Bragg's main army he was to block it until Buell could concentrate. When the Rebel pressure built up to a point beyond McCook's control he was to fall back slowly to Altamont. While this deployment was being made Thomas was posted at Mc-Minnville in command of all the troops in that area. He reached his post August 19 and was prepared to check Bragg if he moved through Pikeville just as McCook would check him at the Therman road. These were proper moves but Buell was handicapped by two shortages which could not be immediately remedied. The first was his lack of food and forage. The second was his lack of cavalry.

Bragg was well served by John Hunt Morgan, Forrest and Wheeler and the Northern cavalry was totally insufficient to cope with them.[21] When Morgan blocked the Gallatin tunnels Buell made two moves to counter him. Unorganized Union regiments were being collected in Louisville for army reinforcements and Buell detached Bull Nelson from his division command and sent him to Louisville with a cadre of infantry and cavalry officers to organize a combat force and open the rail line from Louisville to Nashville. In cooperation with Nelson's prospective move southward from Louisville, Buell assembled all his available cavalry and put them under the command of R. W. Johnson, who had been trained during his service in Texas with the Second Cavalry. This unit he sent into Kentucky to keep Morgan away from the rail line.

Within this framework of plans and counterplans Bragg started his campaign. On the heels of the Gray cavalry Kirby Smith moved northward from Knoxville, turned the Union garrison at Cumberland Gap and on August 16 entered Kentucky. He was on the Wilderness Road following in reverse the route Thomas had planned to use when he was interrupted by the Wildcat Stampede. His was the north prong of a double envelopment with an option as to the route. He made his choice after clearing the mountains and headed for the bluegrass region of central Kentucky.

On August 21 Johnson with his scratch cavalry was shattered near

Hartsville, Tennessee, by John Hunt Morgan. He was taken prisoner and his command ceased to exist as a separate unit.

On August 23 Major General Horatio G. Wright was given command of that part of Buell's District of the Ohio north of the Tennessee border and east of the Tennessee River. This area housed Buell's reinforcements, his base of supplies, most of the rail line which fed his Nashville depot, and his flank guard at Cumberland Gap. All these now came under Wright's control, as did Bull Nelson as soon as he entered Kentucky. Wright cancelled the mission Buell had given Nelson and sent him, over Nelson's strenuous protests, to reinforce the beleaguered garrison at Cumberland Gap. In carrying out these orders Nelson stumbled into Kirby Smith's superior force near Richmond, Kentucky, and was wounded and badly defeated. This was on August 30.

As disaster piled up on Buell, Halleck's dispatch to Wright, which paraphrased the criticisms he had been hearing from Stanton and Lincoln, disclosed the straits into which the Union military command had fallen under the discipline of misfortune.[22] Halleck's dispatch, dated August 25, read, "The Government . . . is greatly displeased with the slow movements of General Buell. Unless he does something very soon I think he will be removed. . . . There must be more energy and activity in Kentucky and Tennessee and the one who first does something brilliant will get the entire command. . . . The Government seems determined to apply the guillotine to all unsuccessful generals. It seems rather hard to do this where the general is not in fault." It was an invitation to chaos, and to Wright's credit it was not taken up.

As a net result, however, Buell's left flank was protected by that imaginary line called a state boundary which was no impediment whatsoever to the Rebels. His army and Nashville were completely cut off from the North and a military defeat of the first magnitude seemed imminent. If Buell received no thanks from the President and the Secretary of War for his military service he should have been credited with retrieving their colossal military blunder of divided command.

Buell had problems to solve besides the one in Kentucky. On August 19 McCook sent word to Buell that Bragg was crossing the Tennessee River in strength. It was false intelligence but McCook acted upon it and started up the Sequatchie Valley for the Therman road. He never saw any sizeable Confederate force but he did get intelligence, which must have been planted, to the effect that Bragg was across the Tennessee in strength and was pouring his regiments into the

Sequatchie Valley through every pass from the Therman road north. McCook never got to the Therman road to test for himself the truth of the reports he credited. Ten miles south of his goal he counter-marched his brigades and returned to Battle Creek.[23] "The failure of McCook's movement up the Sequatchie was unfortunate. It gave a false impression of the enemy's progress and of the route he was to pursue." [24] Such was the mild censure written by Buell twenty-two years after the event.

This was not the only evidence of a deep-seated decay in the ap-paratus of Buell's command. Thomas, at McMinnville, was skeptical of the truth of McCook's report but Buell gave it full credit and planned a concentration at Altamont of the troops of Thomas, McCook and Crittenden. Thomas tried hard to dissuade him. On August 21 and 22 he sent five dispatches to Buell seeking to convince him that Bragg would cross the mountains north of McMinnville rather than south of it.[25] Neither officer could get incontrovertible evidence of Bragg's route. Buell was certain that the move could best be parried farther south and on August 23 he ordered Thomas to Altamont by forced marches.[26] Thomas marched as ordered but took only a token force, found what he wanted to find and returned the next day without orders. What he expected to find was a shortage of water and grass and he gave this as his reason for leaving. McCook, however, main-tained a division there after Thomas had left. The positions of both Thomas and Buell in regard to the Altamont concentration have been justified by historians. They point out that Thomas was proved right by subsequent events but since Buell had to justify his moves by what he knew or conjectured prior to the event his position was more tenable than Thomas'.

But something was wrong. Within three days' time, Buell's two principal subordinates had refused to give him that obedience which is required for a successful military campaign. McCook was chided in a mild way years later but so far as is known Thomas never was. In both cases Buell was faced with an accomplished fact but his mild acceptance of each of them made it easier for both subordinate officers to flout his authority at Perryville. This and other factors which make the Kentucky campaign of 1862 one of the most puzzling of the war will be summarized in more detail in a later chapter.

Thomas' failure to remain at Altamont ruined Buell's plan for a concentration at that point but since his plan had been made on false intelligence no immediate harm resulted from enemy action. The situa-tion, however, did demand a strategic reappraisal. Three events, unrelated in themselves, determined Buell's next move. The conviction was growing in his mind that Bragg would move into middle Tennessee and threaten Nashville. The closer Buell moved his troops to that city the less danger there would be of a supply shortage. Two divisions from Grant's army in north Mississippi were approaching middle Tennessee to reinforce Buell's army. To strengthen his army, ameliorate his supply situation and give better protection to Nashville, Buell ordered a concentration at Murfreesborough to be completed on September 5.[27]

It was during this movement that the news of Kirby Smith's victory over Nelson reached Tennessee and changed the plans of both armies. Bragg had crossed the Tennessee on August 28 and heard the news when he had finished his climb of the Cumberland massif near Sparta. He immediately changed his destination from Nashville to Bowling Green, Kentucky, and moved to cross the Cumberland River at Carthage and Gainesborough. Buell heard the news as his army approached Murfreesborough and he redirected his divisions to Nashville without stopping them. The race was on for the military storehouse at Louisville with Buell three or four march-days in the rear.

Kentucky, Ohio, Indiana and Washington were uncertain and fearful. The Kentucky government fled from Frankfort. The Ohio River towns fortified themselves and mobilized their citizens for defense. Business was suspended in Cincinnati and martial law was declared. Governor Morton went to Louisville bent on destroying Buell and reasserting his influence over the Indiana volunteers. Three times Lincoln queried his worried commanders as to Bragg's whereabouts. He could not rid himself of the nightmare that Bragg was on his way to Virginia to join Lee in his strike northward into Maryland. Fear fed upon fear.

It was on September 10 that Buell knew Bragg was across the Cumberland River. He halted his rear guard under Thomas at Nashville and sent the rest of his maneuverable army northward along the Louisville-Nashville railroad. Somewhere along this stretch of steel he knew he would find Bragg and he intended to bring him to battle. Time was working at last for Buell. Each day's march took him closer to his base of supplies and reinforcements while it took Bragg farther away from his. The frustrations of a game of hide-and-seek amid the blind valleys of the Cumberland Mountains were over. Everything depended now on how high a march cadence his men could hold from dawn to dusk. On the fifteenth, Buell learned that Munfordville was under attack. He directed his advance guard at that point and called Thomas to his side by forced marches.

This hundred-mile march from Nashville to Prewitt's Knob was different from anything Thomas' men had ever experienced. Clothing and shoes were deficient. The pike was hard and dusty. Drinking water was nonexistent for most of the march. Pools of standing water along their route had been deliberately fouled by the enemy or carelessly churned into mud holes by Buell's advance elements. Their diet was thin, for the troops ahead of them had stripped the country of food and fuel. At the end of the march they deployed in front of the Rebel pickets and fought them for the apples growing in the quartermile strip between the lines.

Bragg split his force to reduce the time of crossing the Cumberland River and reunited them at Glasgow, whence four divergent roads continued northward to the strategic Louisville-Nashville railroad. An average march of twenty miles brought his dispersed columns to the Green River bridge, which took the rails across a deep gorge, and its defending stockade. Here was a strong garrison under the command of John T. Wilder.[28] He had little military experience but lots of common sense. He defeated the first Rebel effort to take his position and by a series of ruses he delayed Bragg's entire army for nearly four days.[29] It was enough to let Buell overcome Bragg's lead and both armies began to deploy for battle. But when Thomas' troops came on the field Bragg refused the test and swung his army off to the east, restoring to Buell the control of his vital railroad.[30] The Blue army moved northward, unhindered, to Louisville.

Thomas covered the rear as far as Elizabethtown and then moved straight north to the Ohio River. Here transports picked up the weary, ragged men and carried them to Louisville. The leading elements of Buell's command had reached the city on the twenty-fifth. Many of the regiments, ragged and covered with dust, marched in singing and were greeted with cheers. Girls distributed water, cakes and other food along the streets. Thomas' rear guard came in on the twenty-ninth. The fears of the inhabitants had subsided but confusion was rampant. There were 30,000 raw troops in Louisville, unorganized, unequipped and undisciplined. They could not be used to replenish the manpower of the veteran regiments but were incorporated into the army as complete units with a resultant lowering of morale, discipline and combat power. The 54,000 men that Buell marched in had to be re-equipped and reorganized. For the first time in the history of the western armies, each soldier was provided with individual cooking utensils. The change was not welcomed by the troops, who had successfully improvised a system which required no additional equipment.

Our first glimpse of Thomas' personal housekeeping is recorded at this time. He established his headquarters in the Galt House but replaced the usual hotel bed with his camp cot. The hotel maid's services were refused and her work was done by Thomas' Negro bodyservant. Most officers welcomed the appointments and services that Thomas refused. No one knows at this time why he ordered these changes. It is almost certain that they did not evidence ostentation. Order and habit were strongly ingrained in the man. It may have been that he was merely doing the things to which he had become accustomed. On the other hand, the camp cot may have been especially made to ease his injured back, and the chambermaids may have been barred to prevent the leakage of military information.

The climactic day of the entire campaign came on September 29 when the intrigues of the state governors and some of the ranking officers of the army bore fruit. The army was readying for battle. Nelson had been appointed by Buell as one of his three corps commanders. On the morning of the twenty-ninth, contentious and harsh tongued as ever, he was stopped in the lobby of the Galt House by Brigadier General Jefferson C. Davis,[31] accompanied by Governor Morton, who demanded satisfaction for an insult passed a few days before during a personal quarrel.

"Go away, you damned puppy. I don't want anything to do with you," was the satisfaction which Nelson tendered. Davis snapped a wadded paper ball into Nelson's face and Nelson slapped him across the cheek. Then he turned his blazing rage on Morton, daring the Governor to make a personal issue of the affair. Davis borrowed a pistol and, at a range of not more than a yard, shot Nelson over the heart. The powerful Nelson walked up the main stairway, collapsed at the door of Buell's room and died in less than an hour with the Communion bread unswallowed in his mouth. Davis was placed in arrest and the affair was reported to Halleck with the recommendation that he order a general court martial. A month later Davis was indicted for manslaughter but the case never came to trial.

While some of the troops were cheering for Davis after the murder, and others were being held under close guard to prevent an attempt on his life, a courier from Washington sought out Thomas and Buell and handed them orders from Halleck dated September 23.[32] Buell was relieved of his command and Thomas was to supplant him as head of the newly created Department of Tennessee. Thomas promptly asked that the order be suspended and Halleck complied.

This was the second time that Thomas denied himself a promotion. Among the self-seeking Northern officers this was cause for wonderment and speculation. Most of the speculation had to do with motives. There is evidence that Thomas himself was not certain about his motive. At any rate, it was his vagueness about the subject which caused most of the speculation.

These are the facts of the affair as they are known today. The appointment of Andrew Johnson was one of Lincoln's injudicious and unnecessary steps because it divided the military authority which ruled the state of Tennessee.[33] Next to Virginia, Tennessee was tramped by more soldiers, plowed by more projectiles, plagued by more guerrillas and consequently bred more military problems than any other state. Johnson was a sturdy Unionist and a capable politician. He had done as much as any individual to convince Lincoln that East Tennessee should be freed from Rebel bayonets, but like Lincoln he was militarily ignorant. When Buell refused to move into East Tennessee after Mill Springs, Johnson turned his implacable wrath upon him.

Governor Morton of Indiana was likewise burning with the ambition to get rid of Buell so that he could restore his own authority over the Indiana troops and eventually over the western war. These two men were a potent team and they gathered high-powered support. Buell's military record was too good for them to attack directly so they misrepresented his motives and attacked them. Theirs was a contrived campaign of professional murder.

It was one of Lincoln's policies that the Northern armies should not pillage and abuse the Secessionists. Buell carried it out, perhaps too strictly, although Lincoln never explicitly accused him of it. He implied this, however, when he reversed the verdict of a court martial dismissing Colonel John Basil Turchin[34] for sacking the town of Athens, Alabama. Buell forced his men to return runaway slaves who had sought protection from the army. He refused to take supplies from Secessionist farmers and was forced to rely on what was brought to him from Louisville. Such policies maddened the radical element in the North. Johnson and Morton began to focus this wrath on Buell with charges of disloyalty and Lincoln was unable to resist the pressure.

These charges were all advertised in the newspapers and for one reason or another many of Buell's subordinate officers took them up. From the idea of disloyalty grew the idea that Buell was unfit to lead the army and finally that Thomas, among others, should relieve him. The first recorded charge was made by Alexander McCook at the headquarters of Thomas' division but at a time when it was under Schoepf's command. Bragg had not yet crossed the Tennessee River. Any blame for Buell's failure to fight Bragg up to this moment had to rest on Halleck's order to repair and operate the Memphis and Charleston railroad and Stanton's failure to supply a cavalry command which could ride off the raids of Wheeler, Morgan and Forrest.

"Don Carlos won't do," General McCook said, striking his listener's knee with his open palm for emphasis. "George Thomas is the man and we must have him." [35] The rumor that Thomas was to succeed Buell was circulating through the army when it reached Louisville and much of the antagonism towards Buell spread from Thomas' Mill Springs division. Thomas was conscious of what was happening and formally requested Buell to return the division to his command before it was ruined. [36]

Thomas knew that appearances indicated he was seeking Buell's command, that Buell was being pilloried for political reasons and was being blamed for the mistakes of other men. He took his stand, as he had always done, with the military men against the politicians and his stand was not a passive one. A month and a half before he was offered Buell's place, Thomas had rebuked Johnson for his part in discrediting Buell. "I can confidently assure you and the Government," Thomas wrote Johnson, "that Gen. Buell's dispositions will eventually free all Tennessee and go very far to crush the rebellion entirely. . . ." [37]

Thomas had stepped down from an army command during the Corinth Campaign because he saw that he was being used to hurt Grant. Now he was being used to hurt Buell. This was a reason personal to himself and he could not use it as a basis for refusing the promotion. Buell refused him permission to use any reason which was personal to Buell, so Thomas gave up his idea of refusing the command and substituted a request that Buell be continued in command since he was on the eve of battle and should be permitted to go through with it. Then he added a sentence which has been the cause of speculation ever since.

"My position is very embarrassing," he wrote, "not being as well informed as I should be as the commander of this army and on the assumption of such a responsibility." [38] He was embarrassed by the situation but not because of the lack of military information. Buell promised to give him all the information he had and the officers knew it. This reason did not ring true to the public either, so they supplied their own reason. It was that Thomas was too modest and distrusted his ability to exercise an expanded command. Thomas' vagueness in this instance is similar to his vagueness in his letter declining, just prior to the outbreak of war, Virginia's offer of an appointment as Chief of Ordnance. From this incident grew the question of Thomas' loyalty. From these two equivocal statements the arguments over Thomas' motives became a roaring controversy after his death.

In 1868 Thomas finally got his motive in line with his official words. He said then, "I was once offered the command of the Army of the Cumberland when I thought it should not be taken from a general who had claims for it. I therefore declined it. I would not permit myself to be made use of to do him an injury." [39] But by then it was too late. The war was over. The audience was too small. The damage had been done.

As it turned out, there were others who agreed with Thomas. Lincoln had a change of heart and tried twice to forestall delivery of the orders. Kentucky's Congressional delegation threw their support behind Buell when they heard of his proposed relief and the other corps commanders joined Thomas in urging Buell's retention. But the attacks of Johnson and Morton did not cease. Buell was finally investigated by a military commission. His accusers failed to face him. At least one of his five judges was shown to be biased and vindictive. Yet even after the commission found nothing to censure, Lincoln permitted him to be hounded out of the army.

13

Perryville and the Struggle for Command

Bragg, with an inferior force, had put Buell on the defensive and held him there by superb fencing. But when he refused battle at Munfordville Bragg gave up this advantage and moved to Frankfort where he could concentrate his army with that of Kirby Smith and inaugurate a state government which would justify keeping Kentucky's star in the Rebel flag and Kentucky legislators in the Confederate Congress. While he marked time with these political activities he dispersed his two armies on a sixty-mile front from Bardstown to Frankfort. Buell intended to take advantage of this dispersion but the confusion incident to Nelson's murder and the abortive change in command delayed him one day.

Nelson was replaced by C. C. Gilbert. He had been a captain in the regular army when Buell sent him to Kentucky as a part of Nelson's officer cadre. After Nelson was wounded Wright appointed him major general of volunteers but this was a usurpation of Presidential authority and the whole army knew it was invalid. Less than a week before Buell entered Louisville, Gilbert was appointed a brigadier general of volunteers but was not confirmed.[1] Although his ability may have entitled him to replace Nelson, his rank did not. Sheridan, assigned to a brigade, objected so insistently that he was given a division to keep him quiet. Rank was a touchy matter with most officers and Buell's boost of Gilbert to command of the Third Corps made many of his subordinates resentful.

The First Corps went to Alexander McCook and the Second, to Thomas L. Crittenden. Thomas was named as Buell's second-in-command. This appointment was equivocal for it certainly seemed to indicate an authority greater than that which Thomas was given. Basically Thomas' authority and independence of action was the same as that of the three corps commanders. His rank was the same as that of McCook and Crittenden but the date of his commission made him their superior. He was not given the authority to act as the commander of the army in Buell's absence nor to take responsibility for emergencies beyond Buell's observation. As the general of highest seniority among the corps commanders, Thomas might have been called upon, under certain conditions, to command in Buell's absence, but at Perryville such a contingency never occurred.

While Buell may have been at fault in the matter of organization, his strategy was perfect. He intended to feint at the Frankfort end of Bragg's dispersed force with two divisions while he struck the Bardstown end with eight divisions and defeated Bragg piecemeal.[2] This was the strategy of annihilation, which should have been the primary objective of every Northern general in every battle. It was a difficult victory to win and Buell properly arranged for a limited objective. He would turn Bragg's Bardstown flank, compel him to concentrate as far away from his East Tennessee sanctuary as possible, and get across his retreat route to block his flight.

In the furtherance of these plans Buell pushed four columns out of Louisville towards Bardstown on October 1, 1862. Thomas rode with Crittenden's Corps and was in command of it. While on this march, he received a farmer's complaint that one of his subordinate officers had stolen the farmer's horse. Thomas, who knew the complainant to be a Union sympathizer, had him point out the thief. The officer admitted the charge and Thomas stripped off his shoulder straps with the point of his sword, compelled him to dismount, lead the horse to where he had stolen it and pay the farmer for the trouble he had caused him.

There were sharp skirmishes in front of Bardstown but Thomas reported that the town was in his possession on October 4. From Bardstown the enemy had fallen back towards Harrodsburg, where Bragg hoped to concentrate. Hardee commanded the Rebel rear guard during the march from Bardstown and Gilbert was pressing him hard. Wheeler's cavalry was driven onto the heels of the marching infantry and the rear of the Rebel column had to face about and support the horsemen. At Perryville the pressure had increased to a point where Hardee was forced to halt his two divisions and deploy a heavy skirmish line, probably stiffened with artillery. A division of Polk's wing was countermarched to Hardee's support. Polk's other division had been sent to Kirby Smith's aid as Buell's feint towards Frankfort developed its strategic potential. Gilbert was stopped a few miles west of Perryville.

On the night of October 7 Hardee studied the significance of Buell's skillful dispersion. Gilbert, moving almost due east, had already pinned down Hardee's skirmish line. Thomas was camping that night along the Rolling Fork of the Salt River and would approach Perryville the next day from the southwest. He could reach Hardee's rear just as quickly as he could reach his front. This was a threat which Hardee had to counter. McCook camped that night at a road junction whence he could move east through Harrodsburg to Bryantsville. There all the supplies for the Rebel army were stockpiled and McCook was almost as close to this sensitive point as to the Rebel skirmish line along the height of land east of the Chaplin River. This threat, combined with Thomas', presented Hardee with a choice of difficulties. He could stand and risk annihilation or he could attack Gilbert before Thomas or McCook could get up. He might win this aggressive battle but Buell's other two corps could overwhelm his tired divisions before Kirby Smith's army could move to their support. The choice was finally made by Polk and he elected what he called a defensive-offensive. This was changed after Bragg came on the field a few hours later.

The Battle of Perryville may be America's best illustration of what is meant by the fortunes of war. What seemed before dawn to be a certainty of total Union victory became by nightfall a victory so fragile as to be sterile.

Buell's troubles began about 7:00 P.M. on October 7. They started with a collapse of his staff work which grew cumulatively as the combat progressed. Buell's intelligence arm had convinced him that the Rebels were concentrated at Perryville but this was offset by Bragg's conviction that the Union forces were concentrated at Frankfort.[3] Buell's misconception slowed his assault beyond all reason but Bragg's put him in great danger.

The shortage of water that had plagued Thomas' troops during their forced march from Nashville was now so severe that it became the controlling factor which upset Buell's plans. The Chaplin River flows north through Perryville and a little more than a mile west of it a tributary called Doctor's Creek flows nearly parallel to its parent stream. At this time there was no flowing water in either of these streams but there were drinkable pools in the limestone layers of their beds. Gilbert's men pressed Hardee's skirmishers for some of these pools, first with a brigade and later with two divisions. Hardee was not aware of Gilbert's limited objective so he met force with force until the heavily stiffened skirmish lines were locked in position. At this point the water shortage worked in Buell's favor; but some six miles in Buell's rear it began to work in favor of Bragg. This was at the camping place which Buell had designated for Thomas' corps. It was 6:00 P.M. of October 7 when Thomas reached the spot and found it destitute of water. He therefore moved his troops a five-hour march away from Perryville in order to find it.[4] This was done without Buell's permission, although Thomas advised him of the move and why he had made it.

Coincident with Thomas' unilateral decision occurred a major breakdown in Buell's staff work. Buell, with more favorable odds than he dreamed of, planned a battle to start about 7:00 A.M. on October 8. Before that hour Thomas had to march six miles, deploy, develop the enemy position on his front and report to Buell for battle orders. McCook had to march seven miles and do the same things. The battle line was already established by Gilbert. Thomas was to deploy on his right and McCook on his left. Buell ordered the movements of Thomas and McCook to start at 3:00 A.M. but this was insufficient time. Buell must have known this but his chief-of-staff should have caught the error. To make matters still worse, the orders were delivered to McCook and Thomas too late for the preparation necessary to march at the specified time, although the fact that Thomas was not where he was supposed to be might be pleaded in extenuation.

At daybreak of October 8, Gilbert's troops won the water they had been pushing for all night and Hardee's guns fired on them as they filled their canteens. Overlaying the roar of the batteries of both sides was the sharper crackle of musketry as the enemy skirmishers saw, or thought they saw, each other. This was what the Civil War military experts called desultory firing, which meant that deployed units were in sight of each other but that neither was attacking. It was generally a prelude to an attack.

By 7:00 A.M. Gilbert was the only one of Buell's corps commanders who had reported and presumably received his battle orders. Buell was confined to his headquarters two and a half miles in the rear of Gilbert's battle line by injuries received when his horse fell on him. He was still under the mistaken impression that the bulk of Bragg's armies was facing him and feared its concerted attack on Gilbert before McCook and Thomas could come on the field. At some time before 10:00 A.M. Buell probably reached the conclusion that Bragg would not attack before the bulk of his full strength was in position and at about the same time decided not to launch his own attack that day. He issued no order to this effect because he expected to advise McCook and Thomas when they reported to him. Gilbert had probably been advised.

It was 10:00 A.M. when Bragg reached the battlefield, correctly interpreted the firing, looked at Gilbert's line through his glasses, and weighed the factors Hardee had considered the night before. At noon he ordered an all-out attack by his three divisions. It takes time to arrange an army for battle and develop the full power of its attack. This was accomplished at 2:00 P.M.

At the time Bragg issued his attack order, McCook's corps was approaching the point of its deployment in a long column which followed the turnings of the Mackville road. Already his leading division under Brigadier General Lovell H. Rousseau had been split when part of Brigadier General James S. Jackson's division crowded into his column at a road intersection. McCook's third division, commanded by Brigadier General Joshua W. Sill,[5] had been sent toward Frankfort. Jackson's division was entitled to take the lead of McCook's column but since it was made up of untried troops Rousseau's veterans were given the position. They moved carefully, alert to parry a sudden attack which they expected from the direction of Harrodsburg. The head of this column came within sound of the firing, threw aside their caution and hastened their march. This opened gaps in the column behind them which was supposed to move closed up. Such changes in the march order always occur when large masses of troops are moved over a single road, and an alert staff guards against them as well as it can. They become significant only when they have an effect on the outcome of a battle.

McCook's orders were to deploy when he reached Gilbert's line and make a reconnaissance to his front and left.[6] Then he was to report to Buell. But McCook reported before making the reconnaissance. The ground to which he was assigned was advantageous to the enemy attacking from the east along the Mackville road and particularly so when the troops attacked were in the process of deployment.[7] In addition, all of McCook's men were tormented by thirst.

Thomas' cavalry was on his designated part of the line at dawn. The head of his column was up before McCook but his three divisions were not fully deployed until midafternoon. The failure of Buell's staff to allow sufficient time for McCook and Thomas to get on the field, and Thomas' disobedience of orders in looking for water the night before, accounted for his tardiness.[8] But his animals were watered, his men had full canteens and were ready for a fast march around the Rebel left that was to win for the Union the honors of the Kentucky campaign. Thomas had been instructed to report to Buell for battle orders as soon as his troops were in position. Again he disobeyed.[9] There was skirmishing on his front so he felt that he should not leave his command and sent his aide to report for him. This aide must have reached Buell about the time McCook was leaving him or shortly thereafter.

It was at this time that the result of a series of seemingly unconnected events began to coalesce into catastrophe. Buell was incapacitated. Bragg's attack, ordered two hours before, had found its peak momentum and McCook's failure to reconnoiter had not disclosed it. His men, driven by thirst to the pools in Doctor's Creek, collided with this attack and drew upon themselves its full fury. As they fell back they came upon the disorganization of deployment. The solid Blue ranks which should have been there had been delayed by the breakdown of Buell's staff nine hours before. Polk's defensive-offensive stand had fixed the conviction in Buell's mind that since the Rebels had not attacked Gilbert's men when they were unsupported, they would not attack at all and the desultory nature of the firing which had been kept up since daybreak confirmed him in this view. Perhaps seldom before had the fortunes of war proved so fickle to an American commander.

Here was a situation which called for a tight control of the six-mile-long Union battle line but Buell was not there to exercise it and he designated no one to do it for him. As a result of errors and coincidences the power of Bragg's attack fell mostly upon the two divisions of McCook's corps. The odds, roughly three to two, were in Bragg's favor. These odds were increased because one of McCook's divisions was made up of untried troops seeking to accomplish that most difficult of defensive maneuvers—the formation of a battle line under attack. While Jackson's division was struggling to change its formation from a column to a line over uneven ground and under fire, Rousseau's men had to bear the brunt of the attack. The fact that one third of this division was separated and mixed up with Jackson's green troops lowered the Union odds to the danger point. McCook, who returned from Buell's headquarters just about the time Bragg's attack struck Rousseau, asked Sheridan for help. Sheridan was a little more than a quarter of a mile south of Rousseau's flank across a ravine but he was feeling the fringe of the attack against Rousseau and failed to answer the call. Sometime between

2:30 and 3:00 P.M. McCook sent his second call for help. This went to another of Gilbert's division commanders and was referred by him to Gilbert and then by Gilbert to Buell. It was 4:00 P.M. when the messenger reached headquarters and it was Buell's first information that a battle was in progress.[10] Buell's signal officer knew all about the attack but not having been asked made no report to his superior. This officer and the three lieutenants who assisted him were introducing visual signalling as a method of combat control but they evidently had not been fully integrated with Buell's other staff functions. Buell immediately sent out orders to rectify the situation but it was about 5:00 P.M. when the first reinforcements reached McCook's battle line. The battle spluttered out after 6:00 P.M. when darkness hid the field.

This was one of the audacious attacks of the war. While the divisions of B. F. Cheatham and Patton Anderson maintained pressure on McCook's front and left, the division of Simon B. Buckner wedged into the ravine between Rousseau's division and Gilbert's corps, deployed facing north and, with their back to two-thirds of Buell's army, roughly handled the other third. The situation may be without parallel in combat history.[11] It tore from Buell's hands the prospect of what looked to be a certain and total victory and was evidence of grave blunders on the part of the senior commanders of the Union army. It was also the loss of a magnificent opportunity. Buell saw this and tried to take advantage of it.

All he had to do was to swing Thomas to the left using Gilbert's center as a pivot and trap all three Rebel divisions. Buell sent the order for this movement to Thomas at 4:00 P.M. The aide who carried it, Lieutenant C. L. Fitzhugh, was provided with a guide, so that no time would be lost. The order was verbal. This was unusual and indicated the urgency of the situation. In his own words, while under oath, Fitzhugh told the story.

". . . We reached the right and found Gen. Thomas about half past six. . . . It was about an hour after sundown. I gave him the orders. He asked me if it was intended to advance after dark. . . . I left him to draw his own inference. I came back with him to his headquarters . . . and took tea with him. When I was about to ride home again he told me to tell General Buell that the enemy was in strong force right in his front, and that an advance of 100 yards would bring an engagement of the whole line, but that he would advance the next morning. . . ."[12]

This testimony was given six months after the event. Fitzhugh was testifying in favor of Buell before the Military Commission, which appeared to be packed to ruin Buell's military reputation. The questioning of Fitzhugh seemed to be aimed at impeaching his testimony and the witness was apparently hostile to Thomas. Buell took pains at this point to relieve Thomas of the implied charge of disobedience.

Incredible as it seems now, Thomas did not know before Fitzhugh reached him whether the fighting on the left was the beginning of the offensive which he knew Buell had planned or whether McCook was fighting off an attack. Thomas had received nothing but some minor instructions from Buell since his march order that morning.[13] He had refused Crittenden's urgent request for permission to attack because he did not know Buell's plans.[14] He had spent all of the day some two and a half miles south of the roar of battle without hearing it plainly enough to recognize its significance. Buell spent his time two and a half miles west of the point of attack and heard nothing more than Thomas did. In Civil War days the sound of battle was almost as revealing to a commander as a view of it. On October 8 an unusual atmospheric condition denied to Buell and his senior commander this hitherto dependable aid.

The staff officer sent by Buell at 4:00 P.M. to order Gilbert to send two brigades to McCook's assistance described this atmospheric sound barrier. "I suddenly turned into a road," he wrote in 1884, "and there before me, within a few hundred yards, the Battle of Perryville burst into view and the roar of the artillery and the continuous rattle of the musketry first broke upon my ear. . . . At one bound my horse carried me from stillness into the uproar of battle. . . ."[15]

Even though the delay in the presentation of Buell's last order to Thomas had made it inadvisable to attack, Thomas had not been idle. Two of his brigades made substantial gains against light skirmishing. On the night of the eighth one of them held the high ground three quarters of a mile west of Perryville and watched the Rebel line which had been driven through the town and occupied the high ground east of it. One of Gilbert's brigades had swung with Thomas' troops and was in Perryville that night. This natural drift of battle demonstrated the soundness of Buell's plan. Despite all the errors and mistakes, however, Buell had kept the field and buried the enemy's dead. By the scoring methods in vogue at that time the victory was his, but he never received the credit for it.[16]

Buell's pursuit of Bragg was slow in getting started. He was still under the impression that the bulk of the combined Rebel armies was in front of him, so he waited for his two divisions to join him from Frankfort. The night of the thirteenth the Federal troops with Thomas in command took up the pursuit. The enemy was heading for the Cumberland Gap and Thomas knew every foot of the way.

For an army seeking a negotiated peace, retreat is one of its prime maneuvers. It is always a dangerous one. Bragg's was made more difficult by the drag of his captured supplies. He conducted it skillfully. Leading the retreat were the droves of captured livestock. Following these came a motley of vehicles carrying the families and goods of Kentuckians who had shown too plainly their bias towards the South. Then came the army trains overloaded with captured goods, followed by the close-packed infantry, each soldier burdened with food, extra clothing, bolts of cloth and whatever else might have taken his fancy.

Thrown around this caravan was the protective cordon of Wheeler's cavalry. At every defile, every river crossing, every stone fence, and with artificial barriers when the terrain indicated, they forced Thomas' head of column to deploy and gained the precious hours needed to insure the safety of their captured wealth. Thomas gave up the pursuit some two weeks and sixty-five road miles after it started and began to concentrate the army at Glasgow and Bowling Green.

The biggest puzzle of Buell's campaign is why his staff and army fell to pieces under the pressure of their first battle. What must have happened was that the intricate coordination of Buell's complex machine failed to function under the conditions set up by Halleck's inability to grasp a military problem and the refusal of Lincoln and Stanton to discuss Buell's difficulties on purely military grounds.[17] Rumors of the government's loss of confidence in Buell were sweeping the ranks as the army closed with the enemy in the hills west of Perryville. In the only full dress battle under Buell's command he failed to get the cooperation of a single one of his major subordinates.

Thomas' disobediences were quantitatively greater than those of any other officer but they were not as qualitatively flagrant as McCook's. Thomas' derelictions were motivated in Buell's favor. His three refusals within twenty-four hours to obey direct orders were coincidental.

The concentration at Altamont was contrary to Thomas' judgment and he obeyed his orders reluctantly. When he found only one spring, not enough forage to last a day and the road up the western escarpment so steep that more than twenty-four hours were needed to get up his divisional artillery, he reported the facts to Buell and returned without orders to McMinnville. If he believed that Buell would condone his disobedience, he was correct.[18] On the supposition, however, that Buell had definite knowledge that Bragg was making the attempt and was planning to turn its tactical disadvantages to his own account, Thomas' disobedience could have been tragic.

When Buell's order to make a dry camp the night before Perryville overrode Thomas' judgment he disobeyed, but it was a refusal in Buell's favor. Thomas knew he was moving to battle. His men and animals were dehydrated. On top of this the notorious battle thirst would drive great numbers of his men out of the battle line. There was no way for him to refer the matter to Buell so he did what seemed best to further Buell's known plans.

When Thomas ordered the head of his column to deploy at Perry-ville it ran into resistance. Tension is high and the men are nervous at such a time so Thomas elected to stay on the field and sent a staff officer to tell Buell what he was doing and why. It should be considered that McCook did what Thomas refused to do and ruined Buell's chance for victory.

In the fourth instance, inefficient staff work delivered a battle order to Thomas after the conditions upon which it had been based had changed materially. An officer ordered to attack under conditions which could hazard the safety of the army is expected to make the situation known to his superior before he commits his strength. This was the message Thomas returned by the same dilatory messenger who brought the original attack order.

Thomas may have been unconsciously affected by the general feeling of uneasiness, but it is doubtful if he felt the contempt for his commander that the actions of some of the officers seemed to show.

Buell was now back to the position he had occupied after Thomas' Mill Springs victory. The mountain ramparts of East Tennessee were still securely held by the enemy. They guarded Lee's rear and gave the western Rebel armies a safe jump-off for raids toward the Ohio River towns. Lincoln had had enough. He replaced Buell with Rosecrans.

William Starke Rosecrans was a forty-three-year-old West Pointer from Ohio who had been graduated with the class of 1842 and assigned to the engineers. His military career was successful but he had resigned in 1854 to direct his considerable talents along industrial lines. This move drew him into mining ventures in the Virginia mountains. At the outbreak of the Civil War he was appointed colonel of a regiment of Ohio volunteers and succeeded McClellan in the command of the Union troops in West Virginia. He proved himself as competent in the line as he had been in the staff. After the capture of Corinth he succeeded to John Pope's command and relieved Thomas at Tuscumbia when the latter was ordered east to join Buell. He long had been an admirer of Thomas, had recommended him for a West Point instructorship and had backed him cordially for the position at Virginia Military Institute. Now he was at loose ends, having issued what was almost an ultimatum to Grant and destroyed any cooperation with that officer.[19]

The selection of a successor to Buell had precipitated a battle between Stanton, who favored Thomas, and Chase, who backed Rosecrans. Lincoln decided in favor of Chase, allegedly with the remark, "Let the Virginian wait." Stanton was bilious with disgust. "Well," he said, referring to Rosecrans, "you have made your choice of idiots. Now look out for frightful disaster."

It was a political as well as a military appointment. Rosecrans would not be opposed by the Abolitionists. He was a Roman Catholic and Lincoln wanted to make a friendly gesture toward that church. Thomas had several political liabilities which could have been, and probably were, advanced against his candidacy. They must have been used but overruled a month previously. His Virginia birth made him vulnerable to the charge of disloyalty. He had provoked a large section of the public by his defense of Patterson and aggravated them by his defense of Buell. Furthermore, Lincoln's recently issued Emancipation Proclamation had added a crusade against slavery to the purpose of the war. Thomas, a slave owner, might be unsympathetic. So Lincoln predated Rosecrans' commission to give him the seniority necessary to outrank Thomas and appointed him to the command of the Department of the Cumberland and of its troops, now called the Fourteenth Army Corps.

Thomas was in Lebanon, Kentucky, in active command of the army, when he read of Rosecrans' appointment in a newspaper. The blow almost knocked him down. He wrote the following letter to Halleck:

Soon after coming to Kentucky in 1861 I urged the Government to give me 20,000 men properly equipped to take the field, that I might at least make the attempt to take Knoxville and secure East Tennessee. My suggestions were not listened to but were passed by in silence. Yet, without boasting, I believe I have exhibited at least sufficient energy to show that if I had been entrusted with the command of that expedition at that time (October 1861) I might have conducted it successfully. Before Corinth I was entrusted with the command of the right wing of the Army of the Tennessee. I feel confident that I performed my duty patriotically and faithfully and with a reasonable amount of credit to myself. As soon as the emergency was over I was relieved and returned to the command of my old division. I went to my duties without a murmur, as I am neither ambitious nor have I any political aspirations.

On the 29th of last September I received an order through your aid, Colonel McKibbin, placing me in command of the Department of Tennessee, and directing General Buell to turn over his troops to me. This order reached me just as General Buell had by most extraordinary exertions prepared his army to pursue and drive the rebels from Kentucky. Feeling convinced that great injustice would be done him if not permitted to carry out his plans I requested that he might be retained in command. The order relieving him was suspended, but today I am officially informed that he is relieved by General Rosecrans, my junior. Although I do not claim for myself any superior ability, yet feeling conscious that no just cause exists for overslaughing me by placing me under my junior, I feel deeply mortified and aggrieved at the action taken in the matter. I do not desire the command of the Department of the Tennessee, but that an officer senior to me in rank should be sent here if I am retained on duty in it.[20]

This was a refusal to serve under Rosecrans. It was the second time within a year that Thomas had taken such a step. Next to a resignation it was the strongest action he could take.

Thomas' strongest argument was that he had been the choice for this command thirty days before, that the order had been suspended at his request to give Buell the chance to prove his own right to it and, since Buell had failed, the change should now be consummated. Instead Thomas substituted the weak argument that his seniority was being violated. No one knows the reason for this switch. Perhaps a good guess is that Thomas believed promotion to be the prerogative of the superior and that when it was earned it would be awarded. It was a violation of his code to ask for the award even when convinced that it was earned. It was difficult for him to conceive of a responsible official not doing what he ought to do. So Thomas, angry at being passed over, substituted a defense of his rights for a demand for his reward. Perhaps he considered, too, that a demand would have done him little good without the help of a powerful political sponsor.

On November 1, Thomas and Rosecrans met in Bowling Green and Rosecrans has left a record of this meeting. "You are my senior in years, in the service and in merit," Rosecrans said. "I need the cooperation of every member of the army, especially of its best men. I have not sought this command, and desire and need your aid, and will give you any command you want in this army, whether one of its three divisions or the place of second-in-command."

The appeal won Thomas, Rosecrans went on to say. Thomas expressed the greatest confidence and esteem for his new commander but reiterated his dislike of the violation of the army's regular system of promotion by seniority. He asked the date of Rosecrans' commission and was told about its antedating so as to make Rosecrans his superior. He stated that that ended his last objection, gave up his intention of seeking service in Texas and stated his preference for the command of an army corps rather than the designation of second-in-command.[21]

This report does not agree with that of Van Horne. He states that Rosecrans told Thomas the date of his commission but did not mention the fact that this had recently been changed. Later, when Thomas learned that this was not the original date, his indignation flared in one final, incandescent outburst to Halleck. "I have made my last protest while this war lasts. You may hereafter put a stick over me if you choose to do so. I will take care, however, to so manage my command, whatever it may be, as not to be involved in the mistakes of the stick." [22]

Thomas' Civil War record, in marked contrast to his pre-war record, is studded with instances of neglect or reluctance on the part of the government. Before the war, backed by the political prestige of Virginia, recognition came promptly and unstintedly. Beginning late in 1861, however, came his threatened supersession by Mitchel, followed shortly by the belated and insufficient recognition of his success at Mill Springs and now his rejection in favor of Rosecrans. His friends are unanimous in thinking that these things happened because Thomas' loyalty was questioned by those in high places. Undoubtedly this was true, but the real motive for raising this objection may have been to bring political pressure on Thomas' weak point in order to advance the fortunes of a state favorite.

At the outbreak of the war the political primacy that had served Thomas so well was seized by Ohio. Its Governor maneuvered for more and more power. He was aided by Ohioans in both houses of Congress and in the Cabinet. Late in 1861 it became evident that one of the principal military moves in the west would be the invasion of East Tennessee and it seemed that an Ohio leader for it would be advantageous to the state. Mitchel was chosen by the Ohio politicians as their candidate and the shadowy influence of Chase became discernible in the Cabinet. Chase had nothing against Thomas except, perhaps, his failure to get into Washington at the time of the Baltimore riot, but he had to be shouldered out of the way to make room for Mitchel. The easiest way to rally more political influence to his plan was to question Thomas' loyalty.

Now there was a vacancy in one of the Union's three major armies. McClellan, Ohio's ranking military protégé, was already in command of the Army of the Potomac but he was in deep trouble. Grant was backed by Lincoln's state and offered no opportunity to Ohio, but Ohio would serve itself well by putting a native son into the place of Buell.

Rosecrans was a likely candidate. Chase did the axe work in the Cabinet when he again found Thomas blocking his way. It is conceivable that he swung Lincoln to his support with the remark, "You gave

Thomas his chance and he refused it. Now give Rosecrans his." The President may well have sighed with a feeling of relief when he suggested that the Virginian wait. It is certain that he had no qualms about Thomas' loyalty. He had given him four promotions in less than a year and a half and had named him a month previously as Buell's successor. The appointment of Rosecrans was easily defended. It would change the Governor of Ohio from a critic of the Administration's military policy to a sponsor and there was no political group backing Thomas which would have to be consoled by some concession on Lincoln's part.

The tardiness of official recognition for Mill Springs was not caused, so far as can be discerned, by Ohio's ambitions. Lincoln promptly sent Thomas' name to the Senate but confirmation died in committee for reasons unknown, since no minutes were kept. A surmise is that there was no one to push it. When Thomas came under Halleck's command and Halleck wanted his rank upgraded, confirmation came quickly enough but it was dated as of the time that Halleck asked for it and not back to January 1862 as a reward for Mill Springs.

This theory would indicate that Thomas' loyalty was questioned without conviction by politicians. It was merely an easy means to an entirely different end. The real drag on Thomas' ambition was his statelessness and this makes his abnegation of higher command at Corinth in June and at Louisville in September even more incredible. In the unscrupulous competition which ruled advancement in the Union officer corps Thomas was patient and self-confident enough to await the proper presentation of the honors for which he was so eager. Van Horne says that this was a noble aspiration.[23] He might better have said that Thomas would not accept an unearned advancement nor press for an untendered one. He could treat the twin extremities, triumph and disappointment, with equal composure. Sometimes the wait was long. It was said after his death that he never gained substantial honors until they were forced from the government by the growls of public opinion.[24]

Whether Thomas was aware of this crippling drag on his military career is not known but the irascible, autocratic Andrew Johnson was moving to bring it to an end. In October 1861 Johnson had tried to oust Thomas from his command. During the period just ended, he had come to favor him in preference to Buell for the same job he had been trying to do then. Thomas had grown considerably in Johnson's eyes. "General Thomas," he wrote, "I believe to be truly brave and patriotic and his sympathies and feelings are for [the East Tennesseans]."[25] When Nashville was under threat Johnson wanted Thomas for the defense of that city and expressed the utmost confidence in his capacity. There are on record four requests within ninety days from that absolute ruler of Tennessee for Thomas' services.

Johnson was almost as stateless as Thomas but he was not a political outcast. In the course of time Johnson cured Thomas' lack of state citizenship and the two formed a powerful team which was decisive in working a similar cure on all of the inhabitants of Secessia.

In Buell's ill-starred Kentucky campaign there was no honor to be won by his subordinate commanders but there were many opportunities to improve their military techniques. Thomas took advantage of them all. His ambition was to organize and train an integrated army aimed at destroying in battle the Rebel military power. Step by step with this process he sought to train himself in the handling of larger military units. To this end he did not want to lose control of his own division and it is possible that there were some aspects of divisional command which he wanted to explore before giving it up permanently for a command of three divisions, later designated as a corps.

One outstanding evidence of Thomas' progress in military education was in his intelligence section. He was the first to learn that a Rebel division had left Tupelo for the east and his knowledge came thirteen days after the event. When all other sources indicated that their destination was Richmond, Thomas divined correctly that it was Chattanooga. In August there was a continuing intelligence crisis which sought to fix the time and route of Bragg's invasion of middle Tennessee. Thomas was never able to forecast the time of Bragg's crossing, although he was convinced that Buell's first assumption was in error. He did, however, learn that Bragg would not cross the Cumberland Plateau south of the Pikeville-McMinnville road.

His news came to him from four sources—scouts, cavalry patrols, resident citizens and enemy deserters. It was easy to spread the net that would pick up the news. The problem lay in its evaluation. He was highly suspicious of enemy deserters. He put little faith in reports of enemy strength from informers who could not pass certain simple tests in the handling of figures. East Tennesseans were generally friendly to the North and this gave Thomas a big advantage. It was necessary, however, to crosscheck every piece of their information before relying upon it. At Dick Robinson Thomas did most of the evaluating himself. By early in 1864 he had a superb intelligence organization. It is probable that he was training selected staff members in this work during the Kentucky campaign.

Roads were always first-class indicators of the probabilities of what a Civil War army would do. Thomas made a special study of them, particularly as to grade, fords, water and pasturage. He evidently photographed them on his memory. Four months after the campaign was over, Thomas could give without notes the location and exact mileage of the various roads across the Cumberland Plateau, even to stating the maximum and minimum distances as given by the different maps.[26] He reduced these mileages to march time with corrections for grades, river crossings and surfaces. Before the war ended commanding officers in different theaters used to ask for copies of Thomas' intelligence reports.[27]

The test of the correctness of intelligence reports is whether action based on them would be successful. If Bragg climbed the Cumberland Plateau from the north end of the Sequatchie Valley he had a choice of two routes into middle Tennessee—east by way of McMinnville or northeast by way of Sparta. Thomas reasoned from his use of the theory of probabilities that Bragg would move through Sparta and this is what he did. Buell rejected Thomas' repeated urgings to give him battle there as his weary, hungry, strung-out columns topped the final grades of the Plateau and it is not a criticism of Buell's judgment that he did. It is evidence, however, that Thomas, this early in the war, was able to forecast enemy moves correctly on the basis of his military intelligence combined with his knowledge of the terrain and the probabilities of the enemy commanders' intent. He did this frequently in the succeeding two and a half years without a serious blunder.

Thomas had received a practical education in army logistics at Camp Dick Robinson. At Iuka he took an advanced course specializing in military transportation. Here he compared, under standardized conditions, the assets and liabilities of river, road and rail. He discovered that rail was the most efficient, provided a shield could be erected against the far-ranging, fast-moving, spur-raked horses of Morgan and Forrest. He spent the next year and a half solving this problem and ended with one of America's greatest contributions to the art of war.

The most valuable tactical lesson of Buell's campaign was the sixty-five-mile, two-week pursuit of Bragg by Thomas which ended the campaign. It was the second longest pursuit of a major enemy force. It demonstrated that a smaller force fleeing straight away over a single road could always escape, unless the pursuer had adequate, skillfully led cavalry.[28] Thomas spent the rest of the war preparing for such a tactic. His importunities kept Rosecrans in hot water for nearly a year. His own career barely escaped being wrecked because of his stubbornness in the matter. His tenacity finally won the war's decisive battle.

14

Stones River

The public had confidence in Rosecrans because of his military record. They knew his army to be one of their largest and they began to clamor for victory. Rosecrans soon learned the facts. The new regiments that Buell had picked up in Louisville lacked training and discipline but it was the veterans who presented the gravest problems. They were poorly clad and equipped. Their pay was in arrears. Discipline was relaxed. Their loss of morale was being communicated rapidly to the recruits. With or without cause, one-third of his new army was absent. The damp chill of a Tennessee winter was coupled with the ever-worsening mud that dragged at march-weary feet as they headed toward Nashville over the same route they had already traversed twice within nine months. The single-track railroad was inoperative south of Green River. This meant slim rations, a lack of the sparse comforts provided by army equipment and added burdens for the soldiers' shoulders and hips. The men were dispirited, discouraged and disheartened. These were pressing evils,[1] but another, even more pressing, was awaiting Rosecrans' attention.

What was to be the objective of the Fourteenth Army Corps? Lincoln wanted it to head for East Tennessee. Yet Nashville was beset—practically invested—by Rebel troops and Bragg was moving additional forces toward it. Nashville was the seat of Andrew Johnson's government and that potent politician was demanding help. Buell had

wrecked his military career by disregarding Johnson's wishes. Rosecrans' orders permitted him to do what Buell had been fired for pro-
posing. He was not forbidden to move his army into Nashville but
he was officially discouraged from doing so. Halleck's objections to this
move were specific and itemized. Rosecrans, however, disregarded
Halleck, placated Johnson and adopted Buell's plan. He ordered all his
troops to Nashville except the five divisions comprising the Center.[2]
Thomas was put in command of these troops and given the responsibility for reopening and guarding the Louisville and Nashville railroad. On November 12, 1862, he established his headquarters at Gallatin,
Tennessee, some thirty miles northeast of Nashville.

In this specialized task, Thomas was to make one of the nation's
greatest contributions to the science of logistics. His apprenticeship had
been short in time but compared to that of other military leaders it was
varied and extensive. He had attempted unsuccessfully to unsnarl the
tangle of the Northern Central railroad when Washington's communication with the North had been cut by the Baltimore riots. He had
built up his supplies for Camp Dick Robinson by rail transport from
Cincinnati and Louisville. He had used the Lebanon branch of the
Louisville and Nashville railroad to outfit for his Mill Springs campaign. He had wrestled unsuccessfully with the task of keeping open
the Memphis and Charleston railroad between Iuka and Decatur.
The branch railroad out of Tullahoma, Tennessee, had supplied his
divisions at McMinnville.

The Army of the Cumberland was the only Civil War army that
fought exclusively along the line of a railroad. It adapted its strategy
to this novel form of transportation. The development of railways as
a military tool, worked out at this time, outmoded Napoleonic logistics
and influenced the course of subsequent warfare.

Forrest, Morgan and Wheeler made railroad destruction their
business. They destroyed timber bridges, trestles and tunnel shorings
by fire, tore up tracks, sometimes in twenty- to thirty-mile stretches,
derailed trains, filled cuts with rocks, earth and felled trees, and burned
ties and locomotive fuel piled along the tracks. With a single cannon
ball through a boiler, they could ruin a locomotive.

Thomas spent much of his time seeking to prevent these raids. For
three years he was unsuccessful, mainly because of a lack of cavalry.
Buell had devised a system of blockhouses for protecting the rights-of-
way, which Thomas later redesigned to resist artillery fire. Guards
rode the trains for protection between the blockhouses but the Rebel
raiders broke through these defenses at will. Since Thomas could not

prevent the destruction of the railroad he turned his attention to the problem of quick repairs.

He began his work almost immediately after his arrival at Dick Robinson. When he dreamed of a perfect military machine trained according to his own theories he construed the term broadly. He envisioned not only a fighting force but all the things necessary to its functioning as a self-contained unit. These necessary things included equipment, morale, intelligence, rewards, punishments and even burial.

Since transport was a pressing problem at Dick Robinson, Thomas organized what was probably the first pioneer unit west of the Appalachians. He sought authority for increased pay to attract a highly qualified class of men, whom he put to work repairing roads. He had a battalion of pioneers with him on the march to Mill Springs. It wasn't long before he transferred their energies from wagon roads to railroads.

The federal government never took over the ownership of all the Southern railroads along whose routes the Army of the Cumberland operated. Their management remained the responsibility of their original owners. A civilian superintendent of railroads was responsible for their operation, while a military superintendent of railroads was the over-all authority. It was an awkward arrangement with overlapping controls and shadowy areas of authority. Thomas interpreted as broadly as possible his assignment to restore the railroad communications and to accumulate supplies. He began to study and organize the task of repairing these vital communication lines. He drew upon the mechanical skills of his volunteers for the means.

Thomas formulated one of the first sets of principles governing the military use of railroads: that wagon trains operating more than fifty miles from a base hindered an army more than they helped it; that a railway would sustain an army 300 miles from its base; that no more guards were required for a railway than for a wagon train, while a railway had a tremendous advantage in tonnage and time; that the construction of a railway to supply a force five or ten miles from its base was justified if the force remained there six months and was importantly engaged.[3]

The original construction of the track of the Louisville and Nashville did not give Thomas much help. Cuts were rare, fills were almost nonexistent. Rights of way followed old roads, twisting around farms, skirting the low spots and wandering through the hills looking for the easiest climb, with sharp curves and steep grades the result. Tracks were laid on top of the ground, generally without ballast. Many of the rails were wooden, sheathed on top with iron straps some twenty feet long.

Others were iron U-rails on stringers. Gauges were not standardized. Heavy military traffic combined with poor construction to cause frequent derailments. The strap-iron sheathing would curl up under the weight of the train so that the end would often stab through the bottom of the car. Another trouble independent of enemy raids was caused by steep grades. There was a particularly bad one at Iuka. If the engine, with a running start, could not make it on the first attempt it would roll back to the bottom, drop off a few cars and try again. Wet rails made such a grade almost impassable. The solution which Thomas began and encouraged was a triumph of Yankee mechanical genius.

Thomas gradually built extensive repair shops at Nashville and Chattanooga. Surveyors, engineers, and construction, operation and maintenance men were recruited and detailed for railroad service. Supplies were stockpiled at safe and accessible places. Thomas suggested the construction of a rolling mill to straighten the bent and twisted rails. Construction trains, loaded and fully manned, were held at various points on the tracks. Standardized bridge trusses in sixty-foot spans were dropped into place by cranes mounted on railway cars. Thomas could not prevent the damage, but by his system for repairing it, he was able eventually to lay a new track as fast as a dog could trot. British armies used his railway construction corps as a model.

Thomas' first job was to open the Gallatin tunnels which had been blocked by Morgan in the middle of August. He turned the work over to one of his brigade commanders and 500 men from his Mill Springs division. By November 13, he had the first tunnel open. By the twenty-fourth, the second was passable. A month later he had supplies enough at Nashville to support Rosecrans' advance against Bragg. During this repair period supplies trickled into Nashville by a thirty-five-mile wagon haul. They amounted to only one-fifth of the army's consumption. The Cumberland River could not be used because of low water.

In less than sixty days Thomas had solved Rosecrans' supply problem but during that period his command suffered one of the most disgraceful defeats of the war. It was administered by Colonel John Hunt Morgan. From the Southern point of view it was one of the Confederacy's brilliant blows. History records it as the Hartsville raid, when the garrison was snatched from under Thomas' nose by a numerically smaller force.

Rosecrans was incredulous. Twice in one day he queried Thomas. "Do I understand that they have captured an entire brigade of our troops without our knowing it, or a good fight?" And later, "It seems

The Battle of Wildcat, October 21, 1861. Zollicoffer is attacking from the left. Wolford's dismounted cavalry, in the foreground, was the first mounted unit incorporated into the Army of the Cumberland. They tied their horses in a safe place instead of using horseholders and refused to fight from two serried ranks. *Alfred E. Mathews, Library of Congress.*

Union troops crossing Fishing Creek on their way to Logan's crossroads (Mill Springs). The ammunition boxes on the caissons have been raised to keep them out of the water. There is a rider on each artillery horse to forestall trouble. The infantrymen are crossing by the aid of a rope and there is a line of mounted men downstream to rescue any swept off their feet. The two-wheeled ambulances were seldom used. *A. E. Mathews, Library of Congress.*

The Battle of Mill Springs, January 19, 1862, showing Zollicoffer being shot out of his saddle. The Rebels are attacking from the right. Thomas' counterattack is just beginning to move. The Second Minnesota is at the far left, hidden in the woods. Part of the rail fence can be seen in the foreground. The Ninth Ohio is not yet deployed. *A. E. Mathews, Library of Congress.*

The crisis at Stones River, December 31, 1862. Thomas' batteries are firing at the evenly crossed ranks of the enemy, center right. The railway on the left and the Nashville pike on the right intersect beyond the Round Forest. In the right background are the cedars where the regular brigade took its appalling losses. In the foreground to the right of the road are the overcoats of the regular brigade, discarded as they went into action. Rousseau's exhausted troops are resting to the left of the railway. *A. E. Mathews, Library of Congress.*

Close pursuit by Yankee cavalry near Murfreesborough, Tennessee. There was a significant difference between the North and the South in the use of cavalry. Nearly every Southern army commander was a field-trained cavalryman while the North had only one. *William T. Trego, National Archives, Record Group III.*

Union cavalry being driven away from Reed's bridge by Confederate infantry during the Battle of Chickamauga. The infantrymen are lightly outlined to freeze the action. Later the finished drawing would be made from this field sketch. *Alfred R. Waud, Library of Congress.*

Field sketch of a Confederate assault at Chickamauga, possibly Hood's famous breakthrough. *Alfred R. Waud, Library of Congress.*

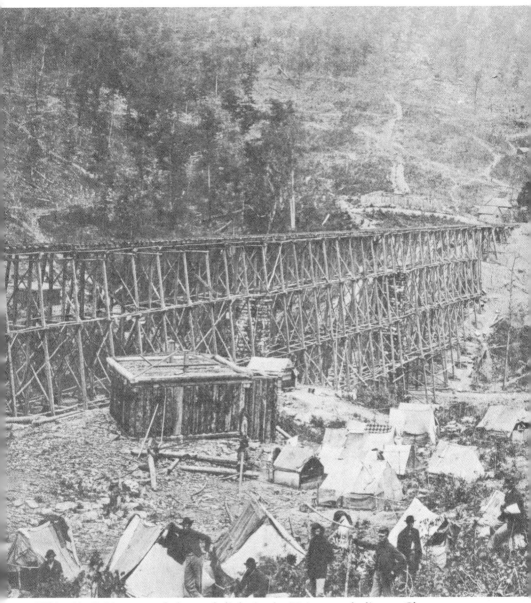

Whiteside Bridge, one of the weak links in the Union supply line to Chattanooga. It was made from green lumber cut nearby and milled on the spot. The two stone piers of the original bridge gave some rigidity to the 113-foot high, quarter-mile trestle. *G. N. Barnard, Library of Congress.*

A Union wagon train trapped by Wheeler's cavalry as it climbs out of the Sequatchie Valley. Such raids nearly starved the Union army. The train guards would be killed or driven off, the mules sabered in their traces and the wagons and their contents burned. *J. F. E. Hillen, National Archives, Record Group III.*

The Union command watching the Battle of Missionary Ridge, November 25, 1863, from Orchard Knob. Thomas is the large figure at the left facing the artist. Grant is on his right with binoculars. Gordon Granger is the third figure. The drawing shows the inexplicable moment just before Thomas' assault when Rawlins had to remind his superior of the responsibilities of command. *T. De Thulstrup, Library of Congress.*

Thomas' attack on Little Kennesaw Mt., June 27, 1864. Big Kennesaw is in the background. The Union officer with upraised sword is Harker. Col. Daniel McCook lies mortally wounded in the right foreground. *Library of Congress.*

Part of the Fourteenth Army Corps attacking at Jonesborough, Georgia, September 1, 1864. Only officers of field grade or above are mounted. The position is defended by Cleburne's tested veterans. *Currier & Ives, Library of Congress.*

Hood's final breakup at Nashville, December 16, 1864. This drawing shows how error crept into the story of the Civil War. The Union cavalry fought dismounted and at the opposite side of the field from the Negro brigades. *Library of Congress.*

A five-gun battery in park with the harness piled on the limbers. The scene is Johnsonville, Tennessee, a week before Hood's destruction. The bleak, muddy terrain shows why Thomas' pursuit failed. *G. N. Barnard, Library of Congress.*

to me impossible that an entire brigade could have surrendered. Are there none left?" [4]

Thomas was embarrassed. Hartsville was a defensible post, adequate for its purpose, with ample supports close enough to insure its safety. Yet the incident disclosed carelessness in the administration of the division and Thomas did not know who was the garrison commander. It was twenty-four hours before he could designate the infantry regiments at that post. It was forty-eight hours before he could advise Rosecrans in detail about the garrison and then he did not know its effective strength. Nor was he able to state definitely where the blame lay. This would indicate inefficient staff work.

Northern reaction was bitter. Halleck was wrathful and wanted someone punished. No official blame attached to Thomas, yet one of the senior officers of the army pointed out that if Thomas had sent a capable staff officer to show the Hartsville commander how to select his position the garrison would not have been surprised.

Less than a month before, Rosecrans had asked Halleck to give Thomas permission to select his own staff. Thomas may already have been aware of weakness in his organization and wanted to cure it. But he was powerless to cure part of the trouble. Ignorance and incompetence on the part of many officers up to and including regimental rank could not be attributed to the army commanders and their ranking subordinates. This defect stemmed from the Administration's policy of selecting these officers and integrating them and their commands with the army. At Thomas' instigation, Dumont's division, of which the Hartsville garrison was a part, was reorganized immediately after the raid. [5]

Early in November, Rosecrans moved McCook into Nashville and relieved that city of its Rebel investment. The rest of the Fourteenth Army Corps moved in piecemeal as Thomas piled up the supplies. While this was going on and within five weeks after Rosecrans assumed command, Halleck's familiar threats were raining down upon him—"the President is very impatient; I have been asked to designate another to your command; one more week at Nashville and I cannot prevent your removal; if you cannot respond to the government's demand for action someone else will be tried." Rosecrans' reply was quick and tart. "To threats of removal I am insensible," he telegraphed Halleck.

On Rosecrans' orders an energetic polishing and refining of his army was under way. Elaborating on Thomas' plan, an engineer detachment of twenty men and three officers was organized in each regiment. The topographical engineers were reorganized. Courier lines were established for carrying dispatches through safe country, operating like the pony express riders of the far west. Rosecrans asked for and received authority to dismiss officers for pillaging, drunkenness and misbehavior in the face of the enemy and set up a more efficient provost guard to put down straggling and marauding and to punish the milder breaches of military discipline. To reduce the appalling number of desertions, he asked for $1,000,000 to take care of pay accounts more than three months in arrears. He wanted more cavalry and he wanted them armed with revolving rifles.[6] He asked for the equipment to organize a mobile striking force—"mounted infantry," Rosecrans called them—forerunners of the paratroopers.

By the middle of November Thomas was sure in his own mind that the railroad soon would be pouring supplies into Nashville. His thoughts began to turn toward combat operations. Bragg had completed his Murfreesborough concentration. Being intimately acquainted with that area, Thomas proposed two aggressive plans. They are noteworthy because they show the trend of his military thinking. Their primary objective was the destruction of the opposing army—the classical principle taught by Mahan. Their final objective was a turning movement against Richmond. In both cases Thomas suggested himself as the commander of the striking force, which would seem to answer the accusation that he lacked confidence in his military ability. His plans had two weaknesses—time schedules were figured too closely to allow for contingencies and both called for the concentration of separated columns in front of the enemy after long marches.[7]

On December 22, Thomas moved his headquarters to Nashville. By this time his command had been given a symbolic individuality. As commander of the Center, he designated his headquarters with a plain, light blue flag. It was carried with him when with his staff and escort he trotted through Nashville toward his camp on the Franklin pike three miles south of the city.[8]

Rosecrans seemed to have revived to an even greater degree his old liking for Thomas. He consulted him habitually on his military problems. Later Rosecrans came to display an almost reverential respect for his chief lieutenant. One day he told his staff, "George Henry Thomas is a man of extraordinary character. Years ago, at the Military Academy, I conceived there were points of strong resemblance between his character and that of Washington. I was in the habit of calling him General Washington." Even before they heard this, Rosecrans' line officers recognized that Thomas was acting as the army's chief-of-staff. The ranks noticed it, too, and felt more confident.

Rosecrans was ready to advance. Essential ammunition and rations for twenty days were on hand. Morgan and Forrest had been detached and Bragg had released a division to go to the aid of Vicksburg. With a view to taking advantage of these detachments Rosecrans called a meeting at his headquarters in the Cunningham home on Christmas night. The room was dimly lighted by candles and fire. The corps commanders and some of the division commanders were present. As was his habit, Rosecrans drew Thomas aside. Rosecrans did the talking. It was in an undertone but it was evident that he was animated and vehement. Thomas listened profoundly, nodded now and then and occasionally dropped a curt sentence. The other line officers were chatting together or watching the grate fire. Garesche, the army's titular chief-of-staff, was flinging off small sheets of manuscript. Staff officers tiptoed in and out.

When the glasses of toddy were brought in there was an eager sentence or two between Thomas and Rosecrans and an acquiescent nod by each. Then Rosecrans' empty glass banged on Garesche's table and he addressed the room.

"We move tomorrow, Gentlemen. We shall begin to skirmish probably as soon as we leave the outposts. Press them hard. Drive them out of their nests. Make them fight or run. Strike hard and fast. Give them no rest. Fight them. *Fight* them. FIGHT, I say!" His right fist smacked his left palm for emphasis.[9]

Rosecrans' advance began the morning of December 26. He moved in three columns through a heavy rain against the Rebel defense cordon stretching east from Triune through Murfreesborough to Readyville. Crittenden with the Left Wing, comprising the divisions of John M. Palmer, Horatio P. Van Cleve and Thomas J. Wood, moved on the Nashville turnpike directly toward Murfreesborough. McCook with the Right Wing, formed of the divisions of Jefferson C. Davis, P. H. Sheridan and Richard W. Johnson,[10] moved toward Triune by way of Nolensville. At the start of his march Rosecrans knew the exact strength and disposition of Bragg's force but for some reason he did not think a stand would be made at Murfreesborough. His intention was aggressive and his wings were instructed to force an enemy concentration but not at the cost of being trapped. Thomas, commanding the Center, was to be Rosecrans' insurance against disaster. He marched with the divisions of Lovell H. Rousseau and James S. Negley. As far as regimental strength was concerned these two divisions were as heavy as the three divisions comprising each wing. In addition Thomas had three other divisions, with an aggregate strength of twenty-six regiments, which took no part in the battle.[11] Thomas moved the first day in the rear of McCook and then swung over to the east. His role was to protect Rosecrans' service of supplies and to be ready at any time to give combat support to either wing. Since the axis of Rosecrans' advance was the railroad from Louisville through Nashville to Murfreesborough, the area which required Thomas' defensive attention was accurately delineated, but it lengthened with each day's march. What he needed was cavalry. Far to the north along the Kentucky-Tennessee border the infantrymen of Fry and Reynolds were trying to fend off John Hunt Morgan's quick-striking horsemen.

At this time Bragg had a cloud of the finest cavalry in the war. Their mounts were of the best racing blood, bred to track and saddle. Their immediate ancestors had never looked through a collar. Double barreled shotguns were the favorite weapon of their riders, who could scout, screen, harry and raid. Joseph Wheeler, Jr., with four cavalry brigades, held a tight picket line south of Nashville. He seemed to read Rosecrans' mind and kept Bragg promptly informed of every Union move. He also kept his promise to delay Rosecrans four days in his thirty-five-mile march from Nashville. His harassment started as soon as the Blue regiments cleared Nashville's defenses. His light forces were brushed aside by the massed Yankee columns but he overran their points, harried their patrols and tore at their flanks. At the end of the first day's march he had forced McCook to deploy two brigades. They were probably two regiments in line on each side of the road with two more regiments similarly deployed behind them. As they labored ahead, trying to keep some semblance of line and interval while climbing over natural obstacles, the rest of the Right Wing sat down beside the road.

On December 27 a dense fog, which was not burned off until noon, and more drenching rain slowed McCook. This in turn slowed the rest of the army, which was under standing orders that neither wing should get out of supporting distance of the other. There was heavy skirmishing but McCook got the head of his column into Triune before dark. Crittenden inched down the Nashville turnpike in step with him. His march was relatively easy on a surfaced road. The troops and trains of McCook and Thomas on dirt roads moved slowly through the sticky mud.

On the twenty-eighth, McCook had to locate Hardee's wing of Bragg's army, which had evacuated Triune, following the roads both south and east. A brigade of infantry solved the puzzle when they reached Shelbyville to the south and sent word that Hardee's main force had gone east. It was late in the day before McCook began his march toward Murfreesborough. Behind the screen of Wheeler's cavalry Bragg was reorganizing his forces but Rosecrans knew neither how nor where. The Union cavalry, split into brigades, was almost useless in front of Wheeler's concentrated units.

On the afternoon of December 29, the head of Crittenden's column reached a point on the Nashville road two and a half miles north of Murfreesborough and received orders to occupy the town that night. Rosecrans' cavalry had never learned that Murfreesborough was thick with Rebel troops and that their battle line was being deployed three quarters of a mile ahead of Crittenden's suspicious advance guard. Rosecrans' order entailed crossing Stones River, which flowed through low banks of limestone, steep and difficult for trains and artillery but at this time passable without difficulty by infantry. At the fords the water was only ankle deep. Still the crossing had to be made in a column, which was a poor formation for fighting off an attack. Wood, who had the advance, protested the order to occupy Murfreesborough. He could tell from the stiffening resistance in front of him what Bragg was doing and knew more about what was going on than the Northern cavalry. The Left Wing risked heavy casualties before it was withdrawn after dark to its own side of the river. Rosecrans had backed away from disaster but his safety margin was near the vanishing point.

Thomas, who had spent most of the twenty-ninth with Rosecrans, was riding Negley's line, through the chill and dampness of the winter twilight, where it was deployed on Crittenden's right. Suddenly heavy firing broke out.

"What's the meaning of that, General?" asked one of his staff.

"It means a fight tomorrow on Stones River," was the reply.

Bragg was of the same mind and his troops were deployed to receive an attack. They were nearly two miles out from town blocking the converging roads leading into Murfreesborough from the north and west. Hardee commanded his left with the divisions of McCown and Cleburne. Bishop General Polk held his right with the divisions of Withers and Cheatham. North of Polk was another division under Breckinridge. He and Polk were protected by fieldworks. Bragg considered that the strength of his position would offset the Union superiority of 43,400 to 37,712. To lengthen the odds in his favor, Bragg called on Wheeler's sleepless men and fagged horses to cut Rosecrans' communications with Nashville.

It was so dark that Wheeler's riders could not see the water as they splashed through Stones River off to the right of Bragg's army and scrambled up the rocky bank on the far side. At daylight they struck one of Rosecrans' trains at Jefferson but were driven off. At La Vergne they had more luck with one of McCook's trains. As far as a man could see from his saddle the turnpike was filled with burning wagons. Disarmed men and liberated horses and mules overspread the country. At Nolensville the destruction was repeated. For fourteen hours Wheeler made himself the master of Rosecrans' rear as he rode around the Northern army. Eleven hundred prisoners and a million dollars' worth of destroyed property was the price the North paid for disregarding Rosecrans' appeals for adequate cavalry. At the same time, by way of strategic help, John Hunt Morgan was raiding the Nashville-Louisville railroad some seventy-five miles to the north.

On December 30 Rosecrans was far from ready for the attack Bragg was expecting. His Right Wing was moving up in route columns on Wilkinson's turnpike with Sheridan in the lead followed by Johnson and Davis and hampered by Rebel skirmishers. As they neared the point where Negley's right flank reached for them through a heavy growth of cedars, the skirmishing grew so brisk that McCook was forced to deploy Sheridan on the left and Davis on his right. These divisions moved slowly ahead through a broken terrain until Sheridan locked onto Negley's line, which rested on the Wilkinson road. For the rest of the daylight the various brigades of Sheridan and Davis jostled the Rebels for the choice positions on their front. The same restless movement was going on north of the Wilkinson road where Negley, then Palmer and then Wood completed the Union line nearly to Stones River.

While McCook's wing was taking its position on the Union battle line, Rousseau's heavy division of five brigades was moving to its multiple assignments. Starkweather's brigade was stationed at Jefferson to protect the bridge over Stones River. Walker's brigade, on loan from Fry's division, was left at La Vergne to guard Thomas' wagon trains. Rousseau's three remaining brigades, commanded by Oliver L. Shepherd, John Beatty and Benjamin F. Scribner [12] were held in mass formation as the army reserve just off the Nashville road at a point three miles from Murfreesborough.[13] A group of the pioneers was improving the Stones River fords to make them more defensible and more easily traversed by Rosecrans' assault columns. Another group was building a temporary bridge farther downstream for the artillery, ammunition wagons and ambulances. A third group was cutting a

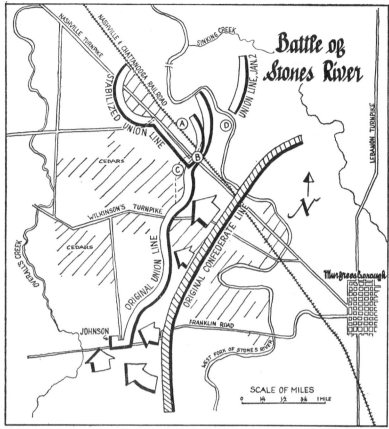

Map 5. Battle of Stones River, December 31, 1862—January 3, 1863. From a sketch drawn on the field which accompanied Rosecrans' official report. (*O.R. Atlas, Plate 30, No. 1.*)

A—Thomas' artillery, Dec. 31
B—Round Forest
C—Access road through cedars
D—Mendenhall's guns, Jan. 2

north-south road through the cedars so that the rear of Negley's division would be accessible from the Nashville road. The sharp cedar stumps left by the axes had to be grubbed out so the fetlocks of the gun teams and those of the ammunition wagons and ambulances would not be injured. Rocks that might break an axle or dish a wheel had to be dug out, rolled aside and the hole leveled. It was a thirteen-hour job, much of it done under fire.[14] Even before it was finished, Thomas watched Negley's foot and guns file through the new road and checked their battle position. These facilities, planned as aids to a Union assault, proved their value in an entirely unforeseen way before the battle was **over.**

Thomas' headquarters the night of the thirtieth were with Rousseau's division. He was protected from the cold, wind-driven rain by
a tent but he had little time to use it. He had been up at 4:00 that
morning superintending the pioneers as they drove Negley's access
road through the heavy growth. In the evening he was summoned to
Rosecrans' headquarters. It is not known when he returned from this
meeting but it is doubtful if he got much restful sleep that night. An
aide, who had occasion to find him, stepped around the fire in front
of his tent and pulled aside its flap. By the light of a couple of candles
he saw Thomas asleep. He was astride a chair, his arms resting on
its back and his head pillowed on his arms. The aide awakened him to
deliver his message and was probably only one of several such messengers. A few hours later Thomas was in his saddle watching in the
pre-dawn light as a thin mist floated up from the surface of Stones
River. As soon as it was light enough, Thomas moved Rousseau's
division southward along the Nashville road to Palmer's rear and
deployed it facing southeastward, its left on the turnpike and its right
reaching toward Negley.

During the night there had been a continual stirring in the Rebel
battle line. The irascible and impatient Bragg, not having been attacked as he expected, had decided late on the thirtieth to launch his
own attack at daybreak. His preparations were audible in the Union
lines and McCook's subordinate officers, aroused from their fitful sleep,
were watchful and apprehensive. All the movements tended toward
McCook's right. That evening, on Rosecrans' orders, he had built a
line of dummy campfires far to the south and rear of his position.
Shortly after 2:00 A.M. McCook was awakened by Sheridan and one
of his brigade commanders from his damp straw bed in the angle of
a worm fence. He shrugged off their news of the Confederate troop
movements, probably from the conviction that the campfire ruse was
working and that Bragg was stretching out his attenuated line to a
dangerous length. Bragg was stretching his battle line southward, all
right, but it was a move from strength and not from weakness.

The opposing battle lines in the early morning of December 31 were
about three and a half miles in length and their direction was approximately north and south. They were half a mile apart along the
Franklin road and twice that distance at their northern ends. Stones
River, meandering northward in the rear of the southern end of Bragg's
line, turned and cut through his line almost due east of Negley's left
flank, thence it continued between the opposing battle lines. The right
of Cheatham's division of Polk's wing rested on Stones River where it

cut through the Confederate line between Cheatham and Breckinridge. Almost even with the north end of Breckinridge's line were the massed divisions of Van Cleve and Wood.

Both Rosecrans and Bragg were committed to an attack and their plans were the same—to envelop the enemy's right while their own right fought a holding action. Bragg intended to get on the turnpike and the railroad between Rosecrans and Nashville, cut him off from his base and destroy him. Rosecrans intended to get into Murfreesborough, cut Bragg off from his base at Chattanooga and destroy him. The advantage, and it could be decisive, would go to the commander who struck first.

Wilkinson's turnpike bisected Rosecrans' line. North of it he had fifteen brigades, comprising his attack force, and south of it were the nine brigades of his holding force. The separation point was at Negley's right flank on the turnpike. To make his attack, Rosecrans had to cross Stones River, deploy for battle and march perhaps three miles. This would require two to two and a half hours with no margin for contingencies.

It was the movement of Hardee's divisions of McCown and Cleburne on the night of December 30 which disturbed the sleep of Sheridan's and Johnson's troops. The Rebels were massing in two lines facing west with McCown in the front line. Their right touched the Franklin road. Their left overlapped McCook to the south by perhaps a mile. This was the murderous combat combination which Rosecrans thought he had beguiled with the worn-out military stratagem of fake campfires.

Rosecrans' unsuspecting line stretched from the left bank of Stones River half a mile north of the railroad at a point two and a half miles from Murfreesborough. In this area there were no deployed troops, but the regiments of Van Cleve and Wood stood massed in columns ready to ford Stones River, deploy and attack. Beginning at the railroad and reaching south was Palmer's division with two brigades in the line and one close up in reserve, then Negley's division with no divisional reserve but with Rousseau deployed close behind him, then Sheridan with the same formation as Palmer. South of Sheridan, Johnson's line thinned out. Davis had all of his brigades deployed in single lines except that Carlin, in his center, occupied a front of two regiments with the other two deployed just behind them. Post, Davis' southernmost brigade, had one regiment in reserve.

The south end of Kirk's brigade of Johnson's division was anchored on the Franklin road facing east. Next to them, facing south with their backs to the Franklin road, were two regiments of Willich's brigade and next to them, facing west, were the other two regiments. Kirk and Willich each had one regiment in reserve. Johnson's third brigade, under Baldwin, was held as a divisional reserve more than a mile northwest of the junction of Kirk and Willich. On this frail box-like structure McCook rested his hopes of containing any attack Bragg might launch against him. He never knew until too late that Bragg's shock troops reached so far south of Willich's puny flank.

Twice Rosecrans questioned the position of McCook's line but in the end left the matter to McCook's judgment after receiving his promise to hold Bragg in his position for three hours, the time Rosecrans estimated it would take him to bring his assault columns into action against Breckinridge's northern flank.

Daylight came about 6:00 A.M. on December 31. An hour earlier the officers and orderly sergeants of Rosecrans' Left Wing had aroused their men. There was no sound of drum or bugle. Forty rounds of ammunition were in each man's cartridge box and forty more in his pockets. Haversacks and canteens were full. At 7:00 A.M. Van Cleve's leading brigade, in a close-packed column, was wading through Stones River. But they were not moving early enough.

Perhaps an hour earlier, Kirk's pickets, 150 yards east of his salient angle with Willich on the Franklin road, could see nothing but they heard the unmistakable noise of a heavy troop movement which seemed to be coming closer. Willich's pickets nearly half a mile south of the Franklin road and watching the open fields still farther south had visual as well as auditory evidence of trouble. An extraordinary number of frightened rabbits were scampering west through the weeds and corn stubble. Out of sight and a little to their right was the unmistakable sound of mounted troops who seemed to be headed the same way as the rabbits.

Fifty yards behind the salient angle, Edgarton's Battery E of the First Ohio Light Artillery was in park, its field of fire masked by the infantry. Edgarton's limbers were dangerously depleted of ammunition. His horses were harnessed but not hitched in and were almost frantic for water. At daylight he discovered a small stream a little more than a quarter of a mile in the rear. All was quiet. He was completely surrounded by veteran troops. He ordered half of his battery teams to be driven to water at a sharp trot.

Many of Willich's men were standing at arms long before dawn. When it was light enough to see, some of them were allowed to cook breakfast. Willich himself was at division headquarters, leaving his brigade temporarily without a commander.

The Rebel attack was aimed at the salient angle on the Franklin road—the weakest spot in the Union line. The attack was expected but its speed and power were a surprise. Some of the Union regiments were engaged before their pickets could get back to their own ranks. One company facing west on the extreme flank was attacked from the rear before it could turn around to face the storm. Edgarton got half his guns into battery and fired a few rounds of canister before he was overwhelmed. As Willich was galloping back to his brigade his horse was shot and fell heavily. He was captured before he could give an order. Kirk was mortally wounded trying to rally support for Edgarton's guns. The brigades of Willich and Kirk were swept from the field.

Bragg was using a complicated assault tactic, attacking by divisions, in succession from south to north. McCown's division, which was entirely south of the Franklin road, moved west in line of brigades. Cleburne, in the same formation, moved closely behind him. Their orders were to outflank McCook's line and roll it northward by changing direction to their own right. The pivot for this giant swing was the right of Polk's command where it touched Stones River. Withers, who commanded Polk's left division, would keep in line with Hardee's men, and Cheatham, commanding Polk's right, would move after Withers had gone forward. It was intended, however, that Cleburne would remain in McCown's rear and move to the front when McCown's attack was spent. McCown moved west nearly to Overall's Creek before turning north and pulled away from Withers, opening a wide gap in the Confederate line. Cleburne promptly filled this hole and established contact with Withers. Ahead of McCown 2,000 of Wheeler's excellent cavalry swung in a wide arc which took them to the point where the Wilkinson road crossed Overall's Creek. It was probably the longest and best executed envelopment of the western war to date. Under its impact the Union brigades were broken off the end of Rosecrans' battle line, first singly, then in pairs and finally by divisions.

The Union reports of the Battle of Stones River are detailed but they reflect the confusion of the field and the coordinates of time and space cannot be reconciled. It is even impossible to determine from them the order in which the various brigades left the field. For nearly four hours the Right Wing fought separate brigade actions without any over-all control.[15] McCook either didn't know that he was routed until

his men were driven off the field or he purposely neglected to keep
Rosecrans informed of what was happening. It was perilously late when
Rosecrans and Thomas between them repaired the damage which
McCook had allowed to go so far. In all this confusion and without
a sequential chronology, it is only possible to divide the story of the
battle into phases.[16] Phase one ended when Kirk and Willich were
driven off the field and Hardee achieved his tactical superiority.

Phase two began with Johnson's desperate effort to form a new
line along the Franklin road from Baldwin's reserve brigade and what
was left of McCook's original line. It was never consummated. Mc-
Cown's whooping troops knocked Baldwin out of the battle by crushing his right flank while Cleburne's fighters, always among the best of
the Confederate assault troops, tore Post's unfortunate ranks to pieces
and spread ruin northward to the Wilkinson road. Meanwhile Davis
and Sheridan struggled through their impossible role of combining a
steadfast defense with a limited retreat. One new line, formed by
Davis' two remaining brigades and one of Sheridan's, fought off three
Rebel attacks by the divisions of McCown, Cleburne and Withers
before leaving the field for the comparative security of the Nashville
turnpike.

The responsibility of combat command now descended upon Sheridan. He tried desperately to hang onto Negley's flank while swinging
his two remaining brigades as a minute hand moves from 11:30 to
11:45. He was under irresistible pressure to form a defense perimeter
on the model of a three-quarter completed British square. His dilemma
was indicative of the breakdown of the Northern combat responsibility.
No ranking officer was concerned with the preservation of the Union
line as a whole. Each beleaguered unit curled back its flanks to save
itself from a fire directed simultaneously against its front and both
sides. To the Blue units on each side, this looked like a retreat and
they made similar efforts to secure their own safety.

Off to Sheridan's right, Hardee's troops were warily crossing the
Wilkinson turnpike. They had overlapped every flank that had been
offered to them but had never gotten far enough to the rear of any of
them to cut off their retreat. Their losses had been heavy and the
survivors were almost fought out. Hardee sent a call to Rebel headquarters for reinforcements and ammunition. It was now about 10:00
A.M. and the beginning of the third phase of the battle.

The mastery of the art of war is given to the few individuals able
to forecast the pattern of battle and take, ahead of time, those steps
which may be necessary to meet the contingencies which will arise.

Bragg's forecast was in error. Hardee's call for men and ammunition reached him just at the time when Polk's remaining brigades had been committed to action. Bragg turned to Breckinridge and ordered him to send two brigades to Hardee's aid.

Breckinridge had seen two Union brigades, dripping water from the Stones River fords, deploy and move toward his right flank. Knowing that other brigades were massing to cross to their aid, he sent word to Bragg that he would soon be under attack. Almost simultaneously Bragg learned from his cavalry patrol farther north that Union infantry in force was moving against him on the Lebanon turnpike. This report was a mistake, but Bragg countermanded his order for Hardee's reinforcement and ordered Breckinridge to attack. It was the best he could do. His reserve was no longer available but he did not intend to lose the initiative. At the climax of the battle, when every factor indicated an overwhelming victory for Bragg, Fortune's needle began to swing from South to North.

Sometime close to ten o'clock, Rosecrans, on his large gray horse, his old blue overcoat buttoned up to his chin and the stump of a cigar clamped between his teeth, learned that his Right Wing was routed, that his attack plan was aborted and that only a new line could stave off disaster. The shock drained the usual ruddiness from his face but he met his problem with energy and courage. He recalled the advance of the assault regiments of Van Cleve and Wood and countermarched them northward along the Nashville road to form the skeleton of a new line which would protect his communications and serve as a rallying point for his routed wing. To gain the time required for this maneuver, he ordered Thomas to take Rousseau's division into the cedars and form a temporary line where Negley's and Sheridan's survivors formed a salient angle on the Wilkinson road.

About daylight Thomas had deployed Rousseau behind Palmer's line in preparation for Rosecrans' assault, which would pivot where Negley touched the Wilkinson road and would include the full weight of his Left Wing and Center. While Rousseau was deploying, a sound like the breaking of a million dried sticks heralded the beginning of the fire fight against McCook's wing.

Thomas often made his dispositions with more than one end in view and this may have been one such instance. Rousseau was in line of battle ready for an advance eastward, yet if trouble developed to the south Thomas could face Rousseau's men to their right, march them through the cedars in a column of twos to the place he wanted them and face them to the right again. The awkward, time-consuming job of deploying a march column into a battle line would be saved. It was an example of Thomas' military foresight. Now the contingency had developed and Thomas moved Rousseau to face the clamor of approaching battle.

Every general officer in the Union army knew that safety lay in forming a new line. A dozen or more counterattacks were ordered with this end in view but were shot down before they could get started. A score of new lines were formed and promptly shattered. The first day of Stones River might well have been called the Battle of the Salients. Thomas, who never forgot what he had once mastered, remembered the tactics which had been proved right at Buena Vista when he had helped hold Taylor's salient against Santa Anna's massive pressure. His gun had served him well on that bright February day. He expected that his batteries would serve him well today. There were twelve guns now, all under the command of Captain C. O. Loomis. Six of Battery A of the First Michigan Artillery, commanded by Van Pelt, were already in firing position at a point on the Nashville road three miles from Murfreesborough. They had been left there when Rousseau's infantrymen moved closer to the front at daybreak. There was no need for the guns in this spot if the battle went as Rosecrans planned it. But Thomas must have been thinking of future contingencies when he kept them there. After the rout of McCook's wing, Rosecrans ordered the six guns of the Chicago Board of Trade Battery, under Captain Stokes, to take a position near Van Pelt and cover the infantry as they retreated from the cedars into the open. They were supported by the three battalions of the Pioneer brigade. Rosecrans was building an anchor for his new line on the spot Thomas had selected four or five hours before. The six-gun battery of Company H, Fifth United States Artillery, under Lieutenant Guenther, accompanied Rousseau into the cedars. When Rousseau was redeployed Thomas ordered them to return to the open field which they had recently left and take a position forward of, but within range of, the batteries of Stokes and Van Pelt so that they could protect Rousseau's infantry when they fell back out of the cedars. These were moves in anticipation of the future.

It was within fifteen minutes either way of 10:00 A.M. when Rousseau faced his men to the right and sent them southward on the trot. The regular brigade was probably in the lead, followed by that of John Beatty, with Scribner bringing up the rear. They took their position facing southwest under a dropping fire from the "overs" which were aimed at Sheridan's men, so that John Beatty was in contact with Negley and the regulars reached westward to support Sheridan. Scribner was held as a reserve behind the center of this line. Sheridan was in front of this line and slightly to its left.[17] It is probable that Rousseau's line extended northwest from Negley's right in order to use the cover of a cedar brake with a quarter-mile open field in front of it over which the Rebel advance would have to move without cover. Within minutes after Rousseau halted his breathless men and faced them left, Sheridan's men, out of ammunition, were instinctively curling back their brigade flanks. Polk's hawk-eyed fighters moved quickly to exploit these openings. Sheridan sought out Thomas and announced that he was pulling his command out of the fight. Almost immediately Thomas' men were looking through their musket sights at the solid Gray ranks.

Sheridan's withdrawal ushered in the crisis of the first day's fight. The enemy rushed into the space they left and, at close range, poured into Rousseau and Negley an unendurable crossfire of musketry and artillery. The "overs" from Withers' muskets dropped into Rousseau's line from the rear while the high shots from Hardee's men did the same thing to Negley's line. It was an intolerable situation and Thomas ordered a limited retreat to the open field about half a mile in his rear, where Guenther's battery had already been sent to protect the men as they cleared the cedars. There was an east-west depression in the open field which would offer additional cover. Here Rousseau was to make a stand long enough to cover Negley's retreat and give Guenther's battery time to move to a position in line with Van Pelt and Stokes, all of whom would then cover Rousseau when he fell back to Rosecrans' new line.

Rousseau made his retirement under a heavy fire but in pretty good order. Rosecrans had told Thomas before sending him into the cedars that he needed half an hour. The time was not yet run out but Thomas resolved to give it to him. A significant part of Rousseau's division was gone. His shot-up line was almost the last hope of the Union army. Rosecrans' right was splintered and many of the splinters demoralized. His center was dislodged. His left was changing front under a heavy crossfire. As soon as the Rebels broke out of the cedars the Nashville turnpike was in range of their muskets. If Bragg could get his men across that road and hold it, the Yanks were finished. The thin Gray lines took fire when they saw their goal.

The Rebels came out of the woods in front of Rousseau several lines deep. As they started downgrade toward the depression where Rousseau waited, he loosed his fire at their terraced bodies at a murderously short range. Over the heads of Rousseau's men, from high ground along the turnpike, fire from the Union artillery was slowing the Rebel advance. The regular brigade took the brunt of this assault and held for twenty minutes. They were beaten down by the leaden hail. Nearly every other man was a casualty. Their losses far exceeded the theoretical breaking point given in all the military treatises of European experts, but their enormous casualties gave Rosecrans the time he needed.

John Beatty, commanding the Second Brigade of Rousseau's division, left a detailed account of this final stand.[18] His four regiments held the western half of the salient angle on the Wilkinson road. The roar of the guns right, left and center sounded like a pounding on thousands of anvils. The colonel of his Fifteenth Kentucky Regiment was killed and the regiment retired in disorder but the flanking regiments closed in to fill the gap. Beatty found a Michigan regiment and attached it to his command to stiffen the weak line where the Kentuckians had been. It was probably the Eleventh Michigan from Stanley's brigade of Negley's division. They had been fighting almost back to back with Beatty's men trying to hold the salient angle. After repelling the second distinct attack against his front and learning that the troops on both sides of him were falling back, Beatty sent a staff officer to learn from Rousseau what the orders were. The officer couldn't find Rousseau but he learned that Scribner and the regulars had both left their positions. Beatty faced his own brigade to the rear and marched north through the cedars. The withdrawal of Rousseau to the west of him and Negley to the east had created the combat vacuum through which Beatty moved to safety. As he came into the open he saw Rousseau's new line in the depression in front of the Nashville turnpike and he took a position beside it. Within five minutes the leaden storm struck them again. Beatty cannot remember how long this line held. When it showed signs of breaking, Beatty hastened to his colors in an attempt to rally his regiments. His horse was hit and fell heavily. When Beatty got to his feet he was alone on the field. Going back to the railroad he found the survivors of his brigade forming on the guns of Stokes, Guenther and Van Pelt. The artillery fire, he concluded, had saved the army.

While the events related by Beatty were taking place, Negley, compromised by Sheridan's withdrawal and a shortage of ammunition, ordered his division to cut their way through the enemy, who practically surrounded them. They accomplished this difficult maneuver by short marches interspersed with stands to slow the enemy's advance. Most of Negley's guns were lost. Two of the regiments of Scribner's brigade

were detached from Rousseau's line in the depression to cover the last
and most dangerous part of Negley's retreat.

The final stand of Rousseau's men in the depression was aided by
help on both his flanks. East of him two brigades of Palmer's division
were breaking up but Hazen's brigade was retaining its grip on the
Round Forest [19] in the acute angle between the turnpike and the
railroad. In the struggle which contorted this portion of the field, the
left flank of Rousseau's final line along the Nashville road was unmolested by a frontal attack. To their immediate right, Rosecrans had
hustled the brigades of Sam Beatty and Charles Harker through the
indescribable confusion which jammed the Nashville road. They came
from the divisions of Van Cleve and Wood. Sam Beatty's men were
still wet from their two crossings of Stones River. These two brigades
clung for the rest of the day to the right of Rousseau's men. On their
right the reorganized elements of McCook's wing were taking their
places in the new line, which now stretched far north of any point
Bragg could hope to reach.

The withdrawal of Negley's division from the original line had left
Palmer's right flank hanging in the air and ushered in the fourth phase
of the first day's fighting. It began about noon. When Negley left his
position north of the Wilkinson road, Cruft's brigade of Palmer's
division was left with its right flank wide open. In his rear, however,
was Grose's heavy brigade of five regiments, which protected Cruft
when he pulled out of the line. Grose then turned his attention to
defending Hazen's right. This he did by forming a temporary link
between Hazen and Rousseau in which he was aided by Batteries H
and M of the Fourth U.S. Artillery.[20] On this pivot of Hazen's right
the entire Union army had swung clockwise from a north-south line
facing east to a northwest-southeast line facing southwest.

Thomas and his staff watched from their saddles the welding of the
new line with the old. Bullets and shells began to seek them out.
Thomas glanced to each side and then half turned to look behind him.
"I guess it's about as safe one place as another," he said to his staff.
He seemed no more disturbed by the confusion, danger and tension
than he would have been at a sudden shower. He was imperturbable
but vigilant. He was watchful of his command. The skulkers shrank
back abashed when he looked at them, even though he said nothing.

Hazen, not as calm as Thomas but every bit as unyielding, was
ordered to fall back when Sheridan's badly used regiments were streaming northward behind him. "I'd like to know where in hell I'd fall back
to," he said to the aide who brought the retreat order, and he kept

on fighting. The heaviest assault of the day was still in store for him.

It was 2:00 P.M. by Bragg's reckoning when he learned that Hardee's men had the Nashville road in their musket sights but were too played out to advance. He ordered Breckinridge's troops, now released from the pressures of Rosecrans' attack and the false intelligence from the Rebel cavalry, into action. They forded Stones River east of where the rail and wagon roads to Nashville crossed each other but instead of coming as a unit, the brigades of Adams and Jackson arrived first, followed much later by the brigades of Preston and Joseph B. Palmer. Polk took command of them as they reached the left bank of the river and formed a battle line with its right on the river and its left extending westward across the railroad and turnpike. Hazen's position directly ahead of them and nearly three-quarters of a mile distant was their objective. This Rebel infantry assault was supported by a concentration of artillery. The brigades of Adams and Jackson struck first and were repulsed. As they streamed to the rear many of their men rallied on the brigades of Preston and Palmer and moved northwestward with them in a second assault. It was about 4:00 P.M.

This was the fourth all-out attack on Hazen. He had changed his position four times, had been reinforced by four regiments which he recognized and by other units which were strangers to him. One after another they reported to take the place of those regiments whose casualties were dangerously high, whose ammunition was shot away or who had fought themselves into a state of exhaustion. Altogether enough regiments to form a division had fought with Hazen in the Round Forest. His tenacious hold on that shattered and burning cedar copse was one of the main factors which saved the Union army.

His repulse of this final attack, the exhaustion of the Rebels and winter's early darkness ended the day's fighting. Later Rosecrans drew back his left about an eighth of a mile to a more defensible position and Bragg's watchful skirmishers promptly moved up to the vacated position. They had then thrown the Yankees off every inch of the line they had occupied fourteen hours before. There was no doubt about its being a Rebel victory. Rosecrans' problem was to decide whether to stand or retreat.

As the firing sputtered out, Thomas rode slowly along the line of his divisions. An army talks excitedly after battle. This is part of its release from tension. Thomas wanted to hear what the men said. He listened to their reports and noted their suggestions. He made the wounded as comfortable as possible. By training or by instinct his eye sought the minutiae of battle wreckage and his mind was busy seeking ways and means of repairing them. The harder and longer an army fought, it seemed, the greater the mass of detail that had to be looked into.

Often a detail supplies the groundwork for speculation. If gun A had not been at point B at minute C, then his line would not have held and the loss might have been irreparable. On the other hand, he was certain now that his volunteers were not subject to unreasoning panic. The next step in his reasoning must have been obvious. If he could combine the leadership that put gun A at point B at minute C with still greater self-confidence on the part of the troops, then no human power could throw them out of a position they were determined to hold.

Such thoughts may have been on Thomas' mind when he was called that night to a council of war. No record was kept of what happened there but the accounts of eye-witnesses and of those who purported to speak for eye-witnesses have made the meeting one of the legends of the war. The meeting was held in a cabin on New Year's Eve. All the officers bore marks of the hard fighting. A young lieutenant who was present at the meeting described their appearance.

"It was a firelit scene. These men looked as if each had been a gunner all day and had taken special pains to get himself smoked and powdergrimed. Battered as to hats, tousled as to hair, torn as to clothes and depressed as to spirits, if there was a cheerful expressioned face present I did not see it. It was no time nor place for the glitter and tinsel of rank; it was a clear case of a demand for nerve and fight to the death on an empty stomach and in wet clothes. Thomas looked, as he always did, calm, stern, determined, silent and perfectly self-possessed, his hat set squarely on his head. It was a tonic to look at the man."

The question to be resolved was whether or not the Union army should retreat. Thomas, who had fallen asleep, was awakened by Rosecrans with the question, "Will you protect the rear on a retreat to Overall's Creek?" "This army can't retreat," Thomas replied, and went back to sleep. Rosecrans decided to hold his ground.[21]

The rear of an engaged army, at best, is characterized by an alarming confusion. At worst this is compounded of panic, hysteria and despair. Experienced commanders are fooled by it and fear that a calamity has taken place at the front. Organized bodies of men seem to be moving aimlessly and at cross purposes; disorganized skulkers relate exaggerated calamities in apology for their own defection. Teamsters and artillery drivers uselessly lashing their animals, who are already striving their utmost, give an impression of fearful urgency; broken equipment, dead and wounded men, the agonized screams or stoic hopelessness of the wounded horses and mules dismay the stoutest. Such was the condition of the Nashville pike until this vital highway became the front and settled down to the relative efficiency of combat.

The fugitives from Johnson's division began to reach the pike in significant numbers within an hour after their rout. Panic swept the pike about the time Sheridan broke in the cedars. The senseless stampeding of thousands of fugitives hampered the movements of Crittenden's brigades hurrying to succor Thomas' defense line in the cedars. It actually brought one of these brigades to a halt. Cavalrymen, couriers, teamsters and fugitives spread the infection along the pike. By afternoon, most of these fugitives had recovered from their fright and were back in action.

At 3:00 A.M. on New Year's Day, 1863, Rosecrans ordered the resumption of the turning movement against Bragg's right that McCook's collapse had postponed the day before. By daylight the first Blue brigade was across the river. It took possession of some high ground near the ford and intrenched. The men were impressed by the way the hoarfrost of the preceding night had whitened the beards of the dead. Skirmishers and flankers kept the enemy interested for the rest of the day while additional infantry and a battery of artillery extended the new lines northward. Thomas spent part of the day riding over the field with Rosecrans. They were inspecting portions of the line and encouraging the troops. The men were already reacting favorably to the decision not to retreat. There were light probings by the Rebels all along the Union line.

Van Cleve's position east of the river, now augmented by a part of Palmer's division, was an increasing worry to Bragg. It enfiladed the right of Polk's line in front of the Round Forest. On January 2, Bragg decided to liquidate these Union forces and named Breckinridge, who obeyed under protest, to lead the attack. Under cover of a diversionary fire from Polk's artillery, Breckinridge struck at 4:00 P.M. The shock threw the Yankees out of their works and rushed them back to the river. Negley's reserve, under Thomas' orders, went in on what had been Van Cleve's right. Davis' reorganized division swung to the east around the fight and took the position that had been occupied by Van Cleve's left. The massed fire from fifty-eight guns, ranged along the high ground on the west side of the river, beat down the attack with its metal flail.[22] In eighty minutes in the dusk of a winter evening,

Bragg's offensive spirit was broken. Breckinridge's losses were appalling. Bragg sought to blame him for the debacle and the strained relations between Bragg and his corps commanders flared into an open quarrel. The Rebels were ready to give up. Rosecrans said he would have gone into Murfreesborough that night except for the rain and darkness.

On the morning of January 3, Thomas' troops were massed at the southern end of the Nashville pike as a general reserve. He was alerted at 10:00 A.M. for an attack that failed to develop. By noon Bragg had already ordered the withdrawal of his trains and the preparation of his infantry for a retreat. His pickets kept up a heavy, constant fire to mask the movement of their army. Toward evening this fire had become so irritating to Rousseau that he obtained permission from Thomas to clear the Rebels from his front. Thomas did not know it at the time, but Bragg had only 7,000 men in line parallel to the Nashville pike and there were no reserves available to them on their own side of the river. Thomas authorized a local attack to be made by two regiments of John Beatty's brigade under the fire of Guenther's battery. Spear's troops, another of Thomas' brigades that was late in reaching the field, were in support. Thomas went along as a spectator. The impact of this attack shook the Rebel command right up to the top. Bragg mentioned it in his official report. In breaking clear of its contact with the enemy an army is always under tension. An attack at such a time increases this tension to the breaking point. But Thomas' thrust had the limited objective of silencing an irritating fire and was broken off as soon as this was accomplished. Rousseau wrote in his report, "This ended the Battle of Murfreesborough."

This little skirmish, fought after dark, convinced the troops concerned in it that night fighting should be avoided. Twice they were fired into by their own men, once by Guenther's battery and the second time by Spear's Tennesseans.

One reason why Thomas wanted to be a spectator of this sortie may have been his desire to know something about the combat morale of his troops. Only seventy-eight hours before, Beatty's troops had broken under pressure in their sacrificial stand in the cedars. Thomas may have wondered whether these troops would carry out their orders to attack the same enemy, now behind breastworks, in the same woods.

Despite this skirmish, Bragg went ahead with his plans. At 11:00 P.M. his infantry began to move out through the sleet and rain.

On Sunday, January 4, Rosecrans heard a rumor of Bragg's retreat, substantiated it with a cavalry reconnaissance and ordered Thomas into

Murfreesborough on the fifth, close on the heels of the Confederate rear guard.

Rosecrans had a victory but he failed to exploit it. Apparently this was no disappointment to Lincoln and Halleck. They had assured him less than a month before that they would be satisfied with a victory in space. Bragg kept his army intact, moved it a score of miles south behind the natural barrier of the Duck River and put it in readiness for another meeting with the Union forces. As one officer put it, "Bragg went off a few miles and camped, while Rosecrans' army went into the hospital for six months." The Administration was satisfied to have Bragg's army in being as long as it was pushed back. This failure to destroy the enemy was a repetition of the mistakes of Shiloh, Corinth and Perryville. The Union commanders seemed loath to press home their attacks. In the west Thomas was one of the two commanders to show evidence of all-out aggressiveness. His counterattack at Mill Springs had dissolved his opponent. Grant, in his Donelson campaign, was the other.

Barren though the victory may have been from a military point of view, it had political significance. Burnside's defeat at Fredericksburg, the destruction of Grant's tremendous supply depot at Holly Springs, Mississippi, and Sherman's failure at Chickasaw Bluffs, Mississippi, had cast an intense gloom over the North. Lincoln was under attack. There was a crisis in the cabinet. The copperheads in Indiana and Illinois felt strong enough to bring their attacks on the Union into the open. France made a formal offer of mediation.

Lincoln believed at the time that the nation scarcely could have survived another defeat. His relief was evidenced by his fervent thanks to Rosecrans. The Administration's interest in the details of the battle ran high. Captain George C. Kniffen had been sent by Rosecrans to Washington with a letter for the President. Lincoln questioned him closely about the battle and Kniffen drew a map to illustrate the various movements, using his sword as a ruler. As he worked, members of the Cabinet and of Congress crowded into the room and peered over each other's shoulders to watch his finger trace the sequence of events. The battle was discussed at a Cabinet meeting. "You see," said Chase to Stanton, "my friend [Rosecrans] has justified all I urged on you in his behalf."

"If you knew as much about Stones River as I do," Stanton rejoined, "you would not feel so cocksure of your friend. But for George H. Thomas, the man I wanted to head that army, Stones River, instead of being a victory, would have been a defeat." [23]

With his habitual restraint Thomas put on record the fact that his command was deserving of the highest praise for its patient endurance and for the manly spirit it exhibited. He might have said that his men captured the only Rebel battle flags that were taken. Soldier and commander were both learning their trade and at Stones River the cost of their education was high.

Recognition of his contribution to Rosecrans' success came to Thomas on January 9 when he was assigned to the command of the Fourteenth Army Corps of the Army of the Cumberland. This was no advance in rank nor was it an actual change in command. But it was official recognition of the command he was already exercising. It entitled him to a larger staff and presumably greater allowances. The same day he announced the names and duties of his augmented staff of nineteen. As commander of the Right Wing, Thomas had carried a staff of five. Rosecrans moved from a corps command to that of an army.

Thomas was twice nominated after Stones River for the brevet rank of brigadier general in the regular army but these were in recognition of Mill Springs. Both nominations died in committee.

15

From Tullahoma to the Tennessee

As a rational appraisal of Stones River revealed the hollowness of that victory, the gleam of hope over Bragg's defeat flickered fitfully and died. Within seven months Rosecrans himself intimated that it had been unnecessary to fight that battle in order to drive Bragg out of Murfreesborough. But justifiably or not, it had been fought and its commander was now faced with the inevitable task of rebuilding his army. Thirty days after the battle, Murfreesborough was a vast hospital filled with the human wreckage of both armies. The 212-mile, single-track railroad that connected the northern army and its base was inoperative because of storms and enemy action. Rosecrans wanted to supplement the railroad by the use of the Cumberland and Tennessee rivers. This would necessitate the construction of a new railroad connecting the disembarkation point on the Tennessee River with Nashville. The vital quadrilateral between the Tennessee, Cumberland, Stones and Duck rivers required garrisoning for self-protection. While his infantrymen were licking their wounds, Rosecrans asked for cavalry for the dual purpose of keeping the Rebel horsemen away from his own supply lines and threatening the supply lines of his opponents.[1]

His requisitions began to flow into Washington. Fresh food was needed to fight off scurvy. Personnel and materiel battle losses needed replacing. He mentioned particularly the regular brigade. He wanted officers and mentioned two by name. He wanted tugs, barges, transports and gun boats for his water communications, and locomotives, cars, rails and bridge iron for his land routes. He wanted horses and mules by the tens of thousands, saddles, bridles, shoes, nails, forage and all the things that went to equip a first-class mounted force. He asked for breech-loading repeating rifles, pay for his men and drastic powers to stop desertion. He asked to have the limits of his department extended to embrace Forts Henry and Donelson, which guarded the water routes to his base. He wanted his commission antedated again in official recognition of his services.

His requisitions were forthright, direct and businesslike but they lacked the official lubricant of "I respectfully request," "If you can see fit," and "I beg leave to propose." If they were not answered promptly he pushed and prodded for action. If they were filled in a niggardly manner he quoted figures to show why the War Department's stand was false economy. If they were turned down he refused to accept the situation and pressed his demands again and again, but always giving valid reasons. If they were ignored he took his case to Lincoln. He assumed that the War Department was basically unjust in its dealings with its field commanders. He was argumentative, contentious and disputatious.

The army loved it. They felt that Rosecrans was fighting for them. An exaggerated story that he had called Stanton a liar went the rounds of the regimental messes.

Halleck had clubbed Buell into resigned acceptance of his official bullying. He tried it on Rosecrans but that officer ignored it. Then he tried a counterattack based on Rosecrans' extravagant use of the telegraph. Rosecrans stopped this with pointed remarks about the forgetfulness and inefficiency in Washington. The result was that Rosecrans achieved a psychological ascendency over Halleck.

Then the General-in-Chief changed his tactics. There was an open major generalcy in the regular army and Halleck notified Rosecrans that it would be given to the field general who first won an important and decisive victory. Rosecrans rejected the offer on the ground that it degraded him. Then he went on to establish a dialectical dominance over his military superior with a question and its answer: "But are all the brave and honorable generals on an equality as to chances? If not, it is unjust to those who probably deserve the most."

The debate climaxed early in August. Halleck had issued a peremptory order to Rosecrans to move forward. This was at variance with Rosecrans' own plans, which he outlined in a dispatch that ended with this sentence: "If, therefore, the movement which I propose cannot be regarded as obedience to your order, I respectfully request a modification of it or to be relieved from the command." Halleck did not modify his order but neither did he enforce it.

Rosecrans' tactics, pressed to a conclusion, would have supplanted civil authority with a military dictatorship. He might never have gone this far but the threat was there and Thomas was the only person in the Army of the Cumberland who did anything about it. It was his presence and influence that prevented Rosecrans from throwing his commission in Stanton's face. It was Thomas who assuaged Rosecrans' growing irritation and who pleaded for an understanding of the heartbreaking problems of the Administration.

Thomas agreed that an advance by the Army of the Cumberland long had been delayed. He could see why the Administration was impatient. But he was of one mind with Rosecrans that the army was not ready for an advance. The only solution he could offer was that Lincoln and Stanton send out a competent investigator in whom they had confidence to judge the situation. He was ready to rest the case upon the facts.

Thomas contended that the army could not move until the vast quadrilateral between the four rivers was absolutely secure in Union hands and that it should not move until it had an adequate force of cavalry. He heartily supported the eight and a half months' delay between the battles of Stones River and Chickamauga.[2]

What Halleck, Stanton and Lincoln apparently did not realize was that, by their leave or not, the Army of the Cumberland was outgrowing Napoleonic dogmas. Railway transportation and lack of good roads presented problems that had to be met in new ways. Maneuvering and fighting over extensive land areas that were thickly wooded and sparsely settled now became the rule rather than the exception. Tangled undergrowth, thick woods, dense cedar thickets made close-order maneuvering almost impossible. When the terrain prevented the use of a battle line of two serried ranks firing by volley, the troops spread out and took cover of necessity and without fear of the taunt that they failed to stand up and fight like men. The ranks tested this in the cedars at Stones River and found they liked it. The step from natural cover to artificial cover was not a big one. The use of trenches lost its odium and became popular. The use of horsemen to carry messages from one flank of a forty-mile line to the other broke down from the sheer weight of time and distance and a signal corps evolved. Crossing major rivers without bridges or boats, and mountain ranges without roads, made engineers as important as infantrymen. McClellan,

Rosecrans and Thomas knew these things. They had fought in the mountains. They had learned the need of armies different in kind from the formal, traditional fighting force. This was one of the things Thomas had in mind when he said that he wanted an army trained by himself that he could multiply in his own hands. This may have been a basic reason for the famous delays of McClellan and Rosecrans.

Halleck was recognized as a military scholar. He was steeped in military history. He specialized in looking backwards. When Rosecrans spoke of mounted infantry he was thinking of a threatened flank twenty miles from his reserve. Mounted infantry to Halleck was a hybrid—neither good infantry nor good cavalry. Their minds did not meet.

But Rosecrans did not permit his irritation with his superiors to halt the work of supplying, equipping and training his army. Buell had organized an army out of a mob. Rosecrans made it into a quality tool with self-contained skills to meet the manifold emergencies of a different kind of warfare. In this work Thomas was his strenuous coadjutor. As one observer put it, Thomas did unknown and unnoticed work in repairs, supplies and communications beyond, perhaps, any other general of his rank.[3] He took personal direction of the supply department of his own corps until his men were properly fed, housed and equipped. This was the unglamorous work of war avoided by most line officers, who believed that their commissions gave them a ready-made army. Thomas compiled a table of the army's requirements of grain for the horses, rations for the men, quartermaster stores, medical stores and contingencies. These were tabulated by weight and then reduced to freight-car loads. The railroad was organized to deliver these requirements. A delay in the quick turnaround of the flat cars delivering pontoons at Stevenson, Alabama, brought quick censure from general headquarters.

The names of outstanding men were inscribed on a roll of honor. Rosecrans wanted to organize them into a special unit, probably with the idea of making them shock troops. When permission was refused he awarded each roll of honor man a red ribbon to be worn as part of his uniform. Battle honors were inscribed on the regimental colors and artillery guidons or on ribbons attached to the staff. Battle dress was prescribed for officers to make them less conspicuous to the enemy sharpshooters. Arms were rearranged so that all the soldiers in a regiment used the same ammunition and the ammunition wagons were marked and positioned to eliminate mix-ups.

Thomas' contributions to the evolution of the army were varied and extensive. Some of them were over and above the line of duty. He initiated a policy change that was basically political. One of his division commanders reported that the Unionist inhabitants northeast of Murfreesborough were being impressed into the Rebel army, their property seized and their families driven out of their homes, while the Federal policy of encouraging Union sentiment in disloyal states protected the rebellious element in the same area from similar treatment. Thomas referred the report for the consideration of the government, noting on his endorsement that the same situation prevailed in Kentucky, that the conciliatory policy had failed and that the expulsion of disloyal persons from behind the Union lines should replace it. Rosecrans, after a week's consideration, endorsed it without commitment and forwarded it. Three weeks later expulsion replaced conciliation as the United States government's policy toward the Rebels.[4]

One of the army's pressing problems was absenteeism, the official name for desertion, which was so widespread as to be uncontrollable. Thomas' corps had a better record on February 20 than either of the others, yet he showed only 56.01 per cent of his total strength present for duty. With few exceptions the officers set their men a poor example. Thomas was one of the few who never left his post. He asked once for permission to visit Nashville for the day but at the last moment he decided not to go, perhaps because of the chance that some fighting might occur in his absence. Or perhaps, as one of his brigade commanders intimated, he felt that his personal example might curb absenteeism.

Thomas' soldiers had a different slant on this well-known trait. Once, when he was riding with Garfield, Thomas was hailed by one of his men.

"Hello, Mister, you . . . ! I want to talk to you."

Thomas rode over to him and the soldier said, "Mister, I want to get a furlough."

"On what grounds do you want a furlough, my man?" asked Thomas.

"I want to go home and see my wife," was the reply.

"How long since you saw your wife?"

"Ever since I enlisted—nigh on to three months."

"Three months!" said Thomas. "Why, my good man, I haven't seen my wife for three years."

"Well," replied the soldier, "you see, me and my wife ain't that kind."

Although the army made no geographical advance during the seven months after Stones River, Thomas saw to it that the Fourteenth Army Corps improved in efficiency and quality. He had early recognized the adaptability of the volunteer to military service. He sought to place his men so that the nation might have the benefit of their breadwinning skills as well as their newly acquired military skill. It was his theory that a volunteer command should be given a variety of service.

Take for example the 105th Ohio Volunteer Regiment. Nine times within five months it raided the right of Bragg's army. These were miniature battles that accustomed the ranks to enemy fire and provided tactical and logistical training for the officers. The regiment scouted the area between Rosecrans' left and the Cumberland River. "Scouting" was a blanket term for skirmishing, enforcing military rule on a hostile population, foraging, picketing, marching, map making, collecting and appraising intelligence reports, learning the necessity of protecting a line of communications and, above all, learning how to keep the men healthy while doing these things. Sixty days later, Thomas proved the value of his training program under the stress of battle when the 105th held off Lee's best shock troops long enough for Thomas' torn flank to reorganize.

Thomas regretted that his own solemn, undemonstrative temperament kept him from getting closer to the men of his command. He loved his men and they apparently reciprocated. He delighted in studying them individually and collectively and there was nothing more fascinating to the men than Thomas' face when it broke into a smile or his rare laugh, soft and musical.[5]

In one way or another Thomas always recognized the outstanding work of his individual soldiers. Stanton once assisted him. His reception room one morning was crowded with favor seekers. In the background was a young soldier obviously just recovering from a severe illness. His uniform was soiled and worn. Stanton called him forward through the crowd of officers and contractors. He asked the boy what he wanted and the soldier in silence handed him a letter. Stanton glanced at it, held up his hand for attention and read it aloud. The letter was from Thomas, asking for the bearer a reward in recognition of his performance of a hazardous duty. He was the sole survivor of a group Thomas had sent deep into Rebel territory prior to the advance on Shiloh. Their mission had been to burn bridges and destroy Rebel communications. The others had been caught and hanged. The survivor had been in a hospital ever since. At the close of the impromptu ceremony Stanton asked the boy what he wanted in the way of a reward.

"Let me go home," was the reply.

In training his men for combat, Thomas eliminated many of the close-order movements intended for display and reviews but stressed the movements needed for deployment, changing front, assault and withdrawal. It was part of his system to keep his men under enemy fire as much as possible. He started with the self-evident proposition that fear is common to everyone. His own experience convinced him that it could be dulled by familiarity and minimized by knowledge. So he tried to accustom his men to the idea that battle was worse in anticipation than in reality and that there were effective counter-measures to every surprise, the breeding ground of that sudden fear that gave way to panic. He stressed the triumph of reason over emotion.

But the riddled body of the lone Comanche warrior beside the waters of the Clear Fork in Texas may have puzzled the matter-of-fact Thomas. Reason told the Comanche that he could not survive this action but that it might insure the escape of his party. Thomas may have acknowledged this rationalization but he also must have had to admit that something else was necessary. If he named it he would have used the word inspiration, or emotionalism. In some way he taught his army at this time what the Indian had taught him. Within four months it was evident that he had successfully harnessed his men's emotional impulses.

Once his troops familiarized themselves with enemy fire and learned the successful defense to a surprise attack, Thomas reasoned that they would stand firm. Once having stood firm and proved to themselves that they could not be driven, the step to driving the enemy was more easily taken. So, to the constant instruction in the school of the soldier that was demanded by army regulations, Thomas added one ingredient; namely, that the troops should become accustomed to doing their work under fire. Troop training had long concerned itself with the symbolism of violence. Thomas substituted the actuality.

He explained his theory one day to his staff. "Put a plank six inches wide five feet above the ground," he said, "and a thousand men will walk it easily. Raise it 500 feet and one man out of a thousand will walk it safely. It is a question of nerve we have to solve, not dexterity," he continued. "It is not to touch elbows and fire a gun but how to do them under fire. We are all cowards in the presence of immediate death. We can overcome that fear in war through familiarity.

Southerners are more accustomed to violence and therefore more familiar with death. What we have to do is to make veterans. Mc-Clellan's great error was in his avoidance of fighting. His congratulatory report was, 'All quiet along the Potomac.' The result was a loss in morale. His troops came to have a mysterious fear of the enemy."

As the warmth of his enthusiasm died down Thomas noticed the attention his staff members were giving him and said, with a tinge of embarrassment, "Well, Gentlemen, we will defer bragging until we capture Bragg."

"This was more of a surprise to his staff than his military comments," writes one observer, "and they recognized it as a hasty retreat from what Thomas thought was an improper utterance." [6]

So his men learned their trade the hard way. They acquired a battle know-how as they survived fight after fight. Such wisdom was an accumulation of the simple things that the books have always taught but that the soldier seldom learns until he has been shot at. In addition, Thomas taught them that no man soft of muscle or short of wind can survive long as a combat soldier. He taught them that the best method of defense was a perimeter and the best psychological defense was self-confidence. As Thomas condensed it, any unit no matter how small could nearly always save itself from annihilation if it would stay in its circle and fight; the troops that were cut up and destroyed were those that tried to make a running fight along narrow roads covered by a hidden enemy; being cut off and surrounded was nothing to cause terror.

Among the less practical bits of troop training widely indulged in around Murfreesborough were the reviews—regimental, brigade, division and corps. They were fine displays but hard on the men and probably an abomination to Thomas. In mid-June, Thomas displayed his more than 32,000 troops and 80 guns in a grand corps drill before Rosecrans and invited guests. Rosecrans—hook-nosed, red-faced, stocky —was accompanied by his staff, a large escort and the national colors. Other officers and their wives and civilian visitors grouped themselves behind the commanding general's post. The corps was like a clumsy giant. Hours were required to execute the simplest movement. Changing front in one evolution, one brigade had to march more than a mile to reach its place in the new line. Banners waved, steel flashed in the sun, mounted aides galloped over the field, the men sweated under their loads in the ninety-degree heat and choked in the pall of dust.

Before the review the various general officers called on Thomas at his headquarters. They found him in a wall tent with the fifteen or twenty more tents of his staff grouped nearby in a geometric pattern. Thomas' blue headquarters flag with its spread eagle and the figure "14" superimposed on a shield was displayed in front of his tent. Thomas received his callers with a grave courtesy and when they left presented each with an abominable cigar.

Often these reviews were followed by a party. Negley was a host at one of these. Food and punch were served in abundance. Rosecrans' face was more red than ever. One division commander was insistently maintaining that the Twenty-first Corps could not be beaten in a horse race. Thomas sat for an hour conversing with a lady over his wine. When he arose much refreshed he proceeded to make himself agreeable to the group. One spectator recorded that he never knew the old gentleman to be so gregarious.

Thomas was not the oldest corps commander with the Army of the Cumberland nor did he have the appearance of being the oldest. He was within a couple of months of being forty-seven. His whiskers and hair were graying, he put on less style than most of his fellow officers. Yet the descriptions of him in that period all carry an intimation of age. To his troops he was "Pap Thomas" or "Old Pap Thomas." Another nickname, which survived from his West Point instructorship, was "Old Slow-Trot." Since neither appearance nor birth date indicated relative old age, it must have been his actions and attitude that gave this flavor to descriptions of him. He was deliberate, mature, grave, unostentatious. He was the antithesis of the juvenile, the flamboyant, the colorful, the extrovert. As an individual he was colorless, yet his career was only slightly less colorful than those of the swashbuckling cavalry chieftains. Even in his shaving Thomas was moderate. Rosecrans and McCook scraped their faces clean. The other corps commanders went for the full whisker. Thomas shaved his upper lip.[7]

Thomas was a regular attendant at the soldier skits that broke the tedium at Murfreesborough. He was not amused by a burlesque of a preacher but he was by an Irish song. At such times he would nod his head and beat time to the music. At the visible absurdities he would roll from side to side and nearly choke with merriment.

On June 8, Rosecrans sent to his corps commanders and most of his division commanders three questions concerning the depletion of Bragg's army to bolster the Vicksburg front and the advisability of an advance by the Army of the Cumberland. The questions were poorly drafted so the replies were predicated upon different interpretations.

Garfield interpreted the answers as being opposed to an advance but his conclusions were as muddled as the questions. A careful reading of Thomas' reply shows him opposed to an attack against Shelbyville, which was the position of Bragg's left flank. He suggested that Rosecrans hold his army where it was, operate upon and threaten the Rebel flanks, and be ready to act at the first opportune moment.

Although there was no cooperative connection between the Army of the Cumberland in Tennessee, the Army of the Potomac in Virginia and the Army of the Tennessee in front of Vicksburg, several of Rosecrans' generals, but not Thomas, considered such a relationship in order to answer Rosecrans' questions. The battle line between the various armies stretched from the Rappahannock River in Virginia to Vicksburg, Mississippi. In the east, the Army of the Potomac, demoralized under Burnside at Fredericksburg, had been humiliated under Hooker at Chancellorsville. Lee was now headed for Pennsylvania. Rosecrans in the center had not moved for more than six months. Grant was stalemated at Vicksburg and his position between two Rebel armies was precarious. Rumors of his intemperance were shaking the public confidence. In addition, much of the country had lost confidence in Lincoln's Administration.

Despite the disapproval of his subordinates, Rosecrans decided to move against Bragg. He must have reached this conclusion sometime between the tenth and twentieth of June 1863. His first movement was ordered June 22. It was a feint at Bragg's left flank.

Two days later, Thomas' heavy corps was moving south on the Manchester road pointed for Hoover's Gap, the key to the Yankee turning movement. Crittenden was swinging his corps through Bradyville far out on Thomas' left. McCook moved down the railroad on Thomas' right and performed a triple role. He gave color to the Rebel belief that the main attack was directed at Shelbyville, he pinned down Hardee's strong corps, which held the country around Wartrace, and he could strike in the flank any force sent to Hoover's Gap to hinder Thomas.

Far off to the east and north, using Thomas' detailed information on roads, forage, water and defenses, Burnside [8] threatened the gaps in the Cumberland, feinting toward that vital East Tennessee area that controlled the inland empire of eastern Kentucky and Tennessee and the northern parts of Georgia, Alabama and Mississippi.

Rosecrans' movement was brilliantly planned. Bragg's forces were perpendicular to the railroad, reaching from Shelbyville on the west— his left—to Wartrace on the east. His cavalry extended his Shelbyville

flank as far as Columbia and Spring Hill and his right flank as far
as McMinnville. The infantry line at Shelbyville was protected by saw-
toothed earthworks obstructed in front by sharpened logs planted in
the earth so that their pointed ends would hinder the attackers. It was
too strong to be assaulted but it might be turned by a movement swinging wide to the west and south. In this direction were the fat farm
lands of middle Tennessee with a surplus of food for men and horses
and with good roads. It was the likely flank for Rosecrans to turn and
Bragg had his cavalry out there in force to delay any such movement until the infantry could come up and stop it. The night of
June 24 the area from Eagleville to Unionville in front of Bragg's lines
twinkled with campfires to simulate the bivouacs of the Blue infantry.

Off to the east of Wartrace, forming the watershed between the
Cumberland and Tennessee rivers, was a range of hills mounting
higher and growing rougher as they approached the Cumberland
Mountains. There were four gaps by which artillery and wagon trains
could move through this range. These were guarded by mixed forces
of Rebel cavalry and infantry. The country was rough and sterile. Its
eastern part was called The Barrens. The roads were few and poor
and made difficult passage for the army. This was therefore the least
likely route for an attack, which was exactly why Rosecrans chose it.
Yet it is unlikely that the choice fooled Bragg. His problem was to
identify the key point of the Union attack and get there first with a
heavier concentration of infantry. The two things that foiled him were
the Yankee cavalry screen and Thomas' brigade of mounted infantry.[9]
Thomas estimated that this combination saved the Army of the
Cumberland a couple of thousand casualties. Yet Rosecrans had had
to wring these troops from a reluctant War Department at the risk of
his professional career.

Hoover's Gap, which was to funnel the columns of infantry into the
rear of Bragg's defense line, was the second one east of the railroad
on the watershed. It was a narrow, dangerous defile, three miles long,
through which flowed the headwaters of the West Fork of Stones
River. At the south end, carrying the headwaters of Garrison's Fork
of the Duck River, was Matt's Hollow, an equally dangerous defile
two miles long. The road was so narrow in places that a broken axle
on a gun carriage or an overturned ammunition wagon could block
the whole army. Two companies of Rebel infantry posted on the high
hills on each side of the defile could delay the advance.

Wilder's splendid brigade of mounted infantry was ordered to trot
through the Gap on June 24. He obeyed his orders literally, driving the

Rebel pickets ahead of him so fast that they tumbled back upon their reserves stationed on the Duck River side of the watershed. The head of Thomas' infantry column was six miles in the rear but Wilder dismounted his troops and held his place by means of his Spencer carbines [10] until the infantry could come up and take over.

Thomas was riding with the rear of Reynolds' division when the head of that column came to a fork in the road about three miles from the north end of Hoover's Gap and halted. Reynolds kept his brigades massed in column but moved them off the road, one column on each side. An oak tree dense enough to keep off some of the pouring rain grew at the fork and Reynolds took advantage of its shelter. Thomas, with his staff and escort, splashed up at a trot and joined him. The two officers talked for a while, then Thomas dismounted, seated himself on a stone under the oak and began to whittle at a shoot he had cut off with his pocket knife. The noise of cannon fire came down the Gap on the wind, supplemented soon by the rattle of musketry. A mounted officer rode up. He was recognized as one of Wilder's aides although he was almost disguised by the mud that covered him. Thomas, still whittling, listened to his report. Then he stood up, threw away his stick, closed his knife, put it in his pocket and turned to Reynolds. The troops were too far away to hear what was said, but they could make a close guess. They saw Thomas swing into his saddle and return Reynolds' salute. The bugles blew. Orders sounded along the massed columns. Reynolds was on the march to stiffen Wilder's mounted infantry and clear the Gap for the Union advance.

Before 9:45 P.M. of the twenty-fourth, Thomas had moved his headquarters up to the vicinity of the Gap and was dictating the orders for the concentration of his corps the next day. Matt's Hollow had still to be secured. If the enemy was going to make a stand that would be the place for it. Thomas learned what was going on by a personal visit to the front and by 3:00 P.M. on the twenty-fifth had formulated his plan for an advance [11] and sent it to Rosecrans. He proposed to complete his concentration at Hoover's Gap that afternoon and advance with two divisions at daylight against Fairfield and with one division against Manchester. Rosecrans approved the plan with one revision. He ordered the main force against Manchester and the lesser against Fairfield.

This was a lordly disregard of the Rebel striking power. Half of Thomas' corps would be closer to Tullahoma, which was Bragg's rallying point, than to either of the Union's other corps. To make it worse, Bragg could pour his troops into Manchester by rail while the head of Crittenden's mud-bound Twenty-first Army Corps was at least a day's march away. If everything worked, however, the muster rolls of the Confederacy would no longer list an Army of Tennessee. The Blue infantry would chop it up as it crossed the Elk River and Rosecrans' cavalry would ravage its lightly guarded trains as they raced for sanctuary over the Cumberland Plateau.

By noon of June 27, Thomas' van marched into Manchester bowing their heads against the driving rain. McCook was close on their heels. Eight hours before, orders had gone out for a Confederate concentration at Tullahoma. The Fourteenth Army Corps had outflanked Bragg and the race was on for the Elk River crossing. It was at 10:00 P.M. on the twenty-seventh that Rosecrans had sure knowledge of what was happening. There was an exultant ring to the dispatch from Manchester that called up Crittenden.

The night of the twenty-seventh, Thomas' headquarters were near Fairfield with that town firmly in his grip. His chief-of-staff was writing up the orders for the next day's movements and sending them off by the dripping couriers as soon as Thomas approved them.

Shortly after noon of the next day, Thomas received the orders he had been expecting—to move his infantry toward Tullahoma with marching rations and no trains. If possible, his orders concluded, cut the railroad.

Thomas strongly suspected by the twenty-ninth that Tullahoma was being evacuated. His headquarters were on Crumpton's Creek halfway between Manchester and Tullahoma. His corps was astride the McMinnville branch railway and McCook was coming up on his right. The country was timbered and inaccessible, the roads terrible. Wilder was back with the report that he had been on the main line of the railroad at Decherd, Tantalon and Anderson (on the Alabama line), had done it some damage but had been driven off by infantry. He reported some reinforcements coming toward Bragg. All that night Thomas could hear railroad trains but he could not be sure whether they were bringing up reinforcements or evacuating the town. At 8:30 A.M. on June 30 he left his headquarters for an examination of the front toward Tullahoma. He could learn little. J. M. Brannan,[12] now commanding Thomas' Third Division, crowded his men two miles closer to the Rebel stronghold. Shortly after midnight Sheridan had pushed to within three and a half miles of the town. All that night and the next morning the Army of the Cumberland probed vainly for news of what was happening behind the tight Rebel lines.

By 2:00 P.M., Brannan's division was in Tullahoma securing what booty it could in the form of ammunition, guns and subsistence stores. Bragg's rear guard had pulled out that morning and was headed south for the Elk River. The railroad bridge was about ten miles away, a vehicular bridge about nine miles, and a good ford about the same distance. Bragg had the advantage of the railroad. Rosecrans' gamble of the twenty-fourth had paid off. If he could catch Bragg's army while it was still divided by the Elk River, victory would be complete.

In his second dispatch about the evacuation Thomas had suggested to Rosecrans a plan of pursuit. It was substantially adopted and Rosecrans' orders were written at 8:10 that evening. Thomas' orders went out that night for the pursuit to begin at 2:00 A.M. on July 2. But it was too late. Bragg's rear guard had crossed the river and burned the bridges about the time Thomas' van was marching out of Tullahoma. Bragg now held the far side of the river, in a strong position to dispute the crossings. Some of the Union cavalry got over but not enough to do any damage. In one or two places the infantry could cross but the heavy rains had raised the river to such a height that their ammunition trains could not follow them without flooding the wagon beds and ruining their powder.

This incessant rain was the most notable feature of the Tullahoma campaign. Rations of bread, meat, sugar, salt and coffee were in each knapsack, but in a few hours they were soaked. The bread became paste, the sugar and salt dissolved, the meat and coffee were ruined. The soldier could eat them, go hungry or "borrow" some rations from a farmhouse.

The infantrymen held their guns beneath their armpits under their shining ponchos. The water ran off the muzzles but the power charge stayed dry. The horsemen had it worse than the infantrymen. Their cloaks sluiced the water off their shoulders into their boots. Gouts of mud thrown back by the hooves of the horses ahead of them stung their faces and covered the front of their clothing. The rain dissolved this mud and the result was a film that thickened day by day. The artillerymen and the teamsters of the wagon trains had the hardest work. Frequently the draught animals had to be unhitched and the vehicles hauled and pushed through the soft spots by hand. There were stories of mules immobilized in the mud and gradually sinking out of sight by the pressure of their own weight.

The advance elements could pass easily over the unbroken roads but each successive vehicle made a deeper impression. Finally the crust broke through and the road was churned up into a bottomless hole impassable to the rear of the column. The train of Palmer's division of Crittenden's corps had the hardest going. They were almost forty-eight hours getting up one grade. At times there were fifty infantrymen lifting one wagon.

Thomas regarded the pouring rain as an opportunity as well as an annoyance. To an officer who complained of the unceasing rain he pointed out that the storms that embarrassed the Union army prevented the enemy from discovering its intent. "We are getting more cold water thrown on our plans than we deserve," he added. He shared discomforts with the men, using the same type of open campfire and the same type of rude shelter. They saw him frequently on the march, bowing his head against the wind-driven rain just as they were. They noticed that he kept his horse and those of his staff away from the marching columns so that the splashing mud from the horses' hooves would not add to the infantrymen's annoyance. This was the first campaign in which his command began to appreciate his true strength and to take pride in executing his orders.

Rosecrans' offensive was a triumph of strategic skill. At the cost of some 500 casualties it forced Bragg out of a strong position and drove him south 100 miles. He outmaneuvered Bragg but several acre-inches of rain kept him from bringing the enemy to battle, which was the real object of the campaign.

There were no congratulations or good wishes from Washington. A businesslike dispatch from Stanton pointedly ignored the whole campaign by pointing out to Rosecrans that his opportunity lay in the future. Rosecrans' sarcastic reply went back to Washington immediately. "I beg in behalf of this army," it said in part, "that the War Department may not overlook so great an event because it is not written in letters of blood."

This was an open challenge to Stanton's strategy of attrition. Stanton was hagridden by the fact that the Civil War was to a great extent being fought in the chancelleries of France and England where a delay in the march toward final victory was damaging to the Union cause. So he decided to capitalize the North's superiority in manpower. He favored the idea of constant attack, of crowding in troops until the enemy was smothered in numbers. He was willing to trade three Yanks for one Rebel. This was a slow, sure, expensive way to win. It required no knowledge and no experience. "Kill Rebels" was his standing order; maintain the butcher's ratio.

There was a contest here between basic concepts of strategy. Attrition was the common substitute for military imagination. It was the historic strategy of the side with the stronger battalions. On the opposite end of the scale was the theoretically perfect campaign that maneuvered the enemy into an indefensible position and forced his surrender by confronting him with overwhelming force. Such a victory, conceivably, could be accomplished without a casualty. Rosecrans was aiming at perfection and came close to its realization. He was thwarted by the extraordinary and relentless rain which retarded Thomas for thirty-six hours at Hoover's Gap and for sixty hours in front of Manchester. Bragg's margin of safety was less than fourteen hours.

In the eleven days that elapsed between the time Thomas trotted out of Murfreesborough on the rain-swept pike and the time he set up his headquarters at the farm of the Widow Winford on the south bank of the Elk River, the almost overwhelming pressure of the Rebel armies had been relieved. Gettysburg had revealed a hitherto unknown hollowness in Lee's army. Grant's brilliant campaign at Vicksburg had not only brought about the surrender of 30,000 troops but it had killed any Rebel hope of breaking the Union blockade by way of the Mexican border. These successes on the flanks, combined with the failure to recognize Rosecrans' campaign in the center, brought Thomas' military status relatively low. Two brigadier general's commissions in the regular army were soon to be available and Thomas was one of five candidates. But Grant's success at Vicksburg had so overshadowed Rosecrans' effort that Grant's recommendations received the appointments.

Rosecrans now was faced with the problem of fighting a successful battle with the Cumberland Mountains and the Tennessee River between himself and Bragg's army. In Napoleon's book these were two of the three most formidable obstacles that an army could be called on to overcome.

As usual, his first concern was supply. His second was whether to force a crossing of the Tennessee River above or below Chattanooga. His railway supply line with Louisville was already within thirty-six miles of the maximum length of 300 miles that Thomas formulated as the safe limit for railway communications.[13] Extending it to the Tennessee River was forcing a dangerous stretch to this vital facility. So far as strategy was concerned, Thomas favored at this time a flanking movement that would cross the Tennessee some 180 miles downstream from Chattanooga, at Tuscumbia, Alabama. This had the double advantage of giving the Army of the Cumberland a practically trouble-free crossing and of substituting water transport on the Tennessee River for the overextended rail line.

Within three weeks after occupying Tullahoma, Rosecrans pushed his first supply train through to Stevenson, Alabama, and established a supply depot there. Sixty carloads of freight were required for the daily needs of the army. A surplus of at least 600 carloads had to be stockpiled for an advance. But the whole 600 carloads were not wanted at Stevenson. There was a branch railroad running east from Cowan, Tennessee, to the little town of Tracy City, which was located on the top of the Cumberland Plateau, and Rosecrans planned to supply the Left Wing of his army from this point. It was this decision that delayed the start of the second giant stride of his maneuver against Bragg. The Tracy City branch line was built to haul coal from the Cumberlands down to the flatlands. It had steep grades and sharp curves. Rosecrans planned to reverse the flow of freight with the loaded trains moving from the lowlands up to the highlands. A peculiar type of engine was required and the only one available was not repaired until August 12. Within six days from that date his marching orders were out.

Meantime the Army of the Cumberland was polishing a staff organization that was prophetic of a modern army. Its medical department was trying to establish the practice of preventive medicine. Cooking methods were improved. To replace the ineffective system of assigning ambulances to the various regiments, brigades and divisions, Thomas worked out an ambulance system which met the acid test of battle more satisfactorily than any other system that had yet been tried in the Army of the Cumberland.

While Rosecrans centered his attention on the design of a new field ambulance, Thomas turned to a more modern medium—the military railroad. He had reached the decision to substitute steam for mule power wherever possible. He envisioned a complete hospital built upon the chassis of a railway train. Just before the movement on Chattanooga began he received permission from the office of the assistant surgeon general to fit out such a train to operate between Louisville and Nashville and immediately started his medical director to work on the project.[14]

Map making was quicker and more accurate. Never again would an American battle commander face the map difficulties Thomas had faced at Mill Springs when he and Schoepf, separated by a day's march, tried to coordinate their movements from different maps, using different place names and showing different roads. Sharp-eyed cavalrymen on Thomas' front reported to his headquarters on roads, streams, fords, forage, bridges, drinking water, defense positions and the other minutiae necessary to rapid maneuver over a strange terrain. This information, supplemented by the steady flow of material from Thomas' scouts and spies and infantry reconnaissances, was correlated at Thomas' headquarters into bulletins and simple two-dimensional maps. One bulletin that he published listed fifty-six fords and ferries crossing the Tennessee River between Chattanooga and Florence, Alabama. Each was located by its mileage from Chattanooga and most of them were described. These detailed studies went to the topographical engineers, who transferred the more important items to maps which were printed in the field and distributed throughout the army. The first edition would be liberally sprinkled with little question marks, explained by a note which read, "Information is wanted where this (?) sign occurs. Engineers and officers are requested to send it in immediately to these headquarters." [15] As fast as this information came in, more complete maps were printed and distributed.

The transition in field signaling from couriers through visual signals to the use of the telegraph took place in this campaign. At Mill Springs Thomas used couriers. At Perryville visual signals were so new that Buell apparently refused to use them. Rosecrans moved around so much at Stones River that the new signal system with its fixed reception center proved impractical. In the Tennessee-Cumberland-Stones-Duck rivers quadrilateral, the Union forces had lost control of all the area except where their troops actually stood. Thomas used visual signals to keep in touch with his scattered outposts and found them much more efficient than heavily guarded couriers. But heavy rains, fog and distance limited this method of communication and the army was turning to the new idea of the field telegraph.

The pioneer organization which Thomas had initiated at Camp Dick Robinson, with promises of extra pay, had now expanded to nearly 1,000 officers and men. Thomas asked for a battalion of them when he was charged with getting the Tracy City branch railroad open. He requisitioned four companies of these experts when he started his march for the Tennessee River. Their duties were manifold. They built bridges, cut cordwood for the railroad locomotives, built storage platforms for the army's supplies, repaired and operated steamboats and sawmills and worked on roads and fortifications.

Bragg was still using the unsuccessful cordon system of defense. The North had breached it the first time with their Mill Springs–Fort Donelson offensive and again with the capture of Corinth. But by means of a campaign of maneuver Bragg had won back in less than thirty days the area that it had taken the North nearly five months to wrest from him in the first place. This thirty-day recoupment had all been lost again and Bragg was back where he had started the preceding August. His defense line was a strong one. It lay behind the Tennessee River from Knoxville on the north, where Buckner guarded the passes through the Cumberland Mountains, to Decatur, Alabama, where Wheeler's horsemen watched the terminus of the railway that ran due south from Nashville. In that long reach every river crossing was guarded and the stretches between the crossings were patrolled. Threat countered threat. Bragg feared a heavy Union cavalry raid deep into Georgia to cut his feedline between Chattanooga and Atlanta. Rosecrans feared two possible breakouts of the Rebel army, one around his left by the same route Bragg had used when he dragged Buell out of Tennessee; the other miles to the west where Bragg could stab at Nashville through the granary of middle Tennessee now bursting with the harvest. To counter these and to guard the Union flanks in case of advance, Rosecrans asked for the cooperation of Burnside and Grant.[16]

But all these problems—supply, staff organization and counter-offensives—were subordinate ones. Battle was Rosecrans' business and he had to cross the Tennessee River to force it.

By August 9, Rosecrans had evidently made up his mind to make this crossing below Chattanooga while he feinted upstream from that city and while Burnside closed down through Knoxville and Kingston to give substance to the feint. The arrangement was for Burnside to be in Kingston when Rosecrans was at the river. From early July to mid-August this was probably the most discussed subject in the army but the official records give only fragmentary glimpses of the discussion. Since it was a top secret matter most of the conclusions must have been kept off the record. On August 15 the orders went out to move.

Rosecrans' first obstacle was the Cumberland Mountains. These are a rocky, lofty land mass rising steeply from the plains of middle Tennessee and dropping precipitously into the narrow valley of the Tennessee River. Its top is between sixty and seventy miles wide, timbered, rough, short of water and destitute of food and forage. From Jasper north for some fifty miles the Sequatchie River cuts the Cumberland from north to south into what is virtually two mountain ranges. The Sequatchie Valley is narrow, three to four miles, with sides just as precipitous as the main range, but it is well watered and fertile. Two poor roads crossed it in 1863, one through Dunlap and the other through Therman. It could be avoided by crossing its head at Pikesville. The narrow slice of mountain lying between the Sequatchie and Tennessee rivers was named Walden's Ridge. Crittenden's

Twenty-first Army Corps, aided by Thomas' brigade of mounted infantry, was assigned to this difficult terrain.[17] Crittenden's men drove all the Rebel pickets from the right bank of the Tennessee River, showed themselves in force first at one place and then at another, dropped their artillery shells into Chattanooga, and fired on every troop concentration they could see. They lit fake campfires to give a false impression of their strength. They pretended to be building in the tributaries of the Tennessee, where they were hidden from sight, boats and bridges for a crossing. They banged boards together, hammered on casks and sawed lumber into small pieces which they allowed to float down to the broad stream of the Tennessee.

And miles to the north a thin flank guard of Blue cavalry stretched for a contact with the patrols of Burnside's cavalry screen coming down from Kentucky.

Thomas' corps was split during this advance. Two of his divisions crossed the mountain by University Place, struck the headwaters of Battle Creek and followed that stream to the Tennessee River. Brannan camped at the mouth of Battle Creek. Reynolds was opposite Shellmound, a few miles upstream. His command covered the mouth of the Sequatchie River.

The divisions of Baird[18] and Negley, accompanied by Thomas, followed the railroad and took their position between Stevenson and Bridgeport. By the evening of August 19 Thomas' four divisions were in position. McCook was up the next day. His river sector was downstream from Thomas, from Stevenson to Bellefonte. Cavalry extended this flank to Whitesburg. Rosecrans established his headquarters a short distance east of Stevenson. Thomas' headquarters were located about one and one-half miles farther east near the little town of Bolivar. His headquarters guard probably selected a site close to a never-failing spring which was the source of a small stream named Benjes Creek. Three and three-quarter miles to the southeast was the Tennessee River. The backdrop for this scene was the green ridge of Sand Mountain. It rose abruptly from the left bank of the Tennessee to a height of some 900 feet and effectively screened the fifty miles of mountains and valleys behind it that the Army of the Cumberland had to cross in order to cut the railway line feeding Bragg's army.

When the first Yankee troops stooped to fill their cupped hands with water from the Tennessee River, the Army of the Cumberland came face to face with one of its crises. Its crossing posed a stupendous engineering problem. The Tennessee was one of the major rivers of the continent. Its bridges had been destroyed. Every boat that was not destroyed had been hidden in a left bank tributary or impounded in Chattanooga under the Rebel guns. The crossing was a hazardous military operation. Grant had crossed it miles downstream in 1862, but then it had been a friendly stream bringing his supplies to him through the sunny farmlands of middle Tennessee and taking away his sick and wounded. Here it was a barrier guarded by forbidding heights from which a determined enemy could turn a crossing into a shambles.

The river presented a psychological barrier, too. Where it gouged its way through the Cumberland range the palisades rose sheer to the sky so that each soldier felt small and weak as he stood beside the water and looked up at the rocky barricade. Its valley was deep and narrow so that the sun reached its bottom late in the morning and left it early in the afternoon. To men from the farmlands of Ohio, Indiana and Illinois it was gloomy and forbidding. The thought of crossing it made them feel that they would be taking a giant stride away from home. Even from the south bank the river would still be a barrier. It would bar their retreat and weaken their supply line. It seemed to increase their distance from the places they knew and with which they were familiar much more in time than it did in space.

Yet it was the gateway to conquest.[19] If the Blue bayonets could get across and stay across, their steel would be in the marrow of the Rebellion.

For ten days the preparation for the crossing went forward without a let-up. In the daytime roads were improved, fieldworks built to cover the points of crossing, fords located, water gauges set up, supplies unloaded and boats and floating bridges built in the tributary streams to be floated down when needed. After dark the pace and tension increased. Patrols crossed the river to drive back the enemy pickets. Behind them men mapped the crossings, cut down the banks to facilitate the landings, marked the fords with buoys and, where islands were handy, built defenses for the sharpshooters. Meantime scouting parties combed the south bank and its tributary streams for boats and rafts, which they hauled across to their own side of the river. Reynolds, opposite Shellmound, had eight or nine of these flatboats in which he could cross 400 men an hour. Brannan, a few miles downstream, built rafts big enough to cross a company at a time.

On the night of August 29 the crossing began. It was made at four points. Two of them, Shellmound and the mouth of Battle Creek, where Thomas was in charge, were made without bridges. Only a few wagons were ferried at these points. A combination of trestle and pontoon bridge was erected at Bridgeport under Sheridan's supervision but it collapsed four times and jammed the roads with waiting trains, artillery and infantry. A pontoon bridge was handsomely laid by the troops under Jefferson C. Davis at Caperton's Ferry. From the top of Sand Mountain it looked like a narrow ribbon stretched across the broad river.

Before this floating bridge was laid, fifty boatloads of fifty men each crossed under cover of night, drove off the Rebel cavalry pickets and secured a bridgehead. Rosecrans did not know it at the time but this little action was the key to the whole crossing. It broke the Rebel picket line so thoroughly that Bragg was blinded for about a week as to the position of the Union army below Chattanooga.

The entire crossing was packed with color but the highest drama took place at the two upper crossings where Thomas' men went over without the benefit of bridges. The boats of Reynolds' division were kept hidden in the brush on both sides of the road that connected Jasper with Shellmound. After dark, one after another was slid down the steep banks into the water. Men trained as oarsmen took their places. The infantrymen were packed in with their colors floating over each boat and the craft were shoved off into the darkness and the rising mist.

Six miles or so downstream, Brannan's crossing was primitive and barbaric with a touch of savagery. He secured his landing by sending over two companies during the night. At daylight there swept out of the mouth of Battle Creek as strange a flotilla as was ever seen on this continent. There were rafts jammed with infantry under their flags and battle ribbons. Other rafts carried wagons of the ammunition train or pieces of artillery. Experienced rivermen and raftsmen from Minnesota manned the sweeps. The drivers hung on to the bits of the rearing, frightened horses while the rafts tipped dangerously and turned slowly from the action of the wind and current. Interspersed among the rafts were jerry-built canoes so crowded with yelling infantrymen that the little waves on the upstream side splashed over the gunwales while their frantic paddlers strove to keep the current from carrying them too far downstream. Behind the rafts and canoes came the swimmers. They were stripped, with their clothing and arms lashed on fence rails. The strong swimmers pushed these individual rafts ahead of them; the weaker ones hung on and drifted with the current. As these floating bundles, accompanied by the bobbing heads, poured out of Battle Creek they spread out as they curved downstream so that they formed the pattern of a two-dimensional cornucopia through which was poured a modern army after a fashion that was old when it was used by the Macedonian phalanxes.

By September 4 the crossing was completed. Thomas and his staff crossed at Caperton's Ferry and moved their headquarters on the evening of September 3 to Moore's Spring on the road from Bridge-port, Alabama, to Trenton, Georgia. On the same day Burnside was in Knoxville.

Thomas' next barrier was Sand Mountain. It was two miles up by road and ten miles across. The roads were rudimentary. It took twenty-four hours for Negley's division to make the top. When the head of the column reached the top it was halted, leaving a continuous column of infantry along the road from the bottom of the mountain to the top. They stacked their arms and piled their equipment well off the road. Then the artillery and train began the ascent with doubled teams, while the foot soldiers on each side of the road acted as a human conveyor, walking the spokes of each wheel and pushing on each vehicle as it came opposite their station. Some of the artillery horses, whipped and spurred past the limit of their endurance, dropped dead on the slope. Some heavily laden wagons broke loose and rolled back-ward down the mountain smashing against trees and rocks.

Rosecrans' principal barrier was Lookout Mountain. This was higher and steeper than Sand but not so wide. At its crest, where the road was most winding, and the grades steepest, 100 Rebel cavalrymen blocked Negley's division for a day. That night a Union sympathizer came into camp and offered to lead a regiment to the top by way of an undiscovered path. The route was thus cleared and the next morning the advance was resumed.

Except for a few scattered gaps, Lookout was impassable to an army. Two of the most usable of these gaps—Stevens' and Cooper's—Thomas was to make safe for the passage of the army. Possession of these gaps would also open Chattanooga to an advance from the south, for this key city lay at the mountain's northern foot. The army's ob-jective was to cut the Chattanooga-Atlanta railroad and force Bragg to fight or retreat. This railroad was still some twenty-five miles straight east of Stevens' Gap but the intervening ridges were lower and the going was easier. McCook's corps was guarding Thomas' flank, two and one-half or three days' march to the south. Crittenden was turning the north end of Lookout to pinch off Chattanooga if he could. He was perhaps one and one-half days' march from Thomas.

By the evening of September 8, Thomas reported that he held the

essential gaps. This turned Bragg's position and the Southern army
evacuated Chattanooga that night. A regiment of Thomas' mounted
infantry trotted into the city at 9:30 A.M. and hoisted their regimental
flag from the third floor of the Crutchfield House.[20] Wood's division
of Crittenden's corps marched in three hours later.

This episode successfully ended Rosecrans' two great turning movements, first to the left and then to the right, which forced Bragg out
of Tennessee. Brigadier General M. C. Meigs considered Rosecrans'
campaign "not only the greatest operation in our war, but a great thing
when compared to any war." It broke Lee's western communications,
freed East Tennessee and gave the North control of one of the five
strategic points in the Confederacy.

It also backlighted one of Thomas' notable characteristics. Brigadier
General Thomas J. Wood was commanding the First Division of
Crittenden's Twenty-first Army Corps. Chattanooga had been the
professed objective of the Army of the Cumberland for nearly two
years and there was an unofficial rivalry to be the first to put foot into
the city. Rosecrans' dispositions after the crossing of the Tennessee
gave the advantage to Wood's division. On the morning of the ninth,
Wood was marching toward the evacuated city over the spurs of Lookout Mountain. He was noticeably upset when he learned that Thomas'
mounted infantry was in the town ahead of him. A courier was sent
to headquarters by the colonel of the mounted infantry with a report
of the occupation. Wood stopped him and endorsed on the envelope
he carried his own claim to the honor of being the first to occupy
the city. Wood's claim ultimately rested on one of his patrols which
crossed the river on the morning of the ninth covered by the guns
of a Union battery posted on the right bank. Thomas made a report
of the facts and let the matter rest. This little episode, considered with
the details of the race to enter Corinth the preceding year, indicates
that Thomas was always aware of these intramural contests and laid
his plans to win them but held aloof from the battle of claims that
inevitably followed.

There developed between Thomas and Rosecrans at this time a
major difference of opinion over strategy. Early in the morning of
September 9 Thomas was awakened by the arrival of a courier. It was
a summons to report immediately to Rosecrans' headquarters to con-
sult about arrangements for pursuit. Thomas dressed, mounted and
rode off through the darkness. He was probably accompanied by an
aide and at least a squad of his cavalry escort. His route lay along the
coves that scalloped the eastern foot of Sand Mountain. To his right

he could see the massive outline of Lookout Mountain against the relative lightness of the pre-dawn sky.

Rosecrans summarized his pursuit plans. He believed Bragg to be retreating for a stand somewhere between La Fayette and Rome, Georgia. He wanted to catch him in the flank while he was on the move or at least to bring him to bay before he could get his army into one of the strong defensive positions that were available to him. Thomas interrupted Rosecrans to present a plan of his own. He favored a temporary concentration of the Army of the Cumberland at Chattanooga until supplies could be built up and communications strengthened for another forward move. The army was dangerously dispersed. The western side of Lookout Mountain was still Bragg's bailiwick. Thomas reasoned that it was an invitation to disaster to push three widely separated corps across that barrier. Besides, Bragg had already been bolstered by reinforcements from Mississippi, Buckner was closing down from Knoxville with more help, and there were persistent rumors that succor was to come from the Army of Northern Virginia.

It was in this connection that Thomas later expounded his theory of military obedience. He believed that Rosecrans, after occupying Chattanooga, should have paid no attention to the pressure from Washington for an advance. "The Army of the Cumberland," he pointed out, "had done a good nine months' work in driving the rebels out of Tennessee and getting a foothold south of the river. Rosecrans should have waited to get another good ready [sic] before he pushed forward again."

But Rosecrans shook his head. The matter was dropped and the details of the pursuit were ironed out. Thomas agreed to do his part but he wanted Wilder's brigade of mounted infantry returned to his command. By 10:00 A.M. the pursuit orders were out. Crittenden would move into Chattanooga and follow Bragg's retreat route. Mc-Cook was to move on Alpine and Summerville and block the retreating army. While Bragg was thus harried from the rear and blocked in front, Thomas was to deliver the knockout somewhere in the vicinity of La Fayette.

Rosecrans was overconfident. He had expected a battle on the sixth and had telegraphed the clergy all over the country soliciting their prayers in anticipation of it. To many of the Civil War generals the Almighty was a personal God. They had no hesitation in asking His aid in slaughtering their brother Americans or in crediting Him for their bloody victories. Lee's dispatches drip with this sentiment. There is no doubt of the source of Stonewall Jackson's military guidance.

None, however, went as far as Rosecrans. Thomas' dispatches never threw off on the Deity.

Thomas was not irreligious; neither was he a church member. "Revealed religion," Thomas believed, "that is given us in the teachings and character of Christ, is clear in all things. I never met an infidel who questioned the goodness of Christ or the purity or divinity of his teachings. Whether they will get us into heaven or not after death, there is one thing certain, and that is to obey them is to make us better and happier on earth. Accepting that I will chance the rest." [21] To Thomas this belief was the basis of human confidence and courage. Without it a man could not be a good soldier. "Above all painful doubts," he said, "we feel that there is an overruling Power ever wise and just." After the war Thomas thought seriously of becoming a communicant of the Protestant Episcopal Church and the idea, though never acted upon, remained with him until the end of his life.

Bragg, however, was not retreating. Like a prudent commander, he did not want his army trapped in Chattanooga. He was moving slowly along his communications looking for a chance to fight. He was being heavily reinforced. Besides those Thomas and Rosecrans knew about, two more brigades were moving in from Mississippi and Longstreet's famous First Corps was moving toward Atlanta from Lee's army. The Georgia militia were being organized and unexchanged prisoners from the paroled Vicksburg army were being recruited.

Thomas went ahead with plans for the pursuit. Negley's troops were at the eastern foot of Lookout Mountain with their skirmishers one and one-half miles ahead of them. Baird was trying to get across Lookout Mountain, much impeded by Negley's trains.

Negley was in a valley known as McLemore's Cove. In a straight line from Stevens' Gap slightly south of east, the valley was seven miles wide. Two streams rose here and flowed northward toward Chattanooga. They were separated by Missionary Ridge, which actually divided McLemore's Cove into two valleys, but this ridge was low on its south end and offered few obstacles to an advancing army. West of it flowed Chattanooga Creek. East of it was Chickamauga Creek. The high ground east of the Chickamauga, which was also the eastern boundary of McLemore's Cove, was Pigeon Mountain and behind it was Bragg's army. This mountain was a natural defense barrier. It could be crossed in three places only—Bluebird Gap in the south, Catlett's Gap in the north and Dug Gap in the middle. Negley was moving toward Dug Gap and La Fayette, which was about four miles farther east.

There was something in Negley's dispatch of the early afternoon of September 9 that aroused Thomas' suspicions. He forwarded it to Rosecrans and early the next morning he left his headquarters, threaded his way up and over Lookout through the tangled trains of Baird and Negley and dropped down into McLemore's Cove to see for himself what was happening. He rode to within one mile of Dug Gap and found an enemy picket line so strong as to indicate a stubborn defense stand. The gap itself was obstructed. From what he could see with his glasses from the low heights of Missionary Ridge the north end of the cove permitted easy access to Negley's left flank. Reports from prisoners and citizens agreed that there were heavy enemy forces just east of Dug Gap and building up in the north end of McLemore's Cove. At 9:00 P.M. on the tenth Thomas dispatched this information to Rosecrans. Its importance lay in what the dispatch did not say. Thomas, as Rosecrans' main striking force, had given no orders to advance. He had not tried to break the Dug Gap picket line to see what it hid. He had acquiesced in Negley's move to put himself on the defensive. True, he expressed the hope that he could drive the enemy beyond Pigeon Mountain within twenty-four hours. But this was stalling and Rosecrans knew it. Thomas was dragging his feet because he smelled danger and not because he disapproved of Rosecrans' program.

Rosecrans' reply was dictated within three-quarters of an hour. Negley's delay, he pointed out, was imperiling both extremes of the army. Rosecrans was disappointed. He showed more irritation at Thomas than he had ever shown before. "Your advance ought to have threatened La Fayette yesterday evening," was his final admonition.

Thomas' reply at 8:00 A.M. on September 11 was firm, hopeful but unyielding. He backed his division commander to the limit. He sent Rosecrans a copy of his orders to Negley. They instructed Negley not to advance except under one condition. He was to defend himself from a flank attack coming at him from the north.

This was almost a defiance of Rosecrans' orders. The information that caused Thomas to take this position came to him sometime between the afternoon of September 10 and 3:25 A.M. on September 11. Whatever way he learned it, it was true. Bragg had set a trap for him. At 7:00 A.M. on September 11, Buckner's corps and Hindman's division were to strike southward between Missionary Ridge and Pigeon Mountain while Bragg struck westward through Dug Gap. This was Bragg's first planned attack for destroying piecemeal the Army of the Cumberland. Thomas learned about this plan almost as soon as it was written. The Fourteenth Army Corps, backed up against the almost impassable bulk of Lookout Mountain, was facing Bragg's whole army. Meantime Crittenden was airily marching and countermarching across Chickamauga Valley utterly unconscious of the fact that the Rebel patrols he lightly brushed aside were the flank guards of the Army of Tennessee.

Thomas had learned enough to make him cautious but not enough to give him the true picture. "We are laboring along as best we may," he wrote on the morning of the eleventh, "and I hope to be able to get into La Fayette tomorrow." He was a master of understatement, but never was he farther under than this time.

Thomas' military intuition possibly saved Rosecrans' army from destruction but Rosecrans was not willing to admit it. He refused to believe the first faint indications that his miraculous success was taking an ominous turn. But by 10:00 P.M. of September 11 the sheer repetition of the warnings began to dent his consciousness. It was not until twelve hours later, however, that he sent out his orders for a concentration on Thomas. At that moment Bragg snatched the offensive. The astute and irreverent observers who manned the military telegraph lines put the situation in a nutshell when they telegraphed Washington: "The enemy are between Thomas and McCook on the south and Crittenden and Granger [22] on the north and the day before yesterday gave Negley a thrashing. . . . We are in a ticklish place here."

16

Chickamauga

Rosecrans' problem was concentration. Crittenden had moved up from the north. The big job now was to get McCook pulled in from the south. Thomas received a verbal order from Rosecrans at about 6:00 A.M. on September 13, instructing him to order McCook and the cavalry to close up and support him. He promptly complied, specifying the detail of McCook's movement. Rosecrans, however, had already sent a written order to McCook which specified a different march detail. As a result, the simple march that should have put Mc-Cook on Thomas' flank in twelve hours was not accomplished for 108 hours. On September 15, Rosecrans moved his headquarters from Chattanooga close to Thomas' position in McLemore's Cove, counter-manded the order that had stopped McCook in his tracks and ironed out the difficulty.

Rosecrans brought with him C. A. Dana, then Second Assistant Secretary of War by appointment but not by confirmation. He was three years younger than Thomas. He was sent as the confidential adviser to Stanton but he was not the experienced adviser that Thomas had hoped for. Under pressure he was hysterical and inexact. He did, however, confirm several facts about the Army of the Cumberland that Washington had refused to believe—that the railway was not adequate to supply the army, that the roads were next to impassable, that the difficulties of maneuver were enormous, that Rosecrans' flanks needed protection, and that the army needed cavalry.

From the twelfth until the sixteenth Thomas remained facing the gaps through Pigeon Mountain and waiting for McCook. On the seventeenth he began a slow movement down the Chickamauga toward Crawfish Springs as McCook's troops began the descent of the east face of Lookout Mountain. On the eighteenth this movement was accelerated.

Meanwhile Halleck was frantically trying to get reinforcements to Rosecrans. He had finally learned that Lee had reinforced Bragg. His telegrams combed the area from Detroit to St. Louis. Evidence that Bragg was expecting to force a battle by a massed attack against the Union northern flank began building up at Rosecrans' headquarters, now at Crawfish Springs. Thomas reached there at 4:00 P.M. on September 18 with the head of his column and was summoned to a conference with Rosecrans. It was here that he got the orders for the famous inversion march [1] that was to move the Fourteenth Corps from Rosecrans' center to his left, overlap Bragg's concentration and put Thomas between the Rebel army and Chattanooga.

Rarely was a Union commander as poorly informed as was Rosecrans that night. Crittenden, the flank guard, failed to keep Bragg from crossing Chickamauga Creek, but, what was worse, failed even to learn that Bragg had crossed. Early on the nineteenth all of Bragg's infantry except three divisions were west of the Chickamauga. They had crossed wherever possible between Reed's bridge and Lee and Gordon's mill and were massed on the left of Palmer's unsuspecting division.[2] The end of Thomas' night march carried him along the front of Bragg's army with nothing but light cavalry patrols to save him from annihilation. Thomas knew it was a perilous march and contrary to all military principles. For that reason he detached one-quarter of his strength, Negley's division, and deployed it as a flank guard on Crittenden's right. Several hours later Thomas learned that the end of his march, which he had thought was the safest, had been reckless to the point of insanity.

The objective of Thomas' march was Kelly's farm on the State road five or six miles north of Crawfish Springs. The distance was not great but night marching under the best conditions is slow and hard on the troops. In the darkness the soldier is unable to judge the unevenness of the surface. At almost every step his foot strikes the ground before or after he expects it to. The impact jars his spine and the suddenly checked momentum of his equipment makes the straps cut into his shoulders or drag at his waist. His pack throws him off balance and he stumbles into the man alongside of him. To make it worse, this particular march was made through clouds of choking dust. The only road was jammed with the corps trains and artillery so the infantry marched through the fields on both sides of it. There was a heavy skirmish line off to the right. It was cold and there were frequent halts while the marching men waited for the troops ahead of them to move. During these halts the men built fires along the fence rows. Toward morning the trains were driving between two continuous rows of fire. By daylight the crisis was past. The marching columns could see brigades and batteries ahead of them leaving the road from time to time and moving off in line of battle toward the Chickamauga. The dusty, sleepless troops of Baird's column halted in Kelly's field long enough to boil some coffee. Brannan's division, hard on their heels, was still marching.[3]

As soon as Thomas came up the deployment began under his personal direction. The battle line faced east and straddled the roads that led to Reed's and Alexander's bridges over the Chickamauga. Brannan was on the north or left end while Baird was on his right with his southern flank refused. There was a wide gap between this refused flank and Palmer's left but Thomas expected to fill it with the troops who were still moving up. Early that morning, Thomas had established his headquarters on the west side of the State road, south of Kelly's field where it was joined by the road from the Widow Glenn's. Sometime before 9:00 A.M., he moved them to the McDonald house, where the road from Reed's and Alexander's bridges came in from the east and the road from McFarland's Gap came in from the west. He was in telegraphic communication with Rosecrans' headquarters at the Widow Glenn's, three miles away, with Granger's reserve corps at Rossville, and with Chattanooga.[4]

Conflicting intelligence came into Thomas' headquarters about the location and strength of the enemy forces on his side of the Chickamauga. Late in the evening of the eighteenth he had heard from Wilder that the Rebels were across in strength. At daybreak the next morning Dan McCook, commanding an infantry brigade of Granger's reserve corps, told him that the only Rebel force west of the Chickamauga was a single brigade trapped on the Reed's bridge road.[5] Thomas did not know where the heart of Bragg's power was located and it was his job to make sure that it was not between himself and

Chattanooga. If he could bag a Rebel brigade while doing this, so much the better. On this skimpy information the Battle of Chickamauga began.

At 7:00 A.M. Croxton's brigade of Brannan's division met the enemy and opened the battle. This was the first positive break for Rosecrans since September 9. Thomas' sudden thrust secured the initiative. Bragg, instead of outflanking Rosecrans, was now out-flanked himself. His army had its back to the Chickamauga, which was impassable except at the fords and bridges. It was a bad tactical position and Thomas immediately improvised a plan to exploit it. The only force Bragg had in the vicinity of Thomas' two divisions was one division of Forrest's cavalry corps. They were dismounted and the absence of the horseholders automatically cut his effective strength by 25 per cent.[6] Forrest immediately called for supports, which Thomas planned to whip in detail as they came up. He ordered Palmer to strike them in the flank while he met them head-on, and he requested Rosecrans to order Crittenden to advance from the south in a coop-erative attack. "We can, I think, use them up," he assured the com-manding general.[7]

But the plan was turned down. Rosecrans did not believe that the enemy was where Thomas said it was. He directed Thomas to take a good defensive position. This order changed the tactical aspect of the battle and returned to Bragg the priceless initiative. It was now a race between Bragg and Rosecrans to build up their northern flanks.

The burden of the Confederate fight fell on Forrest. He, too, was unprepared for it. He had expected to find light infantry patrols in his front. Suddenly he was confronted with the solid lines of Thomas' divisions. He pulled his troopers together and retired fighting. His supports came in piecemeal, first cavalry and then infantry, and the lines swayed back and forth between Jay's mill and Kelly's field as Thomas and then Forrest held the upper hand.

About 10:00 A.M., when Forrest was receiving his first substantial support, Thomas was apprehensive of his ability to hold a defensive line. He sent an order to Reynolds to hurry him into position, ordered his headquarters to pack up ready to move to Chattanooga, alerted Granger and asked Crittenden for a division.

At noon Croxton was fighting southward one-half mile east of Kelly's field. Van Derveer [8] was facing northeast on the Reed's bridge road three-quarters of a mile east of McDonald's house. South of these brigades were the remaining troops of Baird and Brannan, half sur-rounded by an arc of Southern troops made up of the commands of

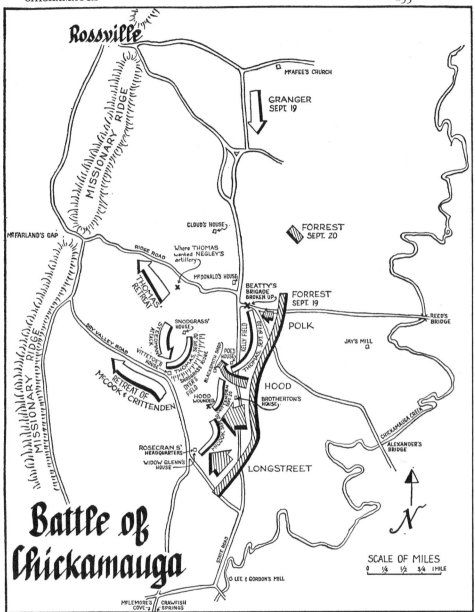

Map 6. Battle of Chickamauga, September 19, 20, 1863. No accurate map of the battle was ever made. Eight months after the battle Thomas had the terrain surveyed but the troop positions were never plotted. This drawing follows the Thomas map (*O.R. Atlas, Plate 97, No. 3*).

Govan, Walthall, Wilson, Ector, Davidson and Dibrell. Cheatham, with the commands of Wright, Smith, Jackson, Strahl and Maney [9] was moving up from the southeast. To balance this pile-up of Rebel strength Johnson [10] was just moving into Kelly's field and Palmer was deployed south of it facing east. Reynolds was coming up on Palmer's right.

This was the crisis of the day's battle for Thomas' wing. He was preparing to meet it with his favorite tactic, a heavy mass of storm troops to pick up momentum with a quick start and deliver their blow with stunning force. The Rebel strike, too, was savage and sudden. Thomas watched the brigades of Scribner and King [11] reel back from it and stream in disorder across the front of his new line. The Gray infantrymen were in close pursuit, their formation shifting constantly as they advanced. When the divisions of Johnson and Palmer were set up in the proper position, Thomas let them loose. Reynolds was held in reserve. At the same time Brannan attacked the Rebels from the north. Outnumbered, surprised and roughly handled, the enemy were driven southeastward a mile and a half to the security of their own reserves, on the west bank of Chickamauga Creek.

It was now in the neighborhood of 2:00 P.M. Baird, badly cut up, and Brannan were pulled out of the line for reorganization and rest. They had marched all night, eaten a scanty breakfast, if any, and charged and countercharged, some units as many as six times, across a three-quarter-mile strip of densely wooded land. Thomas put them on a commanding spot of his own selection between McDonald's house and Reed's bridge. His orders were to hold their position to the last extremity. Thomas expected Bragg to move again, in still greater strength, around his left flank. This was the objective of Bragg's original plan, which had been upset when Croxton and Forrest collided on the woodland road a mile or more to the north. But now Bragg elected to strike at Thomas' right, the gap between Thomas and Crittenden.

Van Cleve's division of Crittenden's corps broke under this attack and the Rebel infantry overran the State road between the headquarters of Thomas and those of Rosecrans at the Widow Glenn's. The telegraph went dead between the two places, and Rosecrans' queries about what was going on came to Thomas by way of Rossville. The breakthrough was in the area under Crittenden's command but Thomas was concerned because his right flank was endangered. He sent Brannan south along the State road on the run, but the damage was repaired before he arrived.

Hazen, who had held the Round Forest at Stones River, and who was now commanding one of Palmer's brigades, was largely responsible for beating off this attack. His men were on the State road filling their pockets and cartridge boxes from the ammunition train when Van Cleve asked for help, saying that he had lost control of his men. Hazen hurriedly got his brigade into line west of the State road, facing south and a little east, and moved them forward until they became engaged, but they were outflanked and began to waver.

Most of the Union artillery was standing by along the State road, since the heavy woods in which the infantry was fighting made it impossible for them to operate. Hazen collected twenty of these guns and put them into position. He could not get his own brigade into place in time to support the guns, so he improvised an infantry support line out of stragglers. The artillery opened with grape and broke up the attack. It was not only quick thinking but also quick acting on Hazen's part that saved the situation. Stragglers are notoriously slow to get back into the fight, yet Hazen accomplished a reorganization in the face of the enemy's fire in two minutes.[12] It was nearly sundown, however, before Crittenden pushed the Confederates off of his section of the State road.

Thomas now began to regroup and reorganize the five divisions under his command—Baird, Brannan and Reynolds of his own corps, Palmer of Crittenden's and Johnson of McCook's. He did this personally with an eye to the morrow's probabilities.

Bragg had in mind the turning movement around the Yankee left that Thomas had prepared for in the middle of the afternoon. To make it, however, he had to move troops from his own left to his right. Cleburne's division led this column in a wide arc to keep clear of the fighting. It got into position after sunset and moved immediately to its work. Thomas heard the racket while he was putting Brannan's division into position near the Poe house. He rode catercornered across Kelly's field toward the fight, picking up Palmer's division on his way. Cleburne's assault was a furious one and threw the Union line into such confusion that one of Baird's brigades fired into another. But the assault could not be sustained in the darkness and order was soon restored.

After the repulse of Cleburne's night attack, Thomas again set about the work of arranging his battle lines for the next day. He knew that the battle would be resumed by an attack against his left, with the design of putting the Gray divisions between the State road and Missionary Ridge in order to destroy the Union divisions in succession

from north to south. At 7:10 P.M. on the nineteenth he advised Rosecrans that he would need supports for his left.[13]

Before he had all of his five divisions in position he was summoned
to Rosecrans' headquarters. It must have been about 8:00 P.M. when
he dismounted in front of the Widow Glenn's, turned his horse over
to his orderly and went inside. All of the corps and division commanders had been ordered to the meeting. There were about a dozen
of them on hand when Thomas arrived. Rosecrans asked each corps
commander for the detail of the present position of his troops and for
his opinion on what to look for the next day.

Thomas reported that he had driven the enemy, and that his lines
had thereby become attenuated. As a result, he had drawn them into
a defensive position on a ridge extending northeastward from Vittetoe's
house to the Snodgrass house,[14] thence to the southeast corner of
Kelly's field, thence to its northeast corner and thence northward to the
Reed's bridge road. He was insistent that the next Rebel attack would
come toward the McDonald house from the direction of Reed's bridge
and that it would turn his left flank. He concluded with a request for
a division to extend his present line in order to block such a movement.

Each corps commander's report and suggestion was discussed, but
Thomas apparently took little part in this portion of the meeting. He
was so exhausted from his all-night march, followed by a day of
battle, that he fell asleep at every opportunity. When aroused by a
direct question from Rosecrans, he would straighten up in his chair
and answer, only to fall asleep again when the commanding general's
attention was directed elsewhere. Each of his answers was the same—
"I would strengthen the left."

After the corps reports, Rosecrans issued his orders for the next
day. Thomas' divisions were to remain as he reported them with one
exception. Brannan, instead of extending Thomas' line westward
along the ridge near Vittetoe's was to be placed in reserve. The right
of Thomas' line would then connect with the left of McCook's, with
Reynolds and Negley at the junction. Negley was acting under Mc-
Cook's command. McCook's line extended south to cover the position
at the Widow Glenn's. This distance was too great for his strength,
a fact that must have been known to McCook and Rosecrans. Crittenden, with the divisions of Van Cleve and Wood, was placed in
reserve. The orders were written, given to each officer, and read in
the presence of all. When everything was understood, hot coffee was

served and McCook was called upon for a song. The meeting broke up about midnight.

Sheridan insisted years later that the meeting was characterized by a feeling of depression, although Dana's frequent dispatches to Stanton filed at this time do not mirror such a feeling. Strangely enough Hood discovered the same feeling at Bragg's headquarters that same evening.

During the day's fighting every Northern unit had been engaged except two brigades and one regiment. Baird had been badly cut up and Reynolds, Davis and Van Cleve had incurred substantial losses. But four miles north of Thomas' position were nearly 8,000 fresh troops under Granger who had not been engaged. Sheridan and Negley had not fought exhaustively. Had the Union commanders known that a substantial portion of Bragg's command had not been engaged on the nineteenth and that more of Longstreet's units were up, they would have been justified in feeling apprehensive.

It was about 2:00 A.M. of the twentieth when Thomas returned to his command to complete the work of adjusting his lines. He had already seen to it that they were stiff enough to prevent a breakthrough. He had been promised the division which he would need to block a turning movement aimed at the junction of the State and Reed's bridge roads. He planned to have his regular brigade, in combination with this promised division, take the brunt of the attack. There was a wooded ridge running north and south across the Reed's bridge road about one-quarter of a mile east of the State road. Here Thomas put the regulars facing east with a fairly good field of fire and the protection of the reverse slope for reloading. Their left, he expected, would touch the Reed's bridge road but there was no natural obstacle there to give it strength. Their right would link up with Scribner, who covered the northeast corner of Kelly's field. From this point Thomas' line ran south 150 yards east of the edge of Kelly's field. Stark-weather, commanding Baird's third brigade, touched Scribner's right. His position was powerful—strengthened by an Indiana battery so placed that it could fire directly upon an assault from the east or could enfilade Scribner's brigade to the north. Baird's line was in two ranks except for the regular brigade, which was more concentrated to give it stiffness, but he had no reserve.

Johnson's division, next in line to Starkweather, faced east. He occupied a front of two brigade intervals, with Willich's brigade kept in reserve. His front line brigades were commanded by Dodge and Baldwin. This was the strongest division in McCook's corps, but

Thomas had replaced it with Negley's division and Wilder's brigade of mounted infantry.

Palmer's division came next. He had two brigades in the line, commanded by Cruft and Hazen, and Grose's brigade in reserve. His men faced to the southeast to cover the southern end of Kelly's field. Their right flank was close to the State road.

Reynolds' division was astride the State road facing southeast. Turchin's brigade was next to Palmer, with Edward A. King on his right. King was not related to the commander of the regular brigade and was succeeded, after being killed by a sharpshooter, by Milton Robinson. Since Reynolds' remaining brigade was detached, he pulled nearly half of his regiments back of the line and held them as a reserve.

Sometime during the night the orders to hold Brannan as a corps reserve were changed and he was put into the line next to Reynolds. Brannan's troops were all west of the State road and faced nearly south. He had two brigades on the line, commanded by Croxton and Connell, and Van Derveer's in reserve. More than half a mile in Brannan's rear, Crittenden's divisions under Wood and Van Cleve were held as the army reserve. To Brannan's right were the divisions of Negley, Davis, and Sheridan and Wilder's brigade, all under McCook's command.

Thomas' line, with two exceptions, was a strong one, and it was further strengthened early in the morning by the erection of log and rail breastworks on Thomas' orders.[15] B. F. Cheatham, who commanded a division in Polk's corps, looking over the battlefield years later in company with some Union officers, pushed at one of these crumbling breastworks with his foot and said, "Only for this little work we would have swept you from the field before noon."

There were weaknesses, however, that set up a chain reaction from which the Army of the Cumberland never recovered. The first weakness was the lack of a corps reserve. There were nearly four brigades of divisional reserves but these were needed close to the line to plug any breakthroughs. Thomas sought to remedy this by having Granger close up. He did not issue an order but requested Granger to advise Rosecrans if he was not in supporting distance of Thomas' left. Granger's reply, sent direct to Rosecrans at 10:30, announced that he was moving toward the battle's roar.[16] The more serious weakness was the defenselessness of Baird's left flank against a turning movement. Thomas had been thinking about it when Cleburne's night attack interrupted him. It was in his subconsciousness while he cat-napped at Rosecrans' headquarters and he was still thinking about it as he rode back along the lines from Widow Glenn's. At 2:00 A.M. he received a report from Baird that the left of his line was too short to reach to the Reed's bridge road, where Thomas had ordered it to be placed. Thomas rode out to take a look. This was the second succeeding night that he had had no chance to restore his drained-off energy. There was already an ominous stir in the woods beyond Baird's lines made by Breckinridge's division moving into position. Thomas could tell from the pieced-together reports of his skirmishers that his flank was overlapped.

At 6:00 A.M. Thomas made his third request for support.[17] This time he asked specifically for Negley's division. He was evolving a defense for his threatened wing. He would mass those batteries of his divisional artillery which could not be used along his barricades, on the shoulders of Missionary Ridge some six or seven hundred yards west of McDonald's house whence they could sweep the clearings over which the Rebel enveloping movement would have to pass.[18] Under cover of their fire, Negley's division would back up Baird's regulars. If pressed too hard both would fall back on the batteries, where guns and footmen would give each other mutual support. Thomas was calling on his cumulative experience. Breckinridge was commanding the attempt to turn Thomas' position. He had tried the same thing at Stones River and been beaten down by Mendenhall's massed guns. Thomas lacked the infantry but he already had the guns. They were strung along the State road—teams watered and harnessed and now standing hipshot, snuffling into their nose bags, caissons and limbers packed with ammunition, drivers with whip and spur waiting to mount at the first sound of the bugle.

Thomas had asked for Negley, probably because he was a part of the Fourteenth Army Corps. But several facts argued against his request. Any infantry division would have answered. Negley was in the line. It was a complex maneuver to pull a division out of the line and move it elsewhere—a dangerous maneuver when the line was under attack. Negley's division was a couple of miles from where Thomas wanted to use him while Van Cleve's division in reserve was closer and could have been sent more quickly. The decision was up to Rosecrans and at 6:30 he ordered it the way Thomas had requested.[19] Five minutes later he ordered McCook to fill the space left vacant by Negley's removal, if practicable.[20] It wasn't practicable and Rosecrans should have known it. McCook's line was already stretched too thin.

At dawn Rosecrans and his staff showed up on the extreme left of Thomas' line. Thomas met them there and pointed out to the commanding general what he wanted. It was at this time that Rosecrans sent the twin orders directing Negley's move to the left. While Rosecrans was waiting for the dispatches to be written he questioned Thomas about his fight of the day before. Thomas told him how he had broken the Rebel attack with the divisions of Johnson and Palmer. It had been a brilliant thrust and Thomas grew animated. "Whenever I touched their flanks they broke, General, they broke," he said. Then, becoming ashamed of his enthusiasm, he blushed and looked at the ground.

Thomas rode with Rosecrans southward along the length of his line. On the east side of Kelly's field Rosecrans directed that Palmer's division be closed up to make it more compact. Thomas issued the necessary orders. This shifted the entire line south of Palmer to the left, stretching McCook's brigades even thinner. Thomas left Rosecrans at the south end of Brannan's position. It would have been just a step farther to Negley's command post, where the whole matter of reinforcement could have been settled at once but the step was not taken. This was the last Thomas saw of Rosecrans for some forty-eight hours. The last word he had from him was a verbal promise to send Negley to his support.

When Thomas returned to his headquarters at the McDonald house he found that Negley had established a courier line. He sent Negley's aide back with another message to hurry up the division. There was firing along his extreme left as the skirmishers ran into each other in the woods. Thomas had moved his troops as near as possible to the road leading from the McDonald house to Reed's bridge, as he was now convinced that the main attack would be delivered at that point. It would be a thrust between himself and Granger, four miles to the north. At 8:30 the popping of the muskets along the skirmish lines had grown into a continuous crackling which meant that the solid lines of infantry were in sight of each other. The sound also confirmed his fears. His left flank was overlapped a quarter of a mile. John Beatty's brigade of Negley's division came on the field just as the Union skirmishers were driven in. Thomas pointed out his position. It must have been with a sinking heart. The Rebels were already pushing at his flank, yet only one-third of his promised reinforcement was at hand. It was a choice now of improvisations and the first was to extend Beatty's thin line west from the left of the regulars, facing it north. It was a refused flank far too weak for the job expected of it.

By 9:30 A.M. the full vigor of the Confederate attack was developed by Breckinridge's three brigades under Adams, Stovall and Helm.

Adams and Stovall drove straight west, north of Kelly's field, and turned south when they reached the State road. They brushed aside Beatty's weak line, overlapped Baird's flank and forced the regulars to wheel backward toward their left and rear. The right half of Helm's brigade went with them but the left half struck that portion of Scribner's brigade which was supported by the enfilading fire of some of Starkweather's guns. Here were two and a half Confederate regiments trapped by two coincidences. The line to their right advanced faster than they could and left them behind while Cleburne's division to their left, attacking in echelon, had not gone forward fast enough. Helm's two and a half regiments were isolated. As these men ran headlong into Scribner's barricade they met a frontal fire delivered by infantry two lines deep and firing alternately by volley. There was a seventy-five-yard cleared space in front of the barricade which gave a fine field of fire for Starkweather's guns firing northward at the close range of one and one half divisional fronts. The place was a death trap. Helm's gallant 700 recoiled from their first attack, re-formed and stormed in again. This time they threw Scribner out of his works but lacked the strength to hold their gains. They fell back again and each crossing of that seventy-five-yard opening took its toll. Again they reformed in the cover of the woods and launched their third attack, too weak this time to be more than a gesture. This was one of the bloodiest encounters of the day, yet eight hours later the survivors, still organized as a brigade, went back into the line, stormed the barricade for the fourth time and chased Scribner's men across Kelly's field in the dusk.

The portion of the Confederate line that had been held by Helm's brigade was never filled during the morning fighting and this tactical error proved to be of inestimable value to Thomas' defense. This crippling of Helm's brigade and the subsequent heavy damage to Cleburne's division, which later struck Thomas' line south of Starkweather, prevented the Rebel envelopment by Adams and Stovall, since Breckinridge did not think it safe to swing them along the State road and into the rear of the Union troops fighting along the east side of Kelly's field.[21]

Bragg was attacking by divisions in succession from his right flank to his left and, like most elaborate tactical combinations, it failed to work smoothly. By the time Johnson was under attack, at ten o'clock, the pressure had been removed from Starkweather until fresh troops could be brought in to replace Helm's shattered Kentuckians. An hour later Bragg's attack had swept southward to Brannan's front. Everywhere along Thomas' barricades east of Kelly's field, his lines held.[22] The Union casualties were remarkably light. Hazen's brigade behind its breastworks in the morning fight took only thirteen casualties, although he thought the fighting more stubborn than any he had faced at Stones River, when his losses had been more than 400.

Meantime Baird had combed the field for unemployed regiments to support his reeling lines. He brought Johnson up to see how things stood and Johnson sent him four regiments under Willich, which backed up Starkweather and Scribner, and Dodge's brigade, which helped hold Baird's flank after Beatty was dislodged. Thomas spent all his time on this flank, trying to get up reinforcements and posting them when they arrived. The division he needed to consummate his defense plan never did arrive but Thomas' hard-riding aides made up for this lack. It was another improvisation which could not have worked if Bragg had moved against Rosecrans' entire line at once instead of attacking by divisions from north to south. This left the south end of Thomas' line relatively unemployed while Breckinridge's envelopment was being checked and from these unemployed divisions Thomas' couriers began bringing up help. Palmer's reserve brigade came up, followed by Van Derveer from Brannan's sector and part of Stanley's from Negley.[23] As fast as his aides brought up the reinforcements, Thomas posted them to bolster his weak spots as the pattern of the fighting changed.

One of Thomas' first reactions to the turning movement against Baird was to call up the men who had broken Zollicoffer's line for him at Mill Springs. This was Van Derveer's brigade of Brannan's division, then in reserve along the State road about a mile south of the left end of Baird's line. They moved northward through the woods west of the State road, deployed in line of battle, and, wheeling to the right when they got north of the Kelly house, crossed the State road facing east. A heavy fire was coming from this direction and it was in this direction that Van Derveer expected to attack. As soon as he came out of the woods he saw his mistake. The force he had to meet was in the north end of Kelly's field, moving south. It was Adams' brigade of Breckinridge's division, four lines deep and advancing on the run. They were Louisiana troops for the most part, with a scattering of Alabamians. There was some musketry fire from the Rebel infantry and two pieces of artillery were firing from a position on the State road. Van Derveer's men were dropping as he wheeled them to the left to face the attack and ordered them to lie down.

When Adams' line had closed to seventy-five yards, Van Derveer's two lines rose to their feet. The first line delivered a volley. The second line stepped through the first and charged. The line with the empty muskets followed close behind them. As Breckinridge put it in his battle report, "After a sanguinary contest, which reflected high honor on the brigade, it was forced back in some confusion." In the confusion, Kelly's field was cleared of the enemy and General Adams was wounded and captured.

It was now about 10:00 A.M. There was a lull in the fighting around the north end of Kelly's field while Breckinridge's hurt brigades were pulled out. Their discomfiture was not altogether due to Thomas' defense. Breckinridge's corps commanders put a large part of the blame on Bragg for ordering an attack against breastworks with a single line of troops without reserves. Whatever the cause, Thomas was grateful for the respite. Johnson and Palmer were now under the full pressure of Bragg's frontal attack and the point of pressure was gradually moving south where it would soon encompass the fronts of Reynolds and Brannan. Thomas left this part of his line to beat back the Rebel assaults in their own way. Unless some crisis occurred along the barricades, Thomas meant to devote his time to solving the defense problem on his left flank.

He had an hour in which to work. The rest of Stanley's brigade came up and Thomas used it to hold the ground where Beatty had stood. Grose, Dodge and Van Derveer were still on hand to strengthen and extend his line. Southwest of where he was working Thomas could see a sizable body of infantry, and he sent one of his aides to direct the officer in command, whoever he might be, to mass the artillery of the Fourteenth Army Corps on the spurs of Missionary Ridge and guard it with his footmen. The guns were to sweep the ground to the left and rear of Baird's flank with canister when the attack developed. It was Negley who got the order. He was sick, undermanned and apprehensive. He put the artillery in the wrong place, never collected enough infantry to properly support the guns, and finally took them off the field, together with most of the infantry of his division. From Rosecrans, Thomas had received many promises but only two brigades. He had no more reserves of his own. Everything he had was in position. There was nothing he could do now but go in search of his reinforcements and bring them on the field.

There was plenty of confusion, too, among the Rebel chieftains in the woods east of Baird's riflemen. They finally got things straightened out. Breckinridge was moved farther north so that his right would now overlap Thomas' left by something like three-quarters of a mile.

It was almost as much as Hardee had overlapped McCook at the beginning of Stones River but Breckinridge had to reorganize his hard-hit brigades before he could move. Between Breckinridge's left and Cleburne's right, Bragg's entire reserve corps was committed. As nearly as can be told from the Confederate battle reports, Govan with his Arkansas fighters moved eastward and then southward on the State road over the same ground where Adams and Stovall had fought an hour before, while Gist's division and Walthall's brigade struck the Kelly field barricades. The stubbornness of Thomas' defense is evidenced by the fact that an hour's fighting compelled Bragg to use all of his reserve strength.

This attack started shortly before 11:00 A.M. and Thomas sent his last dispatch until late afternoon to Rosecrans. It advised the commanding general that the Rebels were on the road leading to the McDonald house and were trying to cut the army's communications with Rossville. "I think, therefore," the dispatch concluded, "it is of the utmost importance that Negley's division be ordered to that point [the hills beyond the center of the army]—the left of my line." This was Thomas' thirteenth call for help since 2:00 A.M. He had done all he could to hold his weak salient on the Reed's bridge road. Where he needed a concentrated body of from eight to ten thousand men he received only driblets of brigade strength which were insufficient to block an all-out attack. If help would not come to him there was nothing left to do but to go for it. He turned his horse southward along the State road. From behind him came the spent bullets of Govan's men. From his left the Minié balls from the muskets of Gist, Walthall and Cleburne slashed through the trees. Ahead of him the gun smoke was rolling upward in billows. Even though the sound was muted by distance, Thomas knew it was an attack of major proportions. As nearly as he could place it, the attack was aimed at Brannan. That meant he had better get up that way and see what the trouble was, but first he had to get some help for his left.

Near the south end of Kelly's field Thomas found it. It was General Wood's division moving northward to support Reynolds. Thomas countermanded these orders and sent him to support Baird.[24] Wood's leading brigade under Barnes moved northward on the run while Wood turned south to bring up his other two brigades. Thomas continued on toward the firing. It was increasing in volume and seemed to be coming from a point farther west than when he had first heard it. This was puzzling. It might be Bragg's line moving westward or Van Cleve's reserve division going into action. Either one meant trouble on Thomas' right flank. If Wood's division moved in to help Baird, the left flank ought to be taken care of. Spurring his horse, Thomas rode southward toward the heaviest fighting.

He had lost all sense of time. He thought it was 2:00 P.M. when actually it was noon. At the height of Govan's attack Beatty had come to Thomas with a plea for another brigade and Thomas had sent Captain Kellogg to hurry Sheridan forward. Now as he rode out of the strip of woodland into the open of Dyer's field [25] he saw Kellogg coming toward him. Sheridan, he guessed, could not be far behind, although the firing ahead of him drew steadily nearer and its volume increased. Kellogg brought astonishing news. Rebel skirmishers had prevented him from reaching Sheridan. He had reported this fact to Harker,[26] commanding one of Wood's brigades, whose troops were deployed in Dyer's field facing south. Kellogg and Harker could both see troops advancing northward in the southern end of the field and they agreed that these were probably Sheridan's men marching to Thomas' relief.

Thomas felt now that he was losing his sense of reality. Harker's was one of the brigades that was supposed to have gone to Baird's support. An apprehension bordering on fear must have magnified his doubts and misgivings. To relieve them he rode on toward Harker, whose answer to his question was inconclusive. The advancing troops had not fired on him. He thought they wore blue uniforms and he had not fired at them. The troops were actually Longstreet's men, uniformed in blue of a slightly different shade from that of the Northern troops.

"Show your colors," Thomas ordered and the ostentatious display brought scattering shots from the south. Thomas' question was answered. There was no help to be had from Sheridan. What was left of the Army of the Cumberland must help itself.

Thomas ran over the situation in his mind. It looked hopeless. Baird's flank had been breaking up when he left it and the reinforcements he needed to stiffen it were not to be had. His front along the Kelly's field barricades was under heavy attack. Brannan's entire division was torn off of his right and now a powerful attack column was within a few hundred yards of his right rear. If the military debacle that now seemed certain became a fact, his Virginian birth would assure his ruin. Ten months before he had boasted to Halleck that he would so manage his command as to protect it from the mistakes of his superior. Now his boast had trapped him. He could not plead in mitigation that the tactics he would have used could have avoided

this pitfall. Fears of wounds, capture or death must have been in-
significant beside the hazard of command, but there were no other
shoulders to carry the load. With a calmness that must have belied an
inner trepidation, he picked up the reins of over-all command.

"I then rode to the crest of the hill referred to above," was Thomas'
sole statement about the crisis.

Laconic he may have been, but only because his emotions were
bottled up. His hat had been knocked off by a low hanging bough and
his face was clearly discernible. His lips were pale and compressed,
his jaw set, his brow furrowed into a scowl, his eyes almost hidden
by his shaggy eyebrows. On each cheek was a small round flush.

The hill "referred to above" was in plain sight half a mile northwest
of where Thomas sat talking to Harker. It was one of the transverse
spurs of Missionary Ridge, steep and heavily wooded except where the
northwest corner of Dyer's field carried a V-shaped clearing up to
the point where now stands the South Carolina monument. Thomas
started for this nameless hill. Six hours later it had become one of the
famous places in American history.

This hill, where Brannan had established his headquarters, was the
northeastern height of Snodgrass Ridge. On its northern declivity,
overlooking the farmlands, was the Snodgrass house. Southwest of it
along the Ridge were two other heights, the westernmost one being
north of Vittetoe's house. It averaged 100 feet in height from its base.
Except on its northeastern end, it was covered with trees and brush.
Between the high points were saddles. Ravines leading up to these
from the foot of the Ridge provided easier gradients and some cover
and these assets fixed the points for the heaviest attacks. This was the
defensive position that Thomas had selected the evening of the nineteenth and that Rosecrans had changed early in the morning of the
twentieth. At noon Brannan, looking for a place to stand with his
survivors, would naturally think of the ridge where Thomas had
posted him eighteen hours before.

On his way to this Ridge, Thomas met Wood, who confirmed the
fact that the advancing troops were Rebels. The strong division that
Wood had had in hand when he talked to Thomas not many minutes
before in the rear of Reynolds' barricades, was shattered. One brigade,
Barnes', was presumably with Baird. What was left of Harker's
brigade was fighting a holding action in Dyer's field. George P.
Buell's [27] brigade had dissolved—wounded, captured, dead or fugitives.
Wood was trying to rally the pitifully few survivors. He was unable
to tell Thomas what had happened. When he had left Thomas to

rejoin his command, after detaching Barnes, he had found the valley to the south of him swarming with the enemy. Nor were the survivors of Buell's brigade much help. They spoke of the enemy as "a host," "a great force," "overpowering numbers." They said the entire right and part of the center of the Army of the Cumberland had given way. Another said that all the Federal forces in view had fallen back.

One articulate officer told what had happened to the rear regiment in Buell's column. His skirmishers were engaged when the order came to pull out of the line and move to the left. He called them in, and their line was immediately occupied by the enemy. He feared that the order was a mistake or a blunder. Stray shots soon came whistling through the trees. Enemy fire increased in rapidity and came nearer. He received the order to move in double time. The brigade artillery was dashing along against trees and over stones at a headlong rate. The growing unsteadiness of the men made him anxious. A mass of fugitives struck his command, and, becoming completely mingled with it, carried it to the rear.

Beyond this, Wood knew little except that Brannan, who should have been near the State road with Reynolds, was now on Snodgrass Ridge with a few troops. Thomas rode on to the Ridge but before leaving he gave two more orders. Wood was to place what was left of his division on Snodgrass Ridge to connect with Brannan's left. Captain Kellogg was to notify Reynolds that his right had been turned and that the enemy was in his rear.

Brannan's division had broken up like Wood's. He had Croxton's brigade with him on the Ridge. He also had news of even worse disaster. The ferocity of the Rebel advance had driven the mass of Connell's brigade—men, horses, guns, caissons, battery wagons—into Sam Beatty's [28] brigade of Van Cleve's division and had disintegrated it. Its remnants, parts of two regiments and stragglers from the other two, Brannan had with him. A short time before, Negley had been on the Ridge with forty-eight guns, Sirwell's brigade and a large part of John Beatty's brigade of his own division and the greater part of Dick's brigade of Van Cleve's division. But now, with the exception of one regiment which Brannan had borrowed from Negley, they were gone and no survivor could tell him where.

Thomas established a sketchy headquarters in the lee of the Ridge just north of the Snodgrass house, and began to take stock of things. To the north and northeast he could see as far as the Ridge road and through one opening almost as far as the Cloud house. A strip of woods to the east blocked his view of Kelly's field. No one knew what

had happened to Rosecrans, McCook, Crittenden or the divisions of
Sheridan and Davis. One brigade of Van Cleve's division was with
Baird. The rest, except for parts of two regiments and a few stragglers,
were gone. One regiment and a few stragglers from Negley's division
were on the field. The rest were gone. One-third of Brannan's and
Wood's divisions were on the Ridge, one-third were with Baird, and
the rest were gone. All was quiet, except for occasional shots, along
the fronts of Baird, Johnson, Palmer and Reynolds, and Thomas assumed that they were all right. Kellogg had brought back word that
Reynolds had survived the Rebel assault in good shape, that he had
pulled back his line so that it faced south along the south edge of
Kelly's field astride the State road, and that the rest of the Kelly's field
force was intact and relatively unmolested. The woods to the north of
Snodgrass Ridge, between Missionary Ridge and Baird's left, were
thick with Forrest's dismounted troopers. Thomas and his men were
apparently cut off from Chattanooga. Baird's left was stronger than it
had been in the morning but it was still weak. There was a gap three-
quarters of a mile wide between the northeast end of Snodgrass Ridge
and the Kelly's field barricades. The 2,700 men under Brannan and
Wood were insufficient to defend the length of the Ridge, so it was only
a question of time before the Rebels would outflank them and drive
them off. All units were short of ammunition. Water was scarce.

Thomas' problem had two possible solutions—first, cut his way
through to Chattanooga; second, stay where he was and hope that the
rest of the army would cut its way through to his relief. His position
was hopeless unless he got some unforeseen breaks. It was desperate
at best. The men could appraise the situation as well as their general.
Victory they could not hope for but they believed they could hold their
ground as long as they had to.

It was the head of Longstreet's column under Hood's command that
had fired on Harker's waving flags in Dyer's field. Hood himself was
down, with a hip hopelessly shattered by a Yankee bullet. Kershaw
had settled the matter of relative rank with Bushrod Johnson on the
field and had taken over Hood's command. Harker made a short
stand along a fence row but Kershaw soon drove him out and Harker
retreated to Snodgrass Ridge. At about 2:00 P.M., Kershaw's line
halted along its southwestern base and looked up at its defenders like
a hunting pack treeing a coon. His left was near the Vittetoe house
and it overlapped Brannan's line on the Ridge by nearly half a mile.
His tactical problem was to get on the Ridge southwest of Brannan's
position and then sweep northeastward driving the Yankees before

him. There was a ravine to the right of Brannan's position and the Rebel assault columns moved into position to take advantage of it.

Thomas received the news of the Rebel preparations for assault at his headquarters. The accepted countermove was to bring up troops from the Kelly's field barricades to support Brannan. But the problem was not quite that simple. A little more than a mile off to the north, in the vicinity of the Cloud house, dense billows of dust were rising from the tree tops. Forrest was known to be in that vicinity. It was from that direction that the two Rebel flank movements had developed against Baird. No troops could be moved from Kelly's field with this threat against their flank. The pattern of the dust cloud indicated moving infantry and this was soon borne out by the flashes of sunlight reflected from the polished surfaces of the rifle barrels and bayonets. While the threat of an enemy column marching up from the north kept Thomas from shifting regiments to Brannan's aid, there grew a dim hope that the troops might be friendly. The divisions of Negley and Van Cleve, with brigades from Wood and Brannan, had been swept off the field in that direction. Some of these troops had rallied after an initial repulse and had fought well in the cedar brakes at Stones River. Perhaps they would do it again. If Granger were answering Thomas' call for help he would come from that direction. A dozen glasses were leveled on the approaching ranks in an effort to read the riddle.

Thomas' self-control was rapidly breaking down under the strain of uncertainty. The greater the tension the more Thomas fussed with his beard. Now it was standing out from his face at all angles. His horse felt the emotional tension and refused to stand still long enough for the general to focus his glasses, so he appealed to one of his staff with a steadier horse to identify the colors of the approaching troops. Finally he requested an aide to run the gauntlet of the Rebel sharpshooters and resolve the uncertainty. The aide was gone some time and the nervous suspense became almost unbearable. When the aide finally returned with news that it was Steedman's[29] division of Granger's reserve corps that was approaching, Thomas' customary taciturnity returned and he smoothed out his tangled whiskers.

Thomas' first order was for Steedman to take his men to the left and fill the gap between the Ridge and Kelly's field, but before this could be executed a report came from Brannan that Rebel artillery and infantry were on the Ridge to his right. The Twenty-first Ohio Volunteer Infantry had discouraged the first Rebel assaults on Brannan's right with their Colt revolving rifles, but the fast build-up of

Rebel strength proved too much for them. Steedman's orders were changed to meet this new threat. This incident illustrates the soundness of Thomas' military judgment. He had to drive off a force dominating his right and he had to plug the hole between Snodgrass Ridge and Kelly's field before the enemy could exploit it. He wavered momentarily between the alternatives. The orthodox solution, to divide Steedman's force between the two spots, would have worked if part of his force had been powerful enough to take and hold the Ridge. Otherwise, division would have been fatal. He did, however, send one of Steedman's batteries to his left to join the two already there. These eighteen guns might check an enemy movement long enough to shift infantry to the threatened point. The correctness of these quiet decisions built up the confidence of the Cumberlanders in Thomas.

Steedman countermarched his brigades, moved them around the north and west sides of the Snodgrass house and, carrying the colors of one of his Illinois regiments, personally led his men up the Ridge against the sheeted fire of the Gray infantry and two batteries. He deployed them four lines deep on a front of seven regiments. His two heavy brigades, numbering some 4,000 men, outnumbered the Rebels at the point of attack, threw them off the crest of the Ridge and chased them down its south slope.

This storming of Snodgrass Ridge by Steedman's men was the most spectacular and profitable counterattack of the day from the Union point of view. It was also the most contrary to reason. There was no artillery preparation, no diversionary attack, no surprise. Every element that would make it a success was lacking but one. That was an energetic ardor that was almost a passion. It accomplished in twenty minutes what Longstreet tried for six hours to do. The Army of Tennessee lost its *élan* on the south slope of Snodgrass Ridge while, on the north slope, the Army of the Cumberland discovered its own latent power.

Before Steedman's men could catch their breaths, the Rebels counterattacked with fresh troops, but unsuccessfully. Steedman's losses were appalling. In twenty-five minutes he lost between one third and one half of his strength. But his strike was so sudden, so savage and so thorough that the Rebel officers had all they could do to keep their troops from panicking. Appeals, commands and physical efforts were unsuccessful in getting all the survivors back in line. Some persisted in skulking behind trees or lying on the ground.

Along the fire-wreathed crest of Snodgrass Ridge, half a dozen brigades of the Army of the Cumberland waged the last desperate struggle of the Battle of Chickamauga against Longstreet's seventeen brigades. The bayonet was frequently used. Men were smashed out of action by the blows of musket butts. Prisoners and colors were captured by both sides. The odds against Thomas on the Ridge must have been in the neighborhood of three to one. Longstreet wasted this advantage in frontal assaults while the northeastern flank of the Ridge lay almost at his mercy. Nor was there any coordination between the wings of Polk and Longstreet. Most of the morning Polk attacked while Longstreet waited. Most of the afternoon Longstreet attacked while Polk waited. When they struck together at 11:00 A.M. the Union line broke. When they struck together at sundown they swept the Yankees off the field.

The attacks on Steedman's sector, for example, were not sustained. There was a three-quarter-hour lull after the Rebels' first counterattack was beaten off. Following this lull there were successive attacks of varying duration but with distinct pauses between. Along other sectors of the Ridge, however, the attacks were furious and unceasing. Steedman had demonstrated to Longstreet that the Ridge defense was vulnerable to a proper assault. Longstreet had watched Lee shatter his army at Gettysburg with unsupported frontal assaults, yet it was nearly sundown before he mounted an all-out attack. Then he put in his reserves against the weak northeastern flank of the Ridge and gained and held the heights. Thomas realized the tremendous advantage he was deriving from Longstreet's poor tactics. "The damned scoundrels," he said, "were fighting without any system."

Thomas often came within speaking distance of the men in the front lines. When he saw a unit that was threatened with being overrun he would strengthen it with help brought from another part of the line which was not so hardly pressed. He was ever mindful of the influence upon the men of his own attitude and that of his staff. Once he sent word to Brannan, who was out of ammunition and under heavy pressure. "Tell General Brannan that his is my old division and that they will hold their position." Another time he called back one of his aides who was dashing off with a message and told him to ride leisurely, as he did not want to get the troops excited. At one crisis of the battle, when it seemed almost certain that the Rebels were about to overrun the crest, another aide who had started on an errand turned back to Thomas, saluted and asked, "General, after delivering your order, where shall I report to you?"

"Here, Sir, here," replied Thomas impatiently.

Harker used volley firing to beat off the attacks launched against the northeastern end of the Ridge. He fought his men in two ranks. While one rank was firing the other would be reloading, well protected by the reverse slope. Then they would step to the top and fire while the other rank reloaded.

Besides winning and holding the key position on Snodgrass Ridge, Granger's advance improved Thomas' position in two other ways. He brought with him 90,000 rounds of ammunition which were immediately distributed to the troops on the Ridge at the rate of about ten rounds per man. He also posted the brigade of Daniel McCook at the Cloud house. This kept open the State road to Rossville and the Ridge road to McFarland's Gap and proved to be of material help in covering Thomas' retreat at sundown.

Immediately after Granger's arrival, Garfield, Rosecrans' chief-of-staff, and two of Thomas' aides who had been sent to the rear for ammunition, came in from Rossville by way of the eastern side of Missionary Ridge. A little ammunition came with them and this was distributed to the men around Kelly's field. Garfield brought Thomas the first reliable information that the right and center of the army had been driven off the field. The other news he brought was even more depressing. He knew of no ammunition closer than Chattanooga, nor were there any reinforcements to be had from Rossville. Negley was there with one battery and some infantry but Garfield had ordered him to stay there to cover the retreat of the trains. There was at least a battalion of enemy troops west of the State road beween the McDonald house and the north end of Kelly's field. The implication was obvious. A battalion now meant a division soon. If this division moved south in conjunction with another moving north between Harker and Reynolds, Thomas' command would be split and destroyed. It was the same catastrophe that had hung over him since one o'clock. Now it seemed imminent.

Garfield had nearly lost his life in the half-mile between the State road and the Snodgrass house but relief over his escape was not his dominant emotion when he reached Thomas. "I shall never forget my amazement and admiration," he said, "when I beheld Thomas holding his own with utter defeat on each side and wild confusion in the rear."

"We have repulsed every attack so far," Thomas told him, "and we can hold our ground if the enemy can be kept from our rear."

Garfield's heart was in his mouth.

Coincident with Garfield's arrival was that of Major Gates P. Thruston. Thomas thought he had come in with Garfield, but Thruston had come to him from the west, from where the Dry Valley road lay along the eastern face of Missionary Ridge just before it plunged through McFarland's Gap. In a straight line this was about a mile and a half from the northeast extremity of Snodgrass Ridge. The trip could not be made in a straight line, however. Thruston had tried it and run into the enemy, but a slight detour to the north cleared them. Thomas was a few steps below the crest of the Ridge, intently watching the battle when Thruston found him and told him that Sheridan and Davis with the remnants of five brigades were within easy supporting distance. Thomas listened to the report, thanked Thruston and requested him to go back and try to bring up Sheridan and Davis with their troops to strengthen his right. Thruston left at 4:00 P.M. on his return trip.

Half an hour after Granger reported to Thomas, Van Derveer's brigade of Brannan's division, consisting of 1,200 men, marched up to the Ridge and was put into position between Brannan and Steedman.

Van Derveer, after helping fight off the eleven-o'clock attack against Baird's left, was picking up his wounded in Kelly's field when he heard heavy firing to his left rear. Having already learned that the remainder of Brannan's division was engaged there he faced his men toward the sound of the guns, ordered out his skirmishers, and gave the command to march. The brigade moved cautiously almost due west through a wooded area that seemed to be a sort of no-man's-land, and cut their way through some enemy forces. When they emerged from the woods into Snodgrass field they were met by one of Thomas' aides, who conducted them into another strip of the woods that was filled with troops. Here Thomas rode up, gave some instructions to Van Derveer and then sat quietly upon his horse watching the regiments file by on their way to the battle line. When the Second Minnesota went by— one of the regiments that had fought with him at Mill Springs—he told their lieutenant colonel that he was glad to see the regiment in such good order. Years later Lieutenant Colonel Bishop wrote, "We did not know how many troops he had seen in disorder during the day, nor did he know that within an hour's fighting we had just lost more than one third of our regiment in killed and wounded, yet we greatly appreciated the compliment at the time."

Along the Kelly's field barricades, except for an occasional shot from the musket of a Rebel sharpshooter, quiet had prevailed for two hours. Everything seemed safe except for the heavy and insistent firing from Snodgrass Ridge in their rear. Thomas had not been seen along the barricades since the eleven-o'clock attack. The troops there had watched Steedman's flags turn west from the State road and heard the crescendo of battle as his men went into action. Thomas, they assumed, was with the engaged flank. He might be wounded. There was a chance that the enemy might drive a wedge between the wings of the Army of the Cumberland and force on them a battle of annihilation. There was a consultation of the division commanders and it was suggested that Palmer, who was the ranking officer on the field, take command of what was left of Thomas' original line and order a retreat. Palmer refused.

As the clamor of battle increased along Snodgrass Ridge the opinion grew among some of these same general officers that help should be sent to their beset comrades. There was more discussion and Palmer ordered Hazen to go. Hazen moved off on the run, deploying in line of battle on a front of two regiments. He lost almost as many men during this half-mile march as he did in four hours behind the breastworks. Palmer heard his volley as he went into action. Hazen's brigade extended Harker's line in an easterly direction and helped close the gap between Snodgrass Ridge and Kelly's field. Baird, at the same time, sent word to Thomas that he had two regiments available if needed and Reynolds inched westward to get a little closer to Hazen. Coordination was finally established between the wings of the army.

Rosecrans, who had left Garfield at Rossville, reached Chattanooga at 3:40 P.M. At 3:45 Garfield sent him the news of the battlefield. It went by courier to Rossville and from there to Chattanooga by telegraph. He reported the hope that Thomas could hold on until dark and would not need to fall back farther than Rossville. There was a hint that he might not need to fall back at all. Garfield urged that all combat troops be stopped at Rossville to hold the roads between Missionary Ridge and Lookout Mountain, and that Rosecrans move up to Rossville with ammunition. At 4:15 P.M., Rosecrans sent an order to Thomas which read, "Assume command of all the forces, and with Crittenden and McCook take a strong position and assume a threatening attitude at Rossville. Send all the unorganized force to this place for reorganization. I will examine the ground here and make such dispositions for defense as the case may require and join you. Have sent out ammunition and rations." [30]

Thomas probably received this order about 5:30 P.M. He had already made up his mind to retreat but for the safety of the army he did not want to begin this movement before sundown. It was a difficult and dangerous military maneuver, for the enemy was in sight or hearing of his lines for every foot of their length. The first sign of withdrawal would start a murderous assault that was bound to break his line at some point and start rolling up the flanks.

He decided to start the retreat with the four divisions around Kelly's field, where the hard fighting had ceased about noon. Reynolds, with the farthest to go, would move first, leading the column northward along the State road and then westward along the Ridge road to Mc-Farland's Gap. He would be followed in succession by Palmer, Johnson and Baird. Daniel McCook, with his brigade at the Cloud house, would cover the withdrawal. An aide was sent to alert the division commanders for the movement. The Snodgrass Ridge forces would hold their lines until the Kelly's field defenders had passed along the Ridge road. Then they would commence their withdrawal.

At 5:30 P.M. Thomas sent an aide to Reynolds with orders to begin the withdrawal. At the same time Thomas rode east towards Reynolds' position.

Unknown to Thomas, three things happened almost simultaneously with his departure from the Snodgrass house. Polk ordered an attack against the Kelly's field barricades, Buckner put his artillery on the State road near the burning Poe house and was firing northward against Reynolds' southern front with eleven guns at 600 yards' range, and Longstreet's reserve, finally being committed to the fight, advanced against Snodgrass Ridge over Kershaw's played-out troops. This was the total assault against the entire line that Thomas had been dreading all afternoon. It left no opportunity to shift men to a threatened point from one that was not so warmly engaged. His ammunition shortage made it probable that his line would be broken somewhere and subjected to the inevitable onset at the broken flanks. This made a Union withdrawal a dubious and bloody maneuver. In Thomas' opinion retreat was inevitable but he hoped to make it at nightfall when he would be relieved of enemy pressure. It was the coincidence of Longstreet's and Polk's attack orders with Thomas' retreat orders that gave the withdrawal the elements of confusion, disorganization and panic.

Thomas learned the news of Polk's attack a little at a time. The first intimation came to him from two of his soldiers whom he met in the woods near the State road between the barricades and the Snodgrass house. They told him that a large Rebel force was in the wood to the north deployed in a line at right angles to the State road and advancing south to occupy the ground on which Thomas' horse then stood. This meant that the enemy had turned Baird's left for the third time that day and were across the army's retreat route.

Just then Thomas saw Reynolds riding at the head of his withdrawal column. Thomas ordered him to form a line perpendicular to the State road facing north. Turchin drew the assignment and his men promptly moved into position. Thomas ordered them forward to clear the woods. The brigade yelled, rushed forward with twin lines of two regiments each, overwhelmed the skirmishers of Govan's column, and cleared the west side of the State road to Dan McCook's brigade a mile and a half north. McCook's artillery added to the discomfiture of the Rebels. Turchin took 250 prisoners and overran two Rebel guns but could not get them off the field because the gun teams were disabled. Thomas and Garfield watched the attack. Garfield was much impressed and made a report of it in some detail when he telegraphed Rosecrans from Rossville that night. Garfield's account doubled the number of Turchin's prisoners. Dana picked up Garfield's account and sent it to Stanton the next day and Lincoln must have read with interest how the officer whose military reputation he had saved a few months before [31] rendered such conspicuous service to the army.

Reynolds' other brigade marched north behind Turchin. These two brigades, in combination with Daniel McCook and Willich's brigade of Johnson's division, formed a defense line which covered both roads leading to Rossville. Behind this protection the tattered divisions that had held the barricades filed westward toward McFarland's Gap.

As Reynolds moved north on the State road, Palmer, Johnson and Baird fell back in succession across Kelly's field. As they went they were pounded by Buckner's artillery from the south and lanced at by Polk's storm troops, who climbed over the barricades and overran their rear guards. Palmer took many casualties. Johnson got his men back in better shape by covering their retreat with his reserve brigade. Baird was under such heavy attack along his front that he hesitated to withdraw, but the retreat of Johnson, Palmer and Reynolds left him no choice. His men took a fearful punishment.

Thomas now began the withdrawal of the troops that held Snodgrass Ridge.[32] Steedman moved first, dropping back to a ridge north of the one he had defended all afternoon. The rest of the force, Hazen, Wood and Brannan, moved northward in a column to the Ridge road and then turned westward towards McFarland's Gap. At 7:30 P.M. the rear guard broke its formation and started for Rossville—Reynolds through McFarland's Gap and McCook along the State road. At 8:40 P.M. the head of Thomas' column was entering Rossville. At 1:30 A.M., September 21, Thomas was at Granger's headquarters at Rossville deploying the army to defend Chattanooga. This was the third successive night he had gone without sleep.

Sheridan later described Thomas as he looked and acted when he reached Rossville. "The General appeared very much exhausted, seemed to forget what he stopped for, and said little or nothing of the incidents of the day . . . his quiet unobtrusive demeanor communicating a gloomy rather than a hopeful view of the situation. This apparent depression was due no doubt to the severe trial through which he had gone in the last forty-eight hours, which strain had exhausted him very much both physically and mentally. His success in maintaining his ground was undoubtedly largely influenced by the fact that two-thirds of the National forces [33] had been sent to his succor, but his firm purpose to save the army was the mainstay on which all relied after Rosecrans left the field. . . ."

Two days after the battle Thomas learned in detail what had happened on his right flank at 11:00 A.M. on the twentieth. Until that time, no consequential fighting had taken place on Brannan's front nor on any of Rosecrans' line south of that point. All the noise, smoke and dust from Thomas' left and his incessant calls for Negley led Rosecrans to believe that Bragg was throwing all of his strength at Thomas' barricades. A dispatch from Thomas shortly after 10:35 A.M. seemed to confirm this conclusion; yet a skirmish line pushed a couple of hundred yards in advance of Brannan, Wood and Davis would, in ten minutes, have demonstrated the falsity of this supposition. In any event, just about the time that Rosecrans learned that Thomas was under heavy pressure, Captain Kellogg rode up with another request from Thomas for reinforcements. In addition Kellogg brought a message from Reynolds that there were no troops on his right. But Reynolds was in error. Brannan was there just where he should have been. Previously, however, there had been an intention of moving Brannan to the left and Rosecrans supposed that this movement had been executed. Without investigation, he sent a written order to Wood, who occupied the line on Brannan's right. The order went by courier and was marked "gallop" and the time was 10:45 A.M. It read, "The general commanding directs that you close up on Reynolds as fast as possible and support him." Wood received this order about 11:00 A.M. Since Brannan's division lay between Wood and Reynolds, Wood had to pull his men out of the line and march them northward behind Brannan until they reached Reynolds' rear. There is evidence that Wood knew he should have protested this order before executing it.

The cessation of the attack on Thomas' barricades and the lack of action against the center of Rosecrans' line was pure coincidence. Hood, opposite the Brotherton house, had not completed his deployment when the time came for him to move. He was ready at just about 11:00 A.M. His troops occupied a front of four divisions—from left to right, T. C. Hindman, Hood's own division, Bushrod Johnson, and A. P. Stewart. J. B. Kershaw was held as a reserve. This was Longstreet's main column of attack. It moved forward just as Wood was pulling out of the line. At the same time Davis was moving north to fill the gap left by Wood, and Sheridan was closing up to fill the gap left by Davis.

Hood's line swept straight ahead through these fluid columns, throwing the broken brigades of Davis and Sheridan onto the shoulders of Missionary Ridge west of the Dry Valley road. Hood ordered a right wheel to direct his striking power against Harker in Dyer's field and Brannan on Snodgrass Ridge behind him. There was confusion in the Confederate ranks while these lines were re-forming and the Texas brigade began to waver. This had been Hood's first command as a general officer and he rode up to it and demanded its colors, the accepted way of showing a loss of confidence in a unit. The Texans rallied and charged. During this interlude a bullet smashed into the upper third of Hood's right leg. He swayed in the saddle as the support of stirrup, knee and thigh failed, and fell heavily into the arms of some of the Texans. His leg was amputated that night in the field hospital of his division and the Texas brigade collected a fund to buy him an artificial one.

When Hood's attack exploded through Brannan's position, Reynolds' division was left hanging onto the south end of what was left of Thomas' original line. It was a perilous situation. Reynolds had to relieve his right flank from the pressure of the victorious Rebel regiments exploiting the breakthrough and he had to do it quickly. To give him the respite he needed, he ordered the 105th Regiment of Ohio Volunteer Infantry to change front to the south and drive back Hood's flank. It was an annihilation order, but the troops obeyed it. Nine hundred men launched their little thunderbolt against an army corps. The suddenness of their movement, the dense undergrowth which hid from the enemy the meagerness of their strength, and the unevenness of the ground which compelled the regiment to extend its front to more than a regimental interval all worked in their favor. The first Rebel line was crumpled back on the second and the 105th came to a halt and opened fire. The audacity of their charge gave Reynolds the time he needed to form his new line and Thomas thanked them publicly for their help after he had heard their story.

When Hood broke through the Yankee line the troops of Davis and Sheridan were driven westward, but Harker's counterattack in Dyer's field kept them from being pursued. They were disorganized, however, and their officers were unable to re-form them. Many of them drifted northward along the Dry Valley road. At 12:15 P.M. Rosecrans considered the situation hopeless and left for Chattanooga to do what he could to counter the seemingly inevitable rout of his army. McCook evidently left between 1:30 and 2:00 P.M. Crittenden left after Rosecrans but before McCook. None of these officers took troops with them. It happened that on the morning of the twentieth Colonel Parkhurst, who was acting as Thomas' provost marshal, was moving south on the Dry Valley road. About 12:30 P.M. stragglers began to appear in front of him. At 1:00 a large body of troops, several batteries and transportation wagons came rushing through the woods and over the road in the utmost confusion. Parkhurst formed his men in a line and stopped the fugitives. At 2:30 P.M., these troops, which made up a sizable command, were within one-half mile of the Vittetoe house. They were ordered to Rossville by Crittenden. Parkhurst's line had blocked the northbound traffic on the Dry Valley road so that at 2:00 there was a jam of ammunition wagons extending as far south as Vittetoe's. The Confederates appropriated the ammunition from these wagons and used it that afternoon against Thomas. The road they were on skirted the southwestern end of Snodgrass Ridge at a distance never greater than two or three miles from the Snodgrass house. Sometime between 2:00 and 3:00 P.M. Davis and Sheridan, with several thousand of their troops, were on this part of the road and the way was open to Thomas' right. Thruston rode it twice. Two medical directors joined Thomas by the same route. When Thruston reached Sheridan and Davis with Thomas' request for aid, Negley was with them. Davis immediately started his troops to Thomas' support and arrived in time to help cover the retreat. Sheridan and Negley ignored the plea and continued on their way to Rossville. J. B. Fry was of the opinion that Sheridan lost his head at Chickamauga. He spoke of him as wandering back to Rossville. His action could not be explained, Fry wrote, upon any theory except that he was dazed.[34]

Negley's conduct was even more inexplicable. Having finally been relieved by Wood and ordered by Thomas to the command of the artillery, he did some good work with his guns in helping turn back the eleven-o'clock attack on the north end of Kelly's field. Shortly after this Brannan met him on Snodgrass Ridge and borrowed his strongest regiment. Before Harker could join Brannan, it became expedient, in Negley's judgment, to remove the artillery to Rossville.[35]

Thomas knew all about what happened when Hood's battle line wheeled to its right at the south end of Dyer's field and started north toward Snodgrass Ridge but he did not know until a couple of days later what happened on Snodgrass Ridge and Kelly's field after Turchin's charge had cleared his army's retreat route.

All during the afternoon of the twentieth Longstreet had been apprehensive of a Yankee cavalry attack on his left and rear, and he held his reserve uncommitted to oppose it. Sometime between 4:00 and 5:00 P.M. he determined to use this reserve in an effort to breach the Snodgrass line. His attack began to move just after Thomas had left the Ridge to lead the retreat of the Kelly's field troops. Gracie's brigade of Alabama troops advanced first, and Kelly followed him after a ten-minute interval. Kelly's men evidently gained the crest of the Ridge first. Gracie came up shortly afterwards. The Union counterattack was delivered with speed and power and it is probable that the locked lines (they were facing each other in places over a twenty-yard interval) swayed back and forth over the Ridge as one side and then the other gained the ascendency. Both Gracie and Kelly called for reinforcements and Trigg's brigade was brought up from its position near the Brotherton house. Trigg had to move nearly a mile and a half and deploy to get into position. Darkness had fallen before the Ridge was finally cleared of its Yankee defenders. The strength of Longstreet's reserve and that of Steedman's brigades were nearly equal. The Rebels went in a brigade at a time and required an hour and a half or more to do the job that Steedman's massed assault accomplished in twenty minutes. Steedman's losses ran about the same as those of the Confederates. The economy of force that Thomas practiced in 1863 is today one of the basic tenets of the United States Marines' assault doctrine.

Chickamauga opened like the Battle of Gettysburg, inasmuch as neither side looked for nor was prepared for battle at the time and place where it happened. Each battle turned out to be the most publicized of its theater of the war. In each the waywardness of a subordinate ruined the plans of his commanding general—Longstreet's stubbornness and Wood's vindictiveness. Lee's army never recovered from its defeat at Gettysburg and Bragg's never recovered from its victory at Chickamauga.

Next to Gettysburg, Chickamauga was the bloodiest battle of the war. Yet only sixty to sixty-five thousand troops were engaged on each side. In percentage of losses, Chickamauga's casualties were heavier than those of any other Civil War battle.[36] In Steedman's charge against the Ridge, Preston's assault farther east, and Helm's fight at the barricades, the losses, both relative and absolute, were cripplingly heavy. The exact casualties of the battle were never known. The best guess put the Union loss at 16,179 and the Rebel loss at 17,804. Preston's Second Alabama Battalion had its colors pierced eighty-three times. In another of his battalions the losses ran to more than 70 per cent. It was this savage mauling that destroyed the *élan* of the Army of Tennessee.

Just after noon, when Forrest reported the approach of Granger's divisions from the north, the commanders of Polk's right elements thought of retiring from the field. At 3:00 it was Bragg's opinion that his Right Wing was fought out. Chickamauga was the only battle in which Hazen saw the opposing lines advance to close quarters and fire in each other's faces. In this battle the Army of the Cumberland learned to take cover. The reports are full of orders for the troops to lie down, although the ranks mostly rose to fire. Along the Ridge, however, some of the men fought through the afternoon using trees for shelter. The greatest lesson they learned was one Thomas had been trying to teach them since the days of Camp Dick Robinson. When the Rebels advanced, the Yanks noticed that they pulled down their hat brims or bent their heads as if they were walking into a storm. They looked at the ground instead of at the enemy and kept their alignment and direction by touching the man on each side of them with their elbows. If enough men could be shot out of the front line to break this physical contact, the survivors became confused, hesitated and fell back. This was one of the great defensive discoveries of the war for the Cumberlanders.

A curious aspect of the Chickamauga campaign was the sudden reversal of Northern fortunes at 11:00 A.M. on the twentieth. From June 23 to the morning of September 9, Rosecrans' movements were flawless. But in that early morning meeting with Thomas, Rosecrans made his first military error. From that time until 11:00 A.M., September 20, nearly everything went wrong. There were the misreading of Bragg's plans, the conflicting orders that delayed McCook's close-up on Thomas, the failure to hold the offensive the morning of the nineteenth, McCook's delay in relieving Negley on the twentieth and finally the astounding cascade of orders that descended upon Brannan,

Negley, Wood, Van Cleve, Davis and Sheridan just prior to 11:00 resulting in the wrecking of Rosecrans' reputation and the loss of the battle.

At the moment Thomas picked up the responsibility which Rosecrans had dropped, the situation began to improve. Granger started his march southward; Brannan picked a strong position on Snodgrass Ridge; Harker fought a delaying action in Dyer's field; Polk broke off his attack against the barricades; Reynolds checked an army corps with a regiment and won time to form a new line.

In two and one half hours the situation had bettered to the point where men talked of defeating the enemy. Thomas had made no flamboyant military moves to bring about this change. He had moved quietly to the spot of greatest danger, approved the orders of Brannan and Wood and sent a warning to Reynolds. A newspaper correspondent who was an eye-witness maintained that the men's confidence in Thomas insured the safety of what was left of the Army of the Cumberland. Other observers have said of the situation, "One of those crises had now arrived, rare in the history of any country, where the personal character and power of an individual becomes of incalculable value to the general welfare. Only the highest qualities in the second-in-command, thus instantly left in charge of the abandoned field, saved the Army of the Cumberland from incredible ruin." [37] One of Reynolds' junior lieutenants, who would have known little about tactics, experienced the psychological uplift that came from Thomas' calm presence and inflexible resolve. He recalled how Thomas gathered up the shattered forces and welded them into an army without regiments, brigades or divisions, where rank counted for nothing but each man grasped a gun and lay side by side in the long line while along it rode Thomas who, without appeals, without words, without clamor, turned doubt into determination and rout into resistance. As he rode the men cheered and their clustered flags dipped in salutation.

It was a soldier's battle. The woods north of the Ridge and west of Kelly's field were filled with stragglers but few malingerers. When the fire grew hot they made their way to the front, by divisions like the men of Granger, by brigades like the men of Van Derveer and Hazen, by regiments, by companies and, surprisingly, singly and by unorganized groups. They took their places in the line, not because they were ordered to fight but for some stronger reason that no description of Chickamauga has ever explained. Wood saw some men pick up their wounded, carry them below the crest for safety and return immediately to take their places in the line. Turchin, whose charge at dusk opened the escape route, said that the spontaneous rally on Snodgrass Ridge was an expression of the character of the American volunteer, who prefers to fight single-handed on his own account rather than as a cipher among thousands.

It was to his men that Thomas gave the credit for the miracle of Chickamauga. "On that sunny, September afternoon," he afterward told Garfield, "as they stood in a half-circle facing the enemy that again and again poured a superior force three lines deep upon our front, not a man of them but knew that our right had been shattered and our left disorganized, and yet the brave fellows plied their guns, cool, firm and determined. They made success possible under all circumstances."

The men had a different story. It was told piece by piece at the G.A.R. encampments and written in the sketches published by the Loyal Legion. One of their spokesmen was James S. Ostrander. Under the title *Two September Days,* he wrote: "The Army of the Cumberland dies hard. Seven skeleton divisions, their dead and living equal, desperately maintain a battle for whose success the entire army was all too weak. There is no hope for aid. Burnside is 100 miles away. Only night is left to pray for. Disaster is closing in everywhere. Yet under the shadow of a spreading oak, near Snodgrass house, is a grizzled soldier, calm, silent, immovable, who resolves to hold the field until night comes—hemmed in by appalling ruin yet supreme above disaster —The Rock of Chickamauga."

From the time Thomas' men walked into Bragg's trap in Mc-Lemore's Cove on September 10, the Army of the Cumberland was under a heavy strain. The enemy was being reinforced from all sides, yet no aid came to them. Thirteen times Burnside was ordered to their support, yet in the end he was farther away than he had been in the beginning. McCook's delay in closing up was nerve-wracking and his forced march of fifty-seven mountain miles wore out his men and animals. Thomas' inversion march on the night of the eighteenth, with little or nothing to eat for twenty-four hours, took a heavy toll of the energies of the Fourteenth Army Corps. Officers began to crack. The cavalry commander left for the railhead in an ambulance. Negley was ill but stayed on his feet. Garfield reported himself as half dead with fatigue. Dana, with no military obligations whatsoever, lapsed into near hysteria.

Rosecrans, with the greatest responsibility, felt the greatest strain. By 11:00 A.M. on the twentieth he apparently lost control of himself and certainly of his army. As he rode to the rear it seemed to his staff that he neither saw nor heard. His nerve and will seemed to have collapsed. When he reached Chattanooga he had to be helped from his horse. Irresolution replaced his former buoyancy. One historian who met Rosecrans occasionally after the war thought he always saw the shadow of Chickamauga on his face.

The battle was unnecessary, since Rosecrans had had a week during which he could have moved his army into Chattanooga unmolested. It was fought on an unknown and unmapped terrain, with visibility, except where a cleared field intervened, limited to a few yards. Undoubtedly the physical weariness and mental uncertainty of the Union's general officers was the cause of many of the unexplainable happenings on that field.

Up to the time of Chickamauga, the army had considered Thomas an artillerist. His reputation from Buena Vista and the way in which his gun blasts helped save the army along Stones River were grounds enough for this belief. He intended using his guns at Chickamauga, but, undismayed by the wreckage of his plans, he showed his versatility by saving the army without them.

Chickamauga was one of the most singular battles of the war in that the commanding generals of both sides left the field in the afternoon of the twentieth giving the impression that they considered the battle lost. At least this was the impression Bragg gave Longstreet, although Bragg may have been sulking because the battle had not worked out the way he had planned. He was temperamentally unfitted for a quick shifting of his plans.[38] At any rate the ranking subordinate became the dominant figure on the field for both armies.

Thomas' ability to shift quickly from a plan that had failed to one that succeeded gave military significance to the Battle of Chickamauga. This happened four times. The first was on the afternoon of the nineteenth when, as at Stones River, the line broke to the right of Thomas' position and endangered his flank. The second was caused by Negley's failure to appear. This was a stretched-out crisis lasting more than three hours and was met by patch-work reinforcements, mostly secured and positioned by Thomas, but aided by two brigades sent by Rosecrans and others dug up by Baird. The fourth came at dusk on the twentieth, when he discovered his escape route blocked and cleared it with Turchin's bayonet charge.

The third crisis was so sudden, so disastrous and so complete that, to many, it seemed insoluble. It came when Thomas rode out of the shade of the pine woods into the noonday glare of Dyer's field and learned in one glance that his left had not been strengthened and that his broken right was threatened with overwhelming force. The shock had stunned Rosecrans and two of his corps commanders into apathetic resignation. At any moment it could resolve Thomas' command into panic. A show of nervousness on his part, a sign of indecision, an order to retreat—any one of these might have been enough to trigger the rout. Years of mental rehearsal on how to meet any conceivable crisis had trained him in what to do. The simple solution was to form a defense perimeter and stand fast. Three quiet orders initiated the movement and Thomas rode without haste to the top of the hill where the defense line was to be formed. He had averted a panic but the problem was still unsolved. His defense perimeter was too long for the number of men he had available. Yet even if Thomas lacked the men to solve his military problem he brought psychological reinforcement to their aid.

From confident hope in the morning, through discouragement, doubt, despair, and back to confident hope again, the morale of the remnants of the Army of the Cumberland swung the full cycle. Thomas, who always regretted his inability to make a successful emotional appeal to his individual soldiers, had discovered that he could overcome mass fear with rational stimuli.

At noon, Thomas' army would have been unanimous in claiming success for itself if it fought off the Rebel attacks until nightfall. Five hours later significant parts of that army began to question such a limited objective. They looked to the ultimate success—the destruction of Bragg's army. But Thomas was not to be caught in a trap of his own making. There had been no consequential margin between survival and destruction. Pure luck had dipped the balance to the favorable side. Thomas decided to retreat. Later he received Rosecrans' order substantiating this decision. His men were wearier than they realized. Their losses in almost every unit had passed the theoretical breaking point. By the time the army reached Rossville, Thomas' decision was justified in the eyes of its chief critic. At 1:30 A.M. on the twenty-first, Garfield advised Rosecrans, "We do not seem to be in the best trim for an early fight."

The irony of Chickamauga lay in the fact that the combat color of defeat impressed the public more than the solid competence of victory. Thomas' role in a battle he would never have fought, compounded of mistakes he would never have made, remains green. His victory a little more than a year later, which shifted the war's center of gravity, is all but forgotten. Legend dims reality.

Snodgrass Ridge lay dark under the heavy foliage of its trees. Early in the afternoon the shadow of Missionary Ridge began to slide along its crest. The powder smoke, trapped by the foliage, was augmented by the smoke from burning leaves. It stung the eyelids of the living and charred the uniforms and blackened the flesh of the wounded and dead. The air was close and stifling. Distance seemed to shrink so that the scene was flattened like a Japanese print. The atmosphere lacked luminosity and seemed filled with foreboding.

In contrast to the somber tones of Snodgrass Ridge, Kelly's field was still filled with sunshine, open sky, distance, panorama and light greens, blues and yellows. Here the grim fighting of Chickamauga displayed a panoply unlike the monotonous slugging along the Ridge. Kelly's field had been the objective of Thomas' inversion march on the night of the eighteenth. Brannan had halted there early the next morning for his men to cook a breakfast they never ate. Baird had left his first dead along its northeast corner. Grose's skirmishers, moving wraith-like along its eastern side, had picked up one of Bragg's orderlies and the army learned for sure that the Confederates were massed in rapidly growing strength. Johnson and Palmer had deployed over its weedy, uneven surface at midday before moving eastward to pull together Thomas' broken lines. A few hours later Palmer had retired to it with his powder-blackened survivors for rest and ammunition. After dark the spitting flames of Cleburne's muskets had winked like angry fire-flies among the trees along its edge. The following day, John Beatty's men had hastened northward along its western side to their disintegration. All morning, clods from Kelly's field had flown backward behind the horses of Thomas' excited aides. Wary infantrymen from seven different Confederate states had breached the field's northern defenses. But a Dutchman, a Russian and a German, leading other Americans from five Northern states, had denied them their gains. Near its northwest corner Brigadier General Adams, Confederate States Army, had slumped to the ground at the foot of a tree, weak and sick from a severe wound. His capture was officially recorded by half a dozen Union regiments. Half a mile to the east, at almost the same time, Brigadier General Helm had gone down with most of his men under the flaming muzzles of Starkweather's cannon and Scribner's muskets, and his widow went to Washington to be comforted at the White House by her sister, Mary Todd Lincoln.

The shadow of Missionary Ridge crept past the eastern edge of Kelly's field. The darkness deepened, the firing died away. Suddenly there arose from its stubbled surface a continuous exultant shouting. The wings of Bragg's army had met. The field of Chickamauga was theirs.

17

Battles for Chattanooga

By daylight of September 21, Thomas had his command sorted out and positioned to make a stand at Rossville. He reported his dispositions to Rosecrans, adding pessimistically that they were the best he could make for the present. Almost before Rosecrans had read this dispatch Thomas' cavalry was driven in and the Rebels threatened to occupy a commanding hill from which the Union lines could be shelled.

Late in the afternoon, Thomas got his orders to withdraw. The movement began after dark and the men were in their new lines by 7:00 A.M. the next day. These followed the works built by Bragg when he was defending the city, extending from the river north of Chattanooga to the river below it in an arc that was about three miles long. Another force occupied the point of Lookout Mountain. Thomas was assigned to the center, the weakest spot in the Union defense system. By nightfall of the following day, he felt that the army was strongly enough intrenched to resist an assault. Within the next twenty-four hours, he strengthened his lines so that he felt confident of holding until reinforcements could arrive.[1]

Dana, however, was not so certain as Thomas. He sent Stanton seven dispatches in two days ranging from despair to hopeful desperation. Rosecrans, Thomas and Dana all agreed, however, that reinforcements were necessary.

Within forty-eight hours after taking his position in Chattanooga,

Rosecrans made his final and nearly fatal mistake. He gave up the point of Lookout Mountain to Bragg without a struggle. This surrendered control of the railway, the river and the wagon roads westward from Chattanooga and cut off the Army of the Cumberland from its supply depot at Bridgeport, except for a difficult sixty-mile road haul by way of Jasper and Walden's Ridge. Rosecrans looked to the rich Sequatchie Valley to supply his army with food and his animals with forage until reinforcements could arrive. Hooker was on his way with 20,000 men from the Army of the Potomac. Grant was moving eastward with 15,000 men from the Army of the Tennessee. Burnside was coming down the East Tennessee valleys with a potential force of 30,000 men.

Hooker's command, which now became a part of the Army of the Cumberland, consisted of the Eleventh and Twelfth Army Corps. The Eleventh Corps was commanded by Oliver Otis Howard. His reputation with the Army of the Potomac had been that of diligent mediocrity, but under Thomas' guidance, he was to make a proud record for himself. The reputation of his command was worse. It contained enough German soldiers to be known as a Dutch command and German immigrants were looked down upon in the East. They were good material but their luck was bad and they were unhappy to have their German commander, Sigel, replaced by Howard. At Chancellorsville they broke under Jackson's slashing flank attack. The ranks took the blame and, although the fault really lay with their superiors, the Army of the Potomac wanted no more of the Dutchmen, especially after they broke again at Gettysburg.

The Twelfth Army Corps, on the other hand, was a hard-fighting, fast-marching, tough-talking outfit. Its commander, Henry Warner Slocum, had fought with distinction in nearly every one of the battles against Lee. At Gettysburg he had gathered additional laurels as the commander of the Right Wing of the Union army. Although he was one of the best corps commanders in the Northern armies his arrival brought another problem to Thomas, for Slocum was a bitter, outspoken enemy of Hooker. Unlike Hooker's command, the armies of Grant and Burnside were not part of the Department of the Cumberland.

Among the officers of the Army of the Cumberland, as in every army after a defeat, there was a widespread discontent. It focused upon McCook, Crittenden and Negley. Strangely enough, it was not extended to Rosecrans. When he rode the lines around Chattanooga the men rushed out to greet him, filling the air with hats and cheers. Thomas was a popular figure with the army but the men seldom threw up their hats for him. Many officers believed that Thomas would have liked it if they had. But in the fight they were always glad to have "Old Pap" looking after things. This they let him know even while they kept their hats on their heads. Months before, the enlisted men of the Fourth Regiment of Kentucky Volunteer Infantry had collected $1,500 for a testimonial sword to be presented to Thomas. No officer had been allowed to contribute. The sword was received from the manufacturer during the siege of Chattanooga. Many of the donors were dead. General Thomas rode down to the regiment for the presentation and replied briefly to the remarks of the quartermaster sergeant who handed him the gift.

The fate of the army now depended upon a smoothly working supply line and Thomas found the problem dumped into his lap with orders to build a wagon road on the north side of the river. Just at this time, Rosecrans' nemesis struck him down. Heavy rains broke the drought that had plagued the army all during the Chickamauga campaign. Within a matter of days the narrow, ungraded, bridgeless roads north of the river became mud traps. It was impossible for the draft animals to drag their loads up the steeps of Walden's Ridge. Soldiers pulling on ropes helped the teams over the worst spots and snubbed the loads while the beasts eased their heaving lungs. At the same time Wheeler trapped one of Thomas' trains in the Cumberland highlands, burned 800 wagons, killed 4,000 mules, and then moved northwestward to cut the Nashville railway. Thomas' simple logistical problem of building a road now became a sizable military operation with brigades detailed to escort forage trains.

The situation moved from bad to worse. The Army of the Cumberland was threatened with starvation or with a retreat without cavalry, artillery, food or ammunition—the infantry strung out along different roads to be cut to pieces. Washington was frantic to escape the blame. Rosecrans was a ready-made scapegoat. If Halleck, Stanton and Lincoln didn't think of it themselves, Dana soon steered them onto the track with a dispatch which read, "I judge from intimations that have reached me that in writing his own report of Chickamauga General Rosecrans will elaborately show that the blame of his failure in this great battle rests on the Administration; that is, on the Secretary of War and the General-in-Chief, who did not see that Bragg would be reinforced, and who compelled him to move forward without cavalry enough, and very inadequately prepared in other respects."

Apparently the idea of changing the command of the Army of the Cumberland arose simultaneously in Washington and Chattanooga. On September 27 Seward suggested the removal of Rosecrans.[2] On the same date Dana expressed the thought that if a change in the command were considered some Western commander like Grant might be a good choice. Gideon Welles told Lincoln on September 28 that he doubted there was anyone in the East suitable for the command or the equal of Thomas.[3] Three days later, and again on October 12, Dana plumped for Thomas. Part of the question was probably settled before this, because on October 3 Grant was sent to Cairo to await orders. A few days prior Stanton had sent a message to Thomas by Dana: "The merit of General Thomas and the debt of gratitude the nation owes to his valor and skill are fully appreciated here and I wish you to tell him so. It was not my fault that he was not in chief command months ago." [4] Thomas returned his thanks for Stanton's good opinion by the same messenger.

Within the week rumors of Rosecrans' relief by Thomas had become so flagrant that Thomas was forced to take notice. He sent a message to Dana that he would accept any command to which Stanton might assign him except that of the Department of the Cumberland, because he would not do anything to give countenance to the suspicion that he had intrigued against his commander. He emphasized also his perfect confidence in Rosecrans' capacity and fidelity. Thomas knew that Rosecrans held the fruits of victory of his Chickamauga campaign by his occupation of Chattanooga, even though he lacked the trophies of battle. Dana transmitted this message to Stanton on October 8.[5]

Rosecrans, of course, had heard all the rumors and knew of at least one private meeting at Thomas' headquarters attended by Dana, Wood and McCook. He learned through Garfield that Thomas was determined to refuse the command of the Army of the Cumberland if it were offered to him and he sent a message back through Garfield that Thomas should have no misapprehension of a misunderstanding on his part.[6]

While the technique of these negotiations seems incredible, it is evident that Thomas took the only means available to make his stand clear on a matter which, although not officially broached, was common property throughout the officer corps of the Cumberland army. Men who knew Thomas and the part he had played in Rosecrans' command knew what he was talking about. Rosecrans had conducted his command in a way that Washington found offensive. For this Thomas had been partly responsible. He believed that the Cumberland command had been properly administered, that Rosecrans had rightly resisted the pressures put upon him by Halleck and Stanton. Except for his failure to move into Chattanooga and prepare for another advance, Thomas held Rosecrans blameless for his failure at Chickamauga. As Thomas put it in later years, "I would have asked to be relieved sooner than act

on compulsion contrary to my judgment. When a general commanding an army is ordered to do what he feels he ought not to do he should
act upon his own opinion and let things take their course." Having
been partly responsible for the difficulty in which Rosecrans found
himself Thomas was loath to contribute to the sacrifice of his superior.[7]

The decision was Lincoln's. He had already made up his mind to
combine the armies of the Tennessee, the Ohio and the Cumberland,
with Grant in command of the combination. The plan was put before
the cabinet. Chase read a letter from an officer with the Army of the
Cumberland to the effect that Rosecrans was unfit for his command.
Stanton suggested the substitution of Thomas for Rosecrans and the
Cabinet approved. Lincoln objected on the ground of injustice to Rosecrans. The issue was compromised by leaving the decision to Grant.
Duplicate orders were prepared. One gave the command of the Department of the Cumberland to Thomas. The other left it in the hands
of Rosecrans. In all other respects they were the same. Both combined
the three departments under Grant.

Lincoln's personal opinion of Thomas is best illustrated by a curious
episode. On September 23 Lincoln received a telegram from a citizen
of New York which asked two questions: "Will Buell's testamentary
executor George Thomas ever let Rosecrans succeed? Is Bragg dumb
enough to punish Thomas severely and disgracingly?" Thomas was
being charged a high price for his defense of Buell and his Virginia
birth. Lincoln pondered the matter for several hours. He knew that distrust and anxiety were widespread throughout the North. The Rebel
papers were unrestrained in their denunciation of Thomas. They pictured him as a fat, beefy, rabid secessionist before the war and so loud-
mouthed that he shamed the other Southern-born officers, who also put
a low estimate on his professional ability. They maintained that he married a Yankee woman old enough to be his mother and that her money
influenced him to change his allegiance. That evening Lincoln handed
the telegraph operator an answer to the New York queries. It read,
"I hasten to say that in the state of information we have here, nothing
could be more ungracious than to indulge any suspicion towards General Thomas. It is doubtful whether his heroism and skill exhibited last
Sunday afternoon, has ever been surpassed in the world." [8]

Grant met Stanton at Indianapolis and the two rode together to
Louisville, where Grant assumed his command on October 18. Stanton
gave Grant all the military news from Washington and talked at length
about the disappointing results of some of the campaigns. There can
be little doubt that Grant understood to the last detail what Stanton

desired in the way of command changes and it was easy for him to make his choice. He disliked both Thomas and Rosecrans but he disliked Rosecrans the more. That evening in Louisville, Stanton received a dispatch from Dana which led him to believe that Rosecrans would retreat unless peremptorily ordered not to. So Grant assumed command of the combined armies and on October 19 ordered Thomas to relieve Rosecrans. About midnight Thomas received a telegram from Grant to hold Chattanooga at all hazards and replied, "I will hold the town till we starve." [9] For Thomas, habitually the master of understatement, this was a sweeping promise. Within an hour his caution had resumed its customary ascendancy and another telegram shot northward to Grant. This one advised him that if the wagons then on the road arrived safely, the Army of the Cumberland was all right until November 1. Thomas gave his army a thirteen-day grace period based upon a doubtful contingency. It was the second time within thirty days that he had assumed the responsibility for a military situation that seemed hopeless. There were officers of discernment in Thomas' command who believed that his acceptance of this responsibility boded no good to his future reputation. The episode explains one of the apparent contradictions in Thomas' makeup. He was a bold leader—witness his plan for East Tennessee and his assumption of risk at Chickamauga and Chattanooga—yet he was reluctant to promise achievement and exasperatingly cautious in perfecting his plans to solve the problems that he had accepted. His critics overlooked his audacity because he failed to whip up their enthusiasms with reassuring promises and stifled their ardor with his scrupulous preparations.

Thomas assumed the command of 154,289 men and 274 pieces of artillery. His army was divided into the Fourth Corps,[10] commanded by Granger; the Eleventh Corps, commanded by Howard, and the Twelfth Corps, commanded by Slocum, both jointly commanded by Hooker; the Fourteenth Corps, commanded by Palmer; and the Cavalry Corps, commanded by Stanley.[11] His regiments were scattered from Chattanooga north to Fort Donelson, Nashville and Gallatin. Only those in Chattanooga were short of rations. The shortage had existed since the first part of October but the condition of the men was not yet serious. It was the lack of food for the horses and mules that was crippling the army. The artillery horses, being the least useful, got little or no food and fell dead in great numbers day by day. The cavalry was ordered out of the city and their mounts were comparatively well fed. The mules on the wagon trains were pressed beyond endurance. The roads worsened from the rains and heavy hauling so that loads had to be lightened and this tonnage loss had to be made up by quick turn-

When Thomas whipped the off horses into their fastest gait at Peach Tree Creek the scene may have looked like this. In the background the driver is turning the lead team of the caisson to follow the gun. *W. H. Shelton, Library of Congress.*

A mule chute used at Camp Nelson, Kentucky. Since the farriers were civilians the work was probably done on a contract basis. *National Archives, Record Group III.*

William Tecumseh Sherman with the corps commanders who made the March to the Sea. Many had served under Thomas. Left to right, Major Generals Oliver Otis Howard, who believed war to be the triumph of right rather than of good soldiers; John A. Logan, whose command appointment was postponed through Thomas' influence; William Babcock Hazen, who rejected the prejudice against artificial cover; Sherman; Jefferson Columbus Davis, Thomas' greatest personnel success; Henry Warner Slocum, whose dislike of Hooker posed a problem for Thomas; and Joseph Anthony Mower, who received his second star for wounding Forrest. *National Archives, Record Group III.*

Brevet Major General John Milton Brannan. His dawn crossing of the Tennessee River without bridges or sufficient boats must have been one of the most stirring sights in American history. *National Archives, Record Group III.*

Major General Patrick Ronayne Cleburne, C.S.A. one of the South's brightest military stars, was frozer in a division command because of his belief that slaves should be used as troops. This frustration may have led to his apparently suicidal death at Franklin

Major General Thomas Leonidas Crittenden. His father did as much as any man to hold the Union together. His brother led the Southern forces at Mill Springs. His son died with Custer on the Little Big Horn. *Library of Congress.*

Brevet Major General John Thomas Croxton. There was a military axiom that mounted troops could not operate successfully in enemy areas. Croxton showed that the generalization need not be specific. *National Archives, Record Group III.*

Major General James Abram Garfield left the field at Chickamauga with Rosecrans but instead of following his chief to Chattanooga he joined Thomas on Snodgrass Ridge. Rosecrans' choice ended his military career; Garfield's eventually led him to the Presidency. *National Archives, Record Group III.*

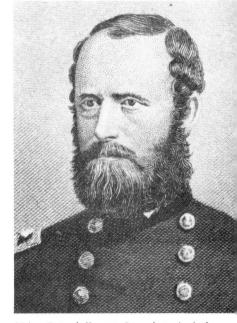

Major General Kenner Garrard received the blame for Sherman's ineffectual management of his cavalry during the Atlanta Campaign, although Garrard furthered Sherman's designs more than any other cavalry leader. *Library of Congress.*

Major General Gordon Granger has always received credit for voluntarily marching toward the sound of the guns on Chickamauga's second day, but there is reliable evidence that Thomas called him to his aid. *National Archives, Record Group III.*

Brigadier General Charles Garrison Harker was one of the best of the regular army officers whose skills were largely wasted by Lincoln. He died on Kennesaw Mt. *National Archives, Record Group III.*

Brevet Major General Edward Hatch in two days of heavy fighting at Nashville dissolved the doubt long held by the War Department that mounted troops could play a decisive tactical role. *National Archives, Record Group III.*

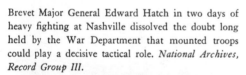

Brevet Major General Daniel Craig McCallum. He and Thomas perfected what was probably the world's first successful movable railway base. *National Archives, Record Group III.*

Brevet Major General Edward Moody McCook, nephew of A. M. McCook, ruined Joe Johnston's plans in Georgia by daring, twice in one day, to attack Hood's infantrymen with his mounted division. *National Archives, Record Group III.*

Major General Alexander McDowell McCook. Twice his command broke yet none doubted his courage. He was an irrepressible juvenile until sobered by the debacle at Chickamauga. *Painting in Cullum Hall, West Point.*

Major General James Scott Negley was a victim of combat pressure. He retrieved his division from disaster in the cedars at Stones River but broke under the sheeted fire of Hood's riflemen at Chickamauga. *National Archives, Record Group III.*

Brevet Major General Emerson Opdycke saved Schofield's military reputation at the Battle of Franklin by refusing to obey the orders of his division commander. *National Archives, Record Group III.*

Major General John McAuley Palmer was one of the few volunteer officers to gain a corps command but he was unable to gain the cooperation of his West Point trained division commanders. *Library of Congress.*

Brevet Brigadier General William Jackson Palmer put the capstone on Thomas' pursuit of Hood two hundred miles from its starting point. *Library of Congress.*

Major General Lovell Harrison Rousseau demonstrated that properly led troops will absorb losses far beyond the theoretical percentage without breaking. *National Archives, Record Group III.*

Lieutenant General John McAllister Schofield was the fifth officer in the service of the U. S. to win that rank. John Pope said of him, "He could stand steadier on the bulge of a barrel than any man who ever wore shoulder straps." *National Archives, Record Group III.*

Major General James Blair Steedman threw the Confederates off Snodgrass Ridge in twenty minutes by launching overwhelming strength at a single point, while Longstreet, using a line of attack, needed six hours for the same job. *Library of Congress.*

Major General David Sloan Stanley commanded the advance guard in the desperate retreat from Columbia and held open the jaws of Hood's trap until Schofield could get through. *National Archives, Record Group III.*

Major General George Stoneman. Although Stanton branded him as a failure, he became the only ranking cavalry commander to play a part in the elimination of all three major Confederate armies. *National Archives, Record Group III.*

Brigadier General Ferdinand Van Derveer. Few men did a better job of accepting the crushing responsibility of command at Chickamauga. *Library of Congress.*

Brevet Brigadier General John Thomas Wilder saved the Union two thousand casualties at Hoover's Gap with what part of the army called his "tadpole cavalry." *National Archives, Record Group III.*

Major General David Emanuel Twiggs, C.S.A. His quarrel with Thomas before the Civil War, reputed to have started over a team of mules, finally involved the Secretary of War. *National Archives, Record Group III.*

Major General Thomas John Wood was a baffling problem in psychology. He wrecked Rosecrans' career at Chickamauga by his vindictive obedience to orders. *National Archives, Record Group III.*

arounds and more speed. The effects of starvation were compounded by overwork. Ten thousand dead mules walled the roads between Bridgeport and Chattanooga. It took ten days for a loaded wagon to make the trip. Two days before Thomas assumed the command, 500 teams were stalled between the mountain and the river with no food for the animals and no prospect of getting any. Forage was more important than riflemen. The same immobilization occurred in connection with the movement of reinforcements from the Army of the Potomac. The troops were hurried forward without their transportation and were unable to move from the railhead.

Thomas' first job was to mend his broken communications. Next to the railway between Bridgeport and Chattanooga, which was cut by the Confederates on Lookout Mountain, the Tennessee River offered the best line of communication except for two things: first, the Rebels on Lookout Mountain prevented its use around the southern end and the western side of Moccasin Point; and second, that portion of the river between Kelly's ferry and Brown's ferry called The Suck was impassable to all except the most powerful steamboats when moving upstream. Others had to be cordelled, which made them particularly inviting to Rebel raiders. Late on October 19, Rosecrans returned to his headquarters from a vain search for a solution to this problem to find Grant's order relieving him from command. One of his subordinates, however, had discovered an answer. This was Brigadier General William F. Smith, chief engineer of the Department of the Cumberland.[12] Smith's plan involved three crossings of the Tennessee—one at Bridgeport, one at Brown's ferry and one at Chattanooga. Brown's ferry was the key to the solution. It was in Rebel hands. It if could be taken and held, supplies could be carried upriver from Bridgeport, unloaded on the right bank at Brown's ferry and transported into Chattanooga by a four-mile wagon haul.

By the twenty-second Thomas had examined and approved Smith's plan, issued his orders for a movement of Hooker eastward from Bridgeport toward Brown's ferry and for the construction of the Brown's ferry bridge and the assault boats, and advised Halleck that he expected to open the railway and wagon road to Bridgeport in a few days.[13]

The next evening Grant reached Chattanooga, lame, wet and dirty. He brought with him a letter from Stanton thanking Thomas and his men in the name of the people of the United States for their magnificent behavior at Chickamauga. "You stood like a rock," Stanton wrote, "and that stand gives you fame which will grow brighter as the ages go by. You will be rewarded by the country and by the Department."

As an invited guest, Grant moved into Thomas' headquarters on his arrival at Chattanooga, and it was here that James H. Wilson, Grant's inspector general, found him a short time later. Grant was sitting on one side of the fireplace and Thomas on the other. Neither had anything to say. Both looked glum and ill at ease. Grant's sodden clothing was steaming on the side nearest the fireplace. Under his chair was a puddle of water that had dripped from his muddy uniform. Discreet inquiry disclosed that nothing had been offered for the visitor's comfort. The tension was broken when Wilson suggested that some member of Thomas' official family might have dry clothing that Grant could use until his own uniform could be cleaned. Once the machinery of hospitality had been set in motion everything was done to remedy the situation and was apparently done cheerfully, but Thomas' initial coolness and neglect had been too noticeable for Grant's staff to overlook.[14]

The reasons for Thomas' aloofness have never been revealed. Personal relations between the two had been strained during the Corinth campaign and seemed to have worsened since. Thomas' feeling was so marked that it was adopted by his staff as the model for their official relations with Grant's headquarters. As a result, transactions between the two chiefs-of-staff deteriorated in several instances to personal rudeness. Friendly cooperation between the staffs was never established.

A mutual friend who tried unsuccessfully to bring about more cordial relations between the two men found that Grant at first was more considerate and conciliatory toward Thomas than was Thomas toward Grant. Both were strong men with different points of view and idiosyncracies and with prejudices and preferences that pulled them in different directions. This temperamental friction, however, was not permitted to interfere with their work.

A detailed description of Thomas at this time was also noted by Wilson, who reached Chattanooga one day ahead of his chief. He went with Dana to pay his respects to the new head of the Department of the Cumberland. He had never met Thomas but Dana had described his courage and composure and Wilson was prepossessed in his favor. Dana introduced the men. "I found him as calm and serene as the morning," Wilson wrote later. "He received me gravely and courteously, but without the slightest show of uneasiness or concern. He expressed a modest confidence in being able to make good his hold upon Chattanooga and at once inspired me with a faith in his steadiness and courage. He intimated that he had never sought command, nor, contrary to the popular impression, declined it when offered, but felt himself fully competent to meet all the responsibility that might be laid upon him. And later, when I came to know him better, he not only confirmed the impression of perfect self-reliance he gave me on that occasion, but made it clear that the need of supervision from any source had never presented itself to his mind."

The morning after his arrival Grant rode with Thomas and Smith as close to Brown's ferry as the Rebel pickets would permit to look over the ground. He approved what had been done and what was planned. Four days later—nine days after Thomas assumed command—the short supply line to Bridgeport was opened and the army was safely past its supply crisis. This was the famous Brown's Ferry Cracker Line. The ferry had been seized at daylight on October 27 by troops floated downstream from Chattanooga. Hooker marched overland from Bridgeport, fought off a night attack at Wauhatchie and linked up with the Brown's ferry bridgehead. Thomas had expected this operation to give him control of the railway and wagon road from Bridgeport to Chattanooga. When it failed to do so it became a makeshift substitute rather than a remedy for his ruptured supply line. Grant was satisfied with the makeshift but Thomas felt that the railway and wagon road should be made secure by breaking the Rebel grip on Lookout Mountain. At least part of the supply job, however, was done. River steamers rebuilt at Chattanooga and Bridgeport by Thomas' engineers began to pile up stores at Kelly's ferry and Brown's ferry for the relatively short wagon haul into the beleaguered city.

Thomas' problems were not all related to supply and to his personal relations with Grant. He had to cure the demoralization which grew out of the Chickamauga defeat. To do this he had to eliminate the bickering and recrimination prevalent among both officers and men and to tighten his discipline by eliminating the unfit and rewarding the deserving. He worked from the top down and began with his own staff. Each member was selected because of his fitness to perform the duty to which he was assigned. His official family was never used to pay a personal debt nor to shelter an incompetent kinsman.[15] There was no place for the officer whose major role was to entertain.

Thomas and Whipple,[16] his chief-of-staff, had many of the same characteristics. Both were studious, reserved, formal and meticulously observant of the punctilios of official relationships. They refused to tolerate the haphazardness which had become characteristic under Rosecrans.[17] Order and punctuality now prevailed. Headquarters became quiet, dignified and solemn.

Some of Rosecrans' staff members who visited Thomas after a few months' absence found him as reserved and undemonstrative as ever. His office was run like a place of business and they missed the clublike atmosphere. Garfield's outgiving habits and hearty politician's welcome were replaced by Whipple's coldness toward any conversation that was not strictly business. Convivial reminiscing was out. The junior staff members damned Whipple for instituting the changes but it probably was not all Whipple's doing. Thomas could hold the respect and sometimes the affection of many different kinds of men and he seemed to do it naturally but when he handpicked this official family, mannerisms became evident in the group which had not been noticeable in the individuals.

One of the visiting officers was a guest at the headquarters mess and was oppressed by its formality and solemnity. Not a word, he said, was spoken during the meal. Phillips, a freed slave, stood behind Thomas' chair looking like the chief mute at a funeral. His role as a formal Negro servant fit exactly the fastidiousness of the new arrangements. In this environment both servant and chief-of-staff seemed to acquire some of Thomas' basic characteristics. Even his horses, the mules around his headquarters and the sleek cat that rubbed against his legs or lay purring at his feet seemed to shape their temperaments in accordance with their master's influence. Thomas even hosted a formal Christmas dinner for which invitations were issued bearing the letters R.S.V.P. The guests were seated according to their rank. Some of them had been unable to decipher the social code until the afternoon of the dinner. It was not Thomas' doing but that of his aide, Captain Kellogg, who evidently thought the formality would be fitting.[18] For a western army camp on short rations this was carrying social correctness to the point of stuffiness. Although it was Kellogg's prescription the unspoken suggestion could well have come from Thomas.

Officer morale needed the salve of Thomas' influence. The division and brigade commanders who had served under McCook and Crittenden were most affected. They resented their desertion at Chickamauga. The War Department solved the basic trouble by combining these two commands into the Fourth Corps. McCook and Crittenden left Chattanooga when this was done. Negley reported for duty but Thomas refused to give him a field command. The unrest was deep-rooted and showed itself in other manifestations. Carlin asked to have his brigade transferred to some other division or to be relieved. Palmer was resentful of the abolition of the Twenty-first Corps and the lies sent out from Chattanooga by letter writers. He wanted to see a reorganization of the army or to have his resignation accepted. Hazen was upset by the public censure he received during the tensions of the Chickamauga concentration. John Beatty was irritated by baseless slander regarding his conduct on that hard-fought field. Sheridan, Wood, Davis and Johnson wanted some guaranty that they would not be forced to face the hazards of incompetent command in the future. Battle was sifting the weaklings out of the Army of the Cumberland. Military incompetence, once re-garded sympathetically, now was recognized as a threat to everyone and Thomas set himself to uproot it. Three of the eleven infantry division commanders at Chickamauga were promoted and five retained their commands. Of the thirty-three infantry brigade commanders at Chick-amauga, two were promoted, seven were casualties and thirteen retained their commands. For one reason or another two corps commanders, three division commanders, and eleven brigade commanders left the Army of the Cumberland. In addition, two of Chickamauga's regimental commanders had been promoted to brigades. Next to this wholesale reshuffling of the general officers, Thomas' major effort toward getting the situation in hand was to recommend a list of nineteen for promotion. He sought to persuade Garfield to return to the army and take a field command. It is probable that he turned loose his personal persuasiveness on Steedman. That deserving officer was in a peeve over the lack of recognition of his Chickamauga services. Typical of the way Thomas handled his officers was his solution of Palmer's request to have Baird transferred from his command. He wanted someone who was not so prone to quibble and criticize. At the close of Palmer's complaint Thomas said, "Well, General, wait until we have a battle, then if you want Baird relieved I will do it." After this test Thomas asked Palmer, "How about relieving Baird?"

"No," Palmer answered, "Baird is a fighter. He devils the Rebs more than he ever did me."

Brigadier General Jefferson C. Davis was another of Thomas' prob-lems. He was a division commander dogged by misfortune and branded as a murderer. His crime had been exculpated by an Administration pliable to political pressures. Twice his division had broken under enemy pressure. One of his brigade commanders was so exasperated he officially demanded relief. One more such piece of hard luck might result in his ruin and the needless sacrifice of many of his men. When Sherman reached Chattanooga, appraised the job ahead of him and asked for more infantry, Thomas sent him Davis' division. In retrospect and on the record, this order is one of the shrewdest personnel moves that Thomas ever made. The brigading of Davis' men with Sherman's veterans gave them a distinct individuality that obliterated their past record. With a little luck they might regain their self-confidence. The plan succeeded beyond Thomas' wildest hopes. At the close of the campaign Sherman officially named Davis' division as one of the best ordered in the service. Thomas endorsed his gratification on Davis' battle report.

Thomas' confidence in the volunteer had been growing since the days at Camp Dick Robinson. He decided it was time that one of his corps commanders be chosen from their number. He selected John M. Palmer for this honor and gave him the command of Thomas' own corps—the famous Fourteenth. This generous recognition erased Palmer's resentment and held him in the army.

Hooker came to the Army of the Cumberland with a reputation for criticizing his superiors almost to the point of insubordination. The Army of the Cumberland was still buzzing with the details of how he had sought to put Grant in his proper place when that officer passed through Bridgeport.[19] Thomas knew that he had on his hands a latent problem in command. Eight days after the Cracker Line was opened Thomas rode out to Hooker's camps to solve it. He found the lines negligently placed and the work on the rifle pits badly done. Hooker seemed to pay little attention to his duties. Howard apparently had never ridden the lines of his corps. What Thomas did about it is unknown but Hooker's men performed to his satisfaction in the Chattanooga-Ringgold campaign and in the end Hooker and Howard became Thomas' admirers.

One of the first of Grant's official moves after reaching Chattanooga was to order Sherman, who was then marching from Vicksburg, Mississippi, toward Chattanooga, to drop the work of repairing and guarding the Memphis-Chattanooga railway and push on toward Stevenson. Sherman had begun the movement toward Chattanooga on September 25 and had been on the road more than a month when he received Grant's peremptory order. He was near Iuka, still 160 miles short of his goal. It was November 23 before he got his divisions into position to force a crossing of the Tennessee River upstream from Chattanooga. This was an average of less than six miles a day for that part of his march after he was relieved from Halleck's crippling order to guard the railway. He may have established the record for the slowest relief march in American history. He was shamed and mortified by his failure. Grant was pressing him to get up and Sherman answered with awkward apologies.

Most of the blame for Sherman's tardiness rested on his own shoulders, but the jumble of hills, valleys, creeks and rivers and the wretched roads were partly to blame. Grant and his chief-of-staff were appalled by the physical obstacles that had been overcome by the Army of the Cumberland in the Chickamauga campaign. Grant felt that while it was barely possible to supply the Army of the Cumberland now, it would be impossible when the winter rains set in. Sherman's arrival would worsen the situation. When he learned that Bragg had moved Longstreet up the Tennessee Valley toward Burnside, who was at Knoxville, Grant considered his whole situation desperate. Thomas refused to share this pessimism. His troubles all stemmed from a long, overtaxed, poorly managed, single-track railway and Thomas was probably the best equipped combat officer in the world for solving such a problem. All he wanted from the War Department was more motive power. The rest he could handle. Nor could Thomas be alarmed over Burnside's situation.

"Longstreet's move," he pointed out, "is a raid upon our lines of supplies. Burnside at this moment has three men to Longstreet's one. We greatly outnumber Bragg's army and, if in our attack we can bring the crushing weight of our full force to bear, we are sure to win." [20] Within a month events had proved him right but Washington shared Grant's alarm and plied him with dispatches urging that something be done for Burnside's relief.

Thomas' solution of his supply problem, which seems simple enough in retrospect, impressed his associates. Grant, who felt the situation to be impossible, Dana, who reported that the Army of the Cumberland balanced on the knife edge of disaster, and Sherman, who had no idea that things could be so bad, watched Thomas bring order out of chaos. Baldy Smith and Meigs [21] alone seemed to share his confident optimism.

From experience Thomas knew that sixty carloads of freight a day could be unloaded at the Tennessee River. He specified that thirty-five of these were to be loaded with subsistence stores. He was also specific in his requirements for fresh meat and ordnance stores. Including Sherman's army, he needed 125,000 daily rations. His orders were issued to reach this goal. The workability of his supply plans, whether by rail, boat or wagon was always based upon his correct appraisal of the potentialities of his communications. Grant, for example, underestimated the capabilities of his Chattanooga communications by 50 per cent.

Once Thomas issued his orders he tackled the second part of his problem, to see that they were carried out. There was vigorous enforcement all along the line. Aid from all over the North came to him in opening his communication line. Ship's carpenters were ordered down from Louisville. Complete shipyards were built, manned and operated at Bridgeport. Prebuilt railway bridges were collected. Every railway in the country was laid under contribution to provide rolling stock. Branch

railways were cannibalized. Units of the construction corps were borrowed from the eastern armies. Substantial aid was rendered by Grenville Dodge,[22] commanding a division in the Army of the Tennessee,
and his 8,000 infantrymen, who rebuilt the Nashville-Decatur railway
in forty days and provided another rail link between Nashville and
Bridgeport. It was the middle of January, however, before the army
in Chattanooga was on full rations.

The link between the Bridgeport-Stevenson railhead and Chattanooga caused Thomas the most trouble. He had expected that Hooker's march eastward would open this rail line. When this failed he insisted that Lookout Mountain be cleared of Rebels. At one time he
swung Grant over to this idea. A few hours later, however, Grant had
changed his mind.

In the midst of these problems Robert Anderson retired from his
commission as brigadier general in the regular army. Lincoln immediately and unofficially gave the appointment to Thomas. Grant was
notified by Halleck and he advised Thomas in a congratulatory letter.
According to Grant, this promotion was in recognition of Thomas'
services at Chickamauga.[23] Lincoln formally proposed Thomas for the
promotion on December 31, 1863, and the Senate confirmed his appointment March 1, 1864. This put Thomas fifteenth on the list of
brigadier generals. He was junior, among others, to Hooker, Meade,
Sherman and McPherson.

Among the thousands of things requiring Thomas' attention, the
most important, after that of supply, was to drive Bragg away from
Lookout Mountain. Bragg's advance lines held the Union forces in a
tight arc around the outskirts of Chattanooga with their backs to the
river, but his main lines stretched from the north end of Missionary
Ridge south to Rossville and thence across Chattanooga Valley to the
point of Lookout Mountain. Except for raiders and defenders against
raids, all the combat troops of both armies were on the left bank of the
Tennessee River but Bragg had the advantage of quicker communication with his flanks. To reach either of Bragg's flanks from Chattanooga
the Union troops had to make two crossings of the Tennessee. Bragg's
defeat posed as tough a problem as that faced by Grant at Vicksburg,
and Thomas turned to Smith, his chief engineer officer, for the solution.
The responsibility, of course, was Grant's but he had neither the time
nor the opportunity to gather the facts. Neither was he an engineer
nor, strangely enough, a close calculator of risks.

Between the time Bragg decided to send Longstreet against Burnside and the time Grant learned about it, Smith had worked out his plan.

He proposed to break through Bragg's advance lines on the Union left and threaten the north end of Missionary Ridge. This, coupled with the activity in Lookout Valley incidental to the opening of the Cracker Line, would, in Smith's opinion, force Bragg to concentrate and so withdraw Longstreet from his movement toward Knoxville. On November 5, Grant and Thomas had the plan under advisement. The following day, Thomas made his first inspection of Hooker's lines and the general situation in Lookout Valley. One result of this inspection was to crystallize his opinion that the first place to strike Bragg was on Lookout Mountain.

Grant, in the meantime, had learned that Longstreet had marched against Burnside. Without balancing the risks, he changed Smith's plan for threatening Bragg and ordered Thomas to make an immediate attack on the north end of Missionary Ridge. Thomas was aghast. To carry out the order was to invite disaster. While he moved his troops out of Chattanooga for the assault there was nothing to stop Bragg from marching into the city, cutting Thomas off from all supplies and putting himself in an excellent position to gobble up Hooker after disposing of Thomas. The suggestion of a threat against the north end of Missionary Ridge was Smith's original idea, so he called his chief engineer to his headquarters and pointed out to him the utter impracticability of Grant's order. Their conversation was protracted. Smith then went to Grant's headquarters and had the attack order countermanded.[24]

Trivial as the incident was, it soured Grant more than ever on Thomas. The countermanding order was verbal so its phrasing is not available. For nearly two months, however, Grant insisted in his official correspondence that the November attack failed because of Thomas' slowness and not because he had withdrawn it.[25]

On November 15 Sherman arrived in Chattanooga ahead of his men. Grant explained the situation to him. Thomas' animals were too starved to haul his guns. His army was so demoralized by the disaster at Chickamauga that it would not get out of its trenches. Sherman's force was needed to spark an offensive and restore the lost morale of the Cumberlanders.[26] There was a meeting that night in an upstairs room at Grant's headquarters. Thomas did much of the talking. His knowledge of the surrounding country was positive, detailed and abundant, his attitude confident. His hearers felt that his information was accurate and his conclusions sound. Grant listened, breaking in occasionally with a pointed remark.

Then Grant announced his attack plan. It was the one worked out by Smith and now strongly favored by Rawlins, Grant's chief-of-staff.

Thomas was to hold Bragg in place along some thirteen miles of front that extended from the point of Lookout Mountain across the valley of Chattanooga Creek to Rossville, thence north along Missionary Ridge to Chickamauga Creek. Sherman was to move secretly on the far side of the Tennessee River to a point opposite the mouth of Chickamauga Creek. From here he would make a night crossing of the Tennessee, fall upon Bragg's unsuspecting right flank and roll it southward along Missionary Ridge. Thomas was to supply the boats, bridges and artillery support for Sherman's crossing. One of his divisions was to be transferred to Sherman's command and Howard's corps was to be pulled out of Lookout Valley and positioned to support either Thomas or Sherman. With one division Thomas was to feint up Chattanooga Valley but the bulk of his troops were to be massed on his far left where they would make a junction with Sherman and cooperate with him. Sherman was to lead the attack and set the pace.

November 21 was set as the date. Sherman, who had examined the ground and expressed himself confident of his ability to execute his share of the work, returned to Bridgeport to bring up his command. His preparatory responsibility was to put his troops into position. He expressed his admiration over the completeness of Thomas' cooperative preparation.

The rivalry between the Army of the Tennessee and the Army of the Cumberland, which was to play so decisive a part in the struggle for Chattanooga, actually dated back to Shiloh. It had begun shortly before dusk of Shiloh's first day when Bull Nelson's leading brigade jostled its way through 15,000 of Grant's demoralized troops at Pittsburgh Landing and helped beat off the last Rebel attack of the day. Grant, in his anxiety, had called Buell's army up to help save the day for him; but, when it arrived, he turned his back upon its commander and ever since he had belittled its efforts. The Army of the Cumberland had never allowed Grant's men to forget the debt they owed them. The stage was set now for its repayment. Grant's men were jubilant at the prospect. With Vicksburg's laurels fresh on their flags, Sherman's men marched cockily into Bridgeport between rows of Hooker's curious troops, now part of the Army of the Cumberland, wearing the Twelfth Corps badge, a five pointed star. The Tennessee army stared in wonderment.

"Are you all brigadier generals?" asked one of the more inquisitive marchers, who had never seen a single military star mark anything less than a brigade commander. The eastern troops explained condescendingly that the star was their corps badge [27] and then inquired loftily, "What's your badge?" From this point on the remarks between the rival armies degenerated into personalities. "Dudes and brass-mounted soldiers," jibed the marchers. "Tramps," rejoined the lookers. This was the first time in the west that troops from the North's three major armies had been brought together for a common effort. All had deep-seated reasons for pride in their own records. Hooker's men had played historic roles on a dozen famous fields. The sound of the names on their battle ribbons had a ring of steel. They had distilled their experience from the hot fire of Lee's veterans. They had been part of an army that had seen more combat, suffered more losses and been mishandled more than any body of troops in the nineteenth century. Sherman's men were part of an army that, as a whole, had never known defeat. It was their boast that they were sure to win any battle that lasted more than one day.

In ten months, Thomas' men had won back all that vast area between the Ohio and Tennessee rivers that had been lost by official incompetence. Military experts were astounded at the physical obstacles they had overcome. They had developed the most advanced strategic competency of the war. But for the first time they had left their dead on the battlefield. Grant said there was no jealousy, hardly any rivalry, between these troops, and perhaps he believed this. Sherman complained about the rivalry. Thomas capitalized on it.

An interesting appraisal of these same units was made shortly after the war. The judge, well qualified on military matters, was the German ambassador to the United States. When the Fifteenth Corps of the Army of the Tennessee passed the reviewing stand where he sat, the ambassador observed that an army like that could whip all Europe. As Hooker's old command went by, he said, "An army like that could whip the world." Then Thomas' famous Fourteenth Corps turned the corner and moved along the avenue between curbs dense with wildly cheering crowds. The ambassador studied them and then, across their brawny shoulders he placed his accolade. "An army like that could whip the devil," he said.

There were plenty of officers who knew the facts about these rivalries and tried to put an end to the bickering. One of the Twelfth Corps generals took official notice of the friction between the Army of the Cumberland and the former representatives of the Army of the Potomac and ordered the quarreling stopped. Sherman complained unofficially to Grant about the sneers of the Cumberlanders.

Thomas sought to heal the sore in a way that was peculiarly his own. Grenville Dodge of the Army of the Tennessee was repairing the Nashville-Decatur railway. He was in Thomas' department but not under his orders, since he reported directly to Grant. Dodge's foragers, who were supporting 12,000 men and 10,000 animals, began to irritate the civilians whose produce they were requisitioning and the officers of the Army of the Cumberland, who wanted the supplies for their own troops. An appalling number of complaints began pouring in on Dodge which made it appear that his command was completely out of hand. The file finally reached Thomas. It put the left wing of Sherman's Sixteenth Army Corps at his mercy, but Thomas, instead of following the suggestions of his subordinates, passed the file along to Grant with the remark that Dodge was so busy with the railway that he probably did not know of the unauthorized depredations of his foragers. Grant killed the charges and Dodge thanked Thomas for his courtesy and commendation.

The old competitive urge that had put the first troops into Corinth and later into Chattanooga was gnawing again at Thomas but this time he was severely handicapped. He was cast in a minor role. His animals were still breaking down, lack of artillery limited his striking power, and lack of transport would prevent a sustained pursuit. He could make sure, however, that no slip-up occurred in the part that his army was to play in the combined operations. Twice between the time of Sherman's arrival and the time scheduled for the attack Thomas convened meetings of his subordinate commanders to be sure that they were letter-perfect in their parts. He pointed out that their role was confined to demonstrations on Bragg's front and the protection of Chattanooga from counterattack. The main attack was to be made by Sherman. He talked, too, about a frontal assault on Missionary Ridge, warned them about the heavy casualties it would demand and the probability of its failure if it were made before the Rebel flanks were shattered. The officers seemed to understand their commander, for their battle reports express the conviction that the Army of the Cumberland eventually was to storm Missionary Ridge.

Thomas' dispositions were made in good time. Howard brought his columns in between Brown's ferry and Chattanooga. Two brigades of Granger's corps were moved into place to support Hooker. Davis was detached to join Sherman. Smith's bridge materials were hauled up the right bank of the river. Brannan's guns—he was now chief of artillery of the Cumberland army—were put into position to cover Sherman's crossing. The cavalry was called in ready for a sweeping raid on Bragg's right flank. The overloaded supply line between Bridgeport and Chattanooga was subjected to still heavier strains. The steamer *Dunbar* was temporarily detached from this important service and moved upstream to ferry Sherman's artillery horses. On November 17 the Army of the Cumberland was ready.

That morning Sherman's leading division left Bridgeport for its rendezvous with battle at daylight on the twenty-first. The distance was thirty-five to forty miles, the roads were bad and they had to cross three frail bridges. But Grant and Sherman agreed that the time was adequate for the movement. Unfortunately, a lamentable blunder that was to postpone the opening of the battle, change all the carefully laid plans and throw away the element of surprise, had already been made.[28] Sherman was unable to move fast enough. The attack was postponed until the twenty-second and then postponed again. The situation was getting out of control. News had come in that fighting had begun at Knoxville. Burnside was cut off from telegraphic communication. Lincoln, Stanton and Halleck were in an agony of suspense. Grant had definitely dated his attack for the twenty-first and Burnside, when last heard from, was coordinating his movements on that time schedule. Grant was plainly embarrassed. It was apparent to the troops that the attack plans had miscarried and that the situation was drifting.

When Thomas was advised of the second postponement he suggested to Grant that Howard's corps be substituted for Sherman's tardy divisions, which in turn would be assigned to Hooker's command for an attack on Lookout Mountain. Thomas was still pounding at his original idea to attack Bragg's left instead of his right. He wanted a trouble-free supply route between Bridgeport and Chattanooga. He also wanted the means of connecting his right flank with his center without two crossings of the Tennessee River. Sherman's difficulty was now pointing out the basic weakness of Grant's idea that a makeshift communication line with Bridgeport was adequate for relieving the investment of Chattanooga. In addition, Thomas counseled against further delay on the ground that Bragg would learn Grant's battle plan. The enemy could see Sherman's troops crossing the bridge at Brown's ferry but soon lost sight of them and Grant hoped they would infer that they were moving upstream after Longstreet. The possible discovery of Sherman's destination worried Thomas. But his advice was rejected.

The night of the twenty-second Grant received a report that Bragg was retreating. Early the next morning Thomas was ordered to make a reconnaissance in force to check on this news. Thomas organized a movement that was a suitable prelude to a battle. He designated the divisions of Wood, Sheridan, Baird and Johnson for the movement, with Howard's corps massed close in their rear as a reserve. It was as heavy a force as Grant had planned to use in his main attack. The terrain Thomas chose for his movement was the almost level cleared ground lying between Chattanooga and Missionary Ridge. It was the floor of a natural amphitheater, the surrounding heights being occupied by the Rebel forces and all the vantage points in his rear swarming with the curious Union troops who were not being used in the assault. This was the first aggressive move by Grant's force in the struggle for Chattanooga. The lead had come by luck to Thomas' army and Thomas did not intend to muff it. From this point on, by luck and foresight, Thomas saturated the Battles for Chattanooga with his military talent.

The Rebels looked down upon his deployment with an air of detached boredom. They thought the Yankees were putting on a grand review or perhaps a raid for firewood.[29] Bragg's pickets were just east of the Western and Atlantic railway, on a north and south line through what is now the national cemetery. A mile and a half to the east, and just about halfway to Missionary Ridge, was the enemy's fortified line —rifle pits and barricades of logs and stones. Between the pickets and this fortified line were the grand guards and the isolated defenses of the picket reserves. The strong point of the fortified line was an abruptly rising elevation the crest of which was some one hundred feet above the Chattanooga plain. It was called both Indian Hill and Orchard Knob. This was the key to the line of Rebel works. Thomas apparently made up his mind to take it although his orders would have been satisfied with much less than this.

Officers of high rank, covered with honors gained on many fields, gathered on the ramparts of Fort Wood, whose cannon covered the advance. All of the infantry units of the Cumberland army, except perhaps a half dozen brigades, were under arms and could see all or a great part of the pageant. A large part of Thomas' cavalry was on hand although most of his artillery missed it. Only Hooker's troops in Lookout Valley and Sherman's troops toiling up the north side of the river were too far away to see what was taking place. Cooks, teamsters, clerks and other non-combatants left their jobs to watch for the first time in the west a battle in its entirety. Each of the Union signal stations that ringed the north side of the Chattanooga amphitheater had its glasses trained on the Union regiments and gave a blow-by-blow account of the proceedings to the rest of the signal detail who gathered to listen. Hooker rode over from Lookout Valley and took his place at Fort Wood. Howard left his massed divisions and made his way to the same point to compare the professional assets of the Cumberlanders with those of the Army of the Potomac. Close to Grant were the Quarter-

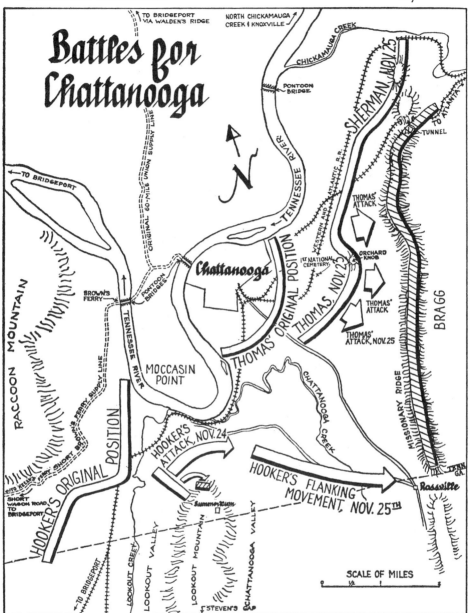

Map 7. Battles for Chattanooga, November 23, 24, 25, 1863. From a sketch made two months after the battle by Brigadier General William F. Smith and used by Grant as a part of his official report. (*O.R. Atlas, Plate 49, No. 1.*)

master General of the Army and the Assistant Secretary of War. Generals of corps, generals of division, generals of brigade, with their staffs and orderlies, crowded deferentially into the best spots of observation to which their rank entitled them.

Thomas put on a show. He mounted his attack under the full panoply of war. Men who saw it were reminded of the famous military shows of Europe. Troops in line and column checkered the broad plain of Chattanooga. In the rear of Fort Wood were the reserve ammunition and ambulance trains. The men seemed to drink in the inspiration of the scene. For the leading roles, Thomas cast Willich's superbly drilled brigade and Hazen's brigade of battle-wise veterans—one of the few at Chickamauga that met the test of both Kelly's field and Snodgrass Ridge. To match the natural setting Thomas employed all the numerous properties of war. Flags were flying. The locked steps of thousands of infantrymen beat equal time. The sunlight flashed from their bayonets. The sharp commands of hundreds of company officers could be heard, and the stirring notes of the bugles. And what had probably seldom been seen before—the tiny drummer boys marched with the troops, their sticks flashing in unison as they beat the stirring tempo of the charge.

At the bugle signal, about 1:30 P.M., the exact lines and serried columns moved forward. It was soon evident that Bragg's troops were still in position. The purpose of the reconnaissance was thus fulfilled but Thomas pressed forward his even, close-spaced ranks. No stragglers raveled their compact lines. First the Rebel pickets and then their reserves were swept out of their way. Without slackening their pace and with hardly a waver in their formations, the assault pressed forward to Orchard Knob. Willich's men drove the Rebels from its base and then hurled them off the summit. Hazen took the works on a lower hill to the right with the bayonet, and the colors of an Alabama regiment were seized as a battle trophy. Sheridan's men moved up on Hazen's right.

"I have carried the first line of enemy intrenchments," Wood signalled to Thomas, who stood with Grant on the eastern parapet of Fort Wood.

"Hold on," Thomas signalled back. "Intrench your position."

This was about 4:00 P.M. Thomas ordered Howard into line on the left of Wood. A six-gun battery was put into position on Orchard Knob and Grant promptly moved his headquarters up to this eminence. Two important military advantages resulted from this attack. It thrust a strong salient toward Bragg's center which was useful for observation and as a starting point for an assault. It also tore out the Rebel wedge which denied the Blue troops the use of the left bank of the Tennessee River upstream from Chattanooga to the point where Sherman was scheduled to make his crossing. From a tactical point of view it demonstrated a technique that must have been of absorbing interest to the thousands of military experts who watched it. Thomas mounted a surprise attack with 25,000 men in full view of the watching Confederate army. It was impudent and audacious. When the 200 Rebel prisoners were sent back for questioning by Thomas' intelligence section, they admitted that they thought the whole movement was a review and general drill. When Thomas' skirmishers suddenly opened fire it was too late to send for reinforcements and the Rebel lines were overwhelmed by force of numbers.

This attack had a psychological result which may have been as important as the military ones. Grant had been compelled to call on troops of the Army of the Cumberland to make his first offensive.

By late afternoon the show was over. The audience dispersed to the comfort and leisure of their permanent quarters to discuss and argue the details of what they had seen. These experts did not overlook the fact that Thomas, under orders to make a reconnaissance in force, had thrown a challenge into the teeth of Bragg's entire army and that his men had backed him up; that the Cumberlanders had set a high standard of military competence and that other units would need to get on their toes to equal it.

A corollary advantage arising from the afternoon's threat against Bragg's center was that the Confederates were forced to withdraw troops from Hooker's front to strengthen Missionary Ridge. Thomas pressured Grant to take advantage of this opportunity by giving him permission to order Hooker against Lookout Mountain. Grant finally agreed, but only conditionally. One of Sherman's divisions was still on the left bank of the Tennessee at Brown's ferry. If it could get across in time to take part in Sherman's assault a dozen miles upstream, Hooker was not to move. If, on the other hand, Sherman's divison could not cross in time, Hooker was to attach it to his command and demonstrate against the western slope of Lookout Mountain. The sole purpose of this movement, Grant pointed out, was to distract the enemy's attention from Sherman's crossing. One of Hooker's aides was stationed at Brown's ferry to keep Hooker advised of the movements of Sherman's division. Early in the morning of November 24, Hooker exercised his option and added Sherman's troops to his command. At 4:00 A.M. he notified Thomas that he was in position and ready to advance. He had one division from the Army of the Tennessee, commanded by Osterhaus,[30] and two brigades of Cruft's division from the Army of the Cumberland in addition to his own command. All were strangers. Before daylight Thomas sent Hooker the order for which both had been waiting. Hooker was no longer tied down to the supporting role for Sherman's crossing. He was authorized to attack the mountain stronghold.

As daylight slowly overcame the gloom of a cold drizzling rain, Lookout was shrouded in mist. By 8:00 A.M. Geary's men had reached the fords of Lookout Creek and were beginning to cross and climb the lower shoulders of the western slope of the mountain. Geary gradually formed his line facing north with his right against the base of the mountain's rocky palisade and his left reaching for the level bottomlands. By 11:00 A.M. Osterhaus had completed a bridge across Lookout Creek. His division crossed, followed by the Cumberlanders, and both aligned themselves on Geary's left. Hooker got some artillery into position and opened on the Rebel rifle pits. Thomas' fixed batteries from the toe of Moccasin Point joined in. The Rebel lines fell back reluctantly before this crossfire.

At midafternoon Hooker halted his advance. The heavy mist shut off his view of the enemy and he was out of ammunition. But he had carried the point of Lookout Mountain and was around on its eastern side. The job Thomas had been sponsoring for two months was done. Grant's army now had open lines of communication from one flank to the other along the left bank of the Tennessee River and enjoyed the inestimable advantage of interior lines. In addition, the rail and river lines between Chattanooga and Bridgeport were safe. The army's supplies no longer depended upon a makeshift communication line of three inadequate bridges.

In response to Hooker's call for ammunition, Thomas sent in Carlin's brigade, each man bent under a load of powder and bullets. At 5:00 P.M. this improvised ammunition train made its contact with Hooker and, as soon as it was relieved of its load, took its place in the battle line.

Yesterday some 120,000 spectators, friend and enemy, had watched the center of the Army of the Cumberland take Bragg's outlying works on the floor of Chattanooga Valley. Now almost as many watched anxiously for some evidence of the progress of the right flank of that same army against the mountain heights. They could hear a battle which they could not see. Occasional rifts in the mist that hid the peak revealed the tiny defenders in flight closely pursued by figures equally tiny. After dark the fog lifted and the night turned clear and cool. The heavy firing had ceased but the watching thousands saw the parellel lines of the campfires of the opposing armies, while the flashes of the pickets' rifles winked in the blackness between them. The next morning the sun climbing over Missionary Ridge at Rossville lighted the colors of Old Glory on the topmost peak of Lookout Mountain.

This was the finale to the second act of a battle such as the Yankee troops in the west had never before witnessed. The swamps around Vicksburg, the fat farmlands of Kentucky and Tennessee afforded no such spectacular battlefield as this. There each soldier's experience had been limited to a small compartment of stinging smoke, searing flame, deafening noise and sights of bloodshed that tied his stomach muscles into retching knots. Here the smoke billowed upward, soft and beautiful as a cloud. Gun flashes winked harmlessly, the noise was muted to a rumbling or a small crackling, men fell down as if they were tired and wanted rest. Here there were only the drama and the spectacular properties of battle. The onlookers were stirred to emulate—to surpass, if possible. They were anxious for their moment on the stage, hungry for the plaudits of the audience.

Since the night of the twentieth, the engineers and pioneers of the Army of the Cumberland had been readying the means by which Sherman's troops would cross the Tennessee. One hundred and sixteen pontoons had been hauled in secrecy to North Chickamauga Creek, seven or eight miles upstream from Chattanooga, where they had been launched and concealed. The citizens living in the vicinity had been put under guard so that no warnings might leak to the enemy. Everything was ready and waiting. At midnight on the twenty-third the boats left their hiding place and floated quietly down the stream to the crossing place opposite the north end of Missionary Ridge. By daylight of the twenty-fourth, two of Sherman's divisions had crossed and established a bridgehead. The pioneers began to lay the bridges. A steamboat came up from Chattanooga to help with the crossing. Simultaneously, Howard started his march up the left bank of the river from Chattanooga. Shortly before noon one bridge was completed. At 1:00 P.M., three of Sherman's divisions were moving toward the right flank of Bragg's army preceded by skirmishers. At 4:00 P.M., his men were on what Sherman thought was his objective and he so reported to Grant. On this misinformation Grant laid his plans for battle.

Sherman had never seen an accurate map of the country in which he was operating. His reconnaissance from the right bank of the Tennessee River a week previously showed him Missionary Ridge as one continuous elevation. In reality the north end of the Ridge was a series of detached hills. At least five of the highest and most formidable of these, flanking the railway tunnel, were occupied by the enemy. Here Bragg's heavily fortified right flank commenced, manned by the troops of Patrick Cleburne's [31] crack division. There were none better in the Confederacy. Sherman's men threw some of Cleburne's skirmishers off two of the outlying hills of Missionary Ridge, but they made no contact with Bragg's main defenses. What was worse, Sherman failed to realize it.

Grant's orders for the twenty-fifth went out the previous night. Sherman was to launch the main attack. Thomas was to cooperate with him and Hooker was to move southward on the east face of Lookout toward the Summertown road. There was some vagueness about these orders. Sherman thought that Thomas was to attack early in the morning. When Grant learned that Sherman was not in the position that he thought he was, he sent out a new set of orders. Under these, Sherman was to attack as originally ordered while Hooker was to move on Rossville and turn the left flank of Bragg's Missionary Ridge line. As soon as the flanks had been turned Thomas was to storm the center. Thomas was with Grant on Orchard Knob and he could not move until Grant gave the word. Sherman, however, never learned of the change and watched vainly for Thomas' attack to develop.

Sherman opened the battle at daybreak. It was the first time in Thomas' Civil War experience that his command had not been positioned to take the brunt of battle. A few moments after 10:00 A.M. the Rossville strike order went to Hooker. At 1:25 P.M. his command was halted by the destruction of a bridge over Chattanooga Creek. After repairing it Hooker moved on toward Rossville, swung his division to the left, carried the south end of Missionary Ridge and swept northward until they came to the front of the earthworks that Thomas had built the day after Chickamauga. Cruft's division, which had formerly occupied these works, stormed them and finally broke through the Rebel line, but by now it was nearly sundown.

Just as Thomas on the twenty-third and Hooker on the twenty-fourth had performed before a critical audience, so Sherman's assault was now the focal point of thousands of eyes. Success, however, did not follow. Grant became apprehensive. He sent an aide to hasten Howard's movement to reinforce Sherman. Later he detached Baird from Thomas' command and sent him to Sherman's aid. This was the eighth division ordered against Cleburne's stubborn defenses, not to mention Thomas' cavalry, which was wrecking Bragg's communications farther off to the north and east. By 3:00 P.M. Sherman's attack was hopelessly stalled even though he had more men than he could use.[32] Grant anxiously watched his left flank as Cleburne made a successful counterattack. He felt that Sherman's condition was becoming so critical that an assault against Bragg's center for his relief could be delayed no longer. It was plain enough to the professional critics watching Sherman's attack from Orchard Knob that the dominant element in Grant's battle plan was not only hopelessly defeated but that its defeat had seriously compromised the position of the entire Union army.

The tensions among these officers had been accumulating all day. By midafternoon they had become almost unbearable. The Army of the Cumberland had suspected since the twenty-third that eventually they would be ordered to storm Missionary Ridge. The waiting was a severe strain on the soldiers' nerves. In addition they were chafing under the calumny of Grant's charges that they were too sluggish to move out of their trenches. The strain on Thomas was even greater. There were nine divisions belonging to his army on the field at this time. Three of them were with Sherman, two were with Hooker. The four under Thomas' command were deployed so that they were covering Chattanooga as well as threatening Missionary Ridge. Every man was in the battle line, leaving him with no reserves. Bragg's center was numerically equal to Thomas' storming columns and had the tremendous advantage of position. The risk of ordering forward 18,000 men under these conditions seemed to Thomas unparalleled. He opposed such a movement until Bragg's flanks had been shattered. If his troops were to retreat from the Rebel works at the foot of the Ridge or if they failed in storming the crest, the Union army's lot might be defeat. Added to these pressures were several other explosive ingredients. Grant and Thomas were normally ill at ease in each other's presence. Grant was overly deferential, Thomas was unresponsive and silent, Rawlins was sullen, the staffs were fidgety. Granger, much to everyone's annoyance, was relieving his nervousness by banging away with one of the field pieces emplaced on Orchard Knob.

The most oppressive burden, however, was Grant's. He had put his victory prospects in Sherman's basket. More than half of all the infantry forces on the field were under Sherman. There were more men from the Army of the Cumberland under him than had been left with Thomas. Hooker's flank march on Rossville, which had been an unexpected gain for Grant, had now dissolved into silence. No word had come from him since 1:25 P.M., when he had announced that he was stalled at the bridge over Chattanooga Creek and would not get across for an hour. Sherman's efforts seemed to be paralyzed by his severe repulse. Grant's subordinates were discouraged. Hope of victory was waning with the day. Grant was anxious, doubtful and indecisive. Strain gave way to embarrassment. Three members of Grant's staff, in the hope of forcing some action, agreed that a demonstration by the center was the best means of breaking the deadlock and they pushed Rawlins forward to urge it upon Grant. Grant's indecision was evident in what followed.

He moved over to T. J. Wood, who was waiting on Orchard Knob for orders to move his division of Thomas' Fourth Corps. "General Sherman seems to be having a hard time," said Grant. "I think we ought to try to do something to help him." Wood replied that he was willing to try if Grant would give the order. "I think," Grant continued, "if you and Sheridan were to advance your divisions and carry the rifle pits at the base of the ridge, it would so threaten Bragg's center that he would draw enough troops from the right to secure his center and insure the success of General Sherman's attack." Wood stated again that he would move on Grant's order. This was at 2:30 P.M.[33]

Grant left Wood without giving the order and walked over to where Thomas was standing about ten paces away. In a conversational tone he asked, "Don't you think it's about time to order your troops to advance against the enemy's first line of rifle pits?" Thomas' reply could not be heard by the staff. He never lowered the glasses with which he was scanning the crest of Missionary Ridge. He believed an attack might succeed only if Bragg's flanks were broken first. As it happened, Hooker had already broken Bragg's left, but Thomas did not know it and refused to give the order on Grant's mere suggestion.

Grant's evident unsureness seemed to rob everyone of initiative. Time moved slowly. Thirty minutes went by. Rawlins' embarrassment had already turned into indignation. Indignation was now giving way to anger and at 3:00 P.M. Rawlins pressured Grant to issue a positive order. This time his emotions communicated themselves to the commanding general. Grant's face blazed and he dropped his conversational tone. "General Thomas," he said, "order Granger to turn that battery over to its proper commander and take command of his own corps." Another order soon followed with all the authority of over-all command—"And now order your troops to advance and take the enemy's first line of rifle pits."[34]

This was an order to demonstrate in favor of Sherman, not to make a frontal assault on Missionary Ridge. Thomas made no reply but he called Granger to him and the two spoke together while Grant listened. Shortly Granger stepped over to Wood and ordered him to move out and carry the rifle pits at the foot of Missionary Ridge. The signal for the execution of the order was to be the firing of six guns in rapid succession from Orchard Knob.

Historians seem to be unanimous in the belief that the orders to the Fourth and Fourteenth corps were to halt and await further orders after they had taken the rifle pits at the base of the Ridge. There is no doubt that this was the understanding of Grant, Granger and Wood. Sheridan, who got his orders from an aide, was doubtful whether his objective was the base of the Ridge or the crest. He sent to Granger for a clarification but the signal guns boomed before the aide returned. Palmer, the other corps commander, made no mention of the order in his battle report but both his division commanders believed their objective to be the crest. Of the eleven brigade commanders engaged in the assault only one stated positively that he was to halt at the foot of the Ridge and await orders. Two seemed to feel that to continue the advance or to halt was optional. Four stated that their commands were under orders from the division commander to continue to the crest of the Ridge. The remaining four considered the top of the Ridge to be their objective.

It was about 3:40 P.M. when the signal guns were fired. Thomas' line moved out promptly. The works at the foot of the Ridge were heavily manned and a mile and a quarter away. Rebel skirmishers checked their advance. Thomas' front was about three miles wide. Along part of this distance all cover had been removed from a strip 300 to 500 yards in width where the Rebel small arms and artillery could play havoc with the assaulting troops. Behind the rifle pits loomed the 600-foot height of Missionary Ridge, its side almost clear of timber and eroded into gullies. In places its gradient was more than 45 degrees. Halfway up was another line of rifle pits. At the top was the main Rebel army and fifty pieces of artillery.

Thomas' men could not linger in the space between their own lines and the crest of the Ridge. Never before in the history of American arms had a frontal assault of this magnitude succeeded. No mathematics could justify an assault that was expected and prepared for and that had to move across a mile and a quarter of level ground, climb 600 feet and take three lines of intrenchment. The Federal dead windrowed along the sunken road at Fredericksburg had given their mute testimony. Lee's shock troops had twice recoiled in a bloody mist from attacks that were less difficult. Now the emotions of the Cumberlanders smothered their rationalism.

At some time unrecorded, in some manner unknown, morale deserted the Southern arms and guided Thomas' flags through the impossible. A leaven swelled the emotions of the Army of the Cumberland. Thomas had seen the flash of its brilliance when a lone Comanche

warrior died in the broken plains of Texas along the Clear Fork. One
of his regiments had picked up the flame at Mill Springs. At Stones
River a brigade had caught the vision. At Chickamauga, when hope
was nearly gone, it burst into a blaze that lighted two divisions. Thomas
tried hard to lift his army into this exalted spirit. But by his own appraisal, he had failed. He thought himself too reserved to stir the feelings of his men.

Perhaps he was wrong. Or perhaps there was something in the
alchemy of time and situation that fired simultaneously the spirit
of his four divisions.[35] An urge to go forward ran through the ranks
like the spark through a powder train. Eighteen thousand troops overran the rifle pits at the base of the Ridge in short order and then moved
upward in the face of the sheeted fire poured down upon them from
the top of the Ridge. Grant was upset at this spontaneous assault.
"Thomas," he demanded angrily, "who ordered those men up the
ridge?"

"I don't know," was Thomas' quiet reply.

"Did you order them up, Granger?" was Grant's next query.

"No," answered the irrepressible commander of the Fourth Corps.
"When those fellows get started all hell can't stop them."

Grant's growled threat about making someone suffer if the charge
did not turn out well was lost in the noise of Thomas' guns. He gave
no more orders. The Army of the Cumberland was winning his battle
for him.

Against the bare, eroded slopes of Missionary Ridge, clearly lighted
by the westerly sun, Thomas' men looked entirely different than in
the correctly aligned ranks of the twenty-third. Now their classical formations were discarded. Where there was partial cover from the murderous Rebel fire the Blue figures packed closely into a small space
as they struggled upward. On the bullet-swept slopes they spread out
and moved more quickly. One observer thought they looked like
migrating birds constantly dissolving from one pattern into another
as they moved upward. There were fifty-three regimental flags on the
slope that afternoon. Their progress measured the rivalry between the
various units. The bright spots of their colors could be distinguished
from Orchard Knob. Occasionally one of their brass-tipped staffs threw
backward a brilliant flash of light. Near the top of the Ridge the assaulting troops coalesced behind these pinpoints of color and flashing
light, generally in the form of a wedge with the point uphill and the
sides straggling unevenly down the slopes. The color sergeants led
these wedges to their victorious destiny. When Thomas saw six of

them break through the Rebel defenses on the top of the Ridge at the same time, he mounted his horse and rode forth to join them.

The divisions on the right and left of Wood and Sheridan came promptly up to their support. Absalom Baird, who had marched northward to Sherman's support, almost immediately countermarched to go into the line on Wood's left, but he was too late. Sheridan's men were part way up Missionary Ridge before Baird's men left their positions in the original Union line. He was also checked by Cheatham and Cleburne, some of whose men turned their backs to Sherman to fire on him. Johnson's division came up on Sheridan's right. On their way they gobbled up a Rebel regiment which had been driven into their arms by Hooker's advance along Missionary Ridge from Rossville.

The brigades holding the center of Bragg's line panicked under the impact of Thomas' assault. It was one of the rare occasions in the war when first-line Rebel troops threw away their arms, turned their backs to the Yanks and ran for their lives—not all of them, though, for the men of Bate, Cheatham and Cleburne held their ground with the usual Rebel stubbornness. The fight for the Ridge was as desperate as any of the war. The range was short. Half a hundred guns poured an enfilading fire of grape and spherical case upon the climbing troops. Near the top, extemporized hand grenades made of artillery shells with short fuses rolled down on the storming wedges. Bayonet wounds were reported by the medical director. Sixty-six days previously Thomas' men had broken Longstreet's assaults against Snodgrass Ridge by shooting enough men out of the front rank so that the survivors lost physical contact with each other. In their breathless rush up the bald slopes of Missionary Ridge, his Fourth Corps was twice decimated. Yet they drove home their attack with full power. Grant and his staff had seen the dramatic demonstration of a new tactic. Thomas' men scaled the heights as individuals, for there was no physical contact between them. They dodged from one piece of cover to the next. They timed their rushes over exposed ground to take advantage of the lulls in the firing tempo of the defenders. They gave to military science that fundamental concept of attack known as extended order. It was the answer of the offense to the overwhelming firepower of rifled barrels, percussion caps and breech loaders.

The victory astounded the military world. One observer called it an accident, another called it a miracle, and still another thought it the most brilliant assault in history. The South's greatest historian said it was incredible. Dana was amazed. "Glory to God! The day is decisively ours," he wired impulsively to Stanton. Grant sourly observed

that the charge of Thomas' men had effectively carried out his orders
of the twenty-fourth.

Missionary Ridge was stormed too late in the day for a general
pursuit, although Sheridan's division and Willich's brigade of Wood's
division followed the fleeing Rebels down the eastern slope and picked
up a few more battle trophies. A fast, integrated pursuit was never
planned by Grant although the instructions he had given to Sherman
in cooperation with Thomas' cavalry raiders might have developed
into one.[36] That night, in compliance with Grant's orders, Thomas
pulled Granger's corps back to Chattanooga to prepare for a forced
march to the relief of Burnside.

On the morning of November 26 the chase was renewed. Sherman
moved upstream along Chickamauga Creek. Hooker and Palmer
moved southeastward toward Graysville and Ringgold.

Sherman, using Davis' division and Howard's corps, pressed toward
the big Rebel depot at Chickamauga Station. Davis reached there at
noon on the twenty-sixth and found it already in flames. He pursued
on the Graysville road but found himself in the rear of Palmer's troops.
Howard got his men through Parker's Gap farther to the east and put
out a column to destroy the railway between Dalton and Cleveland,
which was Bragg's link with Longstreet. Meantime Hooker and Palmer
had been held up by the destruction of bridges over Chickamauga and
Pea Vine creeks. The infantry got across but the artillery was left behind. At the road junction east of Pea Vine Creek the pursuit split.
Palmer took the left road toward Graysville. Hooker followed the right
toward Ringgold.

Palmer caught up with Bragg's rear guard at 9:00 P.M. on the
twenty-sixth and drove it out of Graysville before midnight. Next
morning Hooker and Palmer converged on Ringgold, Palmer coming
in from the north and Hooker from the west. Bragg was making a
stand at the gap where the railroad to Atlanta passed through Taylor's
Ridge. Hooker's artillery had not come up and he tried to silence the
Rebel batteries with rifle fire. Cleburne, who held the gap, was not to
be trifled with. Hooker tried to work a force around Cleburne's right
and was repulsed. He tried again, swinging this time in a longer arc,
and was again repulsed. At noon Hooker's guns came up but Cleburne,
having delayed the pursuit sufficiently, pulled out. Grant came on the
field and ordered the pursuit discontinued.

From the evening of the twenty-fifth until his arrival at Ringgold
on the twenty-seventh, Grant was undecided whether to pursue Bragg
or to move to the relief of Burnside. Thomas was holding Granger on

the leash in Chattanooga but for two days Grant refused to let him move. After reaching Ringgold, however, Grant was convinced that Bragg did not plan to join Longstreet in front of Knoxville and he sent orders for Granger to move at once.

This was Grant's number two job. From Washington's dispatches it seemed at times to be ranked as number one. Burnside was one of the hapless figures of the Civil War. He did fair work as a unit commander in another man's army but twice went to pieces in an independent command.

At the same time that the orders went to Granger, Sherman was ordered to move leisurely back to Chattanooga. That night Grant visited Sherman in Graysville and granted his request that he might make a circuit with his infantry as far north as the Hiawassee River. This was a move of some forty to fifty miles in the direction of Knoxville. Grant says the movement was to prevent Bragg from sending troops to Longstreet's aid. Sherman says that it was to pick up forage for his animals. On November 28 Grant returned to Chattanooga, found that Granger had not moved, that he was planning to move with fewer troops than Grant had specified, and blew up. He permitted Granger to march but he sent orders to Sherman to take command because he had lost all faith in Granger.

Longstreet with 20,000 men was besieging Burnside and his 12,000 men inside the city of Knoxville. Sherman with 30,000 in addition to Thomas' cavalry was advancing upon Longstreet from the south. The Cavalry Corps of the Army of the Cumberland was moving straight against him from the west. Major General John A. Foster with 5,000 men was coming south from the Cumberland Gap. Longstreet was not in an enviable situation. On December 3 Sherman got some of his advance units into Knoxville and the next day Longstreet raised the siege and moved his army up the valley toward Virginia. Two days later Sherman and Granger, leaving their infantry behind them rode into Knoxville. They marveled at the herds of fat cattle they saw there. They found Burnside comfortably housed in a mansion and sat down to a dinner of roast turkey, catered with a complete dining service. In an understandable reaction to the scare stories that had come out of Knoxville and Washington, they were justifiably disgusted.

Burnside asked for and received the Fourth Corps and the Cavalry Corps of the Army of the Cumberland to aid him in driving Longstreet off the soil of Tennessee.

Grant had the best record to date in breaking down the Rebellion. He had knocked two armies out of the war and it would be reasonable to suppose that his inclination ran that way at Chattanooga. It was Washington's frantic insistence on relieving Burnside which precluded the total pursuit of Bragg and it may have been one of Washington's biggest strategic blunders. The cream of military ability was rising to the top of the Northern armies in the persons of Grant, Thomas, Sherman and Sheridan. Here their combined energies were aimed at one Rebel army. There is no telling what might have happened if they had been free of Washington's shackles.

But Grant's official problems were all mixed up here with personal ones. The high drama of the Battle of Chickamauga, the lull in the fighting in Virginia, the heavy concentration of the North's military power along the western approaches to the Great Smoky Mountains pulled the attention of the nation to Chattanooga. Illustrious names began to converge on it. Above them all was Grant. His military fortunes had rocketed from disgrace to distinction in less than two years and, judging from the fate of many other army commanders, neither their direction nor acceleration could be maintained. To a great extent Grant's destiny lay in strange or inimical hands. Lincoln he had never met. Stanton was building a dossier of his shortcomings. Halleck had already evidenced his lack of faith in him and his discernment had bared Grant's basic military weakness. Thomas he could not dominate. Hooker's habit of undermining his superiors by political intrigue was well known. The ill-starred Burnside was more likely to get him into trouble than to help him out of it. In doubt and insecurity Grant turned to the only tested aid he knew—the Army of the Tennessee.

Since Burnside was one of his main responsibilities, he elected to make his assault against Bragg's right, for this put his main striking force between Bragg and Longstreet. Here his reliance on a makeshift line of communications began to bear its bitter fruit.

From this point on Thomas dominated the field of Chattanooga. Grant, hoping to save time by the use of a temporary communication line which delayed Sherman until after the successful assault on Lookout, proved Thomas' contention that Bragg's left, rather than his right, was the place to strike.

Such differences always exist between military geniuses but no matter whose theories prevailed the victory was Grant's and it put him on the path to top command. In looking at the tangled results of a co-operative effort in an uncooperative manner the fact should not be overlooked that Thomas' ambition introduced a personal element into his military thinking and strained the relations between the North's foremost commanders to a point which subsequently threatened to endanger the national welfare.

Thomas had been one of the dominant combat elements in every one of his battles beginning with the Mexican War. Neither Rosecrans nor Buell had resented this and Thomas leaned backward to prove that they had no reason to. Under Grant this trait was accented. Thomas resented being cast in a minor role and Grant and his supporters showed their resentment of his intransigence. Grant cannot be blamed for protecting himself, although some of his subsequent methods carried vindictive overtones.

The basic differences between these two leaders—how to save time and how to calculate military risks—began to crystallize at this time. Later a third and more important appeared. Grant brought to the Union armies something that no other western commander had brought them and the result pleased Lincoln. This was his energetic attempt to do the things that Washington wanted done in the way that Washington wanted them done and with the tools that he had at hand. Thomas had refused consistently and stubbornly to work this way. He quickly specified his needs for any job he was given and refused to move until his specifications were met. Sometimes this seemed like procrastination to his superiors but actually Thomas was acting in accord with a plan agreed upon. His objective was the annihilation of the enemy rather than compliance with superior commands. He realized that no soldier ever misunderstood victory, that he adored the leader who gave it to him and was unconcerned whether the end was achieved by brilliance against great odds or by awkwardness against inferior forces. This esteem for victorious leadership brings to an army a hidden asset that sometimes seems to be its most valuable one. It was a characteristic of leadership that Thomas and Grant understood equally well. They differed, however, in counting the cost of a too-easy compliance with higher authority.

Both Thomas and Grant had tremendous energy but Grant's was more apparent from his dispatches. These rang with an authority that the high command found reassuring. Thomas was as bold in his conceptions but more cautious in expression. This reticence made Thomas seem uncertain. Grant's written orders generally were abrupt, pointed and concise. The Virginian's ingrained courtesy gave his orders a suavity that often bordered on request. Both men got equal results but to the onlooker Grant seemed more sure of himself.

Grant was a brilliant improviser. Any successful military man must have this talent. It is the only way in which a defensive action can be won. But Grant carried his improvising over to the offense, as witness Donelson, Vicksburg and Chattanooga. Thomas always planned his offensive before he struck.

This conflict between planning and improvising may have been the result of Grant's inability to evaluate military risks. His attack order of November 7, later canceled as impracticable, is an example. The Battles for Chattanooga lasted three days, yet until the very end Grant never left his post in the center. Thomas, under similar responsibility, would have been all over the field. Sherman, with the most important role in Grant's attack plan, required attention, especially after his attack bogged down. Several objectives offered themselves for the employment of his unused divisions. If Grant himself had been unable to leave Orchard Knob when Sherman's attack collapsed, one of his competent staff could have been sent instead.

There was another cleavage. Grant seemed uninterested in the staff work that smooths the way for combat activity. Thomas took pains to see that the Army of the Cumberland was proficient in every detail of these supplementary services and he broadened their scope at every opportunity. At this time the army signal corps was struggling for recognition. The army commanders were asked to aid this embryo staff group in reaching its goals. Grant doused these hopes while Thomas threw his influence in their favor. He pointed out how the signalmen saved lives, time and money at Murfreesborough, in the Tullahoma campaign, in the maneuvering for the crossings of the Tennessee River and the concentration at Chickamauga. Thomas did not say so, but during the Battles for Chattanooga he used the signalmen to institute one of the early systems of remote fire control in North America.

Coincident with his support of the signal corps Thomas put into effect a system for providing his army with books and magazines. He was not in sympathy, however, with the work of the Sanitary and Christian Commissions. "They have caused much trouble," he said, "and could be easily dispensed with for the good of the service, as their duties are legitimately those of and should be performed by the Medical Department."

As soon as the Burnside relief column was on its way Thomas sent two of his brigades to Chickamauga to bury the Union dead. A few days later he rode down to Chickamauga himself, taking Grant with him. Always heedful of his dead, Thomas wanted to see how the burials were progressing. Also he had the understandable impulse to show the field to Grant and to live again those tense hours when time stood still and the familiar seemed strange. If the conversations between these master craftsmen during that trip could be read today many historic opinions might need revision.

Less than a week before the storming of Missionary Ridge, Lincoln had gone to Gettysburg to dedicate a portion of that bloody field as a state cemetery. Perhaps Thomas was thinking of Lincoln's words on Orchard Knob as he waited out the strain that precedes battle. The preservation of the dignity of the common soldier in death as well as in life had always been a subject close to his heart. Suddenly he pointed to a small hill just past the curve of the railway and one of his staff was astonished to hear him say that it would make a good cemetery. After returning from Chickamauga Thomas put the idea into effect with an order that a national cemetery be established on the spot that he had chosen in commemoration of the Battles for Chattanooga and to provide a proper resting place for the remains of their dead and such others as might thereafter give up their lives in the vicinity. He invited plans for a suitable monument to crown the little hill and specified that the work on the monument and the cemetery be done exclusively by the troops of the Army of the Cumberland. Later, when the burials were being made, the officer in charge of the work asked if the bodies should be buried in state groups.

"No, mix them up," was Thomas' reply. "I've had enough of states' rights."

This was the first cemetery to be established by military order. Thomas put the responsibility of caring for the battle dead on the Federal government. The Stones River National Cemetery north of Murfreesborough was also established by his orders.

With the raising of the siege of Chattanooga and the relief of Burnside, the Washington authorities once more began to center their attentions upon the Army of the Potomac. Meade felt that his days as its commander were numbered. There was no doubt in his mind about his supersession. The only question was by whom. Meade wrote to his wife, ". . . I understand the President and Secretary Chase are very anxious to bring Hooker back but Halleck and Stanton will undoubtedly oppose this. A compromise may perhaps be made by bringing Thomas here and giving Hooker Thomas' army. . . ." Garfield and Steedman were plugging for Thomas in Washington and Horace Greeley, who believed Thomas to be the greatest soldier in the North, came down from New York to put in a word for the Virginian.

Thomas was upset when he heard what was going on and wrote Garfield, ". . . You have disturbed me greatly with the intimation that the command of the Army of the Potomac may be offered to me. It is a position to which I am not in the least adapted, and putting my own reputation entirely aside I sincerely hope that I at least may not be victimized by being placed in a position where I would be utterly powerless to do good or contribute in the least toward the suppression of the Rebellion. The pressure always brought to bear against the commander of the Army of the Potomac would destroy me in a week without having advanced the cause in the least. Much against my wishes I was placed in command of this army—I have told you my reasons— now, however, I believe my efforts will be appreciated by the troops and I have reasonable hopes that we may continue to do good service.

"P.S.—If you will permit I will suggest that a better commander for the Army of the Potomac cannot be found than General William F. Smith, who is an eminent strategist, a man of firmness and energy and whose name is already identified with that army. His services with this army richly entitle him to advancement." [37]

For once Grant was in agreement with Thomas but the agreement extended to little else.

What came to be known as the Grant Legend grew up around the series of battles which he fought for the possession of Chattanooga. The impression was planted that it was the unique battle of the war, planned from beginning to end and fought as planned, and that Grant's own Army of the Tennessee played the dominant role and led the way to victory. The Legend was conceived in the battle reports of Grant and Sherman. Campaign literature devised to elect and re-elect Grant to the Presidency made full use of it. Some of Grant's unscrupulous biographers sought to rivet the Legend into history. Undoubtedly similar legends grow up around all great military leaders. The only point to be made about this one is that it downgraded Thomas to up-grade Grant and Sherman. It was subtly done at first. There was no denial of the fact that Thomas had initiated and implemented the changes in the battle plans nor was it denied that the Cumberlanders usurped the major combat role on the twenty-fifth. But there began an official campaign to label Thomas as a sluggard which became strident and outspoken after his death.

There is a quintessence of combat energy which sometimes flows from one part of a battlefield to another. No one knows what it is, no one can control it. By its transfer good military leadership multiplies the strength of a command without increasing its fire power. Mahan tried to teach its principles but he never knew what made men defend an indefensible position or carry one that was unassailable. Thomas, with its aid, inspired his men to do both within sixty days at points ten miles apart on the same historic ridge.

On November 25 this emotional energy seemed to flow from the Confederate battle line, with every advantage but one in its favor, to the tense Blue line of the Cumberlanders. It by-passed the Army of the Tennessee yet found lodgement in the one unit of that army temporarily under Thomas' command. No picket marked its passage. No breastwork broke its flow. Grant's bulldog realism never saw that the oriflamme which led the Cumberlanders to the heights might have been born in his disparagement of their combat ability.

With varying intensities similar results are apparent in five of Thomas' battles—enough to nullify the theory of coincidence. It is the key to the mystery of Missionary Ridge.

18

The Atlanta Campaign Under
Grant's Plan for a Professional War

After the relief of Knoxville there was a noticeable combat relaxation among the troops quartered along the Tennessee River. Grant and Sherman went on leave. Thomas stayed in Chattanooga rebuilding his shattered communications. There were nearly 500 miles of them which formed the supply lines of the Armies of the Cumberland, the Tennessee and the Ohio. It was Thomas' job to feed and supply these armies and through his overburdened headquarters in Chattanooga during the winter and spring of 1864 all three armies transacted their business.[1] It was the middle of January 1864 before he could operate a continuous rail line from his base at Nashville to his enormous Chattanooga store sheds.

The distillation of nearly two and one-half years' experience with military railways made Thomas the most thoroughly qualified line officer for this work in either the Union or Confederate armies, but his previous problems were flea bites compared to what he was up against from October 1863 on. All the variables in his problem—time, distance, numbers, tonnage and personalities—were blown up to fantastic proportions. Hazen, driven to desperation by the lack of food, clothing and shelter, asked that his command be transferred to some place where it could be adequately supplied. Foster,[2] who had succeeded Burnside, notified Grant that Thomas' failure to get supplies to Knoxville prevented any aggressive movement on his part and would soon necessitate a retreat. Logan,[3] commanding the Army of the Tennessee in Sherman's absence, was in a relatively good position as far as supplies were concerned but was irritated by the restrictions Thomas placed upon his use of the railroad, restrictions made necessary by the desperate effort to feed and supply the Armies of the Cumberland and the Ohio, Confederate prisoners and deserters and the Chattanooga citizens. It was the backbreaking job of supplying the Army of the Ohio, piled on top of the burdens he was already carrying, that almost broke Thomas down. On January 13 he seemed to give up the job as hopeless. "I do not know," he dispatched to Foster, "how you can be supplied from this place with anything like half-rations. . . . All I can do is to promise you all the aid I can give. . . . My animals are dying of starvation, too, . . . and I have concluded to starve with them until we can better their condition as well as our own. . . ."

Three days later Thomas had climbed out of his depression. "We have managed to feed Sherman's Corps," he wrote Garfield, "about 10,000 destitute citizens, all the prisoners captured in the Battle of Chattanooga and upwards of 8,000 who have come into this post since I assumed command. Now we have another call upon our energies and resources. It is to feed Foster's army when as yet we have not been able to accumulate any surplus here. . . ." Then he assured Garfield that he hoped to overcome eventually the immense difficulties that were staring him in the face.

Thomas was responsible not only for feeding and supplying the military forces but for building up a reserve in Chattanooga which would support a movement southward. Adequate supplies had been collected in Nashville. The problem lay in their distribution by rail. This work was under the control of John B. Anderson, military director of railroads for the Department of the Cumberland. He had been appointed by the Secretary of War and was authorized to restore the efficiency of the railroads and to operate them to Thomas' satisfaction. Thomas had no authority to give Anderson his orders but he put his troops to work cutting ties and fuel and offered Anderson all the men he might require to get the roads in operating condition. Through a series of dispatches to Grant and Halleck, Thomas acquired the services of D. C. McCallum, who had left his job as superintendent of the Erie Railroad to become the director of military railroads early in 1862.[4] In less than two weeks freight deliveries had increased 60 per cent. By the middle of February Thomas had the railroad open from Chattanooga to Loudon and by March 20, from Chattanooga to Ringgold. He was now ready to stockpile the supplies for the next campaign.

This was aimed at Mobile, by way of Atlanta, where a sea-supplied base could be set up to replace the long, exposed railroad from Nashville. The supply shortage in Chattanooga, however, coupled with Longstreet's presence in East Tennessee and with the immobilization of the Army of the Cumberland because of troop furloughs and the recent terrible wastage of horses and mules, forced Grant to devise an interim plan.

Meanwhile the Army of Tennessee, which was the Confederacy's second strongest, was in winter quarters at Dalton, Georgia. Since the end of December it had been under the command of Joseph Eggleston Johnston, who was one of the South's master military minds. Now he was threatening to turn either of Thomas' flanks in a massive raid on the Ohio River. If he turned the eastern flank Longstreet stood ready to help him. If he elected the west, Polk in Mississippi and the incomparable Forrest in West Tennessee would guard him. Grant had the Army of the Ohio protecting his eastern flank and Sherman guarding his western flank from Bridgeport to Decatur, thence northward along the railroad toward Nashville.

But both Johnston and Thomas were having manpower troubles. Johnston was losing men by desertion at the rate of about thirty a day. Because of Lincoln's amnesty proclamation they were giving themselves up to Thomas' pickets. Apparently this was not a net gain for the Union, for these deserters were a heavy drain on Thomas' scanty supplies. They trafficked with the enemy and they were prone to redesert. Thomas offered to turn them over to Governor Brough of Ohio for use as a migrant labor force if the Governor would keep them north of the Ohio River. Thomas' army was weakened by the absence of regiments on veteran furlough under the Civil War's rotation plan. Regiments which had been in service two years or more were invited to re-enlist on the promise of a thirty-day furlough, a $400 bonus and free transportation to and from their homes. Ninety-seven units took advantage of this furlough in January, riddling Thomas' brigades but lessening the burden on his communications.

Grant realized that his best interim plan was one that would keep Johnston off balance by some aggressive move of his own. He thought seriously of driving northeastward up the great valley of East Tennessee which led from Chattanooga to within striking distance of Richmond. He thought that somewhere along this route the final battle of the war would be fought in the spring of 1864 [5] but gave up the idea because it would require more troops than he had available. While he was thinking along these lines, Sherman suggested that he be permitted to make a raid against Polk and his two infantry divisions at Meridian, Mississippi, and against Forrest, who was audaciously recruiting a new cavalry corps in the center of Sherman's defense area.

Raiding was the type of military operation at which Sherman excelled. Somewhere deep inside himself he seemed to back away from terminal combat. His imagination harked back to the days when Andrew Jackson scourged the nation's enemies through the deep South and fed his men on parched corn.[6] This was just the type of action Grant needed to gain time to prepare for his full-scale advance and he granted Sherman's request. Sherman was to select his troops from his powerful Mississippi River garrisons, knock Forrest out of the war, drive Polk out of Meridian, destroy that rail center's military potential and then, if possible, occupy Mobile. Meantime, Schofield, who had replaced Foster in command of the Army of the Ohio,[7] would pin down Longstreet and Thomas would hold Johnston in place at Dalton.

Within this framework was enacted the episode which finally fixed Grant's distrust of Thomas' professional competency. On February 3 Sherman got his raid under way. His footmen marched out of Vicksburg with light packs. There was not enough opposition to force a deployment of the head of either of his two columns. William Sooy Smith[8] moved out of Memphis a few days later to take care of Forrest, who had about half as many saddles, and to join Sherman at Meridian. Polk evacuated the town and Sherman entered it on February 14 and began his destruction. He had no intention of complying with his conditional assignment against Mobile. When Sooy Smith failed to appear Sherman headed his infantry back to Vicksburg. Reaching it on February 28, he learned that Forrest had disgracefully defeated Sooy Smith and driven him into Memphis.

Grant knew nothing about these events until early in March but he had heard plenty of rumors about cooperative attacks by Longstreet upon Knoxville and heavy detachments by Johnston in favor of both Longstreet and Polk. On February 12 he suggested that Thomas make a reconnaissance in force toward Dalton to compel the return of two divisions Johnston was supposed to have sent to Meridian and, when this was accomplished, to occupy Dalton, if possible. Thomas was too weak to make this movement but agreed to go as soon as he received reinforcements. These arrived on February 16. From then until February 20 he was immobilized by rain.[9] Meantime he had

secured and forwarded to Grant all the information that his reconnaissance could possibly develop.[10] At daybreak on February 22
Thomas' troops moved out under Palmer's command, as Thomas
was laid up with neuralgia. There were three days of heavy skirmishing costing more than 300 casualties and the news which Thomas had
sent to Grant a week previously was verified. Thomas, who had now
come on the field, withdrew his force to Chattanooga despite Grant's
urging to maintain the pressure on Johnston.

A by-product of Thomas' reconnaissance had a bearing on the subsequent campaign. His scouts discovered that Dalton could be cut off
from Atlanta by using an unguarded road through Snake Creek Gap.
He wanted to try it and submitted the proposal to Grant shortly after
recalling his troops. From this beginning Thomas requested permission
to move against Atlanta with three army corps and a strong division of
cavalry, but Grant had other ideas for the Atlanta campaign.[11]

Here in the winter of 1863–64 was a situation in which Grant had
given simultaneous orders to two of his subordinates to accomplish
limited objectives and then move, at their discretion, against a final
objective. The subordinates were Thomas and Sherman. Thomas accomplished his limited objective and Sherman accomplished part of
his. Neither attempted to comply with Grant's discretionary order. Grant
was pleased with the success of Sherman's campaign and mildly con-
temptuous of Thomas'. The dispatches from the two fronts were
markedly different. Thomas minimized his successes and bluntly told
his superior that his plan was unworkable but suggested an alternative.
Sherman hid his opinion that Grant's ultimate objective was fantastically
impossible, overplayed his achievements and gave Grant the impression of an eager and energetic subordinate.

By the end of February the military situation around Chattanooga
was still undeveloped but Thomas had managed to work a great improvement in his basic supply problem. He now turned the energies of
his army toward the insurance of its future safety. His chosen method
of railroad defense had always been a concentrated mounted force to
fend off the raids of Forrest, Morgan and Wheeler before they could
reach the line, but his frequent requests for such a force had always
been refused. Now he called the talents of William E. Merrill to his
aid. Merrill was the son of one of Thomas' fellow officers in the Mexican
War, top man in his West Point class of 1859 and now chief engineer and
chief topographical engineer of the Army of the Cumberland. To help
him, Thomas had available what modern armies call combat engineers.
He had been recruiting and training them since the days at Camp Dick

Robinson. He and Merrill decided to solve their problem by means of fixed defenses.

This was not a new concept. Buell had initiated the idea by building blockhouses to defend the vital spots of his rail line but the Rebel offensive power soon outmoded them. Forrest would ride up to one, dismount his troopers and throw a ring of riflemen around the fort while the guns of his horse battery would be trained against the works at a murderous range. Then he would send in a flag demanding the surrender of the thirty or so defenders. The blockhouse was generally given up without a fight and the rail facility it guarded was quickly destroyed. Merrill replaced these blockhouses with ones that could resist artillery fire. At the most important points he built forts where guns could be emplaced, and stocked them to withstand a siege.[12] The winter and spring of 1864 saw 169 of these fixed defenses built.

Two corollary gains resulted from this use of scientific talent to replace military brawn. The available mounted troops, dispersed to defend vital railway installations, were now concentrated and moved to the front where they belonged. Veteran infantrymen were relieved from blockhouse duty by state militia with a resultant gain in combat efficiency.

There were unrelieved stresses resulting from the Chickamauga and Chattanooga campaigns which necessitated changes in command and Thomas set about making them. He preferred efficient colonels to mediocre brigadier generals in the command of his brigades. He asked brevet promotions for sixteen of them. He had made up his mind to replace Gordon Granger and R. W. Johnson as soon as there was an opportunity to do so without embarrassing his subordinates. He offered commands to Buell and Crittenden but both refused them as beneath their dignity. He was beginning to doubt the ability of Palmer to handle the Fourteenth Army Corps.

Hooker's command of two army corps threw the entire organization of the Army of the Cumberland out of gear; yet it was Lincoln's idea and so became Thomas' problem. He solved it by combining the Eleventh and Twelfth corps under Hooker's command. The rank and file wanted the new organization designated as the Twelfth Corps, which had won an honored record in the eastern battles. Thomas, interested in promoting the morale of his command, endorsed their application. Grant, however, ordered their designation as the Twentieth Corps, which had acquired such an unsavory reputation under McCook at Chickamauga that it had been dropped from the army rolls. Thomas thought highly of Slocum and Howard, who were now left at loose ends. He obtained an acceptable command for Slocum in the Department of the Tennessee against the day when he could be recalled to the Army of the Cumberland, and he moved Howard to the command of the Fourth Corps when Gordon Granger left for a leave of absence.

The concentration of his cavalry units, released by the construction of the improved railroad blockhouses, necessitated a sweeping reorganization of that arm. George Crook,[13] who eventually became the nation's ablest Indian fighter, had been relieved of his command of Thomas' Second Cavalry Division and sent east. Thomas tried to replace him with J. H. Wilson [14] or Wilder. When these were refused he asked that Crook's orders be countermanded, but it was seven months before he secured a competent replacement. Thomas requisitioned the animals and equipment needed to put his cavalry in readiness for the campaign. The Quartermaster's Department was aghast at the required expenditure of $4,250,000. Grant sided with the Quartermaster and cut the requisition in half. Thomas unsuccessfully protested.

In the middle of March the news became public that Grant had been called to Washington, promoted to the rank of lieutenant general and elevated to the command of all the Northern armies. Sherman stepped into Grant's shoes as the commander of the Military Division of the Mississippi and McPherson followed Sherman as commander of the Army of the Tennessee. Since Schofield had just received his appointment as commander of the Department and Army of the Ohio, every ranking officer in the Military Division except Thomas, whose record was starred with success, was the recipient of official favor. Thomas made no complaint that can be found today nor did he give any evidence of irritation but in spite of his silence the army was full of rumors of Thomas' discontent at the slight. Civilians close enough to official Washington to be conscious of the implications behind the news had felt that Thomas was sure to have the Western command. "I suppose you will place Thomas in command of the West?" Andrew Carnegie inquired of Grant, who was his dinner guest just after receiving his new commission.

"No," Grant replied, "Sherman is the man for chief command. Thomas would be the first to say so."

Sherman was asked if there were any truth in the rumors that Thomas was dissatisfied. "Not a bit of it," was Sherman's reply. "It don't make any difference which of us commands the army. I would obey Thom's order tomorrow as readily and cheerfully as he does mine today. But I think I can give the army a little more impetus than Thom can." Sherman realized that Thomas complemented his own abilities and "knows how to pull with me, tho' he don't pull in the same way."

At the start of the Atlanta campaign one observer wrote, "The venerable George H. Thomas is in fine spirits and gets along with Sherman better than anyone else can."

Only one voice was raised publicly in behalf of Thomas. This was Andrew Johnson's, now for two years military governor of Tennessee and destined in another year to be the President of the United States.

"The Department of the Cumberland," he advised Lincoln, "ought to be placed under the command of Major General Thomas, receiving his instructions and orders directly from Washington. I feel satisfied from what I know and hear that placing the command of the Department under General Sherman, over Thomas, will produce disappointment in the public mind and impair the public service. General Thomas has the confidence of the army and the people, and will discharge his duty as he has from the commencement of the Rebellion. He will, in my opinion, if permitted, be one of the great generals of the war, if not the greatest. . . ."

Grant's accession to the top Union command was the opportunity for a strategic reappraisal and a long overdue army reorganization. Grant knew that the Rebels' losses in personnel, materiel and territory in the last half of 1863 had crippled them so that the Rebellion was running on the momentum acquired by Lee's victories from Bull Run through Chancellorsville. If he could knock the South's major armies out of the war this momentum would lose both its mass and velocity and the war would slow to a stop. To this end he proposed to subordinate most of the seventeen independent commands, which now wasted much of the North's military effort, and to aim the energies of the rest at a common objective. The war, as far as Grant was concerned, had now professionally begun and he intended to use the North's overwhelming resources to insure its successful conclusion.

Grant returned to Nashville in the middle of March to see that Sherman understood to the final period the part he was to play as his prime lieutenant in the new plan. Grant's plan was simple, complete and strategically sound. His objectives were the armies of Lee and Johnston. The Army of the Potomac would move directly south against Lee, aided by the Army of the James on the left and three columns under Sigel, an early commander of the Eleventh Corps, on its right. Simultaneously, Sherman would move against Johnston while Nathaniel P. Banks, who had relieved Patterson in the Shenandoah, would move from Louisiana against Mobile. Failure to pursue a beaten enemy had been the North's costliest error to date and Grant intended to put a stop to it. Sherman's second objective was to take and hold Atlanta. While Thomas remained with Sherman, Grant took Sheridan east with him and so the North's Big Four took the top roles in the final chapter of conquest—Grant and Sheridan against Lee, Sherman and Thomas against Johnston.

Sherman assured Grant that he would not let side issues draw him off from his two objectives; yet thirty days after this meeting he was beginning to look upon his role as a raid rather than a mission of destruction.[15]

As soon as Grant returned to Washington Sherman went down to Chattanooga to talk things over with Thomas. McPherson was picked up on the way and Schofield was brought down from Knoxville. The four of them agreed on the proven tactic of a movable base. One of the four added a new element—the supplying of a movable base by rail. This was the ultimate adaptation of the railroad to military purposes. Hitherto the Army of the Cumberland had used the railroad to supply a fixed base. First the enemy was pushed back, a new base secured and the railway repaired up to it. Then supplies were stockpiled for another advance. This resulted in costly, exasperating delays, prevented the maintenance of a constant pressure on the enemy and permitted him to rebuild his strength to oppose the next Union advance. The problem was to rebuild the railroad as fast as the army could move and keep it in repair so that the loaded freight trains could supply the skirmish lines.

Thomas and McCallum worked out the details. They set up a ratio of rolling stock per mile of track to forecast the needs of the Atlanta campaign. The rolling mill that Thomas had begun at Chattanooga was completed and machine and repair shops were set up there. The technical problems—cutting and piling locomotive fuel, spotting cars by means of mule or man power, quick unloading, fast turnarounds, establishing division points, securing men and tools for the maintenance of the right of way, and increasing the speed of loaded trains—all were discussed and settled.[16]

They organized efficient construction, maintenance and repair gangs and worked out in advance of the Atlanta movement solutions for the major problems they would have to face. Thomas' intelligence section had already compiled or was gathering detailed information on rolling stock, track, right of way, fills, cuts and bridges from Ringgold to Atlanta. The army marveled when the Chattahoochee bridge, 780 feet long and 90 feet high, was rebuilt in four and one-half days. This was the most spectacular result of their forward planning. Bridge sections built to measure in advance were dropped into place and bolted together. Portable sawmills cut lumber on the site.

The attempt to supply a large army from a point more than 350 miles distant over a single track through hostile territory is believed to have been without precedent in military history. It was a calculated risk and Sherman assumed the responsibility for its failure. But he acted on the advice of Thomas and McCallum and they made the plan succeed.

There were some problems this team could not correct. The telegraph lines were under Stanton's rigid control although 90 per cent of their traffic concerned the operation of the railroad. Stanton refused to let go of them and McCallum was seriously embarrassed. Successful railway operation also depends on men who know the peculiarities of the system—grades, curves, stations, wood yards, water tanks, passing places—and since it was impossible to hold these trained men in the face of civilian blandishments, labor turnover was higher than it should have been. Despite these drawbacks, the record of the United States Military Railroads in the Atlanta campaign was an enviable one. At no time was Sherman's movable base as much as five days behind his forward depot.

The Nashville car shops were one of the high spots in the technical achievements of the Army of the Cumberland. When Thomas' division had arrived there on its transports early in 1862, Albert Sidney Johnston's retreating army had destroyed everything. Thirty-two months later Superintendent George Herrick had the men and equipment that enabled him to service thirty-four locomotives simultaneously and to keep in repair 3,000 freight and baggage cars. In addition he was designing and building hospital cars, armored cars and other special units.[17]

Since it was impossible to meet all the demands of the railroads, Thomas set up a table of priorities and permitted no deviation. Schofield felt that he was not getting the things he needed in preparation for an advance. Logan charged that Thomas was discriminating against the Army of the Tennessee in favor of the Army of the Cumberland. Even Thomas and Sherman were at loggerheads over some details. These frictions were settled by Sherman's taking control of the railroads. Thomas now requested Sherman to issue the orders that heretofore he himself had issued. Sherman personally made several important contributions to the solution of railroad problems. He denied civilians the use of the road and made his ruling stick in the face of political pressure.

He impressed freight cars and locomotives as they arrived at Nashville until he had rolling stock enough to meet his own requirements. Veteran regiments returning from furloughs were marched from Nashville to Chattanooga. This was illegal but none seemed to object. All cattle and horses went south under their own power. He instituted one-way traffic on a single-track line by sending loaded cars from Nashville to Stevenson and returning them by way of Decatur, Pulaski and Columbia. He ordered Thomas to stop feeding the luckless Rebel citizens trapped in Chattanooga by the Union army. Thomas, evidently on his own authority, sent a flag of truce to Johnston suggesting that the Confederates, on the ground of moral duty, take over this responsibility.

Thomas, in command of the Center, was given one of the most difficult roles in the art of war. He was to move straight on Johnston wherever he might be and fight him cautiously but persistently. The complexities of his role arose from the fact that he was to pin down an enemy force equal in strength to his own without knowing exactly where that force was located. While doing this the Army of the Cumberland was to provide an impenetrable wall behind which, in safety, the services of supply could function. Thomas was to hold Johnston so tightly in position that he could not change front to repel a flank attack by McPherson or Schofield. He had the responsibility of keeping Johnston from breaking through the Union line, enveloping it or turning its flank. At all times he was to have a steady, reliable, unshakeable force to be used as a rallying point in case of trouble. In retrospect it seems that Thomas' first concern was to hold Sherman's army safe and to perform his aggressive role only when its safety was assured.

When McPherson and Schofield complained that they should have some of Thomas' infantry, Sherman replied, "You know that the reason I keep you on the flanks is that if the enemy should wipe you out I would have Old Thom left, and they could not move him." Strategically Thomas was constantly on the offensive. Tactically he was in a defensive role as Sherman's base guard but he shifted to the tactical offensive when this base moved forward. The moments of greatest danger and anxiety came during a forward movement after Johnston had broken contact and the location of his various units was not accurately known. Then Thomas' army marched in columns on parallel roads often too far apart for mutual support. At these times Sherman had no protected base and his safety depended on Thomas' ability to foresee danger and to get his dispersed forces into position to meet it in time to avert disaster. Proper reconnaissance and good skirmish lines were the main reliance against surprise at such times. Intrenchments would serve to hold a counterattack until relief could come and infantry units were to intrench every night. There is evidence that Sherman never really understood the tactics imposed upon the Army of the Cumberland, but his chief engineer did and emphasized in his official report that the Union force was never surprised.

With these things in mind Thomas began to pull his army into shape. It was comprised of three infantry corps—the Fourth commanded by Howard, the Fourteenth by Palmer and the Twentieth by Hooker. Howard's division commanders were Stanley, Newton and Wood. Palmer had Johnson, Davis and Baird. Hooker had Williams, Geary and Butterfield. In addition, Thomas had two divisions of cavalry, one under E. M. McCook and the other commanded by Kenner Garrard. Another division, belonging to the Army of the Cumberland and commanded by Judson Kilpatrick, was loaned to the Army of the Tennessee. Fortunately the Cavalry Bureau had reinstated Thomas' original requisition for remounts and equipment and recommended Sharps or Spencer carbines for their arms. There were 98,797 troops and 254 guns in Sherman's army, of which Thomas commanded 60,733 men and 130 guns. Johnston opposed this force with approximately 60,000.

Sherman's plans were based upon information brought in by Thomas' intelligence section. It was a rich harvest resulting from months of training and organization. By the middle of March Thomas had an arc of signal stations observing all roads from points six to eight miles in advance of his infantry lines. These were connected with his command posts by telegraph, visual signals and couriers. Every two or three days information came in from Johnston's headquarters. This information was received by different routes from persons unacquainted with each other. Supplemental reports came in from Atlanta. All of this poured into Thomas' headquarters for appraisal. Digests of it went to Sherman. Even after he had left the western armies, Grant used to ask for Thomas' intelligence reports. Joe Johnston must sometimes have felt that Thomas was looking over his shoulder. One of Johnston's Alabama units had been subverted and Johnston wanted it quarantined. He was dismayed to learn that Thomas already knew of the situation. As the campaign progressed Thomas' intelligence section proved its worth on several occasions. During the blind march after the Etowah crossings, it discovered in time to avert a disaster that Johnston, too, had left the railroad and was planning to meet the Yanks near Dallas. Twelve hours after Johnston received the telegram relieving him of his command Thomas was able to inform Sherman of that fact. Thomas' discovery of Wheeler's concentration for his raid northward was almost simultaneous with Wheeler's orders. Sabotage was an outgrowth of intelligence and Thomas did not hesitate to use it. He struck a deal with some unknown party to burn one of the bridges over the Etowah River for $30,000 Confederate money.

Two other military contributions by the Army of the Cumberland should be noted. It was as important to get combat troops across a river as it was to get a railway train across. But the pontoon trains heretofore available to the western armies were a drag on their mobility. Heavy, cumbersome wagons were needed to carry the twenty-one-foot boats. Rosecrans had suggested building these in two sections but the scheme never worked. Thomas ordered Merrill to perfect the idea. The result was the famous Cumberland Pontoon. Merrill hinged the gunwales so that one end of the boat turned back upon the other. He built an 800-foot bridge on this principle for Thomas' army and then equipped each of Sherman's corps and trained their pontoniers. The bridges were first used at the Etowah River and the rapidity with which they were laid surprised Sherman.

Thomas also turned his attention to map making. Before the start of the Atlanta campaign his topographical engineers secured the best obtainable map of Georgia and enlarged it to a scale of one inch to the mile. Thomas' intelligence section, under Sergeant Finnegan of the Fourth Regiment of Ohio Volunteer Cavalry, amplified and corrected it by skillful questioning of prisoners, deserters, spies, refugees and peddlers. No available map, for instance, showed Snake Creek Gap but Finnegan located it and described it. Captain William C. Margedant, one of Thomas' staff officers borrowed from an Ohio regiment, invented a field reproducing process which placed bound copies of identical maps in the hands of each brigade, division, corps and army commander before contact was made with the enemy. In Merrill's opinion the army that Sherman led to Atlanta was the best supplied with maps of any that fought in the Civil War.[18]

The Cumberland medical units came in for some fundamental reorganization. Previously their ambulances had found more use as private conveyances for regimental commanders than for the sick and wounded. They were now organized into a unit for each army corps and put under the control of the army corps medical director. The order was specific and detailed. It antedated the War Department order for similarly organizing ambulance trains by two and one-half months. Under the gruelling test of the Atlanta campaign it broke down in two respects. Its horses were of the poorest character. They had almost starved at Chattanooga and had not recuperated before being hitched to the ambulances. Regimental and company officers, who designated the stretcher bearers, picked their weakest, most sickly and most trifling men.

Once Thomas had sufficient ambulances to pick up his wounded and get them to the hospitals and eventually to the railway, he turned his attention to the trains that were to take them north. Rosecrans had organized solid hospital trains. Thomas moved to make them safer. He assigned to them the most reliable locomotives and the best crews. He had the stacks, cabs and tenders painted red and had three red lanterns installed below each headlight for identification after dark. The words "Hospital Train" were lettered on each car. There is no record that any of Thomas' marked trains were ever molested intentionally by the Rebels.[19] For the first time in the Cumberland army the use of chloroform became standard practice in the medical units and, closely related to the idea of preventive medicine, cooks were detailed for the first time to prepare the soldiers' food.

By the end of March six regiments of colored troops had been organized under Thomas' direction. Three more regiments and a battery of light artillery were being organized. Negro recruiting was directly opposed to Sherman's policy but in line with that of the Administration. Since the outbreak of the war the government had approved the use of slaves in military labor. The next step was to enlist them into the armies. Thomas marshaled his arguments to cover both eventualities. If slaves were enemy property he said, their use was justified by the Articles of War. If they were free men they should be enlisted like any alien national. In either case, military service would help bridge the social and economic gap between slavery and freedom.

Sherman's army was probably as ready as any Northern army in the west ever was, although it had several grave deficiencies, most of which stemmed from the shortage of supplies at Chattanooga. The worst was its lack of sufficient and adequate transport animals. In addition, scurvy prevailed in most regiments in the Cumberland army and this physical condition was not bettered by the basic diet of coffee, salt meat and flour paste, Georgia's midsummer heat, blue woolen uniforms, unremitting labor and a lack of opportunity for baths and laundry.

It is little wonder that Sherman conceded that Thomas' army was the best provided and contained the best corps of engineers, railroad managers and repair parties as well as the best body of spies and provost marshals. He was compelled to rely on Thomas for staff work as well as combat strength. This quest for an integrated army of high competence was Thomas' lifelong pursuit. He saw it as a two-way responsibility—his to be sure that his men were well supplied, well looked after and brought to the right place at the right time; theirs to carry out their orders. Only by unremitting effort could Thomas perform his part of the contract.

He tried to visit every part of his command daily. On one of these visits he learned that the drunkenness of a commissary officer was depriving some of his men of their proper food. Thomas ripped the straps from his shoulders and reduced him to the ranks. It was his habit to have every piece of equipment complete. There can be no doubt that Thomas was a master of detail. "Something is sure to get out of order if I go away from my command," he once said. "It was always so when I commanded a post. I had to stick by and attend to everything or else affairs went wrong." [20] He was always asking questions, examining minute details. The commander of his headquarters guard was fearful that Thomas would know more about his command than he did himself. Thomas abhorred waste. During one campaign his troops stripped the country of sweet corn. Thomas stopped to watch one of these pillagers who had propped the ears of corn around his fire and was on his knees turning each ear a little at a time as it roasted.

"What are you doing?" Thomas asked.

"Why, General, I'm laying in a supply of provisions."

"That's right, my man, but don't waste them."

In battle, Thomas invariably made his way to the head of a threatened column, then dismounted and walked to the front of the skirmish line, but on the march he kept out of the way of his laboring troops. His subordinates knew they would be commended for their successes and that Thomas would find the causes for their failures, that he would never blame others to shield himself.

Newspaper correspondents were a source of irritation to Thomas as they were to most ranking Union commanders. His habitual defense against their publication of inexact or restricted material was to guard his official correspondence and caution his officers and men against too much talk. While the preparations for the Atlanta campaign were in progress one of Thomas' signal officers broke the Rebel cipher and, in an unguarded moment, mentioned the fact to a division commander in the Fourteenth Corps. The story was soon in the papers and the Rebels changed their cipher, much to Thomas' disgust. The next time it happened Thomas felt that the guilty correspondent should be executed. Sherman had the man arrested and turned over to Thomas but

Thomas had a change of heart and sent him north of the Ohio River instead of to a firing squad. He did require, however, that all correspondents sign their articles.

It was Sherman's ambition to make his army as mobile as possible, which was a proper goal too often overlooked by Union army commanders. The effort could, however, be carried too far. In his attempt to equal the mobility of the Southerners, who had few military supplies as compared to the Yankees, Sherman actually threw away some of his military advantages. He aimed at a ratio of 600 wagons for every 3,500 men. These wagons were reserved for ammunition, cooking utensils and food staples. An officer's personal baggage was cut to the amount he could carry on his own horse. This shortage of wagon transport forced Sherman to cut the grain ration for his horses in half and eliminated their forage ration altogether, expecting them to make up these lacks by foraging. In preparation for his advance he had made a close study of the United States census reports for Georgia (probably those of 1860) and the tax rolls of the various Georgia counties. From these he picked the areas where he had the best chance of getting food for his men and animals, but he made some miscalculations which bore heavily on his command before it reached Atlanta. Johnston's army stripped the country ahead of Sherman's skirmishers and there was a crop shortage in Georgia which historic records did not foretell.

Actually Sherman was moving backward in this part of his military thinking. The North was winning the war with its superior resources. Sherman jettisoned this advantage to prove that his army could do what the enemy did. He seemed intent on meeting the enemy on an equal footing. It must have been the reassertion of his raiding complex.

On April 29, Sherman arrived at Chattanooga to take over the combat command. On May 1, Thomas began his concentration, with Howard on his left at Catoosa Springs, Palmer commanding his center at Ringgold and Hooker at Leet's tanyard six or eight miles to the southwest. McPherson's two corps were moving up to Lee and Gordon's mill on Thomas' right. Schofield's Twenty-third Army Corps, another name for the Army of the Ohio, was coming up on Thomas' left after their march from Knoxville and Sherman and Thomas rode out to meet them. They dismounted on the sloping lawn in front of Doctor Lee's house and watched the occasional puffs of smoke off to the south where Thomas' guns were correcting their ranges on Tunnel Hill. Schofield and his staff rode up and were introduced to the two ranking commanders. Among them was the thirty-six-year-old J. D. Cox, then commanding a division in the Twenty-third Corps. He had a low regard for the narrow education given at West Point and for most regular army officers, whom he felt to be arbitrary, despotic, often tyrannical and poorly equipped for commanding volunteers. Against this background it is interesting to note that he saw Thomas as unlike the typical officers for whom he had so little use. He also saw a man whose intellect was much broader than that of most West Pointers.[21]

In Thomas, Cox had met an army man with a liberal education. He had found a professional soldier with broader interests than his vocation and this choice of interests had led him to significant changes in his professional outlook. At West Point Thomas was indoctrinated with European ideas of warfare. His education was dogmatic. He was expected to memorize and accept other men's theories. But when he exercised the freedom to broaden his education some of the dogmas came into question and were gradually replaced with concepts of his own. Thus we understand how Thomas might disagree with his superiors and have the courage to risk his career on the issue of his disagreement.

Cox saw that the old schoolmate affection between Thomas and Sherman was still warm. Sherman called him Thom and his army was Sherman's chief reliance.

Dalton, where Johnston had his headquarters, was a railway junction. The road north from Atlanta split there, one line going north to Knoxville and the other northwest to Chattanooga. The Rebel supplies came up this railway. West of Dalton on a north-and-south line was a mountainous ridge called Rocky Face Ridge on its northern end, Mill Mountain in the center and Horn Mountain on its southern end. It could be crossed by several gaps, the most usable of which from north to south were Buzzard Roost Gap, where the Chattanooga railway and the main wagon road crossed it, Ray's Gap, some three miles due west of Dalton, Dug Gap, and Snake Creek Gap, which was about five miles west of Resaca. At Resaca the Atlanta railway crossed the Oostanaula River. Johnston was using the declivities of the Rocky Face-Mill-Horn Mountain range to guard his western flank. He had earth works and adequate holding forces at each gap except Snake Creek. The shortest approach to Dalton from the north was by means of Buzzard Roost, but it was also the most heavily guarded. A dozen miles of earthworks extended northward, thence eastward and thence southward in the shape of a fish hook—the barb at Buzzard Roost, the curve three miles east of Tunnel Hill and the end of the shank east and slightly south of Dalton. In February Thomas had stood on the railway fill north of Buzzard Roost, outlined against the sky and within easy range of the Rebel rifle pits. While a sharpshooter fired at him,

Thomas thoroughly examined the works with his glasses and convinced himself that they could not be forced. It was a shrewdly chosen position and was striking evidence of the claim of Johnston's friends that he was one of the foremost military leaders of the South.

Sherman had three options. He could move southward along the Knoxville-Dalton railway and strike Johnston on his weak eastern flank; but this move would uncover the Union base at Chattanooga and was probably never considered seriously. Or he could strike eastward through Buzzard Roost, Ray and Dug gaps. There is nothing in the official records about it, but Thomas must have objected strenuously to this tactic which had almost brought annihilation to Rosecrans in the Chickamauga campaign. Thomas proposed the same plan he had offered to Grant in February. While McPherson and Schofield demonstrated east, north and west of Dalton to hold Johnston in position, the Army of the Cumberland would swing southward and eastward through the unguarded, unwatched Snake Creek Gap and cut Johnston's line of retreat. It was the duplicate of the Tullahoma campaign plan, when the rain had stopped him from bagging Bragg's army. This time Thomas knew how to turn the trick without a slip-up. Johnston would be trapped between Thomas on the south, the rest of Sherman's army on the north, an impassable ridge on the west and the Connassauga River on the east. He would be brought to bay at the point closest to Sherman's base and farthest from his own. The plan also presented an opportunity to prevent Polk, who was moving up from the south with an army corps, from uniting with Johnston.

Sherman adopted Thomas' strategy but refused his tactics, using McPherson's light flanking force for the attack instead of Thomas' heavy striking force. At this time the Army of the Tennessee consisted of the Fifteenth Army Corps, commanded by Logan, and the Sixteenth, commanded by Dodge. The Seventeenth joined them later. McPherson reached the mouth of Snake Creek Gap on the morning of May 9 while Thomas was holding Johnston in place around Dalton, but the trap was never sprung. McPherson, who had no cavalry, hesitated to make the march eastward to the railroad with his left flank exposed to whatever enemy force might come down the roads from the north. The news that McPherson had failed to break the railway was a great disappointment to Sherman. He realized his mistake but Thomas pointed out that there was still a chance to retrieve his fortunes and offered to loan McPherson 20,000 men. On May 10, Sherman began the reinforcement. One of Hooker's divisions started for Resaca first, then Kilpatrick's cavalry, then another division of the Twentieth Corps. By the following day the entire army, with the exception of Howard's Fourth Corps, was at Resaca or on the way there. Thomas remained with Howard north of Dalton until the twelfth and held the bulk of Johnston's army in his works, but Sherman was too slow to take advantage of the opportunity. When Thomas heard that the excuse for not getting on the railway was the thick woods north of Resaca, he is reported to have asked, "Where were their axes?"

By the thirteenth Johnston had concentrated at Resaca and occupied a strong position defending the crossings of the Oostanaula River with both flanks well protected. But it was also a dangerous position because, in case of a retreat, he would have to put his army into a vulnerable column formation to cross the river. Thomas saw the opportunity and urged Sherman to take advantage of it by pushing McPherson's army across the Oostanaula River at Lay's ferry to get on the railway at Calhoun. To add weight to McPherson's threat, Thomas offered the use of the Twentieth and Fourteenth Corps. This proposal was made sometime between 9:00 A.M. and 2:15 P.M. on May 13, but Sherman discarded the idea in favor of throwing his army across the railway between Resaca and Dalton.

Howard entered Dalton at 9:00 A.M. on the thirteenth and immediately pushed south along the railway toward Resaca. He camped eight miles north of the town that night. The next day Sherman developed Johnston's position. Polk, who had come up, held the southern flank at the Oostanaula and Hood held the northern flank with his right anchored on the Connassauga. Hardee occupied the center. Sherman's deployment put McPherson on the right facing Polk, Hooker put in one division on McPherson's left, the Fourteenth Corps extended the line northward on the left of this division and Schofield came in on the northern flank. Between the opposing lines was Camp Creek, which added to the strength of Johnston's position. McPherson opened the battle on May 14 by forcing the passage of Camp Creek, pushing Polk off the hills that commanded the railway bridge over the Oostanaula from the west and moving up close to Polk's intrenchments. Sherman now began to swing the rest of his line to the right with the junction between Hooker and Palmer as the pivot, each Union division starting its own fire fight as it came in contact with the enemy. There was trouble working through the thick brush that bordered both sides of Camp Creek. Keeping alignment and interval on a right wheel of three army corps is difficult enough on a parade ground. Here it was impossible and the sharp fire of the Rebel skirmish line increased the confusion. The division at the pivot crossed Camp Creek and came under the Rebel artillery fire with disordered lines. It fell back to the shelter of the creek banks and went no farther that day. The next division on its left halted along the same line. In front of Baird's division, which was next on the left, and Schofield's, which was to the left of Baird's, were the thick woods that had discouraged Sherman two days before. These slowed the wheeling movement, but the left-most end of the line had open country and went forward without support on either flank until the merciless Rebel fire stopped them and then drove them back. The reserves went in and covered these broken divisions while they re-formed.

Meantime, Howard's Fourth Corps came in on Schofield's left, gained a good position and opened a destructive artillery fire that drove Hood's men temporarily out of their works. To save his army Johnston ordered Hood to counterattack. Howard had no reserve and called on Thomas for help. With this aid the counterattack was beaten off and darkness ended the fighting.

What proved to be the decisive action took place at Lay's ferry where Snake Creek empties into the Oostanaula River—six miles in an air line downstream from Resaca. Shortly before noon on May 14 Sherman had ordered two brigades of the Sixteenth Corps to that point to effect a crossing. Six companies got across that afternoon but withdrew after dark on orders.

On the fifteenth the advance began at noon. The heaviest fighting of the day took place on the Federal left, where Hooker's Twentieth Corps now held the line. The repulse of a Rebel counterattack which began about 5:00 P.M. closed the random fighting around Resaca.

Earlier in the day, the First Brigade of the irascible, one-armed Sweeny's division had been ordered to secure a bridgehead at Lay's ferry. In an hour and a half the brigade was across and intrenched and another brigade came over in support. This spelled the doom of Resaca and any Rebel stand north of the Oostanaula River. As soon as Johnston learned of it he ordered a retreat.

During the night of the fifteenth Johnston got across the Oostanaula without losing a gun or a wagon and in time to destroy the railway bridge and partly destroy the road bridge. Sherman learned of the retreat the next morning and started his whole army in pursuit with Thomas following directly on the heels of Johnston's rear guard. It was Thomas' job to crowd this rear guard back upon Johnston's main forces, make them deploy and bring them to battle. As long as Thomas knew where Johnston's three corps were located and in what formation, he was reasonably safe, but his position was extremely dangerous when

he lacked sufficient knowledge of these two things. Sherman had warned
him to be cautious under these circumstances. Being cautious meant
that he should not be caught marching in column across the front of
the enemy in position, nor with part of his men closer to the enemy
than to their own supports. As a result Thomas had to deploy his leading elements when the signs that he was closing with the enemy began
to multiply. Since the function of Johnston's rear guard was to delay
pursuit these signs multiplied with disconcerting frequency. Where
there were no natural barriers to shield his marching division, Thomas
resorted to heavy skirmish lines or to intrenchments. It was a nerve-
wracking series of decisions between hot pursuit and cautious advance,
either of which had to be made on sets of carefully balanced facts.

McPherson got across the Oostanaula at Lay's ferry and followed
the road through Springtown, Nannie, Hermitage and Woodland.
There was a chance that Johnston might fall back upon Montgomery,
Alabama, instead of Atlanta. This would give him fine protection for
both flanks by parallel rivers approximately thirty miles apart and would
nullify any far-flung flanking movement on Sherman's part. At the
same time it would draw Sherman farther away from his movable railway base. If Johnston made this move, his line of retreat would edge
off to the southwest by way of Rome, Georgia. One of McPherson's
duties was to herd Johnston away from this escape route.

He was aided by Davis' division of the Fourteenth Army Corps,
which was detached at Resaca and sent down the right bank of the
Oostanaula River to Rome. This city was located at the junction of the
Oostanaula and Etowah rivers, an air-line distance of thirty miles
west of the point where the Atlanta-Chattanooga railway crossed the
Etowah. Davis occupied it on the afternoon of May 18, thus breaching
Johnston's third best defense line and putting him on notice that he
must fight or retreat before Davis could march to some point in his rear.
This brilliant little action ruined any hope Johnston might have had
of falling back on Montgomery. The rest of Thomas' army was delayed
at the Oostanaula until the half-burned wagon bridge could be repaired
and a pontoon bridge laid down.

Schofield, meanwhile, made a wide swing to the east and then
moved south on a road parallel to and east of the Calhoun-Adairsville-
Kingston route. Within the area of this dispersion, Thomas moved
eight-ninths of his army southward on two roads which converged
near Adairsville. On the seventeenth Newton's division of the Fourth
Corps was leading the advance about five miles north of Adairsville. To
widen Newton's front, Wood was ordered to take his division off to

the west and to follow the railroad right of way. The rest of the Fourth
Corps and all of the Fourteenth Corps were strung out on the road
behind these two divisions. Newton and Wood had heavy skirmishing
all day. Johnston's cavalry rear guard with a battery of artillery sometimes stiffened by infantry slowed the Union advance by every possible
means. The enemy formed three lines, one behind the other some three-
quarters of a mile apart, barricaded with rails, covered by woods and
with an open field in their front. When the Fourth Corps skirmish line
drove back the first Rebel line it passed to the rear of the third where,
in some new and favorable position, it made another defense line. As
the resistance increased Newton continued to deploy his regiments until
he had a brigade engaged. At 4:00 P.M. these skirmishers began to
come up to the Rebel infantry in force and Howard made preparations
for an assault. In accordance with standing orders, Howard notified
Thomas that the main body of Johnston's infantry was brought to bay.
Thomas weighed the chances of success and decided against an attack.
But the power to select or refuse an engagement had already passed out
of his control. Both sides continued to reinforce their skirmish lines
until they were actually battle lines. The Rebel artillery opened upon
the infantry and the Yanks answered with counter-battery fire. The
usual response to such a situation is to hurry forward the support
columns, clearing the roads of the slow-moving trains, with aides
stationed at every crossroad to keep the hurrying supports from getting
lost. But in this instance Johnston chose to disengage and continue his
retreat southward.

In military parlance, the head of Thomas' column was checked by a
stubborn rear guard action and skirmished heavily until dark. "Old
Pap" Thomas carried with him the faith of his men because they knew
he was trying to save them from being maimed and killed needlessly in
the thousands of little actions such as this that grew into the complex
edifice of a campaign.

Johnston was under pressure from Richmond to stand and fight and
now he was looking for a suitable place. He thought he had it at
Adairsville but changed his mind when he became convinced that the
valley was too wide at that point to secure his flanks. At the little town
of Cassville some twelve or fifteen miles farther south he found what
he was looking for. His position was well taken southeast of the town
on a ridge above Nancy's Creek which extended from the northeast
to the southwest. Its crest was about ninety feet higher than the valley
floor to the north. This valley was half a mile wide and Thomas' troops
would have to cross it and climb the ridge to come to grips with their

enemy. But the basic strength of Johnston's position lay in its relation to Thomas' two advancing columns. The Fourth and the Fourteenth Corps were moving toward Kingston, where Sherman was convinced the bulk of Johnston's army would be found. To reach Cassville they must march on two legs of a triangle and cover almost twice the distance that the Twentieth Corps must march on the direct road from Adairsville to Cassville. Johnston aimed to trap whichever of Thomas' columns reached him first and destroy it before the other could come to its support. He had issued an order of intention to fight. His senior subordinates had agreed to his dispositions. Now his front ranks narrowed their eyelids, took a tighter grip on their weapons and their tension mounted as the waiting period dragged on. Then occurred two unrelated incidents which, being improperly appraised by Johnston's corps commanders, upset his carefully laid plans.

Off to the east of Johnston's battle line, Thomas' First Cavalry Division under E. M. McCook was moving along the Canton road. Men and horses were drooping with weariness after eighteen consecutive days of killing labor and inadequate food. They had averaged only four to six hours of rest out of every twenty-four. Their orders were to overtake, develop and contain the enemy until the Union infantry could come up and relieve them. Four miles from Cassville the tired squadrons ran into a heavy force of Gray foot soldiers. McCook dismounted and deployed but his men fell back before the advance of a Rebel division. In the afternoon McCook received orders to attack. There was nothing but infantry in front of his lines but he carried out his orders. The Second Regiment of Indiana Cavalry, in a saber charge, captured an entire company of the Eighteenth Alabama. This incident alone gives some indication of the character of the fight, for the Alabamians were not a regiment to be pushed around. They were one of ten that had borne the brunt of the heavy fighting at Shiloh. Part of the Eighth Regiment of Iowa Cavalry duplicated the feat of the Second Indiana. One of McCook's guns knocked an enemy gun and caisson to pieces and the enemy abandoned the wreckage to the Yanks. The cavalry division drove the Rebel infantry out of two lines of rifle pits, captured two ammunition wagons and a quantity of flour, corn and bacon. The division they had met in the morning was Stevenson's. The one they cut up in the afternoon was Stewart's. Both were in Hood's corps and Hood was holding the right of Johnston's Cassville line. Hood's intelligence section studied the reports and concluded that a heavy force of Blue infantry was on their right flank and working around to their rear.[22]

While this was going on, Butterfield's division was leading the southward advance of the Twentieth Corps on the Adairsville-Cassville road. The men not only had to march off the road but they had to keep their interval and alignment. Skirmishing started as soon as the march began and continued for two and one-half miles. Here the skirmish line came under artillery fire and halted. They had come upon the enemy in force and the standing orders were to halt and wait for support. The nearest support was on their right and the standing orders were to deploy in that direction. W. T. Ward, commanding Butterfield's leading brigade, soon issued the orders the men were expecting.[23]

Captain M. B. Gary, Battery C, First Ohio Volunteer Artillery, and chief of artillery for Butterfield's division, located a battery position some two miles to the west of the Adairsville-Cassville road. The deploying regiments as they came up soon afforded adequate support to the guns, which opened with case at 1,200 yards. The enemy disappeared and the infantry began to move cautiously ahead. The guns changed position several times that afternoon seeking targets of opportunity most of which were on the crest of the ninety-foot ridge along Nancy's Creek. By 5:00 P.M. the enemy had ceased to reply to this fire. Unknown to themselves, Gary's guns had enfiladed Polk's corps, which held the center of Johnston's line. This threat, coupled with that of McCook's cavalry, brought about the withdrawal of Johnston's army to a position behind the Etowah River.

Here in northwest Georgia on the nineteenth of May were fought two unnamed actions which together proved to be one of the decisive factors in the Atlanta campaign. In the official records they are listed merely as "combats near Cassville." Johnston was forced to give up the second major river on his retreat route. When he gave up the third, Davis removed him. Thomas habitually fought every little skirmish as if his campaign depended on it. He was an observer of trifles, a zealot of detail and a judge of minutiae. There is no record that he gave any orders at Cassville but his training bore its fruit.

The night of the nineteenth, Johnston moved his army south of the Etowah. Again he left nothing behind him and he struck back savagely when Thomas' vanguard pressed him too closely. On the twentieth, having secured two bridges and an excellent ford, Sherman ordered a two-day rest for his hard-driven forces and received from Stanton the thanks of the country for the vigor and success of his operations.

Vigorous his campaign may have been but it could hardly be called successful. On paper the North had conquered Tennessee, Missouri and the northern parts of four other seceded states, but Joe Johnston's army kept the conquest from being real. Territorial victories were an illusion. While Sherman halted along the north bank of the Etowah, Grant was checked at Spotsylvania. More Northern voters were coming to the opinion that the states in rebellion were not worth the cost of conquest.

The two-day rest that Sherman had ordered was a welcome interlude from the incessant marching, fighting and intrenching. Sherman's restrictive transport order was bearing heavily upon his command. There was no way to get sufficient forage up for the horses. The cavalry mounts in particular suffered severely. The housekeeping efficiency of the rank and file was nearly wrecked. Due to the lack of necessary equipment the cooking was of the worst character and least conducive to digestion. Hard bread, salt meat, fresh beef, coffee and sugar were in adequate supply but little if any beans, rice, soup or other small rations were issued. It was the lack of soap and of opportunity to bathe and launder that was most irritating to the troops. Thomas refused to obey the restrictive baggage order as it applied to himself.

No description of Thomas' mess as it was during the Atlanta campaign has been found, but just before the short rations of the Chattanooga siege reduced its quality and variety, it was evidently one of the most sumptuous in the Western armies. One observer tells us that the meal was announced by Thomas' colored servant dressed in a clean white jacket. Coincident with the announcement punch was served. The table was spread under a tent fly. The tableware was silver, elaborately finished. At each silver plate was a white napkin folded in the style of a first-class hotel. Smoked fresh beef, ham, baked potatoes, hot rolls and strong black coffee had been carefully selected and tastefully prepared.[24] Thomas never went on leave and rarely visited a hotel during the war, but he evidently denied himself few culinary luxuries. He was probably a better trencherman than dietician. At Atlanta he weighed 220 pounds.

One evening early in the campaign Thomas saw Sherman and his staff struggling along with tent flies. He detached a company of his own command to act as Sherman's headquarters guard for the remainder of the campaign to pitch the tents Thomas loaned him and generally to look after Sherman's creature comforts. Other officers got tired of using their fingers for forks and their pocket knives for carving, of turning sardine boxes into dishes and preserved meat tins into coffee cups.

The restrictive baggage order might have been proper for a short campaign but it was not a real economy to make it permanent.[25] Thomas had issued the restrictive order to his command but there probably was no strict enforcement of it. He refused to cripple an essential service for the sake of an arbitrary animal-to-man ratio. Schofield, in an effort to obey the order, refused to permit any ambulance to travel with his army. His wounded were left with citizens living near the battlefield who were paid a dollar a day per wounded soldier for taking care of them.

On May 23 Sherman put his armies in motion. Their objective was Marietta. Their purpose was to outflank Allatoona where the railway broke through the Appalachians into the flatlands of central Georgia. Sherman had left the railway at the Etowah River and was supplying his army with wagon trains. His railway base could not move south with him until the Etowah River bridge was rebuilt. McPherson moved well out toward the west heading for Van Wert, and Davis' division came southeastward from Rome to join him. Schofield moved on the east flank in the position of greatest potential risk, for Johnston was thought to be along the railway and presumably he would overlook no opportunity to take Sherman's marching columns in the flank. Thomas covered the stretch between McPherson and Schofield. He was marching directly on Dallas from which point he would turn east and close in on Marietta. Sherman grossly underrated his opponent in this phase of his campaign. He expected his men to swarm along the Chattahoochee River within five days. His time calculation was nearly 800 per cent in error.

On May 24, the head of Thomas' column was covered by McCook's cavalry division. That afternoon they picked up a Rebel courier with a dispatch from Johnston to his cavalry screen. From it Thomas learned that Johnston had discovered Sherman's flank movement and was planning to meet it along the Dallas-Powder Springs road. Thomas stripped the captured courier of his uniform, used it to disguise one of his own intelligence men and sent him with the captured dispatch to complete the original errand. The news of Johnston's intentions was soon corroborated by information sent in from one of Garrard's squadrons.

The following day, the march was resumed. Thomas, instead of Schofield, now had the post of danger. Sherman was converging his columns on Dallas. The Army of the Cumberland was marching on several roads. At 11:00 A.M. Geary's division of the Twentieth Corps came upon the enemy in force. A burning bridge over Pumpkin Vine Creek guarded by a Rebel cavalry outpost aroused Geary's suspicions and he deployed a regiment of skirmishers ahead of Candy's brigade. The pressure against these skirmishers built up rapidly. Suddenly there was a Rebel charge upon his skirmish line and Candy deployed the rest of his regiments. Geary pushed up his other two brigades and the skirmishing spread out east and west as successive regiments came up to the head of the column and went into line of battle. Geary's battle line pushed forward half a mile and picked up enough prisoners to convince him that Hood's corps was in his front with Hardee in close support. Hooker, who was with Geary's column, took command. The situation was critical, as no Union forces were in supporting distance and no single division could hope to live long in front of Hood's aggressive corps. Hooker notified Thomas and ordered Geary to dig in on a hilltop.

Thomas understood the significance of the situation. The head of his column had stumbled over Johnston's army six miles north of where it was expected. It was impossible for the Army of the Cumberland to concentrate before Johnston could strike. He would strike as soon as he learned what was in his front and there was plenty of daylight left in which he could win a full-scale victory. Thomas had to conceal his weakness until darkness brought the time he needed to get up more men. Sherman was on the field by this time but his idea of the tactical situation was different from Thomas'. Sherman contended that he was on Johnston's western flank and proposed to turn it, but Thomas' ideas prevailed in the end. The divisions of Williams and Butterfield came up and the whole Twentieth Corps was thrown against Hood's lines. They pushed them back a mile and a half to New Hope Church, where they were stopped by artillery fire. Thomas had sidestepped a trap.

Johnston had blocked Sherman's attempt to get around his western flank so Sherman linked up his three armies into a continuous battle line and sidled them eastward. He would try Johnston's eastern flank and wedge himself between the Rebel army and the railway. To cover the movement Howard was ordered to assault Johnston's right flank. In a fight at Pickett's mill, Howard was unsuccessful. On the opposite end of Sherman's line, toward Dallas, McPherson was pinned down. Every time he tried to pull out of his trenches and move eastward Johnston attacked. It was June 2 before he was finally able to move.

Thomas was now working in thickly wooded country with inaccurate maps and unreliable guides. The promise of seeing something from the next ridge ahead was never fulfilled. The local inhabitants were more likely to mislead him than to help him. His columns were constantly marching out of the area that had been scouted into the unknown where his opponent knew the lay of every stream, the military value of every ridge and the roads leading to the points of quick concentration. Thomas' job was to develop the Rebel position and this was constantly changing. Johnston's army built nearly 200 fortified lines in defending Dallas and Marietta. There was no sharp line between advance and retreat, between attacking and defending. No one knew when a skirmish line became a battle line or when a front became a flank. The techniques of battle were changing and Thomas was making a major contribution to their evolution.

Thomas' troops learned how to build breastworks while under fire. They would start them, while lying on the ground behind some flimsy shelter, by scraping up the dirt with their hands or tin cups and piling it in front of them. As their little trench deepened the parapet in front of it grew higher. Soon each foxhole would be linked up with those to the right and left. Eventually the trench would be completed by a head log. Between the bottom of this log and the dirt of the parapet was the firing loophole.

In this campaign the individual soldier was not supplied with intrenching tools. These were kept by the pioneers but were evidently loaned to the infantry on orders. When the tools arrived (there were not enough for every man) the infantrymen would alternate in short periods of furious digging. Sherman sought to spare his men from some of this labor by organizing groups of 200 escaped slaves to complete the intrenchments at night. One such group was assigned to each infantry division. Under this system the intrenchments became elaborate. Each parapet was from four to six feet high. The head log which surmounted it might measure twenty inches at the butt. This rested in notches cut in logs lying at right angles to the head log and bridging the trench so that a cannon shot would roll the head log on these supports safely over the heads of the defending infantrymen. Often these head log supports were covered with branches for the double purpose of camouflaging the position and protecting the riflemen from the sun. Between the parapet and the enemy the trees and underbrush were cleared for a distance of 100 yards or more and the slashings built into an abatis or entanglement.

When McPherson finally loosened Johnston's strangling grip on his army in front of Dallas on June 2, Schofield and Hooker were feeling toward Ackworth. The next day Allatoona was evacuated and the first geographical objective between the Etowah and Chattahoochee rivers had been achieved. Johnston had pulled back his right flank to save it from a turning movement, but this maneuver had cost him the control of the railway to a point within six miles of Marietta. Little progress had been made, however, toward accomplishing the destruction of Johnston's army. Sherman's attempt to roll up his western flank had been parried at New Hope Church. By maneuver, Johnston had circumvented a similar attempt on his eastern flank and had taken up a new line in front of Marietta. His right was east of the railway on Brush Mountain, his center on Kennesaw Mountain and his left on Lost Mountain. He had a strong advanced work on Pine Mountain.

On Sherman's orders, the army made no attempt to advance their lines for four days, partly to get a little rest, partly because of the heavy rains, and partly to get up supplies. The railroad bridge over the Etowah was completed and the railway base was moving up to Allatoona Pass. Blair came up with part of McPherson's Seventeenth Corps and compensated for all of Sherman's battle losses and detachments. In defiance of Sherman's limited transport order, he brought with him wagons loaded with iced champagne.

On June 11, Johnston's lines were developed. Given the job of pinching off the Pine Mountain salient, Thomas pushed through a soft spot which he found between Pine and Kennesaw. During the fighting his artillery killed Bishop-General Polk and Thomas' signalers learned about it by reading the Confederate messages. Both of Sherman's flanks moved forward a little with Thomas' advance. He had cracked the main line but, much to Sherman's disappointment, he had failed to break it. For the next eight days Sherman's army maintained an unrelenting pressure against Johnston's entire line and pushed in both his flanks until his position assumed the form of a gigantic V with its apex on Kennesaw Mountain and its flanks trailing southward on both sides of the railway.

It was at this time that Johnston completely bemused Sherman. His defensive salient on Kennesaw Mountain was faced by McPherson on the east, Thomas in the center and Schofield on the west. On the twenty-first of June, Johnston secretly transferred Hood from the eastern to the western end of his line. This left a vacuum in front of McPherson's army and piled up a heavy concentration at the junction between Hooker and Schofield on the west. It was another of those daring Southern tactics that continually amazed the military world. Wheeler and his troopers so successfully concealed this vacuum that McPherson, and Sherman, who was with him, were positive that there was more heavy infantry in front of McPherson than there had been. Thomas demurred and suggested that Sherman take advantage of this opportunity and move McPherson through Johnston's weakened eastern flank on Marietta, but Sherman decided in favor of a move by the right flank.

Meantime, off to the west, Hooker was obeying his orders to get possession of the ground up to Mrs. Kolb's farm. The three divisions of the Twentieth Corps did not occupy a continuous line but each held a hill with open spaces between them. At 2:00 P.M. on the twenty-second, Williams' division on Hooker's extreme right rested its flank on the Powder Springs road at Kolb's farm. Shortly after this, Schofield's line came up on Williams' right and the joint commands pushed eastward along the Powder Springs road. The resistance to this advance began to stiffen. At 4:30 the enemy struck in a heavy counter-attack and Williams' men picked up some prisoners whom they identified as belonging to Hood's corps. Behind the Union lines the telegraph instruments began clicking and the brightly colored signal flags jumped their messages from station to station. "Three entire corps are in front of us," Hooker advised. "I am apprehensive about my right flank." Instead of sending this message to Thomas, Hooker sent it direct to Sherman, which was a violation of military protocol. The episode fixed Sherman's animosity toward Hooker. He had never cared for Hooker since the latter's caustic remarks about his failure at Missionary Ridge. Hooker's efforts to embarrass McPherson, and especially Schofield, since the opening of the Atlanta campaign had irritated Sherman still more. There was a plain implication in Hooker's last message that Schofield was not carrying his end of the load and the statement that three corps were in front of him was, in Sherman's view, preposterous.

Sherman's nervousness had been getting out of control for several weeks. He had advertised the fact that he would be on the Chattahoochee by the end of May. It was now getting on toward the end of June and he wasn't there yet. For nearly a month he had been looking for a place to break through Johnston's line and now he learned through Hooker that he had been looking at such a spot without knowing what it was. Sherman was frustrated by the extent of Johnston's fieldworks. He estimated there were fifty miles of Rebel trenches. The whole country was one vast fort. As fast as the Yankees took one position Johnston fell back to another equally strong. Sherman's campaign was at a standstill.

On June 18 he had relieved his mounting nervous tension by an unofficial letter to Grant. He blamed McPherson for his failure to bag Johnston at Snake Creek Gap, and damned Schofield with faint praise.

One of his cavalry commanders was over-cautious, another was lazy. But his chief blast was aimed at Thomas and the Army of the Cumberland. "My chief source of trouble," he wrote, "is with the Army of the Cumberland, which is dreadfully slow. A fresh furrow in a ploughed field will stop the whole column, and all will begin to intrench. I have again and again tried to impress on Thomas that we must assail and not defend; we are on the offensive, and yet it seems the whole Army of the Cumberland is so habituated to be on the defensive that, from its commander down to its lowest private, I cannot get it out of their heads. I came out without tents and ordered all to do likewise, yet Thomas has a headquarters camp on the style of Halleck at Corinth; every aide and orderly with a wall tent, and a baggage train big enough for a division. He promised to send it all back, but the truth is everybody there is allowed to do as he pleases, and they still think and act as though the railroad and all its facilities were theirs. This slowness has caused me the loss of two splendid opportunities which never recur in war." [26]

To read this private letter as an integral part of the correspondence of the Atlanta campaign is to realize that Sherman could not have meant what he said. The 200 pages of letters and dispatches embracing the official correspondence for three weeks prior to its writing are proof that the Army of the Cumberland was not motivated by a defense psychology. Neither is there any reason for his accusation that Thomas' headquarters camp was so unnecessarily elaborate that it was a drag upon the mobility of his army. Sherman boasted that his headquarters and official records remained in Nashville and that he kept with him a skeleton staff of twelve, one of whom acted as his chief-of-staff with an order book, letter book and writing paper which filled a small chest no bigger than a candle box.

With all three armies relying on Thomas' engineers, railroad managers and repair parties, spies and provost marshals, the vast administrative details of managing the non-combat activities of 100,000 men centered in Thomas' headquarters. When a newspaper correspondent violated McPherson's security he was arrested but sent to Thomas to be imprisoned and tried. The smoothness and dispatch of Sherman's operations were insured by the efficient handling of staff work. A candle-box administration would have resulted in chaos.

On June 24 Schofield reported that he could not advance because he was outflanked. Almost simultaneously Thomas sent word that his Fourth and Fourteenth corps were so extended that he could not mass sufficient troops to make a breakthrough. Sherman sarcastically rejoined, "I suppose the enemy, with his smaller force, intends to surround us."

That evening Sherman issued his orders for the assault on Kennesaw Mountain. It was to begin at 8:00 A.M. on June 27. The three intervening days were for preparation. Thomas was ordered to break Johnston's line on Little Kennesaw. About a mile north, McPherson was to assault. No attack was to be made on Kennesaw Mountain proper. McPherson struck at the angle where Johnston's line turned from an east-west direction to a northeast-southwest direction. Thomas' assault faced almost due east. Each attacking column was to endeavor to break through at a single point, drive two and a half miles to the railroad, split Johnston's army and, turning on either part, overwhelm and destroy it in detail.

This is one of the most criticized movements of Sherman's career. Sometime between June 18 and the evening of June 23 he made up his mind to assault. His reason for an assault instead of a turning movement was because the enemy and his own officers had settled down to the conviction that he would not order an assault on fortified lines. Johnston, Sherman reasoned, looked for a flank movement, and in this Sherman was correct. But what Johnston wanted above all was for Sherman to attack him in his intrenchments.

"An army," Sherman wrote in his official report, "to be efficient must not settle down to a single mode of offence, but must be prepared to execute any plan which promises success. I wanted, therefore, for the moral effect, to make a successful assault against the enemy behind his breastworks, and resolved to attempt it at that point where success would give the largest fruits of victory." Eleven years later, in his memoirs, he wrote, "I had consulted Generals Thomas, McPherson and Schofield, and we all agreed that we could not with prudence stretch out any more, and therefore there was no alternative but to attack 'fortified lines,' a thing carefully avoided up to that time." [27] It is possible that Sherman's jealousy of Grant drove him to the assault.

Thomas left no record of his attitude toward the assault order but there is no doubt that he felt it was a bad tactic and a useless sacrifice. If so, why did he not protest it? One theory is that he had protested so much during the campaign that he feared another would make Sherman think he was afraid to fight. A more believable reason is that he felt as long as there was a chance of success the assault might lead to a victory and the end of the campaign.[28]

Another fact may have had some weight with Thomas. When Grant's attack stalled in the Wilderness he forsook the brilliant tactics which starred his Vicksburg campaign for the ultimate use of the North's superior resources—the strategy of attrition. This pleased Stanton and apparently Lincoln. The public at first construed Grant's terrible casualties as evidence of his military ability. Now Sherman wanted to try the same thing and Thomas' education in violence had not taken him to the point where he was ready to deny this sure but wasteful way to victory.

These inhibitions and forebodings, however, did not preclude careful preparations for the attack. It was to be made in front of Newton's division of Howard's corps and Davis' division of Palmer's corps. Stanley was to support Davis' assault and Hooker's Twentieth Corps was held as a central reserve to go to the support of either or both of the assaulting columns.

The combined attack on June 27 was on a front of four regiments with Wagner's brigade in column of regiments on the left, Harker next, then McCook, and then Mitchell's brigade on the right. Each brigade occupied a front equal in length to a regimental battle line and a depth equal to the number of its regiments. The brigade assault columns were separated by 100-yard intervals. The front of all four brigades was covered by a heavy skirmish line and the corps artillery was placed to command the Rebel position in front of the attacking columns. There was approximately a quarter of a mile between the main line of the Rebel works and the main line of the Union works. Between these lines were the rifle pits of Johnston's skirmishers. On the fronts of Wagner and Harker the Rebel works were protected by abatis. This was a formal assault. Its formation was governed by the book of tactics prescribed by army regulations. It followed the outmoded principle of French tactics which relied upon shock action instead of fire action. Thomas had to get his troops into physical contact with the enemy before any shock action could take place. At Missionary Ridge he had proved that the way to deliver shock action successfully was in extended order and not by columns in mass; but there are no intimations in the official records that any responsible officer considered such a radical departure from the official, stylized formula.

There was an inadequate fifteen-minute preparation for the assault by the Union artillery. The skirmish line moved out in accordance with the time schedule, closely followed by the four columns of massed regiments. The heads of these columns came under fire as soon as they left the protection of their own works. The Union skirmishers overran the Rebel rifle pits and captured most of the Rebel picket line but the blast of fire from the main works drove them to earth, where the front line regiments of the assault columns passed over them. When the survivors in these columns reached the abatis they, too, were forced to the ground to escape the murderous fire. A few men struggled through the abatis only to be cut down on the outer slope of the Rebel parapet. There were attempts to rally the fire-shattered columns for another advance. Harker, for one, got his second advance under way, but he took a mortal wound and the rally lurched forward and then collapsed. Thomas' total loss was 1,580.

Shot, stoned down by the defenders, exhausted by the heat, by the length of the charge and by emotional tension, the Union survivors with bayonets, spoons, tin cups, mess plates and fingers began to throw up a cover for themselves under the enemy fire at ranges of from 25 to 100 yards. In an hour they had protection enough so that they could finally raise their faces out of the dirt. That night they strengthened their works with picks, spades, rails and logs.

At the Dead Angle, where some of the heaviest fighting took place, an unknown Tennessee rifleman in Maney's brigade put his appraisal on the drive and tenacity of the assault when he yelled in the thick of the fighting, "Hell has broke loose in Georgia, sho' 'nough."

"The Yankees seemed," another Confederate later wrote, ". . . to walk up and take death as coolly as if they were automatic or wooden men. . . . I was as sick as a horse, and as wet with blood and sweat as I could be; and many of our men were vomiting with excessive fatigue, over-exhaustion and sunstroke. . . ." Another Tennessean felt that the attack failed because of the impossibility for the living of passing over the bodies of the dead.

Samuel G. French, Thomas' old friend, watched the left of Thomas' assault column falter and stop under a hail of lead. He tells how Colonel Martin of Cleburne's division declared an informal truce during the thick of the fighting. Martin noticed that the brush was on fire in front of his position and that the Union wounded which strewed the ground there were in danger of being burned to death. He tied a white handkerchief to a ramrod and waved it over his head as he mounted his parapet. "Come and remove your wounded," he shouted, "they are burning to death; we won't fire a gun till you get them away. Be quick." And, at the head of his Arkansas troops he leaped over his works and helped with the removal. When the work was done a Union major pulled a fine brace of pistols from his holsters and presented them in appreciation to Colonel Martin.

Harker and Daniel McCook were mortally wounded in the assault. The 125th Regiment of Illinois Volunteers took casualties at the rate of six a minute. In the 121st Ohio three company commanders were killed or carried from the field. One company lost twenty-nine of the fifty-six men it took into action. Another lost all of its sergeants. The 113th Ohio had ten of its nineteen commissioned officers killed or wounded. "We failed," reported its colonel, "only because we attempted impossibilities." Students in the Army Service Schools at Fort Leavenworth were taught, after the turn of the century, that the assault was tactically well made and gallantly delivered. But Sherman felt that Thomas' attack had not been made with sufficient vigor.

Two hours and forty-five minutes after the attack was launched Thomas made his report to Sherman. Harker's brigade had advanced to within twenty paces of the enemy's works and was repulsed with canister at that range. Wagner's brigade was so severely handled it was compelled to reorganize. Mitchell's brigade captured one line of Rebel breastworks and was holding it. Nearly every colonel in McCook's brigade was killed or wounded and the brigade was compelled to fall back and reorganize. "The troops are all too much exhausted to advance," he concluded, "but we hold all we have gained." When Sherman queried his army commanders about another assault, Thomas bluntly replied, ". . . One or two more such assaults would use up this army."

But the remarks of some of Thomas' subordinates were not so temperate. Newton, angered beyond control by the loss of Harker, accosted Sherman while the rage was still on him. "Well, this is a damned appropriate culmination of one month's blundering," he told the commanding general.

McPherson's attack had been equally abortive although his losses had not been as heavy as Thomas'. Schofield, on the far right, had gained the crossing of Olley's Creek and was now within eleven miles of the Chattahoochee River.

Sherman's dilemma is apparent from his dispatches to Halleck, Grant and Stanton. He had tried to turn both of Johnston's flanks and failed. He had forced Johnston to stretch his defense lines out of all proportion to his strength, yet he had been unable to find in them a spot thin enough for a breakthrough. He was far behind his own time schedule. He had just been reinforced to the extent of an army corps. There were few ranking officers left to be blamed for his difficulties. Since he could not destroy Johnston and since he was unable to drive him back, Sherman offered Halleck a compromise. He would pin Johnston in position and keep him from reinforcing Lee. Within fourteen hours Halleck's reply started westward. "Lieutenant General Grant directs me to say," it read, "that the movements of your army may be made entirely independent of any desire to retain Johnston's forces where they are." Two and a half months after promising Grant that he would not be deterred from crushing Johnston, Sherman seemed ready to leave the heavy combat to his friend and senior.

During the interchange of these messages Sherman asked Thomas what he thought about cutting loose from the railroad, capitalizing Schofield's gain on the right flank and making the attempt to get on the railway in Johnston's rear at a point four or five miles north of the Chattahoochee River. Thomas thought it would be decidedly better than "butting against breastworks twelve feet thick and strongly abatised." [29]

Sherman's rejoinder was almost as tart. "Go where we may," he wired, "we will find the breastworks and abatis, unless we move more rapidly than we have heretofore." The next day Sherman visited Thomas to discuss the projected movement. Thomas asked for and received permission to make a personal inspection of the ground over which the movement was to be made and to discuss the matter with Schofield. By the thirtieth, Sherman and Thomas had worked out the details of the flank movement and that night Sherman published his orders for the next day's movement.

That evening one of Thomas' signal officers saw the spires of Atlanta.

Sherman decided to force Johnston across the Chattahoochee by pushing his own right flank toward that river well downstream from the railway bridge. Schofield was ordered to move on July 1 toward Sandtown and he opened a gap of eight miles between his extreme left and the rest of Sherman's army. It was a ticklish situation and McPherson was making a forced march behind the protection of Thomas' intrenched lines to fill it. On July 2 the stretch-out was more than Johnston's outnumbered army could stand. Sherman's right was now closer to Atlanta by several miles than Johnston's left and the Southern troops fell back that night to Smyrna Church.

Sherman sensed his opportunity. The Chattahoochee—150 yards wide with an uneven bottom and muddy banks—was a formidable hazard to a retreating army. There was one bridge where the railway crossed and two more a dozen miles upstream near the little town of Roswell. Between were numerous ferries. If he could catch Johnston in the confusion of a night crossing with the Union artillery thundering at random in his rear, the campaign might well be successfully closed. He urged Thomas to attack regardless of the cost as soon as his continual probing developed a weak spot. In the face of this pressure Johnston dropped back another three miles on the night of July 4. He was holding his bridgehead now while his trains and artillery crossed. It was a formidable position. Both his flanks rested on the Chattahoochee. His left and left center were protected by Nickajack Creek. It was Schofield who made Johnston's bridgehead untenable when he got a division across the Chattahoochee seven or eight miles upstream from the railway bridge.

Sherman, who had now thrown off his uncertainty, appeared at his impressive best during this part of the campaign. Thomas held Johnston tightly in his works from July 2 to July 10 and behind the security of his stout lines Sherman flung his divisions from east to west and west to east much as the bass drummer in a kilted band swings his sticks. It was the perfect example of Sherman's improvisation of using infantry instead of cavalry wings. On July 9 Sherman secured three good, safe points of passage across the river upstream from Johnston and that night the Rebels abandoned their bridgehead, burned the bridge and left Sherman the undisputed master north and west of the Chattahoochee. Atlanta lay before him only eight miles away. Even the enemy was impressed by such sweeping tactics. "Sherman ought to get on a hill," one of them said, "and command, 'Attention! By Kingdoms, right wheel!' "

Thomas was impressed, too, but with opportunity rather than accomplishment. His army was in fine spirits and inspired with fresh hope and confidence. Ninety days' supplies would soon be stockpiled along the Chattahoochee and there were ninety days' more in the Chattanooga warehouses. It was too late for Johnston to divert the Blue army from its goal by raids on its communications. "If we are careful," Thomas prophesied, "and keep our minds to the work before us, securing what we get, and moving to other work with proper precautions and with a will to accomplish what we have to do, I believe we shall be able to present to the Government by fall, the entire territory of the State of Georgia, redeemed from the grasp of the rebels." [30] Thomas was evidently looking for an advance to the Gulf coast and was showing more interest in territorial progress than he generally did.

For the third time in the campaign Johnston had abandoned his lines, crossed a major river and carried safely with him all the lumber that an army drags behind itself. One of the mysteries of the campaign is why Thomas permitted these unchallenged withdrawals. At the Oostanaula and the Chattahoochee, Johnston made his withdrawals after Thomas had developed his position. In both situations all the advantages were in Thomas' favor. When the roles were reversed in front of Dallas, McPherson was unable to break the contact of the opposing battle lines. McPherson's, however, was a daytime effort with the intention of making a hazardous flank march. Johnston's major withdrawals were all made at night to prepared positions directly in his rear. It was the combination of Johnston's skill in these withdrawals and Sherman's desire to accomplish his advances by maneuver rather than combat that made such Rebel successes possible.

In any event, the Chattahoochee River, which had been a hazard to Johnston, was now, July 10, a hazard to Sherman. He had to get his army across without having one or more of his leading elements cut to pieces while he was astride it. The passage was accomplished on July 17 and it sealed Johnston's fate. He was relieved of his command by General John B. Hood.[31]

During the almost continuous fighting between Pumpkin Vine Creek and the Chattahoochee, Thomas several times was caught in the enemy's musketry fire. At one time, with Davis and members of their staffs, he entered a vacant log cabin on the picket line from which they hoped to determine how much force the enemy had in front of them. Their horses had been left with their orderlies in a depression in the rear of the cabin. The Rebel pickets discovered what was happening and poured such a hot fire into the doorless and windowless cabin that the officers were driven out. Thomas was the last to go. At the gate which led from the dilapidated yard he stopped and turned again to look at the enemy. Then he walked slowly to his horse. At another time during the same part of the campaign he was picking and eating blackberries along the road when a Rebel cavalry patrol burst upon the scene. Bullets began to fly, but Thomas, without looking up and without hastening, announced, "This is eating blackberries under difficulties."

Other anecdotes began to gather about Thomas. Four miles south of Marietta, he came up to the advance of the Fourteenth Corps just after an unexpected brush with the Rebels where none were supposed to be. "You are in the advance," Thomas told the senior officer. "Throw out two or three companies as skirmishers and push right along as you have been doing. If the Rebels cause you too much trouble order up some of the artillery and scrawl the canister to them."

A little ten-year-old waif, small enough to live in his drum, beat the long roll for one of Thomas' Michigan regiments. He had been a marker at Chickamauga and indicated the direction to the troops when Steedman swung his regiments from column into line just before his famous assault. Twenty minutes later the little drummer's occupation was gone and he picked up a gun and fought with the men along the crest. His size and pugnacity attracted the attention of Thomas, who later paid for his schooling and eventually got him into West Point.

From the Chattahoochee to Atlanta, Sherman's movement was in the form of a tremendous right wheel with Thomas holding the pivot on the Chattahoochee and a front that extended across the Buck Head–Atlanta road. McPherson was swinging wide on the rim of a circle, the radius of which was approximately fifteen miles. He was aiming to cut the Atlanta-Augusta railway in the vicinity of Stone Mountain. Schofield was between the pivot and the circumference closed up on McPherson. Sherman's numbers were too small for a connected line between these points and there was a gap of two miles between Thomas and Schofield.

In a critique of the battle used at West Point years afterwards, it was stated that the gap in the line was caused by poor maps which located Howell's mill—the pivot—in two different places.[32] In any event, either Thomas or Palmer chose the wrong pivot point. Sherman knew that the gap existed but in his ignorance of Hood's position he was unconcerned.

The Chattahoochee River, where the crossings were made, flows from northeast to southwest. Peach Tree Creek flows from east to west and empties into the Chattahoochee a short distance upstream from the burned railway bridge. It was the combination of Peach Tree Creek and the Chattahoochee below it that Johnston had chosen for his next defense line before falling back to his prepared works in Atlanta. Hood now made use of the same line—not for defense but as a jump-off for an attack.

Thomas' army was on the south side of Peach Tree Creek. Palmer's Fourteenth Corps had its right near the junction of Peach Tree and the Chattahoochee. Newton's division of Howard's Fourth Corps was three or four miles to the west on the Buck Head–Atlanta road. Hooker's Twentieth Corps filled the space in between. Howard's other two divisions had been moved east by Sherman's orders to close on the right of Schofield's army. The gap still existed in Sherman's line, but now it was between two of Howard's divisions. "We must not mind the gap," Thomas told Howard when he sent him east and elected to remain with Newton himself. "We must act independently." Howard thought it was fortunate for him that Thomas was with Newton when the storm burst.

In its initial stages the Battle of Peach Tree Creek was similar to the combats in front of Cassville. In both cases the Rebels had set a trap and Thomas was ordered into it without a cavalry screen, with the other units of the Northern army too far away for support and with his flank open to attack. Sherman expected a battle in front of McPherson with Schofield and Thomas cast in a supporting role. Sherman was with his Left Wing and reported to Thomas that there was abundant evidence that Thomas could "walk into Atlanta capturing guns and everything." Thomas had evidence of his own which led him to believe that the coming battle would be on his front and that he would need help from the left, but he was unable to convince Sherman. Under the circumstances Thomas, as was his habit, followed his own judgment.

Newton's division, because of its exposed flank, was the weak spot in Thomas' line. His orders were to advance along the Buck Head–Atlanta road and feel the enemy. About noon on July 20 he deployed with two of his three brigades in line, one on each side of the road. Four guns of Goodspeed's battery were on the road between them. The two remaining guns and the other brigade were in reserve. Hooker's Twentieth Corps was in column formation on a road about one and one-quarter miles to the west and parallel to the Buck Head road. From this column Hooker made his deployment with Ward on his left, Geary in the center and Williams on his right. The right of Williams' division made contact with Johnson's division of Palmer's Fourteenth Corps.

When Thomas arrived on the field he found Newton's deployed brigades occupying trenches that had been built by some other unit. He ordered Newton to advance just as soon as Hooker came up on his right. This junction being completed about 1:00 P.M., Newton started forward with a strong skirmish line of five regiments. His immediate objective was what appeared to be a ridge some half a mile in front of his skirmishers. It was difficult to see ahead through the thick undergrowth. His skirmish line secured a position along the crest of this ridge and Newton moved his battle line up to it. This was the routine inching forward of an army feeling blindly for an enemy over a rough, heavily brushed terrain. Newton's next move was to get out a skirmish line on his front and flanks, dig in his battle line, place his guns and wait for Hooker to come up on his right flank. The old skirmish line of five regiments was now relieved by a new one of three. Two regiments were sent off to the east where Newton's left flank was inadequately covered by Pea Vine Creek, which flowed northward into Peach Tree. Almost immediately the skirmishers that had moved forward ran into a sharp fire and then into a line of Rebel rifle pits. They sent back word that they had located the enemy in force.

Thomas ordered Newton to remain on the crest of the ridge where he was and intrench. While the pioneers were digging, aided by as

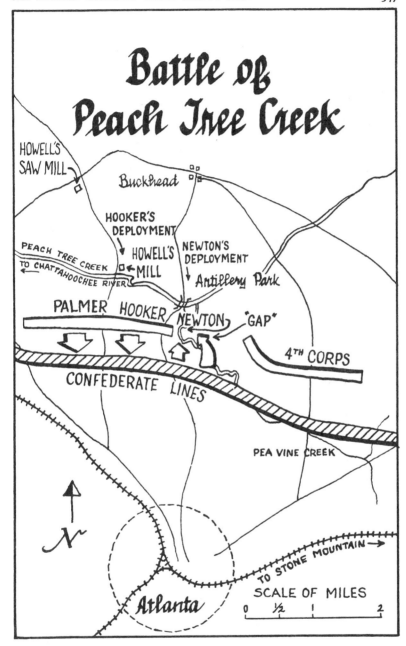

Map 8. Battle of Peach Tree Creek, July 20, 1864. From a sketch used in the Fourth Corps diary and probably made on the field. (*O.R. Atlas, Plate 62, No. 4.*)

many men as could be spared from the battle line, Newton's skirmishers fell back ahead of the Rebel advance, fighting Indian fashion from tree to tree. The two regiments that went out on reconnaissance along Pea Vine Creek were cut off by the Rebel advance and driven across Peach Tree Creek.

Two-thirds of Hood's army was attacking in echelon from their right flank. Hood knew all about the division of Thomas' force and the remainder of his army was held ready for a flank attack against any Yank support moving to Thomas' aid. Hood's objective was to throw his erstwhile cavalry commander and artillery instructor back into the angle between Peach Tree Creek and the Chattahoochee River and destroy him. His assault tactic was the same as that used by Bragg at Stones River and Chickamauga. Its first impact was felt at the weakest point in Newton's line—the unprotected left flank of Blake's brigade. Blake's one reserve regiment was put into the line immediately. The pioneers were ordered to drop their intrenching tools and go to the help of this regiment. Its left flank was refused. Part of Bate's Confederate division flowed around this refused flank and got into the bottomlands along Pea Vine Creek. They were aiming for the bridge across Peach Tree Creek on the Buck Head road where Newton's trains were in park as well as some artillery belonging to Ward's division of the Twentieth Corps. This bridge and the road leading southward from it to Newton's battle line were vital to Thomas' security. To protect them Newton and Thomas began to improvise. The two guns that had been in reserve were faced east and ordered into action. Some of the skirmishers who had been driven in were reorganized and sent to support the guns. Some regiments from Bradley's reserve brigade were thrown in to help.

While this improvisation was going on, the pressure of the Rebel assault was moving westward along the front of Blake's brigade as the Rebel units came successively into action. Kimball's right—he was the commander of the brigade that Newton had deployed to the right of the Buck Head road—was soon under pressure and here there was more trouble because the left of Hooker's Twentieth Corps had not come up. Fortunately, however, Bate's first attack on Kimball's right had gained its greatest momentum. Kimball was forced to refuse his flank and Newton's 2,700 muskets were holding off the divisions of Bate, Walker and Cleburne, who were attacking from the east, south and west. Newton was now partially isolated. If the Army of the Cumberland was to survive, Newton had to have help. Hood had cannily provided for each of his attacking corps to keep one division in reserve, and part of this reserve now came up to stiffen Bate's disorganized lines and drive another attack at Newton's left flank.

The defensive use of artillery was an old and tried formula to Thomas. At Buena Vista and again at Stones River he had seen it accomplish miracles. He now rode back in person to the bridge across Peach Tree Creek where he had seen Ward's guns as he rode to the front at noon. They were Gary's First Ohio Battery and Smith's First Michigan Battery. The teams were hitched, the gunners standing near their places. Before Thomas got his orders out to the battery commanders, the drivers were in their saddles taking up the slack in the trace chains, while the lead drivers got their teams faced toward the bridge. As the battery commanders barked out their orders, the guns began moving. Thomas stationed himself on the off side and used the flat of his sword as the pieces moved past him to help the drivers get the off horses into draft. He followed as the heavy guns bounced from side to side along the uneven dirt road. Thomas put the guns into battery alongside of Goodspeed's two reserve pieces facing east and directed their fire from his saddle. The promptness and energy with which he picked up and performed the combat duties of a brigade commander saved Newton's flank and probably the six divisions to the right of it.

As soon as the batteries were in position Thomas sent an aide to Ward for a brigade of infantry to support them. By this time Ward's whole line was under pressure from the Rebel attack and he begged to be excused from parting with one-third of his force. Thomas listened to the message and scaled down his request to two regiments. Again Ward demurred and Thomas withdrew his request. The record does not show how Thomas' borrowed batteries were finally supported, but their volleys of short range metal heavily dosed with musket balls "relieved the hitch," as Thomas put it.

During the heat of the fighting on Newton's front, a courier arrived from Sherman with a message for Thomas ordering a forward movement since, in Sherman's opinion, there were no enemy troops between Peach Tree Creek and Atlanta.

When the firing first broke out on Newton's front Hooker hurried forward his three divisions. His line of advance, however, was broken and irregular. Geary's division in the center was farther advanced than those of Ward on his left and Williams on his right. Also there were gaps between the division fronts. Geary gave the most complete report of the fighting along Hooker's front. Both of Geary's flanks were overrun and he was forced to change front under fire to make connection with Williams. To cover this hazardous movement, his artillery, supported by five infantry regiments, held his left flank and drove the Rebels out of the pocket between himself and the hard-pressed Ward, who was holding the next high ground to the east. In thirty minutes the crisis of the battle swept westward past Geary's front, although the Rebel attacks continued, as they did along Newton's front, for about three hours.

Geary and his men had seen much hard fighting. At the close of Gettysburg's desperate second day the safety of Meade's army had rested on the burdened shoulders of five of Geary's New York regiments. For three precarious hours they held a corps front on Culp's Hill against four attacks by twenty-two regiments of Johnson's division of Ewell's Second Corps. It was one of the epic stands of the war. These men and their commander were not easily impressed, but this fight on the outskirts of Atlanta reminded them of what they had seen on the rolling land of southern Pennsylvania. Geary thought he had never seen more heroic fighting.

About an hour and a half after the fight began on Newton's flank it moved westward to Johnson's division of the Fourteenth Corps. His men were partially intrenched and preparing for the next step in the advance toward Atlanta. The Fourteenth Corps had been moving south on a road parallel to the Buck Head–Atlanta road and about three miles west of it. They had deployed their marching column into a battle line about a mile south of Peach Tree Creek and were feeling for Hooker's right flank while their skirmishers searched for the enemy. The 104th Regiment of Illinois Volunteers was given the important detail of making the link-up. This was one of those unfortunate regiments that had been penalized by inefficient leadership. It had been cut to pieces by Morgan's dawn attack at Hartsville and had been subject to Negley's inexplicably incompetent command at Chickamauga. Now under Thomas' general tightening up of the Army of the Cumberland it was beginning to find itself. Midway in its reconnaissance it was caught front and flank by Stewart's whirlwind attack. The trapped and isolated regiment, probably less than 400 strong, held its position. It was bolstered by two Wisconsin regiments sent in by the brigade commander and their thin line formed and held the bridge between the Fourteenth and Twentieth corps.

It is easy for the historian to see some significance in the fact that Hood's first battle as an army commander went to pieces when it collided with the battle line of the man who had taught him the fine points of artillery fighting at West Point. There is no comment in the Union reports of any annoyance from Hood's artillery, but Thomas held the left by bringing on the field two batteries and Geary saved the center with his massed guns. It was slow work dragging artillery along the un-bridged dirt roads of Georgia but it paid off for Thomas. Deployment over a brushy, broken terrain undoubtedly slowed an advance, yet at Peach Tree Creek it was Thomas' habitual caution that saved Sherman from the consequences of his own impulsive haste. Sherman put Thomas' losses at 1,710 as compared to 4,976 for Hood.

Another tactical pattern was becoming apparent in this battle, too. The balance between offense and defense was now swinging definitely in favor of the defense. It augured ill for the Confederacy that the man who understood this change was moving toward the top command of the Union forces in the west while the man who denied it had the top command of the forces opposed to him.

There was skirmishing all along Thomas' front on the fearfully hot twenty-first day of July, as his men crowded up to the formidable works the Rebels occupied three or four miles north of Atlanta. That night Hood pulled his troops back inside the city's defenses. Thomas moved up the morning of the twenty-second and the final phase of the struggle for Atlanta began. The Fourteenth Corps was on Thomas' right with its left resting on the Chattanooga railway about two and one-half miles from the center of the city. Hooker's corps continued the line eastward to the Buck Head–Atlanta road where the Fourth Corps joined on and continued to the southeast a mile and a half to link up with Schofield at a point about a mile north of the Georgia railroad. This rail line ran east from Atlanta through Decatur and Stone Mountain to Augusta and Savannah. It was one of the three rail lines radiating from the beset city and McPherson, who held the left of Sherman's line, denied its use to the Rebels.

During the night of the twenty-first Hood swung Hardee's corps from Thomas' front to a position on McPherson's unsuspecting left flank. It was one of the famous battle marches of the war—fast, hazardous and a complete surprise to the enemy. The battle that ensued the next day was called the Battle of Atlanta. Like Hood's first attempt against Thomas this also failed but by only the narrowest margin. McPherson was killed as he galloped into some enemy skirmishers who had in-filtrated his position between Sherman's headquarters and the left end of Sherman's battle line. Thirty-seven hundred casualties, including the only army commander in the Northern armies to be killed in action, was the exorbitant price exacted of the Army of the Tennessee because of its jealousy of the Armies of the Ohio and the Cumberland. "I pur-posely allowed the Army of the Tennessee to fight this battle almost unaided," wrote Sherman in his memoirs, "because I knew that . . . if any assistance were rendered by either of the other armies, the Army of the Tennessee would be jealous."

At the very beginning of the Battle of Atlanta the combat direction of the Army of the Tennessee had fallen on Logan, its senior corps commander, and he did his work so well that it seemed to the Union army that his temporary command would probably be made permanent. It was Thomas, apparently, who upset the plan. He rode over to see Sherman. "What are you going to do about the Army of the Tennessee?" Thomas asked.

"Logan is in command," Sherman answered. "What do you think about it?"

"Well," said Thomas, "that is what I came to see you about. I don't think it is going to do to keep Logan there. He is brave enough and a good officer, but if he had an army I'm afraid he would edge over on both sides and annoy Schofield and me. Even as a corps commander he is given to edging out beyond his jurisdiction. You cannot do better than to put Howard in command of that army. He is tractable and we can get along with him." This is what Sherman wrote in 1886. About this same time Sherman also stated that Thomas' real motive arose from Logan's complaint to Sherman over his high-handed method of running the Nashville-Chattanooga railway. Logan himself believed that Thomas thought the top commands should go to West Pointers, and in his memoirs Sherman seems to agree to some extent.

There is no doubt that Thomas was angered at Logan's complaint to Sherman but he had made a handsome apology to Logan for his unintentional slights of Logan's authority. What angered him was the fact that Logan complained to Sherman before giving Thomas a chance to explain his position and told Sherman that Thomas was actuated by a jealousy of the Army of the Tennessee.

When Howard was moved up to the command of the Army of the Tennessee, Stanley took command of the Fourth Corps. Hooker, hurt because his seniority was overlooked in giving Howard an army command, asked to be relieved and Thomas recommended Slocum for the command of the Twentieth Corps. The President acquiesced in all of Thomas' suggestions.

Sherman lacked the manpower to invest Atlanta but he believed that he could force Hood to evacuate the city if he could cut its third railway line. This line ran south from Atlanta to East Point, where it branched. One line, the Macon and Western railroad, ran southeast to Macon, Georgia. The other, the Atlantic and West Point railroad, ran southwest to Montgomery, Alabama. East Point was really the junction of these two roads which then continued into Atlanta on a common track. A break in this line between East Point and Atlanta would seal the city, but Hood's defense was so tight that Sherman had to cut both roads some place south of East Point.

Early in the campaign Thomas and Rousseau had evolved a plan for cutting the East Point–Montgomery railway by means of a shuttle raid by mounted infantry. Such a raid was an old idea of theirs but in the winter of 1862–63 it had been blocked by Halleck. This time the idea was accepted, its starting date to be contingent upon the crossing of the Chattahoochee. On July 2 Sherman decided that the time was ripe and gave the order as soon as he learned that Thomas was in agreement.

Rousseau, commanding the District of Tennessee, which was one of Thomas' railway defense areas, moved out of Decatur, Alabama, with 2,500 men, two guns and a pack train on July 10. On the fourteenth he crossed the Coosa River, but not before he had thoroughly inspected his command, culled the unfit horses and sent them and the ineffective men back to the Tennessee River. This reduced his force below 2,300 but men and horses were all trained, fit and resolute. The effectiveness of most of the Western cavalry commands had been measured quantitatively by the Northern commanders. Thomas was now applying the standard of quality. Because of the excessive heat and poor roads Rousseau's two guns had trouble keeping up with the column so he ruthlessly destroyed one and added its teams to the other. By the sixteenth the command was showing signs of exhaustion but Rousseau pushed them relentlessly. They reached the railroad on the seventeenth and, after a short rest, spent the next thirty-six hours in wrecking it. On the nineteenth they started for their rendezvous with Sherman's army. This was one of the few successful Yankee cavalry raids in the west. Thomas, who had spent most of the war defending a railroad, had proved that one also could be effectively destroyed by cavalry raids in enemy country. As late as 1943, the army service schools were taught that this could not be done. On July 20, Braxton Bragg reported that the road was badly damaged and would require much time for repairs. Rousseau's loss did not exceed thirty men. Thomas, in his diffident way, showed his pride in the results by detailing the raid in his official report, which ended with this sentence: "Although General Rousseau received his instructions direct from [Sherman], the expedition having been made up from troops belonging to my command, I take the liberty of mentioning their operations officially. . . ."

On July 21, Garrard was ordered to Covington on the railroad forty-two miles east of Atlanta from which point he was to send detachments to destroy the bridges over the Yellow and Ulcofauhachee rivers. This raid, too, was successful. "Since leaving Marietta," Garrard reported, "this division has been so constantly in motion it is now very much out of condition and I would be pleased to have a few days' quiet to shoe horses and repair equipments." He was allowed two days.

Sherman had now destroyed the Augusta railway and the East Point–Montgomery railway. The only supply line left to Hood was the East Point–Macon railway. Sherman determined to destroy this with a cavalry raid and picked Stoneman, who was Schofield's cavalry commander, to lead it. To build up Stoneman's command to 9,000 saddles, Sherman gave him Garrard's division, after its two-day rest, Rousseau's force, which had just come in fatigued from its long and rapid Opelika raid, and McCook's division. It was an elaborate tactic. Stoneman was to circle east of Atlanta with half the force while McCook with the other half circled to the west. On the night of July 28 they were to meet at Lovejoy's Station on the Macon railway and wreck the tracks. Lovejoy's was closer to Atlanta than Covington, which Garrard had raided a few days before. Sherman also gave Stoneman permission to proceed to Andersonville, after breaking the railroad, and release the Yankee prisoners that were being held there.

Everything went wrong with this raid. Sherman, after gathering a massive striking force, divided it into two parts and Stoneman then divided his half into two parts. Wheeler jumped at the opportunity. There were four or five days of running cavalry fights between the Ocmulgee and Chattahoochee rivers. The rendezvous at Lovejoy's was never kept. In the end Stoneman was captured and McCook was cut to pieces trying to get back across the Chattahoochee, while the third unit under Garrard returned almost intact to Atlanta. Sherman took the blame and made his apologies to Halleck. "Nothing but the natural and intense desire," he wrote, "to accomplish an end so inviting to one's feelings [freeing the Andersonville prisoners] would have drawn me to commit a military mistake at such a crisis, as that of dividing and risking my cavalry, so necessary to the success of my campaign." With the Union cavalry out of the way, Hood sent Wheeler north to break up Sherman's communications.

In spite of his official stand, however, Sherman seemed inclined to blame his cavalry troubles upon the hapless Garrard and his complaints to Thomas drew the Cumberland commander into the argument.

"I must have a bolder commander for General Garrard's cavalry,"

Sherman wrote, "and want you to name me General Kilpatrick or some other good brigadier for the command." Thomas had tried to remedy the weakness in his cavalry command before the start of the campaign but Kilpatrick had not been one of his choices.

"I do not know of a better cavalry commander in my army," Thomas advised his superior. "Garrard is more judicious than Kilpatrick, who can knock up his horses as rapidly as any man I know. I think if you will bear with Garrard you will find in a short time he will be the best cavalry commander you have."

Sherman dropped the matter temporarily. "Please do all that is possible," he advised Thomas, "to organize a force of cavalry about Marietta, composed of General Kilpatrick's division and such of General McCook's as have returned."

While the Stoneman raid was in progress, Sherman ordered the Army of the Tennessee to pull out of line east of Atlanta and take up a new position on Thomas' right. Sherman was beginning the stretch-out that eventually drew Hood out of Atlanta. Howard, just confirmed in his new command, got his troops into their new position and had them busy building a parapet of rails and logs. Howard's right rested on Lick Skillet road at Ezra Church and Logan's corps was refused along this road facing south. The enemy made a heavy attack on this flank at about 10:00 A.M. of July 28 and kept up the pressure for six hours. All his efforts were repulsed. This was the last of Hood's sorties out of Atlanta in an attempt to take the offensive away from Sherman's armies.

Sherman had expected to reap fuller results from this movement of Howard's and blamed his disappointment upon Davis' failure to get his division of the Fourteenth Corps up in time. "As usual," Sherman wrote in his memoirs, "this division got on the wrong road." Davis was sick on July 28 and his division marched under the command of James D. Morgan on orders reading as follows: ". . . move to Turner's Ferry and then, by a road leading toward East Point, to feel forward for Howard's right, back into some known point of Turner's Ferry. . . ." A comparison of this order with Sherman's letterbook shows that the copyist left out six words and substituted one preposition for another. Morgan had no guide and no correct map. There were two roads to East Point instead of one and Morgan selected the one that Sherman did not have in mind.[33]

Schofield was the next to move in the Jonesborough stretch-out. On August 1 he gave up the part of the line he was holding east of Atlanta and, marching behind the protection of Thomas and Howard, went into position on Howard's right, extending the Union lines past Utoy Creek towards East Point. Thomas' Fourteenth Corps, under Palmer's command, was temporarily detached to aid Schofield in this movement. Hood's men watched attentively and matched Schofield's southward stretching breastworks yard for yard. Thomas was now holding with two corps the line originally held by Sherman's three armies. He was stretched so thinly that he was unable to mass a force sufficient to try for a breakthrough and ignored Sherman's order for an assault. Hood's lines, of course, were considerably shorter than Sherman's and he had the aid of 5,000 Georgia militia in manning them. They were so cunningly masked by the contours of the ground that Sherman was unable to discover their weak spots. Twice Schofield tried to break through this line and twice he failed. His failures were due primarily to his inability to handle Palmer and the touchy Fourteenth Corps.

The episode was reminiscent of Buell's troubles with Thomas' prima donna First Division during the campaign that ended at Perryville. Schofield was a junior major general who had been pushed up to the command of a department and held there by political pressure. He was outranked by all of the corps commanders of the Army of the Cumberland and by some of its division commanders. Yet he commanded the Department and the Army of the Ohio. Even though this army consisted of but one corps, it put Schofield on the command level with McPherson and Thomas. Schofield's wrangles with Hooker over the use of bridges and roads during the opening phases of the campaign had provided plenty of gossip for the various messes. When Schofield was ordered to extend Sherman's right flank toward East Point, Palmer's Fourteenth Corps was sent to act as Schofield's reserve, but it was not at first intended that Palmer should be placed under Schofield's command. Unknown to Thomas, however, Sherman changed this arrangement. The stiff-necked Palmer notified Sherman that he respectfully declined to report to or to take orders from Schofield and asked to be relieved and sent north. Sherman refused and seemed bent on forcing Palmer to show his subordination. As a result, the right wing of Sherman's army sat down on the hot Georgia farmlands like a team of balky mules.

Sherman threw the responsibility to Thomas and asked for his plans and wishes. Thomas regretted to hear that Palmer had taken this course, recommended that his application to be relieved be granted and that Davis be named to the corps command. With the report of one of his inspector generals as a foundation, Sherman now shifted his criticism. The Fourteenth Corps was of no use for an offensive. If it saw an enemy through a spyglass it would halt and intrench. Unless it would attack, he concluded, he would relieve it in orders and state the reason. Thomas picked up the challenge. "I am surprised to receive such a report of the Fourteenth Corps, for it has always been prompt in executing any work given to it heretofore," Thomas replied. "If General Palmer is an obstacle to its efficiency, I would let him go." That same day Sherman made amends with an acknowledgment that the divisions of the Fourteenth Corps were the strongest and best in the army. Sherman's criticism of the Fourteenth Corps touched a sensitive spot in Thomas. The army called them "Thomas' pets" and he was perfectly aware of the implications of the nickname. After the Battle of Jonesborough, Thomas notified Howard that he had some captured artillery, saying "Thomas' Pets have several guns with Howard's mark on them. He can have them now, having probably loaned them to Hood, who has returned them."

Basically the blame for this lack of cooperation rested on Thomas. For once his plan for personnel redemption had backfired. Palmer was not a West Pointer and every one of his West Point division commanders resented it. Palmer's attempt to replace Baird was indicative of this strife. Thomas tried to adjust the situation before the start of the campaign by giving the corps command to Buell. Palmer was embarrassed and evidently tried to step aside but Thomas refused.[34] It is probable that Sherman knew exactly what was wrong in the Fourteenth Corps and took the opportunity to force Palmer out of the army. This repressed tiff between Thomas and Sherman may have prompted many of Sherman's intemperate remarks. The upshot was that Davis replaced Palmer as soon as his rank could be upgraded to fit the command.

In a few months Thomas had changed the command of each of his three army corps. The replacements of Hooker and Palmer were changes that he had been considering for some time but he had waited for an occasion when they could be made with the least upset to the command. He had noticed that most of the time the troops resisted the removal of their commander, which always made it difficult for the new man. He had first-hand knowledge of this when he succeeded Rosecrans. Hooker never left a command without the troops showing signs of disapproval. In the case of Palmer there was a personal attachment which may have influenced Thomas to delay a change until it could be done with the least hurt to Palmer.

This care for the mental comfort of his officers extended also to his soldiers. At one time, when his headquarters was bracketed by enemy artillery, he issued quick orders to move it to a safer spot and he immediately noticed a flutter of nervousness among the men who were watching him. He determined then never to give his soldiers any inkling of his own inner nervousness. It was probably this same feeling, rather than a show of bravado, that made him so deliberate in removing his person from a dangerous situation.

With his cavalry raids balked and his infantry movements indecisive, Sherman ordered four rifled guns of large caliber down from Chattanooga to see what he could do about forcing the evacuation of Atlanta with artillery. These guns arrived on August 10 and began a continuous fire upon the city—day and night at regular intervals. Thomas was made responsible for them. Sherman suggested a position for the battery but Thomas moved it nearer the city to a spot from which it could enfilade the street in which Hood had his headquarters. Thomas watched the firing with an expert eye but the range was too great to spot the fall of the shot from any position within the Federal lines. Thomas sought to overcome this difficulty by having spies in Atlanta send him the range and traverse corrections to help his gunners get on their target. The artillery bombardment contributed nothing to Sherman's plan for forcing Hood out of Atlanta. The little colored children burned their fingers picking up the hot roundshot to sell to Hood's ordnance department so that they might be fired back whence they came.

A trivial fuss between subordinate officers over the placing of one of these guns was misrepresented to Sherman, who impulsively blamed the Army of the Cumberland for begrudging, in a spirit of jealousy, the use of a single gun to the Army of the Tennessee. For the only time during the campaign, Thomas' concern showed in his dispatches. Again Sherman made his apologies.[35]

The day the big siege guns began firing on Atlanta, Thomas picked up the intelligence that Hood's entire cavalry force was concentrating at Monticello, some fifty miles southeast of Atlanta. It was Wheeler preparing for his raid on Sherman's communications. This was the weak spot in Sherman's Atlanta enterprise but he did not fear any attacks that Wheeler might make upon it. His confidence in Thomas' defense dispositions led him to see an opportunity in Wheeler's departure. This lay in the fact that he would have a cavalry superiority in the Atlanta area as soon as he could get his mounted forces reorganized. At the time, Garrard's division was operating on the left of the Fourth Corps between Roswell and Decatur. Kilpatrick's division was guarding the railway between Marietta and the Chattahoochee. McCook's division was still straggling in from the Lovejoy raid. Stoneman's division of the Army of the Ohio was in the same situation as McCook's. Sherman's cavalry force was really in a bad way. Altogether he could muster 8,261 horsemen.

Sherman and Thomas were diametrically opposed on how to use this cavalry force but in four days they composed their differences and Kilpatrick was ordered out to break the Macon railway. He left the evening of August 18 and returned on the twenty-second having spent six hours on the tracks at Jonesborough. In that time he fought off both infantry and cavalry and made the circuit of Hood's army but failed to carry out the main purpose of his assignment.

While the Kilpatrick raid was being readied, Sherman called upon his army commanders for suggestions for cutting loose from the railway and interposing the heavy Union infantry force between Atlanta and Macon. As soon as the results of Kilpatrick's raid were known, orders were issued to execute the movement agreed upon. Marietta was to be the supply depot for the movement and Thomas was to guard it with the Twentieth Corps. Howard and Schofield commanded the advance, which was to strike the East Point–Montgomery railway between Red Oak and Fairburn. Thomas was to mass the Fourth and Fourteenth corps to the rear to act as a reserve and to cover the trains with their fifteen-day supplies. Kilpatrick was to screen the advance and Garrard was to cover the rear. A standing order was issued to deploy the troops for defense as soon as the railway line was reached, while at least one-third of the force was to destroy the road. Sherman was concerned basically with railway destruction. In reality this was merely a means to an end, but he had his mind so firmly fixed on the means that he overlooked the end altogether.

This was a time of crisis in the maneuvering for the city, yet each of the opposing commanders was controlled by an erroneous idea. Hood believed that Sherman was attempting to retreat northward to get food and supplies and he failed to take the advantage offered him by the strung-out Blue columns marching along his front. Sherman's obsession that his combat infantry must twist rails permitted Hood to march, countermarch and march again with impunity along the front of the Federal army.

Thomas induced Sherman to delay the start of the movement for twenty-four hours so that his cavalry might have time to rest and shoe their horses. "I would like to commence the movement without being hurried," he said. On August 25, this flanking movement began. In three nights Sherman had his army substantially along the line of the

East Point–Montgomery railway with the Army of the Tennessee near Fairburn, the Army of the Cumberland at Red Oak and the Army of the Ohio between Thomas and East Point. Sherman's force was now beginning to swing to its left in a giant circle with Schofield holding the pivot. Thomas in the center was moving from Red Oak toward Morrow's Station on the Macon railway. Howard, swinging wide on the outside arc through Fairburn towards Jonesborough ran into enemy skirmishers on the afternoon of the thirtieth but forced his way to within half a mile of Jonesborough that night. On the morning of the thirty-first he deployed.

Jonesborough was about thirty miles south of Atlanta. Hood's line could not possibly stretch that far so on the night of the thirtieth he moved two corps—Hardee and Lee—to that threatened point with orders to drive Howard westward across the Flint River. During this flank march some of the units of J. D. Cox's division of the Army of the Ohio forced Hardee to make a detour to the east but the interference was unconscious and one of Sherman's great opportunities passed unexploited. The Rebel attack against Howard was unsuccessful and this failure forced Hood to evacuate Atlanta.

For more than a month Sherman had accepted the conclusion that Hood must evacuate Atlanta if the Macon railway were cut. Now he had cut it and maintained his position on Hood's last supply line in the face of Hood's effort to drive him off. Therefore it followed that Hood must retreat and since Sherman had all but one corps of his powerful army closer to each part of Hood's divided forces than either part of Hood's army was to the other, it followed that some part of Hood's retreat must be made across the face of Sherman's army. This, of course, was all military deduction, yet Sherman also had facts to support this conclusion.

Howard knew on the night of August 30 that Hood was pushing troops to Jonesborough. By 2:00 P.M. of the thirty-first Sherman knew that the two corps of Hardee and Lee were at Jonesborough and that Stewart's corps was in Atlanta with Hood. By 4:00 P.M. Sherman knew that Howard had repulsed the effort to throw him off the Macon railway and that Schofield, Stanley and Baird were on the railway south of Rough and Ready.

Hood was now in the predicament that Rosecrans had found himself in during the ten days preceding the Battle of Chickamauga and Thomas clearly saw the opportunity that beckoned to Sherman. At 7:00 P.M. of the thirty-first Thomas proposed that Howard pin down the Rebel force in Jonesborough, that Stanley and Schofield continue the destruction of the railway between Rough and Ready and Jonesborough, and that he be permitted to swing the rest of the Army of the Cumberland through Fayetteville to Lovejoy's Station and trap two-thirds of the army they had so long been seeking.[36] Hardee was the key to Hood's evacuation plan. That night he felt sure that he could hold his position "unless the enemy cross the Flint river below me," which was exactly the thing that Thomas advised. But at 9:00 P.M. on the thirty-first Sherman turned down this proposal.

Sometime near midnight that night, unknown to Sherman, Lee received his orders to return to Atlanta.

Sherman's orders for September 1 aimed at concentrating on Jonesborough but it was impressed upon the Fourth Corps and the Army of the Ohio that they were to destroy the railway as they concentrated. This meant prying up the track, section by section, and piling the sections on enormous fires where the ties were to be burned off and the rails heated enough so that they could be twisted. Thus it was that the concentration order at the crisis of the campaign was made contingent upon the destruction of a railway already useless to the enemy.[37]

Sherman expected the concentration to be completed by noon of September 1. Davis' Fourteenth Corps, with the shortest distance to travel, made this schedule and deployed facing south with its right connecting with Howard and its left resting on the railway. At 4:00 P.M. Davis assaulted and broke the enemy line. Sherman sent repeated orders to Stanley and Schofield to complete the concentration but by the time they got up the Rebel force at Jonesborough had escaped south.

Sherman blamed Stanley's slowness for the failure to bag Hardee at Jonesborough. The information that came to him from two of his staff officers was to the effect that Stanley had remained immobilized in defiance of his orders. But this was inexact. Stanley had remained immobilized for five and one half hours but in compliance with orders —Sherman's orders. The next morning Sherman accused Stanley of losing him the chance to bag a large part of Hood's army.

"If I did so, Sir, it was owing to your orders," Stanley replied.

The assault of the Fourteenth Corps late in the afternoon of September 1 was short and bloody. It excited the admiration of the three armies because it was delivered against Cleburne's troops—intrenched and supported with artillery—whose boast it had been up to this time that no Yankee assault had ever overcome them. The excitement, the strain, the mental illusions that go with an assault were documented by a mounted officer in the Fourteenth Corps. He remembered every detail of his pre-assault movements but nothing of the final, desperate rush to come to grips with the enemy. When the victory cheer went up this officer found himself still mounted, with his horse pressed broadside against Cleburne's log parapet in a tangled group of infantrymen. His hat was gone, the tears were streaming from his eyes. He never knew how he got there. Six climactic minutes in an individual's life left no memory.[38]

Eight hundred and sixty-five Rebels surrendered within their works and a thousand more were captured or surrendered themselves that night and the next day. Eight field guns were captured in position. Seven battle flags and fourteen officers' swords were sent to Thomas' headquarters. It was the only sizable assault upon infantry and artillery behind breastworks successfully made by either side during the Atlanta campaign. The Fourteenth Regiment of Ohio Volunteers lost one-third of its numbers within a few minutes, among them being several men whose time of service had expired but who had volunteered to advance with their regiment. The Thirty-eighth Regiment of Ohio Volunteers, one of the regiments in Thomas' First Division during Buell's command, suffered its greatest loss of the war in this action.

A popular belief grew up after the war that the only time during the Civil War that Thomas ever put his horse to a gallop was when he went to hurry up Stanley for this assault. Sherman was responsible for the story when he said in his memoirs that this was the only time he could recall seeing Thomas ride so fast. While Thomas' injured back led him to restrain his mount from its most violent gait he moved quickly enough when he had to. It is not in the record, but he must have galloped his horse at Peach Tree Creek when he brought up Ward's guns to save Newton's crumbling line.

While the final combat of the campaign was being worked out at Jonesborough, Thomas, on Sherman's instructions, ordered Slocum, now commanding the Twentieth Corps, to make an effort to occupy Atlanta if he could do so without exposing his bridgehead to a counterattack. The dispatch must have been sent after sundown on September 1. Slocum made his reconnaissance the next morning, found the town empty, accepted the surrender of the mayor and occupied the city a little before noon.

On the morning of September 2 the Fourth Corps and the Armies of the Tennessee and the Ohio followed the line of Hardee's retreat. About noon they came up with the enemy two miles from Lovejoy's Station and deployed. The Fourth Corps assaulted and carried a small portion of the enemy works but could not hold possession of the gain for want of cooperation from the balance of the line. That night a note written in Slocum's hand and dated from inside the captured city came to Sherman stating that the Twentieth Corps was in possession of Atlanta. Before making the news public Sherman sent an officer with the note to Thomas. In a short time the officer returned and Thomas followed on his heels. The cautious Thomas re-examined the note and then, making up his mind that it was genuine, snapped his fingers, whistled and almost danced in his exuberance.

The next day Sherman issued his orders ending the campaign and pulled his armies back to Atlanta. The measure of combat efficiency in an indecisive campaign is a matter of personal choice. Sherman laid great store by place captures. Hood refused to notice anything except captured guns and colors. By both standards Thomas had the right to be proud.

Thomas thanked his men for their tenacity of purpose, unmurmuring endurance, cheerful obedience, brilliant heroism and high qualities in battle.

Sherman felt that his own part in the campaign was skillful and well executed but that the slowness of a part of his army robbed him of the larger fruits of victory. He supposed the military world would approve of his accomplishment.

Whatever the military world thought, the political world approved it wholeheartedly. For some time, despondency in some Northern quarters had been displayed in two ways—an eagerness for peace and a dissatisfaction with Lincoln. Proposals were in the air for a year's armistice. Lincoln was sure that he would not be re-elected. In the midst of this gloom, at 10:05 P.M. on September 2, Slocum's telegram to Stanton, "General Sherman has taken Atlanta," shattered the talk of a negotiated peace and boosted Lincoln into the White House. To the Republicans no victory could have been more complete.

Official congratulations showered upon Sherman and his army. Lincoln mentioned their distinguished ability, courage and perseverance. He felt that this campaign would be famous in the annals of war. Grant called it prompt, skillful and brilliant. Halleck described it as the most brilliant of the war.

Actually the Atlanta campaign was a military failure. Next best to destroying an army is to deprive it of its freedom of action. Sherman had accomplished this much of his job and then inexplicably nullified it by his thirty-mile retreat from Lovejoy's to Atlanta. But, so far as its territorial objectives were concerned, the campaign was successful.

Within the narrow frame of military tactics, too, the experts agree that
the campaign was brilliant. In seventeen weeks the military front was
driven southward more than 100 miles. There was a battle on an
average of once every three weeks. The skirmishing was almost
constant. In the summary of the principal events of the campaign
compiled from the official records there are only ten days which show
no fighting. The casualties in the Army of the Cumberland were
22,807, while for all three armies they were 37,081.[39] Men were killed
in their camps, at their meals and in their sleep. Rifle fire often kept
the opposing gunners from manning their pieces. Modern warfare was
born in this campaign—periscopes, camouflage, booby traps, land
mines, extended order, trench raids, foxholes, armored cars, night
attacks, flares, sharpshooters in trees, interlaced vines and treetops,
which were the forerunners of barbed wire, trip wires to thwart a
cavalry charge, which presaged the mine trap, and the general use of
anesthetics. The use of map coordinates was begun when the senior
officers began to select tactical points by designating a spot as "near
the letter o in the word mountain." A few weeks later the maps were
being divided into squares and a position was described as being
"about lots 239, 247 and 272 with pickets forward as far as 196." This
system was dependent upon identical maps and Thomas supplied
them from a mobile lithograph press. Orders of the day began to specify
the standard map for the movement.

    Sherman proved that a railway base could be movable and the most
brilliant feature of the Atlanta campaign was the rapid repair of the
tracks. To the Rebels it seemed as if Sherman carried tunnels and
bridges in his pockets. The whistle of Sherman's locomotives often
drowned out the rattle of the skirmish fire. As always, the ranks
worked out new and better tactics, but there was brilliance in the way
the field commands adopted these methods and in the way the army
commanders incorporated them into their military thinking. The fos-
silized, formalized, precedent-based thinking of the legendary military
brain was not evident in Sherman's armies. Sherman could never be
accused of sticking too long with the old.

    One of Sherman's most serious shortcomings, however, was his mis-
trust of his cavalry. He never saw that it was a complement to his
infantry and not a substitute for it. Then, in some way, this lack of
faith in the cavalry became mixed up in his mind with the dragging
effect of wagon trains and was hardened into a prejudice. A horse
needed twenty pounds of food a day but the infantryman got along
with two pounds. The horseman required eleven times more than the

footman. So Sherman tried a compromise. He would ship by rail five pounds per day per animal and the other fifteen pounds that were needed could be picked up off the country. It failed to work. Already debilitated by the Chattanooga starvation, the quality of Sherman's horseflesh ran downhill as the campaign progressed. Every recorded request by Thomas for a delay in a flank movement or an advance was to gain time to take care of his horses.

Well led, properly organized cavalry, in its complementary role to infantry, had four functions. First, it could locate the enemy infantry, learn what they were doing, and hold them until the heavy foot columns could come up and take over. Second, it could screen its own infantry from the sight of the enemy. Third, it could threaten at all times, and destroy when possible, the enemy communications. It could reach key tactical points faster than infantry and destroy them or hold them as the case might be for the foot soldier. Its climactic role was to pursue and demoralize a defeated enemy but this chance never came in the Atlanta campaign. Thomas tried hard to have his cavalry ready for the test it was to meet, but his plans were wrecked when it was forced into a campaign without optimum mobility and with its commander stripped from it.

Sherman knew the uses of cavalry as well as Thomas but he imagined a moving base with infantry wings instead of cavalry wings. His conception proved workable but slower and it enabled his enemy to make clean, deft, well organized retreats with small materiel losses. Sherman insisted that cavalry could not successfully break up hostile railways, yet Garrard's Covington raid and Rousseau's Opelika raid cut two-thirds of the rail lines he had to break and Sherman lived in mortal fear of what Forrest might do to his communications.

When McPherson pushed blindly through Snake Creek Gap in a potentially decisive movement, the only cavalry in his van was the Ninth Illinois Mounted Infantry, totally inadequate for its role. It stumbled on infantry where no infantry should have been and McPherson's aggressive impulse faded out, overwhelmed by fears of the unknown. A proper cavalry command in his front would have developed the fact that he had run into one division of Polk's Army of the Mississippi moving up from the direction of Mobile to join Johnston at Dalton. From the night of August 30 to the morning of September 2 there was no Union cavalry east of the Macon railway to disclose to Sherman that he was missing the greatest opportunity of his career. A great part of the time, Thomas' infantry never knew the location of the enemy line. At such times Thomas wondered when and where a counterattack would strike him. It was the hard way to fight a war but Thomas did it without making any disastrous mistakes.

Heat during the Atlanta campaign, coupled with unsuitable clothing, caused individual irritation that was compounded by a lack of opportunity to bathe and shift into clean clothing. To relieve the itch and sweat galls, the men got into the water whenever they could and since each sizable stream was generally the dividing line between the armies the pickets declared a private truce while the men went swimming. Johnston believed that Sherman put his naked engineers into the swimming parties to locate the various fords. Lieutenant Colonel James P. Brownlow, who commanded the First Brigade of Thomas' First Cavalry Division, was ordered across one of these fords. The water was deep and Brownlow took his troopers across naked— except for guns, cartridge boxes and hats. They kicked their horses through the deep water with their bare heels, drove the Rebels out of their rifle pits and captured four men. Most of the Rebels got away since they could make better time through the stiff brush than their naked pursuers.

Rank was becoming an explosive issue in all three of Sherman's armies. Merited recommendations from army commanders were passed over in favor of political appointees from civil life. During the campaign two of Sherman's brigade commanders who left the front—one because of illness, the other because of hurt feelings—received promotions as soon as they got to the rear. The uproar when the news got back to the army brought an apologetic explanation from Lincoln. As a result of this episode Thomas was invited to name three colonels for promotion. He does not appear to have fought hard for the deserved promotion of his subordinates. He seemed content to let their cases rest on merit alone although it must have been apparent that this was insufficient to get results. The reason probably lay in his distaste for persuading a man to do what duty plainly indicated should be done.

There is plenty of evidence that during the march to Atlanta the inter-army jealousies which had dominated the battles around Chattanooga were not dead. Their existence built up a dangerous mental block in Sherman's mind. Official charges were made that Thomas, because of it, discriminated against the other armies in the allocation of supplies, the use of the railway and the handling of hospital trains. Stanley felt that Sherman's increasing jealousy and prejudice in favor of the Army of the Tennessee was the basic cause of the failure at Snake Creek Gap. One competent observer thought it more likely that the cause lay in the differences in the characters of Thomas and Sherman which resulted in differences in the organization, discipline and administration of their two armies.[40]

It is possible that a carry-over of this feeling accounts for some of Sherman's unsubstantiated criticism of Thomas and the Army of the Cumberland. At the start of the campaign Sherman seemed satisfied with the Cumberlanders and their leader—a combination which made the superb military tool Sherman required for his intricate campaign. For four months this army pushed an impenetrable barrier into the heart of Georgia behind which Sherman swung his armies of maneuver like a whip around the Rebel flanks. At the end of the campaign, when Sherman culled his army to 60,000, he chose the Fourteenth Corps as one of the best commands available to him.

As the campaign commander, it was Sherman's job to use blame, praise, threats, promises, cajolings or whatever else might be necessary to keep his offensive moving at top speed. There was room, too, for honest differences of opinion about the accomplishments of the Cumberlanders, but Sherman misused his prerogatives. His basic criticism was made behind Thomas' back. Years later, when Thomas could make no defense, Sherman's charge became part of the record. Howard, who enjoyed the confidence of both men and was, therefore, in an excellent position to appraise the situation, felt that Sherman's strictures were undeserved. It is undoubtedly true, however, that, in cases other than emergencies, Thomas was loath to move until he knew where he was going, whom he was going with, what he had with him and what he had against him, and that this thirst for facts arose from his regard for his men. Professionally Thomas came close to being a perfectionist but not so close as to ruin his ability to command. He wanted adequate preparations made for an advance or assault and arrogated to himself the decision as to what was adequate.

Only a few in any profession assume the responsibility for perfection and Sherman was not one of them. He was impulsive. He scorned deliberation because it seemed sluggish and sluggishness was embarrassing. In the rough, heavily brushed country in front of Marietta, soggy with twenty-three days of June rains, he was desperate from frustration. He could turn neither of Johnston's flanks nor find a spot in his line thin enough to break through. His overwhelming strength was stopped by a force half its size. He was morbidly afraid of being accused of making a slower advance than Grant. When he was befuddled by his opponent, when he lagged hopelessly behind his own time schedule, when criticism from his superiors became imminent, his impulsiveness sought release in a spate of words. First he turned to self accusation, but later he put the blame on shoulders where it did not belong.

In the final analysis, there is grave doubt that Sherman meant what he wrote about McPherson and Thomas. He admired them both. He wanted Thomas with him and leaned on his strength, while at the same time he cursed his deliberateness. Thomas thoroughly understood Sherman. He subordinated his rank to Sherman's without any discernible mental reservations, never gave him bad advice and, when Sherman overrode his suggestions, did everything in his power to make Sherman's substitute plan work. Sherman acknowledged that Thomas was a good teammate but he was dubious of his methods.

The basic difference between the two men seems to come down to a divergence in military philosophy. Sherman was a raider to whom mobility was everything. It may have been the compensation for his failure as a fighter. A mobile raiding force living off the country could not stop to fight a battle without risking starvation. After the fall of Atlanta, Sherman found his niche and in it his military fame rests secure.

But at West Point, the world-famous teacher Mahan had given Thomas an eaglet to feather. It was the theory of controlled violence. It was the ultimate economy of force in time, in treasure and in lives. In Thomas' eyes every collision with the enemy was an opportunity for Armageddon and he wanted to be ready for it.

It was during this campaign that Thomas and Sherman received their commissions as brigadier generals in the regular army. Halleck wrote both letters of transmittal and they foreshadowed the future. The one to Sherman expressed the strong hope that he would soon receive the next highest rank. The one to Thomas admitted that the promotion was long delayed but most fully earned.

19

Nashville: The War's Decisive Battle

In the process of the Atlanta campaign, the Confederacy suffered grievous material losses, but its intangible loss was more serious. This was the deterioration of morale in the Army of Tennessee. It threatened the very existence of the Rebellion between the Appalachian Mountains and the Mississippi River.

The numbing effect of a retreat of such magnitude as Johnston's and Hood's is cumulative. The main forces abandon their hard-built, hard-held works. Outposts and pickets furtively break off their contact with the enemy. Trains, ambulances and artillery move out stealthily. Their orders are depressing. Silence must be observed. Wheels are muffled. Movements are made at night. Repetition of these things gives the army a funereal aspect. The wounded and disabled are overtaken by the enemy and cannot return home, buoyant and hopeful, to be nursed back to health. Stragglers and deserters increase—some because they lose hope, others because they want to protect their families. Fresh men refuse to join the ranks. This is the penalty imposed upon the enemy by an aggressive, continuous pressure. It depresses and paralyzes. Eventually it destroys.

In this roundabout way, Sherman was accomplishing his primary objective. He had not destroyed Hood's army but he had battered down its spirit, inaugurated its demoralization and deprived it of its freedom of movement. When, on September 3, 1864, he issued his thirty-mile retreat order he automatically increased Hood's aggressive power by 25 per cent. Of the major Confederate forces in the field, Hood's army alone now had freedom of movement. The South's ablest historian of the western fighting feels that Sherman had no sound military reason for releasing his pressure on Hood's front.

Sherman assuaged his own misgivings by enjoining his army commanders to "take it slow and easy" so that the enemy might not crow over his withdrawal. Thomas pulled back to Atlanta and the other armies were posted at East Point and Decatur. Five days later a ten-day truce sealed Hood's respite so he could begin the long overdue work of reorganizing, refitting and regenerating his army.

During this period, Thomas titillated the Cumberlanders by allowing the impression to get abroad that he had sent for his wife. "He has not seen her since the war commenced," wrote one of his staff, "and can't find time to go and see her." [1]

At any rate, Nathan Bedford Forrest settled the matter for him. Forrest was an old and respected adversary. Thomas had chased him with infantry—on foot, in wagons and on railroad trains—and with cavalry. He had build scores of blockhouses to protect his communications and had perfected a railway construction organization to repair the damage from Forrest's raids. He had met him in pitched battle and in sharp skirmishes. He had accused him of atrocities and had, in turn, been similarly accused by Forrest. He had found him a hard man to stop, an even harder man to whip. And whipping him was one of Thomas' unfinished jobs.

Forrest, when necessary, was a master improviser. He induced local citizens to act as horseholders, automatically adding a third to his firepower. When civilians were reluctant to grant the cooperation he demanded, he hired it with a bribe of salt or some equally scarce, easily carried commodity. Actually he left few things to improvisation. He thought out in advance the best countermove for every contingency. He was adept at reading his opponent's mind.

Intangibles made Forrest great. He could hold men to his will and his will was to "get 'em skeered and then keep the skeer on 'em." "It's the first blow that counts," he believed, "and if you keep it up hot enough, you can whip 'em as fast as they come up." He rewarded his men with intangibles—victory and the undisguised respect of the hard-bitten Rebel infantryman—yet he had a vast practical talent, down to matters of apparently inconsequential detail, for seeing that his command was in constant readiness. These things were incomprehensible to many besides Sherman and, because of them, legends began to gather around his reputation. When Forrest rode to the front of his column, the sight of his silhouette in the darkness and the sound of his strange shrill voice reinvigorated his troopers and their mounts. His men believed in him and when he led they believed in themselves. Forrest's was the power of the handful of truly great captains. He was the one private soldier of the Civil War to rise from private to lieutenant general.

Sherman, who had no confidence in cavalry, was mortally afraid of Forrest. Each was a master of mobility, but they differed as to its function. To Sherman mobility was an end in itself; to Forrest it was the means of joining combat.

Early in September, Wheeler's horsemen had been forced south of the Tennessee River by Thomas' garrisons in the Nashville-Decatur-Chattanooga triangle. The raid took a ruinous toll of Wheeler's force —two of his general officers and at least half of his command; one report said seven-eighths of it. It had been a barren effort. The cost was high, the results nil. The salvage of his command was demoralized and Wheeler was thinking of asking for his relief. So Jefferson Davis decided to play his ace. Simultaneously with Wheeler's retreat he gave Forrest his long-sought permission to wreck Sherman's life line. In ten days Forrest moved from near Meridian north toward the Tennessee River. His mounted men rode. His guns, caissons, ammunition, stores and unmounted men moved in five freight trains loaded inside and out. They made frequent stops while the passengers cut wood for the fire boxes, carried water for the boilers, repaired the bridges and cleared the tracks of roadblocks.

On September 21, Forrest's breakfast guest watched the column cross the Tennessee River as he shared the general's cornmeal and treacle. The mounted men forded in column of twos, following a tortuous underwater track that stretched for two miles from bank to bank at the head of Colbert's shoals, one mile above Waterloo. The wheels were ferried across farther upstream. Forrest's visitor was impressed with the fact that every gun, rifle, wagon and ambulance, as well as all of Forrest's blankets, shoes and ammunition, had been captured from the Yankees. The next day Forrest, mounted on his horse, King Philip, rode through Florence at the head of his column. The streets were lined with cheering inhabitants. Of his 4,500 men, 400 were on foot but hopeful of mounts after the first brush with the enemy. Three days later Forrest had pocketed the garrison at Athens and had cut one of the two railways between Nashville and Chattanooga that supplied Sherman's army.

Troubles began piling up on Sherman. Hood had moved from Lovejoy's to Palmetto and put a bridge across the Chattahoochee River. This removed Hood's communications from the zone of Sherman's immediate threat. The bridge could indicate an offensive move. Sherman was puzzled, but Jefferson Davis arrived at Hood's camp and relieved Sherman's uncertainty by announcing publicly that Hood would break Sherman's communications in Georgia while Forrest broke them in Tennessee. Sherman was still undecided about the best means of countering this threat. He came up with the naive solution that Grant whip Lee while he himself marched to the sea. Grant brushed this suggestion off with an order that Sherman drive Forrest out of middle Tennessee. Sherman tried to comply by organizing, through his chief-of-staff in Nashville, a striking force to move against Forrest as he scattered his command to forage. But Forrest did not scatter and the telegraph wires were hot with messages of Forrest's further triumphs and forecasts of what he would do next.

To solve the problem, Sherman turned to Thomas. His instructions were verbal but Sherman told Halleck that Thomas was being sent north to drive Forrest out of Tennessee. Two divisions of infantry were sent to aid in this work. The Decherd tunnel, the railway junction at Stevenson, and the bridges at Bridgeport and Whiteside were the weak links in the Yankee communications that offered Forrest his greatest opportunity, but Thomas' defenses were adequate and Forrest confined his early operations to the Nashville-Decatur railway.

Thomas reached Chattanooga on September 29. That same day Forrest disappeared from the Nashville-Decatur railway and reports came in that the Nashville-Chattanooga railway had been cut near Decherd. Thomas had no cavalry so he countered with infantry. One detachment under Rousseau moved from Pulaski to Nashville to Tullahoma by rail. Steedman was pulled away from his guard duty on the Chattanooga-Atlanta railway and crossed to the north side of the Tennessee River with 5,000 men. In three days Thomas' trap was set for Forrest. Rousseau with a picked-up cavalry command was to strike him from the north, while an infantry division was to check him at the Tennessee River crossings. Within twenty-four hours Thomas supplemented this effort by moving a cavalry detachment eastward from Clifton and two gunboats up the Tennessee River to block the fords and prevent the laying of bridges. Officially Thomas called his chances of trapping Forrest fair. There is a suspicion that privately he was more sanguine. But Forrest slipped through Thomas' net. He crossed the

Tennessee on flatboats at various places and the Yankee telegraphers reported that Thomas was much chagrined.

Within a week after reaching Chattanooga, Thomas, by energetic improvisation, had forced Forrest out of Tennessee. But Forrest had demonstrated that a few thousand cavalry could paralyze middle Tennessee and enter and leave it at will. To counter such a threat with infantry required the maintenance of a score of heavy garrisons and a mobile force which could be shifted quickly over the railways within the state, but Thomas contended that the most economical deterrent was a well led, well equipped cavalry concentration.

Meantime Hood had put his army between Thomas and Sherman. On October 3 Thomas arrived at Nashville on Sherman's order. There was considerable alarm when the Administration learned that Hood was between Sherman and Chattanooga. Thomas, they realized, lacked the force necessary to prevent Hood from entering Tennessee. They could see that Sherman had failed to anticipate Hood's move and was under the necessity of improvising a course to meet it. Washington's solicitude over the situation was somewhat relieved by the fact that Thomas was at the point of greatest danger.

In spite of constant interruptions in his communication with Sherman, Thomas sensed that Hood had made up his mind to by-pass Chattanooga and to cross the Tennessee south and west of that city, but there was little that he could do to stop it. He was desperately short of troops. He was guarding the railways and loyal citizens of middle Tennessee from guerrillas. At the same time, he was guarding the Tennessee River from Eastport to Tuscumbia against Forrest's re-entry and from Whitesburg to Bridgeport against Hood's. He could watch this long frontier but he could not protect it.

At this time, however, the military crisis along the upper Tennessee abated. Hood moved to Gadsden, Alabama, while Sherman placed his force at Gaylesville, covering the Chattanooga-Atlanta railway and the city of Chattanooga. Hood had been maneuvering, so far unsuccessfully, to force Sherman to divide his army between the opposite sides of the Tennessee River. Now Hood and Beauregard, who had just received the over-all command of the western Rebel armies, sat down at Hood's headquarters to plan the strategy that would bring this about. At this conference Beauregard ordered Forrest to report to Hood as soon as he had completed his current assignment of breaking the communications between Nashville and the Tennessee River.

While the Rebel leaders sought the best way to destroy Sherman, that general seemed to be intent on resigning his obligation to destroy

Hood, the major role to which he had been assigned. His army had already retraced its steps to Dalton. If he chased Hood farther north Sherman would find himself in the same predicament as Buell when he tumbled his weary, breathless men into Louisville after pursuing Bragg from Chattanooga.

Sherman and Hood faced identical pressures. Neither could stand on the defensive and neither could afford to pursue the enemy into his own territory. Both were impulsive men but Sherman's military position had deteriorated so much that he could not stand the strain of indecision. For perhaps the only time during this war Sherman was bankrupt of military imagination. His solution to the problem was a strange one—he proposed to split his power.

One part of the army, under his own command, would march through Georgia to the sea, decoying Hood into following. The remainder, under Thomas, would follow Hood if Hood followed Sherman, or would defend Tennessee if Hood elected to move northward. Hood could make his own choice and Sherman must have known that Hood would not follow him deeper into the South anymore than he himself would chase Hood towards the Ohio River.

Sherman's plan was good as far as it went. If he had added that he would countermarch in the event Hood elected to assail Thomas and join in a battle of annihilation, it would have been complete. The uncertainty of Grant, Stanton and Lincoln hints that they were conscious of some insufficiency about Sherman's proposal. At first their disagreement was unanimous. Lincoln and Stanton put the responsibility squarely on Grant after formally registering their dissents. Grant disagreed, then agreed, disagreed again, and finally concluding that Thomas had ample strength to fend off Hood for ninety days if it became necessary, shouldered the responsibility and gave his official approval to the plan.

Thomas had little relish for guarding Sherman's communications while the march through Georgia was in progress, yet he was the commander of the Department of the Cumberland and middle Tennessee was his responsibility. He tried to get his favorite Fourteenth Corps back in payment of his cooperation, but Sherman refused. Thomas finally agreed to his part of the plan but only on the understanding that he rejected the role of passive defense and would prepare for the annihilation of Hood's army if it should move north of the Tennessee River. To this Grant and Sherman gave their tacit approval.

For nearly 100 years history has referred to Thomas' Nashville campaign and Sherman's march to the sea as unconnected operations.

It should be noted that Sherman's success depended upon Thomas'. If Thomas had won less than a total victory Sherman would have had to retrace his march; but if Sherman had failed in Georgia, Thomas would have been unaffected. This is merely to say that Hood's destruction was decisive in every theater of the war, but with Hood's army in existence Sherman's success in Georgia would have been purely local.

Probably the issuance of Sherman's order on October 26, 1864, dividing his army between himself and Thomas is as good a date as any to mark the beginning of the Nashville campaign. Thomas was then in Nashville. He was ordered to exercise command over all troops and garrisons not absolutely in Sherman's presence. Apparently the order was not as broad as it seemed, for Sherman limited its terms in his official report to the Fourth and Twenty-third corps, three divisions under A. J. Smith,[2] Wilson's cavalry and all the garrisons in Tennessee. This was a potential force of 81,000 to guard an area as large as France against Hood's 40,000 and Forrest's 12,000. Thomas was satisfied with this potential and advised Sherman on November 7 that he would assume the offensive as soon as it was realized. Sherman tried to fix this date definitely—he suggested ten days—but Thomas refused to be pinned down. Finally Grant, Halleck, Sherman and Thomas agreed that Thomas should assume the offensive as soon as possible; and Thomas made clear to Halleck his interpretation of this phrase. Sherman agreed to this interpretation specifically.[3] Halleck agreed that Thomas' offensive should be postponed until A. J. Smith was up but saw no gain in waiting for Thomas' cavalry to be mounted. Sherman, however, refused to press Halleck's view upon Thomas. Presumably Halleck expressed Grant's view. Grant said nothing over his own signature, but he knew exactly what Thomas intended to do and when he intended to do it. Grant had time to change the order or the commander or both but he let Sherman's order stand. The arrival of A. J. Smith's command and the remounting of Wilson's horsemen were responsibilities that centered in Washington, so if Grant wanted Thomas' attack expedited he had the means of doing it.

The timing of Thomas' offensive was contingent upon the arrival of the infantry and cavalry that he required for the destruction of Hood's army, yet Sherman seemed to avoid the issue. As fast as Thomas wrote down the specifications for his campaign, Sherman sought to make an ambiguous settlement between the divergent views of Thomas and Grant. The crowning one went eastward from Sherman's headquarters at midnight of November 11. It was Sherman's last dispatch to army headquarters before he cut his wire for the march

through Georgia. "I have balanced all the figures well," he advised
Halleck, "and am satisfied that General Thomas has in Tennessee a
force sufficient for all probabilities." It would hardly seem possible
that Sherman was deliberately stirring up trouble between Grant and
Thomas but he marched out of the combat zone leaving the distinct
impression in Grant's mind that he did not agree with Thomas and in
Thomas' mind that he did not agree with Grant. James H. Wilson,
who was probably the last ranking officer of the Nashville campaign
to talk to Sherman, discovered that Sherman had no clear idea of the
troops Thomas would be able to concentrate, how long it would take
or when they would be able to confront the enemy.

The change from defense to offense is a delicate military operation
and once adopted it must be maintained. It requires the assembly of
supplies and troops for both defense and pursuit and the selection of
time and place. Thomas was supervising the collection of supplies at
Nashville whence they could be distributed by means of the strategic
railways he was guarding. The troops were being supplied to him by
Washington in categories and in numbers already agreed upon. The
time was contingent upon their arrival. The place was contingent upon
Hood's moves.

So much for the quantitative potential of Thomas' part of Sherman's army. The matter of quality also had a bearing on his campaign
plans. Thomas had asked Sherman to send him the Fourteenth Corps
which Sherman had disparaged so ostentatiously in the Atlanta
campaign. Thomas wanted it because it was thoroughly organized and
completely equipped and because there were strong personal ties between himself and its personnel. When Thomas thought of the Fourteenth Corps he thought of attributes far beyond its combat qualities
—such things as military intelligence, signalling and field telegraph,
mapping, medical service, engineering service. Sherman refused this
request on the ground that the Fourteenth Corps was too compact and
reliable an organization for him to leave behind. It seems evident that
Sherman meant to march out of the western war with the fittest part
of his army, leaving Thomas with the culls to solve the military problem of smothering Hood's freedom of movement.

Sherman took with him a striking force of 60,000 men. It was the
combat core of his army stripped of its trash, malingerers, misfits, the
sickly and the poorly equipped. This was a proper division of his
strength on the theory that Hood would follow him, but it flouted
every military principle if Hood should choose to strike Thomas. This
was the error that brought acute embarrassment to Grant. If Thomas

were defeated Grant could not escape much of the blame. If Thomas destroyed Hood it would set up a military personality that was bound to challenge Grant's military machine.

In place of the Fourteenth Corps Sherman sent Thomas the Fourth Corps—a good veteran organization with a proud record. Stanley commanded it and his division commanders were Wood, Wagner and Whitaker. Sherman put its strength at 15,000, a strength which Grant apparently accepted although this figure was 15 per cent high. The Twenty-third Corps was the weakest unit, quantitatively and qualitatively, in Sherman's field army. It, too, went to Thomas, Sherman reporting its strength as 12,000, another figure which Grant accepted. Schofield, the commander, pointed out its weakness and put its strength at 8,000 men. His division commanders were Cox and Reilly. A. J. Smith's three divisions were first-class troops but they came to Thomas without a corps organization, without hospitals, ambulances, trains or supplies. His division commanders were John McArthur and Jonathan Baker Moore. Wilson's cavalry had been dismounted and stripped to supply Sherman's army. Their morale had been shattered by Sherman's constant, public, unfair censure of their work. Their records were imperfect, the facts concerning them were conjectural, there was no way to accurately determine their numbers. There was no uniformity in their arms. Horses were coming into the remount depots at the rate of 500 per week when 1,500 per week were needed. There was no response to their requisitions for arms and equipment.

Thomas organized one division from the civilian employees of the quartermaster and commissary departments but Forrest's raid had indicated that such troops were not always dependable. A provisional division was being organized at Chattanooga out of what Sherman called the trash of his army and Cruft was trying to work them into some form of military organization. With them went the indifferent wagons, the worthless mules and horses, the sick and wounded, the prisoners of war, and the surplus servants.

Thomas personally was ill-equipped for the campaign. His headquarters train was somewhere between Chattanooga and Atlanta. He missed his expert intelligence section. His engineering department was disorganized. Sherman had taken his pontoon train and its trained pontoniers. His medical director did not reach Nashville until December 1 and the medical department was thoroughly shattered. An incredible amount of confusion had to be straightened out before the work of organizing and refitting could be done. Sherman's chief-of-staff had to appeal to an innkeeper in his effort to locate one of the

corps commanders assigned to Thomas. Chattanooga was so crowded
with unmanageable furloughed troops from Atlanta and way points
that the organized units could not be held together. Some of the Tennessee regiments were fighting the Negro troops assigned to police
duty. With the warehouses overflowing at Chattanooga and Nashville,
the garrisons at Stevenson and Decatur were short of rations.

The new Ohio regiments were as undisciplined as a herd of cattle
and Rousseau refused to receive them into his command. Under the
North's newest recruiting system, cripples, lunatics, criminals, the diseased and the depraved were pouring into the army. The defenses of
Nashville were not completed and work on them had to be resumed.
There were three lines of communication northward from Nashville—
the railway, the Cumberland River, which could not be used now
because of the low stage of the water, and the Tennessee River with
a rail haul from Johnsonville to Nashville. All three ran through Kentucky, yet Kentucky was on the verge of an open revolt. Its citizens
resented the enlistment of slaves. The Negroes had learned that the
consent of their owners was not a condition precedent to service in the
armed forces of the United States and they flocked to the recruiting
offices to escape their bondage. The owners combined to prevent this
loss of their property. The state was overrun with guerrillas. Officially
reported outbreaks of violence averaged nearly one a day. Schofield,
the department commander, was ready to wash his hands of his
Kentucky responsibilities. Frank Wolford, who had commanded one
of Thomas' regiments in the Dick Robinson days and who was one of
the men selected by Lincoln to save Kentucky for the Union, was now
stirring up a revolt. The Governor of Ohio felt that Kentucky's weakness was imperiling his own border. Forays from the relative safety of
Kentucky were being made into Illinois and Indiana. Kentucky's civil
government was impotent. Its military commander was more interested
in collecting votes for Lincoln than in discharging his military duties.
The Judge Advocate General of the army reported that a conspiracy
existed for an armed cooperation with the Rebels. Lincoln had put the
state under martial law.

Tennessee was not in much better shape. Andrew Johnson maintained his own military force and it brooked no interference from
Thomas' garrison commanders. By implication some of the volunteer
regiments of Tennessee cavalry extended this exemption to themselves.
Continuous raids by Forrest and Wheeler incited the guerrillas to
greater activity and cowed the Unionists except where one of Thomas'

garrisons gave them protection. It was unsafe to hold civil courts in Tennessee.

Thomas went to Nashville originally to superintend the reorganization of the troops in Rousseau's district, which he found in considerable confusion. This was an administrative job and the pile-up of administrative pressures, intensified by the continual movement of troops and supplies through the Nashville bottleneck, kept him there. As Hood moved northward these administrative duties merged into a combat responsibility.

The multiple troubles at Nashville were reminiscent of those at Camp Dick Robinson except that in this case Thomas had many more elements in his favor. Outside of some shortages in his mounted arm, he had plenty of supplies. He had one of the best leaders of mounted troops developed by the North during the war. Schofield, Stanley, Smith, Steedman and Rousseau were better than average for their rank and grade. His division commands were well taken care of but the deterioration of officer quality was rapid as rank lessened. Although his staff was scattered and his specialist commands broken up, he knew where to put his finger on men to do the jobs for him. Time was what he needed and it ran in his favor.

With his pick-up army Thomas had to organize an offensive while he defended the line of the Tennessee River from Paducah to the Cumberland Gap—a total length of more than 500 miles. Within this vast semicircle the temper of the civil population was at the point of revolt.

Thomas' defense line was threatened by Hood from the south, Forrest from the west and R. E. Lee from the east. Lincoln wanted something done about the western threat. It was the one nearest to Nashville and to Kirby Smith, commanding the trans-Mississippi Rebel army, who already had his orders to cross the Mississippi and join the attack on Thomas. But Lee's threat aimed at East Tennessee. Failure to control this territory had already ruined three Northern army commanders. To ward off Lee's strike, Thomas had to hold Knoxville. To hold Knoxville he had to hold Chattanooga. To hold Chattanooga he had to maintain adequate garrisons at Dalton, Whiteside, Bridgeport, Stevenson, Tullahoma and Murfreesborough. Until Hood committed his army, Thomas had to maintain a mobile holding force in the Decatur-Pulaski-Florence triangle. To supply this force and insure its mobility he had to keep in operation the railroad lines from Nashville to Pulaski and from Stevenson to Decatur.

Lincoln had put his finger on Thomas' weakest point—his western flank. It was wide open. Thomas tried to strengthen it. He wanted the Memphis garrison to clean out Eastport for him but its commander felt that his force was inadequate. Thomas was assured that Canby,[4] commanding the Military Division of West Mississippi, felt he could prevent any sizable reinforcements from crossing the Mississippi but this fell far short of the support for which Thomas was looking. On November 3 Thomas requested a demonstration from Memphis against Hood's communications but Grant refused to issue the order.[5]

Hood was an audacious man and he had an audacious plan to exploit the political weakness of the North by convincing more of its citizens that the South could never be conquered. He planned a raid in force into Union territory. To be successful he had to keep his army concentrated and hold onto the initiative. It was quite a trick. The three similar excursions made by the South had all been thrown back when their leaders lost the initiative.

On the crucial date of October 26, Hood had accomplished the most difficult part of his self-assigned job. He had regenerated his army, which Stanton now appraised as the best drilled and most formidable Rebel force set on foot during the war. He had taken the initiative and moved northward to a position that unmasked a bewildering number of threats. He could move westward, link up with the trans-Mississippi forces and threaten a combined move north, west or east. He could move north, by-pass Nashville, get into Kentucky and cooperate with Lee's western flank to explode the revolt which seemed about to break out in the Blue Grass state. He could cut off Chattanooga from the north, restore Rebel ascendency in East Tennessee and clear Georgia and Alabama of Federal troops. He could move northeast through Bristol, Wytheville and Lynchburg and threaten Grant at Petersburg. If Sherman moved toward Savannah, Hood could move eastward through the Smoky Mountains and play havoc with Sherman's plans.

Just as the concept of a defense could be stretched to cover many things or relaxed to cover few, the concept of an offensive could cover anything from checking Hood to destroying him. By November 7 Thomas had decided to attempt Hood's destruction and so notified Sherman. He would fight delaying actions until he had his complete striking force of Schofield, Stanley, Smith, and Wilson. Then he would take the offensive. Sherman agreed that same day. The following day Thomas was equally specific to Halleck and a copy of this dispatch went to Sherman but Thomas did not believe it would take as long as it did for Smith to get up and for Wilson to get horses.

The odyssey of Smith's command eastward from the Kansas border was one of the wonderments of the war. He was earmarked for Thomas on October 28. Urgent telegrams from Grant, Halleck, Sherman and Thomas brought no results. Grant's former chief-of-staff, Rawlins, went west to hasten the movement. Somehow the idea got abroad that Smith would report to Thomas around the middle of November. Thomas put enough faith in this schedule to practically promise reinforcements to Schofield by that time. Smith's command finally reached Nashville on December 3 simultaneously with Hood's vanguard.

Cavalry horses had been in short supply since early October but this was chronic with the Army of the Cumberland. In the Atlanta campaign Sherman's horses broke down faster than the cavalry bureau had counted on. Schofield's retreat from Pulaski to Nashville took another heavy toll. For more than a month after the start of the Nashville campaign Thomas' remount situation deteriorated steadily. It was not bettered until he was given permission to impress horses in Tennessee and Kentucky but this permission came only after Hood was in front of Nashville.

On October 1 Grant ordered large reserves to Nashville. By the sixteenth reinforcements were reaching Thomas at the rate of one regiment a day, just enough to replace his losses. His garrison regiments were being mustered out faster than replacements arrived. Regiments that came to him from Kentucky had to be returned to that state. Then Thomas got an order from Washington to furlough all Illinois troops so that they might go home to vote. Thomas refused to obey it but he did send north the Illinois men unfit for service. On the day that Grant ordered Sherman to turn his back on Hood, the Secretary of War ordered all the enlisted men from eight states then in Chattanooga to be furloughed and supplied with transportation over Thomas' railway, already overburdened with the responsibility for supplying Sherman's army for its march to the sea, and at the same time moving the Twenty-third Corps north to Chattanooga. When it was all over, Thomas' net gain in numbers was approximately 7,000 men.

Meantime, Hood had moved westward from Gadsden to Tuscumbia bringing him closer to his line of communication through Corinth and to his expected trans-Mississippi reinforcements. Here apparently Sherman's army, then at Kingston, Tennessee, exerted its last influence upon Hood. The division of Sherman's army was not irrevocable and Hood decided to wait until it was. In addition, neither his supplies from Corinth nor Forrest's command had reached him.

Here were two powerful armies which had been fighting each other continuously for more than six months at a cost of thousands of casualties, preparing to turn their backs on each other and march in opposite directions. It is worth noting that each commander expected the other to follow him; that each hoped the other would not; that each had Richmond in mind as his ultimate objective and that each expected to exploit his opponent's political weakness by a massive raid into enemy territory. The North was vulnerable politically and therein lay the ghost that was to haunt Grant, Stanton and Lincoln.

There was a close similarity between this campaign and the Atlanta campaign, except that the roles were reversed. Both aggressors traveled approximately the same distance following a railway. Both made their major gains by flanking tactics. Both tried one expensive frontal attack. Both missed a golden opportunity. Both came upon a major city at the end of their advance and both lacked the strength to invest it. Both tried to force capitulation by cutting their opponent's communications. Both stripped themselves of their cavalry at the crisis of their campaign. Both defensive commanders came under heavy criticism from their superiors. The main difference between the two campaigns lay in the morale of the defensive force. The Rebel morale sank as they retreated while Thomas, in some unexplained way, pushed the morale of his army to greater and greater heights. Another difference was the celerity of Hood's advance. He made the distance six times faster than Sherman.

On November 12 communication between Thomas and Sherman was broken and Thomas watched with considerable anxiety to see whether Hood would follow Sherman or move northward against his heavily outnumbered holding forces. Stanley's Fourth Corps was at Pulaski, based on the Nashville-Decatur railway, and ready to delay a move by Hood northward toward Nashville or eastward toward Chattanooga. The route that Hood selected would determine the place of Thomas' concentration and the railways he must hold to make it. The Twenty-third Corps, except for two brigades, was on its way to Pulaski. Wilson was in Nashville trying to get the cavalry ready for a campaign that had already started. Hatch, with 4,000 cavalry, had been stopped by Thomas on his way to join Sherman. He had attached Croxton's brigade of 2,500 troopers to his command and had driven Hood's advance units west of Shoal Creek. He was watching for the first sign of Hood's commitment to a specific route and trying to block the roads by which Hood would move away from the Tennessee River. At night, picked troopers were trying to break Hood's pontoon bridge which floated a short distance downstream from the Tuscumbia-Florence crossing.

Thomas' right flank far down the Tennessee River at Johnsonville had been thoroughly smashed by Forrest in one of the amazing episodes of the war. Here he had captured a Union gunboat, manned it, navigated it and fought it against the United States navy. He totally destroyed Thomas' depot at Johnsonville, forced the abandonment of the railway between that point and Nashville, denied to Thomas the use of the Tennessee River upstream from Johnsonville and revealed the undependability of defense forces made up of undrilled and untried troops. What was even more serious, Forrest's attack caused the diversion of the Twenty-third Corps from Pulaski to Johnsonville.

Thomas meanwhile completed the organization of a mobile defense force which he hoped would delay Hood and prevent him from exploiting any breakthrough in the Union defense cordon. Schofield got his instructions verbally from Thomas when he passed through Nashville from Johnsonville to take the command of this field army. He was thirty-three years old. He knew Hood personally and held his military competency to be not much more than average. Thomas briefed him thoroughly. Schofield was to retire slowly toward the reinforcements Thomas was collecting for him, delaying Hood's progress as much as possible and avoiding a decisive battle. Schofield's strength relative to Hood's was about the same as Joseph Johnston's had been to Sherman's. Before Schofield reached Nashville, however, Hood added a psychological domination of Schofield to his numerical one.

Disastrous as it was, Forrest's Johnsonville raid gave Thomas nine additional days of grace. It was November 17 when Forrest's tired horsemen crossed the Tennessee River into Florence and were serenaded by its exuberant citizens. The balance of Hood's infantry crossed three days later and the northward march started on November 21.

Ten days after Sherman's evacuation of Atlanta Thomas learned that Hood had chosen his army rather than Sherman's for his objective. But Thomas was still in the dark as to Hood's route. Capron's brigade of the Sixth Cavalry Division, 1,200 troopers armed with muzzle loaders which could not be reloaded while the horse was moving, moved into position on Thomas' western flank. There was nothing Capron could do except to watch and warn. Forrest's Johnsonville operation had denied the Tennessee River upstream from that point to the United States gunboats. That flank was wide open. Several hundred miles away Thomas' eastern flank, also inadequately guarded, was under severe and what might prove to be fatal pressure from part of R. E. Lee's command.

On November 13, one day after Sherman started eastward from

Atlanta and eight days before Thomas knew that Hood would not
follow him, Breckinridge, Duke and Vaughn, working in concert,
routed the Union force at Cumberland Gap, took its artillery, scattered
the command and drove the remnants back into Knoxville. The military situation was complicated by a political one wherein a clash of
authority threatened between Thomas and Andrew Johnson. Thomas
avoided this pitfall and scraped together a force in Kentucky to repair
the damage. The command went to Stoneman, another of the officers
classified as militarily useless by Grant and Sherman.[6] Thomas had a
face-to-face talk with him in Nashville. Its details are not recorded but
in some way Thomas blocked off Stoneman's weaknesses and made
use of his strengths.

Again another curiously reversed role becomes noteworthy. In 1862
Bragg had been in East Tennessee and threatening an advance into
middle Tennessee or Kentucky. Thomas, at that time relieved of the
crushing responsibility of command, had guessed correctly what Bragg
would do and how he would do it. This time Hood was in middle
Tennessee and threatening a move into East Tennessee or Kentucky
and again Thomas worked out a successful countermeasure. Hood had
two options. He could go up the main valley from Chattanooga to
Knoxville. If he did Thomas planned to check him at Chattanooga.
Or Hood could turn the north end of the Sequatchie Valley and get on
the road to Knoxville. If he chose this route Thomas meant to stop him
at Murfreesborough. Until Hood made his choice, Thomas had to
maintain adequate forces at both places and on the railroads connecting
them. Nor was Hood likely to swing into Kentucky east of Nashville
as long as Murfreesborough threatened his flank.

On November 21 Thomas directed Schofield to move gradually
from Pulaski to Columbia so as to concentrate there ahead of Hood if
Hood should move that way. On November 23, R. S. Granger was
alerted to abandon Athens, Huntsville and Decatur and make a partial
concentration at Stevenson whence he could move toward either Chattanooga or Murfreesborough. On November 25 and 26 the telegraph lines
between Schofield and Thomas were cut. In this period of uncertainty
rumors were thick but facts were scarce. It was sometime after noon
on November 27 that Thomas began to feel sure that Nashville and not
Chattanooga was Hood's objective.[7]

Hood moved north in three diverging columns. His immediate objective was to cut off Thomas' holding force from Nashville and rout
it. Once this was done he would put into operation his long-range objective, which was to checkmate Sherman and support Lee by attacking

Grant in the rear. This was Thomas' old East Tennessee plan, but now aimed at supporting the Rebel Richmond army rather than attacking it. Thomas and Grant were both aware of the implications of Hood's moves. But Schofield, who prided himself on his knowledge of Hood's mental processes, was the one who made the blunder that nearly let Hood achieve his short-range plan. Hood refused to attack at Columbia and permitted Schofield to cross to the north bank unmolested, confident that Schofield, once he had placed the Duck River between himself and Hood, would feel secure and would remain in his position too long.

Hood's western column headed for Waynesborough only a dozen miles from the lower reaches of the Tennessee River while his eastern column moved on Lawrenceburg at the headwaters of Shoal Creek. Forrest sifted his cavalry patrols over every road and trail ahead of these columns, putting an impenetrable screen in front of Hood's advance. Thomas hoped to make a stand along the Duck River, which flowed through Columbia almost due west to the Tennessee. He sent a cavalry reinforcement of 1,000 men and Cooper's brigade of the Twenty-third Corps from Johnsonville to the Duck River downstream from Columbia but even this augmented force was unable to cope with Hood, who was threatening both flanks of Schofield's field army at the same time. Capron's command was typical of the weak spots that exist in a patched-up force. He had been sent from Atlanta to Kentucky in September to be remounted and rearmed but was ordered to a combat assignment before this was done. His final station on Schofield's western flank was isolated. His nearest supplies were fifty-five miles away. He was compelled to forage on a twenty-mile radius to feed his men and animals. Scouting and foraging over muddy, flooded roads sapped the energies of his command until no margin was left for fighting. Many of his horses were without shoes. Their backs were ruined by the constant carriage of their own forage. When they collided with Forrest's cavalry on the morning of November 24 they were neither armed to fight nor able to run. In the nick of time the situation was saved by Cox's infantry. This was the first of a series of hairbreadth escapes that filled the ensuing week.

The weather was unseasonable and worsened steadily. For a week before Hood started north the rain had been almost continuous. By November 21 it had changed to flurries of snow. The next day was so cold that the mounted officers of Schofield's command made part of their marches on foot to keep warm. The cold weakened after a day or two but the rain continued. At Columbia, Hood's central column came

onto the Nashville-Decatur turnpike, which had a macadamized surface and was the axis of Schofield's retreat. Parallel to it was the
Nashville-Decatur railway. Hood's flanking tactics, however, made it
necessary for the bulk of his infantry and cavalry units to use the un-
surfaced side roads where the going was harder.

Cox's opportune arrival at Columbia not only saved Capron but also
prevented Forrest from seizing the Duck River bridges. With Hood's
infantry piling up in front of him, however, his position on the south
side of the river became more and more perilous. Hood planned to hold
Schofield at Columbia with his artillery and a small force of infantry
while his cavalry swung east and then north to cut Schofield's retreat
line at Spring Hill. The plan and its execution, up to the very last,
were faultless. Wilson, who had come from Nashville to take command of Schofield's cavalry, had his horsemen in the proper place but
they could not stand against Forrest's determined onslaught and they
were pushed off to the northeast where Forrest held them in place with
one of his brigades while he led the rest back to a concentration with
the infantry.

James Harrison Wilson, then twenty-seven years old, had changed
his ideas about cavalry tactics since, as the head of the cavalry bureau,
he had helped to get Thomas' horsefighters ready for the Atlanta campaign. Subsequently he had held a field command as one of the able
young officers Sheridan was building up in the east. After Thomas lost
Crook in the winter of 1863-64, the vexatious question of a western
cavalry commander remained unsettled until October, when Grant
picked Wilson for the job. He was junior to many of the officers he was
called upon to command so he was brevetted a major general and assigned to duty at that rank. He was brash, cocky, self-confident and
able. When he laid down the specifications for his command to Grant
they were put in the form of a polite ultimatum. It was intended originally that Wilson would command the raid out of Atlanta into the deep
South but fortunately for the Union, Sherman wanted to do the raiding himself and sent Wilson to Thomas to help with the fighting. With
the exception of the cavalry in Kentucky and along the Mississippi
River, a few units in Tennessee assigned to Andrew Johnson, and
Kilpatrick's division, which accompanied Sherman, Thomas combined
the entire cavalry force of the Division of the Mississippi into what was
to be designated as the Cavalry Corps. The order for the organization
and Wilson's command of it was written by Sherman.

Northern cavalry was inferior to that of the South during the first years of the war but not for the reason that has generally been supposed. Nearly all the top commands in the Southern armies went to cavalry-men. They used cavalry as an offensive weapon. Scott thought that the rifle had outmoded the horseman. In the first call for Northern troops no mention was made of cavalry. The raising of cavalry regiments by the Northern states was discouraged. The mounted regiments that found their way to the front were dispersed and used defensively, or for headquarters guards or couriers.

Thomas now resolved to build something that had never been seen before on the North American continent—a mounted invasion force. It was to be self-sustaining, fast moving, far ranging and hard hitting. It would work in concentration, shatter a flank, cut off a retreat and erase Rebeldom's second strongest army from the war. This was a theory that was proved by Forrest, denied by Sherman, opposed by Halleck and belittled by Grant.

Thomas was the only field-trained cavalryman to hold a major army command in the Northern forces during the Civil War.[8] His appreciation of this arm of the service differed from that of army head-quarters. At the outbreak of the war he was reorganizing the Second Cavalry. A regiment of cavalry was enlisted in Kentucky by special permission but it remained an orphan until Thomas incorporated it into the First Brigade of the Army of the Cumberland. He took this regiment to Mill Springs where its vedettes played an important tactical role. He continually besought Buell and Rosecrans for more and better mounted troops and their cavalry requisitions rasped the stubborn views of army headquarters. Thomas favored the massing of his cavalry force for use as an aggressive tool and opposed frittering away its strength on defensive roles of guarding trains, supply dumps and infantry bivouacs. He departed from the conventional theory about the use of cavalry in the same way that Forrest did. Both believed that cavalry should be mounted for the sake of mobility but should do its fighting on foot. Thomas had seen too many mounted charges on the Texas plains unravel as the faster horses pulled away from the slower ones. He knew from experience that a mounted charge could make no impression on a properly led infantry; that it might break through the enemy line but could not re-form and face about as fast as the enemy could reorganize and take a better defensive position. He proved his theories with Wilder's mounted infantry. He wanted Wilson to do the same thing and Wilson was willing.

A cavalry force had often been organized in the North at a time and place safe from direct enemy pressure. None but Wilson and Thomas ever did the job in the confusion and hurry of a desperate midwinter campaign.

The cavalry situation on October 26 was not encouraging. Wilson was outnumbered more than four to one. He lacked farriers and their tools. In some cases horses were shod by the use of hatchet and pocketknife, regardless of the fact that a badly fitted shoe might be worse than no shoe at all. It was November 6 when Wilson reached Nashville and he remained there until the twenty-third. When he assumed his field command he still found himself outnumbered two to one and opposed by the man he considered to be the most successful of the Rebel cavalry leaders. By this time Wilson was thoroughly acquainted with the differences in organization, training and tactics between eastern and western cavalry. When he inspected Croxton's brigade near Columbia he discovered another novelty. Riding with the staff of the Eighth Michigan Veteran Cavalry was a well mounted, well uniformed woman who made no effort to hide her sex behind a man's clothing. Wilson ordered her to Nashville over the lady's remonstrances. She was the wife of the colonel of the regiment and based her right to remain with the troops on the fact that Thomas had given her permission to do so.

The three unit commanders of his force were Hatch, Croxton and Capron. Wilson may have met Croxton at Chattanooga. He certainly heard of him there, but it is doubtful if he had seen Hatch or Capron before. Croxton was well known to the Army of the Cumberland. He was the lieutenant colonel of the Fourth Kentucky at Mill Springs. Later he commanded one of Brannan's infantry brigades in the Fourteenth Corps. At Chickamauga Thomas received a report that a disorganized body of Rebels was trying to pull itself together under the cover of a piece of woods. He ordered Croxton and his brigade to bring them in. Croxton went after them and immediately his troops came reeling out of the woods under the pointblank fire of a Rebel division moving to the attack. After re-forming his discomfited men he rode to Thomas and reported, "General, I would have brought them in if I had known which ones you wanted." He was an acknowledged favorite of Thomas', tall, handsome, dark eyed and characterized by a fiery zeal, a bitter hatred of slavery, rare discretion, coolness and courage.

Edward Hatch was an Iowa lumberman who probably never saw a uniformed company until he volunteered. He was in his early thirties, had a splendid constitution and a striking figure. He never refused a suggestion for an aggressive movement regardless of the odds or shortages of food, forage or ammunition. He was an irrepressible gascon. "I wish I could live long enough to have Sheridan's cavalry for just one day," he announced to his staff, which rocked with laughter when one of its more impudent members rejoined, "Wouldn't you want to live just another day to brag about it?" He was one of the most successfully aggressive Northern cavalry leaders of the war.

Horace Capron was New England born and enlisted from Illinois. He was attached to the Army of the Ohio when it had the misfortune to be commanded by three different officers over a period of a few months and then, untested and untempered, was thrown into the Atlanta campaign to compete on an equal basis with the veterans of the Armies of the Cumberland and the Tennessee. Capron suffered from Sherman's unconcealed contempt and Schofield did nothing to rebuild his prestige. Like many such officers he gave a better account of himself under Thomas' influence.

Wilson's first job now was to cover the crossings of the Duck River, to forecast Hood's intentions and to screen Schofield's little army from a sudden, disastrous attack. His eastern experience had given him no practical education for dealing with such a situation or for countering Forrest's shrewd thrusts. Wilson got his patrols on the crossings and gave Schofield timely warning of Hood's plan to circle his eastern flank and cut off his retreat at Spring Hill. But his horsemen could not cope with the know-how of Forrest, who drove a wedge between Schofield's infantry and Wilson's squadrons. For thirty-six hours Schofield was at Hood's mercy, but part of his trouble was of his own making. Spring Hill was a five- or six-hour route march north of the Duck River, but Schofield, bemused by Hood's artillery demonstration south of that stream, delayed twelve hours in disengaging his main army and starting its retreat. He was saved by one of Hood's monumental errors.

It was after daylight of November 29 that Schofield started Wagner's division of the Fourth Corps for Spring Hill. Stanley went with it and all of Schofield's trains. The Twenty-third Corps and the remaining two-thirds of the Fourth Corps remained in their works to deny the crossing to one corps of Hood's infantry and his artillery.

Nearing Spring Hill, Wagner's advance discovered Forrest's cavalry approaching that road junction from the east. The infantry double-quicked into position and drove them off about half a mile to give the wagon train room to go into park near the north boundary of the little village. At 4:00 P.M. Wagner's thin line in a semicircle east of the village was attacked and after an hour's fighting its southern flank was forced back to the turnpike, but not before the last of the wagon train had passed. Hood had Schofield in the palm of his hand. One isolated division was at Spring Hill beset by the infantry corps of Cheatham and Stewart and most of Forrest's cavalry. The bulk, trapped between Spring Hill and Stephen Lee's infantry corps to the south of them, could either march or stand. The odds against them in either case were unbeatable. Schofield elected to march. His advance pulled out of their works at 3:00 P.M. His rear guard disengaged itself at dark. Schofield rode with the advance, established communication with Wagner after brushing some of Forrest's men off the pike, and moved to a point about three miles north of Spring Hill called Thompson's Station. There he found Forrest's camp fires still burning. On his way he passed within 800 yards of Hood's sleeping army and picked up some of Cheatham's pickets. Silently and quickly the bulk of Schofield's army filed northward through the darkness behind Wagner's watchful infantrymen and continued on to Franklin. The head of the column reached this pretty little town before daylight. Wagner's rear guard, herding ahead of them the stragglers from one of the war's most exhausting marches, protecting the flanks of the wagon train and, with one brigade on the pike, halting and facing to the rear whenever Forrest's cavalry pressed them too closely, got into position about 11:00 A.M. Wilson had broken out of Forrest's smothering screen and rejoined Schofield. The outnumbered Union force was in a better position than it had been but it was far from safe.

From Thomas' point of view the critical point in Hood's northward march was the Duck River. If he crossed it, Thomas reasoned, his objective would be Nashville or Murfreesborough and Chattanooga would be safe. While he awaited the news that would confirm Hood's choice, Thomas considered two plans. One was to send Steedman to Tuscumbia to cut Hood's bridge of boats across the Tennessee River. The other was to entice Hood across the Duck River on a route that would lead him west rather than east of Nashville.[9] Sometime after 10:00 P.M. of November 29, Thomas learned that Hood had elected to move north. There had been a twelve-hour delay in getting the news, partly due to the malfeasance of Stanton's cipher operators.[10] Thomas' orders went out immediately for a concentration on Nashville. The city was placed in a state of defense, its fortifications manned by the garrison reinforced by the volunteer employees of the quartermaster and commissary departments. Steedman, with 5,000 men, was ordered from Chattanooga to Cowan. All except one of the garrisons on the Nashville-Chattanooga railway south of Tullahoma were pulled back to Murfreesborough. The Louisville-Nashville railway was closed to passenger traffic. The Nashville-Johnsonville railway was abandoned and all traffic between Nashville and Chattanooga was halted. Meantime Thomas had sent to Schofield five more regiments of cavalry and 900 infantry with orders to fall back on Franklin. There is no doubt that Schofield understood what he was to do and there is no doubt that Thomas, still fighting for time to make his concentration, was encouraging Schofield to buy him more of it but not at the expense of losing his army.

At dawn on November 29 Hood led Cleburne's division of Cheatham's corps through the water at Davis' ford on the Duck River and started for Spring Hill. Behind him and to his left he could hear the roar of artillery against Schofield's bridgehead covering the turnpike and railway. The morale of his troops was high. He had forced Sherman to divide his invincible army and now he had tricked Schofield into a subdivision of one of the portions. From where Hood sat on his horse at 3:00 P.M. he could see Schofield's wagons and men passing northward on the pike on the run. He ordered Cheatham to seize the road and then apparently left the front. He had been in the saddle for nine or ten hours. His useless arm pained him almost constantly. The straps that held him in his saddle in lieu of his amputated leg chafed him where his clothing wrinkled under their pressure and cut into him when his horse's movements threw the weight of his body against their restraints. While the executive head of the Rebel army retired to ease his pains and recruit his energies, Schofield's army slipped by almost intact.

But now the Harpeth River blocked Schofield's northward retreat. As he turned over in his mind the problem of getting across it he began to get panicky. There was no bridge suitable for passing his wagons and artillery. The pontoon bridge he had asked of Thomas had not arrived. There were no large reinforcements. He was forced again to stand off Hood's army—this time with the bottleneck of a bridge at his back. His right flank was wide open. His left was vulnerable to an attack by Forrest. His telegraphic communication with Nashville was perilously interrupted. As he compared his harried retreat from Pulaski with Johnston's orderly, unhurried, controlled retreat from Dalton to Atlanta, his self-confidence may have been shaken. Thomas neither expressed nor implied any critcism of the way Schofield conducted his retreat, yet it is evident from the dispatches that he had hoped for more from Schofield's army than he got. Thomas had proved more than once that an army properly led could not be driven. Over the fifteen or twenty miles that separated his field army from Nashville on the morning of November 30 Thomas must have felt that Schofield's troops were close to the breaking point. Before midnight, however, they had proved that his fears were groundless.

At 5:00 A.M. on the thirtieth Thomas informed Schofield that Smith was up but could not reach Franklin that day, and that Schofield must cover his trains and get his infantry into position at Franklin. At 10:25 A.M. he advised that Franklin should be held if Hood could be prevented from turning his position. A few hours later he asked Schofield if he could hold Hood at the Harpeth River for three more days, but when Schofield said he could not Thomas gave him orders to fall back to Nashville.

While the tensions were building up along the Duck River, Thomas prepared and put under way a diversionary strike through East Tennessee to remove any possible danger to Knoxville. During the wait for news from the fighting at Franklin, Thomas received a telegram from Grant that Breckinridge was marching on a campaign that would fill Kentucky with dismay. It was the strike through the Cumberland Gap that Thomas had been expecting. The news was five days old, which put its beginning at the same time that Hood crossed the Duck River. The tight rein that Thomas habitually held over his emotions had paralyzed those necessary safety valves. His staff was conscious of no increased tension or apprehension. Certainly his reply to Grant showed none, yet Kentucky was a tinder box. Threatened by a Rebel invasion from two sides it might easily explode. The situation was worsened by the maladministration of Brevet Major General Stephen Gano Burbridge. By Presidential appointment he was the acting military administrative head of Kentucky but he was alienating large blocs of Union support. Thomas, unsuccessfully, had been trying to replace him. This was the enemy-made climax of Thomas' troubles in the Nashville campaign. At 6:00 P.M. of this early winter evening his difficulties from enemy action began to dissolve. The change was as dramatic and well defined as the one that took place at noon on Chickamauga's second day.

The point of Thomas' greatest danger at the moment, however, was the infantry semicircle holding the bridgehead at Franklin. The troops were intrenched and generally covered by an abatis. Each flank rested on the river. The 800 wagons of Schofield's train and his artillery were choking the streets of the village. Wood's division of the Fourth Corps had crossed to the north side of the river and taken position to guard against a flank movement to cut the Nashville turnpike. Later the bulk of the artillery was crossed at the fords and placed in position to defend the eastern flank of the bridgehead. Schofield and Stanley were on the north bank. The engineers were working feverishly to get some bridges up. Cox, who commanded the bridgehead, had never seen Schofield so disturbed as he was at daybreak in Franklin. He was pale and apprehensive as he issued Cox his orders. "The pontoons are not here, the county bridge is gone and the ford is barely passable. You must take command of the Twenty-third Corps and put it in position here to hold back Hood at all hazards 'till we can get our trains over and fight with the river in front of us." Schofield's apprehensions proved needless. The county bridge was repaired, the pontoons arrived, the railway bridge, which Schofield did not mention, was floored, and by the time Hood's infantry came up most of the wagon train was across the river and on its way to Nashville. The weak spot in Cox's bridgehead was his right flank, but Hood never learned that fact. By noon Cox had completed his plans for receiving the enemy. An outpost of two brigades of Wagner's division of the Fourth Corps was astride the Columbia pike half a mile in front of Cox's breastworks. The intention was that Wagner's men were to come inside of Cox's lines and act as a corps reserve after their outpost duty had been completed. In addition, Kimball's division of the Fourth Corps was holding the downstream flank of Cox's bridgehead.

Among Wagner's brigade commanders was Colonel Emerson Opdycke, a thirty-four-year-old Ohioan who came from a line of fighting men. He enlisted in July of 1861, was mustered in as a first lieutenant and was promoted through the various ranks to that of brevet major general. At Shiloh he carried the regimental colors as he led his command in a decisive charge. At Chickamauga he was prominent with Harker's immortal brigade in Dyer's field and in the afternoon held a sector of Snodgrass Ridge. The losses of his command in that battle were one-third of its total strength. He was one of the first to reach the top of Missionary Ridge. Rocky Face Ridge and Resaca had increased the respect in which the army held him. He had Wagner's advance on the march from Columbia to Spring Hill and deployed his men on the run to drive off Forrest's cavalry. His brigade stood to arms all that night and formed the rear guard on the march to Franklin, where they fended off Hood's pursuing elements, cut the knapsacks from the backs of hundreds of Schofield's dazed recruits and herded them to safety with their bayonets.

When Wagner's division took its outpost position, Opdycke objected so vigorously to its faultiness as to be almost insubordinate. He must have been somewhat of a law unto himself because Wagner let him go his own way. "Now, Opdycke," he said, "fight when and where you think best." So at about 2:30 P.M. Opdycke massed his brigade along the Columbia pike several hundred yards inside of Cox's defense line. He was taking upon his shoulders the responsibility of acting as the reserve of Schofield's field army. He rested his men and let them make coffee.

Cox's semicircle was a solid line of barricades except where the Columbia turnpike passed through it. This was kept open so that stragglers, and eventually Wagner's two outpost brigades, could get within the safety of the works. It was a weak spot in the defense line and was strengthened by artillery planted on each side of the road. Opdycke posted his force as a plug for this gap.

Hood's army came in sight in two columns, one marching on the road close to the Harpeth River and the other along the Columbia pike. The Columbia pike column came into view about two miles from the Federal barricades and thousands of Yankee eyes watched it blot out the white surface of the road as it moved diagonally down the north slope of Winstead's Hill. At the bottom of the hill trees and a fold in the land hid the Rebels from view. It was here that they began their deployment. To pass 25,000 men from columns into line of battle required several hours. By 3:00 P.M. Hood was ready but he had little time for battle since the sun would set in two hours. Again his aides helped him out of his uncomfortable harness. Alongside the pike at the foot of Winstead Hill he lay upon some blankets on the ground. His head and shoulders rested on a saddle. Here he received the reports from his combat commanders and issued his orders for a battle he could not see. Hood was making another major mistake by ordering a frontal attack against troops behind breastworks without artillery preparation and without an effective threat against their flank or rear. It was an order for suicide, induced probably by the incredible failure to spring his trap at Spring Hill. He was counting upon Forrest to crumple Cox's left flank by crossing the Harpeth River and getting behind his bridgehead. But Wilson had learned a lot in thirty-six hours. For one of the few times in his career Forrest was unable to have his way. Thomas' luck was changing from bad to good on the counterattacks of two Blue cavalry brigades in the wintry twilight along the Harpeth.

It was about 3:15 P.M. when Wilson's outposts began to feel the pressure of Forrest's squadrons as they sought to force a passage of the river some three miles upstream from Cox's position. Simultaneously Hood's infantry got within reach of Wagner's outpost. A section of

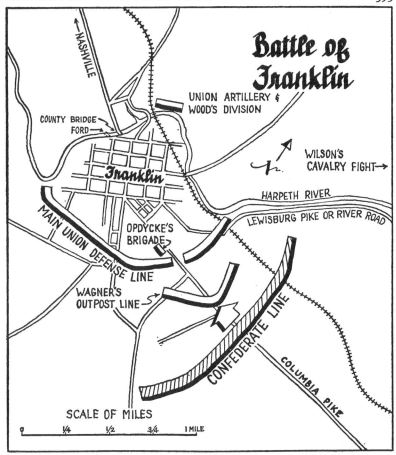

Map 9. Battle of Franklin, November 30, 1864. From a sketch made possibly four years after the battle (*O.R. Atlas, Plate 72, No. 1*).

one of Wagner's batteries pulled out of its position and came into the protection of the barricades at a slow trot. A line of rabbits, flushed out of the grass by Hood's battle line, scampered northward over the plain. The rapid musketry fire of Wagner's two brigades checked the center of Cheatham's advance, but his bands played the troops forward on both sides of Wagner's hopeless position.

Then Wagner's men broke for the safety of Cox's line. It was a rout of panic proportions—2,000 men trying to reach safety through a bottleneck built for one-way wheeled traffic. Most of the veterans made it. Most of the recruits were captured. A mass of fugitives crashed through the barricade several hundred yards to the right of the pike. Cox had already warned the troops at the opening in his barricades to hold their fire until Wagner's men could get in. It was a heaven-sent respite for

Hood's assault line, which smashed through behind the protection of the panicked Yanks, overran both batteries and tore off sections of the brigades of Strickland and Reilly that held the opposite sides of the breach. For the width of a brigade front, the Rebels had opened a hole in Cox's line and the Gray assault troops were pressing the advantage hard to the right and left of the breach.

Cox was not at the point of breakthrough. He had tried to get there but a runaway gun limber had frightened his horse beyond control. The Twenty-third Corps brigade commanders on the flanks of the breakthrough were rallying their broken lines. Stanley was on the field, having started for the point of danger at the beginning of the fire fight. Along the turnpike he found utter confusion. It was a more critical moment than Stanley had ever known in his battle experience. Part of the Twenty-third Corps had broken and was running to the rear in company with Wagner's fugitives. Two caissons, the drivers lashing their already frantic teams, ran interference for the fugitives. Wagner was mounted on his horse inside the line trying to rally his excited troops but the physical pressure of the surging mass of men crowded his mount and himself to the rear.

At this juncture, Opdycke, without orders, got his 1,600 men to their feet and led them at the charge into the breach. His regiments went forward in a wedge-shaped formation, somehow breasted the confusion of the retreat, brushed the fugitives out of the way, tumbled the surprised Rebels over the barricade whence they had come, recaptured the lost batteries, restored the line, took nine enemy flags and recaptured one Union flag and seized nearly 400 prisoners—all in about fifteen minutes. Up to and including Thomas, the army credited his brigade with having saved the day.

But Hood from his saddle pillow ordered the assault kept up. It was one of the bloodiest afternoons of the Confederacy. His losses were appalling. Probably in relation to time and numbers no attack on the soil within the boundaries of the United States ever paid such a price.

Stanley F. Horn compares this assault with Pickett's at Gettysburg and points out that Pickett lost 1,354 men while Hood lost more than 6,000; that Pickett went in after two hours of artillery preparation while Hood went in with none; that Pickett crossed an open space of a mile while Hood's men covered twice that distance; that Pickett was totally repulsed and retired from the field while the men of Brown and Cleburne penetrated deep into the Federal line and, after being thrown back, repeatedly renewed their attack until darkness and an enemy retreat brought relative peace to the torn field. In front of Casement's brigade on the western side of the turnpike was an osage orange abatis. As the Rebels attempted to force their way through it the Yankees with repeating rifles poured a continuous fire into their helpless ranks. It is possible that this brigade killed and wounded more men in a shorter time than had ever been accomplished before in any fight anywhere.

Thirteen of Hood's general officers were casualties, among them the all but irreplaceable Cleburne. In the thickest of the fighting, when Opdycke's brigade and the rallying troops of Strickland and Reilly were overlaying the field with their converging fire, Cleburne came charging down the left of his line on a slight diagonal toward the Federal works. His horse was running at full speed and both rider and animal were heedless of the footmen in their path. Within a few paces of Reilly's barricades horseman and mount went down together. Both bodies were pierced by multiple wounds which probably accumulated as they rode until a fatal spot was torn open in both almost at the same time.

At a different time on another part of the field some Federal officers looked over their barricade during a lull in the fighting. Through the thick smoke the Rebel line was dimly seen with a mounted officer trying to get the men forward. As they watched, man and horse went down. The horse struggled to his feet riderless, leaped toward the barricade and fell dead astride it. His rider, both legs useless, was trying to drag himself out of danger. His body could be seen to jump as other bullets struck it. After dark he was brought into the Federal lines still breathing. It was General John Adams, commanding a brigade in Loring's division. His death came shortly after.

After dark, according to previous plan, Schofield continued his withdrawal. Aside from a skirmish between Forrest and Wilson he met with no interference. Many of his wounded and dead were left behind. Some of his exhausted men fell asleep where they had fought and never heard their companions pull out. The living staggered like sick men along the pike overcome by physical exhaustion and prolonged emotional tension. Stanley, wounded himself, never saw troops more exhausted than those he led into Nashville. The artillery was pulled back with depleted teams. Before noon of December 1 Schofield's advance guard marched into the Nashville fortifications. Cox felt that Schofield could have held the line of the Harpeth River for the three days that Thomas wanted but the argument now had no validity.

A fact of tremendous psychological importance to Thomas was the ascendency the Blue horsemen gained over Forrest during the battle at

Franklin. Both cavalry leaders divided their forces. Cooper's infantry brigade was on the Duck River some thirty miles west of Columbia in accordance with Thomas' orders. He had been ordered to concentrate with the main army at Franklin. This was a threat to Hood's western flank and nearly half of Forrest's command was sent westward to counter it. Wilson, on the other hand, sent one regiment downstream to act as liaison. But to protect Schofield's line of retreat he had sent Hammond's cavalry division [11] to patrol between Triune and Brentwood. Wilson, therefore, with the commands of Croxton and Hatch faced Forrest with the commands of Buford and Jackson along the Harpeth upstream from Franklin and rode off the Rebel threat. This was an important contribution to Schofield's stand and undoubtedly raised the prestige of the mounted arm with the foot regiments.

Two errors bulked large in the determination of the battle. Wagner disobeyed his orders and nearly brought ruin to the Union side. He was relieved of his command by Thomas soon after he reached Nashville in spite of the fact that Cox and Schofield attempted to cover up the true facts. The other error was Hood's failure to reconnoiter Cox's line before ordering his assault. He would have learned, if he had, that his best chance lay in a turning movement against its western end.

Thomas' efforts to concentrate a striking force were now bearing fruit. Steedman reached Nashville with 5,000 troops six hours after Schofield. It was a scratch command made up of fragments from four different army corps and a brigade of colored troops. So heterogeneous was it that Steedman did not know how to make its routine returns. A. J. Smith's entire command was up. It had been started southward piecemeal to reinforce Schofield, and one of Smith's regiments contributed materially to fighting off the Rebel breakthrough. It sustained the greatest loss of any Union regiment in the battle. Scattered units, such as the Johnsonville command and Cooper's brigade from the Duck River, straggled in. The cavalry was sent north of the Cumberland River to reorganize and remount, which Thomas estimated would take five days. The railroad workmen, now that all lines except the one to Louisville were abandoned, went to work to strengthen the fortifications.

A significant part of Hood's invasion plan was done. In ten days he had crowded the Blue frontier back from the Tennessee to the Cumberland. A comparable advance in mileage had taken Sherman's army twelve times longer. There was still hope for trans-Mississippi reinforcements and R. E. Lee's right wing was reaching toward him from southwest Virginia.

Thomas knew the apprehension that such a situation could cause in Washington but he could also see some other factors. Hood was now too outnumbered to storm the Nashville fortifications. He could not cross the Cumberland without receiving reinforcements and Tennessee and Kentucky would not rise to his aid as long as the Army of the Cumberland remained in being. He could not afford to retreat but he could await Thomas' attack, repulse it and perhaps enter the city on the heels of the retreating Yanks. But this very situation robbed Hood of the initiative, one of the two things that Hood must retain if his raid was to be a success. He had one other string to his bow and that was to move into East Tennessee, do what damage he could to the North's military potential in that area and move through Virginia to a junction with Lee. It was to prevent or fatally delay such a move that Thomas had strengthened and maintained the Murfreesborough garrison.

In dispatches to his superiors on December 1, Thomas made a forthright appraisal of the situation. He had retired into the fortifications of Nashville until his cavalry could be equipped. Hood could neither cross the Cumberland nor blockade it. He would be seriously damaged if he attacked, and whipped as soon as Wilson was ready. Murfreesborough was safe and Chattanooga, Bridgeport, Stevenson and the Elk River bridge were strongly garrisoned. The situation around Knoxville was under control. It was a reassuring message from a field commander not given to overstatement and with an unbroken record of success. Thomas' appraisal was passed straight to Lincoln who considered the situation overnight and then had Stanton wire Grant at City Point that the President was solicitous over Thomas' disposition to lie in fortifications for an indefinite period, that he was reminded of the do-nothing policy of McClellan and Rosecrans while the Rebels raided the country, and that he wanted Grant to consider the matter.

Grant was worried, not so much about what would happen if Hood attacked as he was about what might happen if Hood did not attack. From his point of view the situation had passed from a military to a political one (as well as a personal one) and he urged Thomas to attack and try for an inconclusive victory.[12] Thomas balked. He had seen three years of inconclusive victories—Shiloh, Perryville, Stones River, Chattanooga, Atlanta. Each had retrieved a military blunder or eased political tension or both, but by sparing the Rebel army, each of these victories made certain that another battle must be fought. Thomas planned the destruction of Hood's army. This would give Grant more than he asked for. To accomplish it Thomas must be prepared to pursue. To pursue he needed a superior force of cavalry. Again he patiently outlined his plans, guessed that he would need two or three days and reminded Grant that the weakness of his situation was not of his making.

Thomas would accept no change in his plan but he would accept relief if his superiors ordered it. He was stubborn but he was not procrastinating. Procrastination is the escape of an unsure mind. Thomas was anything but unsure of himself. Implicit in his attitude was a hint of contempt for Grant's military leadership. He failed to see that Grant's insecurity made him take the cautious, bloody road to victory.

On December 5 Thomas set the seventh as the conditional date for his attack. That same day Halleck informed Grant that it was safe to assume Wilson would never be mounted. Grant reacted promptly with a peremptory order to Thomas to attack at once. Thomas answered that he would make the necessary dispositions for carrying out Grant's order and recorded his belief that it would be hazardous with the cavalry available to him.

Stanton exploded when he heard this reply and he sent a dispatch to Grant. "Thomas seems unwilling to attack," it read in part, "because it is hazardous, as if all war was anything but hazardous. If he waits for Wilson to get ready Gabriel will be blowing his last horn." Grant rejoined that if Thomas did not attack promptly he would recommend superseding him by Schofield. Grant waited a full day and then wired Halleck, "If Thomas has not struck yet he ought to be ordered to hand over his command to Schofield. There is no better man to repel an attack than Thomas, but I fear he is too cautious to ever take the initiative." Halleck took three and a half hours to sound out his superiors and advised Grant that no one in Washington wanted Thomas removed and that if he (Grant) did then he should issue an order, as the responsibility was his. But Grant was not willing to assume this responsibility so he turned to the milder course of ordering Halleck to remind Thomas of the importance of immediate action.

It was Halleck's dispatch of December 9 that gave Thomas his first explicit knowledge of what was going on in Grant's mind. His reply regretted Grant's dissatisfaction but made no apologies for the course he was pursuing. He would receive his relief order without a fuss and he announced that his army was immobilized by an ice storm.

Thomas' military fate on December 9 was hair hung and breeze shaken. At 11:00 A.M. Grant gave Halleck written orders to relieve

Major General James Harrison Wilson in 1865 took the field command of the largest cavalry force assembled up to that time in North America. *National Archives, Record Group III.*

Brevet Major General Robert Anderson picked Thomas, Sherman and Buell to help him hold Kentucky for the Union. Each turned out to be material for army command. *National Archives, Record Group III.*

General Braxton Bragg, C.S.A. His unsuccessful tactics at Chickamauga and Chattanooga advanced Thomas' military fortunes as much as his friendly aid before the war. *Library of Congress.*

Major General Don Carlos Buell learned in the only battle under his command that discipline was more essential to victory than aggressiveness. *National Archives, Record Group III.*

Lieutenant General Nathan Bedford Forrest, C.S.A., has been called the greatest English-speaking leader of mounted troops. It was the South's misfortune that Jefferson Davis refused to develop his full military potential. *Library of Congress.*

General John Bell Hood, C.S.A., a former student of Thomas' at West Point, was a superb assault commander of infantry but he scorned his guns and seldom used his horsemen to the best advantage. *National Archives, Record Group III.*

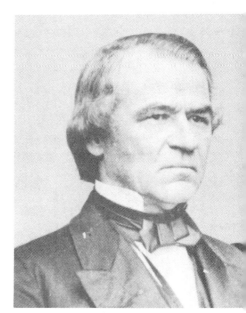

Andrew Johnson. In 1861, as Military Governor of Tennessee, he tried to have Thomas relieved of his command. In 1868, as President of the United States, he tried to make him a four-star general. *National Archives, Record Group III.*

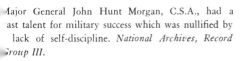

Major General John Hunt Morgan, C.S.A., had a vast talent for military success which was nullified by lack of self-discipline. *National Archives, Record Group III.*

Major General William Starke Rosecrans was probably the only American military commander to attempt to insure a victory by mass prayer. *National Archives, Record Group III.*

Brevet Major Samuel Ringgold takes a fatal wound at Palo Alto, May 11, 1846. He taught a new artillery theory to Thomas and Bragg. Thomas remembered it but Bragg forgot it. *Library of Congress.*

Thomas by Schofield. But Halleck, too, seemed disinclined to obey Grant's order and under this pressure Grant revoked it.

By the eleventh Grant's patience had worn thin again. It was evident that he was hagridden at the thought of Hood breaking through to the Ohio River. He pointed out that Hood could not stand even a drawn battle and ordered Thomas to attack without delaying longer for weather or reinforcements.[13] Thomas notified Washington that he would not attack until the ice melted because of the useless sacrifice of life that would result.

On December 12 and 13 no dispatches for Thomas went out from City Point or from Washington. Behind this silence, however, contingent orders were issued to Logan to relieve Thomas. Logan was cautioned to say nothing about his orders until he got to Nashville. He was not to deliver them then if Thomas had moved but was to communicate instead with Grant. But after Logan had left City Point, Grant became restless and concluded to go to Nashville himself.

On the afternoon of December 15 Grant arrived in Washington on his way west. The wires to Nashville were down. No messages had gone through for twenty-four hours. That evening a conference was held in the War Department between Lincoln, Stanton, Grant and Halleck. T. T. Eckert, chief of the War Department telegraph staff, was present to report on the communication situation. Grant told Lincoln that he was going to Nashville to take personal command of that army but that in the meantime he intended to relieve Thomas by Schofield.[14] Lincoln and Stanton were opposed to the idea but Grant forced their consent. Halleck's position is not known although the impression existed among the cipher operators that his attitude strengthened Grant's unfriendly feeling toward Thomas. With the permission of the President and the Secretary of War, Grant wrote his third order in six days relieving Thomas from his command. It was handed to Eckert for transmission and Grant went to his hotel to prepare for his western trip.

Eckert opened the telegraph line to Pittsburgh, which was the repeating office for Louisville, and learned that he could get through to Nashville. On his own responsibility, however, he decided to hold up the transmission of Grant's dispatch until he could receive the nightly report from his Nashville operator. At 11:00 P.M. cipher dispatches from Nashville began coming in. The first was Thomas' dispatch, now twenty-four hours old, that he would attack in the morning. It was followed by Van Duzer's account of Thomas' success and his intentions of completing the victory the next day. With Grant's order in one hand and Van Duzer's dispatch in the other Eckert ran down to the front door, jumped into the ambulance—the 1864 counterpart of an official car—and drove to Stanton's residence where he aroused him with the battle story. Stanton soon appeared fully dressed and the ambulance turned toward the White House. On the way Eckert told Stanton that he had held up Grant's relief order and his reasons for doing so. Stanton gave Eckert's action his official approval.

Lincoln was aroused and appeared on the second floor landing, dressed in his nightgown and with a candle in his hand. After telling him the news of the first day's battle at Nashville, Stanton handed him Grant's unsent order and told him that its transmission had been purposely delayed. Lincoln, too, approved the action.

From December 2 to December 9 it was the lack of an adequate cavalry command that had deterred Thomas from issuing his attack order. "Had I attacked Hood [during this period]," he wrote to D. H. Mahan, "I should have been unable to have availed myself of any advantage I might have gained, as my troops were not equipped for an advance movement [pursuit]." From December 9 through 14 it was the weather.

On December 7 Thomas had begun to communicate his attack plans to his corps commanders. He did not tell them the time he had selected for zero hour, but they understood it was to be daylight of the tenth. At 3:00 P.M. the following day this time was confirmed, but twenty-four hours later the attack was cancelled because of the sleet storm. Up to this time Thomas' briefing of his subordinates was apparently conducted on an individual basis but after this time there were three formal group briefings. The first was held December 11 at Thomas' headquarters in the St. Cloud hotel. It was evidently at this meeting that Thomas told his subordinates of the pressure from Grant and that he had decided to postpone the attack until the sleet storm abated. This may have been an effort to stop the rumors which were flying through the army.

The men already had heard that Thomas was to be superseded. They demonstrated openly against the high command and there were threats of revolt, both of which Thomas reproved. "The government at Washington has a heavy task on hand," he said. "It has done the best it could under the circumstances. If any officer comes to supersede me, I shall cheerfully report for duty and my officers must do likewise."

"This is Old Pap's fight," the ranks were heard to say, "and we are going to win it for him." That night Thomas sent out a call for another meeting at 3:00 P.M. the next day, and at this meeting the officers were asked for their opinions on the practicability of attacking over the ice. All agreed it would be impracticable. Between the adjournment of the first meeting and the call for the second meeting Thomas had received Grant's order to attack in spite of the weather.

There is some disagreement over Schofield's role in the tense days preceding Thomas' climactic battle. For various reasons Steedman, and perhaps Thomas, became suspicious that Schofield was intriguing with Grant or the War Department for Thomas' command. Steedman records that prior to December 12 [15] Thomas knew someone was using the wires to disparage him with Grant and asked Steedman to find out who it was. Late that night Steedman took Thomas a telegram from Schofield to Grant stating that many officers in Nashville believed that Thomas was too slow. Thomas recognized Schofield's handwriting.[16]

Thomas makes no written mention of Schofield's actions, but in Schofield's detailed account of his Pulaski-Franklin campaign there is evidence of a coolness between the two men. When Schofield reached Nashville after the Battle of Franklin, Thomas greeted him in his usual cordial but undemonstrative way, congratulated him and said that he had done well. But, concluded Schofield, ". . . I did not feel very grateful to him." The contrast with Thomas' greeting of A. J. Smith, who came in about the same time, was apparent.

That story was told by an eye-witness. Thirteen transports and eight armed gunboats, swarming with the veteran troops of Smith's command, were known to be on the Cumberland River. Thomas asked for news of the time of their arrival and, at that moment, Smith entered the door. The undemonstrative Thomas literally took him in his arms and hugged him.

At 6:00 A.M. of December 15 the assault regiments were to move. Smith's command, with the major attack role, was to form on the Hardin pike and strike Hood's left. Two of Wilson's cavalry divisions were to support Smith's right and the third was to clear the Charlotte pike and the left bank of the Cumberland River. The Fourth Corps was to support Smith's left and operate against Hood's salient at Montgomery Hill. This was the center of Thomas' line and it bestrode the Hillsborough pike. This same highway, except for three outlying redoubts, marked the western flank of Hood's battle line. Schofield was in reserve. The Nashville garrison and Donaldson's quartermaster troops manned the interior defense lines behind the assault columns. Steedman's holding attack was aimed at Hood's eastern flank along the Nolensville pike and the Nashville-Murfreesborough railway.

Thomas' infantry divisions were far from organized. Five ranking officers had had less than two weeks to get acquainted with their new commands. Stanley, wounded at Franklin, had been succeeded by Wood in the command of the Fourth Corps. His division commanders were Kimball, Elliott and Samuel Beatty. The latter two were new appointments. Cox and Couch were the division commanders of the Twenty-third Corps. Couch, who had recently been transferred from the Army of the Potomac, had received his appointment nine days prior. Smith's command was not regularly organized. It was designated as Detachment of the Army of the Tennessee. His division commanders were McArthur, Garrard—former cavalry commander from the Atlanta campaign—and Moore. Garrard had had his command eight days and fought the battle without an opportunity to organize his own staff. One of Smith's regiments fought practically without officers since no replacements had been assigned for those mustered out.

Steedman's Provisional Detachment was a hybrid of six brigades from four different corps made up of fragments from 200 ill-provided regiments. A large proportion were unfit for duty. Twenty-five per cent of them were scarcely convalescent. Fifty per cent were recruits. Their officers lacked personal baggage, servants, changes of clothing and money. There were no ambulances or wagons. Some of these troops were not armed until the evening of the fourteenth. Some of the recruits were untrained. Many were unable to speak or understand English. The battalion made up of men from the Fourteenth Corps acted in a cowardly and disgraceful manner during the attack on Rains' Hill, an unheard-of thing to happen in Thomas' crack corps. One of the colored regiments was so badly commanded it had to be sent to the rear. Wilson's troops consisted of one brigade of the First Division, commanded by Croxton, the Fifth Division, commanded by Hatch, the Sixth, commanded by Johnson (one-third of this division was unmounted), and the Seventh, commanded by Knipe.[17] Hammond's brigade of this last division was made up of fragments of unacquainted regiments.

The orders of the corps commanders for the fifteenth indicate that Thomas was planning to exploit a victory. Five wagon loads of ammunition, ten ambulances and the wagons loaded with intrenching tools were all that were allowed to accompany each division of the Fourth Corps. All other wheels remained within the lines. Camps were

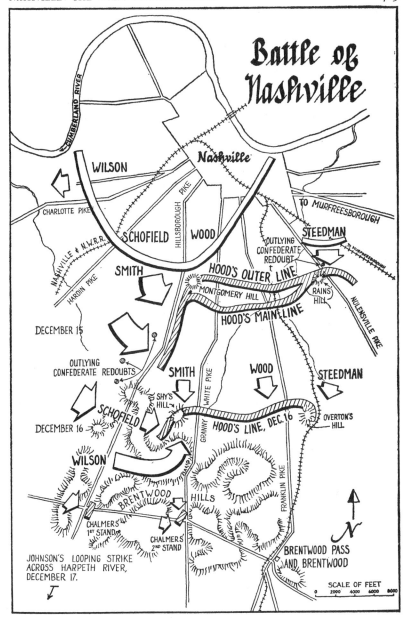

Map 10. Battle of Nashville, December 15, 1864. Drawn from *O.R. Atlas, Plate 73, No. 1,* based on field surveys made immediately after the battle.

broken up, tents were struck and the loaded wagons were parked and ready to move.

Each infantryman carried from fifty to sixty rounds of ammunition, three days' rations, blankets and an overcoat. His gear aggregated a heavy, awkward load and it was never intended that the men should go into action with it. Veteran troops just before deployment would pile their personal gear under the watchful eye of a guard detail and do their fighting unencumbered. But in the Fourth and Twenty-third corps some of the units, probably recruits incorporated into veteran brigades, were ordered to fight in heavy marching order. This indicated a lack of elementary combat training.

The Union forces outnumbered Hood 57,000 to 38,000. Hood had made his third major mistake of the campaign by detaching Forrest to Murfreesborough, so that he fought the two-day battle without him. Considering the tremendous advantage that defense had over offense these were not big odds and Hood had no doubt of his ability to hold his position against attack. With perhaps one exception no frontal assault by either side had succeeded in the Western fighting in more than a year.

Hood was not only without cavalry but he was overlapped by Thomas on both flanks. His line extended from the Nashville-Murfreesborough railway on the east to the Hillsborough pike on the west. It was trisected by the Franklin pike and the Granny White pike. Hood, Thomas believed, was unaware of the impending attack and, more especially, he did not seem to expect any movement against his left.[18] To divert his attention still further Steedman launched his attack at 8:00 A.M. on the fifteenth with two brigades of colored troops, two brigades of miscellaneous white regiments and two batteries. There was a thoroughness about Steedman's preparations that was characteristic of a Thomas-trained officer and Thomas was reputed to have said in later years that Steedman was the best division commander he ever had. He had culled his command and sent his unreliable units back to the interior defense lines. He moved his troops over ground that had been thoroughly scouted and against works that had been observed and evaluated. He began his preparations at 4:00 A.M. His first attack carried a section of the enemy works but his men could not hold their gain. At 11:00 A.M. he struck again and took and held some buildings on Rains' Hill. From this point he maintained a continuous pressure on Hood's right until sundown.

Wood's Fourth Corps linked Steedman's right with Smith's left. In front of him was the advance line of Hood's outer works, which faced north—its left flank anchored on Montgomery Hill. Wood's initial movement was ordered for 6:00 A.M. but it was between 7:00 and 8:00 before the fog lifted enough to permit him to make it. His men were filing into position while Steedman's attack was in progress and gave a cooperative weight to his assault.

While Steedman was preparing for his second attack, Smith began his at 10:00 A.M. It was a gigantic left wheel with Garrard's division on the pivot. The orders were to guide right and close to the left. Johnson's cavalry division was operating against a Rebel battery on the Cumberland River some eight miles below Nashville. In getting into position he came upon Ector's brigade of infantry and Chalmers' cavalry division covering the roads leading southward between Hillsborough pike and the river. He brushed them aside and actually split off Ector from the rest of Hood's army. The debris of this force was streaming from west to east across the front of Smith's line as it moved into position for its advance. Behind a heavy sifting of skirmishers Smith's battle line crossed the Hardin pike facing southeast. Closing in on Smith's right and endeavoring to prolong his line was Hatch's dismounted cavalry division with Knipe's division in reserve.

The western end of Hood's outer line, which faced north, terminated in a redoubt on Montgomery Hill on the east side of Hillsborough pike. Here it turned south 90 degrees and took cover behind a stone wall along the east side of Hillsborough pike. This part of Hood's line faced west and was strengthened by three outlying redoubts. This whole salient from Montgomery Hill to the southernmost of the outlying redoubts was perhaps one of the weakest points in Hood's defense and Thomas intended to exploit it with a frontal attack by Wood while the cavalry got past the Rebel flank and into their rear. Smith's battle line, in closing left, pulled closer to the pivot than Thomas intended and the result was that the infantry and the dismounted cavalry struck the westernmost of Hood's redoubts together and entered it at 1:00 P.M. Almost without a stop the same troops moved on half a mile to the second redoubt, which was stronger than the first. They assailed and captured it, turning Hood's left flank at 2:00 P.M.

While Smith and the dismounted troopers were disposing of these redoubts, Wood assaulted and overran the third redoubt, breaking Hood's outer line all the way north to Montgomery Hill, laying bare Hood's last defensive position, the key to which was the salient where his line bent southward to follow the stone wall along the Hillsborough pike. The right of Wood's line and the left of Smith's

overlapped and Smith's division commander had to pull his troops out
to let Wood's assault teams go in.

Thomas was accumulating irresistible pressure against Hood's left
flank. He was breaking Hood's fortified position by a tactical threat
three miles in its rear. This was the crucial point and time of the first
day's battle. Thomas watched its progress from a position in the rear
of Wood's right. It was also the position of Schofield's reserve and
Schofield was with him. He noticed that when a shell exploded near
enough to cause Thomas' horse to start, his only visible response was
a slight movement of his bridle hand to reassure his mount. The atmosphere was misty and Thomas kept borrowing Schofield's glasses,
which gave him better vision than any others he had found. He said
nothing. He would hand the glasses to Schofield after searching the
right of his line. That simple action seemed to indicate irritation and
impatience. Shortly, without a word, he would reach out his hand
again for the glasses. Finally, at 3:00 P.M., he made up his mind and,
with the energy that battle aroused in him, gave his order to Schofield:
"Smith has not reached far enough to the right. Put in your troops."
The immediate object of Schofield's movement was to put Wilson's
cavalry on the Hillsborough pike some six or seven miles from the city.
One and a half hours were allowed for Schofield to get into position.

It was about 4:30 P.M. when Thomas sent the order for the Fourth
Corps to storm the main salient. The aide who carried it could not
locate Wood so he gave it to the division commander. To this officer
it looked like suicide and he demurred against carrying it out. He did
not know that the salient hill was already untenable, that Hood's
western flank, compromised by the pressure of Smith, Wilson and
finally Schofield, was ready to disintegrate. The attack succeeded with
only light casualties. Hood's line west of the Franklin pike could not
hold and Wood moved east rolling it up as he advanced. His orders
were to seize the Franklin pike, but three-quarters of a mile from that
point he ran into Hood's men behind barricades and they held that
vital facility for their own use. It was 6:00 P.M. The sun had been
down an hour. Thomas missed his maximum objective by three-
quarters of a mile but Hood was forced back that night about two
miles, holding grimly to his retreat routes—the Franklin and Granny
White pikes.

For the first time during the Western war the Northern army used
cavalry as a tactical offensive arm in a major battle. Wilson fought three
divisions. The one under Johnson cooperated with the navy on the first
day of the battle in a semi-independent action. They were clearing the

river roads of all enemy troops. Croxton's brigade was the link between Johnson and Hatch, whose men fought as infantry. Croxton supported Johnson until sundown, when he moved eastward to join the main army on the Hillsborough pike. Knipe's was held all day as a mounted reserve and Hammond's brigade of that division spent the night along the Granny White pike.

Somewhere near 10:30 A.M., Hatch had met an enemy cavalry unit on the Hardin pike where it crossed Richland Creek, drove it off and picked up Chalmers' headquarters train. This was one part of the cavalry's triple assignment. The second part was to cover the right of Smith's infantry and the third was to envelop Hood's left and attack his rear. Hatch performed a major part in all three roles. After disposing of Chalmers, Hatch had to get his troops onto the prolongation of Smith's infantry line. "Touch left and guide right" was evidently an infantry order and Smith's right guide was paying no attention to the dismounted troopers off to his right. This was Datus Ensign Coon's brigade. He was an Iowa volunteer cavalryman. For three miles his men had to run to keep up with the infantry. Nevertheless they maintained their position and crashed into the Rebel redoubts with the foot troops. At the second redoubt, however, some of Coon's men were so exhausted that they had to crawl up the steep slope to the Rebel works on their hands and knees.

While the battle was in progress Brigadier General James L. Donaldson's quartermaster employees and the culls from Steedman's provisional division manned the interior lines of the Nashville defenses from the city water works upstream on the Cumberland River to Hyde's ferry on the river below the city.[19] Their primary role was to block any attempt by the Rebels to enter the city, but as a potential offensive threat they helped Steedman pin the corps of Stephen Lee and Cheatham in their fortifications.

The Union artillery on this first day of the battle was not particularly well handled. Wood put his batteries to good use in preparing for the two assaults made by the Fourth Corps. Kenner Garrard's division of Smith's Detachment of the Army of the Tennessee had three batteries to help it breach the strongest part of Hood's main defense line. But one of these did not fire during the day. The main trouble grew out of the fact that the batteries, except for those in the Fourth Corps, were divided between the various brigades. This faulty artillery organization was not to Thomas' liking. Ever since he had received command of the Army of the Cumberland his artillery had been under the control of one officer. It is indicative of the haste with which his fragmented organization was put into the field that the artillery arm did not receive his customary attention.

Nevertheless the tactical plan and execution of Thomas' strike on December 15 was almost perfect. Steedman, with approximately 3,700 men, pinned one-third of Hood's force in their works while Thomas' massive striking force outflanked, broke and then rolled up Hood's opposite flank. This was the holding or fixing attack—Napoleon's big contribution to infantry tactics. Thomas had never seen it used but he had learned at Buena Vista, Stones River and Chickamauga the boundless opportunity the failure to use it gave to the defending commander. The cavalry for which he had waited so stubbornly played a major role with its six- to eight-mile sweep to seal the wagon road through the Brentwood Hills. It lacked about a mile and a half of reaching its goal.

That night Thomas sent his only recorded message of victory to his wife who was waiting in the New York Hotel. He addressed her as Mrs. F. L. Thomas and said, "We have whipped the enemy, taken many prisoners and considerable artillery." Mrs. Thomas had visited him in Nashville in October but had returned East when Hood began to threaten the city.

Each of Thomas' units on the night of December 15 occupied a favorable position except Schofield's Twenty-third Corps. Instead of rectifying it, Schofield requested reinforcements and received a division from Smith's command. The Union army bivouacked in line of battle prepared to renew the conflict. The orders were to advance at daylight and attack, to pursue if the enemy had retreated. The corps commanders received their orders individually and generally verbally. Their first job was to develop Hood's position on their own front. Once this was done the tactical solution could be executed. It was a repetition of the Atlanta tactics. When the enemy stood, press him; when he retreated, follow him and bring him to bay. Any battle plan for the sixteenth had to be general until Hood's new line could be located.

The army began to move at 6:00 A.M. In front of Steedman and Wood there was no enemy except a light rear guard. Part of Smith's command found the same thing but his right was up against a solid Rebel line and Schofield's reinforced command was in the same situation. Hood's western flank stood on practically the same ground it had occupied the evening of the fifteenth but the rest of his line under cover of darkness had disengaged themselves from the Yankee skirmish line and pulled back to their new positions. He had shortened and strengthened his line—the accepted phraseology for a retreat. He had dropped back close to the Brentwood Hills and prepared positions that would enable him to hold the Granny White and Franklin pikes as escape routes. His trains were sent to the pass still farther in his rear where the Franklin pike ran through a defile in the Brentwood Hills. Both of his flanks were strongly positioned. The eastern one took advantage of the declivities of Overton's Hill just to the east of the Franklin pike. His western flank was secured on what came to be known after the battle as Shy's Hill. Both flanks were refused. About a mile and a half south of Shy's Hill was some high ground that commanded this Rebel strong point and that was not securely defended. For the second day's battle Hood put Cheatham's corps on his western flank, Stephen Lee's on the eastern flank and Stewart in the center.

It was 8:00 A.M. before Wood discovered that Hood had retreated. His corps, which had been facing east, was turned south and moved in that direction following the Franklin pike and driving Stephen Lee's skirmishers ahead of him.

Steedman moved with Wood but to the east of him. As at Chickamauga, he moved without definite orders and, probably with his tongue in his cheek, hoped that Thomas would not be displeased. The Eighteenth United States Colored Regiment moved over ground dotted with their own dead of the preceding day and saw that their bodies had been stripped and left exposed on the field. Steedman's movement uncovered the Nashville fortifications and made them vulnerable to a move by Forrest from the direction of Murfreesborough so Cruft moved out of the inner line of the city's defenses and occupied Riddle's Hill. As Steedman moved southward he closed to his right to make a contact with Wood and swung slightly so that his line was facing almost southwest. He faced ultimately the refused sector of Hood's eastern flank but he did not overlap it.

Smith took position on Wood's western flank and his line extended west of the Shy's Hill salient. Like Wood he faced south.

Schofield, holding the position he had taken the night before, was on Smith's right facing east. His line paralleled the Granny White pike and it was Thomas' intention that Schofield should make the main Federal attack. Hood's center between Overton's and Shy's hills was a weak spot, but a breakthrough would drive the Rebels southward leaving them the free use of both turnpikes. Since Thomas' objective was the destruction of Hood's army he elected to attack from west to east, rolling up Hood's line, cutting both turnpikes and endeavoring to trap Hood by getting Wilson's cavalry across his retreat lines to hold him until the blue infantry could come up. This meant that Schofield had to assault Shy's Hill. To this end he was reinforced by one of Smith's three divisions and the Union cavalry was to help him by getting on the high ground south of Shy's Hill and taking the Rebel defenders in the flank and rear while Schofield struck them in front.

This was a repetition of yesterday's breakthrough. In each case the Rebel defense was so softened by threats against its flank and rear that the Union frontal attacks were overwhelmingly successful with remarkably low casualties. This was the ultimate application of military force but with a deceiving lack of color and drama to the non-military mind.

Hammond's brigade of Knipe's division, which had been in reserve during the fighting of the fifteenth, had its pickets all night along the western side of Granny White pike. Early in the morning they began to skirmish with the enemy and Hammond pushed in more of his brigade as the fighting grew hotter. The remainder of Knipe's division was strung out along the pike south of Hammond. At 9:30 A.M. Hatch's cavalry division, dismounted, was ordered into the line to link up Hammond with the south flank of Schofield's Twenty-third Corps. The cavalry line pressed the enemy back steadily and Hatch was able to get his guns up on the high ground in the rear of Bate's men, who were holding the Shy's Hill salient. By noon the skirmishers of Hatch and Hammond formed a continuous line stretching from Schofield's right across Granny White. This skirmish line was facing partly north parallel to Hood's battle line. Hood's left wing was trapped and Wilson rode to tell Thomas.

It was noon, too, before the Union skirmishers had felt out and located the entire stretch of Hood's lines. At no point were the main lines of the opposing armies more than 600 yards apart. The skirmishers of both sides occupied or covered at point-blank range the no-man's land between the opposing lines. At the point northwest of Shy's Hill, where the western flank of Smith's detachment joined the northern flank of Schofield's Twenty-third Corps, the distance to Bate's works was only a quarter of a mile. Smith waited for Schofield to take the initiative. Meantime his batteries were put into position and, at a range of 800 yards, pounded Bate's guns into silence after two hours. But Schofield's lines failed to move.

Thomas was on the line early. He turned his horse toward the sound of the heaviest firing. This was the skirmish fight in front of the Fourth Corps which lasted from 6:00 A.M. until noon. At that time Thomas joined Wood on the Franklin pike near his most advanced position. Thomas ordered that the enemy be vigorously pressed, that Wood be continually on the alert for any opening for a more decisive effort, that the assault on Hood's left was still the battle objective, and that Wood should coordinate his work with Steedman's. As Wood rode east to carry out this last injunction Thomas turned his horse and rode west. The Union artillery was pounding the Rebel position for its entire length. Thomas kept his eye on these batteries as he rode along. His ammunition supply was inexhaustible while Hood's was limited and Thomas wanted to press this advantage. He saw to it that the ranges were short and accurately taken, that the elevations were correctly given and that the firing tempo was measured and steady.

Sometime before 3:00 P.M. Thomas was with Smith. Word came from McArthur that he thought he could carry Shy's Hill. But Thomas, still wanting Schofield to make the key attack, refused McArthur's request. Schofield was conscious of the role he was to play and tried to get Cox's division to advance but his order was not executed.

Wood's reconnaissance reported at 3:00 P.M. that a successful assault could be made on Overton's Hill. Post's brigade of the Fourth Corps spearheaded the attack, which was made from the north. It was a desperate one, and Post was wounded just as the brigade was about to thrust home its charge. There was a wavering along the assaulting line and then the fatal halt as the men sought cover from the fire that lashed at them. Then the attackers drifted back in defeat. Later in the day the Fifty-ninth Illinois found its dead within twenty feet of the abatis. Some of the Forty-first Ohio got through it. Other men of the storming regiments were too close to the Rebel works to risk retreat.

On the eastern side of Overton's Hill Steedman ordered a demonstration in support of Post's attack. His shock brigade was made up of Thompson's colored troops who had never seen action before. Their attack was made from the east over ground that had not been reconnoitered and in the teeth of a fire such as veterans dread. As the brigade advanced the men became excited and what was ordered as a demonstration turned into an assault. But in their advance the continuity of their line was split by a fallen tree and the troops came up to the Rebel works ragged and broken when they needed a compact mass. To make matters worse, Post had been thrown back and additional fire was turned on the colored fighters, who withdrew without panic. The preparations for Post's attack and Steedman's demonstration drew Cleburne's old division from Schofield's front to bolster the threatened point.

It was probably between 3:30 and 4:00 P.M. when Thomas arrived at Schofield's headquarters. Shy's Hill, and the high ridge south of it dominating the Rebel position, were in full view. Wilson was with

Schofield when Thomas arrived or came up shortly thereafter and was pressing for an infantry advance. The three generals could see Wilson's troopers on the skyline and the puffs of smoke from Hatch's artillery. Thomas was convinced and ordered Schofield to put in his troops. Hood's left was hopelessly beset. Smith faced it from the north, Schofield from the west, and Wilson from the south, and Hood had taken a division away from it to bolster his lines on Overton's Hill. Granny White, one of Hood's two escape routes, was blocked.

McArthur, held in leash by Thomas' refusal to grant his three-o'clock request for permission to advance, fearing that the opportunity might slip by, and rationalizing his resolve on the theory that he had no orders to the contrary, prepared one of his brigades to storm Shy's Hill. The Rebel parapets there had already been leveled by Smith's artillery and Hatch's horse guns. At 4:15 this attack was under way. It carried the key point of the Rebel line and started the dissolution of Hood's army. From here on, Thomas' men saw their opportunity and wrecked the Confederacy. Wood, riding westward after re-forming his shattered troops from their repulse on Overton's Hill, heard the electric shout from thousands of troops—Thomas called it the voice of the American people—as McArthur's men went over the top of Shy's Hill. He immediately ordered his own corps forward for the second attack on Overton's Hill. Coon's brigade of dismounted cavalry struck Shy's Hill from the south as McArthur topped it from the north. Schofield's Twenty-third Corps finally went forward and Thomas' whole line was in motion. The pressure on Hood was intolerable.

The sun set about 5:00 P.M. The rain which had begun in the afternoon was now a downpour and hastened the darkening. Except for the divisions of Clayton and Stevenson there was little organized resistance left in Hood's army. Forrest had been missed for two days. He was sorely missed now and Hood sent an aide with orders to have him join the army at Pulaski.

Hood's retreat orders called for Stephen Lee to hold the Franklin pike while Stewart pulled out of the center of Hood's line and, under Lee's protection, set up another defense line at Brentwood, four miles in the rear. Cheatham was to use Granny White for his getaway and to keep out of the way of Stewart and Lee. His men instead debauched into the Franklin pike, already jammed with troops, in the darkness and drenching rain. It was this disorganized mass that broke up the unpanicked divisions of Clayton and Stevenson.

When Wilson saw the Rebel line fall apart, Croxton was hurried toward Brentwood. Hatch and Knipe were ordered to mount and pursue. Knipe probably moved eastward alongside of Croxton. Hatch pushed south along the Granny White pike whence he was to swing eastward and, if possible, reach and block the Franklin pike. Thomas had jeopardized his professional career to build up his cavalry arm and now it was moving to its destiny. A mile from his starting point Hatch's advance ran into Chalmers' cavalry. They were dismounted and posted across the pike behind a barricade of rails.

Chalmers had the exacting role of covering the western flank and rear of Hood's army. He had taken a position on the Hillsborough pike to guard the road running eastward across Granny White to Brentwood. He held his intersection for three hours while Cheatham's ambulances went south to safety. Late in the afternoon he was ordered to hold the intersection of this crossroad with the Granny White pike. This point was two or three miles east of the Hillsborough intersection. Here Chalmers was under attack from Johnson on the west and Hatch on the north. The barricade was a roadblock to stop or slow Hatch's strike. Hatch broke through it and pushed its defenders back onto Chalmers' main body at the intersection. With three regiments, probably in columns of four, filling Granny White with an avalanche of horses on the dead run, Hatch smashed into Rucker's brigade, which was also mounted. The fighting degenerated into the scramble of hand-to-hand combat, and was not brought to an end until an hour after dark.

It was the troopers of Brigadier General Chalmers that frustrated Thomas' plan for a perfect victory. Their margin was so slight as to be almost non-existent. In time it was perhaps an hour. In space it was less than 900 yards. But that night Thomas was more of a human being than a military machine. Coming down the Granny White pike through the darkness and wet from the direction of the battlefield Wilson heard the ponderous gallop of a heavy horseman and then Thomas' exultant voice. "Is that you, Wilson? Dang it to hell, didn't I tell you we could lick 'em."

The night of the sixteenth, the Fourth Corps bivouacked on the Franklin pike one mile north of Brentwood while Grose's skirmishers covered the Brentwood pass. Hatch pulled up his division one and three-quarters miles west of Brentwood and the rest of the army, except for Johnson's cavalry, was on the arc between these points. Johnson spent the night at the intersection of Hillsborough pike and the Harpeth River. Hood had been able to rally enough men at Brentwood pass to form a rear guard and Stephen Lee took command of it. By 10:00 P.M. Lee was beginning to organize a defense position seven miles north of Franklin. By 2:00 A.M. of the seventeenth it was completed. His pickets at the pass kept the road clear of Grose's skirmishers and watched the remnants of Hood's army file by during the night. The wearied men and horses, strung out without organization between Brentwood and Franklin, made what camps they could in the rain and took a little food and some troubled rest.

There were others who had little rest that night. On the east side of the Granny White pike eight miles south of Nashville in a house owned by a man named Tucker, Wilson and Hatch had set up their headquarters. With them was General Rucker, who had been taken prisoner, after being wounded, less than a mile to the south. Hatch, who had given up his bed to his wounded prisoner, was up and down all night tending to his wants. On the other bed in the same room Wilson sat crosslegged receiving and sending dispatches in preparation for the pursuit that was to begin at daylight.

A short distance to the north, Thomas' staff was drafting his pursuit orders before the cavalry horses were on their picket lines. For two reasons, pursuit was a hazardous tactic. First, it was so complex that success would be almost impossible. Even a barren battlefield victory always brought public plaudits but a failure weeks afterwards in a pursuit cleared the way for a public criticism of the unfortunate general by his enemies. Second, and more basic, was the fact that Thomas' army had never been readied for pursuit. His battle had been fought with a minimum of preparation and he was refused the time required to gird it for a decisive victory.

Even before the necessary railway repair work could be done, the War Department was detaching his railway repair crews for work in the east. Thomas' animals, wheels and equipment were not fit to meet the challenging conditions of a close pursuit in the weather then prevailing. His pontoon train was inadequate, its pontoniers unschooled. The cavalry had no medical equipment and their sick and wounded were left in private homes along the road to be cared for by the infantry surgeons when they came up. There were not enough ambulances, so a motley of make-do vehicles was pressed into service. There was no fast-moving pack train to keep up with the cavalry in their off-the-road work. There were not enough farriers, veterinarians or medicines to keep the horses in proper shape, so that those in the best shape were overworked and broke down in their turn more rapidly than they should have. Thomas, the perfectionist, fought the decisive battle of the war, and staged its longest pursuit, with wornout tools.

Despite these handicaps Thomas had resolved weeks before to hazard the heavy odds against success. His commission was a mandate to destroy the enemy. He had a choice of means but none of objective. Except for Mill Springs, Donelson and Vicksburg, every major Northern victory of the war to date had been sterilized by the failure to consummate it. Nevertheless, pursuit was to start as soon as it was light enough to see. The main force of the cavalry was to move south on the Franklin pike. Johnson was to cross the Harpeth River on the Hillsborough pike and swing east into Franklin, cutting Hood's retreat line where he was slowed by the river crossing. Thomas was trying to trap Hood at the same place Hood had sought to trap Schofield eighteen days before. Wood's Fourth Corps was selected to lead the pursuit with the cavalry. They got their orders before the seventeenth was an hour old but it was 8:00 A.M. before the column was in motion. The day was dark and cloudy. Their route was straight south through the debris of Hood's retreat. Wood's men moved in line of battle, one brigade of each division deployed and the other brigades following the deployed ones in columns. This was not the fastest way to move, but the drive to Atlanta had proved its efficacy.

Steedman followed Wood closely enough to be in support. Smith and Schofield moved north on Granny White to its intersection with the Franklin pike, where they turned south following Steedman. This was a roundabout march of a dozen extra miles but it was quicker in time than a direct route over the unmacadamized side roads. It was evident that the real work of the pursuit was to be done by the cavalry, the Fourth Corps and Steedman's detachment. The wagon trains, laden with ten days' supplies and 100 round of ammunition per man, moved with their respective commands. This was a drag upon the entire movement but it was unavoidable until the railway could be repaired and new rolling stock brought in. The country had been stripped by three sets of foragers within sixty days. Now Thomas' men found root cellars, smoke houses, granaries and barns either bare or partly filled with spoiled stock.

By 5:00 A.M. of the seventeenth Hammond was on the Franklin pike north of Brentwood. Croxton was moving toward that same place from the west. Hammond's advance came up with the Rebel skirmishers just south of Brentwood and drove them southward to an exceptionally strong position at Hollow Tree Gap. Here they ran into the familiar lines of Gray infantrymen and the Northern horse could make little impression upon them. But the Union cavalry was coming into Hood's escape route by every road emerging from the west all the way back to Franklin and there was nothing for the Confederate rear guard to do but to fight its way back through this gathering opposition.

The pursuit pressed southward against stiffening resistance four miles more to Franklin where the rear guard attempted to make another stand at the crossings of the Harpeth River, but Johnson came in from the west on the south side of the river with his Sixth Cavalry Division and hustled the last of the Rebels out of that war-scourged village. Knipe led his horses over the old railway bridge and had his division in the town almost as soon as Johnson got there. Hatch swung east and forded the Harpeth on the Murfreesborough road. Croxton went two miles upstream and swam his command over the place he had forded less than three weeks before. This was a dangerous tactic for untrained cavalry mounts which had been working on farms and pulling the Nashville drays and streetcars ten days before. An unschooled horse forced into a strong current and deep water becomes panicky, paws the air and finally goes over backwards. But it was this or nothing. Incessant rain and snow had every stream bank full and booming. The urgent need was to throw a cavalry flanking column across Hood's retreat route to force a deployment until the pursuing infantry could come up.

The Fourth Corps reached Franklin at 1:20 P.M. Not a bridge over the Harpeth River suitable for trains and artillery was standing, but they built a bridge of salvaged materials, without adequate tools, and the corps was over in sixteen hours.

As soon as the town was secured, Knipe's command moved straight down the Columbia pike. Hatch was east of him and Johnson west, both following parallel routes. These flanking columns forced the Rebel rear guard to keep moving until they found some means of protecting their vulnerable wings. Hood's rear guard made their first stand a mile and a half south of Franklin but were chevied back three or four miles before they could stiffen for another stand. Their opportunity came at the crossing of the West Harpeth River, about five miles south of Franklin. Hatch dismounted and deployed his men to the right and left of the turnpike while the Fourth United States Cavalry Regiment, 200 strong and mounted, formed on the pike in column of fours—a solid plug of horsemen filling the road from side to side and fifty ranks deep. It was dark. Hatch's skirmishers picked up a few prisoners but they were so sullen and disheartened that Hatch thought they were stragglers and wondered if he were not wasting time in his preparations for a fight. In this interval Stephen Lee got his artillery in position to sweep the pike. It was a bleak prospect that faced the Fourth Cavalry. A wounded or stumbling horse in any of the front ranks meant a thrown rider whose chances of survival under the hooves behind him were low. But the bugle sounded and the regiment went into the battery with sabers. They broke through the guns but in the confusion of getting back to their own lines in the darkness their commander was captured three times. He threw away his hat, which made a tell-tale silhouette, and escaped each time by raising the cry, "The Yankees are coming, run for your lives."

Under cover of the darkness the Rebel rear guard re-formed in a three-sided square with its open side toward the south and backed away from Wilson's cavalry to safety. At Spring Hill they picked up another infantry brigade. A mile farther south they escaped the unrelenting Yankee pressure.

This desperate little night action may have been the check that saved Hood from total destruction. His army was strung out along the turnpike from Spring Hill towards Columbia. Stephen Lee, who should know, called the pursuit vigorous, daring, bold, persistent and desperate. In spite of his adjectives the rear guard gained four or five hours for Hood that night. This was the time Hood needed to get his command south of Rutherford Creek. It was 10:00 P.M. when the Federal cavalry ceased their pursuit and 11:00 before order could be restored to their disorganized ranks. Both men and horses were almost worn out.

Thomas established his headquarters near Franklin the night of the seventeenth. It must have looked to him as though his chances for a perfect victory were good. His dispatches to Washington were guardedly optimistic. But he overlooked no chance for bettering his opportunity. Orders for his long-range pursuit plan were put into operation that night. Steedman, who had closed up on Wood at Franklin, was ordered to Murfreesborough to entrain his command for Decatur, picking up some of R. S. Granger's men on the way. Steedman was to cross the Tennessee River at that place and move down its left bank to cut Hood's retreat south of Florence. Working through Halleck, Thomas had orders sent to the garrisons at Memphis and Vicksburg for sorties from the west against this same retreat route. To make doubly sure Thomas requested the navy to send ironclads and gunboats up the Tennessee River to destroy Hood's pontoon bridge.

December 18 was the critical day of the direct pursuit. Hood's army was only a few miles from Thomas' vanguard. Hood's rear guard was under almost unbearable tension and showing signs of collapse. The Union cavalry moved out at dawn and skirmished throughout the day. The rain was torrential. Wood's fast-walking infantrymen overhauled the flagging horsemen just before dark and took the lead. They camped that night in line of battle three and a half miles north of Rutherford's

Creek. Neither Wilson's men nor his horses had had any food for twenty-four hours and there was none to be taken from the country. Cavalry mounts are unable to endure as much as men, and scant forage, constant duty, neglect and the continual wet were breaking them down. Wilson pulled them off the road and put them into camp while the infantry went by. It was a day of disappointment to Thomas' hopes.

The nineteenth was even worse. At 8:00 A.M. Wood started the Fourth Corps south. Again it was raining hard. The surface of the land was flooded and was so soft that loaded wagons could move only on the hard-surfaced pike. It was almost impossible for the infantrymen to get through the mud. At 9:30 A.M. the head of Wood's column reached the north bank of Rutherford's Creek. The bridge was destroyed. The surface of the water was covered with drifting debris, and broken with swirls and eddies. There were no tools or materials for rebuilding the original bridge. A pontoon bridge would be liable to destruction from floating objects and, being at water level, meant that the high, abrupt banks had to be cut down on both sides to get the wheeled vehicles onto and off the bridge. In the holes the water was fifteen feet deep. At no place was it fordable. A portion of Hatch's cavalry division was working along the north bank when Wood's infantry came up. They had silenced the Rebel artillery with their horse battery but this fire had no effect on Hood's sharpshooters.

Wood had put in nineteen and a half years of field service with the army, yet this was the dreariest, most uncomfortable and inclement day he could recall. The military problem was to establish a bridgehead on the far bank. Only then could the engineering work of constructing a bridge be started. As the Blue infantrymen came up to the north bank they came under hostile fire. The only site for a bridge that could handle artillery and trains was at the turnpike so it became necessary to pass troops across the stream either above or below this point and in force enough to drive the Rebel rear guard away from the spot where the south end of the bridge would rest. The first orders went out to build rafts. But when they were loaded with troops and poled out into the stream they proved unmanageable in the swift current. At least one of them capsized and two men were drowned. There was an effort to fell some of the tallest trees growing on the north bank so that their tops would rest on the south bank and their trunks could be used for a bridge. But the limbs on the undersides of the falling trees were caught by the current before the tops could effect an anchorage and the trees were swept away. Hatch got two regiments across on the ruins of the railway bridge but was unable to hold his position and withdrew them at nightfall. Meantime Wood's troops were trying to build foot bridges at two places to cross troops enough to secure the bridgehead.

While Wood and Wilson were stopped at the north bank of Rutherford's Creek, Hood was getting the main body of his army across the Duck River some four miles to the south. Duck River was a formidable obstacle. It had delayed Buell's army several days on the march to Shiloh and at that time there had been no hostile force to dispute his crossing. Now Forrest, who had come up in defiance of his orders, was organizing a rear guard of 1,900 picked men, 400 of them without shoes, to hold the Duck River as long as possible while Hood's main army toiled southward.

On December 20 the Union cavalry and infantry both crossed Rutherford's Creek and pushed on to the north bank of the Duck. Forrest's rear guard could be seen on the opposite side but the rear of Hood's main column now had a lead of twenty-four hours. The river was too deep and swift to be bridged by a structure resting on the bottom. There was little that could be done now until the pontoon train could get up. Perhaps a delay would have been forced regardless of the pontoon train. Hatch's cavalry division was the only mobile unit Wilson had left. The brigades of Croxton, Hammond and Harrison were still in camp drawing supplies. Knipe and Johnson had been dismounted to supply horses for Hatch. A heavy storm of rain and snow lashed the country. That night Hood's headquarters were at Pulaski. Thomas' had been set up at Rutherford's Creek.

It was about noon on December 21 when the pontoon train reached Rutherford's Creek. In the bitter cold of the afternoon the bridge was laid. The untrained pontoniers were unequal to the task and the infantry had to do the work but they were hampered by inexperience. Wood took charge of the operations at that point as soon as the train came up. The canvas boats were assembled, launched and loaded with men of the Fifty-first Indiana. In an hour they had crossed and seized a bridgehead on the south bank and immediately the bridge laying began. Again the work was slowed because of inexperience. The first unit to cross the bridge was the pontoon material for Duck River. It was the night of the twenty-second before the infantry began passing over. They had the use of the bridge for five or six hours, then they were to give it up to the cavalry. The bridge was so inexpertly laid, however, that the artillery and trains were unable to cross in their allotted time.

Thomas knew now in his headquarters at Columbia that his stern chase was hopeless, but as long as there was a chance that Steedman or the navy or the garrisons from the Mississippi might check the Confederate retreat he ordered the pursuit continued by the cavalry and the Fourth Corps. From here on it had little military significance except to illustrate the point that a successful, straightaway chase is one of the most difficult of military tactics. It must be carefully planned and meticulously equipped. The general who tries it runs a much greater risk of tarnishing his reputation than of burnishing it.

Weather, starvation and physical exhaustion combined to ruin Thomas' army as much as battle had ruined Hood's.

The cavalry attempted to travel alongside the highway, looking for a chance to encircle the flanks of the rear guard but the mud was too deep and the horses floundered back to the road, many of them too exhausted for further use. It took twelve hours to haul a wagon six miles. Batteries were left behind so that teams could be increased on those which went along. Ammunition loads were reduced to ten boxes and their teams were doubled. At night the ground froze enough to release the mudbound wheels which could move as long as they kept out of the ruts of those ahead of them. The rivers would be partially covered with thin ice. By noon the mud crust would soften again. The ice would break up, float downstream and jam against the upper side of the pontoon bridges until the pressure carried away one or more of the boats. Steedman took his men south in freight cars and lost five men from exposure. More than 5,000 of Wilson's horses were ruined. During the day their legs were covered with mud which froze into heavy casts at night. They died before dawn on the picket line in the half frozen mud pots scooped out by their hooves as they vainly tried to free their legs from the thick coats of mud. Hundreds lost their hooves and had to be destroyed.

On December 28, Thomas called off the direct pursuit. The gunboats had been foiled. The attack by the Memphis and Vicksburg garrisons, which had been ordered through Halleck, had fizzled. There were still possibilities, however, in Steedman's looping strike from the east. Colonel William J. Palmer with 600 picked men and horses spearheaded this strike. Palmer was a Pennsylvanian and a Medal of Honor winner. He commanded the original company of Anderson Cavalry, a blue-stocking outfit that became so highly favored under Buell's command that Palmer was sent back to Pennsylvania to recruit more like it. This he did, and led them during the Antietam campaign, where he was captured. After his release he reorganized the remains of the mutinous Anderson Cavalry into the Fifteenth Pennsylvania Cavalry and acted as its colonel. Palmer was one of the best of the young crop of battle-tested cavalry leaders.

He crossed the Tennessee River at Decatur and was moving down the left bank in the rear of Hood's retreating army. On December 31 he overtook and destroyed Hood's pontoon train in northwest Alabama. On New Year's day, in Mississippi, he destroyed a supply train of 110 wagons and 500 mules. Two weeks later he captured Lyon, who had been raiding Kentucky and Tennessee in support of Hood, and nearly all his men. To Colonel Palmer and his command, Thomas accorded the credit of giving Hood's army the last blow of the campaign, at a distance of more than 200 miles from where he had first struck the enemy on December 15.

Thomas' was the longest pursuit of the war in time and space. It lasted thirty days. The most famous pursuit—that of Lee by Grant—covered about eighty miles and lasted seven days. Following the arc of a circle, Lee had to travel a mile and a half for every mile traveled by his pursuer and had to make one more river crossing. Hood ran straight away with a railway to facilitate the most perilous part of his retreat.

Meantime Stoneman had broken up Duke's command in East Tennessee, routed Vaughn in southwest Virginia and driven Breckinridge into North Carolina. Wytheville, Virginia, the salt works, the lead works and the railway to Lynchburg were reported destroyed.

In a whirlwind campaign of a little more than two weeks, Thomas had practically annihilated the Confederacy's second strongest army. Lincoln sent him the nation's thanks. Stanton rejoiced and jubilantly spread the news by telegraph to governors, mayors and ranking army officers. Congress engrossed its thanks. Thomas told his army that it had accomplished a brilliant achievement unsurpassed by any other in the war. The victory brought a lift to the flagging morale of the Army of the Potomac. It accomplished half of Grant's eight-month-old plan for winning the war. Thirty-five years later history accepted Thomas' appraisal of his campaign. At first it made no impression on European military thought but by 1892, because of the completeness of Thomas' strike, it was studied in the military schools of Europe. Military critics were saying that there were only two perfect battles in the history of the world—Austerlitz and Nashville.[20]

Thomas did not accomplish this without the help of others. Canby prevented Kirby Smith from crossing the Mississippi and reinforcing Hood, and Sheridan prevented Early from moving toward the Cumberland Gap and making a diversion in Hood's favor. Sherman had begun Hood's ruin at Atlanta. Schofield gave it a push at Franklin. With this aid Thomas finished the work at Nashville. Nearly half a century after the event, selected officers of the United States army were taught that "of all the attacks made by the Union forces in the course of the [Civil] war none other was as free from faults as this one."

Grant was unimpressed. Thomas was not good in pursuit, he wrote to Sherman, because he followed too far behind and left the command of the advance to his subordinates. Two months later he was more pessimistic. He felt that Thomas could never make a campaign, though he was an expert in preparing one.

Grant could have been honest when he called Thomas slow. He was slower by nine days at Mill Springs than Grant had been at Donelson. He was slower by three days at Nashville than Grant had been at Chattanooga. But his strike in 1861 tore out the east anchor of the Rebel defense line and Grant completed its destruction by breaking its center. His strike in 1864 gave Grant the leverage to Appomattox. Together they won the war. Their philosophies differed but their talents were complementary. Grant gave up his genius for command at Vicksburg to follow the unremitting but expensive military erosion which led to the Surrender. Thomas maneuvered consistently to threaten a vulnerable point with an overwhelming power directed from at least two angles and then, when the result of this pressure became apparent, obliterated his enemy with a series of smashing blows.

The tragedy of the last five months of the war was not Hood's despair or Lee's humiliation but Sherman's bankruptcy of military imagination. He marched with a picked command and negligible influence between Thomas and Grant. If Thomas had failed, Sherman's bays would have withered. If Grant had failed Sherman would have had the chance to earn his reputation.

Looked at through Rebel eyes, Hood's army was all but wrecked. Bragg was told that it was a shattered debris. Beauregard was shocked when he saw its ragged, bleeding survivors. Joseph E. Johnston claimed that out of the army he had turned over to Hood at Atlanta only 5,000 reached him in North Carolina.

The degree of the destruction of Hood's army is a debatable question. Hood, who tried hard to minimize his misfortune, reported that he reached Tupelo with 21,000, but subsequent analyses bring no support to this figure. Forrest reported that his command was almost sacrificed. Apparently some 3,500 West Tennesseans went on furlough (which may have been a technical description of desertion), 4,000 men were sent to Mobile and 5,000 to face Sherman in the Carolinas. Under the series of Thomas' savage blows the Confederacy's military strength between the Appalachians and the Mississippi disintegrated. Richmond was desperate to know what could be salvaged from Hood's army, but they asked in vain. Hood's losses by death, wounds and desertion have never been determined.

Thomas listed 13,189 prisoners, including seven general officers, plus seventy-two pieces of artillery and thirty to forty battle flags. In addition he received into his lines 2,000 deserters. His loss in killed, wounded and missing was estimated at less than 10,000. Owing to the lack of organization in some of the units engaged the number of Union wounded never could be tabulated.

Thomas and some of his subordinates stated in their reports that Hood was superior in numbers during the two-day battle. The interpretation of what is meant by "units of fighting" probably accounts for the discrepancy between this claim and that of Hood's protagonists, who estimate that the Confederates fought approximately 23,000 to Thomas' 55,000. One of Thomas' staff officers, writing twenty years after the event, thinks that Thomas had 43,260 men actually engaged. He puts Hood's effective strength on December 10 at 37,937 but not all of these fought in front of Nashville. There is general agreement that Thomas' total strength, including isolated garrisons, railway guards, the East Tennessee striking force and the cavalry detached to drive off Lyon, totalled 70,272. Naval forces were additional to these. Thomas fought the Battle of Nashville without any regular white infantry and convinced himself that the volunteer was adequate for total victory.

Thomas was the severest critic of his failure to achieve perfection. In a talk before a small group in Washington after the war he admitted that he should have blocked the Franklin pike with his cavalry. He maintained that he made a grave error of judgment in not detaching a force to circle Hood's army the night of the fifteenth and get in his rear across the Franklin pike. His listeners, mostly military men, were nonplussed. They had expected the usual mitigation of failure.

The novelty of Thomas' decisive battle grew out of its conventionality. Some of the greatest military commanders of history had proved its principles before Thomas was born. Dennis Mahan, in a series of examinations, had wheedled out of more than 2,000 graduate West Pointers the admission that these were the accepted bases of military operation. Baron Antoine Henri Jomini, who knew everything about tactics and strategy and little about the integrity of command, had reduced them to a compact volume ostentatiously displayed by most Northern officers throughout the war. All gave them lip service. Thomas practiced them. The germ of the concept was to bring overwhelming force to bear on the weakest spot in the enemy's line, break through and destroy the enemy. Three coordinate combat forces had been created to accomplish such a victory—infantry, artillery and cavalry. Nashville was the only battle of the war to destroy one of the two major sources of enemy power but its lack of color obscured its decisiveness. It was the first Union battle in which the cavalry was a decisive factor. Its failure was in the pursuit, not in the battle. It succeeded in its new tactic but failed in its old one. Historically, pursuit was a difficult role when the pursuer had to travel farther than the pursued.

The Union cavalry under Thomas fought dismounted and started the rout of Hood's army. Their mounted pursuit completed it. Most of the men of Knipe and Hatch fought all day on the sixteenth dismounted. By nightfall they were hungry and exhausted. Two small, overlooked factors accounted for part of this. No provision had been made for leaving the sabers on the saddles when the men dismounted, so they dragged them along through the brush and up the steep slopes. Nor were the horseholders properly trained. As a result the mounts were far in the rear when the time came to use them for pursuit. But even these defects would not have been fatal if the cavalry and the Fourth Corps could have crossed Rutherford's Creek and Duck River with celerity. Thomas' pontoon train, which was ordered out of Nashville shortly after the fighting ceased on the sixteenth, reached the Duck River on December 21—more than four days to make some forty miles. Thomas also shouldered the blame for this. He was awakened from a sound sleep and told that the pontoon train was ready to move. He dictated his order to Captain Ramsey of his staff but he misspoke its route and named the Murfreesborough instead of the Franklin pike. The most junior staff officer should have corrected the error. Thomas' staff had made no blunder like this since the Hartsville fiasco late in 1862, but the staff that had been his main reliance was scattered between Sherman's army, Chattanooga and Nashville. A pontoon train is a heavy, cumbersome affair and when it became necessary to cross by rain-sodden, unpaved roads from the Murfreesborough pike to the Franklin pike, hours were lost.

Thomas made official mention of both of these factors. The pontoons, he pointed out, were hastily constructed, incomplete and poorly manned. "I would here remark," he wrote, "that the splendid pontoon train properly belonging to my command, with its trained corps of pontoniers, was absent with General Sherman."

Like all doers Thomas was pre-eminently a teacher. As a disciple of Ringgold he taught the army some new ideas about artillery fighting at Buena Vista. He grounded the army's nascent cavalry in a technique that enabled it to survive two of the greatest improvements in the rifle. He taught an army at Chickamauga the simple self-evident fact that so long as they occupied a given piece of ground the enemy could not occupy it; and at Missionary Ridge the impalpable opposite, that unanimity of will was a more powerful weapon than a bullet.

But strangely enough, bad teaching brought him his greatest victory. Fifteen years earlier Thomas had grounded John Bell Hood in the theories of cavalry and artillery fighting. A few years later he supplemented this academic instruction with practical lessons in the field. But the efforts bore no fruit. Having rejected Thomas' theories on the proper use of guns and horses the student pitted his own ideas regarding the tricky subject of morale against those of his mentor. Two smashing days of defeat ruined his bright hopes of victory. A wounded infantryman saw him in his tent near Brentwood as his broken regiments streamed by and the cold rain sluiced down on the canvas. Hood sat alone. His left arm was crippled and useless. With the fingers of his right hand he combed his tousled hair while the tears ran unnoticed over his beard. Less than a month later Hood resigned his command. Later in Richmond with schemes for raising an army of his beloved Texans, his friends noticed that he sat for long periods silent and with unseeing eyes while drops of perspiration gathered on his forehead. They thought he might be seeing again the piled dead in front of the mock oranges at Franklin and the panic of the routed army that passed his tent at Brentwood.

Like all decisive campaigns, Nashville has been the source of controversy. Thomas' superiors—Grant and Sherman—took the lead in this, aided by Thomas' rival, Schofield. Most of this criticism was unknown to Thomas. Specifically they took the position that Thomas was too slow in attacking and not vigorous enough in pursuit. From this position Grant went on to the untenable theory that Thomas was too inert to mount an offensive. "We used to say laughingly," Young reports Grant as saying, "Thomas is too slow to move and too brave to run away."

20

Thomas Achieves Two of His War-Long Ambitions

Grant in front of Petersburg had closed his active operations for the winter, but he was still faced with the responsibility for completing the conquest of the South. By his own specification this required the concentration of all possible force so as to maintain an unremitting pressure on the enemy. Thomas was part of that force and Grant had two options for his employment. He could use him to mop up resistance south of the Savannah-Atlanta-Vicksburg line or he could call him eastward to resolve his nightmarish fear that Lee might escape into East Tennessee and prolong the war another year. Unknown to Thomas, Grant had already made up his mind to block him off from further combat operations.

On December 27 Thomas ordered Wilson to make a fifty-mile raid to cut Hood's retreat route at the Bear River bridge. Wilson refused the order. Fifty-six per cent of his horses were down and a large part of the remainder were unfit for use. From seventy to ninety days were imperative for the rehabilitation of his command. Wood estimated that he would need ten days to refit his infantry after Thomas could establish and stock a forward base.

The next day Thomas ordered his army into winter quarters for sixty days to prepare for a campaign against Selma and Mobile. When

Halleck learned of this decision he advised Grant that Thomas was too slow to make a campaign toward Selma, that he should stand on the defensive and that his army should be depleted. He suggested the extension of Thomas' administrative command by adding to it Schofield's Department of the Ohio. Grant approved and countermanded Thomas' order for winter quarters.[1]

Schofield, in a letter to Grant that Thomas knew nothing about until the day before his death, claimed the credit for Hood's defeat and asked that the unsatisfactory arrangement of serving under Thomas be terminated. His request was granted and the breakup of Thomas' military command was begun. Smith's divisions and 5,000 of Wilson's troopers were ordered to Canby. Sherman apologetically informed Thomas that his Fourteenth and Twentieth Corps had been organized into the Army of Georgia. The Fourth Corps was all that was left of the Army of the Cumberland. Simultaneously, Thomas was immobilized by the detachment of part of his wagons. A start was made to strip from him his engineers and mechanics. Canby received priority in mounting his cavalry.

Grant's refusal to admit that Thomas' troops were fagged and that it was necessary to "equip up" was the result of his unreasonable anger at Thomas. No specific cause has ever been given for this feeling but it can be guessed at. The two men irritated each other and this widened their professional difficulties. Under Stanton's pressure Grant adopted the policy of attrition. The public welcomed it at first but sickened of it after Cold Harbor, when they became convinced that Grant was wasting instead of using the North's most irreplaceable resource. While Grant was stalemated, no nearer to destroying Lee than he had been nine months before, Thomas in a mid-winter campaign proved that a major Rebel army could be destroyed without using Grant's method. He further aggravated the situation by disobeying Grant's orders.

This was a challenge to Grant's professional career and his habitual insecurity made him acutely conscious of it. If Grant should stumble, hundreds of his subordinates would stumble too. The pressures to curb Thomas brought by these men were probably strong and persuasive. If Grant took official notice of them he needed an official reason and Halleck promptly supplied it. The theory was that Thomas' refit violated Grant's order to maintain a constant pressure on the enemy, but there was a weakness to this position. Thomas, operating from a fixed base, needed time to stock the necessary supplies for a forward movement while Grant, using a movable base, had already closed his active operations for the year. Grant soon realized that he could not rest his case on the denial of Thomas' obvious needs. So, in a chatty, confidential letter to Sherman he gave another reason. Thomas' pursuit of Hood, he said, was too sluggish; Thomas left too much to his subordinates and remained too far behind.

The artistry of Grant's slander rests on his choice of the word sluggish. He was charging that Thomas was habitually idle and lazy, slothful, dull and inert with a hint of stupidity. This was the recorded opinion of the ranking Union general. By the time it was made public Thomas was dead and the crushing authority of the Presidency had been added to this sanction. When Grant repeated the charge from his death bed he molded it into historical fact.

Grant was outspoken to everyone except Thomas. His criticisms were made in writing to Sherman and Halleck, verbally to Lincoln and Stanton. Probably Meade, Schofield and Logan knew all about them. Thomas wrote one letter that has been preserved which noted the fact that Grant was not a friend of his and was not disposed to accommodate him except when compelled to do so by public opinion. The letter contained no criticism of his superior. Thomas also stated his dissatisfaction to Stanton, naming no names. It is probable that Andrew Johnson knew Thomas' version of the affair. At any rate the last few months of Thomas' participation in the war and his part in the Reconstruction were a struggle for prestige between these military titans. Grant had the power of supreme command. Against it Thomas pitted his military foresight. Grant used some of the national leaders to aid his design. Thomas asked for no help until the showdown. He rebuffed Stanton's offer of help when it was made. Yet without being insubordinate, he opposed Grant's military wishes whenever they ran counter to his own judgment. He never opposed him on political issues.

Even though Thomas had no knowledge of the extent of the campaign against him, he sensed its existence. On December 19 Stanton had queried Grant about rewarding Thomas for his Nashville victory with a promotion to major general in the regular army, but Grant demurred. Three days later he withdrew his objection. On Christmas day Thomas received the notification that his name had gone to the Senate. The Senate's executive journal shows, by some clerical error, that Thomas was recommended for promotion in recognition of his Nashville victory three days before that battle was fought. The error might indicate that the original intention had been to promote him for his seniority but someone who blocked that reward agreed later to give him his already merited promotion for his work at Nashville. On the same list and recommended for the same rank were Sherman, Meade, Sheridan and

Hancock. All but the last were to take their new rank ahead of Thomas. If Thomas' name had gone in on the twelfth, as originally intended, the relative ranks of these officers would have been more favorable to Thomas.

Stanton's inquiry to Grant, which read, "What about the major generalship; has it been won?" does not mention Thomas but the context makes it certain that the question refers to him and might indicate a continuing discussion with Grant over the contemplated promotion. At any rate Thomas' name must have been added to the list sometime between December 15 and December 24.

Stanton's covering dispatch to Thomas stated that his appointment filled the only vacancy in the grade, that no official duty had been performed with more satisfaction, and that no officer had more justly earned the promotion. When he finished reading it Thomas sat silent and unseeing. Perhaps he was reviewing the slights of the last few years. When he returned to the verities of his uncomfortable headquarters in a requisitioned church he passed the letter to Surgeon George E. Cooper with the question, "What do you think of that?"

Cooper read it and answered, "Thomas, it is better late than never."

"I suppose it is better late than never," Thomas rejoined, "but it is too late to be appreciated; I earned this at Chickamauga." With that, Thomas' iron self-control gave way and the medical expert watched what no other man ever reported—Thomas' complete loss of emotional control accompanied by the strongest possible indication of intense feeling.[2]

J. L. Donaldson threw a little more light on the affair when he sent a semi-official message on January 10, 1865, to Montgomery Meigs. He wrote, "Thomas left yesterday for Eastport where he is concentrating. I saw him on the boat and he opened his heart to me. He feels very sore at the rumored intentions to relieve him and the major generalcy does not cicatrize the wound. You know Thomas is morbidly sensitive and it cut him to the heart to think that it was contemplated to remove him. He does not blame the secretary, for he said Mr. Stanton was a fair and just man."

Since 1861 Thomas had looked eastward through East Tennessee and southwestern Virginia toward the Rebel army defending Richmond. After calling off the pursuit of Hood he began to examine this situation again and convinced himself that he should be prepared for an advance to the northeast even though he had orders to move southward. Early in 1865 he began to stockpile in Knoxville the manifold supplies that would be needed by a major army initiating a campaign toward Richmond. Grant, however, had other ideas. By a series of orders from January 6 to February 13 he outlined a new role for Thomas. He was to prepare combat forces for other commanders but was to have no combat direction of his own. In lieu of combat duties he was to take over additional administrative work. Thomas complied. He added the Departments of Kentucky and the Ohio to his command area, prepared Stoneman for a raid into South Carolina to cooperate with Sherman, and Wilson for a raid against Selma in cooperation with Canby. Grant gave discretion concerning routes and objectives to the field commanders but none to Thomas. Implicit in Grant's orders was the suggestion that Thomas lacked the knowledge of how many horses were required for his gun teams.

But Grant soon discovered that Thomas could not be insulated from combat. The possibility that Lee might escape into the fastnesses of East Tennessee was the catalyst which combined the plans of the two leaders.

Stoneman was immobilized in Knoxville by a lack of horses, which had been by-passing Thomas' department in favor of Canby's. Grant was disgusted again at Thomas' slowness and he now advised a new objective for Stoneman. To counter Lee's possible move into East Tennessee he wanted Stoneman to break the Chattanooga-Lynchburg railroad and Thomas to collect surplus forage and provisions in that area to support a considerable force there in the spring. Thomas advised him of the steps he had taken in anticipation of such a contingency. "Unless you wish otherwise," he continued, "I shall send General Stanley's entire corps to East Tennessee and shall also concentrate the surplus of new regiments at Chattanooga." Grant promptly approved. With this permission Thomas prepared to expand what started out to be a cavalry raid into a full-fledged campaign which he would lead.

On March 1 Grant learned that Canby, like Thomas, was unable to mount a winter campaign so he ordered Thomas to start Wilson's raid without waiting for Canby. Again Thomas had been able to forecast the military moves and had put his command in readiness to take advantage of them. Grant's original scheme had been a cooperative strike by Wilson with 5,000 troopers. At the end of February, Thomas went down to Eastport to see the state of readiness of Wilson's command. In his pocket was Grant's order for Wilson to demonstrate with a few thousand horsemen against Selma or Tuscaloosa. It was a subordinate role in the main western campaign of 1865. What Thomas found at Eastport was to his liking. He saw the largest body of cavalry ever collected on the American continent, although it lacked 7,000 horses that would have been supplied if Halleck and Stanton had believed in Thomas' idea. Thomas inspected the corps. The horses were groomed, shod and healthy. The equipments were complete, leather cleaned and oiled, buckles shined. Wilson had mounted and equipped the best part of three divisions. They stood to horse as Thomas rode by. The 1,500 unmounted men were organized into battalions and stationed on the left of the mounted squadrons. To the left of these were the pack train, the 250 wagons of the quartermaster's train and the 56 wagons of the pontoon train. One light battery moved with each mounted division. As the inspection was being made Wilson detailed his plan for crossing the devastated country bordering the Tennessee River and the equally destitute hill country south of it—120 miles without food or shelter for man or beast. Each trooper would carry rations for five days, one hundred rounds of ammunition, twenty-four pounds of grain and one extra set of fitted shoes for his horse. The pack animals would carry five days' rations of hard bread and ten of salt, sugar and coffee. The wagon train would carry a forty-five day supply of coffee, twenty of sugar and fifteen of salt with eighty rounds of ammunition per man. He pointed out that all but a few hundred of his men were armed with the Spencer carbine and all-important metallic cartridge.

Then Wilson passed 17,000 troopers before Thomas in review. It was a sight never seen by any other American army commander. It convinced Thomas that a mere demonstration with such a force was a useless waste of strength, that using it as a concentrated mobile force he could break the enemy's last interior railway, destroy their last depots and knock Forrest out of the war. Thomas ordered Wilson to move with his entire force to capture Tuscaloosa, Selma and Montgomery, destroy Forrest and strike against Mobile if possible. He was multiplying violence by velocity. This was to be a campaign in its own right and not in cooperation with Canby's move. Thomas based his right to the combat command of this striking force on Sherman's original orders.

Thomas was ready to put his theories to the test of battle. Today they are axiomatic. In 1865 they were something new in the art of war. He was planning a mounted invasion with the speed and mobility of horsemen unencumbered by heavy trains and lines of communication tying them to a fixed base. Such a force was given the power to fight its way wherever it listed. It was ably led at every level. It was the culmination of Thomas' vision of a complete, trained and self-sufficient army. In the Northern forces the cavalry had been the neglected arm of the service. Cavalry now was all that Thomas had left as a combat force. He aimed to restore it to its historic role, to prevent its dispersion and consequent wastage, to do the thing that Sherman insisted could only be done with infantry. As late as February 13 Halleck tried to wreck this plan but Thomas fought steadily for his convictions. Halleck was able to cripple Thomas' massive raid but he could not stop it.

Thomas and Forrest had evolved a radical switch from the European concept of cavalry tactics. It was the solution Stonewall Jackson had been seeking—the mounted infantryman who could cope with the increased range and fire rate of the new small arms which nullified the cavalry's shock tactics. In addition, this cavalry force could scout, screen and pursue. Through the imaginations of Forrest and Thomas, the cavalry arm became as potent tactically as it had been strategically. Neither had any feel for the swash-buckling romantic and under their tutelage this characteristic of the mounted force was sloughed off.

The exact division of authority between Grant, Thomas and Wilson was never definitely made. Sherman had ordered the capture of Selma and Montgomery. Grant ordered a diversionary strike with 5,000 horsemen against these same points. Wilson felt he could take both places without reference to Canby if Grant's dispersion orders could be nullified. Thomas listened to Wilson's plans, looked at his command and ordered the strike. Wilson later intimated that Grant approved this change. Thomas apparently ordered the movement without reference to Grant and gave Wilson authority to decide tactics and to choose minor objectives.[3] He was using Sherman's three-month-old order as his authority for overriding Grant's dispersion order. No dispatches in the official records show that Thomas ever advised Grant that Wilson was moving with more than 10,000 troopers to take Selma and Montgomery.

Thomas got off both of his cavalry strikes as soon as the roads dried. Stoneman rode out of Knoxville on March 20 with a division of cavalry and one of infantry in support. In reserve was the Fourth Corps and additional forces were earmarked for him at Chattanooga. His route had been chosen in collaboration with Thomas. Sherman was making his concentration with Schofield at Goldsborough, North Carolina. He had just missed his fourth chance to capture Joe Johnston's army and was apologetic over his shortcoming. Stoneman's principal objective was to smash the Chattanooga-Lynchburg railway as close to Lynchburg as possible in order to prevent Lee from slipping past Grant into East Tennessee. In cooperation with this move Sheridan was to strike at

Lynchburg from the east. Stoneman's contingent objective was Danville, Virginia, which would cut the railway line that connected the armies of Lee and Johnston.

Sheridan failed in his part of the assignment but on April 4 Major Wagner led 250 men of the Fifteenth Pennsylvania Cavalry through Salem, Virginia, toward Lynchburg in accordance with Thomas' specific order of March 26.[4] At the same time Thomas held Stanley on the alert at Bull's Gap for Lee's possible move into the mountains. On April 7 Thomas advised Stanton that he was pushing a strong force along Lee's retreat route.

It was on April 5 that Lee, finding his route blocked from Amelia Court House to Danville, turned westward toward Lynchburg. His traverse of the arc of a circle while Grant pursued along the chord lost him his original advantage in time and distance. He ordered a night march to Lynchburg in a desperate effort to shake off Grant's throttling grip. At this critical juncture word came to him that the Federals were advancing eastward along the railway toward that city.[5] Lee was then between Farmville and Appomattox. By less than fifty miles Thomas missed the culmination of his East Tennessee Plan.

Stoneman now directed his attention toward his second objective. This was the railway between Danville, Virginia, and Salisbury, North Carolina. While Palmer's brigade wrecked the railroad northward from Salisbury, Stoneman threw the bulk of his cavalry at that city. At daybreak on April 12 Stoneman's advance came upon the enemy pickets. A few hours later the city was theirs. Late that afternoon Palmer and his hard-riding Pennsylvania troopers entered the town and reported that the railway between Salisbury and Danville had been cut in four places. He was at once sent off to cut the same railway between Salisbury and Charlotte. It was at Salisbury also that Wagner rejoined from his Lynchburg raid.

Meanwhile, on April 5, as Lee was heading toward Lynchburg, Grant telegraphed Sherman, who was then at Goldsborough, ". . . Let us see if we cannot finish the job with Lee's and Johnston's armies. Whether it will be better for you to strike for Greensborough or nearer to Danville, you will be better able to judge when you receive this. Rebel armies are now the only strategic points to strike at." On April 10 Sherman promised again, as he had a year previously, to follow Johnston wherever he might go and he started his army toward Raleigh. It is difficult to see why Grant believed that Sherman was prompt and Thomas was slow in carrying out his orders.

Johnston was forced west out of Raleigh and on the thirteenth

Sherman entered that city. Sherman's cavalry was twenty-five miles farther west at Durham's Station following Johnston's retreat route, the Raleigh-Greensborough railway. That night Sherman ordered them to prevent Johnston's retreat either through Salisbury or Charlotte. This had already been done. The flicker of Northern steel along the western horizon warned Johnston that his end had come. Some hundred miles west of Sherman's advance, Thomas' cavalry division under Stoneman was standing in formation at the heads of the horses awaiting the bugle call to mount. Johnston, trapped between Stoneman and Sherman, asked for an armistice.[6]

At almost the same time that Stoneman had ridden out of Knoxville to play a minor part in the surrenders of Lee and Johnston, Wilson, with three cavalry divisions commanded by Emory Upton, Eli Long and Edward M. McCook,[7] had ridden south from the Tennessee River. His preparations were made on the basis of a sixty-day campaign. To cross the 120 miles of country destitute of food and forage it was necessary to disperse and move fast. On March 30 the three divisions were concentrated at Elyton (now Birmingham). Haversacks were replenished, the loads of the pack train were built up to capacity, and the command started a fast march for Montevallo on the Selma-Talladega railway. The wagon train was left to follow as best it could. News had come in that Chalmers with part of Forrest's command was moving on Tuscaloosa from the west. Not knowing what that meant, Wilson ordered Croxton to move his brigade toward Tuscaloosa from the east. He would cover Wilson's train, turn back Chalmers and threaten destruction to the Rebel military stores and facilities in that city. As a dividend, Wilson hoped Croxton might learn something definite about Forrest's plans. Croxton's was a ride of more than 100 miles along Wilson's exposed western flank and a challenge thrown squarely into Forrest's teeth. Croxton was to rejoin the main force at Selma.

At 4:00 P.M. on March 30 Croxton rode out of Elyton with 65 officers and 1,500 men.[8] Near the little town of Trion they ran into the rear of Forrest's 5,000 men and sent quadruple messages to Wilson detailing Forrest's strength and destination. Next they captured the city of Tuscaloosa, destroyed its military potential and headed south to break the railway at Demopolis. When he heard that Wilson had taken Selma and broken the railway himself, Croxton turned north, threaded his way past a force twice the size of his own and swung a tremendous loop through parts of two states to rejoin the Cavalry Corps at Macon, Georgia, having outridden most of the couriers whom he had sent to Wilson with news of his whereabouts. In thirty days he had marched

653 miles, swum four rivers, fought four times, taken 172 casualties and nearly 300 prisoners. This was the march of Croxton's "lost brigade." His division commander called it "one of the most extraordinary marches on record."

There were other famous cavalry raids into enemy territory. Stuart raided Chambersburg in four days and traveled a little more than 100 miles before returning to the safety of Lee's lines. Morgan rode nearly 500 miles in seventeen days before losing his command and his reputation in the brown waters of the Ohio. Grierson helped advance Grant's plans at Vicksburg by raiding 600 miles from Tennessee to Baton Rouge. He avoided the return trip, which is the riskiest part of such an expedition.

After detaching Croxton at Elyton, Wilson moved his main force southward toward Montevallo. Within three days he knew that Forrest proposed to stop him. On April 1 Upton was told to push the thickening resistance southward and Long's division moved with him on a nearly parallel road. At the junction of these roads Forrest had disposed his troops. His left rested on a high, wooded ridge where four guns were positioned to sweep the Randolph road on which was Long's advance regiment, the Seventy-second Indiana. Forrest's eastern flank was protected by Mulberry Creek and blocked the Maplesville road, which Upton was using. Two guns were zeroed in on this highway. Forrest had 5,000 men in line.[9] Part of them were protected by pine slashings and rail barricades.

Long was the first to come under fire. He doubled his advance force, dismounted it and deployed it to the left of the road. Under this pressure Forrest's first line began to fall back. Four companies of the Seventeenth Indiana, massed for a mounted charge, were turned loose when the line began to sag. They overran the skirmishers, sabering their heads as they went by. They struck Forrest's main line about a mile from where the charge had started, broke through, and with bugles singing and guidons snapping, rode over the four guns. The fire from Forrest's artillery support was too heavy for the horsemen and they veered off to the left and cut their way out. Captain Taylor with sixteen men, leading the advance, did not hear the retreat order, took his men into the heart of the Rebel defenses and engaged in a running fight with Forrest and his escort company. The bass rumble of pounding hooves counterpointed the falsetto rattle of revolver fire. At the head of the Yankee column sabers flashed through the smoke. Taylor chose Forrest for his own opponent and wounded him with a saber slash before Forrest killed him with his pistol. "If that boy had known enough to give me the point of his saber, instead of the edge," Forrest later told Wilson, "I should not have been here to tell you about it." Six of the sixteen troopers died with Taylor, five more were wounded, and the other five were taken prisoner.

Camp that night was nineteen miles from Selma. This was a fortified city of 15,000 persons, protected on the south by the Alabama River and on the other three sides by the concentric arcs of stockaded and bastioned works. Natural defenses commanded by Forrest limited the approaches to these works to two roads. On April 2 Long's division made the main attack down one of these roads, supported by Upton on the other. Long was wounded in the fighting and Minty [10] took the division command. An enemy raid on the pack train and horseholders failed to divert the main attack. The main and diversionary attacks, made dismounted, were stalled temporarily about sunset, but when they picked up momentum again Winslow [11] brought the Fourth Regiment of Iowa Cavalry down the Range Line road in column of fours at a full gallop. It was one of the last boot-to-boot charges of the war. The weight of this attack in the afterglow broke the defense line and carried the Iowans into the city, where they fought by squadrons in the streets.

Wilson regarded the capture of Selma as the most remarkable achievement in the history of modern cavalry and indicative of the new power of that arm of the service. To storm and take in a few hours a fortified city defended by a man like Forrest would have been, he stated, a proud accomplishment for infantry supported by artillery.

Wilson's route from Selma was east along the south bank of the Alabama River toward Montgomery, the third of his specified objectives. La Grange's [12] brigade of McCook's division was given the advance. The road was heavy with mud and several of the bridges had been destroyed. One swamp more than a mile long had to be corduroyed. Montgomery, a city of 12,000, surrendered without a struggle. Early on the morning of April 12 the Fourth Regiment of Kentucky Cavalry planted its regimental standard in front of the capitol of Alabama where the government of the Confederacy had been organized four years before. The buglers of one of Upton's brigades played the regiments through the city. The next forty-eight hours were spent in destroying Montgomery's military facilities.

Wilson now exercised the discretion Thomas had given him and decided to strike eastward instead of southward toward Mobile. His basic idea was the same as Thomas', namely, to get his corps into action against Lee. His next natural obstacle was the Chattahoochee River some eight miles to the east. He needed bridges to make the crossing. The ones he picked were at Columbus and West Point, Georgia. These points were some thirty-five miles apart and Wilson had to disperse his force to reach them, a tactic which had nullified the success of many a raid. La Grange and Upton were picked for the duty and each was successful—La Grange in the teeth of a blockhouse and defending artillery, and Upton by means of a night attack that so confused the defenders they mistakenly allowed a United States mounted regiment to pass through the infantry lines and slash the gun crews from their positions.

On the afternoon of April 17 Wilson ordered Minty's division toward Macon, Georgia, with a detachment sent forward that night to seize the Double Bridges over the Flint River in the direction of Thomaston. The Double Bridges were actually two bridges separated by an island. Minty picked the Fourth Michigan and the Third Ohio, put them both under the command of Lieutenant Colonel Pritchard [13] and told him to gain the Double Bridges by daybreak and take them intact. Pritchard moved out at dusk with light saddles, the files ducking the low-hanging boughs over the narrow, dirt road. There were three housekeeping halts before daylight. Four miles from their objective there was a rattle of carbine fire and a running fight all the way to the Flint River. Pritchard's bugler sounded the charge. His advance surged onto the bridge with their sabers swinging while the bridge guards ducked and ran. A favorite trick of bridge defense was to take up some of the planking, making it rough on the front ranks of a cavalry column. Despite this hazard Pritchard kept his men at a headlong gait until the far bank was reached. He deployed his two regiments to hold off any counter-attack and waited for the rest of the division to come up.

On April 20 the Seventeenth Indiana Mounted Infantry was performing the duties of Minty's advance on the march to Macon. Thirteen miles from that city they were met by a flag of truce and learned that an armistice had been agreed to between Sherman and Johnston. It was 6:00 P.M. when Wilson received the news. His embarrassment was acute. Nominally he was under Sherman's command although Thomas had ordered his operations and was responsible for them. The only way in which Wilson could communicate with Sherman or Thomas was by using the Rebel telegraph lines. To feed 17,000 men and their 3,000 prisoners and 22,000 animals during an extended halt in Macon would devastate the entire country in its vicinity. Wilson put the problem in Thomas' lap.

Thomas received no official notification of the existence of an armistice although he received the unofficial news almost simultaneously from Stoneman and Wilson. Whether his troops were now to be bound by an armistice made several hundred miles from where they were operating and of which they were advised through the enemy was the question Thomas had to answer. Before he could come to any conclusion he received a dispatch from Stanton dated April 27 which informed him that the armistice had been repudiated; that he was to resume hostilities; that he was to direct his officers to pay no attention to orders from anyone except Thomas or Grant; and that he was to spare no exertion to capture Jefferson Davis, who was trying to make his escape southward from Greensborough, North Carolina, with from six to thirteen million dollars of specie. Thomas' orders went out without delay to Stoneman and to Wilson. To free Wilson for Davis' capture, Thomas requested Canby to occupy Selma and Montgomery and alerted the navy to the fact that Davis would attempt to cross the Mississippi if he could elude Thomas' cavalry patrols.

It was a tremendous area for which Thomas was now responsible and Stanton's irascible order restored to him the combat control of it that Grant was gradually placing in other hands. Its eastern boundary reached from the Ohio-West Virginia-Kentucky corner through Abingdon, Virginia, Asheville, North Carolina, Augusta, Georgia and on to the Atlantic coast. Its western boundary approximated the line from the mouth of the Ohio River southeastward through Montgomery, Alabama, and Tallahassee, Florida, to the Gulf coast. He did not have the administrative control of this entire area but the troops under his command were the controlling power within its boundaries. It embraced parts or all of eight of the eleven states in revolt. It was the largest seceded area under the military control of an army commander. The factors that won it for him were Stanton's order and his own powerful cavalry teams which now were proving the truth of Thomas' four-year-old contention. His luck had turned just about as suddenly and completely as it had at Chickamauga, Chattanooga and Nashville.

Thomas' military career, however, lacked the capstone of a major surrender. Grant took Lee. Sherman failed in his attempt to take all the rest of the Rebel forces east of the Mississippi and compromised by taking Johnston. Later Canby would take the rest, including Forrest. Thomas tried to get Forrest's surrender but failed. There still remained Jefferson Davis and the handful of his advisers who constituted Rebeldom's civil government with the specie of the Confederate treasury. It was a capture upon which the attention of the North was focused.

Davis had slipped by Grant under the cover of Lee's fading brigades. In the confusion attending Sherman's attempt at a political truce, Davis passed through North Carolina along the front of Sherman's army. Thomas flung his net over four states. Its meshes were doubly strong at points where there was a strain to be taken. Stoneman was the first to pick up the trail. The three brigades of his cavalry division were on the western slopes of the Great Smoky Mountains when the leash was slipped for the pursuit of Davis.

The field command of this cavalry went to William J. Palmer. In twenty days he blocked Davis from the Mississippi, separated him from his armed escort, picked up the Confederate specie and drove Davis southward through Georgia.

Another mesh in Thomas' net was a detail of twenty men from the First Regiment of Ohio Cavalry under the command of Lieutenant Joseph A. O. Yeoman. Yeoman was bold, quick, resourceful, well educated and a good disciplinarian. He had been mentioned several times in dispatches and Wilson, recommending him for promotion, wrote that there was no more gallant officer in the Northern armies. His orders were to kidnap Davis. He disguised his men and himself as Rebel soldiers and actually spent several days as part of one of the units in Davis' escort. When Palmer separated Davis from his cavalry escort, Yeoman lost his chance to bag the famous fugitive.

Wilson picked up the chase where Stoneman left off. His patrols stretched from the Etowah River in northwestern Georgia to the Gulf coast south of Tallahassee, Florida, an airline distance of some 340 miles. Its midrib lay along the Ocmulgee River. Croxton was responsible for part of this line. He deduced that Davis would move south between Macon and Savannah and try to get through the naval blockade somewhere off the Florida coast. Wilson instructed Croxton to send a battalion toward Savannah to break up such an attempt. Croxton ordered his best unit under Lieutenant Colonel Henry Harnden to move rapidly toward Dublin on the Oconee River and from there to push on to Savannah unless he got some trace of Davis. In that case he was to pursue and capture him. This was the third mesh in Thomas' net. It was the end of the chain of command that stretched from Washington to Nashville to Atlanta to Macon. The 150 men who did the work and took the risk—always dirty, generally tired, often wet, frequently hungry—were carried on the rolls as the First Regiment of Wisconsin Cavalry.

Harnden followed his quarry to Abbeville, Georgia. At this point he was six or eight hours behind the fugitive, who was heading for

Irwinville. At Abbeville he met Pritchard and his regiment of the Fourth Michigan Cavalry. Pritchard's orders were to guard the crossings of the Ocmulgee River between Hawkinsville and Spalding. If he picked up Davis' trail he was to pursue and either capture him or kill him. Here were two of Thomas' young tigers with firm orders that drove them into a clash of authority and with no senior officer near enough to referee the conflict. If Pritchard atempted to pull his forty-one day seniority on Harnden, that officer could have replied that his orders came from Croxton and that only Croxton, or his superior, could change them.

The officers parted without any plan of cooperative action. Harnden rode south on Davis' escape route. Pritchard led his column southeast-ward and early the next morning came onto Davis' camp.

In a surprise attack just as the eastern sky began to lighten, Pritchard captured Jefferson Davis and ruptured the Confederacy's political cohesiveness. In the darkness the Michigan and Wisconsin troopers fired into each other adding six more casualties to the Northern war toll. Once again Thomas had won an inter-army competition.

When the news of Lee's surrender on April 9 was received, Thomas planned a celebration throughout his command. He timed it to coincide with the raising of the old flag over Fort Sumter. It was to begin with a grand review of all the troops at Nashville. The garrison troops were forming for the ceremonies. Various commands were moving into position. Bands were playing. Thomas and his staff were walking their horses toward the reviewing station. The head of the artillery column was just turning into College Street when a horseman appeared galloping toward it. He was Brannan with the news of Lincoln's death. As the news spread, the review broke up. Flags dropped to half-staff. The 200-gun ceremonial salute was now fired as minute guns until sundown ended the Miserere. Thomas' Nashville garrison accepted the news of Lincoln's death as casually as that of some nameless skirmish. It was only in retrospect that the assassination began to assume a significance entirely lacking at the time to the front-line soldier in Tennessee.

On May 9 Thomas put on one of his rare martial shows. It was a farewell review of the Fourth Army Corps, the only unit left to him of the superb Army of the Cumberland. The morning was bright and cool. Thomas rode along the front of the troops. Stanley, the corps commander, who had recovered from a wound taken at Franklin, rode with him, the staffs of both trailing behind. As Thomas passed along the front of the massed battalions the men cheered. When the inspection was over and Thomas was ready for the review they changed direction by the right flank and marched past at quick time, flags dipping in salute. Stanley mustered 19,000 men. It took them two hours to pass. There was no mistake or hitch and Thomas was pleased. After the review a lunch was served with no scarcity of sandwiches and beer.

The Fourth Corps was composed of fighting regiments. It moved over the ground where it had entered upon the struggle that became its crowning triumph. Gordon Granger had been its first commander with Palmer, Sheridan and Wood leading its divisions. Howard had succeeded Granger. Stanley, Newton and Wood were his division commanders. Stanley succeeded Howard in front of Atlanta with Kimball, Wagner and Wood leading the divisions. Wood temporarily took the command for Stanley after the Battle of Franklin and the divisions were commanded by Kimball, Elliott and Samuel Beatty.

Stanley led the march past. He was a difficult man to get along with, as Sherman, Dana, Schofield, Granger, Garfield and scores of others could testify. He had clashed with Thomas over the organization of Wilder's brigade but he liked the way Thomas fought his guns close up to the infantry and he promised to get him some bayonets for them. Then came Nathan Kimball at the head of the First Division. Thomas remembered gratefully how he had held Newton's reeling flank at Peach Tree Creek in those fateful minutes before Hooker came up. His leading regiment was the Twenty-first Illinois. Grant had been its first colonel. Near the rear of Kimball's division marched the Eighty-fourth Illinois. There were thirteen streamers on its colors. One-eighth of its total strength had been killed in action.

Next came Elliott's division with Emerson Opdycke leading its famous First Brigade. Nineteen months before, Steedman had led it against the fire-tipped crest of Snodgrass Ridge. Nearly every regiment in it had a notable record. The Thirty-sixth Illinois had captured ten Rebel flags at the breach in the barricades at Franklin. The Forty-fourth Illinois was one of the first to top Missionary Ridge. The Seventy-third Illinois had fought in twenty-two engagements. Ferdinand Van Derveer rode at the head of Elliott's Second Brigade. As he took his salute Thomas could probably taste again the choking dust that rose from the corn stubble of Kelly's field. Midway in his brigade marched the Fortieth Indiana, which had led one of the assault columns up Little Kennesaw's deadly slope squinting into the blaze of Georgia's mid-summer sun. The survivors could still see, every time they closed their eyes, the yellow spot ringed with green that blinded them that morning to the hazard toward which they moved.

Harker's renowned brigade followed. From the cedar thickets at

Stones River to the bottomless roads of Hood's pursuit they had gathered laurels from every field. Whoever their commander, they clung proudly to the name of the man who made them great.

Thomas J. Wood led the Third Division. His scholarly appearance was belied by the dare in his eye. He was a skillful, deadly combat soldier and his command took on these qualities. But he was ruled by his emotions. He buttressed Crittenden in his corps command for half the length of the war because he liked him. He destroyed Rosecrans in half an hour when a fit of anger was on him. Heading his command marched the cocky, capable veterans of Willich's brigade. There was the celebrated Illinois Railroad Regiment, whose heaviest casualties came at Pickett's mills when Schofield failed to cover their flank; the Forty-ninth Ohio, which had sustained the greatest battle losses of any of the 200 regiments enlisted from that state; and the Forty-first Ohio, which, dog-tired from a forced march, went on the field at Shiloh behind Bull Nelson to stiffen Grant's wavering lines. Battery G of the First Ohio Light Artillery jingled by and Alexander Marshall gave the salute as Thomas thought back to Stones River and Negley's gunner saving his pieces with the prolonges.

The review was over. The official good-bye to the Army of the Cumberland had been passed and acknowledged.

A man of Thomas' imagination must have been conscious of another army that marched that sunny morning. They were uncounted. Many of their graves were unmarked. Many had died in nameless skirmishes under circumstances already forgotten. They marched unarmed in solid ranks with muted footfalls and without preferential trappings—the dead of the Second Minnesota along the rain-soaked fence row at Mill Springs; the regulars who redeemed McCook's blunder at Stones River; the drowned bodies that washed ashore from the night crossing of the Tennessee before Chickamauga; the boyish Michigan gunner who died with his hand on the muzzle shouting at Forrest's troopers; the dusty infantryman beside the road in Georgia killed by the sun; the black bodies in front of Nashville that paid for a freedom already theirs. It was an army of many races that he reviewed, a prideful army that fought for a shining principle and meager reward.

These were the ranks that Thomas would never have filled if there had been any other way. These were the trailing ranks of an army that marched out of an unknown past. Through uncounted centuries they had died blindly in wars long forgotten for a vision they could barely see.

Thomas had completed his education in violence. He knew now

that Americans had little instinct for that formal violence that is called war but that their social energy exploded into the utmost violence under certain provocations. He was once infected by this frontier psychology, but the Comanche arrow pointed out its uselessness as a professional tool and he repudiated the unwarranted expense of attrition.

At Mill Springs, Mahan's cloistered fantasy was clothed with the reality of violence, weariness and fear and Thomas saw the significance of total, economic victory. He saw, too, that battle was only its beginning, not its end. Battle must culminate in pursuit to reach totality. Precedents without number would have permitted him to dodge this difficult tactic but he chose rather to retain his power of decision.

Perhaps the age-old dictum of a poet rang through Thomas' mind. "It is not strength but art that wins the prize and to be swift is less than to be wise." He had fashioned the Army of the Cumberland as the tool for energizing the plan which evolved through the great swinging campaigns of 1863 and the unfinished tactical masterpiece that ended at Atlanta. Sherman's misguided impetuosity broke up his hard-tested tool and Thomas faced his opportunity with its remnant. It was enough.

He refused to let Grant's powerful pressures dull his blade and almost single-handedly gave his countrymen one of the three clear gains to come out of the Civil War.[14] He brought to the torn states of the great midwest surcease from battle and a chance for the grass to green over raw graves.

His looming shadow perplexed and worried the North's other great general at City Point.

21

The Final Years

As the pursuit of Hood's broken forces frayed out along the banks of the Tennessee River, Thomas' mind turned to the problem of unifying the nation. He sent a dispatch from Pulaski on the evening of December 30, 1864, to Andrew Johnson suggesting immediate reorganization of the civil government of Tennessee. The reason he gave was a military one but his motive was political. This was probably the first invitation from a military commander to a military governor of a seceded state to re-establish civil procedures in conquered territory.[1] It was a suggestion that would curtail his own authority.

Thomas' authority at the close of the war extended over the largest area of Secessia under control of an army commander. It was a hodgepodge of indefinite boundaries and overlapping authority. He had at one time military but not administrative control over Kentucky. He had administrative but not military control over parts of the east bank of the Mississippi River. He had complete control over parts of North Carolina, Georgia, Florida, Alabama and Mississippi occupied by his forces but none could tell the boundaries of this domain. He had military control over all troops of the Military Division of the Mississippi not in Sherman's presence, but there was a question of how far Sherman's presence could be extended by staff officers, couriers and telegraph. Thomas had some influence, therefore, in getting more than half of the seceded states back into the ways of peace. His biggest

Reconstruction role, however, was confined to Kentucky and the seceded states of Tennessee, Georgia, Alabama and Mississippi.

Thomas was aware that Tennessee played a peculiar role among the seceded states. It was the last state to secede and the first to have its capital city reoccupied. The courses of the Cumberland, the Tennessee and the Mississippi, and the placement of fertile valleys between the barrier ranges of the Appalachians made it an invasion gateway to the South, and it suffered mightily in consequence. Four hundred engagements were fought within its boundaries. It was the only seceded state not mentioned in the Emancipation Proclamation; the only seceded state in which a considerable body of citizens remained continually loyal to the Union; the only one to escape carpetbag government and military Reconstruction; the only one in which the struggle for power was fought out between factions of its own citizens. A native son headed the Federal government while the Federal Congress refused to seat its senators and representatives.

These individualities brought rewards and penalties. Her voluntary political reorganization won her friends in the North. The strife between her own people caused a bitterness that may have been unequalled in United States history. It was with a full realization of the implications of these facts that Thomas worked out the politico-military problems that brought the first Rebel state into the Union and fixed the procedure for the rest to follow. Among the military commanders in the South, Thomas was pre-eminent in the work of reconstruction.

The form of civil reorganization that Thomas suggested was the ninth to be tried. It succeeded, resulting in the election of W. G. Brownlow as Governor and in the abolition of slavery. Brownlow was a self-educated carpenter, itinerant preacher and editor. A fearless and opinionated man, he stumped against nullification in Calhoun's home district. He favored slavery but opposed secession. He showed the Union flag at his Knoxville home long after it had disappeared from the city. He was tricked into an arrest by the Confederates and charged with treason but, being too hot to hold, was sent into the Union lines. When first elected Governor, he opposed the enfranchisement of the Negro but modified this stand by the time of his re-election.

Between the time of the reluctant departure of Andrew Johnson from Nashville to assume the duties of Vice-President of the United States and Brownlow's inauguration on April 5, 1865, there was an interregnum during which Thomas assumed the political control of the state.[2]

Tennessee, however, was not the only seceded state under his control. After Hood had been driven south of the Tennessee River, a committee of North Alabamians asked Thomas how they might return to the Union. Lincoln was President at this time and the method Thomas suggested was in accordance with Lincoln's theory that reconstruction was an executive function. Thomas made his suggestion on January 21, 1865. On April 13, the day before Johnson became President, Thomas restored the civil authority in those counties of Mississippi, Alabama, Georgia and North Carolina embraced within his military division.[3] He was among the first to make the fateful shift from a military dictatorship to self-government.

One of the worst trouble spots in Thomas' area was Kentucky. He considered Kentucky's political situation at one time more critical than that of Tennessee, Alabama or Georgia. The resentment of the Kentuckians sprang from the freeing of their Negroes and the way in which their protests had been handled by the Federal government. Thomas had the assistance of his friend John M. Palmer, who had been appointed the department commander after his row with Sherman, and he induced him to continue his Kentucky duties long after Palmer wanted to give them up. Kentuckians manifested a hostility toward every exercise of military force and instituted civil and criminal suits against their own elected officers. This set up a vicious circle which Thomas and Palmer contrived to break by personal influence, applied psychology and the common-sense application of force. Thomas relied mainly on the "soothing influence of money earned" to break down Kentucky's animosity.[4] When civil authority proved ineffective Thomas posted troops to afford the needed protection. In this he was given authority by the Washington government to act according to his own judgment. His judgment was apparently good because by October 14, 1865, the President was able to suspend martial law, which had been controlling the state for more than a year.

In Alabama, Georgia and Mississippi, Thomas' problems were different but before the end of the war he was moving to solve them in accordance with the Lincolnian plan. He did this by the use of two innovations. None of these states had a governor so Thomas proposed to act as a provisional governor until one could be appointed. Instead of building a civil government from the top down Thomas began to build it from the bottom up. So far as can be judged from the record these policies were his own. He worked from the self-evident assumption that the population within the state boundaries was not homogeneous in its loyalty or disloyalty. He proposed to rebuild the more loyal counties first and work from this foundation until the entire state was transferred from military rule to self-rule within Lincoln's limitations. According to Thomas' instructions the county officers thus resuming their authority were to be governed by the state laws under which they had operated at the outbreak of the war but with the changes entailed by Lincoln's specifications. At this point Thomas was forced to generalize. Four years of war had affected profoundly the application of the laws of 1861. Some of the inhabitants of even the most loyal county had been active in the Rebellion and were therefore barred from holding office or exercising their suffrage. A large segment of the population which had been slaves was now free and the Rebellion had wrecked the economy of the South. Thomas' instructions to the new county officers to enforce the old state laws "as far as may be found to be practicable" merely put the responsibility for political regeneration on their shoulders.

Orthodox politico-military administration might well have stopped there and ruled upon individual cases as they came up as a result of the natural administration of the civil law. But Thomas sought to identify the areas in which trouble was latent and head off as much of it as he could. The basic problems, political and economic, arose from the Negroes. The rebellious whites had accepted the fact of their freedom but the Negroes had no idea of what it meant. They quit work and gathered in large numbers in the vicinity of Thomas' garrisons, where they had to be fed, clothed and housed. Thomas' new civil governments attempted to solve this problem by forcing the Negroes to work and to assume the fundamental obligations of all human beings. Work statutes were implemented with penalties to enforce their obedience. It was not long before the whites began to see that although the Negroes had been freed from slavery, they could be exploited by peonage. Thomas met this problem by anticipating the Fourteenth Amendment.[5] He limited the sale of ammunition in an attempt to head off violence. He pressured the Freedman's Bureau to make the Negro discharge his responsibilities to himself, his family and his community, and to secure to him the rights of life, liberty and property.

Thomas did what he could to free the movement of individuals so that trade could be restored and a basis laid for collecting taxes. One month after he had suggested the restoration of civil authority in Tennessee he gave some of the Mississippians the authority to operate the railways in their county for their private interests and convenience. This was nearly three months before Lee's surrender and during the time Grant was breaking up Thomas' army. He was getting a running start in his ambition to get his wards among the first to return to their old allegiance. To accomplish this he assumed the authority of governor of the states of Georgia, Alabama and Mississippi. He suggested the organization of a government that was in accordance with neither Lincoln's 10 per cent plan nor the vetoed Wade-Davis Congressional plan. He anticipated by four and a half months Johnson's removal of the restrictions on commerce.[6]

For Thomas these were unprecedented assumptions of power. He asked permission of Stanton to send Steedman to Washington to place before the Administration the details of what he was doing and why. Stanton invited Thomas to come personally instead of sending Steedman and gave as his reason, "I want to see and know personally so good and great a soldier that has served his country so well." This was Thomas' chance to enlist powerful support in the struggle to save his personal prestige from Grant's assaults but Thomas refused it. Before the Steedman mission was settled Thomas went a step further and hinted that it might solve the problem to permit the people of north Georgia to elect their own military governor. The whole matter was referred to the cabinet and for more than twenty-four hours it was debated in Washington. Thomas was granted the permission he asked and Steedman was ordered to make the trip.

In the late spring of 1865 Thomas received unofficial advice from Washington that orders were being drafted for a redistribution of military commands in which, in spite of his rank, he was being relegated to a subordinate role. For the first time in his career he asked for political help. Brigadier General John F. Miller was commanding Thomas' Nashville garrison and Thomas sent for him. He was intimately acquainted with Andrew Johnson. Thomas instructed him to take the first train to Washington with a message that Thomas demanded a command suitable to his rank or he wanted no command at all. Miller reached Washington before Johnson had moved into the White House and was promptly received by the President in his temporary offices in the treasury building. Johnson listened, considered, then traced on a map the outline of the area comprising the states of Kentucky, Tennessee, Georgia, Alabama and Mississippi. "You know of my appreciation of General Thomas," he said. "There is his military division." And pointing to Nashville he concluded, "There are his headquarters."

There followed a scramble on the part of Grant and his friends to find suitable commands for Sherman and Sheridan, whose preferment had been reduced to insignificance by the President's pencil. The Virginian, whose professional career had been nourished for a quarter of a century by the most powerful political clique in the nation, had passed through the period of his political ostracism.

It is doubtful if any citizen of the United States was better qualified by experience for the job of reconstruction than Johnson. He could apply force brutally but, when able to control his temper, he also practiced its delicate application. He had a complete understanding of the impulses of the Southern Unionists suddenly released from the pressure of the bayonet. He knew how to tinker and adjust the political machines of state and local government to keep their operation steady and normal. He was ready to get on with the business of the application of his plan for readmitting the seceded states and the more he thought about it the more his mind came back to Tennessee. The only assurance for the future that Johnson could give to the little group that watched him take his oath of office was to refer them to the past. When he thought of the past perhaps he thought of Thomas—the early misunderstandings of Camp Dick Robinson and Camp Wildcat that grew into mutual confidence as the burdens of combat and administration grew heavier. Both men were basically kind and sympathetic yet both hid these feelings so successfully that one seemed cold and colorless and the other seemed hard and inflexible. Both had physical and moral courage and unlimited faith in the abilities of their fellow citizens. Johnson lacked tact and dignity. Thomas had both and understood the reason for Johnson's shortcomings. He also understood Johnson's plans for reconstructing the conquered areas. Johnson wanted him in Washington and sent him an invitation to come East. Less than three weeks before, Thomas had brushed off a similar invitation from Stanton. This time he accepted.

This was Thomas' first visit to the Capital since the late summer of 1861. Eckert was sent to the depot to meet him and bring him to the War Department in Stanton's private carriage. His baggage was sent to Stanton's home, where he had been invited to stay. Stanton congratulated Thomas on his war record and reassured him of his confidence in him. To this Thomas bluntly replied that he had not been treated as though the Secretary had confidence in him. Stanton repeated his declaration. Thomas receded from his stand and accepted the Secretary's assertion. "Nevertheless," he said, "I have not been treated by the authorities as though they had confidence in me."

There were other meetings with high Washington officials too, not all of them on this same visit, but they indicated a widespread interest in the man. Thomas, with his wife and her sister, called on Secretary

Bates, who thought him a plain, quiet man, exceptionally reticent. Secretary Welles met him in the President's office, was struck by his fine, soldierly appearance and gained the impression that he had no superior in the service—intellectually, as a civilian or as a military man. He took occasion to record that Thomas was not a carpet officer to dance attendance at Washington.

Some of Thomas' friends—Garfield probably was one of them— persuaded him with difficulty to permit them to present him to the House of Representatives. He was escorted to the Speaker's stand. The members and the spectators stood in his honor and greeted him with affectionate enthusiasm. Schuyler Colfax, who stood beside him during the brief ceremonies, noticed that Thomas' hand "trembled like an aspen leaf." Thomas was on the stand when the armies of Meade and Sherman were reviewed by the President. When the bronzed veterans of his favorite Fourteenth Corps swung by, this silent man was heard to say through a mist of tears, "They made me."

To the curious who met him casually, Thomas was not a pleasant person. His cold, quiet manner and extreme reticence made conversation awkward. Deep, thoughtful eyes, heavy brows and a firm chin made the stranger feel that he was looking into the mouth of a cannon and the cannon said nothing. But when a friend who had broken through this reserve came along, Thomas' whole attitude changed. The shyness that had seemed repelling now became a "girlish modesty." Any reference to his merits or successes brought blushes and embarrassment and he sought to minimize his personal contributions by emphasizing those of others.

There is no record of what Thomas and the President discussed at this series of meetings. There is no indication that any of Thomas' assumptions of power were frowned upon. What evidence there is points the other way. Welles noted that the President warmed up and became animated when he spoke of Thomas. Johnson thought that Thomas could make important contributions to the great work of getting the seceded states under a civil government. He told Thomas that the whole South had confidence in him. Thomas disagreed with this appraisal.[7]

One known result of Thomas' visit was that the command marked out for him as a result of his bitter protest, with the addition of Florida, was formalized by military orders. This was a notable expression of Presidential faith. Thomas now commanded a tremendous area stretching from the Ohio River to the Atlantic Ocean and the Gulf of Mexico.

In it was the critical border state of Kentucky and nearly half the states lately in rebellion. Within this vast territory were military, social, political and economic problems of every description.

When Thomas received the general order that fixed his new command, Mississippi was not included. He queried Stanton and the state was added by the direction of the President. In another change, both Florida and Mississippi were transferred from Thomas' command to that of Sheridan. A few months later Mississippi was restored to Thomas' control.

As proconsul of this agrarian empire Thomas came into contact with many of his former enemies and their families. He enforced the Presidential order refusing to permit Raphael Semmes to serve as a probate judge on the ground that he was an unpardoned Rebel. When the friends of Brigadier General Roger W. Hanson, who had been killed at Stones River, wanted to disinter his remains and give them a military funeral, Thomas forbade all military display, the wearing of the Rebel uniform or side arms, the carrying of the Rebel flag or marching by any military organization. When the self-styled Bishop of Alabama insisted on continuing the Rebellion under the symbolism of the church, Thomas suspended him from his professional duties. When some indiscreet young Rebels of Rome, Georgia, hoisted the Rebel flag, Thomas deported them to an Atlanta jail only to release them on the recognizance of the mayor of Rome and some of its leading citizens. The women of Alabama were as recalcitrant as the churchman and the juveniles but Thomas was baffled for a remedy.

Not long after the end of the war Thomas and John B. Hood were stopping at a Louisville hotel at the same time. Through an intermediary Hood asked for a meeting to which Thomas gladly assented. Thomas must have heard the clatter of Hood's crutches along the hotel corridor and had his door open before Hood could knock. He threw his arm around Hood's shoulders and helped him to a seat. "Thomas is a grand man," Hood said after the meeting. "He should have remained with us, where he would have been appreciated and loved." [8]

Not all Rebels were so treated. At Nashville Thomas and his wife occupied a rented house and, like their neighbors, sat on their porch on warm evenings. Next door was an unreconstructed Rebel who porch-sat for six months pointedly ignoring the Thomases. One evening this gentleman approached with the obvious intention of shaking hands, but Thomas waved him off. "Too late, Sir, too late; you have sinned away your day of grace."

Thomas was generally good for a touch by a private soldier of either army. A Confederate soldier from Southampton County who had known Thomas before the war was stranded in Tennessee. He was hungry, ragged and dirty and he had some difficulty getting his name sent in. As soon as these defenses were breached Thomas received him immediately and supplied him with food, clothing and transportation to Virginia. An officer saw two of Thomas' ex-privates, poor and with their property seized under a landlord's attachment as a result of an invalid judgment, approach Thomas for a hearing. They were admitted without delay and Thomas listened to their story, became satisfied of its truthfulness and accompanied them to the dingy office of a justice of the peace. Instead of giving an order that would have interfered with the operations of the civil authorities, Thomas signed their surety bonds. This released their property and, as the men turned to go, Thomas said, "Now boys, don't get me in a scrape about this." [9]

Thomas went to great lengths to help out his Rebel classmate, Lieutenant General R. S. Ewell, one-time commander of Lee's famous Second Corps. Late in the spring of 1865 Thomas was ordered by Stanton to arrest Mrs. Ewell and send her to St. Louis. Thomas protested the order, pointing out that Mrs. Ewell had taken the amnesty oath and believed that she had a right to come to Nashville, manage her affairs and return to St. Louis. He recommended to the Secretary of War that she be permitted to carry out her plans. Stanton turned him down so Thomas sent the file to Mrs. Ewell. ". . . You will readily perceive," he wrote, "that it is made incumbent upon me to direct you to return to St. Louis at an early day. . . ." He sent one of his staff to accompany her and to protect her from inconvenience and annoyance on the way.

From his sisters in Southampton County, Thomas heard nothing. But his youthful friend John Tyler, Jr., whose daughter was postmistress at Jerusalem, kept him advised of what was happening to his family.

All eyes north and south were watching the moves of Tennessee in its blind struggle for recognition of its constitutional sovereignty. The application of military force to this end was Thomas' responsibility. How he applied it within the conflicting limitations laid down by Congress and by the President determined whether there would be bloodshed, civil commotion or a struggle between rivals for political power.

One of the big weaknesses in the new governments was that the loyalty screen eliminated the natural leaders. To some degree Tennessee escaped this penalty, for the natural leaders of the East Tennesseans were not barred from office. Four years of bayonet rule by the representatives of the central and western parts of the state, however, made them harsh and vindictive in their attitude toward Secessionists. The new Tennessee legislature was inexperienced and generally mediocre. The new Governor was too obstinate and vindictive for a politician and too much of a partisan to be a statesman. The ingredients for failure were yeasting in Tennessee. Thomas played a decisive role in preventing it.

There was no doubt of Brownlow's support by the Federal government. Lincoln wanted him, Andrew Johnson had approved him, Thomas backed him. There was some doubt as to Tennessee's actual status in the Union. A month after Brownlow's inauguration Thomas called it a loyal state.[10] Ten days later he got the matter straightened out. Tennessee had not been readmitted to the Union.

Thomas' overriding responsibility in Tennessee was to see that the Brownlow government was not overthrown. He had to parry attacks from within and without. At the same time, his troops were to keep their hands off the administration of the civil government. These general principles were universally understood. His difficulties arose in applying force within these generalities. During the first few months of the life of the new government, latent conflicts threatened to break out as the result of a score of antagonisms. East Tennessee threatened to secede. Returned Confederate soldiers needed food and clothing and protection from the sheriff's posses. The courts needed protection from the legislature. Political dissidents needed protection from those who controlled the state government. Unionists needed protection from their Rebel neighbors. Parts of the state needed protection from guerrillas. Negroes needed protection from the whites. The legislature needed force to enact its legislative program. In all these struggles the final arbitrament was Thomas' troops.

Each of these problems was trapped by pitfalls. What Thomas did not do was often as meaningful as what he did do. The situations were never static. As soon as a workable balance was achieved between two forces, an imbalance with a third would be revealed. Thomas' sagacity showed in the results. He had only one serious outbreak of violence in his command area.[11] In the finespun distinctions between politics and ethics Thomas frequently walked a hairline. But he never violated either principle enough to bring about second-guess attacks upon his decisions.

During the contest between Congress and the President there was intolerable political pressure upon military commanders. A good example of fencing to avoid responsibility by the ranking authorities took place in September 1867. Brownlow and W. Matthew Brown, the mayor of Nashville, were at loggerheads over a municipal election. Each claimed a legal basis for his position. If both went ahead with their plans there would be two elections held to fill the same office. The mayor's polling places would be protected by the city police, the governor's by the state militia. The commander of Thomas' Nashville garrison asked for instructions. Thomas recommended that his force be used to back the governor and asked Grant for his approval. Grant was then the head of the army and the Secretary of War.

Four days before the election Thomas had a reply. He was ordered to Nashville to preserve the peace, but his question was unanswered. Before he started out, another cipher telegram went winging eastward. It asked, "Shall I sustain the governor or the mayor?"

Two days before the election Thomas went to call on the governor, but Brownlow had gone to Knoxville leaving orders that would result in an armed clash if the mayor did not recede from his position. Thomas called on the mayor but he refused to recede. Thomas sent Grant another question. Was he to permit two elections to be held while using his troops to prevent violence? Meantime he ordered the garrisons from seven nearby points into Nashville.

In midafternoon of the twenty-sixth Thomas received a wire from Grant which read, "I neither instruct [you] to sustain the governor or the mayor but to prevent conflict." Thomas summarized the situation for his superior and concluded by pointing out that the use of his troops to prevent violence would be a decision against the state. "Your mission is to preserve peace and not to take sides in political differences," was Grant's prompt rejoinder. At 10:00 P.M. Thomas received the following cryptic disptach from Grant: "I will send you further instructions tomorrow. Nothing is clearer, however, than that the military cannot be made use [of] to defeat the executive of a state in enforcing the laws of a state."

Next morning, the day before the election, Thomas informed the mayor that he would sustain the governor in case of a collision. The opposition to Brownlow's rule collapsed and the discussion died out in a series of acrimonious letters aimed at Thomas by the losers.

As the election of Tennessee's Congressional delegation approached, the President feared that senators or representatives might be named who were not sympathetic to the Brownlow government. Thomas was ordered to keep all illegal voters from the polls, see that the election was conducted fairly, execute the law, and protect the ballot box. Thomas knew the cynical interpretation of these righteous words. He was to make sure that the right men were sent to Washington to speak for the state of Tennessee.

Thomas had learned in Texas that the threat of force was often as potent as its use and left fewer scars. He asked the President for authority to publicize his telegram authorizing the use of force. He ordered troops into the election precincts of twenty-six of Tennessee's counties to protect the legal voters. This was his favorite approach. It stopped trouble before it started. It prevented outbreaks of violence. It hid the iron hand. Most important, it worked. Tennessee elected the right men without violence. The President appreciated a man who could work a policy of expediency and keep out of trouble. When, at another time, the Mississippi legislature attempted to disarm the Negroes, Thomas asked for instructions and Stanton informed him that the President placed full reliance upon his judgment as to the proper action for the military authorities to take.[12]

It was inevitable that attempts would be made to discredit Thomas' administration with the President. Negro troops made up a part of Thomas' police force. Their use was a continual irritant to the Southerners. Word went back to Washington that these troops were out of hand in East Tennessee, that a black uprising was imminent and that outrages were being perpetrated upon the citizenry. Johnson was irritated by a report that his home in Greenville had been turned into a Negro whorehouse. Thomas denied all of these charges and quieted the President's apprehensions. He also took the opportunity to point out to the Commander-in-Chief that the use of Negroes to replace the discharged white troops put additional strains upon the military forces.

Officially, Thomas' role was limited to matters of a politico-military nature, but he could see that successful reconstruction was primarily a matter of bread. The Negroes were trying to live without working while the farms and plantations lacked a labor supply. Returning Confederate soldiers were destitute. The families of the killed and wounded needed help. Having undertaken to care for the ex-Rebels, Thomas could hardly turn down the appeals of the Unionists. The lack of seed, tools and livestock was widespread. Some needed food until their crops could be harvested. Thomas kept an eye on the Freedman's Bureau which looked after the Negroes, gave military help when it was needed and spurred it into greater activity when the situation demanded. But the economic problems of the whites—friend and foe—became part of his over-all responsibility for preventing violence. Thomas must have been desperate for a solution. At one time he suggested to the Union League Club of Philadelphia that they finance a group of Georgia Unionists with a $5,000 loan for food and seed. Eventually the people solved their own problems of production but Thomas could and did do something about those of distribution.

On May 22, 1865, he asked for permission to restore the East Tennessee and Virginia railway to its owners. It was a shrewd move. This was the common carrier for the long, fertile valley that linked Chattanooga with Lynchburg, Virginia. It was the supply line for the dominant political group in Tennessee. Thomas had already tested his idea in northern Mississippi and western Tennessee by loaning short lengths of the railway to the citizens. He had undoubtedly watched the experiment closely and knew what he was about when he recommended the move to Stanton. Seventy-seven days later his request was not only granted but was extended to cover all the railways in Tennessee. The plan for making the restoration was outlined. The roads were to be inventoried. The cost to the government of their expansion and improvement less their charges for the transportation of troops, supplies and mail would set the price to be paid to the United States for the return of the properties. The new directorates had to be purged of disloyal individuals and plans had to be worked out for liquidating the obligations to the Federal treasury. In October 1865 this order was broadened to include all eight railways in Thomas' military division.

Thomas was now faced with complex problems in accounting, law, psychology and administration. The loyalty of the directors was to be established to his satisfaction. Rolling stock, tools, supplies and other property had to be inventoried and separated to show which were originally owned by the railway and which were furnished by the War Department. Bonds had to be prepared setting forth the amounts to be paid to the United States, when, in what amounts, and how the unpaid balances would be secured. Statements of expenditures for repairing each road had to be itemized together with a statement of receipts for all income and the accounts payable by the government for public transportation. Thomas had to decide which buildings erected by the War Department along the rights of way were to be turned over and which were to be retained by the United States.

It took Thomas nearly nine months to set up the machinery for making this transfer. A committee of six men—three army officers and three railroad experts—was appointed to make the appraisals. McCallum was given the responsibility for making up the statements of receipts and expenditures. Thomas wrote the original bonds, which bound the directors personally for the obligations to the United States, but after protests to Stanton they were rewritten to delete this feature. To protect the government against future claims by the railways for use and occupancy, Thomas suggested that Congress pass a resolution denying such an obligation.

Stanton evidently felt that he could leave the problems of railway restoration safely in Thomas' hands. He and Thomas were in agreement on a general policy, but were opposed by Meigs and Sheridan. In approving Thomas' selection of appraisers Stanton wrote, "The department confides in your sound discretion in the executing of the order relating to the railways." Thomas performed the most important part of the job of returning the military railways to their owners. He had foreseen and prepared for this eventuality when the control and operation of the railways first came into the hands of the War Department.

In January 1867 Thomas was called to Washington to give a report of this stewardship to a committee of the House of Representatives. Stanton testified to the same committee, "I have great confidence in the officers whom I had at Nashville and in General Thomas, to whom the whole thing was committed; when General Thomas has recommended an extension I have always, I think, coincided with him; where he has not recommended an extension, I have declined to recommend it; General Thomas' recommendations will be regarded with a proper degree of deference . . . in reference to any facts contained in a report made by him." [13]

Appreciation of Thomas' services was not limited to the President of the United States and the Secretary of War. The state of Tennessee put its approval on the General's work in three ways. On June 22, 1865, Thomas was made a citizen of that state. He had lacked a state citizenship since Virginia seceded so the honor was not an empty one. His will was later probated there.[14] On September 2, 1865, Tennessee voted him a gold medal in commemoration of his services. The medal was presented a year later on the anniversary of the Battle of Nashville. On August 25, 1866, the state commissioned a painting of him which was hung in the library of the capitol building. Three years later, when the political complexion of the Tennessee legislature had changed, some members proposed to sell the portrait. Offers to buy it came from several sources, including Thomas and his brother Benjamin, but they were declined.

Late in 1865 the President's reconstruction plan seemed well along the road to adoption. Most of the conquered states had ratified the Thirteenth Amendment to the Constitution, set up loyal governments and elected senators and congressmen to represent them in Washington.

The President was interested in learning how the lately rebellious populace was reacting to this new state of affairs and he sent Grant, Thomas and Carl Schurz through the seceded area to find out. Thomas completed his trip by the middle of December and reported that the prevailing sentiment in his territory was a desire to restore the Rebel states to their old relations and functions. He did not minimize the unfriendliness of a large minority. Mississippi, he reported, had not ratified the Thirteenth Amendment. He had done what he could to ward off trouble there and recorded a hope that he had succeeded. The people of Alabama, he found, were either more practical or more loyal than the Mississippians and seemed to be in harmony with the Presidential policy. His report on Georgia was perfunctory. He had not been ordered to visit Milledgeville, where the legislature was meeting, and since the Georgians failed to invite him he did not go. He was under the impression that he was not personally acceptable to the new Georgia government.

Thomas' report hardly had time to get into the files before he was called to Washington to report to the joint committee on reconstruction. Congress had upset the President's reconstruction plan by refusing to seat any of the congressmen sent to Washington by the lately rebellious states and served notice upon the executive that they would write the terms upon which the conquered areas would be admitted to the Union. This committee was their instrument for perfecting the details of a Congressional plan. Grant's tour, which had been so brief as to seem indifferent, was limited to the Carolinas and Georgia. His conclusions agreed with Thomas'. Schurz spent three months on his trip, which included South Carolina, Georgia, Alabama, Mississippi and Louisiana. His findings, too, agreed with Thomas', but he went on to analyze the mental processes of the erstwhile Rebels and warned that acquiescence to loyalty was only skin deep.

Guarded questions from the committee brought cautious replies from Thomas. The legislators were probing for details of a mysterious organization, later to be known as the Ku Klux Klan. Early in 1866 in Pulaski, Tennessee, where Thomas had once stacked up his regiments while waiting for Hood to commit himself in the Nashville campaign, the society was born as a social organization of Tennessee juveniles. Its first meetings were held in a lonely, ruined house which the Negroes considered to be haunted. They translated the white, formless, anonymous figures of the Klansmen into ghosts of dead Confederates. The whites learned the secret of their fear by accident. There was a parade one day and one of the shirted marchers dismounted and mutely signaled a Negro spectator to hold his bridle reins. The Negro fled terrified.

In April 1867 the Klan was formally organized in Nashville under Thomas' nose and Forrest was reputedly called as its head. In his report for the year 1867–1868, Thomas named the organization, described its rise and progress and detailed its latent power.

Thomas' examination by members of the joint committee also brought out the fact that he was in substantial agreement with Schurz's idea about lip service to loyalty. He saw no real danger of open revolt but there was no doubt that there existed a smoldering desire to embarrass the government of the United States, to seek to saddle it with the Rebellion's war debt, and to take advantage of any foreign war to strike for the independence of the states lately in rebellion. He thought non-observance of the law and lack of protection for life and property had worsened rather than bettered and felt that the Southerners were bent upon demonstrating that the cause of liberty, justice, humanity and equality had suffered when the Rebellion was broken down. The ex-Confederates, he believed, were bent on hiding the crime of treason under a varnish of patriotism. He called this an amazing effrontery when it was considered that the magnanimity of the North refused to exact the usual penalties in life and property. Thomas also recorded his opinion that the state of Tennessee should be represented in the Federal Congress.

Thomas prophesied exactly the course of history. The South listened to their headstrong minority, sided with the President against Congress and brought down on their luckless heads the vindictive wrath of the Northern radicals. At the same time, these radicals admitted Tennessee into the Union.

Thomas made no contribution to this political inconsistency although the record indicates that he wanted to. Brownlow steered the state in the right direction and circumstances forced Andrew Johnson to accept what finally he had come to oppose. The Thirteenth Amendment gave the slaves freedom. Tennessee adopted it in earnest of their first attempt to regain their position in the Union. The Fourteenth Amendment made the slaves citizens. Congress insisted that this must be a prerequisite to seating the Southern congressmen. Andrew Johnson opposed it and the bulk of the seceded states, making their next greatest blunder after the firing on Sumter, followed him.

Brownlow asked the Tennessee legislature to accept the amendment. The senate complied but the house of representatives balked and refused a quorum. On July 14, 1866, the sergeant-at-arms of the Tennessee house of representatives asked Thomas for a detail of fifteen soldiers to arrest one of the recalcitrant representatives. Thomas' standing orders were to sustain, but not to assume, the functions of civil authority, except where the unsettled state of society required such assumption to preserve peace and quiet. It was this kind of an assumption that Thomas had been making for two years in an effort to stay within the meaning of ambiguous orders. There was a great deal of excitement throughout the state and many persons, including Thomas, believed that an effort would be made to break up the legislature by force. He reported the matter to Grant and asked for orders. There was no doubt from the wording of his dispatch that Thomas favored the use of Federal troops to force a quorum.

His suggestion precipitated one of the minor political crises of the Johnson Administration. Grant turned the dispatch over to Stanton, who withheld it from the President for three days. Gideon Welles, Secretary of the Navy, noted in his diary that on July 17 Stanton read a strange dispatch from Thomas.[15] The President replied that if Thomas had nothing else to do but intermeddle in local controversies he had better be ordered elsewhere. Welles' nose twitched. Stanton, who should have rebuked Thomas, had, the writer thought, a design in bringing the matter to the President, who had a warm personal friendship for the General. Stanton now changed his tone and said that he proposed to tell Thomas to avoid mixing into the matter. "But shall I add your remark?" he asked of Johnson.

"My wish is," replied the President, "that the answer should be emphatic and decisive not to meddle with local parties and politics. The military are not superior masters." Five days after he made his request, the sergeant-at-arms learned that Thomas would not supply the fifteen-man detail. Meantime he had arrested two members who were needed for a quorum, held them by force in one of the committee rooms in the capitol while the speaker put the question, and recorded a vote ratifying the Fourteenth Amendment. In another five days Tennessee had been readmitted to the Union. Brownlow had traded ratification for the seating of Tennessee's Congressional delegation and the indemnification of the loyal East Tennesseans for war damage. In doing so he broke with Johnson's reconstruction plan. With this weapon the Federal Congress forced Johnson into the position of approving the Fourteenth Amendment or of excluding his own state from the Union. It was a galling step for the President to take but he held no grudge against Thomas.

Thomas now considered the major part of his postwar work done. He had mustered out nearly 150,000 troops to break up one of history's great armies. He had reduced drastically his military expenses. Except for one major outbreak, he had suppressed violence in the area of his command. He had marked the road for readmittance to the Union, straightened some of its curves, bridged some of its chasms, tunneled some of its obstacles and brought one of his wards safely through. He wanted to get away from Nashville and he wanted a rest.

Within a week he requested permission to move his headquarters to Louisville. On August 6, 1866, the request was granted and almost simultaneously Thomas' command was changed from the Military Division of the Tennessee to the Department of the Tennessee. This was a change in name rather than in command. Thomas retained his control of the same geographical area, but the sub-commands within his department were reorganized. He applied for and received a leave of absence—the first he had taken since September 1860. His chief-of-staff superintended the moving and the selection of new accommodations while Thomas visited friends in the North and took a trip into Canada.

In the early spring of 1867, Congress put into operation its plan for forcing the conquered states back into the Union. All of them except Tennessee were to be grouped into five military districts under the general officers of the army to be selected by the President. These officers were to control and direct the process of reconstruction which became better known as carpetbag government. Grant was invested by Congress with the power to control these five officers, so that he was practically independent of the President. Thomas was picked by Johnson to command the Third Military District, which embraced the states of Georgia, Alabama and Florida, but Thomas asked that the assignment be withdrawn. The President acceded and ordered him instead to the command of the Department of the Cumberland. This embraced the states of Kentucky, Tennessee and West Virginia. His headquarters were to remain in Louisville. This was an automatic reduction in Thomas' command. Since these three states were already in the Union the order removed Thomas from any part in the struggle over the carpetbag administrations that was to tear the nation to pieces.

On July 23, 1867, Grant ordered Thomas to Memphis to head off an election riot brewing there. Thomas was to use his military force vigorously to prevent the outbreak of violence. When he reached the city he found the residents in a state of excitement. The evening of his arrival he summoned the mayor, the chief of police of the city and the sheriff of the county and found that the civil effort to prevent violence was defeated by a quarrel between the sheriff and the police chief. Thomas effected a truce. The chief was able to use his force untrammeled to preserve order. The election passed off more quietly and more to the satisfaction of all parties than any election in ten years.

Thomas had the power to enforce any decision he might make and the easy path would have been to put in the troops and bloody the heads of the troublemakers. Instead, he took the hard way—a careful sifting of evidence in a night meeting to determine the truth of the situation and then the tough job of persuading a stubborn, antagonistic troublemaker to do what he should do. But this was the constructive way and it had a cumulative value. It was a triumph for the Tennesseans' own civil law and made easier the settlement of succeeding problems.

Thomas' report of this little affair was sent to the Adjutant General on the fifth of August. Two weeks later the President fingered him for a similar job in New Orleans. This was the headquarters of Sheridan's command of the Fifth Military District, embracing Louisiana and Texas. Sheridan's removal had encouraged the opponents of reconstruction and so embarrassed his successor.

The background of this episode was so complex that, at this day, it is impossible to assign motives in explanation of the various moves. The struggle between the President and Congress, which was constantly encroaching upon the executive power, had reached a point where the reconstruction of the South was a secondary effort. All the Cabinet except Stanton backed the President's position that Congress could not strip the Commander-in-Chief of his constitutional supervision of his military subordinates. Grant had become the pliant tool of the radical congressmen. Sheridan, emotionally immature, naive, politically ignorant and bewildered, followed Grant's advice. Sheridan's ineptness drove the Texans frantic and roused to a hurricane the gale of criticism against him in the Northern papers. On July 31, the President fired him. Five days later he asked for Stanton's resignation and, when it was not forthcoming, suspended him from his office. In his struggle, the President turned to Thomas, but Thomas refused the help which Johnson needed. The Fifth Military District, from prolonged mishandling, was difficult to administer. Nor did Grant want him in New Orleans.

Thomas was in West Virginia when the President issued the order for him to relieve Sheridan. Upon its receipt at his headquarters, Doctor Hasson, his medical director, sent to the Adjutant General a telegram concerning Thomas' health.[16] This was unknown to Thomas, who did not use his health as one of the reasons for objecting to the command. Thomas had been under medical treatment and his doctor believed it would be a risk for him to go south at this time. Six days after the medical report was written the President revoked his order and permitted Thomas to remain in command of the Department of the Cumberland.

Thomas described his trouble as "a peculiar sensation which I had in my right side. It was disagreeable and that is all that can be said of it." The diagnosis was an unhealthy action of the liver. The prescription was blue mass. It is probable that Thomas suffered a mild stroke in the early summer of 1867.

Six months after the Sheridan episode the President tried again to bolster his executive powers by the use of Thomas' prestige. It was his sixth recorded effort to tie Thomas to his political machine. He had failed with force. Thomas had been too stubborn to yield to pressure, too nimble to be persuaded. So now the President tried ethical bribery.

The situation within the President's official family was impossible. Stanton, whom he had suspended from office, was now back as a result of Congressional pressure. Grant, caught in the trap that Thomas had avoided, tried to escape by means that laid him open to the suspicion of a moral collapse. Johnson had replaced Stanton for the second time as Secretary of War, but his newest appointee was too much of a light-weight to make the change permanent. He moved to brevet Sherman to four-star rank in order to give him the weight to shove Stanton out of his office, but Sherman refused. Now the President wanted Thomas to replace Grant as General-in-Chief of the army. Grant's political ambitions were making him a focus of infection in the executive group. On February 21, 1867, Johnson sent Thomas' name to the Senate and asked that they confirm him in the brevet ranks of lieutenant general and general. On matters of military principle Thomas fought Grant to a standstill. Over other issues he refused to pick up the gage. Thomas learned of the President's latest move through the newspapers and wired a request that the Senate refuse the confirmation on the ground that the promotion was too late for his war services and unmerited for his postwar services. The next day he thanked the President for the honor and asked him to recall his nomination. The following day, the House of Representatives voted to impeach the President.

Within two weeks after the brevet episode Thomas was being shoved into another political contest with Grant. It was apparent that Johnson would never get a second term as President and that his successor would be a military man. The politicians were testing the susceptibilities and the vote-winning potentials of the successful generals.

Tennessee's state convention declared unanimously for Thomas, but he squelched the move as soon as he heard of it. His self-recorded reasons are given in his various letters of refusal.[17] He gave different reasons to different persons. He had all he wanted out of life, he wanted nothing to do with politics, he wanted to die with a fair record, he lacked the control of his temper necessary for such an office, he was too poor and could not afford it.[18]

Grant's promotion from head of the army to President shook up the high command. Sherman moved into Grant's rank and command after the inauguration. Rawlins succeeded Schofield as Secretary of War. Meade, Sheridan and Thomas were candidates for Sherman's vacated rank of lieutenant general. Sheridan got the honor and was assigned to command the Military Division of the Missouri with headquarters in Chicago. Meade, as a consolation assignment, got the Military Division of the Atlantic with headquarters in Philadelphia.

Thomas at the time was presiding over the Dyer court of inquiry meeting in Washington. He was occupying a room at the corner of 15th and H streets. Sherman was staying with his brother at 1321 K Street. It was Sherman's custom each workday morning to stop at Thomas' room on his way to the War Department to talk of military news and matters of common interest. To the public Thomas was a calm, strong, imperturbable figure, but Sherman records a different picture. He thought that Thomas worried and fretted over what he considered acts of neglect or acts of favoritism. At the time he was concerned, Sherman claimed, over the injustice of Sheridan's promotion and the fact that he could not have the command of the Division of the Atlantic. Undoubtedly these two men did discuss Sheridan's promotion and the assignments to the various division commands but there is grave doubt that Sherman reported correctly the details of their conversations.

Thomas had asked for the eastern command on the ground that he and Mrs. Thomas were both Easterners and that it had been a long time since he had had a command that would permit them to live in that section of the country. In the fall of 1868 Thomas and one of his aides called one evening upon the President-elect. Grant ushered them into the library where Mrs. Grant and her father were seated. At one point in the conversation Grant said, "Thomas, there has got to be a change on the Pacific coast and either you or Sheridan will have to go there; how would you like it?" Thomas replied that he would not like it and reiterated his request for an eastern command on Mrs. Thomas' account.

"Your having a wife," broke in Mrs. Grant smilingly, "is one reason you should go there instead of Sheridan, as he ought to stay here, where he can get one."

It was not Sheridan's promotion to lieutenant general that irritated Thomas. Sheridan outranked him as a major general and Thomas was too much of a stickler for military precedence to object to it. Halleck and Meade were the officers overslaughed by the Sheridan promotion. Halleck evidently made no objection and Meade got the eastern command as a partial assuagement of his injured feelings. Thomas was well satisfied to stay where he was in Louisville if he could not get Philadelphia.

But one day shortly after Grant's inauguration Thomas learned that Schofield was to be sent to San Francisco to relieve Halleck as commander of the Military Division of the Pacific. At Louisville, Thomas commanded a department. A division outranked a department and now Schofield, his junior, was to be jumped over his head.

On his next morning visit to Thomas' room Sherman caught the brunt of Thomas' wrath. He tried to get Thomas to go with him to talk to the President but Thomas refused. Sherman eventually gave Thomas his choice of commands after Sheridan and Meade had been satisfied and Thomas chose the Pacific command.

Halleck was brought east and put in command of a newly created division with his headquarters in Louisville. It was apparent then that Thomas could have and probably would have remained where he was and still have exercised command over a military division. The army command was puzzled over Thomas' outburst and perhaps justifiably so. Thomas had abdicated the command of a military division for that of a military department at the time the Congressional reconstruction plan was put into effect. This was the same thing he had done at Corinth when he gave up the command of a corps to step down into a division. He had told Grant unofficially that he did not want to go to the Pacific coast. But he had also made known his policy that he would resist any order that placed a subordinate over him. In an indirect way this last injunction had been violated and at the first intimation of his dissatisfaction the situation was reorganized to meet his wishes.

Such personality clashes were routine in the Northern army after the war. Grant, Sherman and Schofield had all been victimized in ways that made the Thomas-Halleck affair a comparative pinprick. Biographers and publicists have shown Thomas after the war as a frustrated, embittered individual. There is evidence that this was not so. In 1868 Thomas told one of the officers who had fought the whole war with him that he had all he wanted. Another officer in a position to know says that Thomas was not captious, discontented or disposed to raise questions of rank and precedence. Grenville Dodge, whom Thomas visited on his way to the Pacific coast, thought him happy and contented.[19]

As soon as the Dyer court was dissolved on May 15, 1869, Thomas accepted the Pacific assignment, relinquished his command of the Department of the Cumberland and started for San Francisco. His route of travel was fixed by the Pacific Railroad and he was given a $200 advance for traveling expenses. Five days before he left Louisville the first transcontinental rail line had been linked at Promontory, Utah. At 2:00 P.M. on May 30, 1869, after seven days and ten hours' traveling time, Thomas and his staff stepped ashore in San Francisco from the boat which had brought them from Sacramento. His headquarters were set up in a building on the corner of Kearny and Sutter streets.[20]

Shortly after his arrival Halleck gave a dinner in his honor. During the meal the conversation turned to some of the military highlights of the war and Halleck gave Thomas the details of his near relief before Nashville. He seemed reluctant to name the officer who was to take over the command, but Thomas' curiosity or Halleck's inclination to show off, or both, gained the ascendency and Halleck named Schofield. Thomas' manner revealed his excitement and he exclaimed, "I knew it, I knew he was the man." This little exchange of information set in motion an acrimonious and public discussion on the part of the adherents of both principals that led, indirectly, to Thomas' death.

Within a little more than two weeks Thomas left San Francisco for a tour of his new command. He had been alerted for trouble from three sources—from the Chinese in Nevada, from the British in Alaska and from the Indians everywhere. The trouble over the Chinese did not eventuate. The Indian alert was another false alarm. Neither did any difficulties arise over the alleged habitual encroachments of agents of the Hudson's Bay Company upon the trade and the territory around Fort Yukon.

Thomas started by stage north and east of San Francisco, passing through Nevada, Idaho and Oregon, to Portland. He left Portland on July 6 on the small steamer *Fideleter*, chartered for the trip to Alaska and commanded by Captain J. W. White of the United States Revenue Marine Service. Coasting along southern Alaska, Thomas examined coal diggings and seal fisheries and appraised the troublemaking potential of the Indians.[21] The standing army of the United States had been cut to twenty-five regiments and Thomas recommended the discontinuance of numerous garrisons to make troops available for more important service. He saw no prospect of immigration to Alaska, abundant lumber with no probability that it would be cut, and no future for agriculture. He also reported a rich deposit of iron and traces of gold. The territory had been in possession of the United States less than two years so Thomas' report was one of the earliest ones made on the area. His opinion of Alaska's agricultural prospects disagreed with Halleck's report made a year earlier. His solution of the sealing problem was to permit the natives to do all the hunting and to sell the right to purchase their furs to the highest bidder. This plan was approved by the Secretary of War but the solution offered by Captain White, to turn the seal rookeries into a government reserve, was the one that was adopted. Thomas found time to resume his old interest in botany, zoology and geology and sent to the Smithsonian Institution walrus bones and a box of coal specimens. He also aided science by exploding the story of the Alaska sea cow and by financing one of the Institution's field men to the extent of $50.00. "I have sent you enough [coal] to make a fire for Sumner after you have selected a specimen for the museum," he wrote Baird and later in the same letter gave his unofficial appraisal of the new territory. "Alaska would have been an excellent purchase in 1861," he wrote, "as a kind of water and cold air cure for the hot-headed Southerners who fell into our hands as prisoners of war." Three months in Alaska he thought would be sufficient to cool the most heated brain.[22]

While this inspection tour was in progress Thomas was having made up what may have been California's first road map. It was a table of distances between various points in southern California and Arizona with notes on water, pasturage and Indians. An odometer on an ambulance wheel, with corrections for slippage, measured the mileage.[23]

At the end of September, Thomas, accompanied by three aides, went east by the overland route to bring back Mrs. Thomas and her sister from Louisville.

It was chilly and drizzling a little on the morning of March 28, 1870, when General Thomas left his quarters in the Lick House punctually at 9:20. His portly figure, clad in a blue cloak and high-peaked cap, was by this time familiar to many San Franciscans. Several spoke to him on the block-long walk to his headquarters and the General nodded his acknowledgment. He spoke a cheerful "Good morning" to his aide before entering his private office.

Fifteen minutes later this aide, Colonel Hough, took up with the General the day's current business. It was soon finished in accordance with their usual routine and the two talked for some time about Cox's article in an Eastern paper.[24] The General did not know the name of the author nor did he know that Schofield had inspired Cox's attack upon Thomas' handling of the Nashville campaign. The General seemed to be in his usual health. About 10:30 Hough left headquarters on some private errand and the General went to work upon the draft of his reply to the newspaper attack.

At 1:30 P.M., while writing at his desk, the General slipped from his chair in a faint. A few blurred and disconnected lines were scratched by his pen on the paper as the attack seized him.

One of the General's orderlies heard his commander ask for fresh air. He went to his aid and helped him into the next room. Here the General staggered and fell and was lifted almost insensible onto a lounge. Physicians were called and when Hough returned to headquarters at 1:45 P.M. they had already administered restoratives. The attack was diagnosed as indigestion.

About 2:00 P.M. the General was feeling well enough to get up but, complaining of a pain in his right temple, soon lay down again. One of the doctors told Hough that this was a bad sign. Mrs. Thomas arrived and sat by the General's side. She and Colonel Hough were the only other persons in the room. The General tried to speak. Hough leaned over, put his ear near the General's lips and heard him say that he felt better and had no pain. The General looked up at Mrs. Thomas. She leaned down and listened while he spoke again.

Shortly after this Colonel Hough saw him struggle, with a convulsive movement of his chest. He tried to rise but the effort was vain.

The doctors were called in from an outside room and immediately diagnosed the attack as apoplexy.[25] Both temples were cupped while he lay unconscious on the lounge, but his pulse gradually grew weaker. At 7:25, with a convulsive spasm, he died.

A number of officers by this time had gathered at headquarters but only a few of them had joined Mrs. Thomas, her sister, two army physicians and three members of the General's personal staff in the inner room when the end came.

The body was sent that night to the embalmer and the next day was carried to the Lick House where it lay in state in Mrs. Thomas' private rooms. The coffin was sealed airtight but the General's face was visible through a plate-glass panel. Prominent San Franciscans, army officers and veterans' organizations started plans for a military funeral but Mrs. Thomas vetoed the suggestions. Instead, at 2:00 P.M. on March 30 the Episcopal service was read over the body in the Lick House by the Right Reverend Bishop Kip and the glass panel in the coffin was covered.

That day the flags over the city and the harbor shipping flew at half staff. The law courts adjourned. Thomas' headquarters, the headquarters of the commander of the Department of California and the headquarters of the engineer's department were draped in black.

At 6:30 A.M. on March 31 the coffin was put aboard the Oakland ferry and, as the little steamer left the San Francisco dock, the first of fifty-four minute guns sounded from the fort on Alcatraz Island. Anchored in the stream, her hull hidden by the fog drifting through the Golden Gate, Her Britannic Majesty's frigate *Zealous* answered Alcatraz gun for gun. At Oakland Point the coffin was placed in a special car and at 8:00 A.M. started for Troy, New York.

Mrs. Thomas did not accompany her husband's body. She remained in San Francisco to settle the affairs left unfinished by her husband's sudden death. She took the hotel train for the East on April 5 and reached Troy the fourteenth—six days after the military funeral.

Colonel Hough closed the General's private office after the body had been removed. At Mrs. Thomas' request he examined all the papers it contained to separate the personal ones from the official ones.[26] "This sad duty," Colonel Hough wrote, "occupied me three days. Of course many of the papers were deeply interesting, but all of them only confirmed the strength and beauty of his character; not a paper was destroyed, and not one need ever be by Mrs. Thomas."

Colonel J. P. Willard, one of Thomas' personal aides and a distant relative of Mrs. Thomas, accompanied the body in command of the honor guard. The guard was relieved twice—at Ogden, Utah, and at Omaha, Nebraska—but Colonel Willard went through to Troy.

Sherman had already named the day and hour of the official funeral and Willard was hurrying on a tight time schedule. Originally it was planned to ferry the funeral car across the Missouri River and couple it to the eastbound train, but the river was in flood and the car could not be crossed. So another car, already on the east bank, was remodeled and decorated. The coffin was ferried across and placed in it and the train dispatched near enough to its scheduled time as to occasion no change in the funeral arrangements.

Sherman, immediately after announcing Thomas' death to the army, had wired Mrs. Thomas suggesting burial at West Point. From San Francisco on April 2 he had this reply: "Your dispatch is just received. I regret that I cannot yield to the desire of having the burial at West Point. As Troy will be my future home, I feel that I must bury General Thomas in my family lot at the cemetery there. I will leave to you the arrangements for a military funeral at Troy. On the arrival of the remains there, they will be deposited temporarily in the receiving vault. Colonel Willard knows my wishes. Private services have already been held here. Sincere thanks for your attention. Frances L. Thomas."

George Thomas all through his life had succeeded in keeping his personal life separate from his official one. After his death his widow gallantly tried to follow out his wishes. But two million veterans would not have it so. The funeral had all the trappings that the military, the citizens of Troy and the New York State officials could provide. Congress held a memorial meeting attended by the President, his Cabinet, the Supreme Court, army and navy officers and other officials. The public buildings and many others in Troy were draped. A committee of Troy citizens met the funeral train and saw that the coffin was carried reverently and tenderly to the Episcopal church where the funeral service was to be read the next day.

And now the military took charge. President Grant and four members of his Cabinet attended, as well as the joint committee of Congress, the Governor of New York and his staff, the membership of both houses of New York's general assembly, General of the Army W. T. Sherman and ranking officers of the army and navy, ranking officers of the New York state troops, Troy's municipal officers and those from neighboring towns and cities, and delegates from the Society of the Army of the Cumberland and from the Grand Army of the Republic.

The pallbearers were Meade, Schofield, Hooker, Rosecrans, Hazen, Granger, Newton and McKay. The parade which formed at the church and escorted the body to the cemetery to the tolling of the city bells and the firing of minute guns was a mile long. At Oakwood Cemetery the Episcopal commitment service was read and the coffin was buried [27] in the Kellogg lot while the escort fired three volleys and the massed bugles played taps.

No members of General Thomas' family took advantage of Sherman's pointed invitation to be present, so far as is known. A clipping in the Thomas file in the offices of West Point Graduates names twenty-five members of Mrs. Thomas' family who were present.

But the real homage to a great man's memory welled up spontaneously from the hearts of the people as the funeral train made its way across the country. Minute guns, muffled drums, artillery salvos, tolling bells gave notice of the nation's grief. Floral tributes were put aboard at every stop. Railway stations were draped in black. Memorial arches were built across the track and the train passed slowly under them while the gold and silver letters spelling the names of Thomas' victories reflected the beam of the headlight. Treasured battle flags were carried from their honored resting places to be trooped for the last time before their commander.

But the patient, silent people paid the warm tribute that only a great selflessness can earn. In the cities they came by the thousands and passed slowly by the car, looking wordlessly in the windows at the closed coffin. At Chicago an estimated 50,000 of them lined the tracks as the train rolled slowly through the city. That night another great concourse of them bade it farewell as it left over the Michigan Southern tracks. At Rochester, New York, there was a dense crowd of people at the depot as the train went through at 2:00 A.M.[28]

Through the countryside where the train made no stops it was the same. The silent watchers were there waiting patiently, rain or shine, night or day, singly or in small groups. Some lifted up their children to see it go by. When the train passed they would turn and watch it, the men still with bared heads. When it could no longer be seen, they would turn quietly and move away.

Notes

Abbreviations

The following abbreviations are used throughout the notes for the sake of brevity:

A.G.	Adjutant General
A.G.O.	Adjutant General's Office
A.H.Q.	Army Headquarters
3 A.R.	Monthly Returns, Third Regiment of Artillery
Comdry.	Commandery
2 C.R.	Monthly Returns, Second Regiment of Cavalry
G.O.	General Order [followed by the order number and the name of the command]
H.Q.	Headquarters
L.B.	Letterbook
Let. Rec.	Letters Received File
Let. Sent	Letters Sent File
M.O.L.L.	Military Order of the Loyal Legion
O.I.A.	Office of Indian Affairs
O.R.	*War of the Rebellion: Official Records of the Union and Confederate Armies*
P.O.B.	Post Order Book
P.R.	Monthly Post Return [followed by the name of the post]
R.S.L.	Recruiting Service Letterbook
Regis. Let. Rec.	Register of Letters Received

S.O.   Special Order [followed by the order number and the name of the
                     command]
S.L.B.   Superintendent's Letterbook

Chapter 1

1. Report of the Senate Committee on Pensions, No. 1169, 48 Cong., 2 sess.,
   1885. Filed with Thomas' service record, War Records Branch, National
   Archives.
2. Oliver O. Howard, "Sketch of the Life of General George H. Thomas," in
   War Sketches, New York Comdry., M.O.L.L. (New York, 1890). Howard
   read this paper to the commandery in October 1890. He got most of his facts
   from an eighty-year-old Negro named Artise. The 1850 census for Southampton County lists a free Negro named Artis living with the Thomas
   family.
       Details of the Thomas genealogy have been filed by the author with the
   Virginia State Library, Richmond.
       Among the county records at Courtland is a small ledger containing
   material copied by Miss Bessie T. Shands, deputy clerk of the county, from
   papers left by Mattie R. Tyler (hereafter cited as Mattie R. Tyler Notes).
   Miss Tyler was Thomas' second cousin, granddaughter of President Tyler
   and post-war postmistress at Courtland.
       A Widow's Declaration for Additional Bounty Land, Record Group 15 A,
   National Archives, was called to the author's attention by Mr. Claude Lewis
   of St. Louis, Mo.
       The Rochelle Papers, Duke University Library, give an excellent back-
   ground for Southside Virginia in the early 1800's. Mattie Russell, assistant
   curator of manuscripts in 1951, gave the author some much appreciated
   help in this research.
       Two years after the death of the last of General Thomas' sisters, Mr.
   H. T. Miles of Newsoms, Southampton County, purchased Thomaston. His
   widow contributed many details about the family and marked a photograph
   to show the birthroom, which is now deposited with the Virginia State
   Library.

Chapter 2

1. Hazard Stevens, *The Life of Isaac Ingalls Stevens* (2 vols., Boston, 1901),
   1:37.
2. Sidney Forman, *The Educational Objectives of the United States Military
   Academy* (West Point, 1946).
3. Lt. Col. W. J. Morton, Librarian, United States Military Academy, is the
   authority for the statement that Mahan's notes of 1835 were used by Thomas'
   class. These are owned by the Library but were not available to the author.
   Dennis H. Mahan, *Composition of Armies,* lithographed notes dated 1840
   and used in this book are presumed to be substantially the same as those
   used by Thomas.

Post Order Books, in the West Point Library, give the details of Thomas' cadetship. These are supplemented by the West Point Registers, West Point Regulations and Reports of the Board of Visitors for the years concerned. These were printed annually for the Secretary of War and copies are available in the West Point Library.

Most of the background material for this chapter came from books in the West Point Library authored by men who wrote of the years when Thomas was there. Chief among these was *Cadet Life Before the Mexican War,* edited by Corporal Sidney Forman from cadet manuscripts owned by the Library. It was published as Bulletin No. 1 by the West Point Library in 1945. Dr. Forman, who succeeded Col. Morton as Librarian in 1958, permitted the use of the undated typescript of his Columbia University doctoral dissertation, entitled "West Point, A History of the U.S.M.A.," which appraised it as a school, evaluated its education and gave details of the Rawle controversy.

The West Point Museum displays a few Thomas relics and exhibits of Civil War arms and uniforms. Mr. G. C. Stowe, its curator, initiated the search which located the John N. Hough Papers (see Chapter 8, note 1).

Chapter 3

1. Thomas' military record, except where noted otherwise, will be found in the National Archives in the form of regimental returns, post returns, general orders, special orders, letterbooks, letters received files, and registers of letters received for the various departmental bureaus.

2. Wade's report (file C 106) enclosed in Childs to A.G., Nov. 24, 1841 (C 516), H.Q. Letters, Ninth Dept., Florida Army. The reports of the Seminole War and of the battles of Monterrey and Buena Vista in the Mexican War were taken out of the files, collected and sent to the Secretary of War and by him to Congress. Here they were probably edited and published. When the originals were returned to the War Department they were not refiled in their original places but were kept together and filed under the titles as given here.

Lt. J. C. Ives, in "Memoir to Accompany Military Map of Florida, etc.," compiled in 1856 (Cartographic Bureau, National Archives), details the difficulty of moving troops over the route followed by Wade and Thomas. Three hours were required to get seventeen canoes over a quarter-mile haulover. At the south end of Lake Worth, five days were required to move six miles with twenty men hauling one canoe and sinking in from one to four feet of mud at each step.

3. Worth to A.G., Nov. 24, 1841; Worth to Scott, Nov. 24, 1841; Childs to A.G., Nov. 15, 1841; all in Military Book, War Office, No. 24, p. 252. Senate Executive Journal No. 6, 1841–45.

4. Thomas to Nathan Towson, Sept. 14, 1843, A.G.O., Let. Rec.

Thomas' file in the Records of the Association of Graduates, Officers and Trustees, Cullum Hall, West Point, was made available through the courtesy of Col. Charles N. Branham, Secretary and Treasurer of the Association.

Chapter 4

1. *Ordnance Manual for Use of Officers of the U. S. Army* (Washington, 1841), may have been the one used by Thomas in preparing his section at Corpus Christi.

2. William Joseph Hardee, West Point, 1838, who gave his name to a translation of French tactics used by both armies in the Civil War.

3. Report of Edgar S. Hawkins (175 H 1846) and report of Joseph K. F. Mansfield (286 M 1846), filed with Taylor to A.G., May 19, 1846 (162 T 1846), Mexican War File.

4. Taylor's Collected Reports, Sept. 23, 1846 (38 T 1847), in Mexican War File, Vol. 2.

5. Samuel G. French, *Two Wars* (Nashville, 1901), pp. 63, 66.

6. Report of J. P. Henderson, Oct. 1, 1846, found in Taylor's Collected Reports. Senate Executive Journal No. 7, 1845–48.

7. Taylor to A.G., Nov. 8, 1846, found in H.R. Executive Document No. 60, 30 Cong., 1 sess., 1847.

8. Report of Thomas West Sherman, Mexican War File, 2:203.

9. W. H. French, W. F. Barry and H. J. Hunt, *Instructions for Field Artillery,* approved by the Secretary of War, 1863, states that a piece can throw three aimed canisters per minute. Thomas was firing at such close range that it is doubtful if he was aiming each shot. His rate of fire could have been equal to or better than the average for 1863.

10. Matthew F. Steele, *American Campaigns* (2 vols., Harrisburg, 1943), 1:95. Thomas to James Duncan, March 18, 1847, West Point Library.

11. 3 A.R., Sept. 1848. Senate Executive Journal No. 7, 1845–48.

12. Col. George Gibson to William L. Marcy, May 21, 1847 (270 T 1847), Let. Rec., A.G.O.

13. James Maget to Thomas, Thomas Papers, Henry E. Huntington Library, San Marino, California.

14. Thomas to James Maget, Virginia Historical Society, Richmond.

15. Bragg to John Y. Mason, Nov. 17, 1848, Braxton Bragg Papers, Duke University Library.

16. Slave Census of 1850, Southampton County, Virginia.

17. 3 A.R. and P.R., forts Vinton, Capron and Meade, Oct. 1849—July 1850.

Chapter 5

1. Thomas to Adjutant of U.S.M.A., Nov. 20, 1850, Let. Rec., West Point Library.

2. Henry Brewerton to Joseph G. Totten, March 18, 1851, S.L.B., 2:2, West Point Library.

3. Hartz to Jenny ——, April 3, 1854, E. L. Hartz Papers, Library of Congress.

Oliver O. Howard, "Sketch of the Life of General George H. Thomas," New York Comdry., M.O.L.L. (New York, 1890).

4. The marks in the *West Point Registers* represent the order of merit in artillery. Therefore, the lower the figure, the higher the grade. In 1851 Thomas taught for only two and one-half months. Some of his students and their grades were: Kenner Garrard, 7, who served with Thomas in Texas and in the Civil War; Ben Hardin Helm, 23, Lincoln's brother-in-law, who died in front of Thomas' muskets at Chickamauga; John Mendenhall, 30, whose massed guns shot away Bragg's last hope at Stones River.

In 1852 Thomas taught and graded the following students, among others: Henry W. Slocum, 6, who led an army corps to Thomas' relief at Chattanooga; David S. Stanley, 8, one of the nation's outstanding saddle fighters; Jerome N. Bonaparte, Jr., 10, grandnephew of Napoleon; Alexander McD. McCook, 30, who never learned the elements of successful combat; George W. Crook, 38, who was to become the nation's most successful Indian fighter; and Philip H. Sheridan, who was under suspension for fighting and therefore was not examined.

In 1853 his class included: James B. McPherson, 1, who was blamed for Sherman's failure to follow Thomas' advice at Snake Creek Gap; Joshua W. Sill, 2, who died with his guns at Stones River and gave his name to Fort Sill; John M. Schofield, 11, one of five officers to hold the rank of lieutenant general during the first century of the army's existence; Philip H. Sheridan, 40, who accepted Thomas' instruction but repudiated his philosophy; John B. Hood, 45, who flunked Thomas' final examination at Nashville in 1864.

In 1854 Thomas gave marks in artillery and in cavalry. Some of his better known students were: G. W. Custis Lee, 1, 1, eldest son of Robert E. Lee; O. O. Howard, 8, 24, who got his army command through Thomas' influence; J. E. B. Stuart, 13, 10, Lee's chief of cavalry; Stephen D. Lee, 19, 4, one of Lee's brilliant gunners, later a lieutenant general.

5. Thomas to Totten, April 15, 1853, Let. Rec., Engineers Dept., National Archives.

6. Lee to Jesup, March 17, 1853, S.L.B. No. 3, West Point Library.

7. John Russell Young, *Around the World with General Grant, 1877–79* (2 vols., New York, 1879), 2:296.

8. Wharton J. Green, *Recollections and Reflections* (Raleigh, 1906).

9. Report of Bradford R. Alden, enclosed with Brewerton to Totten, July 8, 1852, Let. Sent File 175, West Point Library.

10. Henry Coppée, *General Thomas* (New York, 1893), p. 23. Howard, "General Thomas." George Meade, *Life and Letters of George Gordon Meade* (2 vols., New York, 1913), 2:253. Edward Bates, "Diary, 1859–1866," ed. H. K. Beale, in *Annual Report of the American Historical Association* (4 vols., Washington, 1930), 4:403.

11. C. W. Tillinghast to Col. Lee G. B. Cannon, April 4, 1870. Tillinghast's letterbook is owned by Alexander L. Darby of Troy, New York, who generously made available his office and his manuscript collection.

12. The catalogs of Troy Female Seminary, 1829 through 1839, owned by the

Emma Willard School, Troy, New York, were made available through the courtesy of Helen J. Marx, the school's executive secretary.

13. Let. Rec., Engineers Dept. The superintendent was responsible to the Chief Engineer of the Army. The Superintendent's Letterbooks, Post Order Books and West Point Registers and Regulations for the years concerned, all in the West Point Library, give the basic facts of Thomas' official record as an instructor.

Chapter 6

1. 3 A.R., April and December 1854. G.O. 8, June 5, 1854, A.H.Q. S.O. 61, April 26, 1854, A.H.Q. Thomas to A.G., April 27, 1854 (24 T 1854), Let. Rec., A.H.Q. See also L.B. No. 6, p. 174, Let. Sent, A.H.Q.

2. Walter H. Harvey to Thomas J. Henley, July 15, 1854; and Harvey to ——, Sept. 3, 1854; both in Yuma Indian file, O.I.A., National Archives.

3. Vols. 12–13 (Los Angeles, 1921–27).

4. Henry Stone, "General George H. Thomas," *Atlantic Monthly,* 68 (Oct. 1891), 506–514.

5. The vocabulary and Thomas' covering letter are in the Smithsonian Institution, Bureau of American Ethnology, Catalog 1107. John P. Harrington, senior ethnologist of the Bureau, appraised the Thomas vocabulary in an undated memorandum to the author. See also the *Annual Report of the Board of Regents of the Smithsonian Institution* (Washington, 1856).

Acknowledgment is made of the help received from the late Dr. F. W. Hodge, Director of the Southwest Museum, Los Angeles, and Leila F. Clarke, Librarian of the Smithsonian Institution, in locating this material.

6. *Organization, U.S. Army,* under Act of March 3, 1855, as published in the Army Register for that year.

7. A.G. to Dr. Richard G. Wood, March 7, 1951, War Records Branch, National Archives.

8. Thomas to A.G., Oct. 20, 1855 (116 T 1855), Let. Rec., A.H.Q. A.G. to Thomas, Let. Sent, L.B. No. 6, p. 403, A.H.Q. A.G. to Thomas, Jan. 14, 1856, R.S.L. Thomas to A.G., Jan. 26, 1856, Let. Rec., A.G.O.

9. A.G. to Thomas, April 12, 1856, R.S.L.

10. Thomas to A.G., April 4, 1856 (27 T 1856), Let. Rec., A.H.Q.

Chapter 7

1. Robert S. Neighbors to O.I.A., May 7 and Aug. 4, 1856, Texas Comanches File.

2. Col. M. L. Crimmins, "Episode in the Texas Career of Gen. Twiggs," *Southwestern Historical Quarterly,* 41 (Oct. 1937), 167. Letter from Office of the Judge Advocate General to the author, October 12, 1951.

3. From north to south, the posts were Ft. Belknap, Camp Cooper, Ft. Chadbourne, and Ft. McKavett. *O.R. Atlas,* Plate 54. The *O.R.* map index will locate the maps by volume.

4. Thomas to A.G.O., July 25, 1857 (181 T 1857), Let. Rec., A.G.O.

5. Neighbors to O.I.A., Feb. 3, 1858, Texas Comanches File.

6. *Annual Report of the Board of Regents of the Smithsonian Institution* (Washington, 1858).

7. File 128 T 1857, Let. Rec., A.G.O., contains the correspondence on this episode: Thomas to H.Q., Second Cavalry, Nov. 13, 1857; Twiggs to Thomas, Nov. 14 and 15, 1857; revocation, by endorsement dated Dec. 9, 1857, of S.O. 146, H.Q., Dept. of Texas.

8. In Oct. 1858, Lee's leave was extended to May 1859, when he received another extension of four months, at the end of which he was ordered to Harpers Ferry to put down the John Brown insurrection.

9. Mattie R. Tyler Notes.

10. The Thomas-Twiggs correspondence relative to the Van Dorn quarrel has been lost as per carbon of letter from E. G. Campbell of the National Archives to Freeman Cleaves, June 27, 1946, filed in Regis. Let. Rec., No. 35 for 1859, A.G.O. The Register, however, gives a summary of the correspondence, beginning on p. 925.

11. Thomas to H.Q., Dept. of Texas, Aug. 31, 1860, with enclosure of sketch map, filed with 185 T 1860, Let. Rec., A.G.O.

12. Robert E. Lee to Lorenzo Thomas, Aug. 13, 1860, filed with 136 T 1860, Let. Rec., A.G.O.

Chapter 8

1. Mrs. Thomas to Col. Alfred L. Hough, Jan. 21, 1876, John N. Hough Papers. Mr. John N. Hough of Boulder, Colorado, is the grandson of Col. Alfred L. Hough, who served under Thomas from 1863 to 1870, most of the time as a member of his staff. Col. Hough's relations with Thomas after the war were close and he continued for twenty years after Thomas' death as counselor to Mrs. Thomas. He was a major contributor to the Van Horne and Coppée biographies and directed the defense of Thomas' reputation during the 1870's and 80's, when the military records of the Grant coterie were being embellished. Mr. John N. Hough helped in the preparation of this work with photostats, typescripts, microfilm, correspondence and verbal recollections.

2. John A. Wyeth, *With Sabre and Scalpel* (New York, 1914), p. 261. This would indicate that Thomas had more than one slave in Texas. Mrs. Thomas not only condoned slavery but apparently found it satisfactory for domestic help.

3. Thomas B. Van Horne, *The Life of General George H. Thomas* (New York, 1882), p. 20. Joseph E. Johnston to J. P. Nicholson, June 28, 1884, Joseph E. Johnston Papers, Duke University Library.

4. *O.R.*, 51:1:311. All *O.R.* citations, unless otherwise specified, refer to Series I.

5. A twelve-page holograph memorandum by Col. Hough, dated Jan. 8, 1876, is an itemized defense of Thomas' loyalty. Eight newspaper clippings of charges and countercharges are pasted in it. This memorandum and its

clippings, with the letter of Mrs. Thomas to Col. Hough, Jan. 21, 1876, give the details of his accident, his letter to Col. Smith, and the various charges concerning his loyalty. Both are in the John N. Hough Papers.

6. Ephraim A. Otis, "General George H. Thomas," a paper read on April 2, 1884, before the Illinois Comdry., M.O.L.L. It was printed in *Military Essays and Recollections* (Chicago, 1891), 1:395.

7. Thomas to S. Cooper, March 1, 1861 (59 T 1861), Let. Rec., A.G.O.

8. James A. Garfield, *Oration on the Life and Character of General George H. Thomas* (Cincinnati, 1870), p. 15.

9. Mrs. Thomas to Col. Hough, Jan. 21, 1876, John N. Hough Papers.

10. Mrs. Thomas to Col. Hough, Jan. 21, 1876, John N. Hough Papers.

11. Mrs. Thomas to Col. Hough, Jan. 21, 1876, John N. Hough Papers.

12. Garfield, p. 13.

13. Mrs. Thomas to Col. Hough, Jan. 21, 1876, John N. Hough Papers.

14. Mrs. R. H. Stevenson of Littleton, Virginia, related these stories to the author at her home on April 4, 1951.

15. Thomas to Grant, Jan. 30, 1864, *O.R.*, 32:2:264. See also *O.R. Atlas,* Plate 93.

16. Mrs. Thomas to Col. Hough, Jan. 21, 1876, John N. Hough Papers.

Chapter 9

1. Fitz John Porter to Lorenzo Thomas, May 1, 1861, Fitz John Porter Papers, Library of Congress.

2. *O.R.,* 51:1:346–56, 363. Adding to the confusion was a difference of opinion between Cameron, who wanted Thomas' troops sent to Washington over the railroad, which he owned, while Gov. Curtin wanted to march them. William B. Hesseltine, *Lincoln and the War Governors* (New York, 1955), p. 150.

3. Newspaper clipping entitled "The Hero of Chattanooga" (name of paper deleted, n.d.), in Records of the Association of Graduates, Officers and Trustees, Cullum Hall, West Point.

4. These were mostly militia in response to Lincoln's first call. The true volunteer enlisted for three years or the duration of the war in response to calls of May 3 and thereafter.

5. John C. Ropes, *Story of the Civil War* (New York, 1933), 2:417, is in qualified disagreement. He writes that the U. S. policy of conquest made a Southern success as decisive as Yorktown an almost necessary condition to achieving independence.

6. W. T. Sherman to James A. Garfield, July 28, 1870, photostat, Manuscript Room, New York Public Library.

7. W. T. Sherman to John Sherman, June 8, 1861, in Rachael S. Thorndike, ed., *Letters of W. T. Sherman* (New York, 1894).

8. Donn Piatt and Henry V. Boynton, *General George H. Thomas* (Cincinnati, 1893). Scattered throughout this biography are details of Thomas' command techniques. See also Garfield, pp. 27 ff.

9. Anderson to his wife, Aug. 6 and 13, 1861, Robert Anderson Papers, Library of Congress.

10. Lincoln to Cameron, Aug. 7, 1861, *O.R.*, 4:255. ". . . make out a commission for Simon Buckner as brigadier general of volunteers. It is to be put in the hands of Gen. Anderson and delivered . . . at the discretion of Gen. Anderson. . . ."

11. Immediately after Thomas' death open charges were made impugning his motives, loyalty and veracity. Garfield was picked by the Army of the Cumberland as the dead man's champion. Sherman, in aid of this defense, wrote Garfield (see note 6 above) that Lincoln was distrustful of Southern-born officers and that he (Sherman) had allayed Lincoln's misgivings about Thomas. Twenty years later Sherman upgraded this endorsement into a guaranty (see Coppée, *General Thomas* [New York, 1893], p. 319). The evidence indicates that Sherman was building up his war record at Thomas' expense.

Thomas M. Anderson, "General George H. Thomas, His Place in History," *War Papers*, Oregon Comdry., M.O.L.L. (Chicago, 1884), 1:345. Anderson, who was the last eye-witness to the event, was dead when this paper was published. Its wording was known to Van Horne before Sherman's death and was used by him on p. 35 of *General Thomas*. Four pages later he used the Sherman version. Van Horne's position is equivocal.

Thomas Anderson was a nephew of Gen. Robert Anderson. This put him in a position to know the facts but the convincing reason for choosing Anderson's version over Sherman's is that Thomas does not intimate in any document found to date that Lincoln lacked confidence in him. Neither do the rambling letters of Mrs. Thomas, although she looked for and generally found criticism of her husband where probably none was intended. Richard W. Johnson, *Memoir of General George H. Thomas* (Philadelphia, 1881), p. 47, and Coppée, p. 42, agree that Robert Anderson's orders were to select loyal Southerners for his officers.

12. Mrs. Thomas to Col. Hough, Jan. 21, 1876, John N. Hough Papers.

Chapter 10

1. Felix K. Zollicoffer was a native of Nashville but had lived in East Tennessee and was popular with many of its citizens.

2. Thomas was traveling on this railway when he strained his back. It transported most of the pork, grain and forage used by the Southern armies.

3. *O.R.*, 52:1:191. Review of Piatt and Boynton, *The Nation*, 57 (Nov. 2, 1893), 334. Van Horne, *The Life of General George H. Thomas* (New York, 1882), p. 41, hints that Thomas originated the East Tennessee Plan and says that he discussed it with Scott. The idea probably occurred simultaneously to many persons. Thomas and McClellan tried to give it military significance. Lincoln saw it primarily as a political end with incidental military value.

4. "Bull" Nelson of Kentucky was drafted from the Navy to help hold Kentucky in the Union. Later he won the rank of brigadier general of volunteers.

5. Thomas to Sherman, Sept. 19, 1861, W. T. Sherman Papers, Library of Congress.

6. Daniel Boone's gateway to the West. It was a toll road in 1861 and Thomas presumably paid toll with I.O.U.'s.

7. Thomas to Oliver D. Greene, Sept. 27, 1861, Andrew Johnson Papers, Library of Congress. This is apparently Thomas' original letter to Anderson's chief-of-staff. That it came to be in Andrew Johnson's personal file is evidence of his influence in military affairs in Tennessee.

8. Lt. Samuel P. Carter was another draftee from the Navy.

9. *O.R.,* 4:284.

10. *O.R.,* 4:302.

11. Ormsby MacKnight Mitchel, West Point, 1829. *O.R.,* 4:303.

12. Manuscript 2902, Andrew Johnson Papers.

13. Whitelaw Reid, *Ohio in the War, Her Statesmen, Generals and Soldiers* (2 vols., Columbus, 1893), 1:602. Reid says that Mitchel was eager to lead an expedition into East Tennessee and that he laid plans before Cameron, who promptly approved them. Piatt and Boynton (p. 112) say that Andrew Johnson planned the replacement of Thomas. Coppée (p. 49) doubts that the question of Thomas' loyalty dictated his attempted removal. John G. Nicolay and John Hay, *A History of Abraham Lincoln* (10 vols., New York, 1890), 5:63, seem to agree with Coppée. They write that the Washington authorities, probably uninformed of Thomas' spirit and confidence, designated Mitchel for the duty.

14. Memorandum, Oct. 13, 1861, Robert Anderson Papers, Library of Congress.

15. *O.R.,* 4:342, 343. There was an element of unreality in the relationship between Thomas and Johnson. Johnson hindered Thomas' appointment as a general officer, maneuvered to put Mitchel in Thomas' command and sought to override his authority over the East Tennessee Brigade. Then, instead of moving to a rupture, their relations began to heal.

16. Albin Francisco Schoepf was a Hungarian with several years' service in Continental armies. He came to the U.S. in 1851.

17. *O.R.,* 4:353, 354. This order was sent by means of a code sentence. Late in 1863 Thomas received the code name Adonis.

Chapter 11

1. Between Nov. 7 (*O.R.,* 4:342) and Dec. 23 (*O.R.,* 7:512) Buell inverted his plans for an offensive eastward to an offensive southward. Thomas kept the eastward idea alive by pointing out that a victory would leave Buell free to choose either option. Buell had no quarrel with Lincoln's yearning to free East Tennessee but he apparently never accepted the premise that the invasion of East Tennessee was primarily a turning movement against Richmond in cooperation with McClellan (*O.R.,* 7:531).

2. Scully to his wife, Jan. 5 and 17, 1862, J. W. Scully Papers, Duke University Library.

3. He was graduated from West Point eight years before Thomas. His brother, T. L. Crittenden, was one of Buell's division commanders. His father, J. J. Crittenden, was a prominent Kentucky Unionist.

4. The original issues of small arms to both sides were identical. Both sides bought what arms they could from abroad. Those from Austria and Belgium were unsatisfactory. The men called them pumpkin slingers. Practically all muskets at that time had been designed as flintlocks but they were converted to the use of percussion caps and at the same time their barrels were rifled. The South had only limited means for making these conversions early in the war. Crittenden's men, deploying through the soaked underbrush, found it almost impossible to keep their priming dry.

5. Thomas' troops stood elbow to elbow and fired by volley. The Rebels broke with military tradition by taking cover and using the prone position.

6. Nicolay and Hay, 5:117.

7. The divided command of the Union forces helped maintain Johnston's bluff. Fremont and Halleck measured the Union forces in Missouri against Johnston's entire force. Anderson, Sherman and Buell measured the Union forces in Kentucky the same way. An organizational fault of the Northern high command appeared to double the Rebel army.

8. He might have pointed out, too, that during this same time one of Garfield's batteries, threading its way through the western Cumberlands, moved sixteen miles in three days. Halleck, Stanton and Lincoln never learned the fundamental difference between fighting in the mountains and fighting in the lowlands. It was this difference which misled Livermore.

9. Senate Executive Journal, 1861–62. Van Horne, *General Thomas,* thinks the delay in confirming his commission was caused by his Virginia birth. Ropes thinks it was because he had no state affiliation. No record has been found indicating that Thomas was dissatisfied with the violation of precedent in not dating the commission back to the day of the battle.

10. Nicolay and Hay, 5:74. They felt that if Thomas had been permitted to march as he originally planned his presence in East Tennessee would have been favored by extraordinary events.

Chapter 12

1. *O.R.,* 7:629.

2. *O.R.,* 10:2:83.

3. *O.R.,* 16:2:663.

4. A more enlightened policy was followed by the navy and it was apparently satisfactory to the public. The Confederates used army rank as it should have been used—a major general commanded a division; a lieutenant general, a corps; and a general, an army.

5. *O.R.,* 10:2:634.

6. Mrs. Thomas to Col. Hough, Aug. 29, 1881, John N. Hough Papers.

7. James H. Wilson, *Under the Old Flag* (2 vols., New York, 1912), 1:273.

8. Piatt and Boynton are the only contemporaneous biographers to discern the powerful influence of ambition in Thomas.

9. *O.R.*, 16:1:123. Piatt and Boynton, p. 167.

10. *O.R.*, 10:1:775.

11. *Battles and Leaders of the Civil War*, ed. Roy F. Nichols (4 vols., New York, 1887–88), 2:704.

12. *O.R.*, 16:2:31.

13. *O.R.*, 16:2:122, 221.

14. *Battles and Leaders*, 2:701. *O.R.*, 16:2:16.

15. *O.R.*, 16:2:119.

16. *O.R.*, 16:2:216.

17. *O.R.*, 16:2:104.

18. *O.R.*, 16:1:5.

19. Howard Swiggett, *The Rebel Raider, A Life of John Hunt Morgan* (Garden City, New York, 1937), p. 60.

20. He was graduated from West Point in 1859 and served in the mounted regiments until he resigned in 1861. Before the war's end he became a lieutenant general.

21. *Battles and Leaders*, 3:38.

22. James Ford Rhodes, *History of the United States from the Compromise of 1850* (5 vols., New York, 1902), 4:174.

23. *O.R.*, 16:1:87.

24. *Battles and Leaders*, 3:40.

25. *O.R.*, 16:2:384, 391–92.

26. *O.R.*, 16:2:399.

27. *Battles and Leaders*, 3:41.

28. The career of this Indiana officer is typical of the way Thomas harnessed civilian skills. He built his own wagons from salvage and mined coal for his forges to make horseshoes and nails.

29. *O.R.*, 16:1:959.

30. *Battles and Leaders*, 3:10, 42.

31. He had enlisted in the army at the age of eighteen to fight in Mexico and had been commissioned for gallantry at Buena Vista. He was in Fort Sumter during its bombardment and surrender. He was an able troop commander.

32. *O.R.*, 16:2:555.

33. John C. Ropes, *Story of the Civil War* (New York, 1933), 2:401.

34. He was a highly trained officer who served on the staff of the Russian Imperial Guards and emigrated to the United States in 1856. He was employed as a construction and maintenance engineer on the Illinois Central Railroad and was appointed colonel of a regiment of Illinois volunteers at the outbreak of the war.

35. *O.R.*, 16:1:134.

36. *O.R.*, 16:2:446.

37. Thomas to Andrew Johnson, Aug. 16, 1862, Thomas Papers, Henry E. Huntington Library, San Marino, California.

38. *O.R.,* 16:2:555.

39. *First Annual Report of the Society of the Army of the Cumberland* (Cincinnati, 1868), p. 84.

Chapter 13

1. Van Horne, *The Life of General George H. Thomas* (New York, 1882), p. 77. Francis B. Heitman, *Historical Register and Dictionary of the U.S. Army* (2 vols., Washington, D.C., 1903), 1:455.

2. *Battles and Leaders,* 3:29.

3. *Ibid.,* 3:47.

4. *Ibid.,* 3:48.

5. West Point, 1853. Sheridan, who was his classmate, named Fort Sill, Oklahoma, in his honor. In 1853 he was Thomas' second best student in artillery.

6. *O.R.,* 16:1:1025.

7. *O.R.,* 16:1:1026.

8. *O.R.,* 16:2:580.

9. *Battles and Leaders,* 3:47.

10. *O.R.,* 16:1:1025, 1040.

11. Van Horne, *General Thomas,* p. 80.

12. *O.R.,* 16:1:667–70.

13. *Battles and Leaders,* 3:48.

14. Van Horne, *General Thomas,* p. 81.

15. *Battles and Leaders,* 3:61.

16. Stanley F. Horn, *The Army of Tennessee* (Indianapolis, 1941), p. 185. Robert Self Henry, *The Story of the Confederacy* (New York, 1936), p. 199. Matthew F. Steele, *American Campaigns* (2 vols., Harrisburg, 1943), 1:312.

17. Ropes, 2:385, 414.

18. *O.R.,* 16:2:425.

19. Rosecrans to ———, Oct. 22, 1862, Sherman Papers, William L. Clements Library, Ann Arbor, Michigan.

20. *O.R.,* 16:2:657.

21. Troy (New York) *Times,* April 6, 1870.

22. Van Horne, *General Thomas,* p. 88. This outburst is evidence of the hot temper which Thomas generally held under tight control. The words were evidently lifted by Van Horne from their context. Freeman Cleaves, *Rock of Chickamauga, The Life of General George H. Thomas* (Norman, Oklahoma, 1949), p. 119, says they were part of a letter to Halleck and Van Horne implies as much, but no such letter is printed in *O.R.*

23. Van Horne, *General Thomas,* p. 76. At least once in his official correspondence Thomas denied that he was ambitious but his military career is studded with evidence that he was, no matter how hard he tried to repress it.

24. Troy (New York) *Press,* April 8, 1870.

25. Clifton R. Hall, *Andrew Johnson, Military Governor of Tennessee* (Princeton, 1916), p. 58. *O.R.,* 16:2:36.

26. *O.R.,* 16:1:189–91.

27. Grant asked for them during the Atlanta campaign.

28. *O.R.,* 16:1:198–200.

Chapter 14

1. It is doubtful if these drawbacks have an adverse effect upon the fighting qualities of any well led fighting force.

2. These were commanded by Lovell H. Rousseau, a Kentuckian who had helped hold that state for the Union; J. S. Negley, a Pennsylvanian who had served with Patterson in the Shenandoah; Speed S. Fry, a Kentuckian who had fought at Mill Springs; Ebenezer Dumont from Indiana, who had come west after fighting in West Virginia; and John M. Palmer of Illinois, postwar governor, senator and presidential nominee.

3. Report of the Committee on Affairs of Southern Railways, No. 34, Jan. 31, 1867, H.R., 39 Cong., 2 sess.

4. *O.R.,* 20:1:41, 42, 43.

5. *O.R.,* 20:2:185. J. J. Reynolds, the new division commander, was graduated from West Point three years after Thomas. He was not the Reynolds who had fought with Thomas in Mexico.

6. Muzzle loaders with percussion caps required sixty seconds to load and fire, but this time increased as the barrel fouled. A breech loader could be fired five times in sixty seconds and a revolving rifle (repeater), from thirty to sixty times.

7. *O.R.,* 20:2:61, 128.

8. A more socially inclined officer with Thomas' rank would have found some excuse for staying in the city. Bassay's Restaurant was housing and feeding the Buell Commission, before which Thomas had been a witness, and Ingomar was playing at the local theater.

9. W. D. Bickman, *Rosecrans' Campaign with the Fourteenth Army Corps* (Cincinnati, 1863), p. 135. Bickman was an eye-witness of the Stones River campaign.

10. Johnson was the luckless cavalryman captured by John Hunt Morgan after the destruction of the Gallatin tunnels. He published the first book-length biography of Thomas.

11. These were the divisions of Speed S. Fry, who shot Zollicoffer, Robert B. Mitchell and Joseph J. Reynolds. Mitchell was stationed in Nashville and Fry and Reynolds were guarding the railroad at Gallatin.

12. Shepherd commanded regular troops. It was Thomas' opinion during most of the war that volunteers needed to be strengthened in this way.

13. *O.R.,* 20:1:377.

14. *O.R.,* 20:1:249.

15. *O.R.*, 20:1 and 2 contain the reports and correspondence relative to the Stones River campaign. It is evident from them that the Right Wing had not yet learned to fight as a team.

16. Thomas B. Van Horne, *The History of the Army of the Cumberland* (2 vols. and atlas, Cincinnati, 1875), Vol. 1, chapter 17, has been followed in the description of the Battle of Stones River. The work was initiated in 1865 by Thomas and until 1870 the author received his personal help. This was supplemented by the recollections of many of the participants.

17. *O.R.*, 20:1:373.

18. John Beatty, *Memoirs of a Volunteer, 1861–1863* (New York, 1946), p. 153.

19. This name was not used in the Union battle reports. It was evidently used by the Rebel commanders to designate a target and was accepted by both sides after the battle.

20. *O.R.*, 20:1:524. *O.R. Atlas*, Plate 30, Map 1, was used for distances, directions and the locations of individual units and was checked with the Confederate battle maps, Plates 31, Map 1, and 32, Map 1.

21. Van Horne, *General Thomas*, p. 97.

22. *O.R.*, 20:1:456. The combined rate of fire from these batteries was 100 shots per minute. Approximately the same number of guns had been massed in support of Rosecrans' new line on the thirty-first. Union artillery played the major role in the Battle of Stones River. Mendenhall, who commanded the fifty-eight pieces, had been one of Thomas' artillery students at West Point.

23. Donn Piatt and Henry V. Boynton, *General George H. Thomas* (Cincinnati, 1893), p. 214.

Chapter 15

1. Thomas had anticipated him by offering to mount Rousseau's infantry division. Rousseau was sent to Washington to press the matter but the change was not authorized. Thomas worked out another plan, which was also turned down. It is significant that Dana, who was acting as Stanton's eyes, backed the contentions of the army commanders before he had been with them a week, *O.R.*, 30:1:184–88.

2. *O.R.*, 23:2:10, 15, 415. See also Coppée, *General Thomas* (New York, 1893), p. 123. John Fiske, *The Mississippi Valley in the Civil War* (Boston, 1900), p. 252, thinks the delay was justified. John G. Nicolay and John Hay, *A History of Abraham Lincoln* (10 vols., New York, 1890), 8:43, and James Ford Rhodes, *History of the United States from the Compromise of 1850* (5 vols., New York, 1902), 4:395, disagree.

3. Coppée, pp. 321, 333.

4. *O.R.*, 23:2:54, 57, 107.

5. J. W. Scully to his wife, May 14, 1862, Scully Papers, Duke University Library. Piatt and Boynton, p. 334.

6. Piatt and Boynton, p. 342.

7. Beatty, p. 176. No photograph has been found showing a shaved upper lip.

8. *O.R.*, 23:2:261. A week before Thomas' battle at Mill Springs, Burnside had landed an amphibious force on the coast of North Carolina to pinch off the Virginia salient in cooperation with Thomas' strike. He was now moving in cooperation with Rosecrans to occupy Cumberland Gap and Knoxville.

9. This brigade of Reynold's division was mounted in February and was commanded by Col. John T. Wilder, who personally secured the mounts for his men and financed the purchase of their repeating rifles. S. C. Williams, *General John T. Wilder* (Bloomington, Ind., 1936).

10. Probably the best of the repeating rifles. They held seven metallic cartridges. The range of military small arms in the Crimean War was 100 yards. In the Civil War it climbed to 500, out-ranged the grape and canister of the artillery, emptied cavalry saddles before the horsemen could close for their saber work, and eliminated the bayonet charge except where the range was reduced by natural cover or trenches. The axe and shovel became the best defense. Extended order replaced close order. Maj. Gen. J. F. C. Fuller, *Decisive Battles of the Western World and Their Influence on History* (London, 1954), pp. 677 ff. E. A. Altham, *The Principles of War, Historically Illustrated* (London, 1914), pp. 211 ff.

11. *O.R.*, 23:2:458. *O.R. Atlas*, Plate 34, Maps 2, 3, 4.

12. John Milton Brannan, West Point, 1841, relieved John M. Schofield in May 1863.

13. Report of the Committee on Affairs of Southern Railways, No. 34, H.R., January 31, 1867, 39 Cong., 2 sess. Thomas testified that the North could not have won without military railways. He pointed out that the South was not like Europe, where an army was certain of finding supplies almost anywhere. There were large areas in the mountains where there were no supplies.

14. Edwin A. Pratt, *The Rise of Rail Power in War and Conquest, 1833–1914* (London, 1915), p. 89.

15. *O.R. Atlas*, Plate 34. Angles were probably measured by a prismatic compass, distances by counting the paces of a man or horse or the revolutions of a wheel. In some cases distances may have been triangulated.

16. Halleck never enforced his orders to Burnside and those that went to Grant were too late.

17. This brigade immobilized one of Bragg's army corps while the Army of the Cumberland made its crossing farther downstream. Thomas was pleased and recommended Wilder for his star.

18. Absalom Baird, West Point, 1849, took command of the division while Rousseau was in Washington.

19. Piatt and Boynton, p. 360. Thomas, before he splashed through the Potomac fords in 1861, had recorded his belief that Chattanooga was the entrance to the vitals of the Confederacy. In words similar to those that Winston Churchill later made famous, he said that the capture of Chattanooga ". . . enables us to strike at its [the Confederacy's] belly where it lives."

20. The site is now occupied by the Reid House, where a plaque details the incident.

21. Piatt and Boynton, pp. 334, 360. Van Horne, *The Life of General George H. Thomas* (New York, 1882), p. 459.

22. Gordon Granger, West Point, 1845, commanded Rosecrans' reserves.

Chapter 16

1. There is a parallel and also a difference between this inversion march and Stonewall Jackson's flank march at Chancellorsville. Although Jackson marched during the day and Thomas at night, both achieved a tactical surprise and exploited it by an immediate attack. The difference was that Lee knew the location of Hooker's army and had arranged the rest of his command to help Jackson in case of need, while Rosecrans was ignorant of Bragg's position and would have been unable to help Thomas.

2. John M. Palmer now commanded Crittenden's heaviest division.

3. Baird, Brannan, Negley and Reynolds were Thomas' division commanders.

4. Chickamauga was the first battle of the Army of the Cumberland, and probably the first battle in the west, to be directed by telegraph. There was a telegraph station at Rosecrans' headquarters, one on the Dry Valley road about two and a half miles west of McDonald's (probably close to Mc-Farland's Gap), which was closed at 9:00 A.M. on the twentieth, and another station at Rossville which was kept open during the battle. The tactical use of the telegraph during the battle was, therefore, rather sketchy. *O.R.,* Series III, 3:863. Charles A. Dana, *Recollections of the Civil War* (New York, 1899), p. 112. Granger was posted on the Rossville-Ringgold road to check any flank movement by Bragg against Rossville Gap.

5. *O.R.,* 30:1:249, gives Thomas' version of his available intelligence. *O.R.,* 30:3:743, gives that of McCook. He gave his information to Thomas verbally but his dispatch shows the gist of his report. It is apparent that he felt his message was urgent. *O.R.,* 30:3:724, 725, contain Wilder's dispatches, the last one dated 8:50 P.M. of the eighteenth. It was after this that Thomas crossed the area of Wilder's fight and, finding no enemy, probably surmised that they had withdrawn.

6. When cavalry fought dismounted, every fourth man was designated to care for the horses of three of his companions. It was his duty to keep them fed, watered, rested and close to their riders. This was a heavy subtraction from a unit's battle strength but the added mobility offset the loss.

7. *O.R.,* 30:1:124. Thomas sent Palmer his orders at 9:00 A.M. Half an hour later he asked Rosecrans to order Crittenden's cooperation with this move.

8. Ferdinand Van Derveer was born and educated in Ohio and ultimately became judge of the court of common pleas of Butler County. He headed one of the assaulting columns at Monterrey and probably knew Thomas at that time. He renewed the acquaintance at Mill Springs.

9. Col. George G. Dibrell and Brig. Gen. H. B. Davidson commanded brigades of Forrest's corps and had been fighting all morning. Brig. Gen. Matthew D. Ector and Col. Claudius C. Wilson, commanding brigades in the division of Brig. Gen. States R. Gist, had been sent in piecemeal to support Forrest.

Col. Daniel C. Govan and Brig. Gen. Edward C. Walthall commanded brigades in the division of Brig. Gen. St. John R. Liddell. Liddell's troops had just come up. Maj. Gen. Benjamin R. Cheatham commanded the brigades of Brig. Generals John K. Jackson, Preston Smith, George Maney, Marcus J. Wright and Otho F. Strahl.

10. Richard W. Johnson commanded one of McCook's divisions.

11. Benjamin F. Scribner commanded one of Baird's brigades. John H. King commanded Baird's regular brigade. Thomas' confidence in the regulars had been unaltered since the days of Dick Robinson. He put them where the enemy pressure would be greatest.

12. *O.R.*, 30:1:762. This unbelievably short time may reflect the common battle phenomenon that makes it impossible to judge correctly the passage of time.

13. *O.R.*, 30:1:134.

14. This was Snodgrass Ridge, then unnamed.

15. Van Horne, *General Thomas*, p. 121. Hazen claims that one of his colonels started the idea.

16. Thomas to Granger, *O.R.*, 30:1:139, is marked 8:00 A.M. Granger to Rosecrans, *O.R.*, 30:1:125, is marked 10:30 A.M., but it was never received.

17. *O.R.*, 30:1:137.

18. Van Horne, *General Thomas*, p. 127.

19. Since Negley never did the job Thomas wanted him to do, second guessing makes this decision look bad. His failure to reach Thomas in time was not caused by the time required to move his division but by the time required to relieve it from the line. Rosecrans may have decided as he did to conserve his reserve.

20. *O.R.*, 30:1:69 is the order to Negley. The order to McCook, *O.R.*, 30:1:70, is conditional where it should have been positive. There is little doubt that Rosecrans was becoming confused.

21. Thomas B. Van Horne, *The History of the Army of the Cumberland* (2 vols. and atlas, Cincinnati, 1875), 1:346.

22. "Held" in the military sense. Baird's men had been thrown out of their position but had regained it by counterattacking.

23. *O.R.*, 30:1:251.

24. This was the fourth division to receive orders to support Thomas' left. Eventually, as a result of the welter of relief orders, he got four brigades, one at a time, from three divisions. Since he got one of these by countermanding Rosecrans' order, the commanding general managed to get only three brigades to the place he wanted them out of the eight he ordered there.

25. Thomas must have entered it near its northeast corner. His aide, Sanford Cobb Kellogg, was a nephew to Mrs. Thomas. A painting of him hangs in the Metropolitan Club, Washington, D.C.

26. Charles G. Harker, West Point, 1858, was one of the few officers to enhance his reputation at Stones River. He was proposed for promotion but Lincoln failed to nominate him.

27. Apparently he was no relation to Don Carlos Buell.

28. Not to be confused with John Beatty.

29. James B. Steedman was nicknamed "Old Steady." He was stout, burly, powerful, bold, honest and confident. He dared to assume appalling responsibilities. He could neither eat nor drink under the tension of battle.

30. *O.R.,* 30:1:140. This was the order Thomas acted upon in withdrawing to Rossville. Rosecrans, *O.R.,* 30:1:61, says Thomas was ordered to use his discretion about retreating. Van Horne, *General Thomas,* p. 140, says Garfield brought Thomas discretionary orders and that Thomas' reply was emphatic. "It will ruin the army to withdraw it now. This position must be held till night." T. C. Smith, *Life and Letters of James A. Garfield* (New Haven, 1925), p. 859, says that Rosecrans sent no orders to Thomas by Garfield. Garfield states plainly in a dispatch to Rosecrans from Rossville, *O.R.,* 30:1:145, that Thomas retired on Rosecrans' orders.

31. A court martial had sentenced Turchin to be dismissed for permitting his troops to sack Athens, Alabama, but Lincoln set aside the sentence.

32. In the vicinity of the Mullis house during the retreat, Thomas learned that Brannan's right was in trouble and sent two Indiana regiments to help him. They followed Brannan's retirement as a rear guard.

33. Thomas had men from every infantry division except Sheridan's. It is possible that on the twentieth more men left the field from the Fourteenth Army Corps than from the commands of McCook or of Crittenden.

34. J. B. Fry to *Century Magazine,* Aug. 8, 1888, Century Collection, Manuscript Room, New York Public Library. Garfield's report to Rosecrans from Snodgrass Ridge started the myth that Sheridan brought his command on the field in time to cover Thomas' retreat. Garfield corrected this error five hours later. Sheridan took advantage of this misinformation in his official report. When he wrote his *Personal Memoirs* (New York, 1888), 1:284, he threw the truth out of the window.

35. It is difficult to tell, from Negley's report on the Battle of Chickamauga and from the testimony taken at his trial, what happened. Beatty's brigade was taken from him at 8:00 A.M. and Stanley's at 9:30. At 10:00, while accompanying Stanley northward, Negley received Thomas' orders to take command of the artillery. As soon as he could detach Sirwell's brigade from the battle line, he used it as support for the guns. The battlefield markers say that Sirwell's troops were the first to occupy Snodgrass Ridge. It might well be that Brannan rallied his shattered division on them. Shortly before 12:15 P.M., Negley sent two aids to Rosecrans for help. Both made the round trip. The verdict of the Negley Court of Inquiry was that, from the facts at hand between 1:00 and 2:00 P.M., the defense of Snodgrass Ridge was impossible.

36. *Encyclopaedia Britannica* (Chicago, 1946), 5:461.

37. Nicolay and Hay, 8:87.

38. Stanley F. Horn, *The Army of Tennessee* (Indianapolis, 1941), p. 266.

Chapter 17

1. *O.R.,* 30:3:794.

2. Carl Sandburg, *Abraham Lincoln: The War Years* (4 vols., New York, 1939), 2:430.

3. *The Diary of Gideon Welles* (Boston and New York, 1911), 1:446.

4. *O.R.,* 30:3:946.

5. *O.R.,* 30:1:211. Dana's last sentence reads, "Besides he [Thomas] has as perfect confidence in capacity and fidelity of Rosecrans as he had in those of General Buell."

6. Troy (New York) *Times,* April 6, 1870.

7. Van Horne, *The Life of General George H. Thomas* (New York, 1882), p. 152, thinks Thomas' reluctance arose from Rosecrans' political complications. Donn Piatt and Henry V. Boynton, *General George H. Thomas* (Cincinnati, 1893), p. 445, think that Rosecrans overcame Thomas' objections to the injustice of the removal by pointing out that his refusal might subject the army to the abuse of some new commander.

8. David H. Bates, *Lincoln in the Telegraph Office* (New York, 1907), p. 169.

9. *O.R.,* 30:4:479.

10. This was a combination of the Twentieth and Twenty-first corps.

11. Hooker's command was an anomaly dictated by Washington. David S. Stanley, West Point, 1852, had returned from the illness which kept him out of the Battle of Chickamauga.

12. West Point, 1845. The troops called him "Baldy" Smith. He was one of the most capable Northern officers.

13. *O.R.,* 31:1:700.

14. Scrapbook in the Chattanooga Public Library. Thomas' headquarters were probably in a plain, wooden, one-story building on Walnut Street near 4th Street. James H. Wilson, *Under the Old Flag* (2 vols., New York, 1912), 1:273, gives a description of Thomas and the details of Thomas' treatment of Grant.

15. Richard W. Johnson, *Memoir of General George H. Thomas* (Philadelphia, 1881), p. 115.

16. William D. Whipple, West Point, 1851.

17. Gamaliel Bradford, "Union Portraits: George H. Thomas," *Atlantic Monthly,* 114 (August, 1914), 224. McKibben to Garfield, Dec. 19, 1863; Gillem to Garfield, Dec. 27, 1863; George Thom to Garfield, Jan. 20, 1864; all in Garfield Papers, Library of Congress.

18. Palmer to his wife, Dec. 27, 1863, Palmer Papers, Illinois State Historical Library, Springfield.

19. Hooker sent an ambulance to meet Grant's train with an invitation to visit his headquarters. This blatant violation of military protocol may have increased Grant's sensitivity to Thomas' slight a few days later.

20. Piatt and Boynton, p. 474.

21. Montgomery C. Meigs, West Point, 1836. He was Quartermaster General of the army and gave Thomas the benefit of his experience and prestige in solving his supply problems.

22. He was one of the few non-West Pointers able to handle large bodies of troops.

23. Piatt and Boynton, p. 467, maintain that it was recognition of Thomas' seniority under the rules and regulations of the regular army.

24. John G. Nicolay and John Hay, *A History of Abraham Lincoln* (10 vols., New York, 1890), 8:130, 131, say that Grant never forgave Thomas for this difference of opinion even though it was the general judgment of military men that Thomas was right. See also *Battles and Leaders of the Civil War*, ed. Roy F. Nichols (4 vols., New York, 1887–88), 3:716.

25. Piatt and Boynton, p. 462, hold the view that Grant never intended his order of November 7 to be obeyed. In their opinion it was meant to convince the authorities at Washington that they had picked a man of spirit and enterprise for their commander at Chattanooga.

26. William T. Sherman, *Memoirs* (New York, 1931), 1:390. G.G. [probably Gordon Granger] to Garfield, Feb. 6, 1864, Garfield Papers, says Sherman's troops were expected to humiliate the Cumberlanders.

27. Thomas' corps badges were a triangle for the Fourth, an acorn for the Fourteenth, and a star for the Twentieth.

28. Lloyd Lewis, *Sherman: Fighting Prophet* (New York, 1932), p. 318.

29. Fuel was as scarce as forage and the Yanks used all kinds of schemes to get it.

30. John W. Geary was a non-West Pointer who was a good troop handler. Peter J. Osterhaus had been trained as a Prussian officer.

31. Hardee commanded Bragg's right, which originally ended opposite Orchard Knob. Thomas overlapped this line on the twenty-third and Cleburne was positioned to extend it to the railroad tunnel. Horn, p. 298, says that this took place on the night of the twenty-third. Van Horne, *General Thomas,* p. 187, says that Cleburne and Walker extended this line on the twenty-fourth and that on the twenty-fifth Bragg detached Stevenson and Cheatham from Lookout Mountain to strengthen his tunnel flank. Bragg moved no troops from Thomas' center.

32. Cleburne bent his line to the east and Sherman never got around this refused flank. Davis wanted to try but Sherman would not permit it. Howard, although available, was never deployed on the twenty-fifth. James H. Wilson, *Major General William Farrar Smith* (Wilmington, 1904), p. 78, says Sherman never reached a point from which he could strike a fatal blow.

33. T. J. Wood, "The Battle of Missionary Ridge," *Sketches of War History,* Ohio Comdry., M.O.L.L. (5 vols., Cincinnati, 1884–97), 4:34.

34. James H. Wilson, *The Life of John A. Rawlins* (New York, 1916), pp. 171–73.

35. Many explanations of this assault have been offered. Van Horne, *General Thomas,* p. 195, was impressed by its unity, which he believed could hardly have been possible without prior instruction. J. F. C. Fuller, *Decisive Battles*

of the Western World and Their Influence on History (London, 1954), p. 284, snorts off the theory of psychological imponderables and says the assault grew out of the soldiers' common sense. They saw the enemy run and ran after them. According to this theory, Thomas' men should have overrun Kennesaw Mountain six months later with Joe Johnston's picket line fleeing up the steep slope ahead of them.

36. John Russell Young, *Around the World with General Grant, 1877–79* (2 vols., New York, 1879), 2:626. William F. Smith, *Military Operations Around Chattanooga in October and November 1863* (Wilmington, Del., 1886), p. 2, states that Grant failed to exploit his victory by throwing Sherman's fresh troops into Bragg's flank.

37. Thomas to Garfield, Dec. 17, 1863, Garfield Papers.

Chapter 18

1. Col. Hough in his Autobiography, typescript from the John N. Hough Papers, points out that this military division was the largest in the United States. Thomas' headquarters in Chattanooga handled practically all the staff work for the three armies while Grant exercised the over-all command from Nashville.

2. John Gray Foster, West Point, 1846. Burnside and the Ninth Corps eventually rejoined the Army of the Potomac.

3. John Alexander Logan of Illinois, soldier, lawyer, congressman and able troop commander. His men called him "Black Jack."

4. *O.R.*, 32:2:43, 63, 88, 237, 248.

5. Sherman, *Memoirs*, 1:414.

6. *Ibid.*, 2:29.

7. Foster had asked to be relieved and Schofield had been shoved into the command over Grant's remonstrances. Sherman was working through Senator John Sherman to get the Senatorial approval that would confirm Schofield in his command. His quarrels with Hovey, Judah, Hooker, Palmer, Butterfield, Stanley and Baird impaired the efficiency of the Atlanta campaign.

8. West Point, 1853. He was an eminent engineer but a poor cavalry leader.

9. Grant to Schofield, *O.R.*, 32:2:434.

10. *O.R.*, 32:2:429.

11. Thomas B. Van Horne, *The History of the Army of the Cumberland* (2 vols. and atlas, Cincinnati, 1875), 2:43. See also *O.R.*, 32:2:489.

12. Van Horne, *Cumberland*, 2:2, 439.

13. West Point, 1852.

14. James Harrison Wilson, West Point, 1860, started as an engineer and was turned into a cavalryman by Grant. He became one of the war's outstanding leaders of mounted troops.

15. Sherman, *Memoirs*, 2:27.

16. *O.R.*, 32:2:88, 131, 143. *U.S. Military Railroads—Report of Bvt. Brig. Gen.*

D. C. McCallum, Director and General Manager from 1861 to 1866, pamphlet with map showing the various gauges of the military railroads. This is apparently McCallum's report to Stanton of May 26, 1866.

17. New York *Times*, Nov. 22, 1864, contains details of the Nashville shops. See *O.R.*, Series III: 3:881 ff., for the operations of the military railways in the Department of the Cumberland. The *Times* states that a headquarters car was being built for Thomas. It is probable that this car is now owned by the Southern Railway System (letter of B. E. Young to the author, Jan. 28, 1953). Thomas may have used such a railway car during his pursuit of Hood and he certainly used it after the war.

18. William E. Merrill, "The Engineering Service in the Army of the Cumberland," in Van Horne, *Cumberland*, 2:439, gives the details of the Cumberland pontoon and of the military maps for the Atlanta campaign.

19. George Edgar Turner, *Victory Rode the Rails* (Indianapolis, 1953), pp. 302, 303.

20. Oliver O. Howard, *Autobiography* (2 vols., New York, 1907), 1:495.

21. Jacob D. Cox, *Military Reminiscences of the Civil War* (2 vols., New York, 1900), 1:165; 2:203.

22. *O.R.*, 38:2:751. Stanley F. Horn, *The Army of Tennessee* (Indianapolis, 1941), p. 328, writes that Hood was surprised by Hooker's infantry, who had lost their way. This is possible, but from the disposition of the Twentieth Corps the preceding night, it seems hardly probable. There is nothing in *O.R.* to indicate that elements of the Twentieth Corps were in this vicinity at this time. Howard, in his *Autobiography*, 1:532, says it was Stoneman's dismounted cavalry and horse artillery that misled Hood. See also Sgt. E. Tarrant, *History of the First Kentucky Cavalry* (Louisville, 1894), p. 330. There are no reports of Stoneman's covering this date in *O.R.*, vol. 38, nor does Schofield make mention of any such action by Stoneman on the eighteenth.

23. The rest of the Twentieth Corps and all of the Army of the Ohio were in the rear of this brigade. When units of the Twentieth Corps deployed, it was away from the Canton road. The 105th Regiment of Illinois Volunteers had the skirmish detail for Butterfield's leading brigade and they were stopped a mile and a half before reaching the Canton road junction. See *O.R.*, 38:2:361.

24. W. F. G. Shanks, *Personal Recollections of Distinguished Generals* (New York, 1866), p. 76. Oliver O. Howard, "Sketch of the Life of General George H. Thomas," in *War Sketches*, New York Comdry., M.O.L.L. (New York, 1890).

25. Cox, 2:233. Blair's two divisions of the Seventeenth Corps also disobeyed the order. There was a shortage of corn in Georgia which Sherman should have known about when he fixed his wagon ratio. The results of this error bore heavily on his cavalry mounts when there was no way of bringing forage to them.

26. *O.R.*, 38:4:507. On the day it was written, Thomas sent a dispatch to Howard, the last two sentences of which read, "Gen. Sherman is at last very much pleased. Our consciences approve of our work and I hope all will go

right." Mrs. Thomas to Col. Hough, Jan. 21, 1876, John N. Hough Papers, makes it appear that Thomas never heard of this excoriation.

27. Lewis, p. 375.

28. Van Horne, *General Thomas*, p. 233. Freeman Cleaves, *Rock of Chickamauga, The Life of General George H. Thomas* (Norman, Oklahoma, 1949), p. 221. David S. Stanley, *Personal Memoirs* (Cambridge, Mass., 1917), p. 173. Horn, p. 335. James Ford Rhodes, *History of the United States from the Compromise of 1850* (5 vols., New York, 1902), 4:454–56.

29. Sherman, *Memoirs,* 2:61, refers to this move against the railway at Fulton and says, ". . . Thomas, as usual, shook his head, deeming it risky to leave the railroad. . . ." *O.R.,* 38:4:611, shows that at 9:00 P.M. of June 27, Sherman queried Thomas, "Are you willing to risk the move on Fulton, cutting loose from our railroad?" Less than forty-five minutes later Thomas sent his approval, *O.R.,* 38:4:612.

30. Thomas to Garfield, July 16, 1864, Garfield Papers.

31. Hood, one of the best combat leaders on either side, was the last commissioned general in the Confederate army. He was thirty-three when he got his fourth star. When he rode to the front of one of his shattered units and demanded their colors, the thinned, bewildered ranks caught fire with energy and resolution. At his best he was an unarmored knight. As such, he scorned the drudgery of adequate preparation.

32. *O.R. Atlas,* Plate 101, Map 7.

33. *O.R.,* 38:5:279; 38:1:650.

34. Palmer to his wife, July 15, 1864, Palmer Papers.

35. *O.R.,* 38:5:456, 471, 472. Rhodes, 4:456, refers to the basic disagreement between Thomas' carefulness and Sherman's recklessness in these words: "In this controversy the layman may not venture a decision, and since the campaign was successful . . . he would like to believe that the differing gifts of Sherman and Thomas wrought together to advantage, and that they accomplished in their union, jarring though it was at times, what neither one alone would have done so completely and so well."

36. *O.R.,* 38:5:718.

37. *O.R.,* 38:5:717–19, 732–34; 38:1:81. Sherman, *Memoirs,* 2:506–12.

38. Maj. James Austin Connolly, "Letters to His Wife, 1862–65," in *Transactions of the Illinois State Historical Society* (Springfield, 1928), p. 361.

39. These were the figures reported by Sherman. In *Battles and Leaders,* 4:289, Major E. C. Dawes concluded that each side had 40,000 casualties.

40. Address of Gen. James H. Wilson in *Report of the Twenty-seventh Reunion of the Society of the Army of the Cumberland,* Sept. 22, 1897.

Before the attack on Kennesaw, Logan boasted that his men would go farther than the Cumberlanders. The day after the battle, Sherman reminded Palmer that Logan had made good his boast. Palmer rejoined that both armies had failed equally and that he had 100 more men than he would have if he had answered Logan's challenge.

Chapter 19

1. Col. Hough to his wife, Sept. 18, 1864, typescript, John N. Hough Papers.

2. Andrew Jackson Smith, West Point, 1838, was one of the few Northern commanders ever to defeat Forrest.

3. *O.R.,* 39:3:685, 686, 697, 704, 718.

4. Edward R. S. Canby, West Point, 1839. On Nov. 7, Lincoln stripped Thomas of all his garrisons on the east bank of the Mississippi, put them under Canby's control and deprived Thomas of his western flank guard.

5. *O.R.,* 39:3:614, 617, 640. Canby's primary responsibility was to keep the Mississippi open. Sherman and Thomas wanted him to smash Hood's communications with 15,000 troops but Grant evidently thought Canby too weak to do both jobs.

6. George Stoneman, Jr., West Point, 1846, commanded the North's first massed cavalry but had done little with it. Sherman failed to use him advantageously at Atlanta. Thomas salvaged his ability. He was the only ranking general officer to take part in the final defeats of Johnston, Hood and Lee.

7. His conviction grew little by little. On Nov. 21, Thomas knew Hood would move against him rather than against Sherman. On Nov. 23, he knew that Hood was moving north instead of east toward Chattanooga. On Nov. 30, he knew that he must make his concentration at Nashville.

8. McClellan is a doubtful exception and Fremont was also a cavalry officer by appointment but not by experience.

9. *O.R.,* 45:1:1108. Thomas' plan is obscure.

10. One deserted, another was drunk, while a third refused to handle Thomas' dispatch to Schofield because he had other duties.

11. John H. Hammond had enlisted in the Fifth Regiment of California Volunteer Infantry as a private.

12. *O.R.,* 45:2:143.

13. *O.R.,* 45:2:143. Grant's order broke the fundamental rule that the commander remote from his superior should be the judge of such things (James H. Wilson, *Under the Old Flag* [2 vols., New York, 1912], p. 73). Thomas' technical position was impregnable. He told Wilson, ". . . If they [Grant and Halleck] will leave me alone I will fight this battle just as soon as it can be done, and will surely win it, but I will not throw the victory away nor sacrifice the brave men of this army by moving 'till the thaw begins. I will surrender my command without a murmur, if they wish it, but I will not act against my judgment when I know I am right. . . ." See *Battles and Leaders of the Civil War,* ed. Roy F. Nichols (4 vols., New York, 1887–88), 4:467. This is a degree of self-abnegation that is hard to understand.

14. David H. Bates, *Lincoln in the Telegraph Office* (New York, 1907), p. 310. Grant, in his *Personal Memoirs* (2 vols. in 1, New York, 1894), p. 569, contradicts Eckert, but *O.R.,* 45:2:194–96, fails to support Grant.

15. Van Horne, *The Life of General George H. Thomas* (New York, 1882), p. 321, names Dec. 14 as the beginning of Thomas' distrust of Schofield.

16. Article in the Cincinnati *Enquirer,* quoting J. B. Steedman, "Robbing the Dead," from the Toledo *Northern Democrat,* U. S. Civil War Newspaper Clippings, Manuscript Room, Library of Congress. Steedman's article is detailed and names a witness. Van Horne quotes Col. Hough as reporting that Thomas merely suspected that Schofield was disparaging him. This suspicion was held by others. See, for example, Sanford Cobb Kellogg to Col. Hough, June 6, 1881, John N. Hough Papers. Kellogg had no doubt that Schofield was secretly disparaging Thomas and that in 1879 the evidence had been removed from the War Department files.

Schofield makes his defense to this charge in *Forty-Six Years in the Army* (New York, 1897), p. 294, but it is unconvincing. Stone maintains that all of Thomas' subordinates at Nashville were loyal. See *Battles and Leaders,* 4:457.

17. Joseph F. Knipe of Pennsylvania was transferred from the infantry to the cavalry during the Atlanta campaign.

18. *O.R.,* 45:1:38. Horn, p. 411, points out, however, that Thomas was mistaken.

19. Donaldson was a West Pointer of the class of 1836 and was now serving as the chief quartermaster of the Department of the Cumberland.

20. Alexander K. McClure, *Lincoln and the Men of War Times* (Philadelphia, 1892), p. 363. John McElroy, "Life of George H. Thomas," *National Tribune,* 1:10 (May 9, 1896), 23.

Chapter 20

1. Wilson, *Under the Old Flag,* p. 158, wrote that rest and refit were imperative but that despite this fact Grant marked out for Thomas an almost impossible winter campaign. When Thomas declared it impracticable he was punished by having his army broken up and scattered.

Cox was another eye-witness to Thomas' troubles. He wrote, 2:385, that the Administration would not believe Thomas when he told them his army was stuck in the mud and that they forced him to pretend to move at the cost of ruining his horses and mules and putting half his men in the hospital.

Thomas' opinions regarding a winter campaign in northern Alabama and Mississippi were corroborated by other on-the-spot experts. Beauregard, *O.R.,* 45:2:637, reported the area drained of military supplies. Hood, *O.R.,* 45:2:656, announced that wagon transport was impossible. Forrest, *O.R.,* 45:2:756, required a minimum of six weeks to refit his cavalry. Chalmers, *O.R.,* 45:2: 758, reported that three or four of the streams that had to be crossed in moving southward were impassable.

2. Van Horne, *General Thomas,* p. 371. This description is typical of Van Horne's prudishness. No one knows whether Thomas cried or cursed.

3. *Ibid.,* pp. 386, 387, is uncharacteristically vague about Wilson's orders.

4. *O.R.,* 49:2:94. Thomas wanted Stoneman to block all of Lee's retreat routes. He was not privy to Grant's plans but he guessed them and alerted Stoneman. There were numerous military combinations that might have preceded the decisive battle which Thomas expected. Thomas was ready for any of them and planned to assume the leadership of his infantry force as soon as

Lee and Grant made their commitments, *O.R.*, 49:1:917. He was preparing
to meet any enemy force moving in his direction, *O.R.*, 49:2:259.

Thomas kept himself informed of what was going on in southwestern
Virginia by means of his intelligence section. He was so thoroughly isolated
by Grant's cold shoulder that he was forced to get his information about the
Union army in the same way he did about the enemy's. His scouts were in
Staunton, Virginia, before Sheridan reached that place and Thomas knew
all about the extent of the cooperation he might expect from Sheridan's
cavalry, *O.R.*, 46:2:896.

5. Douglas S. Freeman, *Robert E. Lee* (4 vols., New York, 1934–35), 4:94, 115.
Grant in his *Memoirs*, p. 646, minimized the results of Thomas' military
activities in 1865, saying, "The only possible good that we may have experienced from these raids [Wilson's and Stoneman's] was by Stoneman's getting
near Lynchburg about the time the armies of the Potomac and the James
were closing in on Lee at Appomattox. . . . His approach caused the evacuation of that city [Lynchburg] about the time that we were at Appomattox,
and was the cause of a commotion we heard there."

6. Grant, *Memoirs,* p. 646. "He [Stoneman] pushed south and was operating
in the rear of Johnston's army about the time the negotiations were going on
between Sherman and Johnston for the latter's surrender." From his perspective, Grant was unimpressed by the 1865 operations of Wilson and
Canby as well as those of Stoneman. Forrest, he pointed out, p. 647, had
neither his old-time army nor his old-time prestige. He would have been
equally correct if he had extended his remarks to Lee, Johnston and the rest.

7. Bvt. Maj. Gen. Upton was a twenty-five-year-old West Pointer with experience
in all three arms of the service. Brig. Gen. Long was a Kentuckian who entered the army from civil life five years before the war. He needed no supervision and few orders.

O.R., 49:1:339 ff., gives the reports on Wilson's raid. An interesting detail
was that a partially-filled Spencer magazine was a danger to horse and trooper
on a hot day. With four inches or more play between the metallic cartridges
in the magazine, the friction from the motion of the horse combined with
the heat of the sun was enough to explode them.

8. Four hundred of his men were guarding the corps train twenty miles in
the rear and did not rejoin Croxton until after the capture of Tuscaloosa.

9. This is Wilson's figure. Robert S. Henry, *"First with the Most" Forrest*
(Indianapolis, 1944), p. 431, puts Forrest's strength at around 1,500.

10. Col. Robert H. G. Minty was born in Ireland, emigrated to the United States
and settled in Detroit. He had served four years in the British army and
entered the Union army in Sept. 1861 as a major in the Second Regiment
of Michigan Volunteer Cavalry.

11. Bvt. Brig. Gen. Edward F. Winslow had joined an Iowa cavalry regiment
late in 1861 as a captain with no previous military training.

12. Col. Oscar H. La Grange was promoted from command of a Wisconsin
cavalry regiment to become one of McCook's crackerjack brigade commanders.

13. Benjamin D. Pritchard quit his studies at the University of Michigan in
1862 to join the Fourth Regiment of Michigan Volunteer Cavalry as a captain.

14. The political gain was the preservation of the Union. The moral gain was the destruction of slavery. The military gain was the technological evolution of the tools of violence.

Chapter 21

1. Van Horne, *The Life of General George H. Thomas* (New York, 1882), p. 370.

2. James W. Fertig, *The Secession and Reconstruction of Tennessee* (Chicago, 1898), p. 59. E. M. Coulter, *William G. Brownlow* (Chapel Hill, 1937), p. 263, says there was no interregnum, that Brownlow acted as governor between the time Johnson left Nashville and his own inauguration. The *Official Records* give no support to this assumption.

3. *O.R.*, 49:2:342, 506.

4. Thomas' Annual Report, September 30, 1867, Let. Sent, Depts. of the Cumberland and Tennessee, vol. 46, National Archives.

5. The Fourteenth Amendment was proposed to the states on June 13, 1866, and declared to have been ratified two years later. In Mississippi, prior to Oct. 1866, Thomas was preventing the enforcement of state laws discriminating against the freedmen because of race or color (see Report of T. J. Wood, Oct. 29, 1866, Let. Sent, Military Division of the Tennessee, vol. 34). In Kentucky he was protecting their rights of life, person and property (see Report of J. C. Davis, April 27, 1866, Let. Sent, Military Division of the Tennessee, vol. 34).

6. Fertig, p. 102. Johnson removed the restrictions on June 13, 1865. Thomas' railway order was dated Jan. 30, 1865.

7. Gamaliel Bradford, "Union Portraits: George H. Thomas," *Atlantic Monthly*, 114 (Aug. 1914), 229, agrees with Johnson.

8. Van Horne, *General Thomas*, p. 406. Freeman Cleaves, *Rock of Chickamauga, The Life of General George H. Thomas* (Norman, Oklahoma, 1949), p. 296, suggests that Hood's remark meant that Thomas was not happy. This is apparently an assumption, but it might be just as reasonable to assume that Hood was expressing a personal conviction about the treatment of Thomas which met with general disapproval among military men.

9. Ephraim A. Otis, "General George H. Thomas," *Military Essays and Recollections,* Ill. Comdry., M.O.L.L. (Chicago, 1891), 1:395. Such judgments were frequent in the seceded states. The victims were ex-Union soldiers accused of murder, robbery or pillage because of acts performed under military orders. All the Southern states except three had men in the Northern armies, but Tennessee had more than the rest of Secessia. The persecution of these individuals had much to do with forming the harsh, vindictive Reconstruction formula.

10. *O.R.*, 49:2:518. Thomas' mistake is understandable. Tennessee had qualified for readmission to the Union under the Presidential plan; its delegates had been seated in the Republican nominating convention; its vote had been tallied for the Lincoln-Johnson ticket and sent to the electoral college; one of its sons was President of the United States; and it had ratified the Thir-

teenth Amendment, which was the principal qualification of the Wade-Davis Congressional Reconstruction plan.

11. The Memphis riot, which took place in 1866, was a bad one, investigated by a Congressional committee and a military commission.

12. Stanton to Thomas, Dec. 13, 1865, Telegrams Sent File, Military Division of the Tennessee, 45:196.

13. Report of the Committee on Affairs of Southern Railways, No. 34, Jan. 31, 1867, H.R., 39 Cong., 2 sess. C. R. Fish, *The Restoration of the Southern Railroads* (Madison, Wisconsin, 1919).

14. Van Horne, *General Thomas,* p. 415. Thomas' will has not been located. The will of Mrs. Thomas is filed at Troy, New York, and those of Thomas' sisters, Francis [sic] and Judith, at Courtland, Virginia.

15. *The Diary of Gideon Welles* (Boston and New York, 1911), 2:554.

16. Alexander B. Hasson of Maryland was Thomas' medical director with the brevet rank of lieutenant colonel. Thomas was grossly overweight, apparently a heavy eater, probably of sedentary habits. His emotional safety valve had been tied down for years. Hasson to A.G., Aug. 21, 1867, Regis. Let. Rec., Dept. of the Cumberland, Book 47, File H25. Coppée, *General Thomas* (New York, 1893), p. 296.

17. The Henry E. Huntington Library owns Thomas' letters to Cist, Bates and Tyler. See also Van Horne, *General Thomas,* p. 422; Richard W. Johnson, *Memoir of General George H. Thomas* (Philadelphia, 1881), p. 234; Stanley V. Henkels and Son, "Catalogue No. 1379 of the Military Correspondence of Major General George H. Thomas," dated Oct. 15, 1925, New York Public Library.

18. *Army Register,* 1868, p. 140, fixed the pay and allowances of a major general commanding a division or a department at $7,445.40 per year. This was larger than the salary of a Cabinet officer or of the Chief Justice of the United States. Grant lived beyond his salary and accepted more than $100,000 from friends to pay his debts. Sherman was supplied a smaller amount by a group of admirers. Thomas accepted medals, swords and spurs, but refused a silver table service, real estate and cash. Early in his career, Thomas fought for an addition to his pay. The only similar request found in the records was made July 3, 1866, when he asked for an increase in his monthly allowance for quarters, Thomas to A.G.O., Let. Sent, Dept. of the Cumberland, p. 144.

19. Johnson, p. 234. Otis, "General George H. Thomas." Grenville M. Dodge, *Personal Recollections of Some of Our Commanders in the Civil War* (Council Bluffs, Iowa, 1914). Willard Warner, *Sherman's Memoirs,* 2:546, notes that after the war Thomas complained on two counts of Grant's treatment. The first was the attempt to supersede him at Nashville. The second was his refusal to give Thomas' old commissary the Nashville postmastership.

20. Microfilm of the *Daily Alta California,* June 1, 1869, March 29, 1870, State Library, Sacramento. Thomas to Col. Hough, April 5 and 14, 1869, John N. Hough Papers.

21. Thomas to Sherman, Sept. 20, 1869 (714 P 1869), and Sept. 27, 1869 (738 P 1869 [filed with 710 W 1869]), Let. Rec., A.G.O.

22. *Annual Report of the Board of Regents of the Smithsonian Institution* (Washington, 1869). Thomas to Baird, Sept. 25, 1869, Correspondence and Records, Smithsonian Institution. The Sumner referred to is probably the Senator from Massachusetts.

23. *Journeys and Itineraries,* pamphlet published by order of Maj. Gen. G. H. Thomas, Bancroft Library, Berkeley, Calif. Robert G. Athearn, ed., "An Army Officer's Trip to Alaska in 1869," *Pacific Northwest Quarterly,* 40:11 (Jan. 1949), 48, 49, 52.

24. J. D. Cox, who had just entered Grant's Cabinet. Stanley attributed the attack to revenge in a letter to Col. Hough, Dec. 10, 1889, John N. Hough Papers.

25. McCormick to Surgeon General, March 31, 1870, filed with S92CB70, National Archives, gives the clinical details.

26. Mrs. Thomas to Col. Hough, April 29, 1870, John N. Hough Papers. She asked for all the writings of General Thomas which were not exactly official, for she did not want them to fall into the hands of the General's successor. This is a reflection of Thomas' lifelong attitude. It made Van Horne's officially accurate biography humanly inaccurate. It discouraged other contemporary biographers and warped the present-day image of Thomas out of all resemblance to the real man.

27. Superintendent, Troy Cemetery Association, to the author, March 30, 1948. The monument, erected on October 26, 1870, was done by Robert E. Launitz of New York City.

28. *Daily Alta California* gives the details of Thomas' death and the trip eastward of his body. It differs slightly from Van Horne's account. The files of the Troy *Daily Budget,* Troy *Times* and Troy *Press* give the details of the funeral and burial and the death of Mrs. Thomas on the night of Dec. 25, 1889, in Washington, D.C.

Selected Bibliography

Bates, Edward. "Diary, 1859–1866." Edited by H. K. Beale. *Annual Report of the American Historical Association,* 4 vols. Washington, D.C., 1930.

Baylies, Francis. *A Narrative of General Wool's Campaign in Mexico in the Years 1846, 1847 and 1848.* Albany, 1851.

Bill, A. H. *Rehearsal for Conflict.* New York, 1947.

Bishop, Judson W. *The Story of a Regiment.* St. Paul, 1890.

Blake, Nelson M. *William Mahone of Virginia, Soldier and Political Insurgent.* Richmond, 1935.

Boynton, Edward C. *A History of West Point.* New York, 1863.

Boynton, Henry V. *Was General Thomas Slow at Nashville?* Cincinnati, 1896.

———. *Chattanooga and Chickamauga.* Reprints of Boynton's war-time letters to the Cincinnati *Gazette.* Cincinnati, 1888.

———. *The National Military Park.* Cincinnati, 1895.

Carleton, James H. *The Battle of Buena Vista.* New York, 1848.

Carnegie, Andrew. *Stanton, the Patriot.* ("Ohio Archeological and Historical Society Publications," vol. 15). Columbus, 1906.

Cline, W. M. *The Muzzle Loading Rifle Then and Now.* Huntington, 1942.

Cox, Jacob D. *The Battle of Franklin.* New York, 1897.

Dawson, G. F. *The Life and Services of John A. Logan.* Chicago, 1887.

DePeyster, J. Watts. *Winter Campaigns.* New York, 1862.

DeVoto, Bernard. *The Year of Decision, 1846.* Boston, 1943.

Drewry, William S. *The Southampton Insurrection.* Washington, D.C., 1900.

Dyer, John P. *Fightin' Joe Wheeler.* Baton Rouge, 1941.

Farley, J. P. *West Point in the Early '60's.* Troy, 1902.

Fieberger, George J. *Campaigns of the American Civil War.* West Point, 1914.

Fiske, John. *The Mississippi Valley in the Civil War.* Boston, 1900.

Fitch, John. *The Annals of the Army of the Cumberland*. Philadelphia, 1863.

Flower, Frank A. *Edwin McMasters Stanton—The Autocrat of Rebellion, Emancipation and Reconstruction*. New York, 1905.

Forman, Sidney. *The Educational Objectives of the United States Military Academy*. West Point, 1946.

———. *Cadet Life Before the Mexican War*. West Point, 1945.

Fox, William F. *Regimental Losses in the Civil War*. Albany, 1889.

Freeman, Douglas S. *R. E. Lee, A Biography*. 4 vols. New York, 1934, 1935.

———. *Lee's Lieutenants*. 3 vols. New York, 1942–1944.

Fry, James B. *Operations of the Army Under Buell*. New York, 1884.

———. *History and Legal Effects of Brevets in the Armies of Great Britain and the United States, from Their Origin, in 1692, to the Present Time*. New York, 1877.

Ganoe, W. A. *The History of the U.S. Army*. New York, 1942.

Geer, Walter. *Campaigns of the Civil War*. New York, 1926.

Gracie, Archibald. *The Truth About Chickamauga*. Boston and New York, 1911.

Greene, Wharton J. *Recollections and Reflections*. Raleigh, 1906.

Hammersley, T. H. S. *The Complete Regular Army Register of the U.S.* Washington, D.C., 1880.

Hay, Thomas R. *Hood's Tennessee Campaign*. New York, 1925.

Hazen, William B. *A Narrative of Military Service*. Boston, 1885.

Heitman, Francis B. *Historical Register and Dictionary of the U.S. Army*. 2 vols. Washington, D.C., 1903.

Henry, W. S. *Campaign Sketches of the War with Mexico*. New York, 1847.

Hitchcock, Ethan A. *Diary—Fifty Years in Camp and Field*. Edited by W. A. Croffet. New York, 1909.

Hood, John B. *Advance and Retreat*. New Orleans, 1880.

Hopkins, Timothy. *Kelloggs in the Old World and the New*. 3 vols. San Francisco, 1903.

Johnson, Richard W. *A Soldier's Reminiscences in Peace and War*. Philadelphia, 1886.

Johnston, Joseph E. *A Narrative of Military Operations and Recollections*. New York, 1874.

Kenly, J. R. *Memoir of a Maryland Volunteer*. Philadelphia, 1873.

Keyes, Erasmus D. *Fifty Years' Observation of Men and Events*. New York, 1884.

McKinney, Francis F. Articles published in *Michigan Alumnus Quarterly Review*. "The First East Tennessee Campaign," 59 (May 23, 1953):213. "The Capture of Jefferson Davis," 60 (August 7, 1954):342. "The First Regiment of Michigan Engineers and Mechanics," 62 (February 25, 1956):140. "The Trial of General Buell," 64 (March 1, 1958):163.

Meade, George G. *Life and Letters*. Edited by G. G. Meade. 2 vols. New York, 1913.

"Military Conditions at the Outbreak of the Civil War." Instructions for cadets, multigraphed, n.d. West Point Museum.

Military Historical Society of Massachusetts. Boston. Vol. 7, 1908; vol. 8, 1910; vol. 10, 1895 [sic].

Military Order of the Loyal Legion of the United States.
District of Columbia Commandery. *War Papers, Nos. 1–25*. Washington, D.C., 1887–1911.

Illinois Commandery. *Military Essays and Recollections.* 2 vols. Chicago, 1891–1894.

Michigan Commandery. *War Papers.* 2 vols. Detroit, 1893, 1898.

Minnesota Commandery. *Glimpses of the Nation's Struggle.* 6 vols. St. Paul, 1887–1909.

New York Commandery. *Personal Recollections of the War of the Rebellion.* 2 vols. New York, 1883–1899.

Ohio Commandery. *Sketches of War History.* 5 vols. Cincinnati, 1884–1897.

Oregon Commandery. *War Papers.* Chicago, 1884.

Palmer, John M. *Personal Recollections.* Cincinnati, 1901.

Park, Roswell. *A Sketch of the History and Topography of West Point.* Philadelphia, 1840.

Patterson, Robert. *A Narrative of the Campaign in the Valley of the Shenandoah in 1861.* Philadelphia, 1865.

Piatt, Donn. *Memories of Men Who Saved the Union.* New York, 1887.

Proceedings of the Massachusetts Historical Society. Boston. Vol. 48, 1882; 50, 1888; 51, 1886 [sic].

Reed, D. W. "National Cemeteries and National Parks." Typescript of an address, n.d. National Park Library, Fort Oglethorpe, Ga.

Reid, S. C., Jr. *Scouting Expeditions of McCulloch's Texas Rangers.* Philadelphia, 1847.

Reid, Whitelaw. *Ohio in the Civil War.* 2 vols. Columbus, 1893. Vol. 1.

Richardson, R. N. *The Comanche Barrier to the South Plains Settlement.* Glendale, Calif., 1928.

Ripley, Roswell S. *The War with Mexico.* 2 vols. New York, 1849. Vol. 1.

Rister, Carl C. *Robert E. Lee in Texas.* Norman, Oklahoma, 1946.

Robinson, Fayette. *An Account of the Organization of the Army of the United States.* 2 vols. Philadelphia, 1848. Vol. 2.

Rochelle, J. H. *Life of Rear Admiral John Randolph Tucker.* Washington, D.C., 1903.

Shannon, Fred A. *The Organization and Administration of the Army of the U.S., 1861–65.* 2 vols. Manhattan, Kansas, 1928. Vol. 1.

Sherman, John. *Recollections of Forty Years in the House, Senate and Cabinet.* New York, 1895.

Sherman, William T. *Letters.* Edited by R. S. Thorndike. New York, 1894.

Society of the Army of the Cumberland. *Reports.* 30 vols. Cincinnati. Vols. 1 and 2, 1868; vol. 3, 1869; vol. 4, 1870; vol. 27, 1897.

Southern Historical Society. *Papers.* 47 vols. Richmond, 1876–1930. Vol. 12, p. 568 gives the Southern version of Thomas' desertion.

Speed, Thomas. *Union Regiments of Kentucky.* New York, 1897.

Squires, W. H. T. *The Days of Yester-Year in Colony and Commonwealth.* Portsmouth, Va., 1928.

Steele, Matthew F. *American Campaigns.* 2 vols. Washington, D.C., 1943. Vol. 1.

Stevens, Hazard. *The Life of Isaac Ingalls Stevens.* 2 vols. Boston, 1901. Vol. 1.

"Study of the Ranges of Civil War Field Guns." Bound manuscript owned by the Manassas National Battlefield Park Library.

Swiggett, Howard. *The Rebel Raider, A Life of John Hunt Morgan.* Garden City, N.Y., 1937.

Temple, Oliver P. *East Tennessee and the Civil War.* Cincinnati, 1899.

——. *Notable Men of Tennessee*. New York, 1912.

Tourgee, Albion W. *The Story of a Thousand*. Buffalo, 1896.

Transactions of the Illinois State Historical Society. "The Diary of Major James A. Connolly." Springfield, 1928.

Partridge, C. A. "The 96th Illinois at Chickamauga." Springfield, 1910.

Turchin, John B. *Chickamauga*. Chicago, 1888.

U.S. Quartermaster General. *Organization of the Army of the Cumberland at the Battle of Chickamauga*. Washington, D.C., 1932.

U.S. Secretary of War. *Cavalry Tactics*. Washington, D.C., 1855.

Williams, T. Harry. *Lincoln and his Generals*. New York, 1952.

Wilson, William B. *A Few Acts and Actors in the Tragedy of the Civil War*. Philadelphia, 1892.

Woods, Joseph T. *Steedman and his Men at Chickamauga*. Toledo, 1876.

Wyeth, John A. *With Sabre and Scalpel*. New York, 1914.

Index